THE IRISH IN AMERICA
JOHN FRANCIS MAGUIRE

TABLE OF CONTENTS

PREFACE

MORE THAN ONE MOTIVE influenced me in the desire to visit America, and record the results of my impressions in a published form.

I desired to ascertain by personal observation what the Irish—thousands of whom are constantly emigrating, as it were, from my very door—were doing in America; and that desire, to see with my own eyes, and judge with my own mind, was stimulated by the conflicting and contradictory accounts which reached home through various channels and sources of information, some friendly, more hostile.

I was desirous of understanding practically the true value of man's labour and industry, as applied to the cultivation of the soil and the development of a country. It has been so much the fashion of the day, either to palliate or excuse even the most grievous wrong done to the poor and the defenceless on the plea that in consequence of their 'want of capital' nothing could be hoped from them in their own country, and that emigration to another country was their only resource; or to despair of any material improvement in the condition and circumstances of Ireland until 'capital'—meaning bullion or bank-paper—was by some means or other introduced, and applied to her soil; that I determined to test this problem, or fallacy, by visiting settlements actually in their infancy, thus going to the very commencement, and seeing how the first difficulties were overcome, and how progress was gradually effected. I have in more than one instance given the result of my own observation in this respect; and where I had not the opportunity of judging for myself, I have relied on the accounts given to me by persons both intelligent and trustworthy. In whatever prominence I have given to this subject, I had another and distinct purpose in view—to combat, by argument and illustration, a sad error into which, from many causes and motives, the Irish are unhappily betrayed; that of not selecting the right place for their special industry—of the Irish peasant lingering in the city until he becomes merged in its population, and his legitimate prospects of a future of honour and independence are lost to him for ever. And to this portion of the volume I earnestly implore the attention of those by whom advice may be usefully given or influence successfully exerted, so that its lesson may be urged upon such as have still the choice of a future before them.

I desired to learn if, as had been confidently and repeatedly asserted, Irish Catholics lost their faith, or became indifferent to religion, the moment they landed in America; or whether, as it had been asserted in their defence, they were at once the pioneers and the pillars of their faith. In this enquiry I was mainly influenced by the conviction that loss of faith or indifference to religion would be the most terrible of all calamities to Irish Catholics; that the necessary result of that loss of faith, or that indifference to religion, would be fatal to their material progress, would disastrously interfere with the proper performance of their duties as citizens, and would be certain to turn the public opinion of America against them. I have devoted a considerable portion of the following pages to this vital subject, and given rather an elaborate sketch of the history and progress of the Catholic Church of America—of that institution by which, humanly speaking, the education, the character, the conduct, the material welfare and social position of the Irish and their descendants are and must be profoundly influenced. And, indeed, in giving a history of the growth and progress of the Catholic Church I was representing the struggles and the difficulties of the Irish emigrant or settler of the present century.

I was also anxious to ascertain the real nature, that is the strength or the intensity, of the sentiment which I had reason to believe was entertained by the Irish in the United States towards the British Government; as I considered, and I hold rightly, that the existence of a strong sentiment or feeling of hostility is a far more serious cause of danger, in case of future misunderstanding or complication, than any organisation, however apparently extensive or formidable. I have given the results of my impressions and information freely and without disguise. What I have stated will necessarily be judged of from different points of view; but of this I feel certain, that did I not write what I know to be the truth, I should not be acting with honesty; and that disguise and concealment would be far more prejudicial than 'open and advised speaking.'

I shall now only express, in one comprehensive acknowledgment, my deep sense of gratitude for the many courtesies, and kindnesses, and acts of friendship, which I received on all sides during a protracted and varied tour.

The book—*The Irish in America*—is now delivered up to the judgment of the reader, with all its imperfections on its head.

LONDON: *November* 27, 1867.

CHAPTER I

Difference of the Position of the Irish in the Old Country, and the New—
Difference in the Countries—Power and Dignity of Labour—The Irish Element
strong in Halifax—Their Progress—The Value of a 'Lot'—No Snobbishness—
The Secret of Prosperity—The Poor's Asylum—Cause of Poverty—Catholic
Church in Nova Scotia—'Sick Calls'—A Martyr to Duty—No State Church—Real
Religious Equality—Its Advantages—Pictou—My Friend Peter—Peter shows me
the Lions—At the Mines—Irish everywhere—A Family Party—Nova Scotia as a
Home for Emigrants.

CROSSING the Atlantic, and landing at any city of the American seaboard, one is enabled, almost at a glance, to recognise the marked difference between the position of the Irish race in the old country and in the new. Nor is the condition of the Irish at both sides of the ocean more marked in its dissimilarity than are the circumstances and characteristics of the country from which they emigrated and the country to which they have come.

In the old country, stagnation, retrogression, if not actual decay—in the new, life, movement, progress; in the one, depression, want of confidence, dark apprehension of the future—in the other, energy, self-reliance, and a perpetual looking forward to a grander development and a more glorious destiny. That the tone of the public mind of America should be self-reliant and even boastful, is natural in a country of brief but pregnant history—a country still in its infancy, when compared with European States, but possessing, in the fullest sense, the strength and vigour of manhood—manhood in all its freshness of youth and buoyancy of hope.

In such a country man is most conscious of his value: he is the architect of his country's greatness, the author of her civilisation, the miracle-worker by whom all has been or can be accomplished. Where a few years since a forest waved in mournful grandeur, there are cultivated fields, blooming orchards, comfortable homesteads, cheerful hamlets—churches, schools, civilisation; where but the other day a few huts stood on a river's bank, by the shore of a lake, or on some estuary of the sea, swelling domes and lofty spires and broad porticoes now meet the eye; and the waters but recently skimmed by the light bark of the Indian are ploughed into foam by countless steamers. And the same man who performed these miracles of a few years since—of yesterday—has the same power of to-morrow achieving the same wondrous results of patience and energy, courage and skill. But for him, and his hands to toil and his brain to plan, the vast country whose commerce is on every sea, and whose influence is felt in every court, would be still the abode of savage tribes, dwelling in perpetual conflict and steeped in the grossest ignorance.

Labour is thus a thing to be honoured, not a badge of inferiority. Nor is the poor man here a drug, a social nuisance, something to be legislated against or got rid of, regarded with suspicion because of his probable motives or intentions, or with aversion as a possible burden on property. In the old countries, the ordinary lot of the man born to poverty is that poverty shall be his doom—that he shall die in the condition in which he was brought into the world, and that he shall transmit hard toil and scanty remuneration as a legacy to his children. But in a new country, especially one of limitless fields for enterprise, the rudest implements of labour may be the means of advancement to wealth, honour and distinction, if not for those who use them, at least for those who spring from their loins. Labour, rightly understood, being the great miracle-worker, the mighty civiliser is regarded with respect, not looked down upon, or loftily patronised; and though birth and position and superior intelligence will always have their influence, even in the newest state of society, still honest industry appreciates its own dignity, and holds high its head amidst the proudest or the best. Therefore America, of all countries, is the one most suited to the successful transplanting of a race which has in it every essential element of greatness—alertness and vigour of intellect, strength and energy of body, patient industry, courage and daring in battle, cheerful endurance of adversity and privation, quickness of invention, profound faith, with firm reliance in the wisdom and goodness of God, and a faculty of thoroughly identifying itself with the institutions, interests, and honour of its adopted home.

And in no city of the American continent do the Irish occupy a better position, or exercise a more deserved influence than in Halifax, which has been well described by an enthusiastic Hibernian as the 'Wharf of the Atlantic.' Forming the majority of the population of that active and energetic city, they constitute an essential element of its stability and progress. This Irish element is everywhere discernible, in every description of business and in all branches of industry, in every class and in every condition of life, from the highest to the lowest. There are in other cities larger masses of Irish, some in which they are five times, and even ten times as numerous as the whole population of Halifax; but it may be doubted if there are many cities of the entire continent of America in which they afford themselves fuller play for the exercise of their higher qualities than in the capital of Nova Scotia, where their moral worth keeps pace with their material prosperity, which is remarkably great, especially when considering the circumstances under which the far greater proportion of them arrived in the new world.

Those who are well off at home do not quit it for a new country; contented with their present position, they never dream of changing it for one which is sure to be accompanied with more or less of risk or hardship. The impelling motive that has driven millions across the Atlantic, and that may drive millions more in the same direction, is the desire, so natural to the civilised man, of improving his condition, of obtaining the certain means of a decent livelihood—in a word, of making a home and a future for himself and his children. It matters little to what portion of

America reference is had: the same impelling motive has added to its population, and been one of the principal causes of its progress and development. Instances there have been of people well-to-do in the old country, deliberately exchanging it for the new, chiefly with the view of turning their means to better account, and thus securing a larger inheritance for their children; but when compared with the vast tide of emigration to which America is mainly indebted for the position she this day holds among the nations, these exceptional cases constitute so infinitesimal a minority as to be scarcely appreciable. The mass came because they had no option but to come, because hunger and want were at their heels, and flight was their only chance of safety. Thus the majority landed from the emigrant ship with little beyond a box or bundle of clothes, and the means of procuring a week's or a month's provisions—very many with still less. Some had education, intelligence, and knowledge of business; but of this class few had money—they crossed the ocean to secure that. Therefore, when in Halifax, as in all other parts of America, Irishmen are to be found in the enjoyment of independence, and even considerable wealth, it must be evident that their success is attributable to their own exertions and their own merit.

Halifax may be described as a city of solid prosperity and steady progress; and the Irish not only share in its prosperity, but assist in its progress. Thus, for instance, a large proportion of the houses of business, several of which would be worthy of the proudest capitals of Europe, have been established by Irish enterprise. One, the most conspicuous for its appearance and extent, is the property of perhaps the most eminent and honoured Irishman in the colony, who bringing with him from his native country, as his only capital, character, intelligence, and industry, has not only realised a splendid fortune, but enjoys a reputation for worth and probity which is the pride of his countrymen. In the rapid conversion of Halifax from a city of timber to a city of brick and stone, the Irish have their full share. Splendid 'stores'—'shops' in the old country —and handsome mansions have been erected by Irishmen; and where the Irish trader adheres to the old place of business or the modest dwelling, it is not because he wants the means of erecting something striking or costly, but that he lacks the inclination to do so, and prefers the simplicity which he associates with his success, and deems indispensable to his comfort.

In Halifax, as throughout America, the Irish necessarily form the large proportion of the working population; and when these men landed on the wharf, they had nothing save the implements of their craft, or the capacity and willingness for labour. But whether skilled mechanics, or mere day-labourers, their condition is, on the whole, admirable; and the best proof of their good conduct is the possession by a considerable number of them of that which, throughout the British Provinces and the States, is the first step in advance —'a lot'—meaning thereby a piece of ground on which a house is or is to be erected.

There is a kind of magic influence in the possession of this first bit of 'real estate.' An evidence of frugality and self-denial, it is an incentive to the continued practice of the same virtues. It is the commencement, and yet something more than the commencement; it may be called 'half the battle,' for the rest depends on perseverance in the same course. The house may be rude in construction, mean in appearance, miserable in accommodation, but *it is a house*, in which the owner and his family can live rent-free, for it is their property—'their own.' With sufficient front and sufficient depth, what is there to prevent the owner, in time, from covering the space with a fine brick house, with its attractive shop, and as many stories as he pleases to raise? Once possess the 'lot' in the town, and the rest is comparatively easy. Every year adds to its value; and if the owner cannot build a good house on it, some one else may, and the owner receives in either case an ample return for his investment. But in thousands of instances throughout America, the Irish, even of the very humblest class, possess lots on which they have erected dwelling-houses which they themselves occupy; and in every city one may daily behold a happy transformation in the character of the dwelling, wherever industry is combined with thrift and frugality. The structure of timber is replaced by a building of brick; and so the family, it may be of the mechanic, it may be of the labourer, move up in the social scale; and the superior education which their children receive enables them to improve the position their father had acquired by his good conduct and good sense. That 'lot' is a wonderful friend to the Irish in America, and this the wise of them know full well.

The majority of those who now constitute the strength of the Catholic element in Halifax came without funds or friends, some literally without a shilling in their pocket; but with honesty, intelligence, and a determination to work. From the humblest occupations, natural to their first efforts in a strange place, many of the Irish in Halifax have risen to wealth and influence. Industry and good conduct— these their all, their sword and buckler, their wand of magic power. And as they rose in the world they carried with them the respect of the community by whom the successful architect of his own position is justly estimated at a higher value than the fortunate inheritors of the wealth of those who went before them.

It may perhaps be too much to assert that the transplanting of the Irishman from his own soil to a new country and a healthier atmosphere has been of unmixed benefit to him in every sense; but in one respect his improvement is unquestionable—he is above that shamefaced snobbishness which he too often displays at home. It is not every one in the old country who will make the story of his own elevation in life a matter of honest pride. In Halifax—in America—it is different. From several of my countrymen, of different degrees of prosperity and social standing, I have heard the history of their early struggles and ultimate success. Some of these had not the advantage of an early education, and were self-made and self-taught; but they were men of great sagacity and fine natural talent, whom cultivation would have well fitted for the administration of public affairs.

One of these gave as his reason for not accepting an office which had been placed at his disposal, his own consciousness of the want of early training, which was unavoidable in his case, owing to the circumstances of Ireland at the time of his leaving it; and yet he dealt with the question of the hour—the proposed Confederation of the British Colonies—with a breadth of thought and a mastery of detail that proved the very fitness which he modestly repudiated.

'Such a man is worth 5,000l.,' 'this man has 10,000l.,' 'that man is worth 20,000l.,' 'this other man is worth 50,000l. if he is worth a penny,' has been repeatedly said to me of Irishmen who made no show whatever; but almost invariably one important statement was added: 'he is a steady, prudent man,' 'he is a good, worthy man,' or, 'there is not a better conducted man in the province.' The golden rule of success in life was thus frequently expressed; 'To get on here, a man must be industrious and well-conducted; with industry and good conduct any man, no matter what he is, or what he has, or how he begins, can get on here; but not without these essentials. But the man who drinks, bid him remain at home—he won't do here.' Spoken in Nova Scotia, as the experience of people of all ranks, classes, and occupations, it is equally applicable to every province of British America, and every State in the Union. Industry, sobriety, good conduct—these, under favourable circumstances, raise the humblest to the level of the great; and favourable circumstances abound in America.

A visit to two institutions of very different character impressed me with a still stronger conviction of the prosperity of Halifax. These institutions, its Poor's Asylum and its Schools.

The number in the Poor's Asylum, according to the record in the book, was 354. This was the gross number; but the number belonging to the city was only 120, which was small for a population of 34,000. The rest had been sent in from various places in the province—some from distances varying from 50 even to 200 miles. Strictly speaking, there was not an able-bodied male pauper in the establishment: those who were there were the aged, the infirm, the sick, the helpless, or those waifs and strays that are stranded on the shore of life, the victims of their folly and infatuation. Deducting the children, 64 in number, the insane or idiotic, about 50 in all, and the sick, infirm, and aged, who were the majority, the remaining were but few. As the Master said, there was not in the house a man who could perform a day's work.

What to do with our workhouse children—how to deal with those who are brought up in such institutions—is one of the most formidable difficulties with which the administrators of the Poor-law in Ireland have to deal. There is no difficulty in Halifax on that score; and if throughout America the children of the poor were treated in one essential respect in the same spirit of fairness, there would be fewer occasions for bitterness than unhappily exist in some of the Northern States. The children being carefully taught, the boys are apprenticed out as early as the age of twelve or thirteen, and are indentured till twenty-one, due precaution being had not only as to the means and character of the master, but for the protection of the religious faith of the child; the latter being secured by binding the Catholic child to a Catholic master, and the Protestant child to a Protestant master—a course which commends itself to every fair and impartial mind. The girls are apprenticed till the age of eighteen. By the conditions of the indenture, the child is to be suitably educated, and to be provided with a Sunday suit, at the expense of the master or mistress. But with very few exceptions, the children, boys and girls, become incorporated with the family, of which, almost from the first, they are looked upon and treated as members.

Of the entire number of inmates in this Halifax institution, about two-thirds are Irish; and according to the united testimony of the secretary and two gentlemen of local eminence, the greater number of them owed their social ruin to the one fruitful cause of evil to the Irish race—that which tracks them across the ocean, and follows them in every circumstance and condition of life—that which mars their virtues and magnifies their failings—that which is in reality the *only* enemy they have occasion to dread, for it is the most insidious, the most seductive, and the most fatal of all—*drink*. Remarking on the fact mentioned, the gentleman by whom I was accompanied, a man of long and varied experience, said:—'All can do well here if they only abstain from drink, or if they will drink in moderation; but drink is the ruin of men here, just as in the old country. No matter how a man starts, though without a cent in his pocket, he can make money here, provided he is well-conducted, and does not drink.' Happily, however, the number of the victims was but small.

My visits to the Catholic schools, which, as is the rule throughout America, are conducted by members of religious communities, were attended with much interest, and left upon my mind the deepest impression, not so much of the excellence of the teaching, for of that I had no doubt whatever, but of the substantial prosperity of the town, and the solid comfort enjoyed by the least wealthy portion of its inhabitants—its working population. I went through the schools conducted by the Christian Brothers, whose system of teaching and discipline is in all respects identical with that so well known in those cities of the old country which are blessed by their presence; my desire being merely to see the children, how they looked, and in what manner they were clad. Nor was my surprise less great than agreeable at the spectacle which I beheld. It was heightened by the force of contrast; as but a few days before I left Ireland I had, with others, accompanied certain distinguished Englishmen to the schools of the Christian Brothers of my own city, and the remembrance of what I there witnessed was strong and vivid. There—in Cork—there was much to gratify, much even to astonish, but there was also too much to sadden and depress. The boys bright, quick, intelligent, exhibiting in every department extraordinary proficiency, to such a degree indeed as to excite the openly-expressed amazement of the strangers; but too many of them exhibited the unmistakable evidence of intense poverty, not only in their scanty raiment but in their pale and anxious faces. What a contrast to this—in this one respect only—was presented by the schools of the Brothers in Halifax! Not a single sign or indication of poverty, not a trace of want, not a tattered coat or trowsers, not a rent, not a patch—on the contrary, every boy, whatever his age, neatly and comfortably clad, and having the appearance of robust health. Indeed such was their appearance that, had I not been repeatedly assured they were the children of working men, I should have taken them as belonging to the middle class. Bright, intelligent, bold-eyed, happy-looking boys, the right stuff for the future citizens of a free country and a progressive community.

In the schools conducted by the Sisters of Charity there was the same air of comfort and neatness in the dress of the female children; and even where a special school might happen to be overcrowded, there was an absence of that oppressive odour too common in free schools frequented by the children of the working-classes, which is mainly attributable to the poverty of their clothing. There was nothing here but comfort and decency of dress; good proofs of the conduct and condition of the class thus favourably represented.

The Catholics of Nova Scotia are estimated at 115,000, being thus divided—30,000 French, 45,000 Scotch, and 40,000 Irish. In Halifax the Catholics form one half of the population, and are almost wholly Irish.

Without going back farther than the commencement of the present century, an incident of pregnant significance will enable the reader to contrast the position of the Catholic Church of that day with the position it now enjoys. The house still occupied by Archbishop Connolly and the clergy who officiate in the cathedral, was built by the Rev. Dr. Burke, or Father Burke, as he was familiarly called. Dr. Burke was a profound scholar, and eminent for his scientific attainments. Following the natural impulse of a learned and zealous priest, he determined to establish a school for the education of the Catholic youth of that day. The Penal Laws were still unrepealed; and though, from the growing enlightenment of the age, this infamous code had fallen into disuse, it still afforded a ready weapon to the caprice or hostility of the bigot. Having been informed of the intention of Dr. Burke to establish a school, and thus, through the most effective means, elevate the condition of his co-religionists, the then Governor of the province threatened to put the law in force against the priest if he persevered in his attempt. In this conjuncture aid came from an unexpected quarter. The leading Protestants of the town exhibited their opposition to the illiberal policy of the Governor in the most effective manner, by sending their own children to a school which they had the wisdom to appreciate and the moral courage to support. The Governor, whatever the perversity of his bigotry, dared not enter into conflict with the influential allies of the Catholic priest; and so Dr. Burke and the cause of education triumphed. Young officers frequented the academy, to learn mathematics and the science of fortification from its accomplished principal. Strangely enough, the Government, whose representatives sought to crush the school and the teacher, afterwards marked its appreciation of the services of Dr. Burke—who, owing to his influence with the Indians, prevented them from joining the French in the war then raging—by conferring on him a pension of 300l. a year. It need scarcely be added, that this money was applied to the advancement of religion and enlightenment in a young and struggling mission.

The progress of the Catholic Church in Nova Scotia was slow, and not over-hopeful, for the first quarter of the present century. In the year 1816 there were about 1,500 Catholics in Halifax, and save in a few towns, where small congregations existed, the faithful were scattered over the province, the greater number hidden in the wilds and fastnesses of an almost unexplored country, and far away from the ministrations or influence of a priest. The Irish carried their faith with them into the forest; and though many of them for years never heard the once familiar voice of their pastor, they cherished in their hearts that strong attachment to the religion of their fathers which is one of the most marked characteristics of their race. As an illustration of this steadfastness in the faith, it may be mentioned that the present Archbishop, when a missionary priest, on one occasion baptised eight children of an Irish family in the midst of the woods.

The father had not seen a priest more than twice in twenty years; and what rendered his fidelity the more remarkable was the fact that he had married a Baptist, who did not regard with much favour the creed of her Catholic husband. This was as late as 1842, when there were but five priests in Halifax, and fourteen or fifteen in the entire diocese. The necessary intermarriage of Irish Catholics with members of various Protestant sects caused many of the former to lose the faith. No chapel, no priest, no mass, no administration of sacraments; nor, from the special circumstances of a country in which education had only ceased to be penal, were the Irish emigrants of the early part of this century remarkable for their literary acquirements—hence what could be more natural than that, while the parent clung passionately to the faith for which, perhaps, he had suffered at home, his children, whom he might not be able to instruct or control, should adopt the religion of their Protestant relatives? Such, at any rate, has been the case in numerous instances; and though these instances are fewer than they have been represented to be, they are sufficiently numerous to exhibit many a strange contrast between the old Catholic patronymic and the modern creed. The same circumstances produced the same result in many parts of America.

In 1820 there were but few priests in the province. The first Bishop of Halifax was consecrated in Rome in 1816, and died in 1820. A little wooden church, dignified by the lofty name of St. Peter's, was his cathedral. On its site a building more suited to the increasing wants and growing importance of the Catholic body was erected in course of time; until eventually that church, which was regarded as a splendid structure by those who first knelt before its altar, gave place to the existing cathedral, which is one of the finest edifices of the kind in America, but which is to be further extended and beautified by the addition of a magnificent facade of white marble from the celebrated quarries of West Chester, in the State of New York. The wooden 'cathedral' of the first quarter of a century was a fitting type of the Catholic Church of that day: the grand stone structure, some 180 feet in length, and with accommodation for 3,000 worshippers, fittingly represents its position at this day. Where a mere log hut was the only temple of the faith in Halifax, four churches are now insufficient for their congregations; and a new building, of the pointed Gothic order, was roofed in previous to the winter of 1866. Where there were but 20 priests in 1820, there are over 70 in the present year. These have the spiritual care of 115,000 Catholics, for whom, or by whom, more than 100 churches have been built. In 1842 the province was erected into a See, and in 1845 it was divided into two Sees, the Western and Eastern. The Western was elevated to the dignity of an archbishopric in 1852.

Bishop Walsh was created the first archbishop; and on the death of that prelate, in 1859, Dr. Connolly, then Bishop of New Brunswick, which is still within the ecclesiastical province, was transferred to Halifax. Since 1830, when first the Catholic element of Nova Scotia may be said to have acquired anything like the appearance of strength, more than 150,000l. has been expended in buildings for religious and educational purposes. Of this amount, by far the largest proportion has been raised by voluntary contribution, under the auspices and through the influence of the second archbishop; a man who, besides possessing a good intellect, considerable power as a writer and speaker, and strong common sense—a valuable quality in one who has at all times to place himself in the front—is endowed with indomitable energy and perseverance. Like his predecessor, Archbishop Connolly is one of the many prelates whom Ireland has given to the American Church. Besides the four churches and that which has been just completed, there are in Halifax three convents—two of the Order of Charity, and one of the Sacred Heart—with a House of the Christian Brothers, whose new schools form one of the most conspicuous of the architectural ornaments of the city. Nor is Halifax without a Society of St. Vincent, which finds the fitting time for its benevolent operations in the depth of the hard winter, when business is usually dull, employment consequently not so general as in the milder seasons of the year, and the feeble, the sick, and the improvident feel its rigour most keenly.

There are likewise more purely religious associations, whose object is to stimulate to the constant practice of piety, and protect the young and inexperienced from the dangers incidental to their period of life. Thus the machinery of the Church is so improved by increased means of usefulness as to be, if not fully equal to the spiritual requirements of the faithful, a complete protection against those contingencies to which loss of faith on the part of individuals or families may be fairly attributable. There is no longer an instance —at least in Nova Scotia—of a Catholic who has been for years without having seen a priest; but there is still hard work for the missionary priest in a territory so widely extended, and whose population is so thinly scattered over a vast space.

Perhaps the hardest and most trying duty which a Catholic clergyman has to discharge is connected with what are so well known to laity and clergy as 'sick calls,' requests made by the relatives or friends of the sick or dying for the attendance of a priest. From this duty the Catholic priest never shrinks. It matters not what the distance, the hour, or the danger, though the sick or dying person was a hundred miles away, though it was midnight, and there was not a star visible in the heavens—though the place to be visited reeked with the deadliest pestilence, the priest should at once obey the solemn summons. The priest who shrinks from this imperative duty is unfit for his mission; happily, an instance of neglect or cowardice is rarely heard of in the Catholic Church. But there are circumstances in which the conscientious discharge of this duty is attended with an amount of individual hardship that can scarcely be appreciated by those who inhabit a country at once thoroughly cultivated and thickly populated.

Father Geary, a Halifax priest—originally from Waterford, and now about four years dead—frequently attended 'sick calls' at a distance of a hundred miles from the city, along the eastern coast of Nova Scotia, and did so without the assistance of horse or vehicle of any kind. He had literally to walk the hundred miles, and this he has done as often as four times in the year. As the tidings of distress reached the city, generally by boat, the zealous missionary at once girded his loins and prepared to set out on his long and arduous journey, frequently in the depth of a Nova Scotian winter, when the snow lay two feet thick on the ground, the thermometer was many degrees below zero, and a cutting blast blew right in his teeth. There was not in his mind a thought of shrinking, a second's doubt as to the necessity of then setting out: a human soul was in peril, and the priest's duty was to reach the sick person's bedside as speedily as possible; and this he did. Twenty miles before breakfast was 'a trifle' to Father Geary.

Within the last ten years a Nova Scotian priest has discharged the duties of a district extending considerably over one hundred miles in length; and while I was in Halifax the Archbishop appointed a clergyman to the charge of a mission which would necessitate his making journeys of more than that many miles in extent. And when a missionary priest, in 1842, the Archbishop would make a three months' tour from Halifax to Dartmouth, a distance—going and returning—of 450 miles; and would frequently diverge ten and even twenty miles from the main line into the bush on either side, thus doing duty for a population of 10,000 Catholics, who had no spiritual resource save in him, and a decrepit fellow-labourer on the brink of the grave.

It is not three years since a young Irish priest, then in the first year of his mission, received what, to him, was literally a death summons. He was lying ill in bed when the 'sick call' reached his house, the pastor of the district being absent. The poor young man did not hesitate a moment; no matter what the consequence to himself, the dying Catholic should not be without the consolations of religion. To the dismay of those who knew of his intention, and who remonstrated in vain against what to them appeared to be an act of insanity, he started on his journey, a distance of thirty-six miles, which he accomplished on foot, in the midst of incessant rain. It is not possible to tell how often he paused involuntarily on that terrible march, or how he reeled and staggered as he approached its termination; but this much is well ascertained—that scarcely had he reached the sick man's bed, and performed the functions of his ministry, when he was conscious of his own approaching dissolution; and there being no brother priest to minister to him in his last hour, he administered the viaticum to himself, and died on the floor of what was then, indeed, a chamber of death. Here was a glorious ending of a life only well begun.

Bermuda is included within the spiritual jurisdiction of the Archbishop of Halifax, and to this fact is owing one of the most extraordinary instances of a 'sick call' on record. A Catholic lady in Bermuda was dying of a lingering disease, and knowing that further delay might be attended with consequences which she regarded as worse than death, she availed herself of the opportunity of a vessel then about to sail for Halifax to send for a clergyman of that city. The day the message was delivered to the clergyman a vessel was to sail from Halifax to Bermuda, and he went on board at once, arrived in due course at the latter place, found the dying lady still alive, administered to her the rites of the Church, and returned as soon as possible to his duties in Halifax; having, in obedience to this remarkable 'sick call,' accomplished a journey of 1,600 miles.

It is the opinion of many candid and unbiassed men in Ireland, that the existence of a State Church, and that the church of the small minority of the population, is injurious to the country in many respects, especially in preventing that social fusion and Christian harmony which are among the happy results of complete religious equality. No one who has been in Nova Scotia but must, if not utterly blinded by prejudice, be convinced that the non-existence of a State Church and a dominant religion is attended with the most beneficial consequences to that colony. There is no cause, no legalised cause, of hostility and ill blood, no provocation to anger—*no grievance.*

The Catholic feels himself to be on an equality with the Protestant, towards whom he does not and cannot entertain a sentiment of hostility; and the Protestant is pleased to know that his Catholic fellow-citizen regards him with a kindly and fraternal feeling. 'We have no occasion to grumble; we are able to meet together and go hand in hand in all matters; and, in fact, we are the happiest people in the world,' said a Catholic Irishman, whose memories of his own country were full of bitterness, but who enjoyed the contrast the more keenly. 'I hold the opinion,' said a Protestant gentleman, the descendant of an Irish father from the south of Munster, 'that if the followers of a church will not sustain it, it is not worthy of being sustained, and the sooner it falls the better.' Few perhaps of this Protestant gentleman's relatives in the old country would endorse his opinion; but he could estimate the advantage to the social harmony of his country of not having in the heart of the body politic a perpetual source of mutual exasperation and bitterness. From persons of all creeds and classes I received the most gratifying testimony as to the good feeling existing between the different churches, and the happy result of the prevalence of this Christian sentiment. 'The Archbishop has done much to promote this feeling,' was frequently remarked by Protestants and Catholics, officials and townspeople. True, the Archbishop has done much to break down the barriers which sect will create under the most favourable circumstances; but had there been in Nova Scotia a State Church, and a dominant party, sworn to maintain it at any cost or hazard, not all the wisdom, tact, and kindliness of so eminent and influential an ecclesiastic as the Archbishop of Halifax could successfully counteract the hostility these would be sure to engender.

It would be foreign to the truth to assert that Catholics in Nova Scotia have not their difficulties to contend with. They have difficulties and troubles, but they are in a position in which they can endure if they cannot overcome them. For instance, unscrupulous politicians will occasionally raise an anti-Catholic cry, that for the time inflames the passions of the unreflecting, and disturbs the good understanding which, as a rule, pervades the colony. But it not unrarely occurs, that the same politician—generally a man who troubles himself but little about religion in any form whatever—who thought it his interest to excite ill feeling against Catholics, discovers that it is more to his advantage to stand well with that body; and instances are told of the same unscrupulous party-leader one day calumniating, and the next making overtures to, those who can at all times materially influence the result of an election, or even the fate of an administration. Nor is this utter dishonesty and shameless want of principle confined to a few unscrupulous individuals in one British Colony; it is much to be regretted that the species— whose chief characteristic is, that they are ready to sacrifice everything, save and except what they think to be their personal interest, for a good 'cry'—are to be found plentifully scattered throughout America. Even the most bankrupt politician finds 'No Popery!' a useful cry—for the time; for the good sense of the community wearies of the folly, or the politician has probably invented something which has the merit of novelty, and he allows Catholics to exist in peace.

The Irish, including Protestants and Catholics, are estimated at 100,000. The larger proportion of the Protestants were originally from the north of Ireland, or had left the United States after they had achieved their independence; and their descendants now possess nearly the whole of the counties of Colchester and Cumberland. They took up most of the lands from which the French Acadians were banished in the year 1755. That they should be prosperous and independent is consistent not only with the sturdy energy of their nature, but with the countenance and support which they received from the colonial authorities and home government. With them, as with their brethren in all the British colonies, things went favourably: not so with the Catholics, who had much to contend with, and everything to do for themselves.

A striking proof of the position of Irish Catholics in Nova Scotia—to which the vast majority emigrated under the most unfavourable circumstances—may be mentioned: namely, that of the 2,000 Catholic voters in the city and county of Halifax, all, or nearly all, own over 50l. of real estate, and but very few of them claim the franchise through the annual payment of a rent of 50l. and upwards.

The necessity of taking passage at Pictou for Prince Edward's Island brought me to that town, which is prettily situated on the shore of the harbour. The Irish do not, at least as yet, form any considerable proportion of the population, the Catholic congregation being little more than one hundred in number. But it would be difficult to behold anywhere a more remarkable instance of generous devotion to their faith than the Catholic Irish have displayed in this place, where they are so numerically weak. To the stranger entering the harbour the most striking object is a well-built brick church, with lofty spire surmounted by a gilded cross. This imposing structure—the *first* actually built in the town, though a handsome Protestant church was being erected in the October of 1866—is the work of the small Catholic congregation, whose zeal and liberality may be estimated from the fact that it has cost about 2,000l., the greatest portion of which was supplied from their own narrow resources.

In an honest compatriot, Peter C——, to whom I speedily became known, I saw the type of the true-hearted Irishman, who not only maintained the character of his faith by his own conduct, but would make any sacrifice for the honour of his church.

Peter, commencing with little indeed, had worked his way with resolute energy, and was then a prosperous man, with something laid by for the rainy day. The new church, which the Archbishop was to consecrate in a few days after my departure, was the delight of Peter's heart; and from Peter I heard how grandly the little congregation responded to the appeal of their pastor, who, his Glengarry blood notwithstanding, had the face of a Spanish saint. Peter gloried in the site, at once beautiful and commanding—in the solid well-made bricks, and the manner in which they were laid—in the buttresses, which he patted with a caressing hand, as if he were encouraging them to do their duty faithfully; but, above all, in the steeple, which could be seen far and wide, 'I collected 100l. myself from Protestants for it; and what is more, they helped to clear the foundations, which was done in a single day. 'Tis the blessed truth I'm telling you,' said my friend Peter, with emphatic triumph.

Peter, like all sober and steady Irishmen whom I have met with in America, had a keen relish for 'real estate,' and being already possessed of an odd 'lot' here and there, he had his eye on other bits in convenient sites,—I shall not say where, as in that case I should be deliberately violating the promise of strict secrecy imposed on me as the condition of his unreserved confidence. I trust Peter will have gratified the object of his honest ambition before these pages reach Pictou; but if not, he may feel sure that the identical 'bits' will never be even indicated by me either to friend or foe.

Among the lions—the live lions—of Pictou to whom I was duly introduced by Peter, was the American Consul, and a most agreeable lion he proved to be; courteous and kindly, as all true American gentlemen are. The Major, for such was his rank, evidently held Peter in high esteem, and Peter repaid the Major's good opinion of him with liberal interest. Peter had previously held out to me the hope, based indeed on his own confident belief, that the Major would be good enough to favour me with an inspection of the many strange and curious things which he had collected, and which had more than once excited Peter's unaffected amazement. I was of course humbly hopeful that, through my friend's influence, I should be deemed worthy of so great a favour, though possessing only the questionable claim of a stranger and a traveller. The introduction effected, the application, made with modest boldness by Peter, met with instant success. 'Didn't I tell you how it would be?' whispered Peter, as we stood in the presence of the accumulated wonders. A nod, which eloquently expressed 'You did, sure enough,' was received by Peter as a satisfactory reply. The collection was really interesting, embracing many natural curiosities, including fossils, shells, minerals, reptiles, animals, birds, fishes, teeth of extinct animals, implements of savage warfare, evidences of bygone civilisation, and a variety of other matters.

All these wonders were explained and rendered intelligible to his visitors by the Major, who favoured us with a sufficient account of each. Peter's genuine admiration as he listened to the Consul, and then glanced at me, as if to witness the effect produced on my mind by the tooth of the megatherium, or the fossil with the impression of a plant, a shell, or a reptile, was every moment becoming warmer and more explosive. His 'Oh, Major!' grew more and more enthusiastic; but when the owner of the treasures exhibited in glass jars the various products derived from a particular description of coal, and Peter was assured that all those beautiful colours were produced by chemical action from a lump of coal such as he held in his hand, his 'Oh, Major!' was largely tinged with awe. He frankly declared that he had never seen the like in all his life, and was profuse in his acknowledgments for the kindness which, at his influential request, had been conferred on his friend, my unworthy self. The Major pleasingly varied the intellectual treat with refreshment of more material kind, to which neither Peter nor his companion proved insensible.

Under Peter's competent guidance, I sauntered through the town and rambled along the shore, and, with Peter as my companion, I sat on a piece of timber within a few feet of the water, which murmured in the tiniest wavelets on the beach, scarcely moved by the soft air of the Indian Summer, that harmonised deliciously with the exquisite colour of the sky, in which grey and blue were blended into an indescribable tint of loveliness; and while the sea murmured as it kissed the beach, and the soft air brought with it a sense of mental repose, I listened to Peter, who told of his trials and difficulties bravely met and manfully overcome, and gave me the benefit of his shrewdly expressed opinions on his race, their many virtues, their few but dangerous defects. 'This is a fine country for any man that's inclined to work, and able to work, and it's a man's own fault if he won't get along, and be respected, no matter who or what he is; but it's a bitter bad place for the drunkard anyhow, whether there is a good place for him in any country, which I am not sure there is,' added Peter doubtingly. Peter had an eye for the picturesque and beautiful as well as for choice bits of real estate, and was fond of the views to be seen from various points. Seated in Peter's comfortable 'trap,' gallantly bowled along by his well-trained and vigorous horse 'Charley,' I enjoyed many charming pictures of land and water, enhanced not a little by my companion's intelligent comments on men and things.

Peter insisted that I should not think of leaving Pictou without visiting what he held to be one of the wonders of the world—the mines at New Glasgow, at the other side of the harbour; and having nothing better to do, I closed with his offer to accompany me in my first subterranean adventure. So up at six, breakfast at seven, on board at eight, at New Glasgow in an hour after, and then on to the mines. As we crossed the harbour, Peter's glance rested lovingly on the red-brick church, the gleaming windows, the tall spire, and the glittering cross. 'Well, surely, it does look beautiful, out and out; and only to think how few of us there were to do it! Glory be to the Lord! It seems wonderful,' said Peter.

Arrived at the Albion Mine, permission to visit which had been previously obtained, Peter and I assumed the requisite but unbecoming costume, and were in rapid yet easy descent, under the cautious guidance of the head banksman, an Irishman from Wexford. To one who goes down into a mine for the first time, the aspect of everything in a quite new world is necessarily strange, and even startling. The meteoric lights, the long and murky galleries, the lofty chambers faintly illumined and replete with dense shadows, the rattle of the cars, the cries of the drivers, the stroke of the pick, and the other noises of a coal mine in active work—all produce for the moment a bewildering effect. Below as well as above were Irishmen employed in every capacity, the majority engaged in the ordinary manual labour, but not a few entrusted with positions of responsibility, or employed in work of a higher class.

The manager, Mr. Hudson, spoke of them in terms of praise, as steady, industrious, sober, and trustworthy. 'There is a man,' said the manager, 'who came here a labourer; he has charge of property worth several thousand pounds. If he was not a good man, he would not be in that position. That man, like many more of his countrymen, has brought up a family with great care; and the young people are now profitably employed, some as engineers, some in other skilled branches.' Go in what direction I might, I met with a countryman. To an emigrant of eighteen years back I imparted the latest tidings from Dunmanway, in Cork county; to a 'boy' of thirty from Connemara I was able to communicate the agreeable intelligence that his old Parish Priest was 'alive and hearty,' which was received with 'more of that to him!' and on assuring another 'boy,' not long from 'sweet Tipperary,' that the 'members stood by the people in Parliament,' he prayed 'that the Lord might strengthen their endeavours, for, faith, the poor people wanted friends, sure enough.' The Irish took great pride in the celebrity of the mine, and the amazing depth of its working seam, over 44 feet; which was to be 'shown to the world' at the Paris Exhibition by the pillar, 37 feet 10 inches in height, which was hewed from this magnificent bed of coal. They were as proud of that pillar as if they were the owners of the mine.

Owing to the increasing number of Catholics at the mines—for there are several others, including the Albion and the Acadian, the latter the property of an American company—an addition was being made to the Catholic Church, which is conveniently and conspicuously placed: nor is it improbable that, in a few years hence, when this mining parish is more perfectly organised, a fine building of brick and stone will replace the neat structure now barely sufficient for its congregation.

In the presence of Peter, and much to the delight of that enthusiastic Irishman, a Scotch gentleman gave an admirable account of our countrymen. Peter glanced at me with a look of radiant triumph, and demanded, in a manner at once corroborative and clinching—'Didn't I tell you, sir, there wasn't a single blackguard amongst the entire of them?' And Peter might well speak with authority, for he knew or was known to nearly every man in the district.

Peter was anxious that I should pay a visit of courtesy to a friend of his in Pictou, but appeared to be somewhat doubtful as to my compliance with his wishes. 'To tell you the truth,' said Peter, with an air of no little mystery, as we were again crossing the harbour, 'he is an Orangeman, or something of that kind, anyhow; but he's from your own part, and I know he'd be glad to see you—indeed he let me learn as much from himself. 'Tis true, he's not one of ourselves, but he's a mighty decent honest man still.' Much relieved by the genuine readiness I expressed to meet 'the Orangeman, but a mighty decent honest man,' our return trip was rendered additionally pleasant to Peter, who enjoyed the appearance of the church on the hill-side with more than usual satisfaction. I paid the promised visit to the sturdy Protestant from Bandon; and not even from Peter himself could I receive a more cordial welcome than from the former inhabitant of that famous borough. The whole family, parents and children—the latter intelligent and nicely reared—were glad to see one from the old country. This 'Orangeman, but mighty decent honest man,' brought with him but his industry and skill as a boot-maker; but being steady, sober, and honest, he was doing an excellent business, and employing several hands. His neat drawing-room, with its piano and pile of music, bore the most pleasing testimony to the comfort and taste of the family.

One other visit I made under the auspices of my friend Peter. That was to the Poor-house, which offered a remarkable contrast to similar institutions at home. It contained *four inmates*! who formed quite a cosy family party, and seemed to take the world and all its troubles, including the vexed question of Confederation, with philosophical indifference, or, as Peter expressed it, 'mighty easy.' A fair percentage of such poor-houses would constitute an agreeable variety in Ireland. The snug family party of four spoke well for the material condition of this part of Nova Scotia; and if it did not prove the existence of great commercial activity, it at least indicated the absence of real poverty.

At a late hour at night I went on board the steamer for Charlottetown, Prince Edward Island, and the last hand I clasped ere I bade adieu to Pictou, was that of Peter C——, who, if allowed to have his own way, would have placed his 'particular friend' in charge of everybody in the ship, from the captain to the captain's 'boy.' Indeed, so considerate was Peter, that, had I only consented to the process, I believe he would have had me labelled as well as my baggage. In the last moment I voluntarily renewed my promise, that I would not disclose to mortal man the slightest information as to the 'bits of ground' upon which Peter had reposed his speculative eye.

Of Nova Scotia, as a home for the emigrant, it is necessary to write in guarded terms. It has the power of absorbing a considerable amount of labour, skilled and unskilled; but it is not, like other of the British colonies, or the States, capable of withstanding a rush. There was a want of labour in Halifax in the autumn of 1866; and in other parts of the province an addition to the labour supply would have been hailed with satisfaction. Nova Scotia does not present the same inducements to the settler that are offered in New Brunswick or Western Canada; still, there is land, even cultivated land, always to be had at reasonable prices. There seems to be a habit of change common to humanity generally at the Western side of the Atlantic. This does not arise either from caprice or unsteadiness, but from a *desire to do better*; in fact, to take advantage of opportunities which a new and yet undeveloped country constantly offers to the enterprising and adventurous. Thus the man who has cleared a farm—literally hewed it out of the forest, hears of something likely to suit him better, and he does not long hesitate about putting his farm in the market, and selling it at a fair price. Or his sons, yielding to the spirit of adventure so common to the youth of the country, have gone to sea, or migrated to Canada or the States, and the father has thus lost the physical means of working his land; and he also sells, in order to realise his capital, and perhaps go into some other business. Thus, by this constant process of change, the path is opened to the new comer, who has only to save a little money, bide his time, and seize the wished-for opportunity of becoming the proprietor of so much land in fee-simple, to have and to hold for ever.

The tendency of the young people, not of Nova Scotia alone, but of most of the British colonies, is to push on to the States. Better employment—perhaps more nominal than real—and a wider field for their energies, appear to be the inducements that lure adventurous youth from the natural attractions of home.

CHAPTER II

Prince Edward Island—How the Irish came—Visit to an Irish Settlement—
Prosperity of the Irish—A Justice of the Peace—The Land Question—What the
Tenant claims—The Tenant League and the Government—'Confiscation'
profitable to the Government, and beneficial to the People—A Scotch Bishop's
Testimony to the Irish—The Irish and their Pastors—The Sisters of Notre Dame—
A graceful Gift.

ONE of the smallest, certainly not the least interesting, of the British colonies of North America is that of Prince Edward Island. Though not exceeding in superficial area the size of an ordinary Irish county, and actually not more than two-thirds that of the county of Cork, with a population not greater than that of the city of Cork, this beautiful little island enjoys the advantages of free representative institutions, and a system of government based upon popular suffrage and amenable to popular control. The authority of the Crown is represented by a Lieutenant-Governor; while in the House of Assembly the leading parties into which the political world of the colony is divided have their recognised leaders and accredited organs. To such an extent is this carried, that the gentleman to whom the party out of office delegates, either formally or by tacit assent, the privilege of speaking in its name, is described in the 'Parliamentary Reporter' (the 'Hansard' of Prince Edward Island), and referred to in debate, as 'the Leader of the Opposition'—the Gladstone or the Disraeli of the colony. It is not, however, with the institutions of the island this work has to do; but this bare allusion to the form of government which its inhabitants enjoy will be found necessary when noticing a movement of rather an important character, fraught with consequences of no small moment to the future of a people whose main resource lies in the produce of their fertile soil.

To the general population of Prince Edward Island the Irish bear a considerable proportion; and not only are they to be found in the principal towns, and scattered over the face of the island, mixed up with the other nationalities—French, Scotch, and English—of which the population is composed, but they form settlements of their own, exclusively Irish in race and Catholic in creed.

People rarely migrate to a strange country, and face the hardships incidental to a new existence, from the mere love of change; nor do the comfortable and the well-to-do usually quit their agreeable homes from a spirit of adventure. Necessity is the grand stimulus which impels the European to sever with rude hand his old ties of home and kindred, and quit his native land to cross the ocean in search of a new home. Of all people in the world the Irish are—rather were—most intensely, even passionately, attached to the land of their birth, and the least willing to leave it for another country, whatever its attractions. But the mass of the Irish who quitted the shores of the old country had no choice left them: what the process of law, too often accompanied with the pomp and parade of armed force, but partially effected, was accomplished by the resistless influence of blight, famine, and pestilence These were the chief impelling causes of that rush across the ocean which has been one of the most extraordinary phenomena of the present century, and which may yet bring about events well worthy of the gravest consideration of the patriot and the statesman.

A wave of this tide of human life broke upon the shores of Prince Edward Island, over whose fair and fertile bosom were scattered thousands of men and women, the majority of them poor, pinched with hunger, scantily clad; but hardy, patient, enduring, and willing to toil. A few, a very few, brought with them a little capital, perhaps half a dozen pounds, probably not more than as many dollars; whereas the majority had scarcely sufficient to purchase their first meal on landing. 'For one who has come out with a dollar, ten have come out with a shilling,' says the estimable Bishop of Charlottetown, Dr. McIntyre, a mild and genial Scotchman, who loves and is loved by his Irish flock. Many of those who thus commenced had been flung on shore from fever-infected emigrant ships in the time of the Irish Famine, and, scattering: over the island, had worked their way by honest labour to the position of independent settlers, even owners in fee of the farms they now occupy.

Wishing to see for myself one or two of the Irish settlements, so as to form a more correct estimate of the actual position of my countrymen in their new home, I readily availed myself of the kindness of one of the shrewdest and ablest of the merchants of Charlottetown—whose capital, when he arrived from Ireland, consisted of a good practical education, keen intelligence, and high principle, and who is now admitted to be one of the ablest and most prosperous among the business men of the island. Through his kindness I was enabled to arrive at a satisfactory conclusion on a subject which to me was one of the deepest interest. From a very early hour in the morning to the dusk of the evening—with the aid of a strong horse, a light vehicle, and a well-informed guide, who knew every inch of the road, and was acquainted with almost every person whom we met during our prolonged tour—I was engaged in visiting and inspecting two Irish settlements, occasionally entering a farm-house, or field in which the work of harvesting was still going on, and speaking with its hospitable and industrious owner. Confining myself to a single settlement—that of Monaghan—I shall state the result of my observations.

The Monaghan settlers, to use the expression of one who knew them well, 'had not a sixpence in their pockets when they landed.' But they took 'green-wood farms,' or tracts of land entirely covered with forest, not a rood of which was cleared when they entered into their occupation. Selecting the most convenient position for his future home, the adventurous settler erected his little log cabin, and having secured that shelter for himself, and perhaps for his family, he commenced to chop away at the trees which overshadowed his lowly dwelling, until the semblance of a field—rather an opening in the forest studded with tree stumps—rewarded his industry, and stimulated him to still greater efforts.

By working occasionally for the nearest farmers, the settlers were enabled to purchase provisions and other necessaries during the first months of their arduous struggle. The next year they burned the timber which they had previously cut down, and used their ashes for manure, and round the stumps of what had been monarchs of the forest, they planted their first crop of potatoes; the following year wheat was added to their harvest, and in a few years they began to have a farm—not, it is true, without hard work, and, occasionally, bitter privation; but the prize—glorious independence—was well worth contending for, while its possession amply compensated for toil and hardship of every kind. These same men who, as a rule, began 'without a sixpence in their pockets,' were then in the possession of 100 acres of land each, with from 50 to 70 acres cleared—much of the land not exhibiting the faintest trace of a tree having ever grown upon it, while the recently cleared portion and the still living forest showed that the island had not long before worn one prevailing livery of green, only varied in shade by the character of the timber and the nature of its foliage. The Monaghan settlers had long since passed the log-cabin stage, and were occupying substantial and commodious frame houses, with suitable offices; and most of them—these Irishmen, who had begun the fight 'without a sixpence in their pocket'—had brought up their families with care and in respectability, could drive to church on Sunday in a well-appointed wagon, with a good horse, or a pair of good horses, and probably had what they would call 'a little money' laid by in the bank.

As a rule, admitting of only a rare exception, I did not for the entire day—during a circuit of nearly sixty miles —see a single habitation that was not decent in appearance or that did not evince an air of neatness and comfort. All were constructed of timber; but they were well glazed, well roofed, and kept as white and clean as lime or paint could render them. We must have seen hundreds of farm-houses during our ten hours' tour; and I can safely assert I did not perceive more than half a dozen which betrayed indications of poverty, or which exhibited an appearance of squalor; and these latter, I am happy to say, were not occupied by the Irish. Substantial comfort was the prevailing characteristic of dwelling and farm building; and cattle and horses and sheep grazed upon broad acres from which the stumps had been lately cleared. And where the forest no longer offered a shelter to the house, or a background to the picture of rural comfort, a cluster of trees, judiciously spared from the levelling axe, or deliberately planted, afforded a pleasing variety to the eye. It too frequently happens in countries which have been recently reclaimed from the wilderness of the forest, war is so relentlessly waged against trees of every kind, which, so long as they interfere with the free use of the plough, are simply regarded as a nuisance, that an air of barrenness, even of desolation, is imparted to the landscapes; and after the lapse of some time, the farmer, whether repenting his desolating vigour, or longing for the shade or shelter of the tree, plants round his dwelling, or the enclosure in which it stands, those beautiful objects, which add a charm and a beauty to the abode of man.

There are people at home who regard the position of the farmer who is without 'capital' as desperate. With them capital—their capital, which is always money— is the one thing necessary, and without which all else is worthless. It were well if these narrow-minded philosophers had an opportunity of estimating at its right value the greatest, the grandest capital of which man could be possessed, especially in a new country, in which nothing has been done, and in which everything is yet to be done. Here is the green forest, the home of the squirrel or the wild cat. For the purposes of human life, of man's enjoyment, that green forest is unavailing. Without the labour of man not all the money in Threadneedle Street or Wall Street will suffice to convert that verdant wilderness into pasture or arable land. The energy, the industry, the endurance of man—of the penniless, or it may be the despised, emigrant, —these are worth any number of millions of money. Lack these, and silver and gold are as worthless as dross, as valueless as if they lay in the depths of the mine, or were still incorporated with their rocky matrix. Those Irish emigrants who landed in Prince Edward Island forty, thirty, or twenty years since, had to go into the forest and fight their way, rood by rood, acre by acre, and win their daily bread by ceaseless labour, until field was added to field, and the encircling forest was driven back by the resistless force of human energy—by the power of the same God-giving capital which is as capable of making the old country—the natural home of that hardy, patient, and laborious race—bloom like a garden, as it is of hewing abundance, beauty, and civilisation out of the wilderness in other lands.

In no one proof of progress or evidence of solid and substantial comfort were the Irish settlers behind their Scotch or English or native-born neighbours. Their land was in as good condition, there was as great activity in clearing, their cattle were as numerous and as valuable, their hay and their potatoes were as good and as abundant; there was not even the suspicion of inferiority in any respect whatever, whether of capacity or in success.

I had the satisfaction of seeing the interior of several of the dwellings of my countrymen—men who were indebted wholly to their industry and energy for all that they possessed; and the interior in no way belied the promise of the exterior. Homely comfort was the prevailing characteristic. In Ireland these men would be described as 'warm farmers,' or 'strong farmers.' Not a few of them had bought the fee-simple of their farms at a moderate price, and they then held them by a title as good as that by which Queen Victoria holds her crown. Were there nothing in the name or in the manner of the settler to denote his origin, the little library—the dozen or twenty of Irish books—stirring prose or passionate poetry —would be evidence sufficient of his nationality. The wrongs, the sorrows, the ancient glories, the future hopes of Ireland—these are the most acceptable themes to the expatriated children of the Irish race.

There was life and bustle in every direction, the farmers being hard at work getting in their potatoes, which were large and perfectly sound; and in this agreeable work men and women were actively engaged.

'Come,' said my companion, 'let us look in upon a friend of mine, who by the way is from your part of the country. He is a justice of the peace too.'

Passing through a spacious enclosure we arrived at the house, a well-built, comfortable-looking dwelling, where we found the wife of its owner, a comely kindly matron, with all the natural courtesy of her country. To the enquiry 'Where was himself?' she replied that he was 'out with the boys, getting in the potatoes.' We proceeded in search of the master of the house, and had not gone far when we saw a sturdy strong-built man of middle age leading a strong horse with a cart-load of potatoes, full-sized and of healthy purple hue. He was one of the many thousands of his countrymen who landed on the shores of America without a pound in their possession. Like them, his capital consisted in his strength, his intelligence, and his capacity for labour; and so successfully had he employed his capital that, as he was leading his horse into his spacious farm-yard that day, he was an independent man, not owing a shilling in the world, and having a round sum in the bank. Rubbing his clay-covered hands in a little straw, and giving them a final touch on the sleeve of his working coat, he favoured me with a vigorous grasp, such as would have crippled the fingers of a fine gentleman; then, after having offered us a hearty welcome, and a cordial invitation to partake of his hospitality, he fondly enquired after the dear old country. He was greatly 'put out' when he learned that we could not stop—that we had to return to Charlottetown before night set in. 'Not stop! Oh, that's too bad entirely! Not take pot luck! not even wet your mouth '. Oh my! oh my! that's hard! Well now, I'm ashamed of you to treat a man so.' But go we should; not, however, before the brief story of his early struggles and their crowning success was had from his own lips.

What a contrast did his air and manner offer to that of the Irish farmer in one particular—in its manly independence of bearing. At home, the tenant is not—at least in too many instances is not—certain of his tenure, of his possession or occupancy of the land which he cultivates, and for which he pays a rent that is absolutely incredible to the farmer of Prince Edward Island—indeed of America throughout; and manly bearing and independence of spirit are scarcely to be expected in his case: possibly any special manifestation of their existence might not be prudent or beneficial. Quite otherwise with his countryman in this little colony, who cannot be disturbed in his possession of his farm so long as he pays the rent—about tenpence per British acre; or who has bought it out, and feels that he stands upon his own property, of which he is the undisputed owner: therefore, while clad in his homely working suit, with the red soil sticking to his strong shoes, and his hands rough with honest toil, he looks at you, and speaks to you, as a man should address his fellow-man, with modest dignity and self-respect.

Strange that in this, one of the smallest of British colonies, very grave and important problems, involving the most cherished of the so-called 'rights of property,' should be practically solved in a manner not only in accordance with the universal public sentiment, but with the sanction of the representatives alike of the people and the Crown.

From the days of the Gracchi to the present hour, the land question—the occupancy or possession of the soil—has been a fruitful source of turmoil and embarrassment. It was so in ancient Rome; it was one of the causes of the most tremendous social convulsions of modern times; and, because of the deep interests it involved, it is destined to play a conspicuous part in popular movements in favour of fundamental changes. Leaving the shores of Ireland, where the land question is the one which most stirs the heart of its people, I cross the Atlantic, and reach a small island of which not very many in the old country have ever heard; and, to my amazement, I find this irrepressible land question *the* question of the colony, though for the moment absorbed in the more immediate and pressing topics of Confederation or Non-Confederation. I had supposed that a 'Tenant League' was one of those things of which I had probably heard the last, at least for some time to come; but I learn with no little surprise that the most troublesome movement, or organisation, which Prince Edward Island had witnessed within recent years was known by that title, and that its origin was owing to a systematic opposition to the payment of rent.

The Irish demand, during the existence of its Tenant League, never went beyond 'fixity of tenure,' possession of the land by the tenant so long as he fulfilled his primary obligation of paying his stipulated rent.

Struck by the similarity of the name, I enquired of an intelligent friend what were the exact objects of the colonial organisation.

'Oh,' replied my friend, 'it was a combination to get rid of rent: the people here don't like the notion of paying rent; they are not satisfied until they have the land in their own possession.' The answer was calculated to put my moderate opinions to the blush.

'Then I suppose the rents are rather oppressive? What are they on the average?'

'As for that, the rent is but a shilling an acre.'

'A what?' said I.

'A shilling an acre—yes, a shilling an acre,' was the tranquil reply, made as much in answer to my stare of astonishment as to the exclamation with which it was accompanied.

'Why how, in the name of common sense, could anyone object to such a rent as that—a rent inconceivably small to one coming from a country where the rent per acre is twenty times, thirty times, even fifty times, nay, in some instances, nearly one hundred times greater?'

'Well, as compared to rents in the old country, it is no doubt low; but you see the tenants took the land in its wilderness state, and they had to do everything to it to make it what it now is. And the rent, small as it may appear to you—5l. the 100 acres—comes heavy enough; and when there are arrears falling due besides, it is a serious thing, I can tell you. But small or large, our people have an aversion to paying rent; they want to have the land *their own*, and they are willing to pay a fair price for it too.'

A shilling an acre! I could scarcely realise to my mind the idea of this being a burden, or its payment a grievance; still to many the burden was felt to be intolerable, and the grievance one of real magnitude. And, as the strangest confirmation of the existence of this feeling, there is the policy of the leading public men of the colony, which is to free the actual cultivators from the obligation of rent-paying, by converting the occupying tenant into a fee-simple proprietor. Already much had been done in pursuance of this popular policy. Extensive properties—mostly held by absentees—had been purchased by the State, and resold to the occupiers on easy terms, ranging from 5s. to 10s. or 12s. per acre. The last great property thus purchased by the Government, with the view of being resold, belonged to the representatives of the late Sir Samuel Cunard. It consisted of 212,000 acres, partly reclaimed and partly in the wilderness state, and was sold for 53,000l. British money; the purchase money including a considerable sum in arrears, generously flung into the bargain, or indeed practically given up. There being no difference of opinion with respect to the *policy* of converting tenancy into fee-simple proprietorship, and the only dispute being as to the best or speediest mode by which this conversion can be accomplished, it is probable that a short time will be sufficient to bring about a satisfactory solution of the 'difficulty' which has its origin in the Land Question of Prince Edward Island.

If the claim to be released from the obligation of paying rent could in any case be regarded as fair and equitable, it would be so when urged by the cultivators of Prince Edward Island; as it was they, and they alone, who by their labour changed the whole face of the country, redeeming it from the forest which at no distant time covered the land from shore to shore. About one hundred years ago the island was parcelled out to about as many proprietors, on certain specified conditions, the principal of which was, to procure settlers, with a view to the cultivation of the soil and the population of the colony, and also to pay quit-rent to the Crown. These obligations, the conditions on which the estates were originally granted, were generally disregarded to such an extent, indeed, were they disregarded, that some forfeitures were made, and these forfeitures would have been extensively enforced had not the defaulting proprietors sufficient influence with the Home Government to retain their property, notwithstanding that they had failed in many and flagrant instances to redeem their part of the original compact. So little was done in the way of obtaining settlers, that at the commencement of the present century the population of the whole island did not exceed 6,000 souls; and it was not until the year 1830-35 that any extensive emigration from the United Kingdom took place. In 1832 the population was 32,000; it was 80,552 by the last census; and in 1866 it was rather triumphantly estimated at or near 90,000.

About two years since the anti-rent feeling resolved itself into an active organisation, having its centre in Charlottetown, the capital and seat of government. Who were its leaders, or by whom it was originated, is of little consequence to know. I have heard it stated that the Irish were not among its active promoters in the first instance, the English and Scotch settlers taking the lead. But the Irish were soon drawn into the League, as they sympathised heartily with its object, which was not so much to abolish the payment of rent, as to compel the proprietors to sell their estates on fair terms. Passive resistance was eventually adopted in certain districts, the representatives of the civil power being coolly set at defiance, or rather laughed at by the sturdy colonists. Seeing the inability of the civil force to cope with what a prosecuting crown lawyer would describe as 'a conspiracy against property at once wide-spread and formidable,' it was deemed advisable to send to the mainland for two companies of infantry, there not then being a single soldier in the colony. Backed by this armed force, the law was vindicated, a few individuals being made the victims of their bold resistance, or legal indiscretion. The Tenant League came to an end; but as proof that the feeling in which it had its origin was still potent, inasmuch as it really represented the universal sentiment of the colony, an extract or two from the public records may be useful.

On the 9th of April, 1866, the Lieutenant-Governor, when opening the legislative session, used these words in his 'speech:'—

The general prosperity of the past year has been marred by the civil disturbances which took place in several parts of this colony. Misled by ignorant or designing men, tenants were induced to form themselves into an association with the avowed intention of withholding payment of their rents, unless their landlords consented to sell their lands on such terms as this association chose to dictate.

The law was openly and systematically set at defiance, and it became necessary to use extraordinary measures to enforce it. A requisition was therefore made for a detachment of her Majesty's troops, to aid the civil power, and the authority of the law has been firmly and impartially maintained.

But, as if to show that the popular demand was not devoid of reason and justice, his Excellency made the following important announcement:—

'I *have recently concluded the purchase of another estate from one of the proprietors. It is my intention to continue to buy out the rights of the landowners, whenever I am enabled to do so on reasonable terms.*'

And on the 11th of May, when the short session was formally closed, the representative of the Crown thus proclaimed the triumph, if not of the League, at least of the popular demand:—

Mr. Speaker and Gentlemen of the House of Assembly:

'The measure by which you have extended my powers of purchasing land, *has my hearty concurrence*; and I trust that, under its provisions, *I may be enabled to purchase large estates from the proprietors.*'

In the 'debate on the address' many things were said on both sides of the House which would have been in the last degree startling if uttered in the senate-chamber of the mother country. A few extracts will suffice.

First from the Hon. Mr. Coles, the Leader of the Opposition, who, referring to a proposition made by the late Duke of Newcastle, as Colonial Minister, says:—

The Duke's own proposals, however, ought to have satisfied the Government. His scheme was that if a tenant had regularly paid his rent, under his lease, for 16 years, he should be entitled to the freehold of his farm at 16 years' purchase; if for 10 years, for 10 years' purchase; and if for 8 years, for 8 years' purchase; that was according to the actual interest which the proprietor had in the leasehold, as evidenced by the amount of rent which he had received on account of it. At the time it was submitted he thought the scheme was a fair one, and he thought so still; but our Government thought otherwise, rejected it, and brought forward and carried their Fifteen Years' Purchase Bill.

The Solicitor-General, the official organ of the Government, defends the Fifteen Years' Purchase Bill, which, though derided for its shortcomings by the Leader of the Opposition, would be regarded in the British House of Commons as a measure of sweeping confiscation worthy of the French Revolution, or the days of Jack Cade. That learned gentleman says :—

In every Session of the Legislature since the passage of the Fifteen Years' Purchase Bill have the Opposition assailed the Government, on the assumed grounds that that Bill was no boon to the tenantry, was unacceptable to a majority of them, and could not by any possibility be made advantageous to them. He, however, confidently maintained that the Bill was a handsome instalment of all the benefits promised to the tenantry, by the party in power, through legislative action with respect to the Land Question. By means of it *large arrears of rent have been expunged from the books of proprietors, and declared irrecoverable, as against all tenants who shall avail themselves of the provisions of the Bill for the purchase of the fee-simple of their farms.* Whilst the tenants' improvements were in existence they were a sufficient security for the recovery of all arrears of rent. On one-third of Lot 34, the property of Sir E. Cunard. the tenants, by having availed themselves of the advantages extended to them by that Bill, had had over 1,000l. of arrears wiped off, every farthing of which could have been recovered by the proprietor, because the tenants were, in reality, men of wealth. It was the same on the Sullivan property. There were many tenants upon the estates affected by the Fifteen Years' Purchase Bill, to whom, before the passing of it the proprietors would not consent to sell the fee-simple of their farms even at 20s. or 30s. per acre; but those proprietors were now compelled to part with the fee-simple of their leased lands at 15 years' purchase.

With the following passage from the speech of the Hon. J. C. Pope, who must be described as the Prime Minister of this sufficiently-governed colony, these extracts may be closed. Nor is it the least significant of the entire. He shows that the purchase and re-sale of the great properties has been a paying speculation for the Government; and he adds his official testimony to the universality of the feeling in favour of the conversion of tenancies into fee-simple—or, as he emphatically expresses it, 'the freeing of the country from the burden of the leasehold or rent-paying system.'

'Nearly all the money which the Conservatives have expended in the purchase of proprietary estates has been refunded. *Every estate which we have bought has proved a paying speculation. We have had a profit upon every one of them. I think the Government will be justified in purchasing all the estates they can, and carrying on, as quickly as possible, the freeing of the country from the burden of the leasehold or rent-paying system*; and whether I may be in the Government or out of it, I will do all in my power to bring about so desirable a consummation.'

So much for the Land Question of the British Colony of Prince Edward Island, which Sir Bulwer Lytton was as anxious to settle on satisfactory terms to the colonists as was the Duke of Newcastle. To statesmen who recoil with dismay from the least invasion of the ' rights of property' it may afford matter for useful reflection.

Before dismissing the subject, I may add, on the authority of men of all parties, classes, and positions, that not only are the Irish amongst the most thrifty, energetic, and improving of the agricultural population, but they are remarkable for their punctuality as rent-payers. I had no opportunity of visiting more than two of the settlements exclusively Irish; but I was generally assured that the other Irish settlements were in every respect equal to those I had seen.

While I was in the island, an Irishman, who had not many years before come out as a labourer, sold a farm for 1,000l., retaining another worth double that amount. 'I came out here with little in my pocket,' said an Irishman from Munster, from the borders of Cork and Tipperary, 'and I thank God I am now worth over 2,000l.' This was said, not boastingly, but in gratitude to Providence for the blessing which had attended his humble industry. 'I had nothing to depend on but God and my own four bones,' said another successful Irishman to me in Prince Edward Island; and this form of phrase, so expressive of self-reliance and trust in the Divine assistance, I heard repeated by men of the same persevering and pious race throughout the United States and the British Colonies. 'I had no one but God to help me,' is a common expression with the Irish everywhere.

The sums mentioned as the results of honest industry, and self-reliance of the most elevated character, though respectable in amount, by no means indicate the position obtained by many Irishmen in the colony. There are instances of success in trade to which the possession of a couple of thousand pounds would be but a small affair indeed. However, the moderate success and modest independence of a considerable number in a community is far more indicative of general prosperity than the extraordinary success and the large possessions of a few; and it is satisfactory to know that the generally good position of the Irish in this small colony is not only a fact well established, but that it is admitted to be the result of integrity, intelligence, and good conduct.

The testimony of their Scotch Bishop is not to be overlooked; it is honouring to them and to him:

'They, the Irish, are a thrifty, industrious, energetic class of people, of a perseverance that would be worthy of imitation. They keep pace in all respects—in intelligence and education, in comfort and independence—with all other settlers.

As for the Irish girls, there could not be a more modest, chaste, and well-conducted class than the Catholics of the town and country. A cause of scandal is of the very rarest occurrence among them.

The Irish are economical when they settle down on the land. They live poorly at first, then save money, and acquire property where they can.

What they are they have made themselves. For one who came out with a dollar, ten have come out with a shilling.'

And testimony such as the foregoing is, to my knowledge, not without the highest official sanction in the colony.

The spiritual provision for the Catholic population of the island, now estimated at 40,000—French, Scotch, and Irish—is steadily on the increase. There are 42 churches and 18 priests, besides three convents of nuns, having the care of academies and schools, in which the children are carefully instructed in their faith.

Two buildings in Charlottetown attest more eloquently than words the history and progress of the Catholic Church in the colony. The one, now used as a school, denotes, by certain lines on its roof, that it had been more than once enlarged while used as the only church for Catholic worship in the capital—in fact, the cathedral. The other is the existing cathedral, a handsome and imposing structure, furnished with a valuable organ, and capable of accommodating the Catholics of the town, in number about 2,500, who, with but a few exceptions, are Irish, or their descendants of the first generation.

To the French, of whom some were the Acadians who had been so ruthlessly banished from their home in Nova Scotia, was the gift of the faith due in Prince Edward Island. Then came the Highland Scotch, strong in their fidelity to the religion of their gallant forefathers; and lastly the Irish, who brought their numbers and their zeal to swell the ranks of the Church and add to its importance and influence in the colony. The first missionary was Dr. McEachern, a Scotch priest, educated at Valadolid in Spain, who came to the island after the first Highland immigration. His was an extensive sheep-fold, and many a weary journey he had to make in looking after his widely-scattered flock. New Brunswick and Cape Breton were included within his jurisdiction, and frequently the faithful from Nova Scotia crossed the sea to seek religious consolation at his hands.

This first Bishop of Charlottetown was a man of energy and resources; for without any aid, save that which the zeal and piety of a small and much discouraged community supplied, he established a school, in which he educated two priests, who formed the nucleus of the future ecclesiastical establishment of the island, which gave eighteen priests and two bishops to the church. It having accomplished its great work, the Seminary of St. Andrews was closed; and in its place there is now an admirable institution, St. Dunstan's College, which was erected by Dr. McDonald, who devoted all his means to that praiseworthy object. This college is supplied with every modern requirement and appliance, and is under the able presidency of the Rev. Angus McDonald, a man well qualified for his important task, and whose title of 'Father Angus' is as affectionately pronounced by the most Irish of the Irish as if it were 'Father Larry' or 'Father Pat.' The Irish love their own priests; but let the priest of any nationality—English, Scotch, French, Belgian, or American—only exhibit sympathy with them, or treat them with kindness and affection, and at once he is as thoroughly 'their priest' as if he had been born on the banks of the Boyne or the Shannon. 'Father Dan' McDonald, the Vicar-General, is a striking instance of the attachment borne by an Irish congregation to a good and kindly priest; and I now the more dwell on this thorough fusion of priest and people in love and sympathy, because of having witnessed with pain and sorrow the injurious results, alike to my countrymen and to the Church, of forcing upon almost exclusively Irish congregations clergymen who, from their imperfect knowledge of the English tongue, could not for a long time make themselves understood by those over whom it was essential they should acquire a beneficial influence. This was glaringly the case in one Western diocese of the United States, where its existence was deplored to me by good men deeply devoted to their faith. But *sympathy* soon renders the most imperfect English intelligible to the affectionate Irish heart, and binds the priest to the congregation in those sacred relations which constitute the strength of the Church, and secure the safety of the flock.

A fact of which I heard, and an incident which I witnessed, will afford an idea of the vitality of the Catholic Church in Prince Edward Island, and exhibit the affectionate respect in which Irishmen in that distant colony hold those religious ladies who devote their lives to the education of the young.

At Tignish, where the Catholic element is very strong, and the Irish are in the proportion of one-third to the French, there is a beautiful church, of stone and brick, which would do credit to any city in the world; and this church was erected, at a cost of 12,000l., in the space of fourteen months! This church, as the bishop stated with just pride, 'was the spontaneous and voluntary offering of the people.' This was not the only effort recently made by the high-spirited citizens of Tignish; for in 1865 a spacious convent, 75 feet in length by 40 in depth, and three stories high, the material of brick, was erected in the same place.

Among the other conventual establishments of Prince Edward Island is a branch of the famous Congregation of Notre Dame. Besides a boarding school and day school for paying pupils, these Sisters also conduct a free school, which is at some distance from the house in which they reside. I here remarked with surprise, from its novelty to one who had just left a country in which religious distinctions are so strongly marked, that Protestants of various denominations, including those most prominent in their hostility to the Catholic Church, send their children to be instructed by the Sisters. As I passed through America, I found that this custom was almost universal. There are very grave reasons which induce parents to obtain for their children the watchful care and salutary influence of religious women, themselves models of gentleness and refinement; and whatever the natural prejudices of the parents, the desire to see their children refined, cultivated, and good, is still stronger. In some communities the motives which impel parents to prefer the teaching of 'the Sisters' are more pressing and powerful than in others; but though the most violent opposition is offered to the practice in many instances, it would appear to be generally on the increase, and even regarded as a matter of legitimate precaution on the part of those who adopt it. In Charlottetown there is no school which can in any way approach in excellence the academy of the Ladies of Notre Dame; which fact is of itself sufficient explanation of what would at first excite some surprise. The Ladies of Notre Dame are not cloistered nuns. Round for life by their vows, like other Orders, they can go about, visit, and teach in schools not under the roof of their convent.

The Sisters in Charlottetown, as I have said, teach in a free school which is not attached to their residence; and when the hard winter sets in, and the snow lies deep on the ground for months, the journey to and from the external school is not a little trying to delicate women. To provide against this inconvenience, and enable the Sisters to visit the sick, and transact their business with greater expedition and safety, the Catholics of the town presented them with an elegant close carriage and harness, all finished in the most admirable style of local workmanship; and this thoughtful present was accompanied with an address, which, written and read by an excellent Irishman (the Hon. Edward Wheelan), was a model of simplicity and brevity. The gift was received in a corresponding spirit to that in which it had its origin, and was acknowledged with graceful warmth on behalf of the gratified community. Among the deputation were such genuine Irish names as Brennan, Reddin, Connolly, Murphy, McCarron, McKenna, Wheelan, Riley, McQuaid, and Gaffney—all 'racy of the soil.'

A poor man might do much worse than turn his face to Prince Edward Island, where land can be had cheap, and where, to use the emphatic words of the Governor, 'the *farmers clamour for help*.' Here, however, as throughout the British provinces, I found the tendency of the young of both sexes was towards the United States, which offered the resistless attraction of higher wages and a wider field for individual enterprise.

CHAPTER III

Scene in the Lords—The Irish Race despaired of—The Settlement of Johnville,
New Brunswick—We enter the Settlement—The First Man and Woman—The
Second Man and Woman—Celtic Energy—Jimmy M'Allister—Mr. Reilly from
Ballyvourney—How the Man of no Capital gets along—One Cause of Success—
Mass in the Forest—Neither Rent nor 'Gale'—Other Settlements

ON a certain evening of March 1866, there was a more than usual attendance of
peers in the House of Lords; and, attracted by the subject for discussion, many
members of the Commons occupied the bar, or that portion of the gallery reserved
for their accommodation. Among the strangers who were present was the Roman
Catholic Bishop of St. John, New Brunswick, an Irishman, but for nearly forty
years a resident in that colony. Earl Grey had given notice of his intention to
submit a series of resolutions in reference to the state of Ireland; and the largeness
of the attendance was owing more to the gravity of the subject than even to the
fame of the statesman by whom it was to be introduced. With that grave and
impressive statement which belongs to the Parliamentary records of the country
this work has no concern, a little incident which occurred during its delivery being
the only justification for its mention in these pages.

Standing immediately near the stranger was a gentleman who displayed marked
courtesy to the 'American'—as the Bishop simply represented himself to be—
pointing out to him the leading peers on either side, and explaining such of the
forms and modes of procedure as were likely to be useful to one who was for the
first time witness of a debate in the Lords. In the course of his statement Earl Grey
necessarily referred to the Emigration movement, which he deplored as a great
calamity—a regret, I may remark, shared in by the wisest statesmen and truest
patriots of the day; though this annual wasting away of the strength and very life
of a nation is regarded, not merely with indifference, but with positive satisfaction,
by shallow thinkers, and false judges of the character and capability of the Irish
race.

'My dear Sir,' said the courteous neighbour of the Catholic Bishop, 'I do not at
all agree with his lordship; on the contrary, my deliberate conviction is, unless the
Irish go away of their own accord, or are got rid of in some manner or other, and
are replaced by our people—I mean the English or the Scotch—nothing good can
ever be done with that unhappy country.'

The conviction thus deliberately expressed was honestly entertained. There was
no hostility, no anger, no passion, but a deep-seated belief in the truth of the
terrible sentence thus tranquilly pronounced on a whole nation. A similar opinion
has been too frequently expressed or insinuated in the public press of England, not

perhaps so frequently of late as in former years; and, shocking as the fact may appear to be, there have not been wanting those who call themselves Irishmen to indorse this insolent slander by their unnatural verdict.

Now, if any man in that assembly could most practically and completely refute the scandalous proposition, it was the Catholic Bishop to whom, in the dusk of the evening, and while the gorgeous chamber was yet in the shadows of twilight, his courteous informant thus vouchsafed this candid opinion. That same day, a few hours before he listened to this sweeping condemnation of the Irish race, Dr. Sweeny had described to me the extraordinary success which had attended his efforts to settle the Irish on the soil of New Brunswick; and how, in the midst of the most trying difficulties, which scarcely any one in the old country could imagine, much less appreciate, the same Irish, of whom the gentleman in the House of Lords so utterly despaired, had, in an almost incredibly short space of time, won their way to rude comfort and absolute independence. In that interview I acquainted the Bishop of my intention to make a tour through the British Provinces and the States; and before we separated it was arranged that I should specially visit his latest settlement of our unjustly depreciated countrymen. The appointment made in London in the month of March was faithfully kept in New Brunswick in the month of October; and on the morning of Thursday, the 25th of that month, the Bishop and I were *en route* for the settlement, a distance of nearly 200 miles from the city of St. John.

After having passed the first evening at Frederickton, the capital of New Brunswick, where many Irish are comfortably circumstanced, and steadily increasing in wealth, and the second at Woodstock, where there is also a fair proportion of the race equally thriving, we set out at an early hour on the following morning for the settlement of Johnville, a distance of thirty-five miles, not of rail or water, but of rough road; and about noon on Saturday we were entering the forest avenue which led to the uttermost boundary on the western side. The road over which we travelled had to me all the charm of novelty, and would have appeared picturesque and striking to anyone from the old country, for it resembled rather a cutting through a vast and ancient wood than an ordinary highway.

The Bishop was, as I thought, unnecessarily enthusiastic in his praise of the new road, which, I must confess, I thought altogether fatal to personal comfort, and in the last degree trying to the safety of the springs of our vehicle, though the carriage had been specially adapted to meet such trifling contingencies as deep ruts, profound hollows, occasional chasms, with an abundant variety of watercourses roughly covered over with logs, not always matched with the nicest care. I appreciated the road from a European point of view, and as it affected my individual comfort; but the Bishop retained a vivid remembrance of the mere lumberman's track of three or four years previous, and could estimate at its right value the facility which this new highway afforded to his settlers for the transit of their produce and provisions. As we proceeded through our couple of miles of dense forest—in which the dark green of the pine and the brighter verdure of the spruce contrasted with the prevailing sombre hue of the hard wood, occasionally relieved by the bright yellow leaves of the beech, and the gleaming crimson of the frost-tinted maple—we were met by two or three of the country wagons, laden with grain, and driven by strapping young fellows, roughly but comfortably clad, their stout horses trotting briskly along the Bishop's model highway. These young men were delighted to see their good Pastor, whom they saluted with a mixture of respect and affection, and with whom they chatted with the most perfect freedom. They promised to spread far and wide the grateful intelligence that Mass would be celebrated at eight o'clock the following morning in the little chapel of the settlement.

Before we enter the Irish settlement of Johnville, it will be necessary to explain briefly its origin and the conditions under which it was established.

Deploring the tendency—the ruinous tendency—of his countrymen to congregate in masses in cities, or to 'hang about town,' as it is generally described, and being thoroughly conversant with the many evils resulting from this prevailing habit of the Irish immigrant, the Bishop of St. John determined to employ his influence to induce numbers of his people to settle on the soil, and thus, amid the simplicity and safety of a rural existence, create for themselves a happy home and an honourable independence. Availing himself of the facilities afforded by the Labour Act, he applied to the Government for tracts of unoccupied land on certain conditions, one being that he should find settlers for this land within a limited time. His first application was for 10,000 acres, which were to be occupied in twelve months. For this quantity of land settlers were found within the prescribed period. A second 10,000 acres were then applied for, and similarly occupied; and an additional 16,000 acres, also obtained by the Bishop, were yet to be occupied by those who possessed the requisite courage to face the difficulties and temporary hardships of a new existence. There were then in actual occupation 170 lots, of 100 acres each; and allowing for the settlers with families, and the young men who had not yet entered into the bonds of wedlock, the number of souls in the settlement of Johnville might be fairly estimated at 600 at the very lowest,—a terrible responsibility to the Bishop, if his influence had been unwisely used, but a triumph and a consolation to him if it had been exercised in a spirit of wisdom and humanity. Of this the reader can form a judgment from what follows.

Each settler was required by the State, as the principal condition of obtaining 100 acres of land, to give work, to the value of sixty dollars, on the public road that was to pass by his own door, and was intended for his own advantage; but while, if so inclined, he could perform this amount of work in one year, he was allowed four years for its completion. Before he could obtain the registry of his grant, somewhat analogous to a Parliamentary title in Ireland, he should be returned by the Commissioner as having executed this required amount of work, cleared five acres, built a house at least sixteen feet square, and actually settled as a resident on the land assigned to him. These conditions had been complied with, in all cases, within the four years allowed, but in most they had been satisfied in two years, and by a considerable number of the settlers in a still shorter time. When the return is made by the Commissioner, who visits the settlement once a year, the grant is then formally registered and issued, and the settler becomes the fee-simple proprietor of 100 acres of land, the property of himself and his family, and of which no power on earth can deprive him or them. Should a poor man be fortunate enough to be the father of one, or two, or more sons, of the age of eighteen or upwards, he can procure 100 acres for each of them on the same conditions; and though a large family is regarded with horror by your Malthusians of the old country, it is a blessing of inestimable value in a new country, in which human labour—that grandest of fertilisers and mightiest of civilisers—finds its true appreciation.

The first tenement which the settler in the forest contrives for himself is a camp, or shanty. It is constructed of logs rudely put together, the interstices filled up with moss, leaves, or clay, whatever can best keep out the wind and the cold; the roof consisting of the same materials, further protected by a covering of bark, eked out, it may be, with branches of the pine, the spruce, or the cedar. Warmed by a stove, or carefully prepared fireplace, the camp or shanty is considered to be a dwelling of surpassing comfort by the settler who commences his first winter in the forest. In a year or two, perhaps a longer time, the rude camp is abandoned for the more spacious and elaborately constructed log cabin, or log house; and when the settler arrives at the 'frame house' and the frame barn, he looks upon himself as having reached the climax of earthly comfort, and even the highest point of luxurious accommodation; though possibly in a few years after the frame house gives way to the substantial brick dwelling, porticoed, and pillared—the glory and delight of its hospitable owner.

Jolting and jumping over many an agreeable variety in the surface of the road, which the Bishop and I regarded with quite opposite feelings, we came to the end of our verdant avenue, and reached a little eminence crowned by a chapel of modest dimensions and unpretending architecture. From this vantage ground the first portion of the Irish settlement of Johnville opened out before us; and though, on that sharp October day, the sun but occasionally lit up the landscape with its cheerful beams, one could easily imagine how beautiful it must appear in summer, when the wide valley is filled with waving corn, varied with bright patches of potato, and the surrounding woods are clad in all the varied verdure of the living forest.

Bounded on all sides by a wall of trees, which in one direction cover a range of mountains as beautiful in their outline as those that are mirrored in the sweet waters of Killarney, an undulating plain of cleared land extends about two miles in length by a mile in breadth, dotted over with the most striking evidences of man's presence and the progress of civilisation,—comfortable dwellings, substantial and even spacious barns—horses, cattle, sheep, hogs, and poultry of all kinds, from the loud-crowing 'rooster' to the puddle-loving duck and the solemn goose. Even to the eye of an Irish farmer, the vast plain before us would have presented a rough and rather unpromising aspect, for not two acres of the many hundred already 'cleared' were yet free from the stumps of the great trees whose lofty branches had waved and moaned in the storms of ages. The road, bounded by rude log fences, and the limits of each holding marked out in the same primitive manner, and stumps a couple of feet high plentifully scattered over every field,—this at the first glance would not favourably impress the Irish farmer, to say nothing of the English Yeoman or the Scotch Lowlander; but were he to overcome his first impressions of the strangeness of all he saw, and enquire into its details, he would soon discover much to astonish and much to gratify him. The stumps, that impart so strange and rough an appearance to an early settlement, cannot be destroyed or eradicated for some years to come; yet, from the first year that the trees had been laid low by the settler's axe, abundant crops of grain and potatoes had been raised with comparatively little trouble; and large quantities of hay, priceless as winter food, had likewise borne witness to the fertility of the soil on which a constant succession of leaves had fallen and rotted through countless ages.

In the fall of 1861 the first settlers, a man and his wife—Mr. and Mrs. Hugh M'Cann—entered the forest, bringing with them provisions for the winter, and a very moderate stock of furniture and other valuables, which the prudent pair had accumulated by their industry in the city of St. John. Through a mere track, the oxen, lent by a kindly Irish family, slowly dragged after them the entire worldly wealth of this stout-hearted couple, the pioneers of the civilisation so soon to follow in their footsteps. Right in the midst of the forest—never before trodden save by the Indian, the lumberman, or the wild animal—the M'Canns settled down, resolved to brave the severity of the approaching season. The first thing to be done was to erect a log cabin, and for the rougher portion of this indispensable work the thrifty pair were able to pay; but they had to cover their dwelling by their own labour, which they did with great pieces of bark and branches torn from the trees under whose shadow they took up their abode. Here then they were, in the heart of what to them was a wilderness, more than two miles from a human habitation, and even uncertain of the way by which they could reach the outer world; their only guide being either a faint track, or an occasional mark, or scar, made on the bark of a tree. Still they were not in the least degree discouraged.

Mrs. M'Cann had pluck and cheerfulness sufficient for a more hazardous enterprise. With a good stove, and an occasional quilt or blanket, suspended on the walls as tapestry, the cold was effectually kept out, and the lonely hours made comfortable during the bitter winter. Armed with his keen axe, Hugh cut and chopped through the months while the snow covered the ground; and so resolutely did he work, that when the white mantle vanished from the earth before the warmth of the spring, the M'Canns had cleared several acres of their land; and in the autumn of 1862 they gathered in their first produce—an abundant harvest of potatoes, oats, and buckwheat. A proud woman was Mrs. Hugh M'Cann, as she did the honours of her forest home to the settlers of 1862; and prouder still as she afforded hospitality and the shelter of her warm roof to many who had yet to raise a dwelling over their heads.

I could well appreciate the brave and cheery nature of this humble Irishwoman, as the Bishop and I—after a lengthened and somewhat laborious tour through the settlement—sat before the well-replenished stove which had so often warmed the limbs of the wayfarer, and smiled its ruddy welcome to the heart of the exile; and I listened to Mrs. M'Cann while she chatted gaily to her guests, making light of trials and difficulties that would have daunted many a lord of the creation. She laughed, as she told of her furniture being flung by a surly captain on the shore of the river; how she lost her temper 'with the fellow,' and did not recover it for ever so long; how tartly she replied, in a spirit not of the mildest theology, to the kindly-intentioned queries of a Free-will Baptist; how 'it was as good as any theaytre' to see Hugh and herself tramping after the lumbering oxen, and all their cherished property nodding and shaking on the jolting wagon; how Hugh spent a portion of his first Sunday—'after saying our prayers, Bishop, by all means'—in making the frame of the door, while she constructed the door 'with her own two hands;' how happy they felt as, the cold being effectually barred out, they sat down before their bright stove, and drank a rousing cup of tea; how, as time rolled on, and the forest receded before the resolute axe, and the fields grew in dimensions, and cattle lowed round their house, and hogs grunted in the piggery, and roosters and their wives strutted and clucked, she had a tremendous battle with a skunk that assailed her chickens, and how, single-handed, and appealing in vain to unheroic or sleepy Hugh, she slew the invader of infamous odour, and then nearly fainted through fatigue, excitement, and the overpowering stench it emitted; how as many as sixteen used to lie at night on every available spot of the floor, and the priest was curtained off by a quilt in a corner to himself; and how, with the help of God, the more she gave the more she had to give. A pleasant hour's chat was that with Mrs. M'Cann, who did the honours of her log cabin with the ease of a duchess.

The second woman settler merits special notice, were it only to prove, to would-be sceptics, that the relations between the landlord and the tenant in the old country have really something to do with the Irish peasant's migration to the New World.

Mr. and Mrs. Crehan, of Galway, had been tenants on a certain property in that county; and this property having, in some way respecting which Mrs. Crehan was a little bewildering in her explanation, come into the possession of a gentleman with a fine old Galwegian name, the tribulation of the Crehans commenced. The first thing done by the new landlord was to raise the rent on his tenants, the second to deprive them of their mountain pasture, the third to cut off the shore and its seaweed from their free use, and the fourth to persecute a cherished pig with degrading pound, and its indignant owners with harassing fines. It is the last drop that causes the glass to overflow; and possibly the wrongs inflicted on the mend of the family and traditional rentpayer filled to overflowing the brimming measure of their woes; for the Crehans made up their minds to go somewhere—anywhere— 'to the end of the world'—rather than remain in a state of abject vassalage, dependent on the caprice or avarice of the gentleman with the fine old Galwegian name, 'and a holy Roman, too, if you plaze,' as Mrs. Crehan scoffingly assured me. The Parish Priest was consulted by the afflicted pair; and he, having seen the letters of the Bishop of St. John, which had been published in the Irish papers, advised them to proceed at once to New Brunswick, and take land for themselves and their children in the Johnville settlement, 'where no man or no law can take it from you or them,' added their counsellor. The advice was instantly adopted by the Crehans, to whom the now wiser landlord would have been glad to let a much larger farm than that whose rent he had so arbitrarily raised. But it was too late; and so, after paying, 'to the last farthing, everything they owed in the world,' they took ship for St. John with their large family of children, their hard-earned savings, and, what they prized scarcely less, a letter from their Parish Priest to the Bishop.

On their arrival in St. John they lost no time in seeking the Bishop, to whom they presented their only credential, the letter that was 'to make a landlord of Dinny.' The wife at that time spoke English imperfectly, while the husband understood no other language than that which is the sweetest to the ear and the softest to the tongue of the Connaught peasant; and clustering round this seemingly helpless couple was a swarm of young children, some little more than toddling infants. As the Bishop heard their story, and glanced at the group of young creatures, he looked upon the case as almost desperate: the husband, who had to rely on his wife's somewhat questionable powers as an interpreter, might not be able to make himself understood, and probably the struggle would be too severe for the children. Therefore he sought to dissuade them from the attempt which they were so anxious to make. But to go into the forest they were determined, and go into it they did—with a result which is pleasant to narrate.

Their entire worldly means consisted of 20l., with which they had to provide every necessary for a large family until the first crop could be reaped and gathered in. There was, however, the right stuff in the poor Galway emigrants, although they were of the purest type of that Celtic race of whose capacity your self-complacent Anglo-Saxon stupidly affects to despair. In an incredibly short space of time the Crehans had a sufficient quantity of land cleared, fenced, and cropped, a spacious log house and ample barn constructed; a horse, and cows, and hogs, and sheep, were purchased, or raised on this farm in the wilderness; and when the Bishop and I walked through their property, and inspected their wealth in barn and field, these despised and persecuted peasants were in possession of 200 acres of land, and such independence as they never dreamed of in Galway.

Volubly did Mrs. Crehan—a dark-haired, sharp-eyed, comely matron—tell of her treatment in Ireland, and her trials in her new home, as she welcomed the Bishop and 'the gentleman from the ould country' into her log cabin, which, in a few days, she was to abandon for a grand frame house, constructed on the most approved principles of American domestic architecture. This mansion was evidently an object of the most intense pride to Mrs. Crehan, who was much complimented by the expression of our desire to see it. As we proceeded towards the new building, which was then receiving its protecting coat of 'shingle,' I remarked that she must have felt somewhat lonely on her first entrance into the forest.

'Thrue for you, sir, it was lonely for us, and not a living sowl near us, but the childer. Indeed, sir, 'twas only by an ould stump that I knew whether I was near home or not; and other times we couldn't find our way at all, only for a cut on a tree. And 'twas the owls—the divils!—that would make a body's heart jump into their mouth. Oh, sir, they screeched and screeched, I declare, like any Christian, till they frightened the childer out of their sivin sinses. The little boy—he's a fine fellow now—would catch hould of me by the gownd, and cry out, "Oh mammy, mammy! what a place daddy brought us to!—we'll be all ate up to-night— mammy, mammy, we'll be all ate up tonight!" You know, sir, it's easy to frighten childer, the craychers,' apologised the mother.

'But, Mrs. Crehan, I suppose you don't regret having come here?'

'Deed then no, sir, not a bit of it. No, thanks be to the Lord, and blessed be His holy name! We have plenty to ate and drink, and a good bed to lie on, and a warm roof over our heads, and, what's more than that, all we have is our own, and no one to take it from us, or to say "boo" to us. The grief I have is that there's only the 200 acres—for I'd dearly like another hundred for the second boy. And, sir, if you ever happen to go to Galway and see Mr. Blank (the gentleman with the fine old Galwegian name), you may tell him from me that I'm better off than himself, and more indipindent in my mind; and tell him, sir, all the harm I wish him is for him to know that much. 'Twas the lucky day he took our turf and the sayweed— and a bad weed he was, the Lord knows.'

'Mrs. Crehan, where's the ould man?' asked a crabbed little fellow, who seemed anxious to do the honours of the settlement to the strange gentleman, and who would keep us company 'for a bit of the road.'

'Where is he gone, is it? Why then, Jimmy, he's gone to sell a cow,' was the good woman's reply.

'Gone to sell a cow!' exclaimed Jimmy, with an expression of affected horror. 'Yea, Mrs. Crehan, ma'am, what do you want partin' with your beautiful cow?'

'What do I want partin' with the cow, is it? Then, Jimmy, it's to pay what I owe, and I don't like to be in debt; that's what it manes, Jimmy.'

'Bravo, Mrs. Crehan!' said the Bishop; 'I admire your principle. Never be in debt, if you possibly can avoid it.'

Jimmy was silenced, thinking perhaps that Mrs. Crehan had the best of the argument, the more so as his lordship was on her side.

Jimmy M'Allister may not be the wisest or most sagacious adult male in the settlement; but, fortunately for him, he has a better half who looks sharply after all things, Jimmy included. Mrs. M'Allister is of so thrifty a turn that she would pick a feather off the road; and indeed so successfully had she picked up and bartered this article of comfort and commerce, that she was then after selling four good beds for the respectable sum of 16l.—no small addition to the annual revenue of the M'Allisters. Jimmy was of a different turn of mind: he would rather pick up a grievance than a feather; and the want of a priest for the settlement was a topic on which he dilated with persistent eloquence, notwithstanding the Bishop's repeated assurances that there would be a resident priest in the course of the following spring.

'But, my lord,' persisted Jimmy, 'he's wanted bad; and that's no lie. Faith, my lord, a body may die three times over in this place before he could send for the priest; and as for that, a poor fellow mightn't have the dollars convaynient to send for the doctor—two dollars goin' and two dollars comin' —Be dad, my lord——'

'Well, Jimmy, please God, you shall have the priest next spring,' said the Bishop.

'That may all be thrue, sir—my lord!—but, after all, a body may die three times over before he could send for him, and then, my lord——'

'Very well, Jimmy, you will be *sure* to have him,' said the Bishop with additional emphasis, in the hope of satisfying the unappeasable grievance-monger.

'And, my lord, sure this settlement is well able to support its own priest, and I tell you he's much wanted—and, for the matter of that, a poor body may die three times over before he could be able to send for him——'

A rumour that Mrs. M'Allister was in sight had a marvellous influence on Jimmy, who asked for and obtained a ready leave of absence from the Bishop, on the plea of 'urgent private business,' which, in his zeal for the spiritual welfare of his fellow-sinners, he had altogether forgotten. Jimmy rapidly fell behind, and was not seen till the following morning.

Amongst other settlers whom we visited was a Cork man, named Reilly, from beyond Macroom, and who, 'every day he rose in the old country saw Ballyvourney before his two eyes.' Reilly was a man of middle age, grave countenance, handsome features, including a marked aquiline nose, of deliberate utterance, the richest of Munster brogues, and a splendid faculty for rolling the 'r' like the rattle of a drum under the hands of a Frenchman; and it would seem as if honest Reilly had a preference for words that enabled him to display this faculty to the greatest perfection. The manner in which he pronounced 'your lordship,' 'your-r-r lor-r-rdship,' was grand.

Reilly had come out in the May of 1862; and all he had, besides an immense family—there were eleven children in the settlement in October 1866—was a little money for provisions, and an axe. But the man, and the axe, and the will and power to use it, were 'with God's help,' equal to the work to be done; and so resolutely did he set to his task, so vigorously did he and his eldest boy hew away at the forest, that he was enabled to gather in 100 bushels of potatoes that fall. These, and what remained in the flour-barrel, kept the wolf from the door of Reilly's little sheepfold. And so the stout Cork man and his sturdy boy toiled on, season after season, and year after year, until, in October 1866, the settler of 1862 had cleared between forty and fifty acres of land, and was the owner of two yoke of oxen, six cows, several sheep and hogs, a good log house, to which he had just added a commodious loft, a fine barn, a piggery of suitable strength and dimensions.

'Well, Reilly, I congratulate you,' said the Bishop. 'What you have done in the time is most creditable to you.'

'Well, my lord, I am getting along purty well, I thank my Maker for it. We have raison to be grateful and contented, your lordship, with what we've done. There is a good prospect for us and the children, the Lord be praised! Sure enough, 'twas a great change from the ould country to this. Glory, too, to the Lord for that same!'

It may be remarked, that my excellent countryman secured to himself in this short speech ample opportunity for the display of his r's, which came magnificently into play.

A glance into the comfortable and spacious house, where Mrs. Reilly was employed in dressing a plump representative of the Reillys, afforded material for pleasing speculation; for near the big table at the opposite side of the room stood a pair whose conscious manner—the same kind of thing one may see in a drawing-room—evidently portended speedy employment for the resident priest for whose advent Jimmy M'Allister so ardently sighed.

Having visited many of the houses in the first great clearance, we drove through the forest, a distance of two miles, and came to a plain or valley of far greater extent, stretching five miles in one direction, but similar in its leading features to that which we had just left. It may be remarked, in order to be accurate, that the Crehan family were among the occupiers of this portion of the settlement; but as Mrs. Crehan was the second woman who had braved the difficulties of a life amidst the woods, I somewhat anticipated in her case. The vast tract stretching out before us was reclaimed, or cleared, on the low ground, and on the gentle elevation, and up the side of the mountain range that ran parallel to the plain.

Here, as in the first clearance, were the same evidences of the presence of man and the power of that most effective capital of all—human labour well directed. Decent houses and ample barns were to be seen in every direction; and, what was the most hopeful indication of the thrift and energy of the settlers, was the fact that, in very many instances, while the family still remained in the primitive log house, the barn for the reception and storage of grain and other produce was large, substantial, and built in the best style common to the province. In numerous cases we found settlers to possess two frame barns, with spacious piggeries constructed of logs, from which the well-known melodious sounds unceasingly issued. In a very rare instance was the original camp or shanty tenanted; but where it was still the dwelling-place of the family, a fair proportion of the land was cleared, and a good barn was filled with the produce of a prosperous season.

One of the settlers, named M'Mahon, had just completed a frame house which, for extent, outward appearance, and interior comfort and accommodation, was equal to almost any farmer's dwelling I had seen in New Brunswick, from Shediac to St. John, or from St. John to Johnville—a distance of 300 miles. M'Mahon had brought some capital into the forest, the result of his industry as a blacksmith. His new trade appeared to thrive with him, as he was surrounded with the most convincing evidences of prosperity and comfort.

It must not, however, be supposed that all who came into the settlement brought more or less pecuniary capital with them. Many—indeed, the majority—commenced without any capital save that comprised in their health, their strength, and their willingness to work. 'Nothing, sir, but my own four bones, a sharp axe, and the help of the Lord,' was the pithy and pious response of more than one toiler in the forest, as he was asked of his struggles and success. This is how the settler with no capital save that indicated in the reply mentioned, managed to 'get along.' Having earned, by working for others, as much as enabled him to procure an axe and provisions for a month or two, he boldly faced the forest, perhaps with a wife and one or more children. Fortunate was the settler if he could obtain the friendly assistance of a neighbour to raise the first rude shelter for his young wife and her infants; but in the earlier period of the short history of the settlement such assistance was not always procurable, and the pioneer of future civilisation had to construct his shanty 'any how he could.' Satisfied that he had thus secured a home for his wife and little ones, he laid about him vigorously with his keen axe, smiting many a tree which would have formed the proudest ornament of an English park, and prostrating pine, beech, oak, and maple, with the same unsparing energy. The rapid decrease of the scanty provisions would but too soon warn the breadwinner that he must linger no longer in the camp; and, leaving his loved ones to the protection of Providence, he would again go out in search of work, which was always to be found.

On the Saturday night the poor fellow might be seen—by the owls, were those grave birds on the lookout, or by a casual wayfarer like himself—trudging along the rough highway, or rude track, bearing on his shoulders the grateful burden of the next month's provisions, won in the sweat of his brow by honest toil. Thus he would work occasionally for others, and then slash around him with his trusty axe, until he had cleared a few acres, and planted them with grain and potatoes, built a barn, and gathered in the first blessed fruits of his industry. And so on, from the shanty to the log cabin, from the log cabin to the frame house, and the couple of barns, and the yoke of oxen, and the milch cows, and the flock of sheep, and the great breeding sow and her clamorous offspring,—so on to independence, comfort, and content. This is literally the substance of many a simple tale, gratefully volunteered, or easily elicited by a few leading questions.

The settlers of Johnville are invariably kind to each other, freely lending to a neighbour the aid which they may have the next day to solicit for themselves. By this mutual and ungrudging assistance, the construction of a dwelling, or the rolling of logs and piling them in a heap for future burning, has been quickly and easily accomplished; and crops have been cut and gathered in safely, which without such neighbourly aid might have been irrecoverably lost. This necessary dependence on each other for mutual help in the hour of difficulty draws the scattered settlers together by ties of sympathy and friendship; and while none envy the progress of a neighbour, whose success is rather a subject for general congratulation, the affliction of one of these humble families brings a common sorrow to every home. I witnessed a touching illustration of this fraternal and Christian sympathy.

Even in the heart of the primitive forest we have sickness, and death, and frenzied grief, just as in cities with histories that go back a thousand years. A few days previous to my visit a poor fellow had become mad, his insanity being attributed to the loss of his young wife, whose death left him a despairing widower with four infant children. He had just been conveyed to the lunatic asylum, and his orphans were already taken by the neighbours, and made part of their families. One of them peered curiously at my companion and myself from under the peak of a huge fur cap that almost rested on his little nose, as the Bishop was enquiring after the family of a fortunate settler, named Murphy, who had brought the eldest of the orphans to his comfortable home. How long these tender sympathies and beautiful charities may resist the influence of selfishness, or civilisation, I know not; but that they then existed in strength and holiness I was abundantly convinced.

To one cause may be attributed some of the success which has crowned the labours of these Irish settlers, and the wishes of their Bishop and his zealous co-operator, the Rev. Mr. Connolly, the good priest of Woodstock,—the absence of intoxicating drink, or the prevention of its sale in the settlement. What village in England or Ireland with a population of 600 souls—that of Johnville in the autumn of 1866—is without its 'publick?' Scarcely one; while the probability is that many villages of an equal population in the old country possess two of such establishments. Against the sale of spirits in the settlement the Bishop has resolutely set his face, and in this salutary policy he has the hearty co-operation of the pastor of Woodstock, to whom much of the merit of the organisation and fortunate progress of the colony belongs. Rarely is spirituous liquor of any kind brought into the house of a settler, and, save in some special instance, after a hard day's work, in which many persons are necessarily joined, it is as rarely tasted by this simple and sinless people. I must, however, admit that, on our return through the entrance avenue, we did meet with an elderly gentleman, who must have been enjoying himself while visiting a friend beyond the limits of the settlement; for not only were his powers as a charioteer considerably impaired, but his damaged articulation imparted a still more bewildering intricacy to 'the explanation of his discreditable conduct,' with which, on demand, he favoured the Bishop.

The material progress of this Irish settlement may be illustrated by a significant fact—that fat cattle to the value of 200l. were sold to buyers from the States the day of my visit. What were the feelings of Jimmy M'Allister, as he heard of this tremendous sacrifice of live stock, and which included the cow of Mrs. Crehan, that excited his special interest, it would be difficult to depict; but the fact of this remarkable sale of the surplus stock of a young colony was mentioned with pride by one of the most intelligent and energetic of the settlers, Mr. Boyd.

Boyd was one of the few who brought a little capital with them into the settlement. But by far his best and most useful capital consisted of four well-grown, healthy, active sons, and an intelligent and hard-working daughter, who adds the functions of post-mistress to the more laborious and profitable duties of housekeeper. Each of the young Boyds has 100 acres of land in his own right, though they all wisely keep together as one family, and probably will continue to do so until circumstances, over which young people generally have 'no control,' compel them to prepare for events by no means unlikely in an Irish colony. One of the 'boys' was finishing a splendid barn, another barn being filled to bursting with grain of all kinds. The father admitted that the property then possessed by the family—himself and his four sons—was fairly worth 1,000l.

According to the census, taken at the instance of the Bishop, the estimated value of the land cleared, with the stock, the produce, and the buildings, up to the fall of 1865, was 14,500l.—an immense sum, when it is remembered that up to May 1862 there had been but one family (Hugh M'Cann and his wife) in the settlement, and it was not until 1863 that the greater number of the residents had ventured into the forest. It was supposed that the estimate for 1866 would have reached 20,000l. And if such be the result of a few years—three or four at the very utmost—of patient industry, stimulated by the certainty of reward and the security of its possession, what may not be looked for ten years hence, when science and matured experience are brought to the aid of human toil and manly energy?

Early on the Sunday morning the roads presented an unusually animated appearance, as groups of settlers moved towards the little chapel in which the Bishop was to celebrate Mass at eight o'clock. Keen was the wind and sharp the air as the faithful appeared in view, issuing from the forest in various directions, some with horse and wagon, but the greater number sturdily completing a smart walk of five, six, and even ten miles. Bright and cheerful and happy they all appeared on this auspicious occasion, when they were to hear the voice of their pastor, and join in the most solemn act of Christian worship.

There was no tawdry finery among the women, no dressing beyond their condition with the men; both were decently and suitably clad, good strong homespun being rather common with the latter. That the ladies had not exhausted the wealth of their wardrobes, or brought out their best at so unfavourable an hour for legitimate display, I was impressively assured; and more than one of the sex— in each case a matron of mature years—volunteered an apology for alleged inelegance of costume, the result, as they urged in extenuation of their sins against Fashion, of the haste required in order 'to overtake Mass.' As a proof that there is no lack of sympathy between the occupant of the palace and the tenant of the wilderness, I may mention, as an interesting fact, that on the wall of the bedroom in which I enjoyed my first and last night's repose in the midst of an American forest, I observed a specimen of that intricate arrangement which is said to have had a royal origin, and is known to the world, admired or execrated, by the name of crinoline. This is given as an instance, not alone of the omnipotent rule and universal sway of Fashion, but of the progress of an Irish settlement in the path of modern civilisation.

Beneath the groined roof of lofty cathedral there never knelt a more devout congregation than that which bowed in lowly reverence before the rude altar of the little rustic chapel of Johnville. Here was no magnificence of architecture, no pomp of ceremonial, no pealing organ, no glorious work of the great masters of sacred song; here were no gorgeous pictures glowing from painted windows, no myriad lights on the altar and in the sanctuary, no priests in golden vestments, no robed attendants swinging silver thuribles filled with perfumed incense,—none of these; but a little structure of the simplest form, covered with shingle, and as free from ornament or decoration as the shanty of the settler—with an altar of boards clumsily put together, and covered with a clean but scanty linen cloth. But those who knelt there that morning felt no want, missed no accessory, sighed for no splendour; their piety required no aid to inflame or to sustain it. Exiles from a Catholic land, they were once more under a sacred roof, once more listening to the voice of their Church—once more assisting at the celebration of Mass. And when the Bishop addressed them in simple and impressive language, such as a father might fittingly address to his children, and promised that he was about to gratify the wish of their hearts by sending a priest to live amongst them, a deep murmur of delight evinced the joy and gratitude of the devoted people. These, indeed, were tidings of gladness, the fulfilment of their fondest hopes, wanting which, material comfort and worldly prosperity would be in vain.

Through one door the women passed out, through the other the men. By the latter sex I was at once surrounded, and I was soon satisfied that every province and most of the counties in Ireland had a representative in that congregation. For a good hour they talked and chatted outside the little church, though the air was keen and the morning still raw. They eagerly enquired after places as well as persons, priests or politicians, and 'how the old country was getting on,' and 'whether anything was really to be done for it?' One gave a case of oppression, another of hopeless struggle against rack rent or insecure tenure, as the reason of his flight from the land of his fathers. But of their new home not one had a desponding word to say. They spoke with pride of their hard work, and their steady progress, and the future which they confidently anticipated.

'Well, thank God, 'tis our own, any how, and nobody can take it from us,' said one of the settlers; to which there was a general chorus of 'amens,' and 'true for you.'

'Take care, Mick, you haven't the half-year's rent ready; so don't be crowing.'

This pleasant sally from a wag much tickled the audience, who, to do them justice, were willing to laugh at the smallest joke.

"'Tis true, Dan, boy; but there's nobody lookin' for it,' replied Mick, who added, in a voice of affected commiseration that was 'as good as a play,' and was rewarded with an approving shout— 'but, faith, I'm thinking the agint has the mazles, or the rhumatiz, poor man! or he'd be here before now for it.'

'Jimmy'—to my friend of the day before—'is your gale to the fore?' asked a pleasant-looking Tipperary boy.

'Little we trouble ourselves with gales, or storms aither, in these parts,' replied Mr. M'Allister, whose innocent wit was rewarded with such vociferous applause that I dreaded the effect on his naturally abundant vanity.

'True for you, Jimmy, the misthress attends to the rint, and that kind of business. I hope she'll be sure and keep the resate,—'tis bad to lose the writin'—as I know, to my cost.'

'There's a boy,' said Mr. M'Allister, pointing to a vigorous young settler of some six feet in his vamps, 'and I ask you, sir, this blessed morning, wasn't it a mortial sin to turn his father, and three boys as likely as himself, out of the ould country? Sheep they wanted, indeed! Christians wouldn't do 'em. Well, the Lord had a hand in it, after all, for here they are, all the boys, with their hundred acres apiece; and what do you think, sir—eh, Terrence, my buck! Faith, sir, he's looking out already.

Don't mind the boys laughing, Terry; you'll never do it younger. But, sir, there they are, them four fine lads, and every man of them the lord of his own estate. After all, there's nothing like being a man's own master.'

'He doesn't always be that same, Mr. M'Allister, when once he's married,' suggested one of the bystanders, with a sly twinkle in his eye.

Mr. M'Allister did not seem to have heard the observation; nevertheless he rapidly changed the conversation, and, plunging deep into the politics of Europe, appeared immensely interested in the intentions of the Emperor Napoleon towards the Court of Rome. Jimmy was in high spirits that sharp morning, influenced not a little by the knowledge that his excellent wife was then enjoying 'a comfortable snooze in her best feather bed' at the safe distance of half a dozen miles from where her husband stood, the centre of an admiring circle. It was not the right occasion for ailing a grievance; and, indeed, his pet grievance—the want of the resident clergyman—had been so completely demolished by the assurance publicly given by the Bishop, that it was hopelessly past use. The temporary delay in establishing the second school in the settlement afforded him both a theme and a consolation; but even of this text for an occasional harangue he was soon to be deprived. Jimmy may now be in search of a grievance; and, when found, it is to be hoped it may not be a very serious one—barely sufficient to afford a gentle provocation to amicable discussion.

To my humble self, I must gratefully admit, Mr. M'Allister did the honours of the settlement in a manner at once affable and patronising.

When we took our departure, which was not achieved without vigorous and repeated hand-shakings, and prayers and blessings unnumbered, we were accompanied a couple of miles of the road by the Resident Magistrate of the settlement, who also combined in his own person the additional dignities of Captain of Militia and Councillor of the Parish. Mr. Cummins was himself one of the settlers, and he recounted with modest pride the story of his early efforts and his daily increasing prosperity.

On our return to St. John we met the Post-Master-General—a Scotchman—who had recently paid an official visit to the settlement; and he was loud in the expression of his astonishment at the progress which the people had made in so short a time, and at the unmistakable evidences of comfort he beheld in every direction.

The settlement of Johnville is but one of four which Dr. Sweeny established within a recent time. He has thus succeeded in establishing, as settlers, between 700 and 800 families, or, at an average of five persons to each family, between 3,500 and 4,000 individuals. The description given of Johnville would generally apply to the other settlements: the difference, whatever it might be, arising more from the quality of the land than any other cause.

CHAPTER IV

Irish who settle on the Land—Their Success—Their Progress in St. John—
Three Irishmen—A Small Beginning—Testimony of a Belfast Independent—
Position of Irish Catholics—The Church in New Brunswick—A Sweet Bit—
Missionary Zeal—Catholicity in St. John—Past and Present

THERE are large districts in New Brunswick almost exclusively occupied by
Irish Catholics, who have been from twenty to forty years in the province. Many
and anxious were the enquiries which I made in every quarter, from persons in
various conditions of life, and holding opposite opinions on most public questions;
and it is but simple justice to the representatives of the Irish race in that portion of
the American continent to state, that the universal testimony was in favour of their
thrift, industry, energy, and honesty. This was the testimony, not merely of
members of their own Church, who might naturally be inclined to exaggerate the
merits, or to deal leniently with the demerits, of those of their own faith and
country; it was the testimony of Scotch Presbyterians, English Protestants, and the
aristocratic descendants of the original colonists. I have been repeatedly assured
that the Irish were amongst the best settlers in the province; and were I, from a
feeling of false delicacy, to refrain from repeating this creditable judgment in their
favour, I should be doing them a grievous wrong, and denying them a merit freely
accorded to them by those who, however individually just and fair-minded,
entertain no special love either for their country or their creed.

As a rule, then, admitting of rare exceptions, the Irish *who settle on the land*, and
devote themselves to its cultivation, do well, realise property, accumulate money,
surround themselves with solid comforts, and bring up their families respectably.

Hundreds of cases could be mentioned of Irishmen, originally of the very
humblest condition, who, when they came out first, worked as farm-labourers for
others, and now occupy, as owners, the very property on which they toiled for
their daily bread. On the one hand, there was waste and extravagance; on the other,
thrift and industry; with the natural result, that the latter took the place which the
former could not hold.

There are millions of acres yet unoccupied, which have never been visited save
by the lumberman and his assistants; and of this land any quantity may be had
from the State on easy terms. Thus, for instance, for a sum of 60l., a property
consisting of 500 acres may be purchased in New Brunswick—may be held as
long as grass grows and water runs. But, altogether independent of the land that
may be had from the State, either by purchase or under the provisions of the
Labour Act, there are cultivated farms which, like all other descriptions of
property, are constantly in the market; and the thrifty man—the sober and prudent

man—who watches the opportunity of purchasing to advantage, may do so at almost any time.

The Irish, Protestants and Catholics, hold a most important position in St. John, and may be said to own fully half the property and wealth of that bustling active city. Of this property and wealth, the Catholics, who, with scarce an exception, are Irish, possess a considerable share. And what they possess they realised for themselves. The majority of those who are now respected for the position they occupy, and which position is enhanced by their character for honour and integrity, came out poor—in many instances absolutely penniless; but they stripped to the work before them, and climbed, with steady energy, from the lowest rung of the social ladder to wealth and independence. Rare indeed is the instance of a young man having come out with a tolerably well-filled purse. 'I had not a pound in the world when I landed here,' is the boast of nine out of ten who owe their present proud position to their own unaided exertions. And when describing how several of the wealthiest of the modern emigrants succeeded in life, some one who knew the city well would say: 'Such a man first worked as a labourer; I remember this man in a sawmill; that man commenced as a lumberman; one was a gardener, another a porter, another a pedlar: and now such a man is worth 2,000l; such a man, 5,000l; such a man, 10,000l; such a man, 20,000l.; such a man, 50,000l.: but, sir, all made by honesty, energy, and good conduct.' This is literally the history—the noble history—of many a man in St. John, who is a credit to the country of his adoption, and an honour to the land of his nativity. Even those who enjoyed the advantage of a good education had, when they started, little more of worldly goods than those whose only possessions were their strength, their honesty, their strength or their skill; and in the hard struggle upwards, that incalculable advantage necessarily told in their favour. But in all cases, education or no education, whether the young adventurer brought with him the well-won honours of Old Trinity, or the learning picked up in a village school, steadiness, sobriety, and good conduct were essential to success.

The possession of 'a little money' is very useful to any man who emigrates to a new country, especially when he has a family to provide for. But it has been confidently asserted, by experienced observers of the early struggles and successful career of their countrymen, that the most fortunate men came out 'without a pound in their pocket,' or, as they phrased it, without 'anything worth speaking of.' This may be accounted for by the necessity which compels a man without money, in a strange place, to set to work at once, *and at anything that offers*; whereas the man with a small capital is perhaps inclined to look about him too long, expecting, like Mr. Micauber, that 'something will turn up,' and may thus lose the opportunity, or fritter away the energy essential to success.

I was much struck with the histories of three Irishmen whom I met while in New Brunswick. One was a sturdy Independent, from the neighbourhood of Belfast; the others were Catholics—one from 'Sweet Glanmire,' near the city of Cork, the other from the county Fermanagh.

The Cork man's first enquiry was, 'Why, then, how's Beamish and Crawford?'

Having satisfied my cheery acquaintance on that head, by assuring him that Beamish and Crawford were as well as he could wish them to be, I suggested a leading question—

'I suppose, Mr. McCarthy, you had to fight your way, like the rest of our countrymen?'

'Faith, and that I had, sir, and no mistake. All I owned in the world, when I got as far as Frederickton, was twenty-five cents, and sure enough that same was not left long in my pocket, as I'll tell you—and it makes me laugh now when I'm telling it, though it was far from a laughing matter then. I took the twenty-five cents out of my pocket, and I put them in my hand, and I looked at them and looked at them, and I thought to myself they were mighty little for a man to begin the world with; but faith, sir, there was no help for it, and I had my health and strength, and all I wanted was work to do, for I was equal for it. Well, sir, small as the twenty-five cents looked in my hand, they looked smaller soon. I felt myself very dry entirely, and I wanted a drop of tea bad; so I went into a house, and said to a woman I met there, "Ma'am, I'll feel much obliged for a cup of tea, if you'd be pleased to give it to me." "Certainly, young man," says she, for she was civil-spoken enough, and I was quite a young fellow in them days; "certainly," says she, "you must have a cup of tea, young man; but you must pay me twelve cents for it." "Beggars can't be choosers," says I to myself, "so here goes for the tea." That cup of tea made a large hole in my twenty-five cents, and the bed and the breakfast next morning put the finish to my capital. But, sir, as the Lord would have it, I got a lucky job from a good gentleman that same day; and when he saw that I was steady, and didn't want to spare myself, he gave me more to do. From that day to this I've never been idle, and always steady, and keeping away from the drink, unless a little in reason, once in a way; and now, glory be to God for it! I have enough for myself and my family, and I'm doing a good business, and have something put by. But, sir, wasn't it a small beginning? Faith, I can't help laughing when I think of the twenty-five cents, and the big hole that cup of tea made in it.'

The Fermanagh man was then living upon his income, which was still considerable, though he had educated and provided for a large family. It was his boast that 'all he had in the world when he landed from Ireland was a dollar and a shilling.' Industry, perseverance, and good conduct did the rest.

I shall allow the Belfast Independent to speak in his own words, his testimony in favour of his countrymen being too valuable to be omitted. He is—or was in October 1866—a member of the Government, though without a portfolio, his important private affairs requiring his principal attention.

'I had to work my way up, with no one to help me but myself. I literally had nothing when I began—nothing in the shape of money or friends; but I got on from one thing to another, and I am now, thank God, all right and getting along. I think it does a man good to be obliged to work his own way in life; I know it did me good, and I am happier than if my father or grandfather had done everything for me, and I nothing for myself but to eat and drink what they left me. My dear sir, some of our best men hadn't a cent when they started; and what are they now? Faith, sir, they are better off than if they'd been left fortunes—for in that case they might be only anxious to spend them. Why, when I was first elected to our Parliament, there were seven of us who began as poor boys—yes, sir, poor boys; and three of them were Irish, like myself.'

'Irish!' I repeated.

'Yes, sir, Irish; and I tell you what, sir, it's not because I am an Irishman myself that I say it, but still I do say it—that our people get along in every way as well as any others. They are as smart, and as industrious—yes, and as saving; and they get property too as well as the rest—English, Scotch, or "Bluenoses." All they want is just to keep away from the liquor—not, sir, that others don't drink as much, and perhaps more, if the entire truth was told, than they do; but when the Englishman will be stupid, or the Scotchman will hide himself in a corner, the Irishman will go out in the street, and make a noise, and call attention to himself—that's just the difference. But, sir, when the Irishman is steady and sober, he has no superior; and I don't say this because I happen to be an Irishman, but because I see it every day of my life. Why, look at them when they get on the land; see how comfortable they are, and what stock they have! I wish you'd come to the Irish settlement near me, in St. Stephen's, Charlotte County; there is not a poor man among them all— yet they all came out poor—as poor as mice—without a cent in the world. Yes, sir, and though they are not of my Church, I say there isn't a more moral or virtuous people in the world,—that I say without fear of contradiction.'

'You must know your countrymen well,' I suggested.

'That I ought. I am in this country nearly forty years, and I saw the first of their coming here. They have gone on wonderfully, surely—all must admit that. And there isn't anything like the drink there was among them. I have experience of that in my own business. I am perhaps as largely in the lumber business as any man in the Province, and I employ a great many men. Some of it is very nice work, I assure you; and for skill and judgment, when once he gets to know his business, I say I prefer the Irishman. And, sir, there isn't that danger that ever was that will frighten him; I've seen him as steady as a rock in the midst of the rapids. As to the drink, when a party went into the woods formerly, they could do nothing without the whiskey, and the keg of spirits was as necessary to the lumberman as the barrel of flour or meat, or the store of groceries; but lately it is not thought of—and so much the better; people get along as well and better without it, and they save their money into the bargain. And let the sober Irishman alone for saving!—faith he scarcely has his equal for that in this Province.'

I remarked that it was pleasant to hear so good an account of one's countrymen, especially as there were too many in the world not inclined to think favourably of them.

'Well, that is true; there are too many who bother themselves about people's religion, and who won't give Catholics a good word; but, for my part, I live in the midst of them, and I find they are in every way equal to any others that you can mention. Then as for the priest, why, I always see him going among his flock, settling differences when they happen, and taking the greatest care of the children. I haven't a better or a faster friend than Father ———, though I am not of his Church. But for the Irish, I know them well, and what I say of them is before my eyes every day.'

That the Irish Catholic has had the hardest battle to fight, not only in New Brunswick, or the other British Provinces, but throughout the States, must be obvious to anyone who considers the circumstances under which he left his own country, and the prejudices, national and religious, which beset his path in the country of his adoption. An Irishman and a Catholic, poor, and perhaps illiterate— the latter the result of vicious laws rather than of any indifference on his part to learning—he had little in his favour, and almost everything against him. Many of the older settlers were the descendants of the Puritans of New England, and the sectarian prejudices of their fathers still survived in the breasts of their children. Indeed, it would be difficult to decide whether the feeling against the Irish Catholics was stronger when they were few in number, and their strength was altogether insignificant, or when they grew into an important section of the population, and their influence became perceptible in the politics as in the trade and commerce of the Province.

The prejudice which they had to encounter was neither latent nor slumbering—it was open and active; it met the Catholic Irishman in every rank of life and in every branch of industry, and nothing short of the indomitable energy which, throughout the American continent, the race have shown themselves to possess, could have raised so large a number of them in New Brunswick above the rudest . employment or the humblest fortune. And yet, while labour, rude or skilled, is the lot of the majority of the Irish in St. John, and throughout the province generally, a considerable proportion are to be found in every department of business, and enjoy, as merchants, traders, and manufacturers, the highest position which character and wealth can secure to their possessor. And not only is it true that the mercantile and trading class among the Irish Catholics are equal in enterprise, and even 'go-aheadishness,' to the most advanced of those who have caught the right spirit from their neighbours of the States, but there is a large amount of property held by the working classes. And this applies with equal accuracy to Frederickton, Woodstock, Chatham, Chediac,—wherever the Irish have established themselves in numbers, or had a fair opening for the exercise of industry, intelligence, and thrift. The Irish Protestant had fewer difficulties to encounter than his Catholic countrymen, and he is generally to be found in flourishing circumstances. Similarity of religion with that of the wealthier portion of the mass of the population was always of great assistance to the Protestant emigrant to America.

The history of the Catholic Church throughout America is also the history of the Irish race in the New World. This is as true of the British Provinces, with the exception of Lower Canada, as of the United States. From this point of view it may prove interesting to describe briefly the growth and progress of the Church in New Brunswick.

It is little more than fifty years since a Kilkenny collegian was ordained in Quebec by the Bishop of that city, whose spiritual jurisdiction then extended over New Brunswick and other maritime provinces of North America. Father Dollard— for that was the young priest's name—was sent to Cape Breton as a missionary among the Indians, who, having been originally converted by the Jesuits, those faithful and fearless soldiers of the Cross, adhered with remarkable fidelity to the religion taught them by the 'black gowns.' While with this simple flock the young Irish missionary led a life of the severest hardship. Living with them in their camps, he shared with them all the privations to which they were peculiarly exposed. Many years after, when Bishop of Frederickton, the venerable priest would take delight in narrating anecdotes of his mission among the 'Red Skins.'

Father Dollard was summoned on one occasion to visit an Indian who lay at the point of death far away in the forest—a distance of twenty-seven miles. It was midwinter, and the ground was everywhere covered with deep snow. Accompanied by his guide, armed with a stout staff, and his feet protected by snow shoes, the priest was soon on his way. Before starting he shared his breakfast with his companion, who, with commendable forethought, but much to the disgust of his reverend friend, coolly took from the table the remnant of the meat, rolled it in a rag of most uninviting appearance, and placed it in his pouch, which he hid away in his breast. When the travellers had accomplished ten miles of their arduous journey, they sat down on a fallen tree to rest. Here the Indian drew forth his treasure from its hiding-place, unrolled the unpleasant-looking rag with much solemnity, and, cutting off a portion of the meat, politely handed it to the missionary, saying, 'Father, you take bit of this?' The young priest shuddered at the proffered dainty, but quietly declined the courteous invitation, on the plea of not being hungry. 'Then me eat it, Father,' said the Indian, who devoured the morsel with every appearance of the most intense relish.

At the end of five miles more of weary trudging through the snow, the pair again rested, the priest feeling faint as well as tired. Again the Indian drew forth his treasure, which the priest now viewed with somewhat different feelings to what he had beheld it on previous occasions, and not with the same involuntary rising of the gorge. Cutting off a liberal portion, the Red Skin, with an insinuating manner, and in the softest voice, said, 'Father, maybe you take some *now*?' 'Yes, my child, I think I will,' replied the priest. 'And, my dear sir,' said the Bishop of Frederickton, 'I can assure you I never ate anything sweeter in all my life.'

While still among the Indians of Cape Breton, Father Dollard had to remain for the night in a strange wigwam, and there being no kind of bed in the miserable dwelling, a couch, formed of fresh green boughs, torn from a neighbouring tree, was constructed for his use. On this he lay down to rest, but he was awakened in the middle of the night by excruciating pains in his back and shoulders, and in the morning he was throwing up blood. Compelled to return to Montreal, where he could obtain medical assistance, he was for two years an invalid, half the time being spent in the hospital. Restored at length to health—so fervently prayed for by the zealous missionary—he was sent to Miramichi, in New Brunswick, this new field of his labours extending over an immense tract of uninhabited country, his flock consisting of tribes of Indians, and a few scattered French, Scotch, and Irish. When on sick or missionary duty, he travelled along the river and its tributaries in a canoe, always accompanied by an Indian; and many a time, when neither wigwam nor log-hut was within possible reach, the priest and his faithful guide had to pass the night on the bare ground, under the welcome shelter of their upturned canoe.

From Miramichi Father Dollard was transferred to Frederickton, the capital of New Brunswick. While here the smallpox, that awful scourge of the uncivilised races of man, made its dreaded appearance among the neighbouring Indians in whose camps it committed deplorable ravages. It was at such a moment that the Irish priest displayed the courage and self-devotion which formed so noble a feature in his character. When the timid savages fled in horror from the mysterious enemy that was hourly striking down their stoutest braves, and making desolate their wigwams, Father Dollard knelt by the rude couch of the sufferer, nursed him, and prayed with him, and consoled him; and when death released the soul of the poor Indian from its swollen and ghastly tenement of clay, the dauntless priest took that festering body in his arms or on his back, and with his own hands placed it in the grave which he had previously dug for its reception. Is it to be wondered at that the Church should have made the progress it has done, when such was the spirit of its early missionaries?

Father Dollard remained at Frederickton until 1842, when he was consecrated Bishop of New Brunswick. At the time he commenced his mission there were not more than four or five priests in the entire province.

Father Gagnon, a French Canadian, was one of these spiritual pioneers, and his duty took him along that portion of the northern shore of which Shediac may be described as the centre. And rough times they were with the missionary, who had to encounter the wild blast and the perilous wave, as he skirted the dangerous shore in an open boat, which he was himself often obliged to row. Not unfrequently did he experience the inconvenience of being wrecked; and more than once had the tall gaunt priest to wade to land, some cherished article of property or provision held high above the raging waters, to save it from destruction. Depending a good deal on this uncertain means of communication, Father Gagnon paid irregular visits to the widely scattered settlements of his extensive mission. In the same district in which the Canadian priest thus pursued his sacred calling, there were in 1866 six large and populous parishes, with good churches and resident clergymen.

We now turn to St. John, the centre of a great and growing diocese. There are men still living—I have spoken with some of them—who remember the time when they could name every Catholic then in that city. One of these, a Catholic magistrate, informed me that when he arrived from Ireland, in the year 1818, there was but 'a mere handful' of the faithful in the town; and he well remembered how 'one Andy Sullivan, a tailor from Bandon,' had to read prayers for them in the church of St. Malachy—a little timber structure, which the poor congregation were years trying to cover in from the rain and the wind, and had no means of warming for fourteen bitter winters, until their numbers and their resources were increased. There was another reader besides the worthy tailor from Bandon—'one Flanagan, a college-bred man;' and the visits of a priest being then of only occasional occurrence, the congregation were glad of the services of one who could read with befitting impressiveness the Epistle and Gospel of the day, such prayers as were suitable to the occasion, with perhaps a chapter from the work of some pious divine, or a sermon from one of the lights of the Church. From a dozen, or at most twenty Catholic families, the number gradually increased, though to a still scanty congregation and feeble community; but from the year 1820 the tide of emigration commenced to flow in, slowly at first, eventually with greater strength and a fuller current, until, in a few years after, Catholics began to feel themselves to be an important portion of the population.

Slowly, laboriously, and amidst much difficulty and marked discouragement, the Irish Catholics grew year by year into a position both prominent and influential. The early Catholic settlers carried with them the impress of their civil and religious degradation; and even for a considerable time after the passing of the Emancipation Act the newcomers were regarded with aversion and mistrust by the old colonists, who likewise, and not unnaturally, looked upon them as interlopers and intruders. But, manfully and steadily, the Irish Catholics won their way, though not without many a hard fight and many a keenly-felt mortification, to political influence and social consideration. Now they kneel beneath the lofty roof of their magnificent cathedral, 200 feet in length, of solid stone, and built at a cost of 30,000l.; and among them, white-haired and venerable, a few of those who, in the wind-scourged shanty of 'the church of St. Malachy'—for which a stove could not be procured for fourteen long North American winters —listened with devout attention to the voice of Andy Sullivan, the tailor from Bandon, and to the more skilful elocution of 'one Flanagan, the college-bred man.' Forty years since, an ordinary room would have afforded sufficient accommodation to the Catholic worshippers of that day: now congregations of 2,000 or 3,000 pour out on Sundays and holidays through the sculptured portals of the Church of the Immaculate Conception. On All Saints' Day I beheld such a congregation issuing from an early Mass, filling the street in front of the splendid building; and from the appearance of the thousands of well-dressed, respectable-looking people, who passed before me, I could appreciate not only the material progress of the Irish in St. John, but the marvellous development of the Catholic Church in that city.

On a plot of land, four acres in extent, and right in the heart of the town, are clustered the Cathedral, the Palace of the Bishop—of cut stone, and one of the finest structures of the kind in the British Provinces, indeed in America—the Convent of Charity, the Convent of the Sacred Heart, an Asylum for Orphans, and a Classical and Commercial Academy under the patronage of the Bishop. There are other churches, convents, and schools in the city, including the admirable schools of the Christian Brothers.

When the present estimable prelate first came on the mission in 1844, he had to travel distances of from sixty to eighty miles to attend 'sick calls,' and was frequently absent for more than six weeks at a time, travelling from mission to mission, saying Mass in log huts, and administering the sacrament to flocks scattered throughout a wide and thinly-populated district. There are now several resident clergymen in that district—outside St. John: and instead of the rude log hut of the past, there are now sixteen good churches, with large congregations. And all this change in the comparatively short space of two-and-twenty years.

There are two dioceses in the same province in which, fifty years since, there were but four missionaries. That of Chatham is presided over by Dr. Rogers, that of St. John by Dr. Sweeny. In the two dioceses there were in 1860 ninety churches and forty-five priests; and as rapidly as priests can be ordained, or obtained from the colleges in Ireland, there are missions awaiting their labours. When Dr. Sweeny was consecrated, in 1860, he had but nineteen priests in his diocese, whereas in 1866 the number had increased to thirty, and two young candidates for the ministry were to be ordained before the spring of 1867.

'Bishop, when we were boys, and when the old church of St. Malachy took so long in building, and when it was so many years before it could be closed in, little did the Catholics of that day think of building cathedrals and palaces for their bishops, and schools and convents.' This was the remark made in 1866 by an Episcopalian clergyman to Dr. Sweeny, as they stood near the group of buildings that present the most eloquent evidences of the numerical strength, material progress, and devoted zeal of the Irish Catholics of St. John. Little did those who listened to the Sunday readings of Andy Sullivan, the tailor from Bandon, or of 'one Flanagan, the college-bred man,' dream of the possibility of a revolution so miraculous. And yet it has come to pass.

CHAPTER V

The Irish in Quebec—Their Progress and Success—Education entirely Free—
Montreal—Number and Position of the Irish—Their Difficulties and Progress—
Beneficial Influence of good Priests—St. Patrick's Hall

ENTERING Canada at Quebec, the presence of a strong and even influential Irish element is at once observable. In the staple industry of this fine old city—the lumber trade —the Irish take a prominent part. About 700,000 tons of shipping are annually loaded at Quebec; and in this vast business the Irish perform the principal part. This trade is divided into several branches, some requiring different degrees of skill and judgment; others calling for physical strength, endurance, or dexterity; more necessitating the possession of capital. Thus, for instance, there is a valuable class of men employed in sorting and measuring timber, who are called 'cullers,' whose business requires special skill and aptitude; and these men are principally Irish. Cullers can make as much as 300l. a year; the very same class who in Ireland would think themselves fortunate if they could earn one-sixth of that income. Then there are 'cove-owners,' who purchase, store, and prepare timber for exportation—who, in fact, sell to the shippers. The cove-owners are principally Irish. The cove-owner does a large business, and enjoys a good credit, and he generally lives well, keeps his country house, and even drives his own carriage. Nor are there wanting Irishmen in the ranks of the shippers, men of large means and good standing in the commercial world. Then for that extensive department in which strength, dexterity, and endurance are all essential, the Irish command the best position, and, as a necessary consequence, they receive the highest rate of payment. On an average, the working men employed in the various branches of the lumber business of the port earn from 6s. and 8s., even to 10s. a day; but it must be remembered that there is a considerable portion of the year during which employment becomes scarce, and even ceases altogether; therefore the man whose sole capital is his labour must determine to save for the hard weather, which is sure to come, or he must be ready to go into the woods as a lumberman, or seek employment wherever it can be procured.

It is pleasant to know that not only are the Irish in Quebec, and indeed along the St. Lawrence, among the most industrious and energetic portion of the population, but that they are thrifty and saving, and have acquired considerable property. Thus along the harbour, from the Champlain Market westward to the limits of the city, an extent of two miles, the property, including wharves, warehouses, and dwelling-houses, belongs principally to the Irish, who form the bulk of the population in that quarter. And by Irish I here mean Catholic Irish. There are many Irishmen of other persuasions, eminent in trade and commerce, men of the highest standing and repute; but not only are there many Catholic Irishmen, who came out to Canada with little more than their skill as mechanics, or their capability as labourers, now in positive affluence, but the larger proportion of those who live by their daily toil have acquired and possess property of more or less value. This property usually consists of the plot of land on which they have erected a house for their own occupation, and another to let to tenants. As the fortunes of the family increased, so did the house, until at length a decent dwelling, of at least two storeys, was secured; then the house for the tenant was constructed. It is ascertained that the Catholic Irish—the Irish of the working classes—have 80,000l. or $400,000, lodged in the Savings' Bank of Quebec; and that in all kinds of bank and other stock, they own something like 250,000l. or $1,225,000. Thus in the Union Bank, of 400 stockholders in Quebec, 200 are Irish. And this is but one of three local banks in that city. Besides possessing extensive house property, and having accumulated money, they are generally engaged in business, of which they enjoy a fair share. Whatever the Irish possess, they have made by their own unaided industry; for, as a respectable Irishman, who had himself worked his way to independence, said to me: 'You could scarcely trace one that brought a sovereign with him.' He added that he had brought out four himself, but that he might as well not have done so, for he lent them to a person who never took the trouble of paying them back. 'And perhaps, after all, it was so much the better for me that I lost the money, for I had to work the harder.'

Among those who came out 'poor,' as working mechanics, is an Irishman who is now in the enjoyment of an income of 10,000l. a year, made by successful contracts, natural ability, and good conduct. This case may be regarded as a somewhat remarkable one in Canada, if the magnitude of the result be regarded; but there are many instances in which sums of 20,000l., 30,000l., and 50,000l. have been realised by the industry and perseverance of Irishmen who came to the British Provinces 'without a shilling.' The secret of the success or failure of Irishmen may be summed up in a sentence, spoken by a countryman of theirs in Quebec; words which I have heard expressed hundreds of times in all parts of America, and which could not be too often repeated: 'Where the Irish are steady and sober, they are sure to get on; where they are drunken, reckless, or improvident, why, of course they fail.'

In Quebec, as in too many places in America, there are instances of drunken, reckless, and improvident Irishmen; but, happily, these cases are exceptional, for, as a rule, the Irish of that city are sober, prudent, and thrifty. And one fact, the exact parallel to which may be told of the Irish in Montreal, is in the highest degree creditable to the moral tone which they maintain,—that there is not in the Irish portion of the town a single house of bad repute, although as many as 10,000 sailors are frequently at one time in the port, and although the Irish keep lodging-houses, and places of entertainment, which are frequented by a class whose influence is not always the most favourable to public or private morals.

The Irish Catholics in Quebec, who number about 12,000, possess Church property of their own creation to the amount of 40,000l.; and the manner in which they respond to appeals made to their charitable feelings was strongly impressed on my mind from hearing the Pastor of St. Patrick's announce from the pulpit that the bazaar just held in aid of an hospital for old and infirm people had realised the net sum of 800l. To this handsome amount the wealthier classes had contributed a fair proportion; but the larger amount came from the pockets of the working people. Indeed, to employ the language of a gentleman long connected with Quebec, 'they form an exhaustless resource in every charitable or religious undertaking.'

I was afforded a favourable opportunity of seeing at one time a large body of the working class of Irish, that is Irish-born, or born of Irish parents. The occasion was a funeral of a young man who had fallen victim to a daring feat, which resulted in his death. The nature of the death created a lively sympathy among his class, who might be described as 'ship-labourers,' engaged in various departments of the great lumber industry of the port. The procession occupied a considerable time in passing the place at which I stood, and the papers of the following morning estimated the number who 'walked' at 1,200. There was not of that large body of working men a single one badly or shabbily dressed; all were well and comfortably clad, while many were attired with a neatness and even elegance that could not be seen in the same class at home. They seemed to me to bear themselves with an air of manly independence, as free citizens of a free country, in which the laws make no distinction between man and man. And taking into consideration the dangers and hardships to which most of those engaged in the principal work of the river and harbour are necessarily exposed, and the temptations to which the very nature of their employment gives rise, these men are, as a body, temperate and well-conducted; the contrary being the exception.

The Irish Catholic who must depend upon himself for 'getting along' has more difficulties to contend with than the Irish Protestant, or the Englishman or Scotchman. The majority of the population are French; and not only does the Irishman speak a different language to that of the majority of the population, but he absorbs a large and valuable portion of the employment, and pushes his way into active rivalry with the more wealthy class in various branches of business. Then he has a certain amount of national jealousy or sectarian feeling to encounter amongst the English-speaking section of the community. So that when he does rise above the mass, and acquire wealth and position, it is at least certain that his struggle has been hard, and that his success has been well earned. But whenever an Irish Catholic in Quebec or Montreal told me of his hard up-hill fight, he was sure to add—'The laws are good and just, and we enjoy everything we have a right to hope for. We have nothing to complain of here; and all we wish is that you were as well off at home.' To which sentiment, I need hardly say, I invariably responded with a cordial 'Amen!'

Education in Lower Canada is entirely free. Each denomination enjoys the most complete liberty, there being no compulsion or restriction of any kind whatever. And the magnificent Laval University, so called after a French Bishop, enjoys and exercises every right and privilege possessed by the great universities of England. This University, which is eminently Catholic, obtained a charter conferring upon it all the powers that were requisite for its fullest educational development.

The rights of the Protestant minority are protected in the amplest manner, as well by law as from the natural tendency and feeling of the majority; for there are no people more liberal and tolerant, or more averse to any kind of aggression on the faith or opinions of others, than the French Canadians; and the Irish Catholics too well remember the bitterness caused by religious strife in the old country to desire its introduction, in any shape or form, or under any guise or pretence, into their adopted home. There are abundant means of education within every man's reach; and it is his own fault if his children do not receive its full advantage. But the Irishman, whatever may be his own deficiencies as to early training, rarely neglects that of his children; and in Canada, as in the States, the fault attributed to him is not that he neglects to educate them at all, but that he is tempted to educate them rather too highly, or too ambitiously, than otherwise.

In no part of the British Provinces of North America does the Catholic Irishman feel himself so thoroughly at home as in the beautiful and flourishing city of Montreal. He is in a Catholic city, where his religion is respected, and his Church is surrounded with dignity and splendour. In whichever direction he turns, he beholds some magnificent temple—some college, or convent, or hospital — everywhere the Cross, whether reared aloft on the spire of a noble church, or on the porch or gable of an asylum or a school. In fact, the atmosphere he breathes is Catholic. Therefore he finds himself at home in the thriving Commercial Capital of Lower Canada. In no part of the world is he more perfectly free and independent than in this prosperous seat of industry and enterprise, in which, it may be remarked, there is more apparent life and energy than in any other portion of the British Provinces. It is not, then, to be wondered at that the Catholic Irish are equal in number to the entire of the English-speaking Protestant population, including English, Scotch, and Irish. It is estimated that the Irish Catholics are now not less than 30,000. Of these a large proportion necessarily belong to the working classes, and find employment in various branches of local industry. Their increase has been rapid and striking. Fifty years since there were not fifty Irish Catholic families in Montreal. It is about that time since Father Richards, an American, took compassion upon the handful of exiles who were then friendless and unknown, and gathered them into a small sacristy attached to one of the minor churches, to speak to them in a language which they understood. In thirty years afterwards their number had increased to 8,000, and now they are not under 30,000.

The Irish of all denominations represent a vast proportion of the wealth and commercial enterprise of Montreal; and though the majority of the Catholic Irish came out at a later period, and under far less favourable circumstances, their position on the whole is in every way excellent. They are not in the least behindhand in industry, energy, and active enterprise, when compared with any other portion of the community. As merchants, traders, and manufacturers, Catholic Irishmen, who commenced without any capital, other than a moderate share of education, natural intelligence and good conduct, are steadily yet rapidly rising to wealth and social position; and instances without number might be recorded of men who could scarcely write their names when they landed on the wharf of Montreal, who, thanks to their native energy and resolute good conduct, are this day rich and independent.

The Savings' Bank is the strong-box of the prudent man of moderate means and humble position; there he places his little surplus capital, generally after having built for himself a house or 'store,' as a shop is termed in America. The position and character of the Irish working classes in Montreal may be fairly estimated from the fact, that of $1,000,000 deposited in the Savings' Bank of that city, four-fifths, or $800,000, belong exclusively to them. A large portion of the stock of the Ontario Bank also stands in their name. Then they possess considerable house property, two-thirds of which is insured. Griffintown, the principal Irish quarter, is almost entirely owned by the working classes; and here, as in Quebec, not a single house of ill-fame is to be found in the entire district. In Griffintown, poverty and wretchedness, miserably clad children and slatternly women are occasionally to be seen; but they are comparatively rare; and in almost every case the drunkenness of the father, or the tippling of the mother, is the sole cause of the wretchedness and degradation which, happily exceptional, form a dark contrast to the prevailing sobriety, thrift, and good conduct distinguishing the Catholic Irish of Montreal.

While it is true that the Irish Catholic feels himself more at home in Lower Canada than in the other Provinces, Upper Canada especially, it must not be supposed that he has not had many and serious difficulties to contend against. Whatever may now be the feelings of the French Canadians towards the Irish, they were strongly hostile to them at one period; for in the rebellion of 1837, the Irish, influenced in a great measure by two eminent priests of their own country—Father M'Mahon, of Quebec, a man of surpassing power as an orator, and in every respect one of the most remarkable men of his time; and Father Phelan, afterwards Bishop of Kingston—generally sided with the British Power, and against the insurgents of that day. This was one and a very natural cause of prejudice against them. Difference of language must at all times, even under the most favourable circumstances, create a barrier against international fusion, or thorough sympathy between races: added to which, the humbler class of the new-comers soon began to occupy situations and even monopolise branches of industry previously occupied and monopolised by the French Canadians. Then, as may be supposed, the Catholic Irish were not much befriended by the English-speaking portion of the population; so that here, as in most other places, the Irish emigrant had to fight his way up under circumstances sufficient to daunt any other people, but which difficulties seem to have had the effect of bracing their energies and ensuring their success. It is nearly a quarter of a century since Francis Hincks, now Governor of the Bermudas, and Louis Drummond, now an eminent and highly respected Judge of the Supreme Courts of Lower Canada—the one a Unitarian, the other a Catholic, and both Irishmen—infused life and spirit into the Catholic Irish of Montreal, and gave them a sense of pride and consciousness of strength, which they much required. Now they form a large and important section of the population of the finest and most prosperous city of British North America, and they are thoroughly conscious of their strength and legitimate influence.

I had the pleasure, on several occasions in Montreal, of meeting the very *élite* of my countrymen of all denominations; and I found among those who, when they commenced, had to rely altogether on their own exertions, more of the American spirit than in almost any other city in the colonies. There is greater manufacturing enterprise in Montreal than elsewhere in British America; there are therefore larger sources of employment throughout the year for the working classes, to many of whom, indeed to most of whom, the winter is a season of trial and privation.

Among those whom I met was an enterprising manufacturer, who boasted of his being 'a Cork boy,' a pupil of the Christian Brothers, and an apprentice of the Messrs. Hegarty, the eminent tanners of his native city. He was doing a thriving business, his orders being over $100,000 in advance of his means of supply. He had left the States some dozen years before, being anxious to afford his young family the advantages of a sound Catholic education, which at that time was not of such easy attainment in the city where he then resided as it has since become. Prosperous himself, he was enthusiastic in his description of everything in Montreal, particularly the position occupied by his co-religionists. 'We Irish Catholics,' he said, 'are in a strong position in this city. There is no city in the States in which we occupy a more favourable position than we do here. We feel ourselves at home here; we are not foreigners, as we are sometimes considered elsewhere. The laws are good, and we have all that we can fairly desire, and we can educate our children in the best manner, and just as we please. In fact, we could not be better off. This is the place for an honest and industrious man, but not for the idler or the drunkard. There is no fear, in this country, of a sober man, who is willing to work; but he must be sober and industrious.'

My worthy friend was himself a rigid teetotaller—to which fact he attributed most of his prosperity.

It is foreign to the purpose of this book to describe the public institutions and buildings of any place; but I cannot refrain from expressing my admiration of Montreal, which is in every respect worthy of its high reputation. It has an air at once elegant and solid, many of its streets being spacious and alive with traffic and bustle, its places of business substantial and handsome; its public buildings really imposing, and its churches generally splendid, and not a few of them positively superb. This description of the churches of Montreal is not limited to the Jesuits' Church, the stately *Paroisse*, and the grand church of St. Patrick, of which the Irish are deservedly proud; it applies with equal propriety to the Episcopalian Cathedral, and more than one church belonging to the Dissenting bodies. Montreal is rich in all kinds of charitable, educational, and religious institutions; and such is the influence and power of the Catholic element, that this beautiful city, which is every day advancing in prosperity and population, is naturally regarded by the Catholic Irishman as a home. The humble man sees his coreligionists advancing in every walk of life, filling positions of distinction—honoured and respected; and, instead of mere toleration for his faith, he witnesses, in the magnificent procession of Corpus Christi, which annually pours its solemn splendour through the streets, a spectacle consoling alike to his religious feeling and his personal pride.

The influence of really good priests, who combine wisdom with piety—who, in their zeal for the spiritual welfare of their flock, do not overlook their temporal interests and material progress—is at all times most serviceable to the Irish; and nowhere is that influence more required, or more potent when exercised, than in America. Happily for the race, it is exercised very generally throughout that country, and in no instance without the most beneficial results, in their improved tone, their greater industry, and their habits of thrift and saving. The good priests of St. Patrick's—the Sulpitian Fathers of Montreal—employ this salutary influence with results most cheering to witness. It lifts the Irish up; it raises their social condition; it induces them to acquire and accumulate property—in fact, by the very improvements which they are induced to effect, to identify themselves with the progress of the community. To acquire this most desirable influence over an Irish congregation, the priest need not be an Irishman; but he should be wise and pious, and his people should feel that he has *sympathy with them*. The lack of this essential sympathy is often fatal to the best intentions of the best men: where it exists, it supplies or compensates for the want of many qualities, if not actually essential, at least very valuable in a priest. The good Fathers of St. Patrick's in Montreal—and fortunately they have their like in every direction—in every Province and every State—combine all these requirements; they are wise as well as pious, and they have a profound sympathy with their flock.

St. Patrick's Hall—of which I only saw the broad foundations—is creditable alike to the enterprise and public spirit of the Irish of Montreal. The Hall itself will be as spacious as a cathedral—134 feet long, by 94 feet wide, within the walls, and 46 feet high. The national sentiment is gratified in the architecture of the building, which is 'purely Irish, copied from Cormack's Chapel on the Rock of Cashel.' The design is really grand and imposing; and when fully realised in cut limestone, St. Patrick's Hall will form one of the most striking architectural ornaments of the city. With a front of 144 feet on Victoria Square, and 100 feet on Craig Street, it is in the very centre of the business portion of Montreal; and the fine shops which are to form the ground flat, and the show rooms on the second flat, together with sundry rents derived from the great concert-room and other portions of the building, will render St. Patrick's Hall not only pleasing as a monument grateful to national sentiment, but satisfactory as a speculation.

CHAPTER VI

Upper Canada—Number of the Irish—How they came and settled, and how they got along; illustrated by the District of Peterborough—Difficulties and Hardships—Calumnies refuted—What the Settlers did in a few Months—Early Trials—Progress and Contrast — Father Gordon—Church-building in the Forest—An early Settler—A Sad Accident—A Long Journey to Mass—A Story strange but true—The Last Grain of Tea—Father Gordon on the Irish and their Love of the Faith

THE Irish form fully half the population of what still, Confederation notwithstanding, may be designated as Upper Canada. Of these the Catholics may be said to be nearly one half. Fortunately for the Irish in Canada, they have generally adopted the kind of industry best suited to their knowledge and capacity, and do not, as it is too much the habit of their brethren in the States, crowd into the large towns, for which, by habit and education, they are not suited. They are scattered over the land in great numbers, either in settlements, in groups, or singly; but in whatever manner distributed over the face of the country, they are, as a rule, doing well. The Catholic Irish are in many instances to be found in almost exclusively Catholic settlements; but they are also to be met with in the midst of Scotch and English, and mixed up with their Protestant countrymen, who have mostly come from the north of Ireland. There are Catholic settlements of every date—from six, ten, and twenty years, to thirty and forty years, backwards—generally in a . flourishing condition, and in every one of which are to be seen extraordinary examples of courage, energy, and endurance, such as may well make an Irishman proud and hopeful of his race.

It would not serve any useful object were I to ask the reader to accompany me through various counties or townships of Canada; my purpose is rather, by the aid of an occasional sketch, to show how and in what manner the humbler and poorer Irish emigrants have succeeded in making a home for themselves in their adopted country. In order to appreciate what they have done, it is necessary to afford some idea of the difficulties that lay in their path. That they have succeeded in rendering themselves independent, and in laying the foundation of a prosperous future for their descendants, is undoubtedly true; but we may profitably glance at the past, to see how all this has been accomplished. I prefer rather to deal with those who came out poor, without capital, depending for their daily bread on the labour of their hands, than with those who, emigrating under more favourable circumstances, were never called on for the display of the qualities essential to the rude pioneer, whose chief capital consisted in a strong arm, a keen axe, and a bold heart. I cannot better commence than with a brief sketch of the settlement of one of the most prosperous districts in Canada—Peterborough.

In the year 1825, now forty-two years since, a considerable number of emigrants, consisting of 415 families, or 2,000 individuals, sailed from Cork Harbour on their way to Canada, where, under the auspices of the Government, they were to establish a home for themselves in what was then a forest wilderness, the abiding place of the wolf and the bear. These 2,000 people were all from the south of Ireland, genuine Irish in birth and blood. Let us follow the footsteps of those humble people, and learn how they battled with the difficulties of a new and trying position, and what they accomplished for themselves and the country of their adoption.

The voyage across the Atlantic was wonderfully prosperous. Heaven seemed to smile upon the poor exiles, and give them courage for what they had soon to meet. In a few weeks after their arrival at Quebec, they were found encamped on the shores of Lake Ontario, near Cobourg, waiting for means of transport to their intended settlement, in what is now the rich and fertile county of Peterborough, then mostly a verdant wilderness. These people were the pioneers of civilisation, for their future home was fully forty miles distant from the frontier settlement of that day. There was not then even the semblance of a track through the wooded country which they had to traverse, and a kind of road had to be cut from Lake Ontario to Rice Lake, a distance of twelve miles through the tangled forest. Rice Lake had then to be crossed, and the rapid and turgid Otanabee, for the distance of twenty-five miles, was to be ascended by this little army of settlers.

In order to cross the lake and ascend the river, three boats were constructed, and propelled on wheels over the rough track from the one lake to the other; but when this part of the difficulty was got over, and the baggage and provisions were brought so far in safety, it was found that, owing to the dryness of the season, and the consequent shallowness of the waters of the Otanabee, it was impossible to proceed without additional means of transport; so a great boat of light draught, sixty feet in length, by eight feet in width, had to be at once constructed, and with the aid of stout rowers, frequently relieving each other, this vessel was steered through the rapids, and got somehow over the shallows.

After difficulties and hardships enough to fill the poor adventurers with despair—which difficulties and hardships were aggravated by fever and ague, that alike unsparingly attacked the robust and the delicate, the strong on whom the weak relied, and the weak who were thus rendered still more helpless—they arrived at what is now known as one of the most beautiful and prosperous towns in Canada, and was then but a trackless wilderness. Those who arrived first commenced immediately to put up rude huts, or wigwams, made of great strips of bark, branches of trees, and sods; and as batch after batch of emigrants arrived, after successfully passing the rapids and shallows of the river, the landing-place presented an animated appearance, which gave some idea of a new home to the exiles, and cheered their drooping spirits. Here they remained encamped until they proceeded to settle on the lands in the neighbourhood. The proportion of land granted to each family of five persons was 100 acres; but each grown-up son was also allowed the same quantity for himself. Soon the temporary huts made their appearance here and there in groups, as the attractions of friendship or acquaintance induced families to seek each other's neighbourhood, or as greater facilities for shelter or comfort suggested; and it was not long before this Irish camp assumed the air of a place of business.

The novelty of the present and the uncertainty of the future must have deeply impressed the most thoughtful and observant of the settlers; but that which gave them the greatest uneasiness was the absence of a spiritual director and comforter—of the priest, to whose guidance and ministrations they had all their lives been accustomed. They embraced the first opportunity of appealing to the Governor-General of the Province to supply this great want; and in their memorial, which is touching in its simple earnestness, they display their traditional love of education and devotion to their faith. They say: 'Please your Excellency, we labour under a heavy grievance, which we confidently hope your Excellency will redress, and then we will be completely happy, viz. the want of clergymen to administer to us the comforts of our Holy Religion, and good schoolmasters to instruct our children.' What a comment is this on a comical absurdity which I heard uttered in no less important a place than the House of Commons—that the Irish were rushing to America in order to get rid of their priests!

Calumny and slander had followed these poor exiles across the ocean, and tracked them to their new home in the wilderness. When first the people in the frontier settlement—for the most part immigrants themselves, or the sons of immigrants from the United States, who refused to abandon their allegiance to the British Crown at the time of the American Revolution—heard of the arrival of these 2,000 'Irish Papists' in the neighbourhood, they became alarmed for their property, and even for their personal safety. This alarm and prejudice were caused by stories circulated by those who, unhappily, had brought the old unnatural hatred with them to a new country. However, such was the order maintained in the colony, and such the excellent conduct of the settlers, that it became quickly apparent that these stories were false and unfounded. A person then residing near the colony bears testimony to their industry, energy, and good conduct, in a letter dated January 1826, a few months after their arrival. The letter is written to a friend:—

I am here in the very midst of them; from twenty to thirty pass my door almost daily. I visit the camp frequently, and converse with them on their affairs, and find them happy and contented. *In general, they are making great exertions in clearing land, and their efforts have astonished many of the old settlers.* Not one complaint has been made against them by any of the old settlers, and it is the general opinion that when so large a body of people are brought together none could conduct themselves better. When we heard of their coming amongst us, we did not like the idea, and immediately began to think it necessary to put bolts and bars on our doors and windows. All these fears are vanished. These fears, I must acknowledge, were in consequence of *stories that were put in circulation before their arrival in that part*, which have all turned out to be equally false.

Let us now see what were the results of the energy and industry of this colony of Irish settlers in the short space of a single year. Remember, these people were not what it is the strange fashion in some parts of America to describe as, and the shameful fashion to admit as being—'Scotch-Irish;' they were genuine Irish, in feeling as in blood. These 2,000 'Irish Papists,' whose path of exile was tracked by wicked lies, sailed from Cork in May 1825; and in November 1826 they were proved to have done this work:—they had cleared and fenced 1,825 acres of land, and raised off the land so cleared 67,000 bushels of potatoes, 25,000 bushels of turnips, 10,000 bushels of Indian corn, 363 acres of wheat, 9,000 pounds of maple sugar; and they had purchased, by their labour, 40 oxen, 80 cows, and 166 hogs; the total value of the single year's work, literally hewn out of the wilderness, by the sturdy energy of these Celts, being estimated at 12,524l.!

These figures represent amazing energy and marvellous success, but they do not do full justice to the people by whom this work was done; for while they were engaged in the novel labour of cutting down the lofty and ponderous trees of the virgin forest, they were assailed by those enemies to the first settlers—Fever and Ague—that seem to resent man's invasion of the solitudes of nature, and endeavour to drive back his daring footsteps. Dr. Poole, a resident physician, writing of the sufferings of these early colonists, says that the fever and ague assailed them almost from the first moment they arrived in the country; and many strong hearts were unmanned, and many vigorous forms prostrated, during the earlier seasons of their forest life. Scarcely a family escaped, and sometimes entire families were afflicted with the ague for months together; and such was the violence of the disease, and their utter helplessness, that, at times, they were hardly able to hand each other a drink of water! It is a wonderful instance of energy and perseverance; and it may be well doubted if a greater amount of work has ever been accomplished during the first year by an equal number of persons, under equally unfavourable circumstances, in any part of America. It must be also borne in mind, that not one of these settlers had ever felled a tree until he set his foot in Canada.

The immigrants or settlers of forty years since suffered from inconveniences that are comparatively rare in the present day, and among the chief and most serious of these was the want of mills to grind the produce of their fields. The difficulty was not to raise the grain, but to convert it into flour, and thus render it fit for the food of man. It is recorded that, at an interview of a Scotch settler with the Governor, he told his Excellency—'We have no mill, sir, and, save your presence, sir, I have to get up at night to chew corn for the children.' Possibly the settlers from Cork were not subjected to a toil so fearful as that endured by the devoted Scotchman; but the only grist mill within reach being at a distance of between fifteen and twenty miles, it was necessary for the person who desired to get his corn ground to convey it to that distance on his back, and to return with it the same distance when it was converted into flour; and frequently would some sturdy Irishman shoulder his bag of grain, and bear it on his back those long and weary miles, his only food some potatoes which his wife had prepared for his toilsome journey. In the winter a hand-sleigh, that could be pushed over the snow, would afford facilities for taking corn to the mill, or for the transport of provisions; but there were states of the weather when the snow, which at other times afforded an easy track, was a source of impediment and danger. For many years the skin of the hog was made into covering for the feet, the hairy side being turned inwards; and as a substitute for tea, which was then a costly luxury, attainable only by the rich, or those within reach of towns, wild peppermint and other herbs were made to take its place.

What but the manly vigour for which the Irish race are now proverbial in the countries to which they have migrated, could have so speedily overcome the difficulties of a first settlement in the wilderness? Not a few of those who sailed from Cork in 1825 have passed away, after a life of hard and ceaseless toil, and others now stand, as it were, on the brink of the grave; but their sons and their grandsons, their daughters and their granddaughters, flourish in the midst of prosperity and comfort, of which those who went before them were the creators. The shanty and the wigwam and the log hut have long-since given place to the mansion of brick and stone; and the hand-sleigh and the rude cart to the strong wagon and the well-appointed carriage. Where there was but one miserable grist mill, there are now mills and factories of various kinds. And not only are there spacious schools under the control of those who erected and made use of them for their children, but the 'heavy grievance' which existed in 1825 has long since been a thing of the past.

The little chapel of logs and shingle—18 feet by 20—in which the settlers of that day knelt in gratitude to God, has for many years been replaced by a noble stone church, through whose painted windows the Canadian sunlight streams gloriously, and in which two thousand worshippers listen with the old Irish reverence to the words of their pastor. The tones of the pealing organs swell in solemn harmony, where the simple chaunt of the first settlers was raised in the midst of the wilderness; and for miles round may the voice of the great bell, swinging in its lofty tower, be heard in the calm of the Lord's Day, summoning the children of St. Patrick to worship in the faith of their fathers. Well may the white-haired patriarch, as he remembers the sailing from Cork, the passage across the mighty ocean, the journey up the St. Lawrence, the cutting of the road between the two lakes, the difficulties of the shallows, and the dangers of the rapids of the Otanabee, the camp in the wilderness, the fever and the ague that racked his bones in the early years, the hard toil and stern privations; well may he be surprised at what he now beholds—at the wondrous change wrought by the skill and courage of man, animated by the most potent of all incentives—the spirit of hope and the certainty of reward.

Twenty-five miles west of Peterborough, another town has sprung up within a few years—sprung out of the forest, as if by enchantment; and of this town a majority of its inhabitants are the descendants of those who left Cork in 1825, and of their friends or relatives who followed them in a few years after. There is not in Canada a prettier town than Lindsay, in which may be seen a curious structure, rather out of place in the midst of brick and stone. Carefully fenced round, and kept in a state of preservation, is an old log shanty, which is regarded by a considerable portion of the inhabitants with affectionate veneration. This was the temple in which they worshipped God when the soil on which the prosperous town of Lindsay now stands was covered with juniper and pine. Near this 'old church' is seen its successor—a splendid brick edifice of Gothic architecture, erected at a cost of $20,000. And not a gun-shot's distance from the old church is a fine block of shops, equal in style to any buildings in Montreal, which cost their owner some hundred thousand dollars. Twenty-five years ago he was a poor lad, not worth sixpence in the world; but he possessed what rarely fails in the long run—industry, honesty, intelligence, and steadiness.

To finish the history of these Irish immigrants, it may be mentioned that the discovery of gold in their neighbourhood has amazingly enhanced the value of real estate; so that those who desire, in the true American spirit, to push on, and seek a more extended field for their operations, may part with their property at prices which would enable them to purchase whole tracts of land in other places.

Proceeding farther West, we may behold the first hard struggle of people and of pastor, to reclaim the soil from the sterility of nature, and maintain the faith in the midst of the wilderness.

There is still living in Hamilton, Western Canada, as Vicar-General of the diocese, an Irish priest—Father Gordon, from Wexford—who has witnessed astonishing changes in his time. He has seen the city founded, and the town spring up; the forest cleared and the settlement created; the rude log chapel, in which a handful of the faithful knelt in the midst of the wood, replaced by the spacious brick church in which many hundreds now worship. And not only has he witnessed astonishing changes, but he has himself done much to effect the changes which he has lived to see accomplished. It is now about thirty-seven years since he came to Toronto, then a small place, and known by the name of Little York. Bishop McDonnell, a Scotchman, was the first Catholic Bishop of the diocese, at that time of immense extent. Father O'Grady, a Cork man, was stationed at Little York, and though even at that time the position of the Irish Catholic was miserable in the extreme, Father O'Grady was a favourite with the authorities: and indeed such were his social qualities and charm of manner, that no dinner party was considered complete without his genial presence. Father Gordon had charge of the back townships, twenty-four in number. We may appreciate the extent of his spiritual jurisdiction when we learn that a township comprised an area of twelve miles square; and Father Gordon had to attend twenty-four of these!

Irish Catholics there were, scattered through this vast territory—very nearly all of which was in its natural state, as it came from the hand of God; but they were few and far between, hidden in the recesses of the forest, most of them not having seen a priest for years, perhaps since they left their native home. Many of these had worked on the Erie Canal, and had come to Canada and taken land to settle. The fewer in number brought some little money with them, but generally their wealth consisted of provisions, which they had to carry on their backs through the woods, a distance of thirty, forty, even fifty miles. So long as the provisions lasted, they cut away and cleared; but as soon as the stock was near being exhausted they returned to the States, and went again on the public works. And thus they worked and laboured until they raised sufficient food to be independent of the merchant and the storekeeper. At this day these men are amongst the most prosperous in Canada.

The townships of Adjala and Tecumseth, in the county Simcoe, are amongst the most Irish and Catholic of any in Upper Canada. When Father Gordon became acquainted with them, there were in both but thirty or forty families, and these were scattered in every direction. Few were the visits which he could make in each district of his far-extended mission; he was in one place this Sunday and a hundred miles in an opposite direction the following Sunday. But the visit of the clergyman was an occasion of jubilee, in which all participated. About the time his arrival was expected, scouts would be on the watch to give the first notice of his approach, and if there were a hill-top in the neighbourhood, a signal fire would spread the glad intelligence to the anxious colony. With joyous cries, and clapping of hands, and eloquent sobs, the pious people would hail the priest, as his wearied horse bore him into their midst; and catching the contagion from them, the travel-worn missionary would forget his long journey and his many privations at the spectacle of their devotion and the cheering accents of their Irish welcome. Sheep and poultry, and even oxen, would be sacrificed by the prosperous settler, who was proud to have his home selected for the 'station;' and after confessions had been heard and Mass celebrated, and Communion received, then would follow the abundant breakfast, of which all partook, and then the grand dinner, for which such slaughter had taken place; and those whom long distance had kept for months apart would now rejoice in the opportunity of talking of the old country and former times, while the priest was appealed to on every side, as the best and surest authority as to what was going on in the world at the other side of the Atlantic, especially in Ireland—that spot to which every heart turned with unceasing love.

In 1833 Father Gordon determined to commence the work of church building in the forest, and his first effort was successfully made on the confines of Adjala and Tecumseth, where he resolved on erecting a log church. Assembling the people, he asked them to assist him in the good undertaking. They were delighted with his proposal, and willingly placed themselves at his command.

'There is one thing, boys, you must also promise me,' said the priest.

'Why, then, whatever it is, your reverence, we'll promise it, sure enough.'

'Well, boys,' continued Father Gordon, 'whiskey is like the devil—it is the father of mischief, and you know it is one of the greatest enemies of our race and country. It makes the best friends fall out, and it is the cause of violence and murder.'

A chorus of voices—'True for your reverence—'tis the blessed truth.'

'Well, then,' continued the good pastor, 'I want you to join me in performing one of the most acceptable works which man can perform for his Creator; that is, to raise a temple to His honour and glory, in which you and your children can worship the Great Being who has watched over you, and protected you and yours in the midst of this forest. I ask you to consecrate this great work by an act of self-denial which will be pleasing in His sight. I want you to promise me that you will not drink a drop of anything this day but water from that beautiful spring, fresh and sparkling from the hand of God, while you are engaged in erecting the temple to His honour. Promise me this, and you will have a blessing on your work, and you will bring gladness to the heart of your priest.'

The promise so solemnly solicited was given with one impulse, and it was religiously kept. Animated by the right spirit, the brave fellows addressed themselves to their labour of love; and so earnestly did they work that they cleared an ample space, as if by magic, and before the night set in they had erected a log church, 50 feet by 30, on the same spot on which now stands one of the finest ecclesiastical buildings in Canada. While the work was proceeding the poor priest was attacked with ague, and he was compelled to lie at the foot of a great tree on a couch constructed of the coats of the hardy church-builders. When the crisis, passed he was again in their midst, assisting them by advice or cheering them by a kindly word; but during that clay he was frequently driven beneath the pile of clothing by a new paroxysm of his disorder. In a similar manner the same indefatigable priest erected six other churches in the course of three years: and so careful was he in selecting the best sites, as to position, convenience, and conspicuousness, that in every case these primitive structures have been replaced by good churches, solidly built, with comfortable dwellings for the priests attached. These churches, erected in the midst of the forest, are now every Sunday surrounded by forty or fifty 'wagons,' many of them with a pair of good horses, the property of the substantial yeomanry, nay the gentry of the country, who, little more than a quarter of a century since, were penniless emigrants, with no friend save Providence, and no capital other than their strength, their industry and their intelligence. Let us take one of these pioneers of civilisation as an instance of what in those days they had to endure.

It is now about thirty years since an honest hardworking Irishman determined to go into the woods, and there make a home for himself and his wife and infant child. He had not, as he afterwards used to declare, 'as much as a half-crown in the world.' He however managed to take, and pay for by instalments, 100 acres of land, then covered with forest. Hiring himself to a farmer at some distance, he was enabled to purchase a stock of provisions and an axe; and, thus provided, he resolutely faced the wilderness, and there erected a shanty for himself and his little family. Like others similarly circumstanced, he then commenced to hew down the trees that overshadowed his primitive dwelling. Having effected a certain amount of clearing, he would again seek for such employment as enabled him to renew his stock of provisions; and thus alternately working abroad for others and at home for himself, this sturdy settler gradually succeeded in making a home for his now increasing family. His first crop of wheat, raised from the small patch which he had then cleared, he was compelled to carry on his back to the nearest mill, to be ground into flour. The distance was thirty miles—not of road or river, but through the dense forest, at that time but rarely intersected by open paths.

Returning on one occasion with the customary bag of flour on his back, the night overtook him while he was still far away from home. Blindly stumbling about in every direction, he fell, and, perhaps owing as much to the burden he carried as to the manner in which he came to the ground, broke his leg. Here was indeed a sad position!—in the midst of a lonely forest infested with wolves, away from all human assistance, and writhing in exquisite pain. There he lay for the whole night, moaning helplessly in agony of mind and body, as he thought of his young wife and his little children, far away from friendly assistance, and of the wild terror which his unaccountable absence would be sure to occasion. He was fortunately discovered next morning by a settler, who was attracted by his cries of distress, and who assisted in conveying him to his almost distracted family. For some months he lay helpless in his cabin, full of anxiety as well as pain; but no sooner was he once more able to be on his legs than he was again at work.

That man never ceased his hard toil till he had cleared his first lot, of 100 acres, and added time by time to his property; and he is this day the possessor of 900 acres of as good land as any in Canada, as well as the owner of saw mills and grist mills, in which the inhabitants of the neighbourhood may grind their corn. Toronto was over twenty miles distant from his log cabin, and when he first settled in the bush it was only at rare intervals that he had a visit from the priest. It was his custom to go to the city as often as he could, to perform his religious duties; and as, for the first years of his settler's life, he could not afford to purchase a horse, he was compelled to walk the whole of the way. When he brought one of his children with him to Mass, which it was his habit to do, in order, as he said, to make a strong religious impression on their youthful minds, he would divide the journey into two stages, and making the house of a friend his resting-place for the Saturday night, would set out at break of day on Sunday morning, holding his boy by the hand, or bearing him on his back. He would thus arrive some time before Mass commenced, so as to prepare for Communion, which he received with edifying piety; and after a brief rest and refreshment he would face towards his friend's house, his resting-place for the night. Nor was the good Irish father disappointed in his hopes of his children, all of whom grew up strong in the faith. Three of his sons received a collegiate education, and are now amongst the most respected members of the society in which they creditably move.

Father Gordon spent half his time in the saddle; and though he spared neither himself nor his horse—but himself much less than his horse—it was with the utmost difficulty that he could visit the more distant portions of his mission oftener than twice or thrice a year. Many a time did the active missionary lose his way in the midst of the woods, and after hours of weary riding find himself, in the dusk of the evening, in the very same spot from which he set out in the morning! His safest plan was to leave himself to the discretion of his trusty companion, that rarely failed him; thus, when puzzled as to the path, or rather track, he would throw the bridle on his horse's neck, and at the end of some time he was sure to be brought up before a cottage door, which was generally opened to him in welcome, for even those not of his faith respected the zealous 'Irish minister.' There was, however, one occasion when his reception was of a very different nature; and as the circumstances of the case are remarkable, it deserves to be told. I may say that I heard it the first time in Toronto from a warm admirer of the fine old priest, and afterwards in Hamilton from his own lips.

Returning to Toronto after a hard day's work, Father Gordon was about entering his modest residence, to obtain some necessary refreshment, when a countryman rode up to the door. He proved to be an Irishman from the township of Tecumseth, in the county of Simcoe, about forty miles from Toronto. 'Father, I'm glad to meet you; I want you to come with me to near my place, where there's a man dying, and there's not a moment to be lost.' This was agreeable news for the poor priest, who certainly had had his fair share of the saddle for that day. 'Who is the sick man? ' he asked. 'Oh, he's one Marshall, from the North—a Protestant, and all his people the same—and he is asking for the priest. I'm a neighbour of his, and I heard it from one of his sons, and I thought I couldn't do better than come for your reverence; and so here I am, just in time, thank God.' 'Very well,' said the priest, 'I will take a cup of tea, borrow a fresh horse, and be off without delay. Come in and join me, and I will be ready to start at once.' In half an hour after the two horsemen rode from the door on their journey through the forest, and it was not until late at night, thoroughly tired, that they pulled up before the house of the sick man, who was said to be at the point of death. Father Gordon dismounted, and knocked at the door, which was immediately opened by an elderly woman, at whose back stood two young men. 'What do you want here, at this hour of the night?' demanded the woman. 'Is there not a sick man in the house?' inquired the priest. 'There is—my husband—he is dying.' 'Well, I was sent for to see him—I am the priest.' 'Priest!' shrieked the woman, as if the Evil One stood revealed before her. 'Yes; I am the priest, come all the way from Toronto to see him, as he wished me to do,' was the quiet rejoinder. 'Then you may go as you came, for no priest will cross this threshold, if I can help it, no matter who wants to see him;' and saying this, the mistress of the house shut the door on Father Gordon and his guide, who was overwhelmed with confusion at the untoward result. 'To think that I should bring your reverence all this distance, and only to have the door shut in your face! I can't forgive myself; but I did it for the best.' 'To be sure you did, man—you did your duty, no more; and I respect you for it. But,' added the priest, 'I must be turning my horse's head homewards.' 'No, your reverence, not a step you'll go back this blessed night, if my name is Spillane (Spillane or Sullivan, I am not certain which); you'll stop at my house—'tis only a mile off—and we'll try and make you as comfortable as we can. It will be time enough to think of returning to-morrow.' 'Be it so, in God's name,' said Father Gordon.

They soon reached the house, where a good supper and a clean bed made some amends for the long ride and the keen disappointment. The tired missionary was soon in a deep slumber, in which perhaps he may have beheld again the group in the doorway, lit up by the flickering candle, and heard the words, 'No priest will cross this threshold if I can help it,' when he was suddenly awakened by a great noise or clatter in the house. At that moment his host entered the room. 'What is the matter, Spillane?' 'Why, then, your reverence, it is a strange matter—the strangest matter I ever heard of;—young Marshall has brought his father to you, as you wouldn't be allowed to come to him,' replied the host. 'You jest, man; 'tis impossible,' said the priest, in his first impulse of astonishment. 'Faith, then, 'tis no jest at all, your reverence, but the truth, as I'm a sinner, and that's no lie, any way,' said Spillane. It was the literal truth. When the dying man heard how the priest had been denied admission, and driven from his door, he was intensely afflicted; but he in vain sought to move the stern obduracy of his wife. 'Not one belonging to me ever disgraced himself by turning Papist, and you shan't be the one to commence.' The poor woman believed she was only doing her duty, and in this tranquillising conviction she soon forgot her troubles in sleep. But the dying man was inconsolable, and he moaned and wept in a manner to touch the heart of one of his sons, to whom he addressed the most earnest entreaties that he might be allowed to die as he wished to die. Moved alike by the tears and importunities of his father, the son at length yielded. But what was to be done?

The priest could not enter the house—his mother would not allow that; how, then, could his father's wish be accomplished? There was only one way of doing it, and that was quickly resolved upon and adopted. Carefully wrapping the dying man in the clothes in which he lay, the son raised him gently on his back, and, stealing softly with his precious burden, he crossed the threshold with noiseless step, and bore it a mile through the dark forest to the house in which the priest found shelter for the night, and there laid it down in safety. Whether it were that

Nature rallied her failing resources, or that the spirit rose superior to the frailty of the body, it may be difficult to say; but the father preserved strength enough to be received into the Church, and prepared for death, and to be brought back to his own home, in which he shortly after breathed his last. For several years, or as long as his mother lived, the son did not separate from her communion; but he afterwards became a Catholic, and is now the wealthy head of a large Catholic family, all good and religious, and full of worldly prosperity.

Father Gordon tells many anecdotes of his missionary life among his Irish flock; and however apparently trivial some of them may appear, they afford glimpses of the early condition of the settlers in the wilderness. Drenched to the skin one day in spring, he was compelled to seek shelter in a shanty; but such was the state of that dwelling that it afforded a friendly welcome to the rain, which entered wherever it pleased through the roof; and as the priest lay on the bed, composed of two logs placed in a corner, while his clothes were being dried at the fire, he was amused at witnessing the enjoyment of a brood of young ducks that were disporting themselves in a stream that ran through the cabin.

It was in a short time after that he rode up to the door of Mrs. Macnamara, 'all the way from the county of Cork.' 'Well, Mrs. Mac, have you anything for a poor traveller?' ''Deed, then, your reverence, there's a hearty welcome, and you know that; and I have a grain of tea, and the makings of a cake—and sure they're yours with a heart and a half, and so they would if they were ten times as much,' said Mrs. Mac. The good woman at once set about making the cake, which was soon in a forward state of preparation, and then, with much solemnity, she proceeded to 'make the tea,' which, in order to 'draw' it in the most scientific manner, she placed in its little black pot on a corner of the fire, away from the blaze. Mrs. Mac's stock of candles had long been exhausted, and she was obliged to be content with the light from the hearth; but Father Gordon had to 'pay his debt to the Pope,' and, in order to read his closely-printed breviary, he was constantly poking the fire with the end of a stick. 'Take care of the teapot, Father Gordon, dear—take care of it, for your life!' remonstrated the good woman, as she observed the reckless vigour with which the priest used the improvised poker. 'No fear, ma'am—no fear, ma'am,' he invariably replied. But there was every reason to fear, as the result proved; for, in one desperate effort to shed light on the small print, the priest brought down the entire superstructure, and with it the cherished teapot, which rolled, empty and spoutless, on the floor. Here was a disaster! The poor woman clapped her hands, as she cried, 'Oh, Father Gordon, jewel! what did you do? You broke my teapot, that I brought from Ireland, every step of the way, and I so fond of it! But, Father dear, 'tis worse for you, for there isn't another grain of tea in the house—and what will you do? Oh dear! oh dear!' Father Gordon had, as penance for his involuntary offence, to wash down the cake with the water of a neighbouring spring.

No one was more surprised at the changes wrought in comparatively a few years after, than was Father Gordon, who witnessed the infancy of the Irish settlements of the county of Simcoe.

'My dear sir,' said he, 'I could scarcely credit my eyesight, it was all so wonderful—like a dream. Fine roads, and splendid farms, and grand mansions, and horses and carriages, and noble churches with organs and peals of bells, and schools—yes, my dear sir, and ladies and gentlemen, the aristocracy of the country! What a difference between what I beheld on my last visit, and what I remember when I saw the young ducks in the stream running through the cabin floor, and when poor Mrs. Mac's last grain of tea was lost in the ashes. Dear, dear! what a wonderful change! God has been very merciful to our poor people. I never,' continued the good priest, who could speak with authority as to his countrymen, whom during his long life he loved and served with all the zeal and earnestness of his nature—'I never knew one of them that did not succeed, provided he was sober and well-conducted. Drink, sir, drink is the great failing of our race; and if they had a hundred enemies, that's the worst of all. But, thank God, on the whole, our people are good and religious, and every day advancing. It is a great change from what they were in the old country, and a greater change from what I remember they were thirty years ago in this.'

To my suggestion that he had had his own share of toil in those distant days, he replied: 'Well, my dear sir, no doubt I had many a hard ride through the forest, and I often had to depend on my poor horse, as my heavy eyelids closed while I sat in the saddle, overpowered with fatigue and want of sleep. But no matter what labour I had to undergo, I always received my reward in the faith and love of the people—their delight at seeing their priest, and hearing his voice—why, sir, it would raise any man's spirits. And how they kept the faith!—it was surprising. For years some would not see a priest; but still the faith was there in the mother's heart, and she would teach it to her children. We have lost some, for there were sheep without shepherds; but that we did not lose more, and that we saved so many in times long gone by, is only to be attributed to the mercy of God, and the tenacity with which the Irish cling to their faith. Oh, sir, their devotion, and their affection, and their gratitude, cheered me many a time, and made me forget fatigue and trouble of every kind. God bless them! they are a good people.'

These were almost the last words I heard from the lips of that true-hearted Irish priest, for it was of his people he loved to speak. Father Gordon has lived to see his church thoroughly organised, divided into several dioceses, each diocese having an efficient staff of clergymen, with numerous institutions, educational and charitable, under the care of the religious orders. Of the Bishops, four are Irish, and about one hundred of the clergy are either of Irish birth or descent. The religious orders also owe much of their strength to the same great national well-spring of the faith.

CHAPTER VII

Woolfe Island—Jimmy Cuffe—A Successful Irishman—Simple Pat as an
Agriculturist—The Land Question in Canada—Wise Policy of the Canadian
Parliament—Happy Results of a Wise Policy

THERE is an island in the St. Lawrence, forming the two channels, the English and the American, through which the majestic river flows from Lake Ontario to the sea. Woolfe Island—for that is the name by which it is known—is several miles in length, and about half as many broad. It is principally occupied by Irish Catholics, who settled upon it at different periods, not very remote. For a time the land was held partly by lease, and for a term of twenty-one years—a description of tenure altogether exceptional in a country in which freehold or fee-simple, in other words, absolute ownership, is almost universal.

In other countries a lease for twenty-one years might be regarded with favour, and under certain circumstances would be considered a security for mere outlay in cultivation. It is so in Scotland; but in America, where absolute and undisputed ownership is the rule, a tenure of this limited nature is rather a discouragement than a stimulus to exertion. And it may be remarked, that by proprietors of large tracts of land, who desire to see them occupied and cultivated, letting by lease is not much approved of; they prefer to sell it in lots, on such terms as may suit both parties, and possibly enable the person who sells to turn the purchase-money to other purposes. And when land falls into the possession of creditor or mortgagee, the new owner generally finds it more convenient and profitable to get rid of it by sale than to let it by lease of whatever term, and thus assume the responsibility and incur the risk incidental to the position of a landlord. The genius of the people, the very instinct of the community, is in favour of entire and unrestricted ownership, through which alone the forests have been turned into fields of grain and pasture, and America has been civilised and peopled.

The proprietor of a vast property in Woolfe Island determined to announce it for sale; and no sooner did he do so, than the Irish tenants put forth the most extraordinary energy, in order to become the owners of their farms. It seemed as if new life had been infused into them by the hope of possessing as proprietors the land they rented as tenants; and such was the success of their exertions that they, or the great majority of them, were enabled to purchase their lots.

As the island, with the exception of such portions of it as had been cleared, was covered with forest, like most of the land of Canada, the settlers of Woolfe Island had to undergo the ordinary hardships incidental to all similar efforts; but as they were not many miles from a fine town and a good market, they possessed advantages not usual with the genuine pioneer of civilisation, who buries himself in the depths of the woods, and is himself the author of everything that follows. Still the advantages of the thriving town and the unfailing market were not unattended with countervailing risk; for the nearness of the town offered to the settlers of the island temptations which many lacked the necessary fortitude to resist. It frequently occurred that the profits of a good season were sacrificed to the fascinations of boon-companionship, and the indulgence of a passion especially fatal to the Irishman. The evil was assuming alarming proportions, when, some dozen years since, an Irish priest—the Rev. Mr. Foley—resolved to grapple with it; and so powerfully and persuasively did he plead the cause of prudence and sobriety, so strenuously did he wrestle with the veteran drinkers—the 'hard cases,' as they were called—and such was his influence with the young, that he succeeded in a short time in enrolling 800 male residents, of all ages, from the vigorous stripling to the grey-haired grandsire, in the ranks of temperance. The result was magical. Soon there was not in all Canada a more prosperous or progressive settlement than that of Woolfe Island. The good priest died in the midst of his labours, and, as was customary, would have been buried in the Cathedral of Kingston; but so beloved was he by the people to whom he had been father and pastor, that they would not permit his honoured remains to be removed from the island; and the grave in which they rest is regarded with veneration by those who remember his holy life, and the zeal with which he watched over the temporal interests as well as the spiritual welfare of his flock. The islanders remain faithful to the advice of their pastor, and, as a consequence certain to follow from the avoidance of a fruitful cause of danger, they are happy and contented, and every year they are advancing in prosperity. The case of one of these settlers will illustrate that of many.

It is now about seventeen years since a little Irishman from Roscommon, named James Cuffe, settled in the island. Low-sized, but broad-shouldered, well-knit and vigorous as a 'four year old,' Jimmy Cuffe, like thousands of his race in America, possessed only that species of capital which may be easily carried across ocean and over mountain—which rust cannot consume nor moth devour, but which, although the wonder-worker of civilisation, is often blindly despised by those who will alone believe in bullion or bank notes;—it consisted of his strong pair of arms and his brave heart. Literally, he had not a penny in his pocket; nor indeed—at that time at least—could he 'take a shine' out of his reading and writing. But so resolutely did the little Connaught man—in whose composition, it may be remarked, there was not the faintest suspicion of the Anglo-Saxon—labour at his calling, 'morning and night, early and late,' that he rapidly became a thriving man; and Jimmy Cuffe is now the proprietor in fee-simple of 800 acres of rich land, which it would be difficult to match in Roscommon; with a fine house, a stable full of good horses, spacious barns, cattle and stock of every kind—in a word, everything that the heart of any rational Irishman could desire. He drives his family to church in a spring wagon, drawn by a pair of good horses, 'as grand as the Lord Mayor of London, or as any real gentleman in the ould country.' I happened to be in Kingston the day Jimmy Cuffe came in to take up the bill on which he had raised the purchase-money for his latest acquisition of 200 acres. It was rather a large sum, but the produce of his harvest enabled him to do so without embarrassment. And Jimmy's sharp grey eye glistened, as he told how he had got along, and succeeded not only in 'making a man of himself, thank God,' but— what pleased him quite as much —in buying out the old settlers—a class rather inclined to think little of what the Jimmy Cuffes can do. It is much to be doubted if Jimmy Cuffe would change places with a lord in the old country. The lord, as is usually the case, owes his position to his ancestors—Jimmy Cuffe, under Providence, owes everything to his industry, energy, and self-denial. Possibly, in the estimation of some people, the balance of merit may be in favour of the sturdy settler from Roscommon. Thankfully be it said, there are many Jimmy Cuffes in America.

Cases of a somewhat similar nature might be multiplied to any extent, all illustrative of the manly vigour of the Irish race, and of what great things they are capable when they have a fair field for their energies.

Living near a thriving city in Western Canada is a hale and vigorous Irishman, well advanced in years, who, as a day labourer, broke stones on the public road not far from the very spot on which stands his splendid residence, one of the most elegant in the country. Like a wise man, he took the first work that offered, and it prospered with him. He rejoices in an unmistakable Irish name, smacking of the 'ould ancient kings;' and there is not in all Canada a stauncher adherent to the ancient faith. When he came out to America—more than thirty years ago—a priest was rarely to be seen near where he settled, and it was only by great effort, at no small sacrifice of time and labour, that he could avail himself of the consolations of religion; but he was determined that, above all things, he would transmit to his children the precious deposit which he had himself received from his simple but pious parents.

Between the Saturday evening, when his week's work was over, and the Monday morning, when another week of labour commenced, this devoted Catholic would constantly walk a distance of between forty and fifty miles, to attend Mass and perform the duties enjoined by his Church. And when his children grew in strength, he would make them the companions of his journey. Not a few of this good man's descendants have abandoned a home of luxury to devote themselves to a religious life, and are now diffusing among the youth of their own race and faith the lessons of piety which they learned from the lips of an honoured parent. Men of his stamp are the glory of their country.

A recent striking instance of progress made by the Irish may be mentioned. The Bishop of Kingston—Dr. Horan—in visiting a settlement, of which the first tree had been cut only five years before, was received by one hundred of the settlers, each driving his own wagon and pair of horses. Preceded by a green banner, and a band of music obtained from a neighbouring town, these sturdy Celts conducted their good Bishop in triumph into the heart of their prosperous settlement. That was a day of well-earned jubilee.

In fully twenty of the counties of Upper or Western Canada there are thriving settlements either exclusively or principally occupied by Irish Catholics; while the Catholic Irish are to be found in every direction, often in the midst of Protestant settlements, whether Irish, Scotch, or English.

Something may here be said of the Irish agriculturist, as compared with his brethren from the sister kingdoms. As may be supposed, by those who know anything of the state of things in different parts of the United Kingdom, the Scotch and English farmers who settle in America bring with them—have brought with them—besides more or less capital in money, a knowledge and skill not possessed by those who emigrated from Ireland. It must be admitted that in Great Britain the science of agriculture has advanced to a degree of perfection to which, even under the most favourable circumstances, Ireland cannot aspire for many years yet to come. Thus it necessarily follows that while the Irishman is in no way inferior to the Englishman or Scotchman in industry or energy, capacity for labour or power of endurance, he is so in theoretical knowledge, and the management of land on the principles of 'high farming.'

Considering the relative condition of the three countries, this is what may be looked for. But the Irishman, even though he may not be able to write his name, is wonderfully shrewd and observant; and before his self-complacent neighbour imagines that simple Pat has even perceived what he was about, simple Pat has borrowed his improvement, and actually made his own of it. It is amusing to hear a poor fellow, who had little inducement for enterprise in his own country, dealing in the most daring manner with scientific terms, picked up from his Lothian or Yorkshire neighbour, and calling things by names that would puzzle a Liebig. But still there is no mistake in his application of the principle; for though he makes a fearful hash of the name, simple Pat has caught fast hold of the thing, as witness the appearance of his land and the abundance of his crops. It occasionally happens that townships belonging to the three nationalities adjoin; and wherever this is the case, the result is a healthful rivalry, productive of general advantage. In the new county of Victoria, in Central Canada, there is an instance of this propinquity. Three townships, almost exclusively belonging to English, Scotch, and Irish settlers, lie alongside each other; and between the three there exists a spirit of emulation, keen but amicable, as to which produces the largest crops, and cultivates the land in the most skilful manner. The result is told by an eminent Irishman, a man much respected in his district, and whose most cherished ambition is to see his countrymen raise themselves higher In the estimation of the world by the exercise of their great natural gifts:—'I am happy and proud to say that our countrymen have proved themselves to be equal in every respect to those from the sister kingdoms. To my mind, the Irish township, according to its numbers, produces the largest crops.' And he adds, 'Rely on it, if your countrymen at home had the same freedom of action, the same sense of security and certainty of reward, that they have in our free Canada, they would enjoy in their own country the same prosperity which they enjoy here.'

To me, the proposition seems consistent with reason and common sense, though fanatical sticklers for imaginary 'rights of property' may regard it as little better than rank blasphemy.

It will be interesting to see how the Canadian Parliament dealt, not long since, with the Land Question of the Lower Province. Fortunately for the public welfare, the earnest attention of the Canadian Legislature was directed to the tenure by which the cultivators occupied the soil, and especially to the obligations and restrictions imposed by its conditions upon that most important class of the community; and in 1861 an Act was passed, which has had, and must continue to have, a marked influence on the prosperity of the Province.

The land had been originally parcelled out among a number of great proprietors, who derived their vast estates directly from the Kings of France. Without entering into the history of these grants, or the manner in which the land was gradually occupied by the cultivators, who came as settlers, it is sufficient to state that the evils with which the Legislature had to deal did not arise so much from the burden of the rent, or the duration of the tenure, as from the 'rights' which the proprietors reserved to themselves.

The rent was so small as to be merely nominal, in fact a few halfpence per acre; but the 'rights'—which restricted the liberty of the tenant, interfered with the free transfer of property, and prevented the progress of the country—were the cause of the discontent that existed, and which it was the object of the Legislature to allay. One of the so-called 'casual rights' was the exclusive mill and water-power reserved to himself by the feudal lord. Not only was the *censitaire*, or tenant, compelled to grind his corn at the landlord's mill, but the latter monopolised the water-power within his territory, thus hampering the industry and enterprise of the district. The other 'right' was that by which, on every sale and transfer of property, the one-twelfth of the amount of the purchase-money was paid to the landlord. Say that A bought property from B, to the value of 120l., A, in addition to paying B the sum of 120l. as the purchase-money for his interest, had also to pay another one-twelfth, or 10l. more, to the landlord; and what rendered the exercise of this 'right' more oppressive and detrimental was the fact that on *every* re-sale of the same property the same process of paying one-twelfth to the seignior had to be gone through. If the property were improved in value, the seller would no doubt receive a larger price for his interest; but the seignior's one-twelfth would be the greater in consequence of the increased value of the whole. This one-twelfth so reserved to the seignior was termed a 'mutation fine.'

To get rid of this intolerable grievance, which was properly regarded as a grave public evil as well as individual oppression, the Canadian Legislature passed a law alike vigorous and comprehensive. The 'casual rights,' specially including those mentioned, were bought by the State at a cost little short of One Million Sterling; and an arrangement was made for the capitalisation and purchase of the rent by the tenant, and its compulsory sale by the landlord. Here was an instance of serious danger wisely averted by a measure which in the British Parliament would possibly be considered revolutionary, if not altogether confiscatory in its character. But statesmen in new countries are either more vigorous or more far-seeing than statesmen in old countries, who are trammelled by traditions and enfeebled by prejudices; besides, the very instinct of a young nation is to remove from its path every visible impediment to its progress.

The spirit in which this beneficent law was conceived will be best understood from a passage taken from its preamble, and another from its concluding clause.

The preamble says: 'Whereas it is expedient to abolish all feudal rights and duties in Lower Canada; and whereas, in consideration of the great advantages which must result to the Province from their abolition, and the substitution of a *free tenure* for that under which the property subject thereto hath heretofore been sold,' &c.

The concluding clause is still more emphatic. It proclaims that—'The Legislature reserves the right of making any provisions, declaratory or otherwise, which may be found necessary for the purpose of fully carrying out the intention of this Act; which in intent is declared to be, to abolish as soon as possible all feudal or seignorial rights, duties, dues, &c. .... And to aid the *censitaire* out of the provincial funds in the redemption of those seignorial charges *which interfere most injuriously with his independence, industry, and enterprise*; and every enactment and provision in this Act shall receive the *most liberal construction possible*, with a view to ensure the accomplishment of the intention of the Legislature as hereby stated.'

The wise action of the Canadian Parliament at once arrested and removed the deep-seated feeling of discontent which was hourly increasing in intensity. From the example of the Canadian Legislature even the Parliament of the mother country may derive a valuable suggestion as to the abolition of those 'seignorial rights, duties, dues,' &c., and the redemption, or at least adjustment, of those charges 'which interfere most injuriously with the independence, industry, and enterprise' of the *censitaire* of Ireland. The parent need not be ashamed to learn a lesson from the child, especially when the wisdom of that child's policy is proved beyond the possibility of doubt.

CHAPTER VIII

*The Irish Exodus—The Quarantine at Grosse Isle—The Fever Sheds—Horrors
of the Plague—The 'Unknown'—The Irish Orphans—The good Canadians—
Resistless Eloquence—One of the Orphans—The Forgotten Name—The Plague in
Montreal—How the Irish died—The Monument at Point St. Charles—The Grave-
mound in Kingston—An illustrious Victim in Toronto—How the Survivors pushed
on—The Irish in the Cities of Upper Canada—The Education System—The Dark
Shadow—The Poison of Orangeism—The only Drawback*

I HAVE more than once referred to the unfavourable circumstances under which
the vast majority of the Irish arrived in America, and the difficulties with which, in
a special degree, they had to contend; but the picture would be most imperfect
were not some reference made to the disastrous emigration of the years 1847 and
1848—to that blind and desperate rush across the Atlantic known and described,
and to be recognised for time to come, as the Irish Exodus. We shall confine our
present reference to the emigration to Canada, and track its course up the waters of
the St. Lawrence. A glance even at a single quarantine —that of Grosse Isle, in the
St. Lawrence, about thirty miles below Quebec—while affording a faint idea of
the horrors crowded into a few months, may enable the reader to understand with
what alarm the advent of the Irish was regarded by the well-to-do colonists of
British America; and how the natural terror they inspired, through the terrible
disease brought with them across the ocean, deepened the prejudice against them,
notwithstanding that their sufferings and misery appealed to the best sympathies of
the human heart.

On the 8th of May, 1847, the 'Urania,' from Cork, with several hundred
immigrants on board, a large proportion of them sick and dying of the ship-fever,
was put into quarantine at Grosse Isle. This was the first of the plague-smitten
ships from Ireland which that year sailed up the St. Lawrence. But before the first
week of June as many as eighty-four ships of various tonnage were driven in by an
easterly wind; and of that enormous number of vessels there was not one free from
the taint of malignant typhus, the offspring of famine and of the foul ship-hold.
This fleet of vessels literally reeked with pestilence. All sailing vessels,—the
merciful speed of the well-appointed steamer being unknown to the emigrant of
those days,—a tolerably quick passage occupied from six to eight weeks; while
passages of ten or twelve weeks, and even a longer time, were not considered at all
extraordinary at a period when craft of every kind, the most unsuited as well as the
least seaworthy, were pressed into the service of human deportation.

Who can imagine the horrors of even the shortest passage in an emigrant ship
crowded beyond its utmost capability of stowage with unhappy beings of all ages,

with fever raging in their midst? Under the most favourable circumstances it is impossible to maintain perfect purity of atmosphere between decks, even when ports are open, and every device is adopted to secure the greatest amount of ventilation. But a crowded emigrant sailing ship of twenty years since, with fever on board!—the crew sullen or brutal from very desperation, or paralysed with terror of the plague—the miserable passengers unable to help themselves, or afford the least relief to each other; one-fourth, or one-third, or one-half of the entire number in different stages of the disease; many dying, some dead; the fatal poison intensified by the indescribable foulness of the air breathed and rebreathed by the gasping sufferers—the wails of children, the ravings of the delirious, the cries and groans of those in mortal agony!

Of the eighty-four emigrant ships that anchored at Grosse Isle in the summer of 1847, there was not a single one to which this description might not rightly apply.

The authorities were taken by surprise, owing to the sudden arrival of this plague-smitten fleet, and, save the sheds that remained since 1832, there was no accommodation of any kind on the island. These sheds were rapidly filled with the miserable people, the sick and the dying, and round their walls lay groups of half-naked men, women, and children, in the same condition—sick or dying. Hundreds were literally flung on the beach, left amid the mud and stones, to crawl on the dry land how they could. 'I have seen,' says the priest who was then chaplain of the quarantine, and who had been but one year on the mission, 'I have one day seen thirty-seven people lying on the beach, crawling on the mud, and dying like fish out of water.' Many of these, and many more besides, gasped out their last breath on that fatal shore, not able to drag themselves from the slime in which they lay. Death was doing its work everywhere—in the sheds, around the sheds, where the victims lay in hundreds under the canopy of heaven, and in the poisonous holds of the plague-ships, all of which were declared to be, and treated as, hospitals.

From ship to ship the young Irish priest carried the consolations of religion to the dying. Amidst shrieks, and groans, and wild ravings, and heart-rending lamentations,—over prostrate sufferers in every stage of the sickness—from loathsome berth to loathsome berth, he pursued his holy task. So noxious was the pent-up atmosphere of these floating pest-houses, that he had frequently to rush on deck, to breathe the pure air, or to relieve his overtaxed stomach: then he would again plunge into the foul den, and resume his interrupted labours.

There being, at first, no organisation, no staff, no available resources, it may be imagined why the mortality rose to a prodigious rate, and how at one time as many as 150 bodies, most of them in a half-naked state, would be piled up in the dead-house, awaiting such sepulture as a huge pit could afford. Poor creatures would crawl out of the sheds, and being too exhausted to return, would be found lying in the open air, not a few of them rigid in death. When the authorities were enabled to erect sheds sufficient for the reception of the sick, and provide a staff of physicians and nurses, and the Archbishop of Quebec had appointed a number of priests, who took the hospital duty in turn, there was of course more order and regularity; but the mortality was for a time scarcely diminished. The deaths were as many as 100, and 150, and even 200 a day, and this for a considerable period during the summer. The masters of the quarantine-bound ships were naturally desirous of getting rid as speedily as possible of their dangerous and unprofitable freight; and the manner in which the helpless people were landed, or thrown, on the island, aggravated their sufferings, and in a vast number of instances precipitated their fate. Then the hunger and thirst from which they suffered in the badly-found ships, between whose crowded and stifling decks they had been so long pent up, had so far destroyed their vital energy that they had but little chance of life when once struck down.

About the middle of June the young chaplain was attacked by the pestilence. For ten days he had not taken off his clothes, and his boots, which he constantly wore for all that time, had to be cut from his feet. A couple of months elapsed before he resumed his duties; but when he returned to his post of danger the mortality was still of fearful magnitude. Several priests, a few Irish, the majority French Canadians, caught the infection; and of the twenty-five who were attacked, seven paid with their lives the penalty of their devotion. Not a few of these men were professors in colleges; but at the appeal of the Archbishop they left their classes and their studies for the horrors and perils of the fever sheds.

It was not until the 1st of November that the quarantine of Grosse Isle was closed. Upon that barren isle as many as 10,000 of the Irish race were consigned to the grave-pit. By some the estimate is made much higher, and 12,000 is considered nearer the actual number. A register was kept, and is still in existence, but it does not commence earlier than June 16, when the mortality was nearly at its height. According to this death-roll, there were buried, between the 16th and 30th of June, 487 Irish immigrants 'whose names could not be ascertained.' In July, 941 were thrown into nameless graves; and in August, 918 were entered in the register under the comprehensive description—'unknown.' There were interred, from the 16th of June to the closing of the quarantine for *that* year, 2,905 of a Christian people, whose names could not be discovered amidst the confusion and carnage of that fatal summer. In the following year, 2,000 additional victims were entered in the same register, without name or trace of any kind, to tell who they were, or whence they had come. Thus 5,000 out of the total number of victims were simply described as 'unknown.'

This deplorable havoc of human life left hundreds of orphans dependent on the compassion of the public; and nobly was the unconscious appeal of this multitude of destitute little ones responded to by the French Canadians. Half naked, squalid, covered with vermin generated by hunger, fever, and the foulness of the ship's hold, perhaps with the germs of the plague lurking in their vitiated blood, these helpless innocents of every age—from the infant taken from the bosom of its dead mother to the child that could barely tell the name of its parents—were gathered under the fostering protection of the Church. They were washed, and clad, and fed; and every effort was made by the clergy and nuns who took them into their charge to discover who they were, what their names, and which of them were related the one to the other, so that, if possible, children of the same family might not be separated for ever. A difficult thing it was to learn from mere infants whether, among more than 600 orphans, they had brothers or sisters. But by patiently observing the little creatures when they found strength and courage to play, their watchful protectors were enabled to find out relationships which, without such care, would have been otherwise unknown. If one infant ran to meet another, or caught its hand, or smiled at it, or kissed it, or showed pleasure in its society, here was a clue to be followed; and in many instances children of the same parents were thus preserved to each other. Many more, of course, were separated for ever, as these children were too young to tell their own names, or do anything save cry in piteous accents for 'mammy, mammy!' until soothed to slumber in the arms of a compassionate Sister.

The greater portion of the orphans of the Grosse Isle tragedy were adopted by the French Canadians, who were appealed to by their curés at the earnest request of Father Cazeau, then Secretary to the Archbishop, and now one of the Vicars General of the Archdiocese of Quebec. M. Cazeau is one of the ablest of the ecclesiastics of the Canadian Church, and is no less remarkable for worth and ability than for the generous interest he has ever exhibited for the Irish people. Father Cazeau had employed his powerful influence with the country clergy to provide for the greater number of the children; but some 200 still remained in a building specially set apart for them, and this is how these 200 Irish orphans were likewise provided for:

Monsignor Baillargeon, Bishop of Quebec, was then curé of the city. He had received three or four of the orphans into his own house, and among them a beautiful boy of two years, or perhaps somewhat younger. The others had been taken from him and adopted by the kindly *habitans*, and become part of their families; but the little fellow, who was the curé's special pet, remained with him for nearly two years. From creeping up and down stairs, and toddling about in every direction, he soon began to grow strong, and bold, and noisy, as a fine healthy child would be; but though his fond protector rejoiced in the health and beauty of the boy, he found him rather unsuited to the quiet gravity of a priest's house, and a decided obstacle to study and meditation. In the midst of his perplexity, of which the child was the unconscious cause to the Curé of Quebec, a clergyman from the country arrived in town. This priest visited M. Baillargeon, who told him that he had 200 poor orphan children—the children of 'the faithful Catholic Irish'—still unprovided with a home, and he was most anxious that his visitor should call on his parishioners to take them. 'Come,' said he, 'I will show you a sample of them, and you can tell your people what they are like.' Saying this, M. Baillargeon led his visitor upstairs, and into the room where, in a little cot, the orphan child was lying in rosy sleep. As the light fell upon the features of the beautiful boy, who was reposing in all the unrivalled grace of infancy, the country cure was greatly touched: he had never, he said, seen a 'lovelier little angel' in his life. 'Well,' said M. Baillargeon, 'I have 200 more as handsome. Take him with you, show him to your people, and tell them to come for the others.' That very night the boat in which he was to reach his parish was to start; and the cure wrapped the infant carefully in the blanket in which he lay, and, without disturbing his slumber, bore him off to the boat, a valued prize.

The next Sunday a strange sight was witnessed in the parish church of which the curé was the pastor. The priest was seen issuing from the sacristy, holding in his arms a boy of singular beauty, whose little hands were tightly clasped, half in terror, half in excitement, round the neck of his bearer. Every eye was turned towards this strange spectacle, and the most intense curiosity was felt by the congregation, in a greater degree by the women, especially those who were mothers, to learn what it meant. It was soon explained by their pastor, who said:— 'Look at this little boy! Poor infant! (Here the curé embraced him.) Look at his noble forehead, his bright eyes, his curling hair, his mouth like a cherub's! Oh, what a beautiful boy! (Another embrace, the half-terrified child clinging closer to the priest's breast, his tears dropping fast upon the surplice.) 'Look, my dear friends, at this beautiful child, who has been sent by God to our care. There are 200 as beautiful children as this poor forlorn infant. They were starved out of their own country by bad laws, and their fathers and their poor mothers now lie in the great grave at Grosse Isle. Poor mothers! they could not remain with their little ones. You will be mothers to them. The father died, and the mother died; but before she died, the pious mother—the Irish Catholic mother—left them to the good God, and the good God now gives them to you. Mothers, you will not refuse the gift of the good God! (The kindly people responded to this appeal with tears and gestures of passionate assent.) Go quickly to Quebec; there you will find these orphan children—these gifts offered to you by the good God—go quickly—go to-morrow—lose not a moment—take them and carry them to your homes, and they will bring a blessing on you and your families. I say, go to-morrow without fail, or others may be before you. Yes, dear friends, they will be a blessing to you as they grow up, a strong healthy race—fine women, and fine men, like this beautiful boy. Poor child, you will be sure to find a second mother in this congregation.' (Another embrace, the little fellow's tears flowing more abundantly; every eye in the church glistening with responsive sympathy.)

This was the curé's sermon, and it may be doubted if Bossuet or Fenelon ever produced a like effect. Next day there was to be seen a long procession of wagons moving towards Quebec; and on the evening of that day there was not one of the 200 Irish orphans that had not been brought to a Canadian home, there to be nurtured with tenderness and love, as the gift of the *Bon Dieu*. Possibly, in some instances that tenderness and love were not requited in after life, but in most instances the Irish orphan brought a blessing to the hearth of its adopted parents. The boy whose beauty and whose tears so powerfully assisted the simple oratory of the good curé is now one of the ablest lawyers in Quebec—but a French Canadian in every respect save in birth and blood.

As soon as good food and tender care had restored vigour to their youthful limbs, the majority of the orphans played in happy unconsciousness of their bereavement; but there were others, a few years older, on whom the horrors of Grosse Isle had made a lasting impression.

A decent couple had sailed in one of the ships, bringing with them two girls and a boy, the elder of the former being about thirteen, the boy not more than seven or eight. The father died first, the mother next. As the affrighted children knelt by their dying mother, the poor woman, strong in her faith, with her last accents confided her helpless offspring to 'the protection of God and His Blessed Mother,' and told them to have confidence in the Father of the widow and the orphan. Lovingly did the cold hand linger on the head of her boy, as, with expiring energy, she invoked a blessing upon him and his weeping sisters. Thus the pious mother died in the fever-shed of Grosse Isle. The children were taken care of, and sent to the same district, so as not to be separated from each other. The boy was received into the home of a French Canadian; his sisters were adopted by another family in the neighbourhood. For two weeks the boy never uttered a word, never smiled, never appeared conscious of the presence of those around him, or of the attention lavished on him by his generous protectors, who had almost come to believe that they had adopted a little mute, or that he had momentarily lost the power of speech through fright or starvation. But at the end of the fortnight he relieved them of their fears by uttering some words of, to them, an unknown language; and from that moment the spell, wrought, as it were, by the cold hand of his dying mother, passed from the spirit of the boy, and he thenceforth clung with the fondness of youth to his second parents. The Irish orphan soon spoke the language of his new home, though he never lost the memory of the fever-sheds and the awful death-bed, or of his weeping sisters, and the last words spoken by the faithful Christian woman who commended him to the protection of God and His Blessed Mother. He grew up a youth of extraordinary promise, and was received into the college of Nicolet, then in the diocese of Quebec, where he graduated with the greatest honours. His vocation being for the Church, he became a priest; and it was in 1865 that, as a deacon, he entered the College of St. Michael, near Toronto, to learn the language of his parents, of which he had lost all remembrance. He is now one of the most distinguished professors of the college in which he was educated; and, in order to pay back the debt incurred by his support and education, he does not accept more than a small stipend for his services. Of his Irish name, which he was able to retain, he is very proud; and though his tongue is more that of a French Canadian, his feelings and sympathies are with the people and the country of his birth. The prayers of the dying mother were indeed heard; for the elder of the girls was married by the gentleman who received them both into his house, and the younger is in a convent.

Absorbed thus into the families of the French-speaking population, even the older Irish orphans soon lost almost every memory of their former home and of their parents, and grew up French Canadians in every respect save the more vigorous constitution for which they were indebted to nature. It is not, therefore, a rare thing to behold a tall, strapping, fair-skinned young fellow, with an unmistakable Irish name, and an unmistakable Irish face, who speaks and thinks as a French Canadian. Thus genuine Irish names—as Cassidy, or Lonergan, or Sullivan, or Quinn, or Murphy—are to be heard of at this day in many of the homes of the kindly *habitans* of Lower Canada.

Though it was the humane policy of those who took care of the orphans of Grosse Isle to keep the same family in the same neighbourhood, so as not to separate brother from sister, it has happened that a brother has been reared by a French family, and a sister by an Irish, or English-speaking, family; and when the orphans have been brought together by their adopted parents, they could only express their emotions by embraces and tears—the language of the heart.

In some, but rare instances, visions of the past have haunted the memory of Irish orphans in their new homes. One of these, a young girl who bore the name of her protectors, was possessed with a passionate longing to learn her real name, and to know something of her parents. A once familiar sound, which she somehow associated with her former name, floated through her brain, vague and indistinct, but ever present. The longing to ascertain who she was, and whether either of her parents was still living, grew into an absorbing passion, which preyed upon her health. She would frequently write what expressed her recollection of the name she had once borne, and which she thought she had been called in her infancy by those who loved her. The desire to clear up the doubt becoming at length uncontrollable, she implored the cure of her parish to institute inquiries in her behalf. Written in French characters, nearly all resemblance to the supposed name was lost; but through the aid of inquiries set on foot by Father Dowd, the Parish Priest of St. Patrick's, in Montreal, and guided by the faint indication afforded by what resembled a sound more than a sirname, it was discovered that her mother had taken her out to America in 1847, and that her father had never quitted Ireland. A communication was at once established between father and child; and from that moment the girl began to recover her health, which had been nearly sacrificed to her passionate yearning.

The horrors of Grosse Isle had their counterpart in Montreal.

As in Quebec, the mortality was greater in 1847 than in the year following; but it was not till the close of 1848 that the plague might be said to be extinguished, not without fearful sacrifice of life. During the months of June, July, August, and September, the season when nature wears her most glorious garb of loveliness, as many as eleven hundred of 'the faithful Irish,' as the Canadian priest truly described them, were lying at one time in the fever-sheds at Point St. Charles, in which rough wooden beds were placed in rows, and so close as scarcely to admit of room to pass. In these miserable cribs the patients lay, sometimes two together, looking, as a Sister of Charity since wrote, 'as if they were in their coffins,' from the box-like appearance of their wretched beds. Throughout those glorious months, while the sun shone brightly, and the majestic river rolled along in golden waves, hundreds of the poor Irish were dying daily. The world outside was gay and glad, but death was rioting in the fever-sheds. It was a moment to try the devotion which religion inspires, to test the courage with which it animates the gentlest breast. First came the Grey Nuns, strong in love and faith; but so malignant was the disease that thirty of their number were stricken down, and thirteen died the death of martyrs. There was no faltering, no holding back; no sooner were the ranks thinned by death than the gaps were quickly filled; and when the Grey Nuns were driven to the last extremity, the Sisters of Providence came to their assistance, and took their place by the side of the dying strangers. But when even their aid did not suffice to meet the emergency, the Sisters of St. Joseph, though cloistered nuns, received the permission of the Bishop to share with their sister religious the hardships and dangers of labour by day and night.

'I am the only one left,' were the thrilling words in which the surviving priest announced from the pulpit the ravages that the 'ocean plague ' had made in the ranks of the clergy. With a single exception, the local priests were either sick or dead. Eight of the number fell at their post, true to their duty. The good Bishop, Monsigneur Bourget, then went himself, to take his turn in the lazar-house; but the enemy was too mighty for his zeal, and having remained in the discharge of his self-imposed task for a day and a night, he contracted the fever, and was carried home to a sick-bed, where he lay for weeks, hovering between life and death, amid the tears and prayers of his people, to whom Providence restored him after a period of intense anxiety to them, and long and weary suffering to him.

When the city priests were found inadequate to the discharge of their pressing duties, the country priests cheerfully responded to the call of their Bishop, and came to the assistance of their brethren; and of the country priests not a few found the grave and the crown of the martyr.

Among the priests who fell a sacrifice to their duty in the fever-sheds of Montreal was Father Richards, a venerable man, long past the time of active service. A convert from Methodism in early life, he had specially devoted his services to the Irish, then but a very small proportion of the population; and now, when the cry of distress from the same race was heard, the good old man could not be restrained from ministering to their wants. Not only did he mainly provide for the safety of the hundreds of orphan children, whom the death of their parents had left to the mercy of the charitable, but, in spite of his great age, he laboured in the sheds with a zeal which could not be excelled.

'Father Richards wants fresh straw for the beds,' said the messenger to the mayor.

'Certainly, he shall have it: I wish it was gold, for his sake,' replied the mayor.

A few days after both Protestant mayor and Catholic priest ' had gone where straw and gold are of equal value,' wrote the Sister already mentioned. Both had died martyrs of charity.

Only a few days before Father Richards was seized with his fatal illness he preached on Sunday in St. Patrick's, and none who heard him on that occasion could forget the venerable appearance and impressive words of that noble servant of God. Addressing a hushed and sorrow-stricken audience, as the tears rolled down his aged cheeks, he thus spoke of the sufferings and the faith of the Irish:—

'Oh, my beloved brethren, grieve not, I beseech you, for the sufferings and death of so many of your race, perchance your kindred, who have fallen, and are still to fall, victims to this fearful pestilence. Their patience, their faith, have edified all whose privilege it was to witness it. Their faith, their resignation to the will of God under such unprecedented misery, is something so extraordinary that, to realise it, it requires to be seen. Oh, my brethren, grieve not for them; they did but pass from earth to the glory of heaven. True, they were cast in heaps into the earth, their place of sepulture marked by no name or epitaph; but I tell you, my clearly beloved brethren, that from their ashes the faith will spring up along the St. Lawrence, for they died martyrs, as they lived confessors, to the faith.'

The whole city, Protestant and Catholic, mourned the death of this fine old man, one of the most illustrious, victims of the scourge in Montreal.

The orphan children were gathered to the homes and hearts of the generous Canadians and the loving Irish; and most of them had grown up to manhood and womanhood before either monument or epitaph marked the spot in which the hones of their dead parents were mingling with the dust. But there is a monument and a record, the pious work of English workmen, inspired by the humane suggestion of English gentlemen. In the centre of a railed-in spot of land at Point St. Charles, within a hundred yards or so of the Victoria Bridge, that wondrous structure which spans the broad St. Lawrence, there is a huge boulder, taken from the bed of the river, and placed on a platform of roughly hewn stone; and on that boulder there is this inscription:—

TO
Preserve from desecration
THE REMAINS OF SIX THOUSAND IMMIGRANTS,
Who died of Ship-fever,
A.D. 1847-8, This stone is erected by the
WORKMEN OF MESSRS. PETO, BRASSEY, AND BETTS,
Employed in the
Construction of the Victoria Bridge,
A.D. 1859.

In the church of the Bon Sécour one may see a memorial picture, representing with all the painter's art the horrors and the glories of the fever-shed—the dying Irish, strong in their faith—the ministering Sisters, shedding peace on the pillow of suffering—the holy Bishop, affording the last consolations of religion to those to whom the world was then as nothing: but, in its terrible significance, the rude monument by that mighty river's side is far more impressive.

Let us follow the Irish emigrant—'the faithful Irish'—farther up the St. Lawrence.

In the grounds of the General Hospital of Kingston there is an artificial mound, of gentle swell and moderate elevation, the grass on which is ever green, as if owing to some peculiar richness of the soil. When verdure has been elsewhere burned up or parched, on this soft-swelling mound greenness is perpetual. Beneath that verdant shroud lie mouldering the bones of 1,900 Irish immigrants, victims of the same awful scourge of their race—the ship-fever. With the intention of pushing on to the West, the goal of their hopes, multitudes of the Irish reached Kingston, 350 miles up the St. Lawrence from Quebec; but the plague broke out amongst this mass of human misery, and they rotted away like sheep. So fast did they die, that there were not means to provide coffins in which to inter them. There was timber more than sufficient for the purpose, but the hands to fashion the plank into the coffin were too few, and Death was too rapid in his stroke; and so a huge pit of circular form was dug, and in it were laid, in tiers, piled one upon the other, the bodies of 1,000 men, women, and children: and even to the hour when I beheld the light of the setting sun imparting additional beauty to its vivid greenness, there was neither rail, nor fence, nor stone, nor cross, nor inscription, to tell that 1,900 of a Christian people slept beneath the turf of that gigantic grave.

Twenty years ago Kingston was a small place, with little more than half its present population; and the Irish, who now form an important portion of its community, were then comparatively few in number. But in no part of British America did the Irish display a more heroic devotion to humanity and country than in that city, from which the greater number of the inhabitants had fled in terror, at the presence of the migratory hordes who brought pestilence with them in their march. The Irish of the town stood their ground bravely; and not only were their houses thrown open to their afflicted countrypeople, and their means placed unreservedly at their disposal, but they tended the sick and dying, and ministered to them in the holiest spirit of charity. Among the best and bravest of those who succoured the plague-smitten of that dreadful time were three Irish Protestants— Mr. Kirkpatrick, then Mayor of Kingston; Alderman Robert Anglin; and Mr. William Ford, afterwards Mayor—who were in the sheds both day and night, and by their ceaseless efforts to relieve the sufferers inspired others with increased courage and still greater self-devotion.

Father Dollard, an Irish clergyman, had to bear the chief share of the priestly duty; and from the first moment that the fever broke out, until the earth was beaten down on the top of the grave-mound, he was in the midst of the danger. So shocking was the condition in which the unhappy people reached Kingston, the last resting-place of many of them, that the clergymen, three at the most, had to change their own clothes repeatedly in the day. One of the three priests, who had been only just ordained, died of the contagion.

When the plague abated, and the danger no longer existed, the inhabitants returned; and now there began an unseemly scramble for the orphan children of the Catholic parents who slept beneath the mound in the grounds of the Hospital. The Irish Catholics of the surrounding locality strained every resource in order to afford a home to the orphans of their native country and religion, and through their charity the greater number of them were well provided for; but others of a different faith secured a certain proportion of the children, who are now perhaps bitter opponents of the creed of their fathers.

The same scenes of suffering and death were to be witnessed in the city of Toronto, as in the other cities of Canada during those memorable years 1847 and 1848. Sheds were constructed, and hearses and dead-carts were in hourly requisition. The panic was universal; but the humane and high-spirited, of all denominations, did their duty manfully. Two and three coffins were constantly to be seen on the hearse or wagon used for bearing the dead to the grave-pit outside the town. One day the horse drawing this hearse got restive, and, breaking from his conductor, upset the three coffins, which, falling into pieces, literally gave up their dead. This occurred near the Market Square, about the most public thoroughfare in Toronto, and at once a crowd assembled, horror-stricken but fascinated by the awful spectacle. Every effort was made to repair as speedily as possible the momentary disaster; but it was some time before the three wasted bodies of the poor Irish could be hidden from sight. The priests, as in all similar cases, were ceaselessly at work, with the usual result—the sacrifice of several of their number.

Among the losses which the Catholic Church had to deplore during this crisis was that of a venerable Irishman, Dr. Power, Bishop of Toronto. He was implored by his people not to expose a life so valuable to his flock; but he replied, that where the souls of Christians, and these the natives of his own country, were in peril, it was his duty to be there. 'My good priests are down in sickness, and the duty devolves on me. The poor souls are going to heaven, and I will do all I can to assist them,' said the Bishop. And, in spite of the most earnest and affectionate remonstrance, he persevered in performing the same labours as the youngest of his priests. The Bishop prepared for his post of danger by making his will, and appointing an administrator. The letters of administration were lengthy, and of much importance, embracing necessarily the financial and other concerns of the diocese. This document, most precious from its association with the voluntary martyrdom of the venerable Prelate, is preserved among the episcopal archives of Toronto. It was commenced with a bold firm hand; but as it proceeded amid frequent interruptions—his visits to console the dying being their chief cause—the writing became more and more feeble, until one might mark, in the faint and trembling characters of the concluding lines, the near approach of death, which soon consigned him to the tomb, another martyr to duty. Rarely, if ever, has a larger funeral procession been seen in Toronto, and never has there been a more universal manifestation of public sorrow than was witnessed on that mournful occasion. Every place of business in the streets through which the procession passed was closed, and Protestant vied with Catholic in doing honour to the memory of a holy and brave-hearted prelate.

Partridge Island, opposite the city of St. John, New Brunswick, was the scene of more horrors, more destruction of human life. In fact, wherever an emigrant ship touched the shores of the British Provinces, or sailed into their rivers, there is the same awful carnage to be recorded.

A portion of the survivors pushed on to the West, their march still tracked by fever, and marked by new-made graves. The majority stopped at various places on the way, or spread over Central and Western Canada, many settling on Crown lands placed at their disposal by the Government, but others hiring themselves as farm labourers, not having, as yet, the energy to face the forest, and engage in a struggle for which disease and sorrow had rendered them for a time unequal. But in half a dozen years after might be seen, along the shores of the lakes, and on the banks of the great rivers and their tributaries, prosperous settlements of those fever-hunted exiles, who, flying in terror from their own country, carried plague and desolation with them to the country of their adoption. It was remarked of them that, though they bravely rallied, and set about their work as settlers with an energy almost desperate, many seemed to be prematurely old, and broke down after some years of ceaseless toil; but not before they had achieved the great object of their ambition—made a home and realised a property for those who, with them, survived the horrors of the passage, and the havoc of the quarantine and the fever-shed.

Even to this day the terror inspired in the minds of the inhabitants through whose districts the Irish emigrants passed in the terrible years of 1847 and 1848 has not died out. I was told of one instance where, little more than a year since, whole villages were scared at the announcement, happily untrue, that 'the poor Irish were coming, and were bringing the fever with them.' It was scarcely a subject for the pleasantry of the wag.

As explorers and pioneers, the Irish have been as adventurous and successful as any others in Canada. As lumbermen, they have pushed far in advance of the footsteps of civilisation. Twenty-five years since they were to be found in the forests along the banks of the Moira, which empties itself into the Bay of Quinte, cutting down the great trees, 'making timber,' then guiding it down the rapids, and bringing it to Quebec. And among the most fearless and daring, as well as skilful, of the navigators of the tremendous rapids of the St. Lawrence are the Irish. The Canadian, though dexterous with the axe, is occasionally rather apt to depend on his prayers in a moment of emergency; whereas the Irishman, who, to say the least, is fully as pious as the Canadian, acts on the wise belief that Providence helps those who help themselves. At the head of the Ottawa, which is the great lumbering centre of Canada, the Irish have principally settled the town of Pembroke, in which reside many who, once enterprising lumbermen and bold raftsmen, are now living at their ease, in the enjoyment of their hard-earned wealth. There is one in particular, who went miles up the river beyond Pembroke, and brought his family into the almost impenetrable forest. Twenty years ago he was a raftsman, earning 16 dollars a month, and he is now one of the richest men on the river. Within twelve miles of Pembroke, at Fort William, a station belonging to the Hudson Bay Company, the keenest competitors with the Company in the purchase of furs are Irishmen. Following up the Ottawa, to French River, which empties itself into Lake Huron, along that river and the small tributaries of the Ottawa, are to be found thriving Irish settlements of not more than six years' date. In fact, the Irish have penetrated everywhere, and have proved themselves bold and self-reliant, and, even perhaps in a greater degree than the other nationalities, have displayed the most wonderful faculty of adapting themselves to every possible circumstance. This faculty, whether of adapting themselves to natural circumstances or to political institutions, specially distinguishes the Irish race.

Throughout the cities and towns of Upper Canada the Irish hold an eminent position in every profession, and in every department and branch of industry; and in the professions, as in mercantile life, the Catholics already enjoy a fair share, especially when their former poverty and religious faith are taken into account. Indeed, considering the circumstances under which so many of the Catholic Irish of the towns emigrated to Canada, not only with little means, and few friends to help them, but with all manner of prejudice arrayed against them, they have done more and succeeded better than those of any other creed or nationality. They have done more in a shorter time, and in the face of an opposition which neither the English nor Scotch nor their Protestant brethren knew anything of. There is not a town in Canada in which there are not to be witnessed instances, equally striking and honourable, of the progress of young Irishmen, who, bringing out with them a few pounds at most, but more probably a few shillings, are now extensive traders, enterprising manufacturers, and large employers. It is not necessary to particularise by individual cases; but were it right to mention places and persons, I could give a long list of the most gratifying instances of the results of unaided industry and unbefriended energy. I was much struck, when walking with a friend through a city in Western Canada, at observing the fine ranges of buildings for commercial purposes recently erected, or being then put up, by Catholic Irishmen, with whose history I was made acquainted. To industry, integrity, and sheer mother wit, they—not a few of them poor but intelligent lads, who came out to seek their fortunes—owed everything; to human favour or patronage they were not indebted to the value of a shilling. One of these Irishmen had studded the country with young traders, whom he established in various directions, and nearly all of whom were prospering. Another was then on his way to Europe to purchase his goods direct from the manufacturers, instead of buying them through Canadian houses; and his calculation was that he would save from 1,500l. to 2,000l. a year by adopting this plan. When he landed in Canada he was not master of twenty dollars in the world. This is what I saw in a single city, and that by no means the most extensive in either business or population.

There are new generations of Irishmen rising up every day in Canada, the sons of men of humble origin or modest beginning, who, having pushed their way successfully in their new home, sent their boys to college, and 'made gentlemen of them.' As lawyers, doctors, engineers, architects, these young men are bringing to the various professions the sturdy energy of the class from which they sprang, and are vindicating by their ability and their genius the intellectual prestige of their race. The well-authenticated stories told of the fathers of young men whom I saw dressed with all the elegance indicative of wealth and good position, and whose manners corresponded with their external appearance, sounded like a romance, they were so marvellous. How these Irish fathers crossed the Atlantic in a timber ship, and landed perhaps at Quebec or St. John, with scarcely enough to support them for a week; how they resolutely turned to the first work that offered, caring little for hardship or drudgery; how they never looked back, but ever onwards; how at length money seemed to grow under their touch, until they accumulated property, built mansions, possessed horses and carriages, lived in splendour, and carefully fitted their children, by education and training, for the position they were to occupy, as the gentry of the country! But in their histories we learn, that these self-made Irishmen, these successful founders of prosperous families, the creators of all this prosperity and splendour, never clouded their bright Celtic intellect, or brutalised their genial and kindly nature, with drink. Not that they totally abstained from the use of stimulants, perhaps few of them did; but they were 'sober, well-conducted men.'

'As a rule,' said a well-informed friend, 'till within the last ten or twelve years, few Irish Catholics of respectable position, or with even moderate means, immigrated to Canada. Under these circumstances it tells favourably for the country, for the government and the laws of Canada, and for the enterprise, industry, and perseverance of our people, that so many are independent, and that the vast majority enjoy all the comforts and many of the luxuries of life.'

The educational system of Upper Canada is in every way calculated to develop the intelligence and stimulate the energies of the rising youth of the country. The teaching is practical and comprehensive, and the administration appears to be, so far as I could ascertain, just and impartial. The superior colleges of Canada turn out as highly cultivated young men as are to be found in any part of America, or in the oldest universities of Europe. And in every educational institution—from the university of Toronto, in which, under the presidency of a distinguished Irishman, I witnessed Irish students bearing off several of the highest prizes of the year, to the humblest village school throughout British America and the United States—the brightness of the Irish intellect is remarkable; indeed, it is a subject of universal observation in all parts of America.

The facilities which the public school laws of Upper Canada offer to the Catholics for obtaining elementary education, strictly denominational, may be thus briefly stated:—

Two or more Catholic heads of families, by giving notice (with a view to exemption from the public rate) to certain local officers, may claim the right to establish a school of their own, and elect their own trustees for its management. The supporters of this school are not only exempt from the payment of all rates for the support of the public schools, but the law guarantees to them the right to share, half-yearly, in the legislative grant, in proportion to the number of children they may educate. They also receive an equal amount to whatever sum they send to the Government department of Education, for the purchase of maps, globes, school-prizes, and library books. These library books are selected by a Council, of which the Catholic Bishop of Toronto is a member. Many of the books are exclusively Catholic in their character, and the trustees have the right to select only such books as they may prefer. The schools are, of course, subject to official inspection, and are required to report to the department; which is only right and fair, considering they receive assistance from the State, through officials responsible for the proper administration of the public money. Every Catholic school may claim an area of country for its supporters of six miles in diameter, or eighteen miles in circumference—that is, three miles in all directions from its school-house, as a central point. All supporters of the school within that area are exempt from public school taxation. Here is the practical admission of a just principle—respect for conscientious convictions in a matter most vitally affecting the interests of mankind.

There is a shadow, a dark shadow, in this bright picture of prosperity and progress—the spirit of bigotry—the spirit of unnatural hate. It is expressed in one pregnant word—Orangeism. Pity indeed that it should exist in that land of free institutions and good laws. Pity that it should mar its peace, or retard its progress. Pity that, from any reason, motive, or object, it should be encouraged by any class. Pity that it is not trampled inexorably under foot, not by harsh enactment, but by the good sense and right feeling of the wise and the patriotic, acting on the public mind of the Protestant portion of the community. Its influence is felt in every department of public and private life, if not in all, at least in too many districts of Upper Canada. Its baneful presence is perceptible in the heart of the country as in the city and the town. I know that many good and enlightened Protestant Irishmen—men who are staunch to their faith, for which they would face any danger or endure any sacrifice—deplore the existence of this, one of the deadly curses of our Irish people, and do all they possibly can to neutralise its venom, and counteract its evil influence. I believe it to be a barrier to the progress —the more rapid progress—of Canada; it not only checks emigration, but it also induces migration; it prevents many from coming, and—often unconsciously—it impels many to leave. What Canada requires, in order to realise the hopes of her statesmen and her patriots, is more men and women, more millions—not of the kid-glove school, but of the strong, the vigorous, and the resolute—of the same class as those who have reclaimed her wastes, built up her cities, and constructed her highways—those sons and daughters of toil, without whose fructifying labour there can be no progress, no civilisation. Undoubtedly great and prosperous as is this sturdiest of the offspring of the mother country, she requires some additional millions of human beings ere she expands in reality to the full measure of her new-coined designation—the Dominion of Canada. And it is neither wise nor patriotic, in any class or section of the population, from any motive or object whatever, to foster or encourage, in the very heart of the body politic, a source of evil which bears sufficiently bitter fruit at the other side of the Atlantic and at both sides of the Boyne—but which, by the waters of the St. Lawrence and the Ottawa, should be doomed to wither beneath public contempt.

Though the hearts of Irishmen in the New World instinctively turn to each other, this pestilent Orange virus keeps them apart. There is their old country, which they love in common, with which their fondest and dearest memories are associated; but this evil thing is so vicious, so full of rancour, that it poisons the very fountains of patriotic emotion, and stimulates to hatred rather than to love.

Under ordinary circumstances, when there is nothing to give life to this Orange feeling, the Irish live in harmony together. They are friends and neighbours, and would willingly assist each other in adversity or distress. The families visit and blend together; the young people grow up in companionship, most likely in friendship; the old people gad and gossip together; births and marriages and deaths are matters of common interest—nay, not a sorrow or pain is felt in one home but excites compassion and sympathy in the other. But, lo! as the period of the Orange festival approaches—as one of those anniversaries of past strife, of battles fought nearly two hundred years ago in Ireland, comes round—then a cloud seems to grow and gather on the brow, and a strange transformation takes place: the open-hearted, kindly neighbour of yesterday is not to be recognised in that downcast, sullen fellow, who meets the Catholic with a scowl, if not a curse; and in his wife, or daughter, or sister, who hurries past the house of the Catholic as if there were contagion in its door-posts, one finds it hard to trace a likeness to the genial matron who so agreeably discussed the nameless trifles that constitute the theme of friendly gossip, or the pleasant damsel whose laughter made music in the family circle. When the day of celebration does come, the Catholic had better avoid his Orange neighbour—for quarrels, blows, bloodshed, may possibly come of their meeting; and if so, alas! deeper hate and greater scandal—sadder shame to those who bear an Irish name. Possibly the crisis passes without collision or disturbance. Happy for all if it be so; and in a few days after, not however without some preliminary shame-facedness, the former relations are re-established, and all goes on as before—until the accursed anniversary again darkens the brow and fills the heart with hate. Terrible, if not before man, certainly in the eyes of God, is the responsibility of those who keep alive the memories of strife and contention which should be left to slumber in the grave of the past.

Canada has a splendid future before her, whatever may be her form of government, or whatever the relations which, in the course of time, she may bear to the mother country, or to her neighbour the United States. She abounds in natural resources. Millions and millions of acres of good land are yet unoccupied, more are still unexplored; and such is her mineral wealth that a vast population should be employed in its development. Thus, with land almost unlimited in extent, mines of unquestionable productiveness, and capabilities within herself for almost every description of manufacturing industry, what does Canada require in order to be really great, but population—*more millions of men and women*? But she must rid herself of this Orange pestilence; for though she pays her workers liberally, and in hard silver, which knows no depreciation; and though they live well, taxation being small and prices of all necessaries being moderate, still their tendency is towards the other side of the Lakes and the St. Lawrence.

I have met and spoken with too many of my Catholic countrymen in Canada not to know that this Orange feeling is a cause of more than dissatisfaction—even of lurking discontent: it is the one thing which, reviving the recollections of old persecution, makes the Catholic Irishman think less fondly of the home of his adoption; it is likewise, I believe, one of the causes which for many years past has diverted emigration into another and a broader channel. For Catholics, I can say their dearest wish is to live in amity with their Protestant neighbours. They admit and feel that the laws are just and good, that the Government is wise and paternal, that the institutions are favourable to the fullest liberty; therefore the more do they deplore the existence of an organisation which keeps alive an evil feeling that is neither suited to a Christian people nor favourable to the fuller development of a youthful State. I write this in the warmest interest in a country to which so many of my own people have directed their wandering footsteps, and where so many of them have won an honourable independence by the exercise of the noblest qualities.

CHAPTER IX

Newfoundland—Monstrous Policy—Bad Times for the Irish Papists—How the Bishop saved the Colony—The Cathedral of St. John's—Evil of having but one Pursuit—Useful Efforts—The Plague of Dogs—Proposal to exterminate the 'Noble Newfoundland'—Wise Legislation—Reckless Improvidence—Kindly Relations—Irish Girls

THERE is not within the circle of the British Empire a more interesting colony than Newfoundland, or whose inhabitants have had to struggle against a more stupid and perverse policy than that deliberately adopted towards it by the Home Government, and faithfully enforced by its willing representatives. The policy of this day is to stud the earth with vigorous offshoots from the parent stock, and foster them into sturdy growth by the gift of free institutions; and the natural result of a policy so wise and enlightened is this—that there being no wrongs to avenge, no bitter memories to cherish, no galling restrictions to chafe or irritate the public mind, the colony cheerfully bears the light yoke of loyalty to the mother country, whose manufactures it consumes, whose commerce it extends, whose resources it develops, and whose people it enriches and employs. But the policy pursued towards Newfoundland was the very opposite to everything wise and enlightened. To say that it was discouraging would not express its character in adequate terms: it was rather repressive, if not actually crushing. The absurd idea of the wiseacres of that day was to make of Newfoundland a mere fishing-station, and of St. John's a landing place. By the Treaty of Utrecht the British obtained the island from the French in 1713. When the island thus came into possession of its new masters it contained a not inconsiderable French population, to whom freedom of worship had been guaranteed by treaty 'as far as the laws of England permitted;' and so successfully did the Governor of the day take advantage of this dangerous proviso, that the disgusted French Catholics and their clergy sold their property and 'abandoned' the questionable protection of the conquerors. The French Catholics having been effectually got rid of, their Irish brethren became the objects of special proscription.

The following order was issued by several Governors down to so late as 1765. It shows the spirit against which the Irish Catholic had to contend:

For the better preserving the peace, preventing robberies, tumultuous assemblies, and other disorders of wicked and idle people remaining in the country during the winter, *Ordered*—

That no Papist servant, man or woman, shall remain at any place where they did not fish or serve during the summer.

That not more than two Papist men shall dwell in one house during the winter, except such as have Protestant masters.

That no Papist shall keep a public-house, or sell liquor by retail.

That the masters of Irish servants do pay for their passage home.

Another order, addressed to the magistrates about this time, exhibits the fierce spirit of persecution in a manner still more striking:

Whereas you have represented to me that an Irish Papist, a servant, a man without wife or family, has put up mark posts in a fishing-room within your district, with an intent to build a stake and flakes thereon, and possess the same as his right and property, which practice, being entirely repugnant to the Act 10 and 11 Wm. III.:

I do therefore authorise you to immediately cause the post marks above-mentioned to be taken down, and warn the person so offending not to presume to mark out any vacant fishing-room again as his property, as he will answer the contrary at his peril. You are also to warn other Papists from offending in the like case, as they will answer to the contrary.

(Signed) T. BYRON, Governor.

But Pat was irrepressible. He would come and remain, and prosper too, notwithstanding that he was fulminated against in order and proclamation, and though the fecundity of his race was officially deplored as a great and embarrassing evil. The fact was, the Irish were hard-working and useful, and those who appreciated their value encouraged their coming and remaining, despite of Governor, and Fishing Admiral, and Home Government. Wisdom slowly dawned on the benighted authorities, who were compelled to tolerate what they could not prevent. But such was the state of things in the colony for a long series of years, and actually within the memory of living men, that a house could not be put up, or even thoroughly repaired, without the sanction of the Governor! The wonder should not be why Newfoundland has not made more rapid strides than it has, but that it has progressed so rapidly as it has done. 'Let no one blame Newfoundland, then,' says Dr. Mullock, 'for not having hitherto advanced as rapidly as other colonies. I boldly assert that there was never more energy shown by any people than by the inhabitants of this island. The Government that should foster them considered them intruders, and banished them when it could.' The gifted Prelate thus completes the picture:

They had not the liberty of the birds of the air to build or repair their nests—they had behind them the forest or the rocky soil, which they were not allowed, without licence difficultly obtained, to reclaim and till. Their only resource was the stormy ocean, and they saw the wealth they won from the deep spent in other lands, leading them only a scanty subsistence. Despite of all this they have increased twenty-fold in ninety years, have built towns and villages, erected magnificent buildings, as the cathedral in St. John's, introduced telegraphs, steam, postal, and road communications, newspapers, everything, in fact, found in the most civilised countries, and all this on a rugged soil, in a harsh though wholesome climate, and under every species of discouragement.

We have seen that the 'Irish Papist' could not be discouraged out of the country, in which he was not without the ministration of the priest, who, though he had no fixed abode in the island, usually came out in a fishing-boat, and so disguised as to escape the vigilance of the hostile authorities. Protestants suffered from no such disadvantage. Their's was the recognised religion of the State, and its ministers were stationed in the principal settlements. This indeed was the state of things throughout the continent of America, wherever, in fact, the British power was recognised. Catholics were under a ban, hunted, persecuted, or grievously discouraged, while Protestants enjoyed in its fulness the advantages of a protected Church and a dominant religion. This should be always taken into consideration when estimating the progress of those who were guilty, in the eyes of their jealous rulers, of the double offence of being Catholic and Irish.

In the year of grace 1784 liberty of conscience was proclaimed in Newfoundland, and the Catholics at once , took advantage of the boon. In that year the Rev. James O'Donnell, 'the founder and father of the Church of Newfoundland,' landed in the island. A native of Tipperary, he had spent a large portion of his life in the Irish Franciscan Convent of Prague, in Bohemia, and afterwards presided over the convent of his order in Waterford, and subsequently as the provincial of the order in Ireland. He was the first regularly authorised missioner in Newfoundland since it had been ceded to the British in 1713; and to his wisdom, firmness and sagacity are due the practical settlement of the Irish in that colony. The following document is rather a strange commentary on the proclamation of liberty of conscience and freedom of worship of six years before. It was written by Governor Milbank, in answer to an application by Dr. O'Donnell for leave to build a chapel in one of the outports:—

The Governor acquaints Mr. O'Donnell that, so far from being disposed to allow of an increase of places of religious worship for the Roman Catholics of the island, *he very seriously intends, next year, to lay those established already under particular restrictions.* Mr. O'Donnell must be aware that *it is not the interest of Great Britain to encourage people to winter in Newfoundland,* and he cannot be ignorant that many of the lower order who would now stay, *would, if it were not for the convenience with which they obtain absolution here, go home for it at least once in two or three years*; and the Governor has been misinformed if Mr. O'Donnell, instead of advising their return to Ireland, does not rather encourage them to winter in this country.

On board the Salisbury, St. John's, Nov. 2, 1790.

What a proclamation of intolerance and stupidity! We doubt if, considering the period at which the world had arrived, there was ever penned a more discreditable epistle. We shall now see how this cruel mistrust was repaid by the distinguished minister of religion who was its object.

It was in the year 1799, shortly after the memorable Irish Rebellion, that the circumstance occurred which exhibited in the most conspicuous manner the value of the influence and authority of a zealous and courageous pastor, and the wisdom of encouraging, rather than discountenancing, the presence of a Catholic clergyman in the midst of an Irish population. Many who had been compelled to fly from their native land in consequence of the rising of 1798 found refuge in Newfoundland, bringing with them the exasperated feelings engendered by that disastrous conflict: nor was the state of things in the colony such as to soothe the bitter hatred which they cherished in their hearts. Amongst them a conspiracy was formed, its object being the destruction of the Protestant colonists; and such was the success with which the conspirators pushed their machinations that they secured the sympathy and promised co-operation of a large portion of the regiment then stationed in St. John's. Their plans were laid with great secrecy and skill, and the day was appointed for carrying their fatal designs into execution.

The time chosen was when the people had assembled at church, and, it not being then the custom for the military to carry arms into the sacred building, it was considered by the conspirators that those who would thus go unarmed could not offer much difficulty in the execution of the fearful plot.

Had the intended rising taken place the consequences would have been awful; but happily, through the vigilance and prudence of Bishop O'Donnell—he had been appointed Vicar Apostolic in 1794—the conspiracy was defeated. Having been apprised of what was contemplated, he at once informed the General in command of the danger impending, urging him to deal with the soldiers, and undertaking himself to deal with the misguided civilians who had been involved in the guilty project. The necessary steps were taken, the contemplated rising was effectually prevented, and Newfoundland was saved from a scene of horror and bloodshed that would have formed a dark blot on the page of its history. The Protestants regarding Bishop O'Donnell as their preserver, under Providence, naturally felt towards that prelate an intense feeling of gratitude; and the British Government, whose representative but nine years before wrote him the miserable letter just quoted, recognised his great services by a pension—a very small one it is true—which was continued to his successors for some time. 'How often,' remarks the friend to whom I am indebted for the recollection of this important incident in the life of the good Bishop, 'have the clergy of the Catholic Church, as in this instance, heaped coals of fire on the heads of their opponents, and rebuked the blind intolerance of the persecutors of their faith!'

The days of systematic discouragement had passed for ever. 'The English Government,' says Dr. Mullock, 'tacitly recognised the population of Newfoundland as having a right to live in the land they had chosen.' But there was hard work in store for the zealous missionary; and, indeed, it required all the efforts of the ministers of religion, Protestant and Catholic, to extirpate the poison of infidelity which the works of PAINE, then extensively circulated and read, had spread through the colony. The mission was a laborious and a rude one at best; and in the seventieth year of his age Dr. O'Donnell resigned his charge to Dr. Lambert, and sought repose in his native land, where he died four years afterwards, and was buried in the parish chapel of Clonmel. Drs. Scallan and Flemming succeeded Dr. Lambert, and preceded the present Bishop, Dr. Mullock, a man of great energy of character, highly cultivated mind, intense zeal for the promotion of religion and education, and ardently devoted to the material progress of his people. There is now a second Bishop in the island, Dr. Dalton, whose cathedral is at Harbour Grace.

The population, being chiefly engaged in the fisheries, are necessarily scattered along the sea coast. The labours of the missionaries are consequently very arduous, they being often compelled to travel by water in small boats at the most inclement seasons; while in many parts of the island, owing to the imperfect nature of the roads, land travel imposes on priestly zeal penalties no less severe. Still, so great and increasing are the efforts made by the clergy, that there are few of their flock beyond the reach of their ministrations. The devotedness of the pastors is thoroughly responded to by the fidelity of their flocks. It is no exaggeration to say that in no part of the world is there a more complete union of clergy and people than exists between the Catholic people and clergy of Newfoundland. If we consider the vast undertakings which have been brought to a successful termination by a Catholic population not much exceeding 60,000 souls in all, we cannot but be surprised at the wonderful liberality and zeal of the people, and at the influence exercised over them by the Bishop and his clergy. The value of the Church property, including churches, parochial residences, convents, &c., is little short of 200,000l. In St. John's alone the value of their property is estimated at over 150,000l. In this is included the cost of the cathedral, one of the noblest structures to be found at the other side of the Atlantic. To raise this magnificent temple, the generous colonists subscribed the enormous sum of 120,000l. Were Governor Milbank now in the flesh, and were he to stand on the floor of that great cathedral, glance up to its lofty roof, cast his eyes round at the beautiful works of art brought from the most famous studios of Rome, and then remember his famous letter to Dr. O'Donnell—so coolly insolent and so haughtily contemptuous—he might well feel ashamed of himself and the Government whose miserable policy he represented; and also learn how impossible it is to destroy a living faith, or crush a genuine race.

It was only fifty years after that letter was written that the idea of erecting this stupendous cathedral was conceived by the Bishop of that day, the Right Rev. Dr. Flemming. Few save the Bishop himself dared to hope that anyone then living would ever worship within its walls; but, strange to say, from the commencement of the work its progress was never interrupted from want of funds, and in the comparatively short space of ten years it was so far advanced as to admit of the Holy Sacrifice being offered up under its roof. Dr. Flemming lived long enough to see all doubts removed—not from his mind, for he never entertained one on the subject—as to the ultimate accomplishment of his object; and in leaving the completion of the great work to his successor, he knew that in the piety and indomitable zeal of Dr. Mullock there was the best guarantee for its speedy and splendid completion. Dr. Mullock received it a mere shell—a magnificent exterior, it is true, but nothing more; everything within remained to be done. Taking hold of the work, as it were, with a strong hand and a determined will, Bishop Mullock went forward with such vigour that in the year 1855 its completion was inaugurated by a solemn consecration, at which several of the most eminent prelates of the American Church were present. The Bishop not only completed this grand edifice, but, in the true Catholic spirit, he enriched it with the choicest works of art, rightly thinking that the efforts of human genius cannot be more fittingly employed than in doing honour to the Creator of man—the Author of his power, and strength, and genius; and that by the aid of the productions of the painter and the sculptor the mind may be lifted, or assisted to rise, above the worldly cares and vulgar thoughts which are too often brought to the very porch of the temple.

Within the area of the ample space on which the cathedral stands, are erected the Presentation Convent and the schools attached, the Orphanage, the Convent of Mercy, the College of St. Bonaventure, and the Episcopal Palace—all worthy of being associated with the noble structure which is the centre of the whole. These institutions, now entirely free from debt, have been erected during the spiritual rule of Dr. Mullock, who thus completed the great design of which the cathedral was only the practical commencement.

At River Head another imposing church, only second in grandeur to the cathedral of St. John's, is now in progress of erection; and at Harbour Grace, Dr. Dalton is engaged in the serious undertaking of enlarging his cathedral, which has long since been too small for his increasing congregation. In his diocese, and with smaller resources and a more limited field of action, this zealous prelate is rivalling the successful energy of his distinguished brother of St. John's. Besides the two convents in the capital, there are twelve branch houses in other parts of the island, and these are in a great degree devoted to the training of the female children of the Catholic population. The Catholics of St. John's have no educational grievance to complain of. The principle on which the system is based is that of allowing to each religious denomination the education of its own youth—an arrangement which marvellously simplifies matters, and removes every possible excuse for mischievous meddling, or collision of any kind. More than one hundred students are receiving a first-class collegiate education in the College of St. Bonaventure, such as to prepare them to maintain an honourable position in the various walks of life for which they may be destined; and in the same institution the candidates for holy orders are prepared for the priesthood, the design of the Bishop being to recruit the ranks of the clergy from amongst the natives of the colony, Ireland having hitherto supplied all the priests for the mission.

The zeal and fidelity of the Irish Catholics of Newfoundland may be estimated by the great things they have done for their Church, notwithstanding limited resources and original discouragement. Whenever a great work is to be done, every one assists according to his means; and where money cannot be subscribed, the full equivalent is freely given in work and labour. So thoroughly identified are the people with the cause to be promoted that in a whole parish a single defaulter is rarely to be met with! But if the Bishop calls on his flock to assist him in one of those useful undertakings in which he is so constantly engaged, he himself is the first to afford a signal example of liberality, having contributed the munificent sum of 10,000l. out of his own resources towards the works of his promotion.

Perhaps the great evil of the colony is the almost exclusive devotion of its inhabitants to the one engrossing pursuit. So long as the fisheries are prosperous the evil is not so manifest; but should this grand resource of the island prove less productive than usual, intense distress is the immediate consequence, there being little else to fall back upon. What agriculture is to Ireland, the fisheries are to Newfoundland; and while Ireland requires the extension of manufacturing industry on a large scale, not only as a means of constant employment, but as a resource in case of failure of crops, Newfoundland has equal need of the cultivation of its soil as a certain source of prosperity, as well as a means of compensating for the casual falling off in the staple industry of the colony. The number exclusively engaged in agriculture is small, and is principally confined to residents in the neighbourhood of St. John's; not that the land in that vicinity is better than elsewhere, but that a valuable market is at hand for the consumption of every kind of animal and vegetable produce. It is found that a judicious combination of fishing with the cultivation of the soil best rewards the labourer; and efforts are now being made to induce the people to give more attention to the latter pursuit. A whole family can seldom find full employment in connection with the fishery, and one of the advantages of the other mode of occupation is that it provides employment for labour that would otherwise be waste.

The importance of cultivating the soil was never fully estimated until in 1847 the mysterious potato disease appeared in Newfoundland, as it did in so many regions of the earth. The distress caused by this event showed how valuable had been that fruitful crop, for which the nature of the soil seems peculiarly adapted. So virulent was the disease in the year mentioned that it appears to have left its sting ever since; for blight, or partial failure, has been of frequent occurrence since then, and even as late as the season of 1866 it assumed a marked character. Good oats and barley are raised in the island, but they are not cultivated to the extent they might be. In fact, farming in Newfoundland is still in a primitive state, few persons being regularly devoted to it as a profession, it being regarded rather as a useful auxiliary to the great staple industry of the inhabitants, than as a valuable source of general wealth. The Government fully appreciate the importance of encouraging the people to adopt the cultivation of the land as a fixed and settled pursuit. In former times it was difficult to obtain a licence from the Governor of the day to till any portion of the soil; but in 1866 an Act was passed offering to the poor cultivator a bonus of eight dollars for every acre up to six acres cleared and fitted for crops, besides a free grant of the land itself. As thousands of acres, suited for cultivation, may be had in various parts of the island, it is to be hoped that the liberal policy of the Colonial Government may be crowned with success. Fisheries, however bountiful, or even inexhaustible, are, from natural causes altogether beyond the control of man, necessarily more or less precarious; and it is wise statesmanship as well as true patriotism to try and lay the foundation of a great branch of industry which, while adding to the wealth of the community, may form the best resource against unexpected calamity.

Efforts are also made to encourage the breeding of sheep, for which the climate and soil seem eminently suited. The attention of the Agricultural Society is being devoted to the subject, and with some success. But Bishop Mullock insists that unless relentless war be waged against the dogs of the colony, sheep-farming will be a matter of impossibility. To destroy, at one fell swoop, the noble breed of dogs which have done much to make Newfoundland known to the world—to annihilate the splendid brute so remarkable for courage, sagacity, and fidelity—may appear to be a proposal worthy of a Draco, and might well stimulate the indignant genius of the poets of the universe; but the Bishop makes out a strong case, which he may be allowed to put in his own words:—

We have, says Dr. Mullock, the means of raising on our wild pastures millions of that most useful animal to man—the sheep. On the southern and western shore, indeed everywhere in the island, I have seen the finest sheep walks; and, what is better, the droppings of the sheep in this country induce a most luxuriant crop of white clover, and prevent the spread of bog plants. If sheep were encouraged, we should have fresh meat in abundance, and their fleece would furnish warm clothing in the winter for our people, of a better quality than the stuff they now buy, 'half waddy and devil's dust,' and which impoverishes them to procure it. Domestic manufactures would be encouraged, the people would become industrious and comfortable, and every housewife in our out-harbours would realise, in some sort, that sublime description of a valiant woman by Solomon, Prov. xxxi., 'She hath put out her hands to strong things, and her fingers have taken hold of the spindle; she has sought wool and flax and hath wrought by the counsel of her hands; she shall not fear for her house in the cold of snow, for all her domestics are clothed with double garments; she hath looked well to the paths of her house and hath not eaten her bread idle; her children rose up and called her blessed; her husband had praised her.' But, unfortunately, this great blessing of sheep pasture is marred by one curse, and idleness and poverty are too often the accompaniments of the poor man's fireside in the long winter—*as long as a vicious herd of dogs are allowed to be kept in the country, so long will poverty be the winter portion of the poor. In no other part of the world would such an iniquity be permitted.* There is a law offering 5l., for the destruction of a wolf, and I never have heard of 5l. worth of mutton being destroyed by wolves since the days of Cabot; but why do not our legislators, if they have the interest of the people at heart (and, according to their election speeches, every member is actuated by the most philanthropic and patriotic motives), pass and enforce a law against dogs, which devour every sheep they can find, and have almost exterminated the breed altogether? *for no one will keep sheep while his neighbour is allowed to keep wolves.*

Nor are the Bishop's reasons for thus preaching a war of extermination exhausted in the passage quoted; he condemns the use of dogs in drawing firewood, the dogs being assisted in their labour by stalwart men yoked to the same car. The Bishop wisely remarks that one horse would do the work of one hundred dogs, and be always useful; and the man who could not keep a horse might hire his neighbour's for a few days, at an expense far less than what he wastes in boots and clothes. The Bishop apprehends that his remarks may prove unpalatable; but he has the interests of the people too much at heart to conceal his sentiments on a subject of such vital importance to them, and he asserts that 'religion, education, civilisation are all suffering from this curse of dogs, worse than all the plagues of Egypt to this unfortunate country.' The lectures from which these strong passages are quoted were delivered in 1860; but I am not aware how far he was successful in turning the public sentiment in favour of sheep and against their implacable enemy, 'the noble Newfoundland.' The reader will perceive that this Irish Bishop is as vigorous as a reformer of abuse and promoter of material improvement, as he is energetic as a founder of religious and educational institutions, and builder of cathedrals. There is a genuine ring in this comprehensive counsel: 'My earnest advice would be, kill the dogs, introduce settlers, encourage domestic manufactures, home-made linen and home-spun cloth, and Newfoundland will become the Paradise of the working man.'

The mineral capabilities of the country are now attracting attention, and promise to prove an important element in its resources. A mineralogical survey, instituted by the Government, is in progress, and the results already established justify considerable expectations. A copper mine is in successful operation; and besides copper, lead and coals are known to exist in several parts of the island. The Government afford every encouragement to mining enterprise. For a fine of 5l. any one may obtain a licence of search over three square miles, and at any time within two years he can select from the tract over which his licence extends one square mile, for which he becomes entitled to a grant in fee, the only further charge being a royalty of 2½ per cent, for the first five years' working. With such liberal terms on the part of the Government, aided by the valuable information which their survey is likely to diffuse, it may fairly be expected that the latent mineral wealth of Newfoundland may ere long afford employment to many thousands of its population.

The Irish portion of the colonists are not in any respect inferior to their neighbours of other nationalities. Whether in the professions, as merchants and traders, or as daring and successful fishermen, they enjoy an enviable position, and maintain the highest character. For their numbers the Irish men of business represent as large an amount of wealth as any other class in the colony, and in influence and general repute they are not second to those with whom they are associated. In the Government the Catholic element is adequately felt, and the right of Catholics to the enjoyment of their legitimate influence is not questioned even by the most extreme of their opponents. 'They have,' says a distinguished Catholic layman, 'their full measure of equal privileges, and neither their country nor their creed is a bar to advancement in any of the walks of life.'

In daring and energy in the prosecution of their adventurous pursuit, the Irish are in every respect equal to the other fishermen who hunt the seal, or capture the cod and ling of the great bank. Indeed it would be difficult to see anywhere a body of men more full of life, vigour, and intelligence, than may be found issuing from the Catholic cathedral any Sunday in those portions of the year when the fishermen are at home. There is, however, one thing to be regretted—that the money so gallantly earned is not always wisely spent. It is a matter of regret that the nature of the fisheries is such as to leave long intervals of unemployed time at the disposal of those engaged in them, and this is especially felt when the fisheries are unproductive. In prosperous seasons the earnings of the men are sufficient for their support for the year; but this facility of earning money has its disadvantages, particularly in inducing a spirit of recklessness and habits of extravagance, which not unfrequently tend to much misery. It is no uncommon thing in the seal fishery for a man to earn 20l., 30l., or even more, in a month or five weeks; but, alas! it often goes as rapidly as it is acquired. This, unfortunately for the world at large, is a common result with money so rapidly earned; but in Newfoundland there is the superadded evil of long intervals of idleness, during which the once jovial sinner mourns, in sackcloth and ashes and unavailing repentance, the follies of his prosperous hours. The Irish, perhaps, are not worse than others in their spirit of recklessness and their habits of baneful indulgence; but certainly they are not better than their neighbours in this respect. Social, impulsive, and generous, there are no people in the world, Newfoundland included, whom self-restraint would benefit more than those of Irish birth or origin.

Even so far back as the commencement of the century, the Irish merchants had taken a prominent position in the colony; and in 1806 the Benevolent Irish Society was formed—an institution which had for its object the relief of the distressed without any distinction, and the fostering of national feeling and spirit. The promoters were some of the foremost men in the colony, Protestants and Catholics, between whom the most friendly relations existed; and the meetings and proceedings of this body did no little to influence the tone and temper of the community at large. Its annual celebrations of St. Patrick's Day, in which men of all creeds and countries participated, were held in great esteem, as much for the kindly sentiments they encouraged, as for the social enjoyment they were always certain to afford. This society, after a life of sixty years, is still in existence; and not only does it fulfil its mission of benevolence in the same spirit in which it was founded, but its annual reunions continue to be an agreeable feature in the festivities of St. John's.

Newfoundland may look in vain for a grievance; but should it discover one, it has the means within itself of quickly setting it at rest. Its inhabitants of all denominations enjoy in unimpaired fulness the blessings of civil and religious freedom: there are no harassing and vexatious meddlings with education; and if a considerable portion of the population do not occupy the soil by the best of all tenures, the fault does not lie with those who legislate for and govern them. That a good understanding between all classes of the community is the result of just laws wisely administered, we may take the conclusive evidence of Dr. Mullock, who thus bears witness to its existence:—

Allow me to say a few words of my experience of the people: I have found them, in all parts of the island, hospitable, generous, and obliging; Catholics and Protestants live together in the greatest harmony, and it is only in *print* we find anything, except on extraordinary occasions, like disunion among them. I have always, in the most Protestant districts, experienced kindness and consideration—I speak not only of the agents of the mercantile houses, who are remarkable for their hospitality and attention to all visitors, or of magistrates, but the Protestant fishermen were always ready to join Catholics in manning a boat when I required it, and I am happy to say that the Catholics have acted likewise to their clergymen. It is a pleasing reflection that though we are not immaculate, and rum sometimes excites to evil, still, out of a population of over 130,000, we have rarely more than eight or ten prisoners in gaol, and grievous crimes are, happily, most rare, capital offences scarcely heard of.

From a communication which I have received from an eminent citizen of St. John's, to whose kindness I am much indebted, I take the following passage:—

The Irish girls, 'to the manner born,' are almost extinct in this island, emigration for many years past having almost entirely ceased. But the Irish of native growth are, as a class, intelligent, well-developed, and industrious. Immorality is rare among them, as may be shown by a record of last year's births in St. John's, from which it appears that of 725 births, 12 only were illegitimate, or less than 2 per cent, of the whole. This, too, is not an exceptional year, but may be taken as a fair criterion of the morality of the Irish girls. The educational labours of the Nuns are doing much to preserve the virtue of the female youth; and nowhere are these holy women more valued than here.

CHAPTER X

The Irish Exodus—Emigration, its Dangers by Sea and Land—Captain and Crew well matched—How Things were done Twenty Years since—The Emigration Commission and its Work—Land-sharks and their Prey—Finding Canal Street— A Scotch Victim—The Sharks and Cormorants—Bogus Tickets—How the 'Outlaws' resisted Reform—The New System—The Days of Bogus Tickets gone— A Word of Advice—Working of the System—Intelligence and Labour Department—Miss Nightingale's Opinion—Necessity for Constant Vigilance— The last Case one of the Worst

THERE are few sadder episodes in the history of the world than the story of the Irish Exodus. Impelled, to a certain degree, by a spirit of adventure, but mainly driven from their native land by the operation of laws which, if not opposed to the genius of the people were unsuited to the special circumstances of their country, millions of the Irish race have braved the dangers of an unknown element, and faced the perils of a new existence, in search of a home across the Atlantic. At times, this European life-stream flowed towards the New World in a broad and steady current; at others, it assumed the character of a resistless rush, breaking on the shores of America with so formidable a tide as to baffle every anticipation, and render the ordinary means of humane or sanitary precaution altogether inadequate and unavailing.

Different indeed, in most of its features, is the emigration of to-day from that of thirty, or twenty, or even a dozen years since. A quarter of a century since, and much later still, the emigrant seemed marked out, as it were, as the legitimate object of plunder and oppression; and were not the frauds of which these helpless people were made the constant victims matters of public record, and against which Legislatures at both sides of the ocean struggled, and for a time ineffectually, one could scarcely credit the lengths to which those who lived upon plunder carried their audacity. Little did the intending emigrants know of the difficulties and dangers that lay in their path in every stage of their momentous journey by land and water, by city and by sea. Little knew the poor mother, as she imparted her last benediction to her 'boy and girl'—the adventurous pioneers of the family—the perils that lay in her children's way; how fraud and robbery, and in friendly guise too, would track them across the ocean, perhaps sail with them in the same ship, even lie with them in the same berth; and how nothing short of the interposition of a merciful Providence could save them from utter and irremediable ruin.

The ships, of which such glowing accounts were read on Sunday by the Irish peasant, on the flaming placards posted near the chapel gate, were but too often old and unseaworthy, insufficient in accommodation, without the means of maintaining the most ordinary decency, with bad or scanty provisions, not having even an adequate supply of water for a long voyage; and to render matters worse, they, as a rule rather than as the exception, were shamefully underhanded. True, the provisions and the crew passed muster in Liverpool—for, twenty years since, and long after, it was from that port the greater number of the emigrants to America sailed; but there were tenders and lighters to follow the vessel out to sea; and over the sides of that vessel several of the mustered men would pass, and casks, and boxes, and sacks would be expeditiously hoisted, to the amazement of the simple people, who looked on at the strange, and to them unaccountable operation. And thus the great ship with its living freight would turn her prow towards the West, depending on her male passengers, as upon so many impressed seamen, to handle her ropes, or to work her pumps in case of accident, which was only too common under such circumstances. What with bad or scanty provisions, scarcity of water, severe hardship, and long confinement in a foul den, ship fever reaped a glorious harvest between decks, as frequent ominous splashes of shot-weighted corpses into the deep but too terribly testified. Whatever the cause, the deaths on board the British ships enormously exceeded the mortality on board the ships of any other country. For instance, according to the records of the Commissioners of Emigration for the State of New York, the quota of sick per thousand stood thus in 1847 and 1848—British vessels, 30; American, 9 3/5; Germans, 8 3/5. It was no unusual occurrence for the survivor of a family of ten or twelve to land alone, bewildered and broken-hearted, on the wharf at New York; the rest—the family—parents and children, had been swallowed in the sea, their bodies marking the course of the ship to the New World.

But there were worse dangers than sickness, greater calamities than death and a grave in the ocean, with the chance of becoming food for the hungry shark. There was no protection against lawless violence and brutal lust on the one hand, or physical helplessness and moral prostration on the other. To the clergyman, the physician, and the magistrate, are known many a sad tale of human wreck and dishonour, having their origin in the emigrant sailing ship of not many years since. Even so late as 1860, an Act was passed by Congress 'to regulate the carriage of passengers in steamships and other vessels, for the better protection of female passengers'; and a single clause of this Act, which it is necessary to quote, is a conclusive proof of the constant and daily existence of the most fearful danger to the safety of the poor emigrant girl. Every line of the clause is an evidence of the evil it endeavours to arrest:—

That every master or other officer, seaman, or other person employed on board of any ship or vessel of the United States, who shall, during the voyage of such ship or vessel, under promise of marriage, or by threats, or by the exercise of his authority, or by solicitation, or the making of gifts or presents, seduce . . . any female passenger, shall be guilty of a misdemeanour, and upon conviction shall be punished by imprisonment for a term not exceeding one year, or by a fine not exceeding one thousand dollars; provided that the subsequent intermarriage of the parties seducing and seduced may be pleaded in bar of conviction.

It is further provided, by the second clause, that neither officers, nor seamen, nor others employed on board, shall visit or frequent any part of such ship or vessel assigned to emigrant passengers, except by direction or permission of the master or commander, 'first made or given for such purpose.' Forfeiture of his wages for the voyage is the penalty attaching to any officer or seaman violating this wholesome rule; and the master or commander who shall direct or permit any of his officers or seamen to visit or frequent any part of the ship assigned to emigrant passengers, except for the purpose of performing some necessary act or duty, shall, upon conviction, be punished by a fine of 50 dollars for each separate offence. And the master or commander who does not 'post a written or printed notice, in the English, French, and German languages,' containing the provision of the foregoing or second section, in a conspicuous place on the forecastle, and in the several parts of the ships assigned to emigrant passengers, and keep it posted during the voyage, shall be liable to a penalty not exceeding 500 dollars.

This is a wise and humane Act, passed at any time; but what lives of shame and deaths of misery would it not have prevented had it been in active operation for the last quarter of a century as a restraint upon lawless brutality!

Before leaving the ship for the land, it may not be out of place to afford the reader, through the testimony of a reliable witness, Mr. Vere Foster, a notion of the manner in which emigrants were treated in some vessels, the dishonesty of whose owners or charterers was only equalled by the ruffianism of their officers and crews. The letter from which the extract was taken was published in 1851 by order of the House of Commons; but facts similar to those described by Mr. Foster have been frequently complained of since then. The ship in question had 900 passengers on board, and this is a sample of the manner in which the luckless people were supplied with a great necessary of life:—

The serving out of the water was twice capriciously stopped by the mates of the ship, who during the whole time, without any provocation, cursed and abused, and cuffed and kicked, the passengers and their tin cans, and, having served out water to about 30 persons, in two separate times, said they would give no more water out till the next morning, and kept their word.

A very simple mode was adopted of economising the ship's stores—namely, that of not issuing provisions of any kind for four days; and had it not been for the following remonstrance, it is probable that as many more days would have passed without their being issued:—

RESPECTED SIR,—We, the undersigned passengers on board the ship .... paid for and secured our passages in her in the confident expectation that the allowance of provisions promised in our contract tickets would be faithfully delivered to us. Four entire days having expired since the day on which (some of us having been on board from that day, and most of us from before that day) the ship was appointed to sail, and three entire days since she actually sailed from the port of Liverpool, without our having received one particle of the stipulated provisions excepting water, and many of us having made no provision to meet such an emergency, we request that you will inform us when we may expect to commence receiving the allowance which is our due.

It may be interesting to know in what manner this application was received by the mild-mannered gentleman in command. It appears that captain and mate were singularly well-matched; indeed, it would be difficult to decide to which of the two amiable beings the merit of gentleness and good temper should be awarded. Mr. Foster thus describes the agreeable nature of his reception:—

On the morning of the 31st October, I presented the letter to Captain ——. He asked me the purport of it, and bade me read it. Having read out one-third of it, he said that was enough, and that he knew what I was; *I was a damned pirate, a damned rascal, and that he would put me in irons and on bread and water throughout the rest of the voyage.* The first mate then came up, and abused me foully and blasphemously, and pushed me down, bidding me get out of that, as I was a damned b————. He was found by one of the passengers soon afterwards heating a thick bar of iron at the kitchen fire; the cook said, 'What is he doing that for?' and the mate said, 'There is a damned b——— on board, to whom I intend giving a singeing before he leaves the ship.'

As a single example of the treatment to which the helpless and the feeble are exposed from brutes who luxuriate in violence and blasphemy, this incident, the more impressive because of the homely language in which it is told, may be given:—

A delicate old man, named John M'Corcoran, of berth No. 111, informed me that on Sunday last he had just come on deck, and, after washing, was wringing a pair of stockings, when the first mate gave him such a severe kick with his knee on his backside as he was stooping down, that he threw him down upon the deck, since which he has been obliged to go to the watercloset three or four times a day, passing blood every time.

These extracts, quoted with the purpose of illustrating the harsh, brutal, and dishonest conduct too often practised against emigrants in some ships—-mostly *sailing ships*—are relied on as accurate, being vouched for by the signature of a gentleman whose name has long been associated with deeds of active humanity and practical benevolence.

Within sight of the wished-for land, the trials of the emigrant might be said to have begun rather than to have ended: or, rather, the trials on land succeeded to the trials on sea.

Previously to the year 1847, the alien emigrant was left either to the general quarantine and poor-laws, or to local laws and ordinances, varying in their character or in their administration. A general tax on all passengers arriving at the port of New York was applied to the support of the Marine Hospital at Quarantine, where the alien sick were received and treated; but this was all that the humanity of that day provided for the relief of those whom necessity had driven to the shores of America. By the local laws, the owners of vessels bringing foreign emigrants were required to enter into bonds indemnifying the city and county in case of their becoming chargeable under the poor-laws. These provisions were found to be inconvenient to the shipowner, owing to the great increase of emigration from the year 1840 to the year 1847, and were altogether insufficient as a means of protection to the emigrant against the consequences of disease or destitution. The bonds were onerous to the respectable shipowner, and a rope of sand to the fraudulent. The shipowner, too, adopted a means of evading his responsibility by transferring it to the shipbroker, a person generally of an inferior class; and the shipbroker thus consenting to stand in the place and assume the responsibility of the owner, the ship and her living freight were unreservedly surrendered to him. The shipowner had the alternative either to give bonds of indemnity to the city against possible chargeability, or compound for a certain sum per head, and thus rid himself of all future responsibility; but he found it more convenient to deal with the broker than with the city authorities. The broker freely gave his bond; but when tested, it was in most instances found to be valueless, he generally being a man of straw. To the tender mercies of the broker the emigrant was thus abandoned.

Private hospitals, or poor-houses, were established by the brokers on the outskirts of New York and Brooklyn; and from the results of an inquiry instituted by the Board of Aldermen of New York in the year 1846, an idea may be formed of the treatment received by the wretched emigrants whose hard fate drove them into those institutions. The Committee discovered in one apartment, 50 feet square, 100 sick and dying emigrants lying on straw; and among them, in their midst, the bodies of two who had died four or five days before, but who had been left for that time without burial! They found, in the course of their inquiry, that decayed vegetables, bad flour, and putrid meat, were specially purchased and provided for the use of the strangers! Such as had strength to escape from these slaughter-houses fled from them as from a plague, and roamed through the city, exciting the compassion, perhaps the horror, of the passers-by(4); those who were too ill to escape had to take their chance—such chance as poisonous food, infected air, and bad treatment afforded them of ultimate recovery. Thanks to the magnitude and notoriety of the fearful abuses of the system then shown to exist, a remedy, at once comprehensive and efficacious, was adopted —not, it is true, to come into immediate operation, but to prove in course of time one of the noblest monuments of enlightened wisdom and practical philanthropy. In the Preface to the published Reports of the Commissioners of Emigration, from the organisation of the Commission in 1847 to 1860, the origin of the good work is thus told:—

This state of things was becoming more distressing as emigration grew larger, and it even threatened danger to the public health. A number of citizens, to whose notice these facts were specially and frequently brought—to some from their connection with commerce and navigation, to others from personal sympathy with the children of the land of their own nativity,— met about the close of the year 1846, or the winter of 1847, and consulted on the means of remedying these evils. They proposed and agreed upon a plan of relief, which was presented to the Legislature of the State of New York, and was passed into a law in the Session of 1847. The system then recommended and adopted was that of a permanent Commission for the relief and protection of alien emigrants arriving at the port of New York, to whose aid such emigrants should be entitled for five years after their arrival, the expenses of their establishment and other relief being defrayed by a small commutative payment from each emigrant.

Figures, however gigantic, afford but an imperfect notion of the work, the self-imposed and disinterested work, of this Commission—of the good they have accomplished, and, more important still, the evil they have prevented. When it is stated that from May 1847 to the close of 1866, the number of passengers who arrived at the port of New York was 3,659,000—about one-third of whom received temporary relief from the Commissioners—we may understand how wide and vast was the field of their benevolent labours. But in order to appreciate the protection they afforded to those who had hitherto been unprotected, and the villanies they successfully baffled, it is necessary to describe some of the dangers which dogged the footsteps of the emigrant after landing in New York.

As voracious fish devour the smaller and helpless of the finny tribe, so did a host of human sharks and cormorants prey upon the unhappy emigrant, whose innocence and inexperience left him or her completely at their mercy; and scant was the mercy they vouchsafed their victims. These bandits—for such they literally were, notwithstanding that they did not exactly strike down their victims with pistol or with poignard—assumed many forms, such as brokers, runners, boarding-house keepers, commission agents, sellers of 'bogus' tickets, and others; and from their number and audacity they appeared to set all law and authority at defiance. To such an extent had their daring depredations been carried, that the Legislature, in 1846, appointed a Select Committee to investigate their practices. But, in their first annual Report, the Commissioners are compelled to acknowledge how little was the practical good resulting from the inquiry and its consequent disclosures; for they say—'It is a matter of almost daily observation by persons in the employ of the Commissioners, that the frauds exposed in the Report of the Select Committee, appointed last year to examine frauds upon emigrants, continued to be practised with as much boldness and frequency as ever. A regular and systematic course of deception and fraud is continually in operation, whereby the emigrant is deprived of a large portion of the means intended to aid him in procuring a home in the country of his adoption.'

To do the Legislature justice, it freely passed laws to guard the poor alien from 'those enemies of the emigrant' —agents, runners, forwarders, and brokers, and also invested the Commissioners with considerable powers; but the best intentions of the Legislature, and the most earnest exertions of the Commissioners, were baffled by unexpected obstacles; and it was not until after having encountered difficulties and borne with disappointments which would have daunted benevolence less courageous than theirs, that, in the year 1855, the Commissioners succeeded in securing the grand object of their persistent efforts; namely, the possession of an official landing-place for all the emigrants arriving at the port of New York. They were from the first fully alive to the importance of obtaining this landing-place; and in their second Report they express their regret that, being unable to obtain the use of a pier for this purpose, and consequently being unable to reach the emigrant before he falls amongst those who stand ready to deceive him, frauds, which formerly excited so much indignation and sympathy, are continued with as much boldness and frequency as ever.

The law also attempted to regulate the charges in boarding-houses, and protect the luggage of the emigrant from the clutches of the proprietors of these establishments; but it appeared only to render the lot of the emigrant one of still greater hardship; for what could no longer be legally retained was illegally made away with. In their Report for 1848, the Commissioners refer to the new system adopted in these houses:—'Of late, robberies of luggage from emigrant boarding-houses have become of frequent occurrence, so as to have excited the suspicion that in some instances the keepers of the houses are not altogether free from participation in the robbery. If the tavern keeper has reason to apprehend that the lodger will not be able to pay his bill, and knowing that the law prohibits his retaining the luggage, he may think it proper to secure his claim without law.'

I must confess to being immensely amused at hearing from one who had passed through the ordeal how he had been dealt with in the fine old time of unrestricted plunder, when the emigrant was left to his fate—that fate assuming the substantial form of the runner and the boarding-house keeper. My informant was a great, broad-shouldered, red-haired Irishman, over six feet 'in his stocking vamps,' and who, I may add, on the best authority, bore himself gallantly in the late war, under the banner of the Union. He was but a very young lad when, in 1848, he came to New York, with a companion of his own age, 'to better his fortune,' as many a good Irishman had endeavoured to do before him. He possessed, besides splendid health and a capacity for hard work, a box of tools, a bundle of clothes, and a few pounds in gold—not a bad outfit for a good-tempered young Irishman, with a red head, broad shoulders, grand appetite, and fast rising to the six feet. The moment he landed his luggage was pounced upon by two runners, one seizing the box of tools, the other confiscating the clothes. The future American citizen assured his obliging friends that he was quite capable of carrying his own luggage; but no, they should relieve him—the stranger, and guest of the Republic—of that trouble. Each was in the interest of a different boarding-house, and each insisted that the young Irishman with the red head should go with him—a proposition that, to any but a New York runner, would seem, if not altogether impossible, at least most difficult of accomplishment. Not being able to oblige both the gentlemen, he could only oblige one; and as the tools were more valuable than the clothes, he followed in the path of the gentleman who had secured that portion of the 'plunder.' He remembers that the two gentlemen wore very pronounced green neckties, and spoke with a richness of accent that denoted special if not conscientious cultivation; and on his arrival at the boarding-house, he was cheered with the announcement that its proprietor was from 'the ould counthry, and loved every sod of it, God bless it!'

In a manner truly paternal the host warned the two lads against the dangers of the streets; and so darkly did he paint the horrors, and villanies, and murders of all kinds, that were sure to rain down upon their innocent heads, that the poor boys were frightened into a rigid seclusion from the world outside, and occupied their time as best they could, not forgetting 'the eating and the drinking' which the house afforded. The young Irishman with the red head imparted to the host the fact of his having a friend in Canal Street—'wherever Canal Street was;' and that the friend had been some six years in New York, and knew the place well, and was to procure employment for him as soon as they met; and he concluded by asking how he could get to Canal Street. 'Canal Street!—is it Canal Street?—why then what a mortal pity, and the stage to go just an hour before you entered this very door! My, my! that's unfortunate; isn't it? Well, no matter, there'll be another in two days' time, or three at farthest, and I'll be sure to see you sent there all right—depend your life on me when I say it,' said the jovial kindly host. For full forty-eight hours the two lads, who were as innocent as a brace of young goslings, endured the irksome monotony of the boarding-house, even though that abode of hospitality was cheered by the presence of its jovial host, who loved every sod of the 'ould counthry;' but human nature cannot endure beyond a certain limit—and the two lads resolved, in sheer desperation, to break bounds at any hazard. They roamed through the streets for some time, without any special ill befalling them.

Meeting a policeman, the young fellow with the red head suggested to his companion the possibility of the official knowing something about Canal Street; and as his companion had nothing to urge against it, they approached that functionary, and boldly propounded the question to him—where Canal Street was, and how it could be reached? 'Why, then, my man,' replied the policeman, who also happened to be a compatriot, 'if you only follow your nose for the space of twenty minutes in that direction, you'll come to Canal Street, and no mistake about it; you'll see the name on the corner, in big letters, if you can read—as I suppose you can, for you look to be two decent boys.' Canal Street in twenty minutes! Here indeed was a pleasant surprise for the young fellows, who had been told to wait for the stage, which, according to the veracious host, 'was due in about another day.' Of course they did follow their respective noses until they actually reached Canal

Street, found the number of the house in which their friend resided, and discovered the friend himself, to whom they recounted their brief adventures in New York.

Thanks to the smartness of their acclimated friend, they recovered their effects, but not before they disbursed to the jovial host, who 'loved every sod of the ould counthry, God bless it!' more than would have enabled them to fare sumptuously at the Astor. And as the great strapping fellow—who had since seen many a brave man die with his face to the foe—told the tale of his first introduction to the Empire City, he actually looked sheepish at its recollection, and then laughed heartily at a simplicity which had long since become, with him, a weakness of the past.

As a companion picture to the foregoing, the story of a Scotch victim, who was driven crazy by the vigorous application of the fleecing process, will exhibit the manner in which things were done before the Castle Garden era. This was part of the evidence taken in 1847:—

Testimony of the St. Andrew's Society. We, the undersigned, officers of St. Andrew's Society, in the city of Albany, do hereby certify that on or about the 2nd day of August last it was represented to us by a manager of our society that a Scotch emigrant, by the name of James Heeslop, had been grossly defrauded and swindled out of his money by the runners, or the robbing concerns for whom these runners do business. We immediately went on the dock, and made inquiries after Heeslop, when we were informed that he had been despatched on a boat to his destination; we had him followed to Troy, and brought back. The story he told the police justice, Cole, in our presence, in asking for a warrant against the notorious Smethurst, was in substance as follows:—That he arrived in New York from Scotland a few days previous; that his destination was Port Washington, in the State of Ohio; that he was accosted by a person in New York near the Albany steamboat, who represented himself as a forwarding agent, and with whom he (Heeslop) agreed for the passage of himself and family (three persons), from there to his destination, and paid the said agent therefore four British sovereigns, the agent consigning Heeslop to the care of Smethurst and Co. He gave Heeslop tickets which the agent told him would carry him through. That a short time after the boat started, Heeslop was accosted by a second person, who likewise represented himself as forwarding agent, and having learned the destination and particulars of Heeslop's affairs, asked to look at his tickets; that Heeslop showed him the tickets, and the agent told Heeslop that the other agent had *mistaken*, that these tickets were only good as far as Buffalo, and that in order to make sure his passage, it would be necessary for him (the said Heeslop) to pay him (the said second agent) a further payment of *three sovereigns* which Heeslop had to pay when he arrived at Albany. They told Heeslop at the office of Smethurst and Co., that he should pay in addition the sum of *eight sovereigns*, together with *fifteen sovereigns more for his luggage*; that the said Heeslop being rendered almost crazy by these repeated plunderings, and wishing at all hazards to proceed to his destination and true friends, he paid down the further demand of twenty-three sovereigns, and was then put on board a canal boat, where the undersigned found him and brought him back as aforesaid. That the police justice, on hearing the poor plundered man's tale, immediately issued a warrant for the arrest of Smethurst, but he was nowhere to be found; and when Smethurst made his appearance again, the *Scotch emigrant was missing*—the instruments and associates of Smethurst having in the meantime cajoled or sent him from the city.

Thus it will be perceived, that *thirty sovereigns, or one hundred and forty-five dollars*, were extorted from this poor man for fare, and to a place the *ordinary price to which from New York is two dollars and eighty-seven cents a passenger, or eight dollars and sixty-one cents for Heeslop and his family*, thus leaving those rapacious forwarders the swindling profit of one hundred and thirty-six dollars in this single case. All of which is respectfully submitted.

So long as the Commissioners were unable to obtain the compulsory landing-place for all emigrants arriving at New York, the runners, and brokers, and ticket-sellers, and money-changers, had everything their own way; and terrible were the consequences of their practical immunity. Swarming about the wharves, which they literally infested, all—the emigrant passenger, his luggage, his money, his very future—was at their mercy. The stranger knew nothing of the value of exchange, nor how many dollars he should receive for his gold; but his new-found friend did, and gave him just as much as he could not venture to withhold from him. Then there were the tickets for the inland journey to be purchased, and the new-found friend with the green necktie and the genuine brogue could procure these for him on terms the most advantageous: indeed, it was fortunate for the emigrant that he fell into the hands of 'an honest man at any rate'—'for, Lord bless us! there are so many rogues to be met with now-a-days.'

An instance of ready reckoning, most favourable to the ingenious arithmetician, is recorded in the evidence taken in 1847. Pat had but a poor chance against such a master of finance. The writer says, 'I was in a boarding-house in Cherry Street; a man came up to pay his bill, which the landlord made out 18 dollars. "Why," says the man, "did not you agree to board me for sixpence a meal, and threepence for a bed?" "Yes," says the landlord, "and that makes just 75 cents per day; you have been here eight days, and that makes just 18 dollars." At three-quarters of a dollar per day, the bill should have been *six* dollars: so the ready reckoner made *twelve* dollars by his genius for multiplication.

Among the most fruitful means of fraud was the sale of tickets. These tickets were of various kinds—tickets sold at exorbitant prices, but good for the journey; tickets which carried the passenger only a portion of his journey, though sold for the entire route; and tickets utterly worthless, issued by companies that had long before been bankrupt, or by companies that existed only in imagination. These latter are called 'bogus' tickets; and these were sold in Europe as well as in America—in village and country town, as in city and in seaport; and not rarely were they palmed off on the confiding passenger, as 'a great bargain,' by a sympathising, good-natured fellow-passenger, who, by the merest luck, had bought them cheap from a family he knew at home, that had 'changed their minds, and wouldn't cross over, being afeard of the say.'

In 1848 the Commissioners of Emigration issued a circular, in which these passages occur:—

As may be supposed, there are many people engaged in the business of forwarding these emigrants, and the individuals or companies thus engaged employ a host of clerks or servants, called 'runners' who try to meet the new-comer on board the ship that brings him or immediately after he puts his foot on shore, for the purpose of carrying him to the forwarding offices for which they respectively act. The tricks resorted to, in order to forestall a competitor and secure the emigrant, would be amusing, if they were not at the cost of the inexperienced and unexpecting stranger; and it is but too true that an enormous sum of money is annually lost to the emigrants by the wiles and false statements of the emigrant runners, many of them originally from their own country, and speaking their native language.

Of late the field of operations of these 'emigrant runners' is no longer confined to this city; it extends to Europe. .... They generally call themselves agents of some transportation, or forwarding bureau, and endeavour to impress the emigrant who intends going farther than New York with the belief that it is for his benefit, and in the highest degree desirable, to secure his passage hence to the place of his destination, before he leaves Europe. .... He is told that, unless he does so, he runs great risk of being detained, or having to pay exorbitant prices. ....

Instances have come to the knowledge of the Commissioners, where the difference amounted to three dollars a person. But this is not all. The cases are by no means rare in which the tickets prove *entirely worthless*. They bear the name of offices which never existed, and then, of course, are nowhere respected; or, the offices whose names they bear will be found shut up, and are not likely ever to re-open: or the emigrants are directed to parties refusing to acknowledge the agent who issued the tickets, and in all these cases the emigrant loses the money paid for them.

A profitable fraud is not to be suppressed without much difficulty; and even in 1857—nine years after—we find the iniquity of the bogus ticket in active operation. In a letter addressed to the Secretary of State, the Commissioners assert that the chief operators in this system of fraud have not only opened offices in the several seaports where emigrants usually embark, but have also established agencies in towns in the interior of those countries, and in the very villages whence families are likely to emigrate. Excluding Hamburg and Bremen from their observations, the Commissioners add that 'very many of those from other ports are first defrauded of their means by being induced to purchase tickets for railroad and water travel in this country, at high prices, which, when presented here, are found to be either quite worthless, or to carry the holders to some point in the interior far short of their destination, where they are left destitute.' Mr. Marcy, in reply, states that he has addressed a circular letter to the diplomatic and consular agents of the United States in those countries of Europe from which emigrants chiefly proceed, and instructed them to bring the subject to the notice of the Governments to which they were accredited, or of the authorities of the place where they reside, and to ask for the adoption of such measures 'as may be required by the claims of humanity and the comity of nations.'

What a gauntlet the helpless emigrant had to run before he was fairly on the road to his land of promise! Many were strong enough to break through, or fortunate enough to slip through, this net-work of fraud; but it may well be doubted if, for some years at least, those so strong or so fortunate were the greater number. It is lamentably true, that many, many thousands had their wings so effectually clipped—nay, so utterly plucked were they by the patriotic gentlemen with the green neckties, or the ladies with the green ribands, that they could not get beyond New York, into which, though perhaps altogether unsuited to the life of a city, the miserable victims of heartless fraud and pitiless robbery sank down to a lot of hardship, it might be of degradation and of ruin. It is heartrending to think of the tremendous consequences of these systematic villanies, and to reflect how thousands of people were thus fatally arrested on their way to places specially suited to their industry, and where, most probably, after the usual probationary hard work, they would have established themselves in comfort and independence. Better for many of them, old and young, the high-spirited boy and the innocent girl, that they had become the prey of the sharks of the deep, than that they had fallen into the clutches of the sharks of the land.

At length, in 1855, the Commissioners succeeded in establishing Castle Garden as the landing-place for all emigrants arriving at New York; and among other benefits which, in their Report of that year, they enumerate as resulting from the possession of this grand convenience, they include 'the *dispersion of a band of outlaws, attracted to this port by plunder, from all parts of the earth.*' The 'outlaws' were perhaps not so effectually dispersed as the Commissioners fondly imagined them to be; for so persistent were the attacks upon the system established at Castle Garden—attacks made generally through the public press—that the Grand Jury of the County of New York was formally appealed to. Nominally investigating certain charges made against the *employés* of the railway companies doing business in Castle Garden, the Grand Inquest really enquired into the entire system; and the result of that timely investigation was of the utmost consequence, in strengthening the hands of the Commissioners, and confounding their interested maligners.

On inquiry (they said) into the causes of certain published attacks on the Emigrant Landing Depôt, the Grand Inquest have become satisfied that they emanate, in the first instance, from the very interested parties against whose depredations Castle Garden affords protection to the emigrant, and who are chiefly runners in the employ of booking-agents, boarding-house keepers, and others, who have lost custom by the establishment of a central depôt, where the railway companies have their own business done by their own clerks, without the intervention of passage-brokers, &c.

This class has thrown great difficulties in the way of the proper development of affairs in Castle Garden, by constituting a noisy crowd outside the gates, whose behaviour is utterly lawless, and endangers the personal safety, not only of the passengers who have to leave the Castle Garden to transact business in the city, but also the *employés* of the Landing Depôt, and of individual Commissioners of Emigration, who are continually insulted in the public grounds surrounding the depôt, and have been obliged to carry loaded fire-arms in self-defence against the violence which has frequently been offered to them.

The Grand Inquest, after administering some hard hits to the local authorities, for the culpable remissness of the police in preventing the disorders which they describe, thus conclude:—

Having become satisfied that the Emigrant Landing Depôt, in all its operations, is a blessing, not only to emigrants, but to the community at large, they would feel remiss in the performance of a sacred duty if they failed to recommend this important philanthropic establishment to the fostering care of the municipal authorities; and they had dismissed the complaints preferred against certain employers of the Castle Garden, satisfied that they are not sustained by law, and have their origin in a design to disturb, rather than to further, the good work for which the establishment has been called into life by an Act of Legislature of April 1855.

This triumphant vindication of an institution which is to none more important than to the Irish who seek a home in America, bears the signature—'Howell Hoppock, Foreman of Grand Jury.'

With a full knowledge of the evils with which the Commissioners of Emigration had to contend, we shall be better able to appreciate the leading features of the system pursued at Castle Garden, and how far it realises the intentions of its benevolent founders.

The emigrant ship drops her anchor in the North River, or upper part of the Bay, where she is compelled to await the arrival of the steamer and barge belonging to the Commissioners, by which passengers and their baggage are landed at the wharf of Castle Garden; which to the alien is the Gate of the New World—the portal through which he reaches the free soil of America. Passengers and their baggage are under the protection of the Commissioners from the moment they are thus transferred to their charge; and though the brood of cheats and harpies may grind their teeth with rage as they remember the time when they were the first to board the emigrant ship, and, as a matter of undisputed right, take possession of her freight, living and inanimate, they know that their anger is unavailing, for that their day of license has passed. No sooner is the ship's arrival notified at Castle Garden, than the officer on duty obtains at the proper office a list of the passengers for whom letters, or remittances, or instructions, have been received by the Commissioners from friends who expected their arrival by that vessel. The officer boards the ship in his steamer; and the first thing he does on reaching her deck is to read aloud to the expectant hundreds, by whom he is quickly surrounded, the names of the passengers on his list, and announce that letters, or news, or money, await them at Castle Garden. Cheering to the heart of the anxious or desponding emigrant—probably a wife who has come out to her husband, or a child in search of a parent—is this joyful proclamation, it sounds so full of welcome to the new home. Too many, perhaps, feel their isolation or their disappointment the more poignantly from there being no word of love, no sign of welcome to hail their arrival.

The passengers are transferred to the steamer, and their baggage to the barge, and landed at Castle Garden, where their names and destinations are entered in a book kept for that purpose. In the large building at the disposal of the Commissioners the emigrants may obtain the luxury of a thorough ablution, and the comfort of the first meal on solid land; and those who have brought out money with them, or for whom their friends have sent remittances in anticipation of their arrival, and who desire to push on—North, South, or West—may at once start on their journey. They can change their money for the currency of the country, and purchase railway tickets to any part of the United States or Canada, and do so without going outside the building, or risking the loss of its salutary protection, They and their baggage are conveyed to the railway depôt, from which they start on their inland journey, fortunate indeed in not having a single feather plucked from their wing by watchful harpy.

Of many important and valuable departments of this Landing Depôt, those for the exchange of money and the sale of railway or steamboat tickets are not the least important or valuable. In the exchange department various nationalities are represented; and for a small percentage, sufficient to remunerate the broker without oppressing the emigrant, English and Irish, Germans, French, Swedes, Danes, and others, may procure reliable money—not flash notes—for their gold and silver and paper currency. The exchange brokers admitted to do business in Castle Garden are men of respectability; but were they inclined to take advantage of the simplicity of the emigrant, their prompt expulsion would be the certain result. Here then, in a most essential matter, is complete protection afforded to the inexperienced and the helpless.

The sale of railway tickets, the fruitful source of robbery and actual ruin in former days, is entrusted to responsible railway agents, over whom the Commissioners, as in duty bound, maintain a watchful control, necessary rather to prevent delay and inconvenience to the emigrant than to protect him against positive fraud. It is the interest of the railway companies represented in this bureau to fulfil their engagements with honesty and liberality; as if they fail to do so, the Commissioners have sufficient power to bring them to their senses. Of bogus tickets there need be no apprehension now, as in former times, when they were sold at home in the seaport town, and even in the country village; on board-ship during the voyage, or on the wharves and in the streets of New York. The mere loss of the purchase-money did not by any means represent the infamy of the fraud or the magnitude of the evil. Not only was the individual or the family effectually plundered, but, being deprived of the means of transport, they could not get beyond the precincts of the city in which they first set foot, and thus all hopes of a future of profitable industry were lost to them for ever. The sale of railroad tickets in Castle Garden is therefore a protection of the very first importance to the emigrant.

The baggage of the emigrant, which had been so long the prey of the lodging-house keeper, the runner, and the 'smasher,' is now not only retained in safe custody in compartments well adapted to that purpose, but is frequently held as a pledge for the repayment of advances made by the Commissioners to assist their owners to proceed on their intended journey. There is, however, no charge made for its custody, neither is interest required to be paid for the loan or advance. I have seen quantities of boxes, trunks, and packages of various kinds, duly marked and lettered, and safely stowed away, to be kept until the owners found it convenient or necessary to send for their effects, or, in case advances had been made on their security, until they were in a position to redeem them.

This plan of making advances on the security of the baggage, or portions of the baggage of the emigrant, which protects it from being plundered, and enables the individual or the family destined for the interior to proceed on their route, has now been in practice fully ten years, and has been attended with great good. The advance does not in any case exceed a few dollars; but the possession or the want of these few dollars may, at such a moment, determine the future fate of an entire family. In their Report for 1865 the Commissioners bear testimony to the good which these advances have done. Assistance has been rendered to many who might otherwise have become the prey of fraud, or have fallen into destitution, 'whilst,' as they state, 'the character of the assistance was such as not to lessen the feeling of independent self-reliance.' The small amount of $112 was advanced in 1856 to nineteen families, or about $6 ½ per family. This had been punctually repaid. The total amount advanced from August 1856, when the system was first adopted, to the end of 1865, was $23,215; the number of advances, whether to individuals or families, being 2,394. Of this amount, there remained unpaid but $1,376.

Another important department may be described as the letter or correspondence department, the value of which is becoming every year more fully appreciated, as well by emigrants as by their friends in America and at home. Suppose an emigrant, on arrival at New York, to be without the means of proceeding inland, or disappointed in not receiving a communication from a friend or member of his or her family, a letter, announcing the person's arrival, and asking for assistance, is at once written by a clerk specially appointed for that purpose; and in very many cases the appeal so made is promptly responded to, and the emigrant is thus enabled to proceed onwards. In the year 1866, there were nearly 3,000 such letters written, stamped, and posted, free of all charge to the parties interested. Of these letters 2,516 were written in English, the balance in German and other languages. The value of this admirable system may be shown by the fact, that the amount of money received in 1866, in reply to letters from the Landing Depôt for recently arrived emigrants, and applied to their forwarding, was $24,385.

It is of the utmost consequence that attention should here be directed to what has been, and must ever be, a source of bitter disappointment, if not of the greatest affliction to individuals and families; namely, the misdirection of letters, owing to the habit of not giving the full address, or the custom common with Irish women of the humbler class, of calling themselves by their *maiden* instead of their *married* names. It would be an act of great humanity on the part of those who are in a position to advise the emigrant, or the friends of the emigrant, whether at home or in America, to see that names are written accurately, and that addresses, especially American, are given fully—that is, that the city, county, or state, should be mentioned; and, lastly, that the envelope, which bears the post mark on it, should be retained as well as the letter. An instance or two in point, and which I select out of many, will exhibit the necessity of this advice being attended to at both sides of the Atlantic.

Mary Sullivan has come to America in search of her husband. Having some vague notion of his whereabouts, letters are despatched to various persons in the direction supposed to be indicated. No such person as Daniel Sullivan, 'who came to America four years ago,' is to be found. Poor Mary Sullivan is in despair. But at length, owing to some chance observation which drops from the afflicted wife, it turns out that Sullivan was her maidenname, and that her husband was Daniel M'Carthy, and not Daniel Sullivan. Letters are again despatched, and Daniel and Mary are once more united.

A woman arrives with her family. She has a letter from her son in Washington, or Jacksonville, or Newtown, and she desires to inform him that she is in New York, awaiting him. There is his letter, and she can tell no more about it; all she knows is, that her son is in the place mentioned; and 'why shouldn't he be there, she'd like to know?' But what Washington? what Jacksonville? what Newtown? There are hundreds of places with similar names in the United States; and which is it? Where, she is asked, is the envelope of the letter; for that would have the post mark, which, if not obliterated or indistinct, would be the best of all possible guides. 'Oh, sure,' the simple woman replies, 'I lost that: but there was nothing on that but where I lived when I was in Ireland; sure 'tis all in my son's letter.' The envelope lost, and there being no address in the letter, the Commissioners have to communicate with all the Washingtons, or Jacksonvilles, or Newtowns in the country; and probably it is owing to the enquiries of the priest of the locality in which the son resides or is at work that the family are ultimately brought together.

A young woman, Ellen T——, arrived early in the present year to join her brother, who was in a certain town in Pennsylvania, whence he wrote to her. She was sent to Ward's Island, and her brother was written to. No answer. Another letter was sent, but with the same result. The sister is safe in the Refuge at Ward's Island, but anxious and impatient. Time passes—still no tidings. At length she abandons all hope of finding her brother, and determines to do something for herself; and actually as she is leaving the office with this intention, the brother makes his appearance. What was the cause of the delay? His explanation is simple enough—he had left the place from which he had written to his sister and gone to another place, and 'he hadn't the gumption' to leave his new address with the postmaster.

Shortly before I left New York an instance occurred which impressed me with the value of the present system, under which such care is taken of the interests of the emigrants. A young girl arrived out by a certain steamer, and being taken sick of fever was sent to the hospital at Ward's Island. She said her father was in Boston, but she did not know his address. Her father, expecting her arrival, telegraphed to the agents in New York, enquiring if his daughter had come. The agents, whether ignorant or careless, replied by telegraph—'No.' The father, not satisfied with the answer, wrote to the Commissioners of Emigration, and they at once notified to him that his daughter had arrived, and was then in hospital at Ward's Island. He started from Boston without delay; and I had the assurance of the admirable physician by whom she was attended, that the interview with her father saved the daughter's life, which was at the time in danger.

Innumerable cases might be given in proof of the inconvenience and suffering—oftentimes the gravest injury—entailed on emigrants, especially young girls, through this neglect of sending the address accurately and fully, and retaining it when received; also of women giving their maiden instead of their married name; of not having the name written distinctly, and of saying the name is O'Reily when it is Riley, or Donnelly when it is O'Donnell. Mistakes, perhaps apparently trifling, are quite sufficient to keep the nearest and dearest relatives apart, and deprive the young and inexperienced girl of the much-needed protection of a brother or a father.

The titles by which the General Superintendent is addressed are very varied. At one time he is styled 'The Mayor of Castle Garden,' at another 'The Commander,' at another 'The Keeper,' and not unfrequently 'Head General!' The mistake of 'Blackbird's Island' for Blackwall Island, in which there is a penitentiary, is not altogether inappropriate; but that of mistaking a General officer for a Police officer was much more serious, as witness the following:—

Two country girls, recently arrived from 'Sweet Tipperary,' with the painting of nature on their healthy cheeks, received from one of the clerks a written card bearing the address of their friends in the upper part of the city, and were directed to apply for information on their way to the first policeman they met; and one of these blue-coated brass-buttoned dignitaries, on duty at the Depôt, was pointed out to them for their guidance. 'Thank your honour kindly, we'll be sure not to mistake the pelliceman when we want him,' said the rosiest, who did all the talking. It was at the early part of the war, when the streets were full of blue Federal uniforms. The two country girls set off rejoicing, but had not been gone many minutes when they were back again, out of breath and greatly flurried. 'Well,' said the clerk, 'what brings you back?' 'Oh, sure your honour, we did just as your honour tould us. We went up the wide sthreet ye call Broadway, and when we kem to the big church beyant, with the cross on it, sure there we saw a gintleman with a blue coat and gould buttons, and a cocked hat on his head, and a fine feather in it, and a swoord by his side; and Mary and meself thought he must be the head of all the Pellice. So we made bould to tell that your honour tould us to ax him which was the way to the third Avany cars, and sure he tould us to "go to the Divil"—so we kem straight back to your honour.' The clerk, who was a good judge of a joke, looked steadily at the speaker; but she seemed utterly unconscious of having perpetrated a *bon mot*.

There is another department at Castle Garden, which has proved of immense advantage to emigrants of both sexes—an Intelligence Office and Labour Exchange. Fortunately for the interests of those who desire to employ and to be employed, this is becoming every day better known, and consequently more generally availed of; and through its operation employment is obtained for all kinds of labour, agricultural, manufacturing, and domestic. There are two such offices in the building, one for men and the other for women. A register, which I had the opportunity of examining, is carefully kept, in which the names of persons requiring employment, or wanting to employ hands, are entered; and in which, in case of hiring, all necessary particulars are likewise set down. This register is thus not only a means of affording useful information respecting individuals to friends who seek intelligence of them, but also of protection to the parties employed; inasmuch as if the employer violates his contract—which is embodied in his proposal—he may be sued on the part of the Commissioners, to whom the emigrant is an object of official care for five years after his or her landing at New York. It frequently happens that, through the operation of this bureau, persons are enabled to procure employment on landing, and go off at once to those who hired them by anticipation. But it must be understood that the chances of employment are generally more in favour of females than of males; and that they are terribly against the latter, if they come out at a wrong season—which is towards the Autumn, and all through the Winter. The girl or woman, assuming that she desires to work and is capable of it, may come out at any season of the year, Winter or

Summer; but the man who looks for out-door employment *should come out when the Spring work is opening —certainly not sooner than March, or later than October*. The total number of males provided with employment last year—1866—through the Intelligence Office and Labour Exchange, Castle Garden, was 2,191; of females, 6,303; of both sexes, through the Commissioners' agents, at Buffalo, Albany, and Rochester, 1,289; and at the office of the German Society in New York, 988—making in all, 10,771.

I saw a number of women and girls, generally young, in a large apartment of the building, employed in knitting or sewing, waiting to be hired for various purposes, whether in factories, in stores, or in domestic occupations.

One of the latest improvements in the Emigration Depôt at Castle Garden is its direct connection by telegraph with every part of the United States and the British Provinces; so that an emigrant, on landing, may at once communicate with expecting friends in any part of North America.

Having referred to some of the most salient features of the establishment at Castle Garden, I may briefly glance at Ward's Island, which is the crowning feature of the whole, combining everything necessary for the care and comfort and protection of the stranger which enlightened benevolence and practical experience could suggest, or the most liberal expenditure could provide. When one remembers the bed of broken straw, the rotten flour, the decayed vegetables, the putrid meat, specially procured for the sick emigrants of 1847 and 1848, by the ship-brokers of that day, one may well invoke a blessing on the noble-hearted men to whose humanity, courage, and perseverance the existing system is mainly due.

Removed, by its insular position, from all contact with the city, its shores washed by the ever-moving tide of the Sound, lies Ward's Island, 110 acres of which are now in possession of the Commissioners, and devoted to the varied purposes of the institution. The stranger is astonished at beholding the splendid groups of buildings that, as it were, crown the island—asylums, refuges, schools, hospitals; the latter for surgical, medical, and contagious cases. These buildings were capable last year of accommodating more than 1,500 persons, and they are added to according to the means at the disposal of the Commission. On the 10th of August, 1864, was laid the foundation stone of an hospital with accommodation for 500 patients; which hospital, designed and furnished with all the latest improvements, is admitted by competent judges—including Miss Nightingale—to be one of the most complete in the world. I visited this hospital in March, 1867, and though not qualified to pronounce an opinion which would be of any practical value, I cannot refrain from expressing the admiration with which I beheld so noble an institution, equal in every respect to the best I had seen in London, Rome, Paris, or Vienna; and, from its peculiar position, especially its entire isolation from other buildings, and being erected on an island, more favourable to the treatment and recovery of the patient than any hospital in a great city. The Commissioners have been careful to provide an unlimited supply of the pure Croton for the inmates of the different establishments under their charge; and to another essential requisite of health—a thorough system of drainage and sewerage—they have devoted considerable attention. The result is a low rate of mortality in hospital and asylum, among infants and adults; which contrasts most favourably with institutions of a similar nature, but not enjoying the special advantages that distinguish those of Ward's Island. The staff, surgical and medical, is equal to the necessity, and consists of men eminent in their different branches of the healing art.

It may be interesting to contrast the number of persons, patients or inmates, at Ward's Island on the 30th of June, 1867, with the number at the corresponding periods of the three previous years. It proves two things—the increased demand on the resources of the institution; also the difficulty of procuring employment, arising not only from the continued overcrowding of New York, but from the inability of these emigrants to push on to the West. The total number of inmates in 1864, while the war was raging, was 1,000. In 1865 it fell to 851. But since then the number has been seriously added to. In 1866 it was 1,251, and on the 30th of June, 1867, it rose to 1,428. The number of able-bodied working men on the island, at a time when the best chances of employment are offered to those inclined to work, is still more significant. In 1864 the number was 42; in 1865 it fell to 34; in 1866 it rose to 100; and in 1867 it was as high as 123. The sick average at least 600, the balance consisting of women and children.

There may be other features of this *unpaid* Commission to which I should have referred, inasmuch as it has afforded to the whole country an example of what practical benevolence and public spirit are capable of accomplishing; but other subjects of interest demand my attention. It is, however, satisfactory to know that the active attention of Congress and the Government of the United States has been directed to the protection of foreign emigrants, and that an efficient organisation may be expected in the most important of the seaports. From the Report of the Government Commissioner of Emigration, presented to Congress on the 28th of February, 1866, one may learn how formidable is the evil against which it is necessary to combat with unabated energy, as well for the protection of the helpless stranger, as for the interests and the honour of the great country to which, from many motives and causes, he is attracted. The Government Commissioner states that upon entering upon the duties of his office he found himself in conflict with a host of persons who had been long accustomed, in the various ports, to prey upon the immigrant.

Companies, boards, and agencies, with sounding titles and high professions, were ready to deceive and plunder him at every turn, and it required prompt and decisive action to meet this great and growing evil. Many organisations, proper in themselves, but representing special interests, were simply subserving their own plans and the views of some single locality, regardless of the welfare of the immigrant. He states that through the appointment of a superintendent at New

York, his bureau has been enabled to break up many swindling agencies with their runners, and protect thousands of emigrants; and he adds: 'This work, however, never ceases. New schemes of fraud spring up whenever occasion offers, and they require continued vigilance to suppress them.' The 'passenger laws' would appear, from this Report, to be systematically violated, indeed boldly set at defiance; and more stringent powers are demanded for their enforcement.

It is satisfactory to perceive that, at least up to the time of the publication of the Report in question, the policy of the Government Bureau of Emigration was to act in harmony with the unpaid Commission in New York; and for the interests of humanity I may venture to express an earnest hope that no change, however apparently beneficial, may have the effect—the fatal effect—of interfering with the operation or impairing the efficiency of an organisation which has rendered inestimable services to the poor, the feeble, the unprotected, and in a special degree to those of the Irish race. The words of Florence Nightingale, when acknowledging, in 1866, the annual Reports which had been sent to her, may fittingly conclude this branch of my subject: 'These Reports are most businesslike. They testify to an amount of benevolent and successful efforts on behalf of the over-crowded old States of Europe of which America may well be proud.'

CHAPTER XI

Evil of remaining in the great Cities—Why the City attracts the new Comer—
Consequence of Overcrowding—The Tenement Houses of New York—Important
Official Reports—Glimpses of the Reality—An inviting Picture—Misery and
Slavery combined—Inducements to Intemperance—Massacre of the Innocents—
In the wrong Place—Town and Country

IRELAND, whence a great tide of human life has been pouring across the Atlantic for more than half a century, is rightly described as 'an agricultural country;' by which is meant that the far larger portion of its population are devoted to the cultivation of the soil. In no country have the peasantry exhibited a stronger or more passionate attachment to the land than in that country from which such myriads have gone and are still going forth. And yet the strange fact, indeed the serious evil, is, that, notwithstanding the vast majority of those who emigrate from Ireland to America have been exclusively engaged in the cultivation of the soil— as farmers, farm-servants, or outdoor labourers—so many of this class remain in cities and towns, for which they are not best suited; rather than go to the country, for which they are specially suited, and where they would be certain to secure for themselves and their families, not merely a home, but comfort and independence. I deliberately assert that it is not within the power of language to describe adequately, much less exaggerate, the evil consequences of this unhappy tendency of the Irish to congregate in the large towns of America. But why they have hitherto done so may be accounted for without much difficulty.

Irish emigrants of the peasant and labouring class were generally poor, and after defraying their first expenses on landing had little left to enable them to push their way into the country in search of such employment as was best suited to their knowledge and capacity; though had they known what was in store for too many of them and their children, they would have endured the severest privation and braved any hardship, in order to free themselves from the fatal spell in which the fascination of a city life has meshed the souls of so many of their race. Either they brought little money with them, and were therefore unable to go on; or that little was plundered from them by those whose trade it was to prey upon the inexperience or credulity of the new-comer. Therefore, to them, the poor or the plundered Irish emigrants, the first and pressing necessity was employment; and so splendid seemed the result of that employment, even the rudest and most laborious kind, as compared with what they were able to earn in the old country, that it at once predisposed them in favour of a city life.

The glittering silver dollar, how bright it looked, and how heavy it weighed, when contrasted with the miserable sixpence, the scanty 'tenpenny-bit,' or the occasional shilling, at home! Then there were old friends and former companions or acquaintances to be met with at every street-corner; and there was news to give, and news to receive—too often, perhaps, in the liquor-store or dram-shop kept by a countryman—probably 'a neighbour's child,' or 'a decent boy from the next ploughland.' Then 'the chapel was handy,' and 'a Christian wouldn't be overtaken for want of a priest;' then there was 'the schooling convenient for the children, poor things,'—so the glorious chance was lost; and the simple, innocent countryman, to whom the trees of the virgin forest were nodding their branches in friendly invitation, and the blooming prairie expanded its fruitful bosom in vain, became the denizen of a city, for which he was unqualified by training, by habit, and by association. Possibly it was the mother's courage that failed her as she glanced at the flock of little ones who clustered around her, or timidly clung to her skirts, and she thought of the new dangers and further perils that awaited them; and it was her maternal influence that was flung into the trembling balance against the country and in favour of the city. Or employment was readily found for one of the girls, or one or two of the boys, and things looked so hopeful in the fine place that all thoughts of the fresh, breezy, healthful plain or hill-side were shut out at that supreme moment of the emigrant's destiny; though many a time after did he and they long for one breath of pure air, as they languished in the stifling heat of summer in a tenement house. Or the pioneer of the family—most likely a young girl—had found good employment, and, with the fruits of her honest toil, had gradually brought out brothers and sisters, father and mother, for whose companionship her heart ever yearned; and possibly her affection, was stronger than her prudence, or she knew nothing of the West and its limitless resources. Or sickness, that had followed the emigrant's family across the ocean, fastened upon some member of the group as they touched the soil for which they had so ardently prayed; and though the fever or the cholera did not destroy a precious life, it did the almost as precious opportunity of a better future: the spring of that energy which was sufficient to break asunder the ties and habits of previous years — sufficient for flight from home and country—was broken; and those who faced America in high hope were thenceforth added to the teeming population of a city—to which class it might be painful to speculate.

It is easy enough to explain why and how those who should not have remained in the great cities did so; but it is not so easy to depict the evils which have flowed, which daily flow, which, unhappily for the race, must continue to flow from the pernicious tendency of the Irish peasant to adopt a mode of livelihood for which he is not suited by previous knowledge or training, and to place himself in a position dangerous to his morals, if not fatal to his independence. These evils may be indicated, though they cannot be adequately described.

This headlong rushing into the great cities has the necessary effect of unduly adding to their population, thereby overtaxing their resources, however large or even extraordinary these resources may be, and of rudely disturbing the balance of supply and demand. The hands—the men, women, and children—thus become too many for the work to be done, as the work becomes too little for the hands willing and able to do it. What is worse, there are too many mouths for the bread of independence; and thus the bread of charity has to supplement the bread which is purchased with the sweat of the brow. Happy would it be for the poor in the towns of America, as elsewhere, if the bread of charity were the *only* bread with which the bread of independence is supplemented. But there is also the bread of degradation, and the bread of crime. And when the moral principle is blunted by abject misery, or weakened by disappointments and privation, there is but a narrow barrier between poverty and crime; and this, too frequently, is soon passed. For such labour as is thus recklessly poured into the great towns there is constant peril.

It is true there are seasons when there is a glut of work, when the demand exceeds the supply—when some gigantic industry or some sudden necessity clamours for additional hands; but there are also, and more frequently, seasons when work is slack, seasons of little employment, seasons of utter paralysis and stagnation. Cities are liable to occasional depressions of trade, resulting from over production, or the successful rivalry of foreign nations, or even portions of the same country; or there are smashings of banks, and commercial panics, and periods of general mistrust. Or, owing to the intense severity of certain seasons, there is a total cessation of employments of particular kinds, by which vast numbers of people are flung idle on the streets. If at once employed and provident, the condition of the working population in the towns is happy enough; but if there be no providence while there is employment, one may imagine how it fares with the family who are destitute alike of employment and the will or capacity for husbanding its fruits. It is hard enough for the honest thrifty working man to hold his own in the great towns of America, for rents are high, and living is dear, and the cost of clothes and other necessaries is enormous; but when the work fails, or stops, terrible indeed is his position. Then does the Irish peasant realise the fatal blunder he has made, in having chosen the town, with all its risks, and dangers, and sad uncertainties, instead of having gone into the country, 110 matter where, and adopted the industry for which he was best suited. Possibly, the fault was not his, of having selected the wrong place for his great venture in life; but whether his adoption of the town in preference to the country were voluntary or the result of circumstance, the evil is done, and he and his family must reap the consequences, whatever these may be.

The evil of overcrowding is magnified to a prodigious extent in New York, which, being *the* port of arrival—the Gate of the New World—receives a certain addition to its population from almost every ship-load of emigrants that passes through Castle Garden. There is scarcely any city in the world possessing greater resources than New York, but these resources have long since been strained to the very uttermost to meet the yearly increasing demands created by this continuous accession to its inhabitants; and if there be not some check put to this undue increase of the population, for which even the available space is altogether inadequate, it is difficult to think what the consequences must be. Every succeeding year tends to aggravate the existing evils, which, while rendering the necessity for a remedy more urgent, also render its nature and its application more difficult.

As in all cities growing in wealth and in population, the dwelling accommodation of the poor is yearly sacrificed to the increasing necessities or luxury of the rich. While spacious streets and grand mansions are on the increase, the portions of the city in which the working classes once found an economical residence are being steadily encroached upon—just as the artisan and labouring population of the City of London are driven from their homes by the inexorable march of city improvements, and streets and courts and alleys are swallowed up by a great thoroughfare or a gigantic railway terminus. There is some resource in London, as the working class may move to some portion of the vast Metropolitan district, though not without serious inconvenience; but unless the fast increasing multitudes that seem determined to settle in New York adopt the Chinese mode of supplementing the space on shore by habitation in boat and raft on water, they must be content to dwell in unwholesome and noisome cellars, or crowd in the small and costly rooms into which the tenement houses are divided.

As stated on official authority, there are 16,000 tenement houses in New York, and in these there dwell more than half a million of people! This astounding fact is of itself so suggestive of misery and evil that it scarcely requires to be enlarged upon; but some details will best exhibit the mischievous consequences of overcrowding—not by the class who, at home in Ireland, have lived in cities, and been accustomed to city-life and city pursuits, but by a class the majority of whom rarely if ever entered a city in the old country until they were on their way to the port of embarkation—by those whose right place in America is the country, and whose natural pursuit is the cultivation of the land. Let the reader glance at the tenement houses—those houses and 'cellars' in which the working masses of New York swarm—those delightful abodes for which so many of the hardy peasantry of Ireland madly surrender the roomy log-cabin of the clearing, and the frame house of a few years after, together with almost certain independence and prosperity. I have entered several of these tenement houses, in company with one to whom their inmates were well known; I have spoken to the tenants of the different flats, and have minutely examined everything that could enlighten me as to their real condition; but I deem it well to rely rather on official statements, which are based on the most accurate knowledge, and are above the suspicion of exaggeration.

The Commissioners of the Metropolitan Board of Health, in their Report for 1866, say:—

The first, and at all times the most prolific cause of disease, was found to be the insalubrious condition of most of the tenement houses in the cities of New York and Brooklyn. These houses are generally built without any reference to the health or comfort of the occupant, but simply with a view to economy and profit to the owner. The provision for ventilation and light is very insufficient, and the arrangement of water-closets or privies could hardly be worse if actually intended to produce disease. These houses were almost invariably crowded, and ill-ventilated to such a degree as to render the air within them continually impure and offensive. . . . The basements were often entirely below ground, the ceiling being a foot or two below the level of the street, and was necessarily far more damp, dark, and ill-ventilated than the remainder of the house. The cellars, when unoccupied, were *frequently flooded to the depth of several inches with stagnant water*, and were made the receptacles of garbage and refuse matter of every description. ... In many cases, the cellars were constantly occupied, and sometimes used as *lodging-houses*, where there was no ventilation save by the entrance, and in which the occupants were entirely dependent upon artificial light by day as well as by night. Such was the character of a *vast number* of the tenement houses in the lower parts of the city of New York, and along its eastern and western borders. Disease, especially in the form of *fevers of a typhoid character*, was constantly present in these dwellings, and every now and then became in more than one of them *epidemic*. It was found that *in one of these twenty cases of typhus had occurred during the previous year*.

The poor Irishman in New York is not without experiencing the tender mercies of 'middlemen,' to whom in many instances the tenement houses are leased. These middlemen are generally irresponsible parties, with no interest in the property except its immediate profits, and who destroyed the original ventilation, such as it was, by the simple process of dividing the rooms into smaller ones, and by crowding three or four families into a space originally intended for a single family.

In 1864, the Citizens' Association of New York was organised, its main object being the promotion of Sanitary Reform. It has already effected much service through the information it has afforded in its valuable publications, which exhibit in a striking manner the enormous evil of overcrowding, and its consequences to the morals and health of the community. Associated with this organisation are many eminent physicians, who constitute the Council of Hygiene, whose report forms one of the most important features of the volume. Having divided the city into districts for the purpose of inspection, the Council appointed competent medical officers for that task; and from the detailed reports of these inspectors an accurate notion may be obtained of the sanitary condition of each district.

That the overcrowding of New York is far in excess of all other cities may be shown by a comparison of that city with London. In the English metropolis, the highest rate of population to the square mile is in East London, where, according to the report of a recent Royal Commission, it reached as high as 175,816. Whereas in certain portions of the Fourth Ward of New York, the tenant-house population were in 1864 'packed at the rate of about 290,000 inhabitants to the square mile.' Nor is it at all probable that things have come to the worst in this respect. The Council of Hygiene, in their Report, take rather a desponding view of the future. Not only has New York already become one of the most populous and densely crowded cities in the world, 'but it is plainly its destiny to become at once the most populous and *the most overcrowded* of the great maritime cities.' The evils, therefore, which now imperil health and morals in consequence of overcrowding, will increase with the increase of the population.

That there are several tenement houses constructed with a due regard for their intended object—the comfort and accommodation of their inmates—is true; but such houses are rather the exception than the rule, and the rent demanded for cleanly and commodious apartments in a tenement provided with the requisite appliances, places them beyond the means of the mass of the working population. It is not with houses of this class, but of the kind which are occupied by the poorer portion of the community, including of necessity those who have made the fatal mistake of stopping in New York, instead of pushing on to the country and occupying the land, that I propose to deal. A few extracts, taken at random from some of the Reports, will place the reader sufficiently in possession of the evils of overcrowding, and the perils, alike to soul and body, of the tenement system, which is now, though late, arousing the alarmed attention of statesmen and philanthropists.

Dr. Monnell, to whom the inspection of the 'First Sanitary District' was entrusted, states that the inhabitants of this district, which comprises part of the First and the whole of the Third Ward, are largely of foreign birth—about one-half Irish, one-quarter Germans, and the remainder Americans, Swedes, Danes, &c. Two-thirds of the resident population consist of labourers and mechanics with their families. The general characteristics are, 'a medium grade of intelligence and a commendable amount of industry, intermixed largely with ignorance, depravity, pauperism, and dissipation of the most abandoned character.' As an illustration of the evil of overcrowding, and the perilous characteristics of a large class of the floating population—consisting in this district of 'travellers, emigrants, sailors, and vagabonds without a habitation and almost without a name'—that mingle with the more permanent residents of this lower district of the city, Dr. Monnell thus makes the reader acquainted with a certain squalid old tenant house in Washington Street:—

Passing from apartment to apartment, until we reached the upper garret, we found every place crowded with occupants, one room, only 5 ½ by 9 feet, and a low ceiling, containing two adults and a daughter of twelve years, and the father working as a shoemaker in the room, while in the upper garret were found a couple of dark rooms kept by haggard crones, who nightly supplied lodgings to twenty or thirty vagabonds and homeless persons. This wretched hiding-place of men, women, and girls, who in such places become daily more vicious and more wretched, had long been a hot-bed of typhus, seven of the lodgers having been sent to the fever hospital, while permanent residents on the lower floors had become infected with the same malady and died.

In the construction of many modern tenant houses, it would appear, the Inspector states, 'that hygienic laws and sanitary requirements have been estimated as of only secondary importance, the great problem being how to domicile the greatest number of families on a given area. And in the practical solution of that problem, in this district, lies the great overshadowing cause of insalubrity, before which all others combined sink into insignificance. The most marked feature of the tenant houses is the small size of their apartments, whereby ensues overcrowding in each family.' Having described a group of tenement houses, which are represented by the aid of photography, and designated as 'a perpetual fever nest,' the Report thus proceeds:—

And in addition, the street throughout this whole neighbourhood presents habitually the vilest condition of tilth, and reeks with most offensive odours. Typhus fever and measles were very prevalent here in the early part of the summer. In my weekly reports of 'pestilential diseases and insalubrious quarters,' I have had frequent occasion to describe the condition of families and disease in the premises that are here photographed. The beautiful work of the artist renders unnecessary any further description of these squalid and pestiferous tenements, and their noisome fronting of dilapidated and overflowing privies, and a dismal, narrow, flooded court. That eruptive fevers, typhus, and physical decay may always be seen here is certainly not surprising.

The worst effects upon the inmates of the poorest class of tenant houses are exhibited not so much in the more acute form of disease, as 'in the pale and sickly countenance of their occupants, with lax fibre and general absence of robust health; we see it also in the pining and wasting of infants, and in the general prevalence of strumous, ophthalmic, and eruptive disorders. All these appearances indicate unmistakably the want of those great indispensible necessities of health—pure air and light.'

Let us follow Dr. Pulling, the 'Inspector of the Fourth Sanitary District' in his visits of inspection, and, without straining probability, assume that the miserable picture so graphically drawn is that of an *Irish* family, the victims of the one great and fatal mistake of the husband and the father—that of having remained in New York, instead of carrying his strength and his industry to the place where they were most required, and were sure to be appreciated:

Through a narrow alley we enter a small courtyard which the lofty buildings in front keep in almost perpetual shade. Entering it from the street on a sunny day, the atmosphere seems like that of a well. The yard is filled with recently-washed clothing suspended to dry. In the centre of this space are the closets used by the population of both front and rear houses. Their presence is quite as perceptible to the smell as to the sight.

Making our way through this enclosure, and descending four or five steps, we find ourselves in the basement of the rear-building. We enter a room whose ceiling is blackened with smoke, and its walls discoloured with damp. In front, opening on a narrow area covered with green mould, two small windows, their tops scarcely level with the courtyard, afford at noonday a twilight illumination to the apartment. Through their broken frames they admit a damp air laden with effluvia which constitute the vital atmosphere imbibed by all who are immured in this dismal abode.

A door at the back of this room communicates with another which is entirely dark, and has but one opening. Both rooms together have an area of about 18 feet square, and these apartments are the home of six persons. The father of the family, a day labourer, is absent; the mother, *a wrinkled crone at thirty*, sits rocking in her arms an infant, whose pasty and pallid features tell that decay and death are usurping the place of health and life. Two older children are in the street, which is their only playground, and the only place where they can go to breathe an atmosphere that is even comparatively pure. A fourth child, emaciated to a skeleton, and with that ghastly and unearthly look which marasmus impresses on its victims, has reared its feeble frame on a rickety chair against the window sill, and is striving to get a glimpse at the smiling heavens whose light is so seldom permitted to gladden its longing eyes. Its youth has battled nobly against the terribly morbid and devitalizing agents which have depressed its childish life—the poisonous air, the darkness, and the damp; but the battle is nearly over—it is easy to decide where the victory will be.

The cellar tenements of this district are fearful abodes for human beings. They were occupied, in 1864, by 1,400 persons, and their floors ranged from ten to thirty feet below high-water mark! 'In the sub-tidal basements nineteen families, or 110 persons, live beneath the level of the sea.' 'In very many cases the vaults of privies are situated on the same or a higher level, and their contents frequently ooze through walls into the occupied apartments beside them. Fully one-fourth of these subterranean domiciles are pervaded by a most offensive odour from this source, and rendered exceedingly unwholesome as human habitations. These are the places in which we most frequently meet with typhoid fever and dysentery during the summer months.'

Matters are not much better in 'the Sixth Inspection District,' where the tenement population is about 23,000.

In some of the cellars and basements water trickled down the walls, the source of which was traced to the foulest soakage. One cannot be surprised to learn that the noxious effluvia always present in these basements are of a sickening character. Many of these cellars are occupied by two or three families; a number are also occupied as lodging-houses, accommodating from twenty to thirty lodgers! What an abode for those who, leaving home and country, crossed the ocean in the hope of bettering their condition!

The Inspector of the Eleventh District, Dr. Brown, states that nearly one-fifth of all the tenements are rear buildings, some of them of the lowest grade. They are generally contracted in size, shut out from the sunlight, and commonly are obstructions to light and ventilation in the front buildings. The interval between the front and rear house is frequently so small and sometimes so completely enclosed on all sides by the adjacent houses 'as to constitute a mere well-hole.' Referring to certain houses in Hammond and Washington Streets, the Inspector describes their inhabited cellars, the ceilings of which are below the level of the street, 'inaccessible to the rays of the sun, and always damp and dismal. Three of them are flooded at every rain, and require to be baled out. They are let at a somewhat smaller rent than is asked for apartments on the upper floor, and are rented by those to whom poverty leaves no choice. *They are rarely vacant.*'

Under the heading 'Rents,' we find the Inspector of the Fourth Sanitary District stating that 'in regular tenant houses the rent of each domicile (generally consisting of two rooms—a "living room" and a bedroom) at present averages $9 per month, or $108 the year.' The cellar is, we are informed, 'let at a somewhat lower rate' than the average mentioned.

From the Report of Dr. Furman, the Inspector of the Seventeenth Sanitary District, the following passage is extracted:—

Most of the larger tenant houses are in a state of muckiness, and as a rule, overcrowded, without ventilation or light. These are offensive enough (and incapable to preserve a normal standard of health); but the crowded rear tenant houses, completely cut off from ventilation and perhaps light, are still worse. They abound in dark, damp, and noisome basements and cellars, converted into *sleeping apartments*. In these the invigorating and health-preserving sunlight and fresh air are *never accessible*.

An illustration is given of one of these habitations, the 'living rooms' of which are nearly dark, and the dormitories' dark and *damp*.' The Report thus continues:—

Here we have low, damp, dark, and unventilated bed-rooms, whose inmates respire a murky air, *and consort with snails, spiders, and muckworms*. These underground habitations are most pernicious in laying the foundation for and developing strumous ophthalmia, hip-joint, and certain diseases of the spine, diseases of the respiratory organs (the chief of which is consumption), rheumatism, which in turn produces organic disease of the heart.

The picture would not be perfect without the following:—

They—the houses—are in many instances owned by large capitalists by whom they are farmed out to a class of factors, who make this their especial business. These men pay to the owner of the property a sum which is considered a fair return on the capital invested, and rely for their profits (which are often enormous) on the additional amount which they can extort from the wretched tenants whose homes frequently become untenantable for want of repairs, which the 'agent' deems it his interest to withhold. These men contrive to absorb most of the scanty surplus which remains to the tenants after paying for their miserable food, shelter, and raiment. They are, in many instances, *proprietors of low groceries, liquor stores, and 'policy shops' connected with such premises,* — the same individual often being the actual owner of a large number. *Many of the wretched population are held by these men in a state of abject dependence and vassalage little short of actual slavery.*

And this is in the greatest city of the Great Republic of the New World! The poor Irishman who leaves his own country to escape from the tyranny of the most grinding landlord, and becomes the slavish vassal of one of these blood-suckers, makes but a poor exchange. The 'improvement in his condition might be fittingly indicated by the homely adage,—'from the frying-pan into the fire.' The rudest hut in the midst of a forest, the loneliest cabin on the prairie, would be a palace to one of these abodes. Health, energy, independence, self-respect—the hopeful family growing up as strong as young lions, and fleet as antelopes—plenty for all, and a hearty welcome for the stranger and the wayfarer,—this is the country. What a contrast is it to the squalor, the debasement, and the slavery of the town—as described by a competent authority!

How intemperance, the author of so many ills to mankind, and in a special degree to those who live by their labour, has its origin in these abodes of misery, to which the working population are condemned through poverty and the want of cheap and healthful homes, is thus accounted for by the Commissioners of Health:—

This we know from observation, and from the testimony of dispensary physicians and other visitors among the poor, that the crowded, dark, and unventilated homes of the classes from which pauperism springs are driven to habits of tippling by the combined influences of the vital depression and demoralising surroundings of their unhealthy habitations. Pertinent was the reply of a drunken mother, in a dismal rear-court, to a sanitary officer, who asked her why she drank: 'If *you lived in this place, you would ask for whisky instead of milk.*'

Dr. Burrall, Inspector for the Twelfth District, touches in his Report on the same point:—

It may be that the depressing causes existing in such a neighbourhood prompt to the use of some 'oblivious antidote,' by which for a time the rough edges of life may be smoothed over. It may be, too, that these stimulants excite a certain degree of prophylactic influence, but the quality of liquor obtained in such places is injurious to the digestive organs, the brain becomes unduly excited, and quarrelling or even murder results.

Dr. Field, Inspector for the Eighteenth District, enters fully into the demoralising influences and results produced by the low class of tenements on those who inhabit them:—

Moreover, it is an accepted fact that to live for a long time deprived of pure air and sunlight will not only depress a man physically and mentally, but will actually demoralisehim. The atmosphere is precisely adapted, through its properties and constituents, to the wants of the beings designed to breathe it.

A man gradually loses ambition and hope; concern for the welfare of his family, by slow degrees, loses its hold upon him. Loss of physical vigour attends this corresponding condition of the mind, until at length lassitude and depression of spirits and constant ennui get such control over him that no power or effort of the will can shake them off. With this decline of energy and vigour, both of mind and body, is set up an instinctive yearning for something which will give a temporary respite to the dragging weariness of life. Hence we find the children even, who are brought up without the stimulating influence of pure air and sunlight, will learn to cry for tea and coffee before they learn to talk; and they will refuse the draught unless it be *strong*. One would hardly credit, unless he has visited considerably among the tenant-house population, how general this habit is among the youngest children. *As they grow older, they acquire the appetite of their parents for alcoholic stimulants*: and we need not go further to account for any extreme of immorality and want.

Nor are abundant opportunities wanting for the indulgence of this fatal passion. Of the twenty-nine Inspectors who report on the sanitary condition of New York, there is not one who does not deplore the existence of the lowest class of 'groggeries' in the midst of the very poorest district. One statement as to this fact will suffice. Dr. Oscar G. Smith, reporting on the Ninth District, says—'The number of dram-shops to be met in those localities where a tenant-house class reside, is surprising.' Dr. Edward W. Derby, in his Report on the Fourteenth District, gives a painful picture of the prevalence of this unhappy vice:—

The low groggeries and groceries, in all of which liquors are sold, are constantly thronged, I am sorry, to say, with members of both sexes, youth and old age vieing with each other as to their capabilities of drinking, enriching the proprietors of these places, spending their last penny in gratifying their morbidly-debased appetite, rather than purchasing the necessaries of life for their families, and then issuing forth or being thrust out upon the streets in various stages of intoxication, half crazed with the vile and poisonous liquor they have swallowed, fit subjects for the committing of the many crimes which are daily chronicled in our papers. Such are the places which stare you in the face at every step, a disgrace to the city, and a prolific source of corruption to the morals of the surrounding inhabitants.

'Poison,' 'vile poison,' 'noxious and deleterious compounds,' are the terms generally applied to the description of liquor for which so many sacrifice their means, their health, and the happiness of their families.

With such a state of things—affecting at least a very large portion of the tenement population of New York—it cannot be a matter of surprise that *the destruction of infant life* in that city is something prodigious. The total number of deaths 'in the first year of life,' for the *nine months* ending the 30th of September, 1866, was 6,258! This is a Massacre of the Innocents with a vengeance. The Commissioners of the Board of Health remark:—

The rate of mortality in children under five years of age in New York is greater than in any city with which this Board has correspondence, and the cause of this excess will best be sought in the miserable housing and habits of the labouring classes, and in the multiplied sources of foul air in our two cities. . . . From various data now in hand, the conclusion is warranted, *that death has in each of the past two years taken nearly one-third of the total number before the first birthday.*

Dr. Derby takes rather a philosophical view of this tremendous death rate, and is inclined to regard it as a providential counterpoise to the fecundity of the poor, which, he states, has long been a matter of remark. He adds:—

The number of diseases which menace and destroy infantile existence seems almost a providential interference to prevent an excess of population over and above that which the means of the parents could possibly support. Nor, when we reflect upon the condition in which these unfortunate children are found to exist, and the many circumstances, moral and hygienic, by which they are surrounded, do we wonder less at the amount of sickness and mortality among them, than that it is not greater; less that they die than they survive.

Dr. Monnell thus concludes his remarks on the destruction of life caused by the miserable dwellings of his district: —

In the deadly atmosphere of some low basement, or close unventilated bedroom, or in the wretched squalor of some dilapidated garret, those little ones so numerously born amongst this class first draw their breath, and in an atmosphere surcharged with poison they battle for life; but in the unequal strife *very few survive, and thus are yearly sacrificed whole hecatombs of living souls.* They fall victims not of necessity, nor of the decrees of inevitable Fate, but of ignorance and avarice, and are lost to parents and friends, to society, and to usefulness in the world.

These poor immature blossoms, that perish so miserably in the foul air of an overcrowded city, how they would have thriven in the pure atmosphere of the country! where the young cheek, 'pasty and pallid' in damp and dismal cellar, or the fusty sleeping-hole of the tenement house, would bloom with health, and the eye, so dull and languid in the haunts of misery or vice, would sparkle into life and hope! In the country, throughout America, children are, next to his own industry and health, the best capital of the parent. What they are under the circumstances described in the passages just quoted the reader may easily imagine.

My own previously formed convictions, which for years had been strong in favour of the Irish selecting the right place for their special industry, were, if possible, confirmed by a visit to tenement houses of different classes. I remember one in particular, occupied principally by Irish. It presented none of the revolting features common to the dens already described. There was no squalor, no dilapidation; the place appeared to be in fair order. But the tenants were *not* the class of people who should have remained in New York. In Ireland they belonged to the rural population; and when I lifted the latch and entered an apartment, it was just as if I had walked some miles into the country at home, and entered the cabin of the labourer, or the cottage of the farmer; for in the accent and manner of the inmates there was no difference whatever. They were all racy of the soil. You could not visit any house inhabited by a number of Irish in which instances of the beautiful charity by which the race are distinguished would not be displayed. Here, for instance, was a great strong fellow, not long from the old country, and not able to get work, listlessly leaning against the door-post of a lower apartment, the tenants of which had given 'the poor boy' a hearty welcome, and a 'shake-down,' and 'a bit and sup;' though they themselves had a hard struggle to keep want from their humble hearth. There was in another room a mother, with her own young brood, yet who found a corner in her woman's heart for the orphan child of a neighbour that died some months before.

In one of the upper 'domiciles' there were then six persons, a mother, four young children, and a female relative, who was engaged in washing. The husband, the seventh inmate, a labouring man, was out at work. The principal apartment measured about 9 feet by 12; the dimensions of the other, the bedroom, allowing little more than the space occupied by a fair-sized four-post bedstead. A stove, necessary for the season, occupied no small portion of the chief apartment. There was no actual want of essential articles of furniture, such as a table and chairs , and the walls were not without one or two pious and patriotic pictures, Catholic and Irish. The children were tolerably clean, but pale and sickly; and a poor little fellow, of wonderfully bright countenance, hopped about on one leg, from an injury which, owing to neglect, was likely to cripple him for life. For this house accommodation, for this confined space, in which seven human beings were pent up for so many hours together, there was paid $7 a month, or $84 a year. Work or no work—and it was not unfrequently the latter—this rent should of necessity be met. In English money, even at the present rate of 3s. 3d. the dollar in 'greenbacks,' a year's rent would come to 13l. 13s.; as much as would enable the tenant of these apartments to purchase the fee-simple of more than 50 acres of good land in a Western State.

The mother of the children was quiet, well-mannered, and respectable in appearance; and though the freshness had long since faded from her face, she retained the traces of a kind of grave and pensive beauty. She was the daughter of a decent farmer in West Carbery, county Cork, and her husband, now a day labourer in New York, had also held some land in the same locality. They had come to America 'to better themselves,'—'to be more independent than they were at home;' and here they were, stuffed into a little room in a tenement house, with four young helpless children depending on them for support, their only means consisting of the earnings of the father of the family—about $9 a week; out of which everything had to be provided, and at prices so excessive as to leave but a small balance en the Saturday night. A month's idleness, or a fortnight's sickness, and what misery! Necessaries to be had on credit, at a rate equal to the vendor's supposed risk; and to be paid for on a future day. in addition to the never-ceasing outlay for the daily wants of a young and growing family. Here then were intelligence, practical knowledge, special aptitude for a country life, madly flung away; and the all but certainty of a grand future, that is, a future of comfort and independence, sacrificed for the precarious employment of a day-labourer in New York . A few years of hopeful toil, not more trying, but less trying to the constitution, than that which he went through every clay, would have enabled the tenant of that stuffy apartment in a desperately overcrowded city to provide his wife and children with a happy, healthful, prosperous home, which would have been theirs for ever, and from which neither factor, nor agent, nor groggery owner could have driven them. But, alas for them and for him! the ready employment and its apparently large reward, and the attractions of a city, were more than a match for his good sense; and now, like so many of his countrymen, he is as thoroughly out of his legitimate sphere as man can possibly be. I regretted I could not see the husband; but I did, as a matter of conscientious duty, endeavour to make the wife and mother comprehend the magnitude of the mistake which had been made, and urged her to counsel him to free himself at the first opportunity from a position for which he was not suited, and which was not suited for him.

I saw much in other tenement houses—whether houses specially built for the purpose, or houses adapted to that purpose—to justify the accuracy of the descriptions given in the Reports from which I have quoted; but though I witnessed much misery and squalor, and in a few instances glanced into places scarcely fit for the shelter of animals, I must confess to have been more impressed by the sad blunder of these young people—who would have made such splendid settlers in some fertile region, whether of Canada or the States—than with all I saw or heard during the day.

Even where there is sobriety, industry, good conduct, constant employment, the city is not the place for the man bred in the country, and acquainted from his boyhood only with country pursuits, whether as farmer or farm labourer. The country wants him, clamours for him, welcomes him, bids him prosper, and offers him the means of doing so. But suppose there is not industry, sobriety, good conduct, or constant employment, is it necessary to depict the consequences? The once simple peasant is soon smirched by the foulness of such city corruption as too frequently surrounds him or lies in his daily path; and the dram shop, so ruinously convenient to the dwellings of the toiling poor, finds him one of its best customers. If his children escape the perils of infancy, and grow up about him, what is their training, what their career, what their fate? Possibly they are saved, through some merciful interposition; perhaps by the tears and prayers of a good mother, perhaps by the example of a sister who has caught the mother's spirit.

Possibly they grow up in industry and virtue, but the odds are fearfully against them; and it is not at all improbable that the quick-witted offspring of the father, who become intemperate and demoralised, fall into the class known as the Arabs of the Street, those victims of parental neglect or unprovided orphanage, that, as they arrive at manhood, mature into a still more dangerous class—the roughs and rowdies of the city, who are ready for every kind of mischief, and to whom excitement, no matter at whatever expense it may be purchased, becomes the first necessity of their existence.

Let it not be supposed that, in my earnest desire to direct the practical attention of my countrymen, at both sides of the Atlantic, to an evil of universally admitted magnitude, I desire to exaggerate in the least. From the very nature of things, the great cities of America—and in a special degree New York—must be the refuge of the unfortunate, the home of the helpless, the hiding-place of the broken-down, even of the criminal: and these, while crowding the dwelling-places of the poor, and straining the resources and preying on the charity of their communities, multiply their existing evils, and add to their vices. Still, in spite of the dangers and temptations by which they are perpetually surrounded—dangers and temptations springing even from the very freedom of Republican institutions no less than from the generous social habits of the American people—there are thousands, hundreds of thousands, of Irish-born citizens of the United States, residing in New York and in the other great cities of the Union, who are in every respect the equals of the best of American population—honourable and upright in their dealings; industrious, energetic, and enterprising in business; intelligent and quick of capacity; progressive and go-ahead; and as loyally devoted to the institutions of their adopted country as if they had been bom under its flag. Nevertheless, I repeat the assertion, justified by innumerable authorities — authorities beyond the faintest shadow of suspicion—that the city is not the right place for the Irish peasant, and that it is the worst place which he could select as his home.

The Irish peasant, who quits his native country for England or Scotland, may be excused for hiding himself in any of its great towns, manufacturing or commercial, inland or seaport; for not only may he find employment for himself, and have some chance for his young people in them, but there is no opportunity of his much bettering his condition by going into the county. But there is no excuse whatever for his remaining in the cities of America, crowding and blocking them up, when there are at this hour as many opportunities for his getting on in the country—that is, making a home and independence for himself and his children—as there were for the millions of all nationalities who went before him, and who now constitute the strength and glory of the Republic. The Irish peasant who goes to England or Scotland has little chance of being accepted even as the tenant of a farm in either of those countries—a remote one, indeed, of ever becoming a proprietor of English or Scottish soil; but the most miserable cottier of Connemara or the worst-paid day-labourer of Cork or Tipperary, who has the good sense to push on from the American seaboard towards those vast regions of virgin land that woo the hardy vigour of the pioneer, may in the course of a few years possess hundreds of acres of real estate by a more glorious title than has been too often acquired in the old countries of Europe, his own included—by the right of patient industry, blessed toil, and sanctifying privation.

CHAPTER XII

The Land the great Resource for the Emigrant—Cases in Point—An Irishman socially redeemed—More Instances of Success on the Land—An Irish Public Opinion wanted—Irish Settlements in Minnesota and Illinois—The Public Lands of America—The Coal and Iron of America—Down South—A Kildare Man in the South—Tipperary Men in the South—The Climate of the South—California an Illustration of the true Policy

EVERY mile I travelled, every man I met, every answer I received, tended the more to convince me that the land was the grand resource for the Irish emigrant, as well as the safest and surest means of his advancement. It mattered not whether it were Canada or the States, it was equally the same; and, save industry, energy, and strength, little was necessary to enable the humble man to make a home for himself and his children.

Walking one day with a friend in a city of Upper Canada, I was attracted by the gentlemanly air and manner of a young man whom my companion saluted; and on my asking who he was, and remarking that he had the appearance of a gentleman, my friend replied, 'Yes, he is a nice fellow, thoroughly educated and accomplished, and a smart man in his profession, too. He, sir, is the son of an Irishman—an Irish labourer—who came out here without a penny in the world, and yet who died a rich man, after bringing up his children as well as the first gentleman in the land. He was a labourer on the canal; and instead of doing what too many of our people are so fond of doing—stopping in the town—he contrived to buy a bit of land, which he cleared from time to time, taking an occasional job to procure provision for the winter; and so he got on, adding to his property year after year, until you see the result in his son, who is now a rising professional man, and who takes his place among the aristocratic classes. *Do, in God's name, advise your countrymen to stick to the land—what they know most about.*'

'Ah! sir,' said an Irishman, who had been many years in the States, and whom I met in a great central city, 'I made a sad mistake when I came out here first. I am from the west of the county Cork, and I was engaged in farming before I left Ireland; it was my business. But I don't know how it was, I allowed myself to stay in the town, and the time passed, and then it was too late, and I hadn't the heart to make a new effort. I am sorry for it now. Thank God, I am able to live, after educating my family, and doing for them; but if I went, as others did, to the country, and took a farm, and stuck to the business I knew best, I'd be an independent man now in my old age. It was a great mistake, sir, and the more I think of it, the more I regret it. My heart sinks in me at times when I think of what I might be this day, if I had only the sense to do the right thing at the right time.'

Spending a Sunday not far from the Falls of Niagara, I was speaking with a number of respectable Irishmen who had been many years from Ireland, and to whom the circumstances of their countrymen in the surrounding districts were thoroughly known. I turned the conversation in the direction most interesting to me—the position of the Irish, and the manner in which they had got on. The subject was one which excited the sympathies and aroused the recollections of my new acquaintances, who detailed as many instances of successful thrift and patient industry as would fill several pages.

Two Irishmen were working as helpers in a blacksmith's shop at Niagara Docks in 1844, and, having saved some money, they each purchased 100 acres of land, at a dollar an acre. One in particular, after bringing his family with him to their new home, and purchasing an axe, had but three-quarters of a dollar in his possession. These men divided their time between working for themselves and others; at one time chopping away with the ever-busy axe, at another hiring their labour to the neighbouring settlers, who were anxious to obtain their services. In the summer months they earned as much as enabled them to live during the winter, when they were hard at work at home, clearing and fencing; and when they had cropped their own land they went out to work again. At the time of which their story was thus told, they were each in the possession of 200 acres of cleared land, with horses, cattle, good houses, and every comfort that reasonable men could desire. It may be curious to speculate what would have been their destiny, had they continued at the drudgery from which they emancipated themselves by their own energy.

These were individual instances, casually mentioned, and only remarkable from the fact of the two men having mutually agreed to do the same thing; but there were numbers of other cases of equally successful industry. There was, for instance, a labourer who left work on a canal for a contractor, for work on the land for himself; and he also was the proprietor of 200 acres of fee simple estate, having given to his children—both of whom were members of learned professions—a first-class education. In fact, there were as many as a hundred Irish families in the surrounding district, who, in the opinion of the experienced gentleman to whom they were well known, had not brought with them altogether 500l., and yet who occupied good farms of their own creation, then their own property, and were looked upon as otherwise independent in their means.

One of the most experienced men in Canada, who has been long connected with emigration, thus gives his opinion as to the best mode by which an emigrant who is resolved on turning his attention to agriculture, and who possesses no other capital than what he has received from Providence, can get on in the new world:—

'One or two years' service with a farmer, particularly one who has himself earned his competency and comforts through trials and from a hard beginning, should be deemed an indispensable preparation for the settler before undertaking the clearing up of land on his own account. With that knowledge, he could obtain through the year, in the favourable months, enough of cash to buy provisions and necessaries for his family; and in the winter and early spring months, before hired help would be required, he could work to much real advantage for himself.' What applies to Canada applies equally well to the same work and the same circumstances in the States.

An Irishman, observing the marked difference in the circumstance and position of the same class of his countrymen in America in town and country, might be excused for supposing there was something specially sacred in the cultivation of the soil—in man toiling in the sweat of his brow to raise from the fruitful bosom of the Great Mother food for the sustenance of the human family. Whether this be a fanciful notion or not, it is certain that, in a moral point of view, agricultural occupations not only preserve the simplicity and even purity of life so usually to be found in the rural districts of almost every country, but even restore to primitive tastes and regularity of life those who return to them as a change. The easy-going haunter of the tavern and the grog-shop in the town becomes a steady and abstemious man when on his farm; and even the loose purposeless idler of the city hardens into unwonted energy when he exchanges its enervating atmosphere for the bracing air and wholesome pursuits of the country. I have had many proofs that this is so in America; but one case, though presenting no remarkable features, particularly impressed me at the time.

I was stopping with a genial countryman in a thriving town in the State of Illinois, which was surrounded by a rich farming country, the land mostly prairie. My host was one of the most prosperous men in the town or district, and enjoyed the highest character for energy, probity, and benevolence. Like most Irishmen in the same locality, he was the sole architect of his own fortunes. In his intelligent company I visited several farms owned by our countryman, and situate from within five to ten miles of the town. 'Now,' said my companion, as his stout horses struggled through the heavy soil of the road, 'I will show you one of the best farms hereabouts; and there is not a better or a steadier man in the whole country than its owner. He is doing well, too, and has brought up his children nicely, though he had little enough when he commenced, as I could tell. Here we are at the gate, and, sure enough, there is himself in the midst of his boys and girls.' The farm, the house, the barns, stable, and out-offices all fully justified the description given of them; and the owner, whom we found hard at work, affording an example of industry to his young people, was in keeping with everything around him,—respectable and substantial.

It is not necessary to dwell on the cordiality of his reception, or to tell of his mortification when he found that his hospitable offers of bed and board could not be accepted by his visitors: with an Irishman, hospitality is almost a matter of course, and no one is more rejoiced than the Irish-American to welcome one who is 'fresh from the dear old country.' During our drive home my friend assured me there was not in the neighbourhood, and for a long way round, a man more respected or more generally looked up to than the Irishman we had just quitted.

'His opinion,' he added, 'is asked, and taken moreover, upon many important questions; and when disputes arise about various things, they are frequently referred to him, and he settles them.'

The next morning I had a long and interesting conversation with an American gentleman largely connected with property in the locality. The conversation happening to turn upon the point respecting which I was ever on the look-out, if not for information, at least for confirmation of my own conviction,—that the right place for the Irish peasant was the land,—the American said: 'It has often surprised me how it is that an essentially agricultural people like the Irish will not invariably turn to the same pursuit in this country, where they can have all they desire—land cheap and abundant, with an undisputed title, and no one to trouble or disturb them. However, we have a good many of your countrymen employed in what I regard as their legitimate and natural avocation, and I am glad to tell you they are all doing well. I know Irishmen who have been doing nothing, or worse than nothing, in the town, and who became altogether different men when they went into the country. I remember one of them'—and he mentioned the name of the well-known farmer I had visited the day before—'and so long as he remained in the town he was doing very little good; in fact, he was falling into vicious habits, and was losing himself day by day. Fortunately for himself, he had the good sense to see that that kind of thing wouldn't do much longer, and so he resolved to change his mode of life. He left the town—cut it altogether—shook its dust from his sandals; he got a small bit of land, worked at it like a man, —I know how hard he worked,—and soon increased his farm, until, ere very long, it became a large one. And not long since he purchased a considerable property in addition; and, what is more, he has paid nearly every dollar of the purchase-money. I was asked by a gentleman of this place whether this property was sold, and I said it was—that Mr. So and So had bought it. "What!" said he, "did you trust him? Why, when I remember him, he was an idle do-nothing loafer, whom nobody would trust with the price of a bushel of apples. I am amazed at your having any business dealings with a person of his class."

"My dear sir," I said, "you are altogether mistaken in the character of the man: he may have been what you say he was when you knew him—that was many years ago; but I tell you there is not a more worthy or respectable man in the country than he is. And not only have I sold the property to him, but I got half the purchase-money the day of the sale, and there is little left to pay, and that little I can have at any moment—to-morrow, if I please." "Well," said the gentleman, "I am glad to hear it; I spoke from my remembrance when I used to see him in the town, and I knew him to be rather a loose fish, and generally in some kind of row or other. Though I can't have the property, I rejoice it is in good hands." Now, sir, you see how quitting the town and going on the land has saved him, as it has many other Irishmen, to my personal knowledge.'

It may be mentioned that the Irishman who was the subject of this conversation found in his young and growing family one of the surest sources of his prosperity. They sprang up about him, strong and vigorous as oaks, accustomed to out-door work, which imparted health alike to mind and body. Nor did he neglect their education —it must be a worthless Irish father who will do so; and in their industry, intelligence, and vigorous health, to say nothing of his own respectability and the quiet happiness of his wife, who had her troubles in the outset—he finds the best reward of his moral courage and perseverance. He might have remained all his life a mere drudge in the town; now he is the absolute owner of 500 acres of land, and is the founder of a prosperous family.

From the following passage of a letter received from a dignitary of the Catholic Church, himself an Irishman, who anxiously desires to see his countrymen in America devote themselves to a congenial pursuit, it will be seen how lack of mere money-capital is no insuperable bar to advancement, so long as there is land to occupy, and there are men and women with strength and intelligence to cultivate it. The writer goes on to say:—

'Once, in visiting the diocese of Pittsburgh, I heard that there were some Irish Catholics living in the extreme end of —— county, Pennsylvania, which was also the extreme point of the diocese. I resolved to try and see them. I arrived there late in the afternoon, and the arrangements already made did not permit me to stay longer than the afternoon of the next day. The poor people were delighted to have Mass, and an opportunity of approaching the Sacraments. I found about twenty families *who had settled there during the previous three or four years*. They had all farms of their own; nearly all had paid for them, and had their land enough cleared to be able to support themselves well on it thereafter. They had taken up the land at a low price, and were able to give time enough to work for hire amongst the older settlers, while they had time enough remaining to clear and cultivate each year an additional portion of their own land. It was the realisation of a system which I had often recommended, and which might be carried out almost to any extent, *that would enable our countrymen to be proprietors of the soil, instead of remaining drudges in our towns and cities.*'

In support of my assertion, that the country is the right place for the Irish peasant, and that in the cultivation of the soil he has the best and surest means of advancement for himself and his family, I cannot do more, in a work of this kind, than prove, by a few cases in point, that the advice I earnestly give to my countrymen on both sides of the Atlantic is for their benefit, and for the honour of their race and country. There is not in America a better man or truer Irishman than the writer of the words I have just quoted; and I may add, that there are not twenty men in the whole of the States who, from long and varied experience, and intimate knowledge of their countrymen, can speak with greater weight of authority than he can.

Turning from Pennsylvania to Minnesota, we have a picture of progress as like as possible to many which have already appeared in these pages. I take it from the valued communication of a zealous and able Irishman in the latter State, who—associated with other Irishmen, including a good priest—is successfully labouring in what I believe to be the most practically patriotic cause that could engage the attention and enlist the active sympathies of my countrymen in America—such Irishmen as, by worth, education, or position, can exercise a salutary influence over those who stand in need of guidance or, if necessary, assistance to secure for themselves a home and an honest independence. Advice, guidance, information, influence—these are even more valuable than pecuniary aid; and these require little sacrifice, even of time. What is required for the uplifting of thousands and thousands—nay hundreds of thousands—of Irish in America, is an active, energetic, out-spoken Irish Public Opinion, that will make its voice and influence heard and felt in every direction, warning those who will take warning, and saving those who can be saved from misery and degradation.

To be potent for good, every organisation should be, like that in Minnesota, free from the taint of speculation or the suspicion of robbery; and there is not a State in the Union, or a great city, in which there should not be found a few honourable and influential Irish gentlemen, who would join together for a purpose which concerns their own reputation, inasmuch as it concerns the reputation of the race to which they belong, and cannot repudiate. It is considered by Irishmen in America a noble and patriotic object to regenerate, by arms and revolution, the millions at home; but surely to lift up the millions who are in the States—to regenerate them morally, materially, and socially—to give them greater power and influence through rightly directed industry—to elevate the race in the esteem of the enlightened and generous-minded of the American people,—this is an object more practical, in no way hazardous or injurious to any interest or individual whatever, and certainly not less noble or patriotic.

But all this while the brief picture of an Irish Settlement in Minnesota is pressing for attention. The writer is the Honorary Secretary of the Irish Emigrant Society of St. Paul, who, by no means indifferent to the value of a little money capital, thus shows what Irishmen have done with the God-given capital of strength, skill, and patient industry:—

'Men who commenced the very poorest are to-day well off. Let me give you an instance. Sixty miles west of St. Paul, on the Minnesota river, Sibly county, is the Irish Settlement of Jessen Land. About thirteen years ago the first steamer that went up the Minnesota landed two brothers of the name of Doheny, and a man of the name of Young, all from "gallant Tipperary," at this place, then an unbroken wilderness. Perhaps they were the first white men who ever stood there. Well, they set to work, cut down a tree here and there, put in a few hills of potatoes, planted a little corn, put a few sticks and logs together, and called them houses. This was all necessary at the time to fulfil the requirements of the law. In this way they made claims, not alone for themselves, but for friends in the East, and became owners of a large tract of splendid land. When all this was accomplished their money was run out; so they returned to St. Paul, and went again to work. In the following spring they again went up the Minnesota, this time bringing their families, and the friends for whom they had made land entries, with them. To-day this settlement, and Walter and Tom Doheny, who started it, are a credit to us all. The settlement has two-storey handsome farm-houses and barns, its church, priest, and school. Its people are what the Irish peasant can become even in the first generation—intelligent, industrious, open-hearted, generous, brave, and independent. When I want to be reminded of my dear country, I spend a day in Jessen Land.'

Here is a mere glimpse of the Irish in Illinois:—

An excellent Irishman, residing in Chicago, whose business, as a commission agent, has for the last ten years brought him into constant communication with his countrymen of the farming classes, not only throughout Illinois, but several other of the Western States, says: 'There is not a county of the one hundred counties of which Illinois is composed, that has not representatives from Ireland among its farming population; and I am proud to say to you, and the world, that where the Irish farmer once gets settled down upon his farm, in this his Western home, that he shows as much energy and go-aheadishness as emigrants from any other part of the world. We have, in almost every county, what are known as Irish settlements founded by some early adventurous Irishman. Several are of great extent; that, for instance, founded by Mr. Neill Donnelly, in M'Henry's county, is one of the finest in the State. There are three good-sized Catholic churches and several excellent district schools in this settlement, in which there is much comfort and prosperity.'

After referring to the harmony in which the Irish live with all nationalities, and the mutual willingness to assist and serve each other, my excellent friend adds: 'Nothing less than 80 acres of land is worth while to have out here, although occasionally you will find a small farm of 40 acres; but it is looked upon as nothing in this part of the world. Some of my Irish friends in Donnelly's and other settlements have 640 acres each, and almost all at least 120 acres. Farmers divide their crops often in this way; say 20 acres of wheat, 10, or 20, or 40 acres of corn, so many acres of oats, rye, barley, potatoes, &c., according to the size of the farm. To afford you an idea of the prosperity of our Irish farmers, I will mention that often, in the course of my business, I have at one time sold as high as one thousand dollars' worth of pork, butter, and wheat, for one Irish farmer; and I can tell you he had not much when he began the world here. But industry, and, above all, *sobriety*, will carry an Irishman through any difficulty. We should not have to see a poor man in any of our big cities while there is a glorious State like this, with the best lands to be had for little. What I say of Illinois can also be said of Wisconsin, Iowa, and Minnesota, as well as of Indiana, Missouri, Kansas, and Nebraska. All this vast country offers inducements to thrifty, honest settlers, such as no other country can offer; and our people, many of whom are wasting their energies in eastern cities, would do well to avail themselves of them. I tell you it would benefit them soul as well as body to do so.'

To one who hears so much as I have heard of the less than 21,000,000 acres of Ireland, and the 77,000,000 of the whole of the United Kingdom—including England, Wales, Scotland, Ireland, and every island adjoining or belonging thereto—the idea of the acreage of the United States is simply bewildering. One would require a gigantic mind to grasp or comprehend a thing in itself so gigantic. Practically speaking, the public lands, or those which have not passed into individual ownership, are illimitable. Millions and millions of square miles, hundreds of millions of acres, never yet surveyed—millions and millions of square miles, and hundreds of millions of acres surveyed, but not occupied, and capable of absorbing, for centuries, the surplus population of Europe. Almost any one of the new Territories—which will be the States of to-morrow—would swallow, at a bite, as a child would a cherry, all the agricultural population of Ireland, with its proprietors, resident and absentee, included. One thing, however, is indisputable—that the Irish who have emigrated, or who may emigrate to America, ought to find no difficulty in suiting themselves; also, that there are as good chances to-day for the bold and adventurous as there were ten, or twenty, or fifty years back.

Though it is difficult to afford a sober idea of what is of itself well nigh incomprehensible from its very vastness, I must endeavour to represent, and that as briefly as possible, the extent of the Public Lands of the United States.

The total extent of the Public Lands of the United States is 1,468,000,000 acres; of which 474,160,000 acres had been explored and surveyed up to the close of 1866. The surveyed land is generally well suited for agriculture, and in the most favourably circumstanced localities, on the banks of streams, and in the neighbourhood of trunk roads. There remain unsurveyed, and open to any settler under the Pre-emption Laws, 991,308,249 acres. In Colorado, a rich mineral and agricultural State, only 1,500,000 acres are surveyed, and 65,000,000, or nearly the extent of the entire of the United Kingdom, unsurveyed. In Washington Territory 3,500,000 are surveyed, 41,000,000 unsurveyed. In Oregon, a State into which immigrants pour at the rate of 20,000 a year, only 5,000,000 acres are surveyed, while 55,000,000 are unsurveyed. In Kansas, a partially settled State, the surveys extend over 16,000,000 acres, leaving 35,000,000 unsurveyed. Nebraska, 13,000,000 out of 48,000,000. California, with 27,000,000 acres surveyed, has 93,000,000 unsurveyed! This one State, to which the Irish have added so large a portion of its population, is six times larger than Ireland, or has six times more than the number of acres respecting which it appears—at least, up to the time these words are written—to be so impossible to deal with or legislate for according to the dictates of man's wisdom and the principles of God's justice. In Arizona, Dacota, New Mexico, Utah, Montana, Idaho, there are enormous tracts, to be counted by hundreds of millions of acres, of every variety of soil, and richly endowed with minerals, open to the emigrant.

In Minnesota, into which immigration has been strongly flowing for years, there are 31,000,000 of unsurveyed land. In the older of the still modern States there are vast tracts of land open to the purchaser, and all surveyed. Thus, in Wisconsin there are 33,000,000 acres; in Iowa, 35,000,000; Missouri, 41,000,000; Alabama, 32,000,000; Ohio, 25,000,000; Florida, 26,000,000; Arkansas, 33,000,000; Mississippi, 30,000,000; Louisiana, 23,000,000; Indiana, 21,000,000; Michigan, 36,000,000; and Illinois, 35,000,000 acres. In the new mineral States, such as Colorado and Nevada, the mining population afford a ready market for all surplus agricultural produce. A couple of years since there were prices for agricultural produce in Colorado which would remind one of the state of things in California during the first rush to the gold mines; but cultivation has now so much increased that the prices, though most remunerative, have been considerably reduced. In the course of time mining enterprise will extend more to Arizona, Montana, Idaho, &c., all the new Territories and States being rich in minerals; and as mining operations advance in any locality, the agricultural population will be correspondingly benefited. In fact, with mining enterprise, all kinds of manufacturing industries gradually spring up; and those who are thus engaged form the readiest and best customers to the farmer, who finds with them a profitable market for his surplus produce of every kind.

The Government surveys not only follow the course of immigration, but meet its requirements. But there is always a large quantity of surveyed land in each of the new States, as indeed in the others, available for immediate settlement. Much of it is prairie, which does not present the difficulties of timber land in cultivation. The total thus available—offered or unoffered—in 1866, was sufficient to make 831,250 farms of 160 acres each.

Under the Homestead Law a farm may be had at an almost nominal price—little more than the cost of its survey. Upon the unsurveyed lands any person may enter, and proceed to appropriate and cultivate a tract; and when the survey reaches and includes his land, he will have the right of pre-emption—purchasing its fee simple—at a small price, which may be somewhat enhanced by a neighbouring improvement, such as a railroad passing within a certain distance. The settler may have occupied his farm for years, it may be two or it may be ten, before the survey comes up to him, and he can therefore well afford to pay the very moderate price which the Government charges for what is then carefully and accurately defined, and for which his title is made good against the world. Under the Homestead Law the limit of the farms which each individual can obtain is 160 acres; but under the Pre-emption Law it appears the settler may purchase any quantity in proportion to the number of acres cleared at the time of the survey.

The amazing vastness of the land or territory of the United States may be indicated by a single fact in reference to her mines, which, in addition to her agricultural resources, offer an immense field for human labour. *Her coal lands alone cover an area of two hundred thousand square miles*; while the combined coal fields of Europe cover but 16,000 square miles—that is, the coal fields of the United States are more than twelve times more extensive in area than all the coal fields of Europe! Iron, that metal more really precious than gold, is found in the neighbourhood of coal. With respect to this valuable mineral, America maintains her supremacy of vast-ness; and any one who travels some hundred miles from the splendid city of St. Louis may behold a huge mountain of solid iron, rising many hundred feet above the plain, and presenting a striking feature in the landscape.

It is not at all necessary that an Irish immigrant should go West, whatever and how great the inducements it offers to the enterprising. There is land to be had, under certain circumstances and conditions, in almost every State in the Union. And there is no State in which the Irish peasant who is living from hand to mouth in one of the great cities as a day-labourer, may not improve his condition by betaking himself to his natural and legitimate avocation—the cultivation of the soil. Nor is the vast region of the South unfavourable to the laborious and energetic Irishman. On the contrary, there is no portion of the American continent in which he would receive a more cordial welcome, or meet with more favourable terms. This would not have been so before the war, or the abolition of slavery, and the upset of the land system which was based upon the compulsory labour of the negro. Before the war, the land was held in mass by large proprietors, and, whatever its quantity, there was no dividing or selling it—that is willingly; for when land was brought to the hammer, the convenience of the purchaser had to be consulted. But there was no voluntary division of the soil, no cutting-it up into parcels, to be occupied by small proprietors.

Now, the state of things is totally different. Too much land in the hands of one individual may now be as embarrassing in the South as in the North, especially when it is liable to taxation. The policy of the South is to increase and strengthen the, white population, so as not to be, as the South yet is, too much dependent on the negro; and the planter who, ten years ago, would not sever a single acre from his estate of 2,000, or 10,000, or 20,000 acres, will now readily divide, if not all, at least a considerable portion of it, into saleable quantities, to suit the convenience of purchasers. He will do more than divide; he will sell on fair terms, and he will afford a fair time to pay—he will, in fact, do all in his power to promote the growth of the white population, while yielding to the necessity of the times, which compels him to part with what has become rather burdensome and embarrassing to himself.

This is a subject on which I could not venture to write without the fullest authority; but I have spoken with hundreds of Southerners of rank and position, men identified with the South by the strongest ties of birth, property, and patriotism; and I know, from unreserved interchange of opinion with them, that the general feeling of the enlightened and the politic is in favour of inducing European settlers to come to the South, and come on easy terms. 'The experience of the past year (1866),' said a well-informed Southern gentleman to me, 'leads most of our people to see *the absolute necessity of dividing and sub-dividing the large plantations.*' I heard almost the same words used in several of the Southern States, as well by owners of large estates as by persons extensively engaged in the sale and management of property.

There is a prejudice, and a somewhat ignorant prejudice, against the South; the prevalent idea being that no one but the negro can venture to brave its climate— that open-air labour in the South is death to the white man. I know of Irishmen who cultivate farms in all the Southern States, and who work at them themselves; and that they and their children are strong and robust. But not only are some of the Southern States temperate and genial, but in almost all those States there are portions which are most favourable to the industry and longevity of the white man. I was anxious to obtain reliable information on this point, and I received from the Bishop of Charleston—the honoured son of a good Irishman—a statement respecting a State that, perhaps of all others, is the one to which prejudice would first point as the most unsuited to the labour of the European. South Carolina, like all the Southern States, has its belts, of soil as well as climate, favourable and unfavourable to the European immigrant. Dr. Lynch says of his State, that it is 'probably the most Irish of any of the States of the Union.' 'Irish family names abound in every rank and condition of life; and there are few men, natives of the State, in whose veins there does not run more or less of Irish blood.' He adds, 'While its inhabitants have always had the impetuous character of the Irish race, nowhere has there been a more earnest sympathy for the struggles of Irishmen at home, nowhere will the Irish immigrant be received with greater welcome, or be more generously supported in all his rights; and I do not know any part of the country where industry and sobriety would ensure to the immigrant who engages in agriculture an ampler compensation for himself and family in a briefer number of years.' In his communication, written in compliance with my request, the Bishop points out the healthy and the unhealthy, the favourable and the unfavourable, belts or districts of his State.

In reference to the Southern States I had the opinion of an eminent Irishman, one who laid down the highest dignity in the Church for an humble position, in which he is honoured and beloved. His knowledge of the country is intimate and extensive, and his experience goes back more than thirty years. I was anxious to have his opinion as to the suitability of the South for the Irish emigrant, as I knew he had recently been in most of its States; and it is thus given:—

'During my late trip to the South I made various enquiries regarding the prospects there for Irish emigrants. The result of these enquiries was, that a great field was open for them; but I feel convinced that it could scarcely be made useful for them in a temporal or spiritual point of view without more combination and organised efforts than I think it at all likely, at least at present, to be obtained amongst our people, or any parties that could be induced to act for them or to direct them. If such organisation *could* be effected, I believe the South would offer a better field for emigration than any other part of the country.'

Bishop Lynch insists on 'industry and sobriety' as the grand essentials to the Irishman's success in the South: and when I was in Charleston he afforded me the opportunity of witnessing, in the person of a countryman from the county Kildare, as good an illustration as I could desire to behold of the happy exercise of these noble qualities. Some three or four miles outside the city we arrived at a snug prosperous-looking place, a good house surrounded by a farm of rich land, in which acres of vegetables and green crops of various kinds were then in luxuriant growth, being cultivated in a manner that would satisfy even a London market gardener. Twenty-three years ago the owner of this valuable property—worth more than $20,000—arrived in America, with little money in his pocket, but with some knowledge of farming, and a speciality for the cultivation of vegetables. He remained 'knocking about' the northern cities for six months, living from hand to mouth, taking such day work as he could obtain. 'This won't do,' said the boy from Kildare to himself; 'it's all well for the day, but there's nothing for the morrow or the next day; I must try and get something to make me independent.'

So in pursuit of independence he came down South, where he entered the employment of a gentleman of famous name in America, but whose parents were both 'full-blooded Irish,' and whose approbation the boy from Kildare won by the success with which he cultivated vegetables and green crops. Had there been a priest or a church within convenient distance, the young Irishman would have willingly remained in his good employment, continuing to lay aside the greater portion of his wages; but as many as eight months would pass before he could gratify the pious longing of his Catholic heart; and so, at length, and much against his will, he quitted the great man's service. With his earnings he came to Charleston—not into the city, unless to say his prayers and make necessary purchases or sales—and set to work, like a sensible Irishman, at the business he best knew. But without entering into the details of years of honest and sober industry, it is sufficient to say that his fine farm is his own property, and that he has given to his children a liberal education. Kindly, good-natured, active and full of health, this man, though now of middle age, is as simple in manner—as natural and as Irish—as he was the day he saw the last of 'Kildare's holy shrine.'

Possibly I am somewhat prejudiced in his favour; for a more pleasant cup of tea I never drank in America than that which I received from the hands of his wife— the more pleasant because of a previous and somewhat extended exploration round and thround the famous city of Charleston. A sober man, he was 'not a bit the worse of the climate;' and his looks fully justified his words. This man's capital was industry, intelligence, and good conduct: and in America, perhaps more surely than in any country under the sun, this kind of capital is sure to create the other capital—the dollar and the dollar's worth.

When in Augusta, Georgia, I fell in with perhaps one of the best persons to offer a practical opinion as to the suitability of the South for the settlement of the Irish. Names are not necessary to be mentioned in most instances, but in this instance the name of my authority for the following statement may be given. Mr. H. C. Bryson, from the north of Ireland, has been engaged for forty years in the cotton trade; and he holds that the temperate portions of Alabama, South Carolina, Georgia, and Mississippi, are well suited to the settlement and healthful labour of the Irish. He mentioned many cases in point, where the Irish had settled, gone on prosperously, and maintained the most robust health. One illustration, and that a very striking and comprehensive one, will, however, suffice. In the year 1850, about fifty Irish families, all from the county Tipperary,—Burkes, Keilings, Keatings, Hyneses, Hartys, Mahers, &c.,—made their way down from the North, and settled in Talliafero county, Georgia. They were hard-working, sober people, but amongst them all they did not possess a hundred dollars. One of the men had to bring one of his children on his back, while the other little ones trotted alongside him. In a very short time after, these hard-working, sober people, who would not 'hang about the cities,' were in comfortable circumstances, entirely the result of their labour and industry—that capital which money cannot always purchase. These Irishmen in the South raise corn, cotton, and stock; and in all they do, they are more careful and particular than many of the people around them. Mr. Bryson has often sold from five to ten bales of cotton for each of them, at $125 the bale. 'They are more particular,' says Mr. Bryson, 'and take more pains with their corn and their cotton, than most of their neighbours. They are all strong and hearty; in fact, I never heard of one of them being ill—and I know every man of them well. But this I attribute rather to their frugal life and temperate habits than to any other cause. They have a fine school of their own, and can go to their church as well as the best people in the country; they have good houses, abundance of everything they can desire—and I assure you they could entertain you as well as any men in the State. They are a credit to any country. But the Irishman, when he comes out here, is among the most industrious of all.'

'I think,' adds Mr. Bryson, 'that the cotton raised by men of this class—men who work at it themselves, and who have an interest in what they are doing—is the finest grown of any. It is better handled, and more carefully picked, None of these men owned a slave, and so much the better for them; for they have lost nothing by the change, while others lost the greater part of their capital.

I spoke of the health enjoyed by the Irish who are farming. In Locust Grove there are a good many of them, and for the last ten years I don't know of an adult among them dying, save one—for I don't count a poor fellow who came home from the Army of Virginia to die; and that one that I do count was Murdoch Griffin, but he was sixty-eight years old when he died, and he had hard work in his day. Griffin started, about thirty-five years since, without a dollar in his pocket;

and when he died his property was worth $70,000 in gold. Any Irishman that goes into the country with his family can do well, and make a fortune.'

This was the testimony of a shrewd observant Northern Irishman,—as good an authority on the subject of which he spoke as could be found in the whole of the United States.

And in the city of Augusta, in which there are several Irish doing a good business, and holding a good position, there is an Irish settlement, known by the name of Dublin, which is occupied by a hard-working, industrious, thrifty, and sober population, to whom the houses and the land on which they stand belong.

An able and experienced Irishman—himself one of the most successful citizens of Memphis, Tennessee—remarked to me one day: 'The trouble is, that the Irish don't go on the land as much as they ought. I never knew an Irishman that pulled up pegs, and went on the land, that did not do well. All have done well that went into the country. It is now the easiest thing in the world to get land, and good land too, at fair terms. Take an example in a man from your own part of Ireland, to show you how an Irishman may purchase a good property here. A man from Cork, a mere labourer, went out to Brownsville, ditching—in other words, fencing, to keep in cattle. That was in 1862. I know that man to have $3,300 in bank, and $1,500 besides; that is, nearly $5,000 in all. He has not yet invested in land, but he intends doing so. He is looking about him, and he will be sure to pick up a splendid thing for the money. This Cork man of yours now hires a couple of negroes, and does work by contract.'

'But the climate?' I enquired.

'Climate!—all nonsense about the climate. Climate! Why, you have more sunstrokes in one month in New York than there are for a whole year in the entire of the South. If a man drinks, the climate will tell on him—may kill him; but if he is a sober man, there is no fear of him. That is my experience; and I have a pretty long one, I can tell you. The land, sir, is the thing—the country the place for our people. The land will give a man everything but coffee, tea, or sugar; these he can buy, and live like a king. I know an Irishman, who was a porter in a hotel, at $25 a month. He went five miles out of the city, and leased forty acres, took a dairy, bought cows, and brought his milk into the city. He is now the owner of eighty acres of valuable land, with a fine house, and every comfort for himself and his family. The land, sir! the land, sir! is the place for our people; tell them so.'

I do not venture to suggest to the Irishman in America, or the Irishman who intends to emigrate to America, to what State of the Union he should go in search of a home. All I say is this: if he is a farmer, a farm-labourer, *a peasant—that is, a man born and bred in the country—let him go anywhere, so that he goes out of the city.* Turn where he may, he is always sure to find a market for his labour; and having obtained the employment best suited to his knowledge and capacity, he can put by his dollars, and look around him to see if anything in the neighbourhood would suit him, or is within his reach; or if there be no fair opening for him, no prospect of making a home there, then he has only to push on farther, and he will be certain to find the land and the home to his liking. With money in his pocket and strength in his arms, and a determination to employ both to the best advantage, surely there is little fear of the Irishman who desires to make a home for himself in the New World.

In a word, the peasant—the man of the spade, the plough, and the barrow—for the country, the land, the soil. So the artizan, the mechanic, the handycraftsman, for the city, the workshop, the factory—for the place and occupation which are best suited to his skill, his capacity, and his training. One would not, at least ought not, recommend a watchmaker, or an engineer, or a gas-fitter, or a house-painter, or a boiler-maker, to go into the forest and hew down trees, or to the prairie and turn it up with a plough and a team of oxen. The city is their right place. But, even with the mechanic, discrimination is necessary. Young and rising cities may offer better opportunities to the skilled workman than old cities, in which the competition is fierce, the special trade may be overdone, and the cost of living is out of all proportion to the payment, however liberal that may be. In new places the prudent man may secure his lot, or his two lots, even a block, on reasonable terms; and as time goes on—a short time in the States—the town extends, the population increases, and property rises in value; and thus, with comparatively little outlay, a prudent man may become rich, with small trouble and no risk. Then, in rising places, the demand for certain classes of skilled labour is greater, and its remuneration larger, than in places already built and long settled. The prudent artizan may thus have two strings to his bow, and both of them serviceable: he may work at greater advantage, and speculate with greater certainty of profit. There are in America thousands of Irishmen—not a few of them 'millionaires'— who, prudent and far-seeing, have risen with the fortunes of new places, in which they secured a large interest by timely and judicious investment. I have met with several of these men, and I heard from their own lips the story of their good fortune.

Taking all things into consideration, I do not know of any of the States which affords a more favourable illustration of the policy I desire to urge on my countrymen than California; where the Irish, besides being engaged in many profitable pursuits, are also found largely distributed over the land, and where the knowledge of farming which they brought with them from the old country has been turned by them to the best account.

I shall therefore glance at that magnificent State, to ascertain in what position the Irish are there to be found.

CHAPTER XIII

California of the Past and Present—Early Irish Settlers—Death amid the
Mountains—Pat Clark—But One Mormon—The Irish wisely settle on the Land—
How they Succeeded in the Cities—Successful Thrift—Irish Girls—The Church in
San Francisco—What a poor Irishman can do

THERE is not a State in the Union in which the Irish have taken deeper and stronger root, or thriven more successfully, than California, in whose amazing progress—material, social, and intellectual—they have had a conspicuous share. For nearly twenty years past this region has been associated in the popular mind with visions of boundless wealth and marvellous fortunes; and it may be interesting to learn under what circumstances the Irish became connected with a country of such universal repute, and of whose population they form a most important and valuable portion.

Long before the discovery of the precious metal attracted the adventurous from every quarter of the globe to the golden shores of the Pacific, Irishmen had made their home in California, where they had been hospitably received by the kindly Spanish race, with whom they freely intermixed, and amongst whom they were in the enjoyment of abundant means, won by honest industry, or the result of no less honourable public service. And how different the California of a quarter of a century since from the California of the present day! It retains but a faint resemblance to what it was when the sole occupants and lords of the soil were the good missionary priests, the rancheros, and the Indians. Then the peaceful dweller amidst the beautiful solitude beheld nature in its most lovely and attractive form; a wide expanse of undulating plain and charming valley, rich and well watered, unfenced and untilled; groves and noble forests of oak, pine, cedar, and other trees of majestic size, some growing singly or in groups, as if planted by the hand of taste; large and numerous herds of horses and cattle roaming over the luxuriant pastures, the only living objects giving evidence of the presence or proximity of man. But a few years have passed since then, and what a change! The landscape chequered with smiling farms, homesteads, and villas—dotted over with towns and villages—life and movement everywhere—evidences of the energy and industry of man in all directions. Where there stood a few huts on the sea-shore, there is now a great city, with bustling wharves and crowded thoroughfares and busy population—a majestic cathedral, and the rival churches of almost every diversity of religious belief. The rancheros and the Indians have passed away, never to return; but the Cross is still there, thanks, in a great measure, to those islanders who have been so wonderfully selected by Providence as the most successful missionaries of the Faith in this century, as in others now remote.

Among the few, not of Spanish origin, who settled in California prior to 1848, were many Irish, of every class, who proved, by their presence in a distant and then almost unknown country, to the possession of those qualities so essential in the pioneer of civilisation—courage, enterprise, and love of adventure. The first sojourners were the mountain trappers, whose knowledge and education extended little beyond the woodcraft so necessary to success in their perilous occupation. The trapper's chief thought was of the trail and the Indian ambush; his constant study, the habits and the haunts of game; his wealth and his defence, a rifle and a horse. This was a wild and dangerous, occasionally a remunerative calling, which too often terminated in his being a victim to the bullet or the knife of the treacherous savage, who adorned his wigwam with the scalp of the white invader of his hunting grounds. To one of this class, an Irishman, Captain J. S. Smith, is due the credit of having led the first party of white men over land to California. At the head of a band of some forty trappers, in the service of the American Fur Company, he had the courage to cross the lofty ridges and formidable barriers of the Sierra Nevada. Smith, who was a native of the King's County, emigrated at an early age to the United States, joined the Fur Company, and ultimately became chief trader at their post on Green River. In one of his excursions, exploring the county south and west of Salt Lake, he crossed over to California, visited San Diego and San José, where he encamped with his party for some time. There is a letter of his extant, written in May 1827, to Padre Zuran, the missionary priest of San José, in which he gives an account of himself, and his reasons for remaining so long in the vicinity. On his return trip he and most of his party were slain by the Indians east of the Sierra. But few escaped—four or five at most; and among them was an Irishman who, from his great stature, was known as Big Fallen. He remained in the country.

Between the years 1825 and 1836, some few Irishmen arrived by sea, and settled in California. These were principally masters or other officers of American trading vessels, or seamen before the mast, with an occasional adventurer in search of a home; and being wise enough to appreciate the advantages offered by a lovely country and a fine climate, and liking the character of the inhabitants, they resolved to abandon the deep and its dangers, and cast anchor for life on shore. Generally settling in the different seaports, they soon, owing to their knowledge and industry, became independent; and having married and become naturalised, they were recognised and treated by the kindly and hospitable people amongst whom they came as belonging to themselves. Their similarity of religion was greatly in their favour with the Spaniards; and this important advantage was in no small degree enhanced by the ease and quickness with which they acquired the language of the country, as well as by their natural politeness and their deference to the fairer portion of the creation, traits for which the Irish are at all times honourably distinguished. These qualities and accomplishments rendered them great favourites with the descendants of the Castilian hidalgo, and facilitated their worldly success.

Many of these early settlers were men of fair education and good manners, and came principally from the Southern provinces of Ireland. Among them were to be found Reads and Dens of Waterford, Allens of Dublin, Murphys of Wexford, Burkes of Galway, Coppingers of Cork, and others. Some became extensive proprietors of land and raisers of stock, others practised as physicians, while more acquired wealth and repute as enterprising merchants; and they with their families, that quickly sprung up around them—vigorous in body as in intellect—formed the nucleus of that Irish and Catholic element which was to be so wonderfully strengthened by subsequent and continuous emigration.

I might be inclined to linger over the history and fortunes of Don Timoteo Murphy, who, arriving in 1829 from Peru, where he had spent two years, rose to an eminent position, as Administrator of the Mission, and Alcalde for the district of San Rafael, acquired vast estates, and was universally esteemed and honoured during a residence of a quarter of a century in the country. He is thus spoken of by a fellow-countryman and friend, himself one of the most fortunate and respected of the Irish settlers in California: 'Murphy was a splendid specimen of a man, tall, powerful, and well-built, a good horseman and keen hunter. He imported the first greyhounds to California, and kept a kennel of twenty to thirty hounds; the abundance of deer, elk, and antelope afforded material for the chase, and Murphy gave them little rest. He was hospitable, kind, and generous, and looked up to as a father by the people of the country.'

About the year 1838, the trail across the Sierras to California began to be travelled more frequently by hunters. In two years after a small party of emigrants arrived by that route; and from that date to the present each succeeding year has brought with it bands of hardy and adventurous men and women to develop the resources of that portion of the American continent. In the exploring expedition of John C. Tremont many Irishmen joined, and remained afterwards in the country.

The year 1844 witnessed a remarkable arrival—that of a body of immigrants from Canada and Missouri, mostly Irish, including a single family numbering no less than five-and-twenty individuals. This party formed a valuable addition to the community, consisting of respectable and intelligent men, who, from their previous training, were well fitted to cope with the difficulties incidental to a settlement in a new country. The leader of this party was Mr. Martin Murphy, a native of Wexford, who brought with him his family of sons, daughters, and grandchildren. Mr. Murphy had originally emigrated to Lower Canada, from which he passed to Missouri; but, not finding that the Missouri of that day realised the anticipations which he had formed of it, he decided, old as he was—he was then in his sixtieth year—on seeking a home more suited to his habits and feelings. He gathered together the different branches of his family, and joining with other Irish families in their neighbourhood, thus formed a numerous party, or train, to cross the plains to California, whither they were destined. Martin Murphy must have had considerable pluck, fortitude, and confidence in himself and his associates, to start on a journey of 2,500 miles over a trackless prairie, inhabited by fierce and hostile Indians, bound to a land then little known, and that only from the vague accounts afforded by trappers and others, who from time to time returned to the settlements in Western Missouri. The party, however, reached their destination in safety, having met with no casualty beyond the loss of their wagons, which they were compelled to abandon in the defiles of the Sierras. The gallant leader, with his unmarried sons and daughters, settled in the valley of San José, where the family purchased large tracks of land, and became extensive owners of stock, counting the one by the league, and the other by the thousand. It is little more than a year since Martin Murphy died, at a grand old age, the founder of a prosperous race.

That Martin Murphy's venture was full of peril, notwithstanding its fortunate result, may be learned from the story of the terrible disaster which overtook the Donner party, among whom were some Irish—one of them now an extensive proprietor in the county of Monterey. This party, consisting of over eighty persons, crossed the plain in the summer of 1846. On the 31st of October they were caught in a snow storm in the Californian mountains, in which all their cattle perished; and having consumed the last of their provisions, and even eaten the leather of their saddles and harness, they were driven to the dreadful extremity of feasting on the remains of those who had died of cold and hunger. A gallant band was despatched to their relief from San Francisco; but, owing to the high state of the waters of the Sacramento, and the heavy snowfall in the mountains, they were delayed several weeks before they could reach the sufferers. On the 1st of March 1847, relief arrived, but too late for many of their party; for, out of a company of eighty-one, not more than forty-five were found alive, the remaining thirty-six having perished horribly. One of the band sent to their aid, an Irishman, was in time to save a poor famished and frenzied mother from laying deadly hands on her own infant, to which he gave the shelter of his coat and the warmth of his honest breast all the way to San Francisco. The Ranch owner, who was one of the survivors, is now living in San Juan, South, with his wife and grown-up children, who shared the privations of that terrific trip across the plains. The old gentleman, though now in his seventy-fifth year, is in the most robust health, and looks several years younger than his actual age.

In the following years many families of Irish, as well as young single men, came by every train that then regularly arrived in the fall. Some had means, others had education without means, and more were deficient in both; but if some lacked both of these important advantages, they had shrewdness, intelligence, vigour of body, and a determination to allow no obstacle to stand long in their path.

The daring adventure of a poor labourer from the county Meath affords a splendid instance of pluck and perseverance.

Patrick Clark, seeing so many of his countrymen leaving Missouri, and pushing on for the new land, of which such promising accounts were given by returning trappers, was resolved, if possible, to imitate their example, and, like them, better his condition. Pat had energy and ambition sufficient for any undertaking; but to get over between two and three thousand miles of ground, and with provisions enough to support life on the journey, required such ordinary appliances as a wagon, a team of oxen, and other matters, all entirely beyond Pat's reach. What was he to do? Go he would, but how? As a landsman offers to work his passage in a ship, so did Pat Clark proffer his services as a teamster. He was willing to feed himself, and he would not demand a cent for his services. But no one required his services, or would have them. Pat was checked, not defeated; go he was resolved, though he had to trudge every step of the weary way. And this he very nearly did. He purchased a hand-cart, in which he placed his blankets, some flour, bacon, and a few other necessaries, and manfully set out on his tremendous journey, now pushing before him, now dragging after him, his hand-cart with his precious stock of provisions: and in this manner he had actually traversed 1,800 miles, when he was overtaken by some compassionate traveller on the same route, who gave the poor foot-sore but brave-hearted Irishman a lift in his wagon, and enabled him to accomplish the remainder of his journey in a manner the comfort of which he could keenly appreciate. The Meath man settled down on Cache Creek, and was soon independent. Irishmen of his stamp cannot fail in what they undertake.

There was in the year 1847 a migration of a peculiar character, in which the Irish had a very small share indeed. The ship 'Brooklyn' arrived at San Francisco in the summer of that year, with 150 Mormons, composed principally of English, Scotch, and Welsh, with a few Americans. Of the whole number *one* was an Irishman—a young fellow named Fergusson, said to be from Waterford. The party pushed on to the Salt Lake, the single Irishman going with them. 'What his end in *this* life was, or may be, is uncertain,' says the friend who mentions the arrival of the ship and its godly freight. From this arrival California gained nothing; but the same year came Stevenson's regiment of New York Volunteers, who held possession of the country until it was ceded by treaty to the United States; and of this regiment not a few of the Irish officers and privates remained in California, and in time became distinguished citizens of the new State.

Shortly after was the headlong rush to the recently discovered gold-fields, causing an immediate and immense accession to the population. In this headlong rush came Irishmen, not only from Ireland, but from every part of the States; from Mexico as well as the British provinces, from Australia equally as from England and Scotland. Animated by the same passion, impelled by the same thirst for gain, all nationalities were merged in one great confusion of races and tongues; while in the universal scramble for gold, every social distinction was trampled underfoot, individual superiority depending, not on good breeding or intellectual cultivation, but on the greater capacity for labour, or the tougher power of endurance. For a time, at least, simple manhood carried the day against all artificial gradations in the social hierarchy; the hodman and the doctor, the labourer and the lawyer, standing upon exactly the same level, provided that the doctor and the lawyer happened to be endowed with thews and sinews as strong and as serviceable as those of his brother gold-seekers, the hodman and the labourer. In such a competition there was a glorious chance for the humblest or most recently-arrived of the Irish new-comers. With the pick and the shovel they were a match for any workers under the sun, and their luck was on the average as fortunate as that of others. It was a fair start, and no favour—just what best suits the true Irishman: and the result at this moment is, that one-half, or nearly one-half, of the entire mining property of the country is in the hands of Irishmen or the sons of Irishmen. The mine known as the Allison Ranch, which is considered to be one of the richest in the world, and which last year employed between 500 and 600 workers, is owned by five Irishmen and an American.

Fortunately for their ultimate and permanent success, many Irishmen either failed in their mining operations, became dissatisfied with the wearisome monotony of the daily drudgery, or desired to engage in some more lucrative employment; and they wisely turned their attention to what was more certain to reward steady industry —the cultivation of the soil. The moment, too, was singularly propitious. During the height of the gold fever, when the one pursuit absorbed almost every thought, all kinds of garden produce were sold at fabulous prices; and even in a year or two after, 12 or 15 cents for a pound of potatoes was regarded as a moderate price for that essential article of food. The hourly increasing demand for the produce of the field and the garden imparted a wonderful stimulus to agricultural industry, to which the Irish brought both energy and experience. When they had made money in the mines, they purchased a convenient piece of land, and soon rendered it productive and profitable; or had they been unlucky in their hunt after the precious metal, they hired themselves as farm hands, and being paid enormous wages—wages which would render high farming in Europe an utter impossibility—they in a short time accumulated sufficient capital to purchase land for themselves. Employment was to be had in every direction by those who were willing to work; and none were more willing than the Irish. Everything had to be built up, literally created—cities and towns as well as communities.

Labour, which is not estimated at its true value in older countries, where the great work has long since been accomplished, and in which society has its grades and classes and distinctions, was highly prized and reverently regarded in California; for without it nothing could be done, where everything had to be done; and the humble Irishman laid the foundation of his own fortunes while rendering to the infant State services which were priceless in their value. Happily, the cities and towns did not seduce the Irish from their legitimate sphere, and the dollars made in the mine, or in ditching and digging, or in hard toil of various kinds, were converted into land; and indeed with such success did they pursue this sound policy—which it would be well for the race were it more extensively adopted in America—that one-fourth of the farming of the State of California is in the hands of Irishmen. This is remarkably so in the counties of Santa Clara, San Joaquin, Marin, Sonoma, Almeda, Contra Costa, and Santa Cruz. As agriculturists and stock-raisers, the Irish are the leaders in almost every county in the State, more particularly those counties lying on the sea-coast and adjacent to the bay and waters of San Francisco.

Inasmuch as it is more interesting to note what the humble man—the Irish peasant—has done through his unaided industry, than what the gentleman has accomplished through the possession of capital, or with the advantages of education, an instance of this nature may be mentioned.

There are two townships in Marin county—Tumalis and San Rafael—largely owned and occupied by Irish. The former of these is as extensive and as rich as any tract of land in the State, and is almost exclusively possessed by Irishmen, nearly all of whom a few years ago were *labourers*, working for monthly wages on the ranches of the old proprietors, or delving in the mines. They worked and they delved until they saved enough to purchase a piece of land; and now these men, who at home were poor peasants, and, perhaps, would have been little better had they remained in the old country, are the proprietors of estates ranging from 160 to 1,000 acres of the best land in California! Here are three Irishmen, two of them 'boys' from Tipperary, who in 1850 worked on Anally Ranch; one of these is the owner of 800 acres of land in Tumalis, well-stocked and cultivated; and the Tipperary boys are rich farmers, and surrounded with every comfort. There are, and will be, among the children of these successful settlers those whose special genius or whose bent of mind will naturally lead them to the city and its pursuits; but their parents adopted the wisest and safest course for themselves and their descendants—they planted themselves on the soil, and thus laid the foundations of a prosperous and independent race. Many of our people are, from special aptitude, knowledge, or experience, best suited to a town life, where alone they may find employment for their trained skill, or a suitable field for their talents; but the vast majority of those who leave their native country fur America were born on the land, were reared on the land, were employed on the land; and the land is the right place for them, whether in America or at home.

We may now see what the Irish have done in the cities of California. San Francisco, the most famous of the fair cities of the United States, will suffice as an illustration of the position and progress of the children of Erin. It is rather a singular coincidence that an Irishman, Jasper O'Farrell, laid out the city which his countrymen did so much to build up; and that in 1850, while all was still in chaos and confusion, and license was the order of the day, another Irishman, Malachi Fallon, was called on by a vote of the assembled citizens to leave his position at the mines, and assume the administration of the police affairs of the city; which he did with admitted success. It was two Irishmen—James and Peter Donahue—that erected the first foundry in San Francisco, which enterprise led to the rapid increase of mechanical industry. The same firm projected the gas works; and with such success was this important undertaking crowned, that the stock of the Company has increased to six million dollars. The same firm erected the largest hotel in the city, at a cost of more than half a million. The first street railway— from the City to the Mission of Dolores—was projected by an Irishman, Col. Thomas Hayes. Among the private bankers of San Francisco, Donahue, Kelly, & Co. take the lead; their firm, established in 1864, does a larger amount of business than that of Rothschild, which dates as far back as 1849.

But a still more interesting item—the first public donation to a charitable purpose was made by two distinguished Irishmen, Don Timoteo Murphy and Jasper O'Farrell, who 'donated' the lot of ground now occupied by the Orphan Asylum, and which is at present worth 200,000 dollars. The greatest ovation ever offered by the citizens to an individual was given to John G. Downey, an Irishman, who for two years ably filled the office of Governor of the State. Irishmen held a prominent position in the convention by which the constitution was formed; and in both branches of the Legislature Irishmen, or the sons of Irishmen, are to be found. Among the largest holders of city property, the most extensive merchants, the most successful men of business, the ablest engineers, the most accomplished architects, and the most reliable contractors, are Irishmen; and in all branches of the legal profession, whether practising in chamber, or in civil or criminal business in courts, Irishmen enjoy an enviable repute.

In fact, as soon as society, which, from the special circumstances of the country, had been in a somewhat chaotic state, settled down into its ordinary grooves, the Irish took their place among the foremost in the battle of life; and in the eager struggle for wealth and distinction they held their own with their co-labourers of every other nationality.

It may be questioned if in any part of the Union the Irish of the working classes are better off in all respects than they are in San Francisco. The immense and continuous employment, as well as the liberal rate of remuneration, have had much to do with this; but to the thrifty habits and admirable conduct of the Irish is the happy result equally attributable. Though wages of all kinds are liberal at present, and employment is constantly to be obtained for the greater portion of the year, still the rate of remuneration is not equal to what it was when the work to be done was more pressing, the hands to do it were fewer, and the mines attracted almost universal attention. From 1849 to 1853 skilled labour ranged from 6 to 10 dollars a day, while unskilled labour commanded from 3 to 5 dollars a day. Washing was then as high as 6 dollars per dozen! Women in domestic employment were paid at from 50 to 70 dollars a month. From wages such as these it was not difficult for an industrious and economical person to save money. Many did so, and bought lots on the outskirts of the town, which soon extended in every direction, and so enhanced the value of the property thus honourably obtained, as to render its owners rich without any further exertion on their part. I am happy to know of many, many instances of such successful thrift and forethought on the part of Irishmen in every part of the United States, and also in the British Provinces.

Mechanics now earn from 4 to 5 dollars, while labourers receive from 2 to 3 dollars a day. This, taking the present value of the dollar, would be, on an average, 14s. 6d. a day for the mechanic, and 8s. a day for the labourer. Being so amply remunerated, almost every working-man, whether mechanic, labourer, or drayman, owns the house in which he lives, and the lot on which it stands. Different indeed from the state of things in New York, where the well-paid mechanic, who but rarely owns the house in which he lives, has to pay 100 or 120 dollars a year for two or three rooms in a tenement house. Women servants receive from 20 to 40 dollars a month, according to their occupation or proficiency, or the class of people in whose houses they reside.

If any further proof were required of the condition of the Irish in San Francisco, it is to be had in the facts connected with the Hibernian Savings' Bank and Loan Society, now nearly completing its eighth year of usefulness. The deposits in this bank to January 21, 1867, were 5,241,000 dollars. I perceive by the returns for 1866 that the depositors receive interest at the rate of eleven per cent., and that the earnings that year amounted to 244,000 dols. But it is more important to learn that seven-eighths of the depositors are Irish, and that of the amount deposited by the Irish fully three-fourths belong to the working classes, including mechanics, labourers, and girls in various employments.

Of the Irish girls in America I have spoken elsewhere; but any notice of the race in San Francisco, in which special mention of the Irish girls of that city was not made, would be most incomplete. They form a considerable and valuable portion of its population, and are deservedly esteemed by all classes of its citizens. They are industrious, intelligent, faithful, generous, high-spirited, and intensely devoted to their religion, of which they are the proudest ornaments and best examples. So justly esteemed are these Irish girls for purity and honour, that some 2,000 of them have been well married—fully half of that number to men of substance and good position. It may be remarked that a considerable number of them had been tenderly reared at home, where they received a fair education; but, driven by circumstances to emigrate, they were of necessity obliged to accept even the humblest situations in a foreign land. They soon, however, rose above the lowly condition which they dignified by their intelligence and worth, and found in an honourable marriage ample compensation for all their former trials.

It is estimated that seventy-five per cent, of the Irish girls in domestic employment in San Francisco can read fairly, while more than fifty per cent. can both write and read well. The rate of wages for domestic employment ranges from 20 to 40 dollars a month. The average would come to 60l. a year. Out of this income they save a certain portion, indulge their Celtic love of finery, gratify their charitable and religious instincts by generous contributions to church, to convent, to orphanage, and to asylum; and the balance is devoted to the twofold purpose, with them almost equally sacred—to assist their parents or aged relatives in the old country, or bring out a brother or a sister to their adopted home. It is calculated by those who have every means of ascertaining the fact, that the Irish girls employed in San Francisco annually remit to Ireland, for the purposes stated, the sum of 270,000 dollars! What eulogium can equal the mere mention of this fact?

Whatever religious indifferentism there may be in other parts of America, there is none in San Francisco among its Irish Catholic population. In their hard struggle for the good things of this life they did not forget their interests in the next; and such was the liberality with which they co-operated with the zeal of their pastors, that, in little more than a dozen years after the new city began to rise above the huts and shanties that once occupied its site, the Church property, including buildings and real estate, was valued at 2,010,000 dollars. This includes the cathedral and five other churches, convents, asylums, and hospitals. Giving Catholics of other nationalities full credit for their liberality, and allowing for the generous assistance afforded by those of different denominations, it is admitted that three-fourths of what has been done for the Church in the city and county of San Francisco has been done by the Irish. In fact, without them little could have been done; but with them everything was possible. It is superfluous to state that the Irish women of San Francisco are famous for their piety and zeal for religion— that, indeed, is characteristic of the race throughout America; but it has been particularly remarked by those who have had opportunities of observation in many of the States, that in few places, if in any, did they notice a greater number of men, in the prime of life, and actively engaged in the pursuits of business, so constant in the performance of their religious duties, as penitents in the confessional, and communicants at the altar, than in this noble city. With every charitable and benevolent undertaking men of this class are instinctively identified, either as leaders and promoters, or as zealous and liberal supporters; and should they shrink from a position too prominent for their modesty, they more than compensate for their sensitiveness by the abundance of their generosity.

As an evidence of the progress and present position of the Irish in San Francisco, a few significant items might be quoted from the record of the Assessor of Taxes; but it is sufficient to state that, with the exception of four others, not Irish, six Irishmen are the highest rated of its citizens. One fact, however, renders further details unnecessary—namely, that while the Irish constitute one-fourth of the population of San Francisco, or 30,000 out of 120,000, they are considered to possess one-fourth of the entire property of the city, or 20,000,000 out of 80,000,000 of dollars. And yet of every 100 Irish who came to San Francisco, as to California generally, 75 were either poor or scantily provided with means. Few, indeed, brought any money capital with them, but they had energy, industry, with capacity for all kinds of work; and though they came from a country in which enterprise had little existence, and industry not at all times a fair field or a right reward, these men and women of Irish race soon caught the spirit of the American—the right spirit for a new country, the genuine 'Go-ahead'—that which always looks forward and never looks back.

With the mention of a single case—of an Irishman who was certainly one of the seventy-five per cent, who brought with them to the land of gold but little of the world's goods—I may usefully conclude this sketch of the Irish in California. It may be given in the words of my informant, a gentleman who left Ireland for America in 1849. He says: 'There is one circumstance in connection with my coming to America that has always, and will always, give me great pleasure. I mention it with a view to enable you to judge of what a poor Irishman can accomplish in this country with a fair field before him. About the time I was making up my mind to come to California, I was then engaged in building some public works in the town of Sligo. I had then in my employment, and for a short time before, a confidential labouring man. At that time he had a wife and six children in the poor-house in Tullamore, in the King's County, to which he belonged, having been dispossessed of a small piece of land in that neighbourhood. When I mentioned to him that I was going to California, he fell on his knees and implored me to take him with me. I was at first thunderstruck at the idea of his willingness to leave his family, and go to so distant a country, and I so expressed myself to him. But he answered me—"If I remain here, I lose my employment, and I, too, must go into the poor-house, and then all hope is over." I felt too keenly the truth of his reply. I could make no further objection, and I told him I would take him with me. In a year after his arrival in this country he sent home money, took his family out of the work-house, and sent his children to school. They are all now here, his daughters well married, his sons in good situations, and the old couple, with two of their younger children, born in California, living in a comfortable way on a good farm, from which no bailiff can eject them. The simple statement of the history of this family speaks volumes, in my mind, of what the Irish can do in America.'

In this language speaks another Irishman, a Californian resident of long standing, whose name is held in merited respect by all who know him: 'Thus, in general with but a poor beginning, in a manner friendless, strangers in a strange land, have our people struggled and fought, and been victorious. Their bones will lie far away from the hallowed dust of their kindred; yet every mountain, hillside, and valley in this favoured land will give evidence to posterity of their toil, enterprise, and success. Their footprints, marking the genius and traditions of their race, their love and veneration of the old faith, and the old country from which they were such unwilling exiles, shall endure in the land for ever.'

As this sheet was going through the press, my attention was attracted by an article in the *Monitor* of San Francisco, from which I quote the concluding passage, written, as I believe, in the right spirit:—

It is our interest to have as many of our countrymen here as possible; and, moreover, we honestly believe no other country holds out such advantages for their coming. They have not the prejudices of race or religious bigotry which exist in some parts of the East to contend with; unskilled labour is more respected here than there, and finally, the natural resources of the country are greater, and the population less dense than in any of the Atlantic States. Why cannot the Irishmen of this city form a society for diffusing a knowledge of California's resources among our countrymen, and communicating with employers throughout the State, for securing immediate employment on their arrival? We almost feel a scruple about encouraging emigration from poor depopulated Ireland, where the fortunes of our race have yet to be retrieved; but in England and Scotland there are nearly a million of Irishmen from whose ranks we could easily obtain an annual immigration of many thousands by a system such as that we have just proposed. We know by experience the state of feeling existing among our countrymen in Europe, and we believe that by a plan such as we have described, an immense Irish population could be drawn here, to both their own and our advantage. The Irish of California are wealthy and liberal, and surely such a society as the one we have proposed could be easily started among them. We hope our suggestions may turn the attention of some of them to the practical development of Irish immigration from England and the Eastern cities.

CHAPTER XIV

Drink more injurious to Irish than others—Why this is so—Archbishop Spalding's Testimony—-Drink and Politics—Temperance Organisations—Hope in the Future

WERE I asked to say what I believed to be the most serious obstacle to the advancement of the Irish in America I would unhesitatingly answer—*Drink*; meaning thereby the excessive use, or abuse, of that which, when taken in excess, intoxicates, deprives man of his reason, interferes with his industry, injures his health, damages his position, compromises his respectability, renders him unfit for the successful exercise of his trade, profession, or employment—which leads to quarrel, turbulence, violence, crime. I believe this fatal tendency to excessive indulgence to be the main cause of all the evils and miseries and disappointments that have strewed the great cities of America with those wrecks of Irish honour, Irish virtue, and Irish promise, which every lover of Ireland has had, one time or other, bitter cause to deplore. Differences of race and religion are but as a feather's weight in the balance; indeed, these differences tend rather to add interest to the steady and self-respecting citizen. Were this belief, as to the tendency of the Irish to excess in the use of stimulants, based on the testimony of Americans, who might probably be somewhat prejudiced, and therefore inclined to judge unfavourably, or pronounce unsparingly, I should not venture to record it; but it was impressed upon me by Irishmen of every rank, class, and condition of life, wherever I went, North or South, East or West.

It was openly deplored, or it was reluctantly admitted. I rarely heard an Irishman say that his country or his religion was an effectual barrier to his progress in the United States. On the contrary, the universal admission was this: 'Any man, no matter who he is, what country he comes from, or what religion he professes, can get on here, if he is determined to do so; and he will be respected by Americans, if he will only respect himself. If the Irishman is a sober man, there is no fear of him—he cannot fail of success; but if he is too fond of the drink, it is all up with *him—he* is sure to fail.' Expressed in these simple words, this is the matured and deliberate verdict of every experienced or observant Irishman, from the most exalted dignitary of the Catholic Church to the humblest workman who maintains his family in comfort by his honest toil.

The question here naturally arises,—do the Irish drink more than the people of any other nationality in America? The result of my observation and inquiries leads me to the conviction that *they do not.* How, then, comes it that the habit, if common to all, is so pernicious to them? There are many and various reasons why this is so. In the first place, they are strangers, and, as such, more subject to observation and criticism than the natives of the country. They are, also, as a rule, of a faith different to that of the majority of the American people; and the fact that they are so does not render the observation less keen, nor does it render the criticism more gentle. Then, be it constitution, or temperament, or whatever else, excess seems to be more injurious to them than to others. They are genial, open-hearted, generous, and social in their tendencies; they love company, court excitement, and delight in affording pleasure or gratification to their friends. And not only are their very virtues leagued against them, but the prevailing custom of the country is a perpetual challenge to indulgence.

This prevailing custom or habit springs more from a spirit of kindness than from a craving for sensual gratification. Invitations to drink are universal, as to rank and station, time and place, hour and circumstance; they literally rain upon you. The Americans are perhaps about the most thoroughly wide-awake people in the world, yet they must have an 'eye-opener' in the morning. To prepare for meals, you are requested to fortify your stomach and stimulate your digestive powers with an 'appetizer.' To get along in the day, you are invited to accept the assistance of a 'pony.' If you are startled at the mention of 'a drink,' you find it difficult to refuse 'at least a nip.' And who but the most morose—and the Irishman is all geniality—can resist the influence of 'a smile?' Now a 'cocktail,' now a 'cobbler'—here a 'julep,' there a 'smasher;' or if you shrink from the potency of the 'Bourbon,' you surely are not afraid of 'a single glass of lager beer!'

To the generous, company-loving Irishman there is something like treason to friendship and death to good-fellowship in refusing these kindly-meant invitations; but woe to the impulsive Irishman who becomes the victim of this custom of the country! The Americans drink, the Germans drink, the Scotch drink, the English drink—all drink with more or less injury to their health or circumstances; but whatever the injury to these, or any of these, it is far greater to the mercurial and light-hearted Irish than to races of hard head and lethargic temperament. The Irishman is by nature averse to solitary or selfish indulgence—he will not 'booze' in secret, or make himself drunk from a mere love of liquor; with him the indulgence is the more fascinating when it enhances the pleasures of friendship, and imparts additional zest to the charms of social intercourse. In his desire to gratify his friends, and stand well with his acquaintances, he is too likely to overlook the claims of those at home—the wife and children, who are the sufferers, if others are the gainers, which is very questionable—from his generosity and his geniality.

It must be admitted that, in some cities of America—by no means in all, or anything like all—the Irish element figures unenviably in the police records, and before the inferior tribunals; and that in these cities the committals are more numerous than they should be in proportion to the numerical strength of the Irish population. This is undoubtedly the case in some instances, But, painful as this fact is to the pride of those who love and honour their country, it is not without a consolatory feature—namely, *the character of the offences* for which the Irish are made amenable to the law. These offences are irritating to the sensitiveness of the orderly, the decorous, and the law-abiding—to those whose position in life raises them above the region in which such offences have their origin—and they are damaging to the reputation of those by whom they are committed; but they are not of a heinous nature—not such as cause a shudder to the heart and a chill to the blood. The deadly crimes—the secret poisonings, the deliberate murders, the deep-laid frauds, the cunningly-masked treachery, the dark villany, the spider-like preparation for the destruction of the unwary victim—these are not common to the Irish.

Rows, riots, turbulence, acts of personal violence perpetrated in passion, are what are principally recorded of them in the newspapers; and in nine cases out of ten, these offences against the peace and order of the community, and which so deeply prejudice the public mind, not only against the perpetrators, but, what is far worse, against their race and country, are attributable to one cause, and one cause alone—*drink*. The American may drink from morning to night without injury to his country, without peril to his nationality; the German may snore himself into insensibility in a deluge of lager beer, without doing dishonour to Faderland; the Englishman and the Scotchman may indulge to excess—as both do indulge to excess—without compromising England or Scotland thereby; but the Irishman, more impulsive, more mercurial, more excitable, will publish his indiscretion on the highway, and will himself identify his nationality with his folly. Were it possible to induce Irishmen, if not to abandon drink altogether, which is not at all likely or probable, at least to be moderate in its use, the result would be a blessed one. It were impossible to imagine any result more blessed, more glorious. It would lift up the Irish race in America as with a miraculous power, simply because Irishmen would then have an opportunity of exhibiting, without flaw or blemish, those qualities which, whenever they are allowed fair play, excite the admiration and win the affections of the American people.

A dozen years since, while the Know Nothing fury raged through the country, and Irish Catholics, especially the multitudes of emigrants who were then pouring into the States in numbers sufficient to inflame the jealousy of certain classes of Americans, were fiercely assailed from pulpit, press, and platform, the venerable Archbishop Spalding thus wrote, in answer to the charges made against them:—

But (it is said) the Irish emigrants are vicious and immoral. That a portion of them have their faults—grievous and glaring faults—we do not deny; but all firm and impartial men will admit that the charge made against them as a body is obviously unjust. They have their faults, which are paraded and greatly exaggerated by the public press; but they have also their virtues, which are studiously kept out of view. They have their faults; but have not the corresponding class in our own population their vices also as great, if not greater, than those of the class which are now singled out as the victims of a virtuous public indignation? They have their vices, but these are often faults of the head more than of the heart; of imprudence and thoughtlessness more than of deliberate design and malice. *If you look for the accomplished forger, the cold-blooded midnight assassin or murderer, the man who goes always armed with the destructive, bowie-knife or revolver, ready for any deed of blood, you will in general have to seek elsewhere than among the class of Irish emigrants whom you so fiercely denounce.*

The Irishman's vices are generally the result of intemperance, or of the sudden heat of passion, sometimes aroused by outrages upon his country or religion; he is easily misled by evil associates, *but his heart is generally in the right place.* The Irishman has no concealment in his character; what he is, he is openly and before the world.

Since the Archbishop wrote, events have greatly modified the feelings then entertained towards the Irishman and his creed; but the enemy of the Irishman's own creation and his own fostering is as rampant and as deadly as ever.

The 'liquor business' is most pernicious, either directly or indirectly, to the Irish. Requiring little capital, at least to commence with, the Irish rush into it; and the temptation to excess which it offers is often more than the virtue of the proprietor of the business can withstand. If the evil were confined to the individual himself, the result would be a matter of comparatively trifling consequence; but the Irishman attracts the Irishman to his saloon or his bar, and so the evil spreads. Almost invariably the lowest class of groggery or liquor-store—that which supplies the most villanous and destructive mixtures to its unfortunate customers—is planted right in the centre of the densely-crowded Irish quarter of a great city; while too often the name on the sign-board acts as a fatal lure to those who quaff ruin or death in the maddening bowl. In America, as in Ireland, there are men in the trade who are a credit to their country, indeed an honour to humanity—generous, high-spirited, charitable and religious, who are foremost in every good work, and who are never appealed to in vain in any cause of public usefulness; but, on the other hand, there are others whose connection with it is injurious to themselves and prejudicial to their countrymen. The bad liquor of the native American or the Dutchman is far less perilous to poor Pat than what is sold by the bar-keeper whose name has in it a flavour of the shamrock.

A feeling of clanship, if not a spirit of nationality, operates as an additional inducement to the Irishman, who probably requires little incentive to excess, beyond his own craving for momentary enjoyment and dangerous excitement. Here, too, the working man is seduced into that most tempting, yet most fatal of all moral maelstroms—the whirlpool of pothouse politics, in whose accursed depths of mud and mire many a bright hope has been wrecked, many a soul lost. Here, fascinated by the coarse Sirens—Drink and Politics—many an Irishman, fitted by nature for better things, has first become a tool, then a slave, then a victim: helping to build up the fortunes of some worthless fellow on his own ruin, and sacrificing the legitimate gain of honest industry for the expectation of some paltry office, which, miserable at best, ever eludes his desperate clutch. It requires no little moral courage on the part of the eager and impulsive Irishman to avoid being entangled in the fatal meshes of the pothouse and its politics; yet if he has the good fortune to resist the temptation, or the energy to break through the toils, he is amply rewarded in his safety and independence. An enlightened interest in public affairs becomes the freeman; thankless drudgery and inevitable debasement are only worthy of the willing slave.

Formerly there were inducements to excess which either no longer exist, or do not exist to the same extent as they did. The principal inducement was the low cost of whisky. Even of the best quality, it was so cheap as to be within the means of the poorest; while whisky of an inferior, and therefore more deleterious description, was to be had at a price almost nominal. And with this poisonous stuff—this rot to the entrails and devil to the brain—many thousands of Irishmen were deliberately slain by contractors engaged in certain public works. The sooner the task was done the more profit to the contractor. It was a free country, and the white man could not be made to work against his will; but advantage was taken of his weakness, and with red-hot whisky the liberal contractor lashed and goaded the toiler to superhuman efforts—before which the embankment grew up, and the huge earth-mound vanished, and the great ditch widened and deepened, as if with the celerity of magic; but ere that work was done—ere the train rattled along the iron highway, the boat floated in the canal, or the ship was moored in the dock—there were widows and orphans to mourn the victims of a fatal weakness, and the reckless greed and wicked cruelty of their taskmasters.

Instigated by the devil whisky, the old insane and meaningless jealousies broke out—not the Catholic against the Protestant—not the Green against the Orange; but Munster against Connaught, and Connemara against Cork. And out of these shameful feuds sprang riots, and bloodshed, and murder, as well as deep national scandal. The Catholic Church spared no exertions to avert this evil, and put an end to a cause of such just reproach; but though immense good was done, and much evil prevented, the active devil was at times too potent for its mild authority. Happily, these are things of the past, which must yet be remembered with a blush of sorrow and of shame.

If even still there is much to deplore, there is more to rejoice at. Not only are the vast majority of Irishmen in all parts of America as sober and temperate in their habits as any men to be found in any community or country, but in many parts of the United States the Irish enjoy the reputation of being among the best, the most orderly, and the most sober portion of the population. And where this happy state of things exists, the Irish of the working-classes are sure to possess property, to have their 'house and lot,' and to be frugal, thrifty, and saving. Nor, as I can testify, are the Irish without meeting with ready and generous appreciation from Americans of long descent. 'The Irish here, sir, are amongst our best citizens; they

189

are sober and industrious, moral, orderly, and law-abiding—sir, they are a credit to their native country.' This testimony I was proud to hear in various States. But, unhappily, in some of the large cities, the evil habit of the minority casts a certain amount of discredit, however unjustly, on their Irish populations.

In every large city and in most of the considerable towns of America there is a temperance organisation, which offers the usual advantages to those who belong to it. On Monday, March 18th, I had an admirable opportunity of witnessing the display made by the temperance societies of New York; and rarely did I behold a spectacle which was in itself so cheering and consolatory, or of which I felt more truly proud. In the heyday of the temperance movement in Ireland I had more than once seen processions quite as brilliant and imposing, after their fashion, as that which I scanned with eager scrutiny in New York. There was therefore nothing novel in the display, whether in its banners, its decorations, its music, or even its numbers. What did delight me—what I know delighted others, who, like myself, had a national interest in the festival of the day—was to witness so large a body of Irishmen, and the children of Irishmen, presenting in the face of the American people a striking and beneficial example of courage and good sense to their own race; in a city, too, which probably has within it more of risk and danger to sobriety than any other city in the States. Their dress was admirable, even conspicuous where respectability of attire was the rule; and there was that in their air and manner and carriage which elicited universal admiration, and deeply gratified the Irishmen—many of them the most eminent in the city—by whom, on that occasion, I happened to be surrounded. In that enormous procession, roughly estimated, at 30,000 persons, men and boys, there were thousands of sober self-respecting men who were not members of a temperance organisation—not 'teetotallers:' but there were also, I must admit, not a few who displayed in their maundering looks and tottering gait an over-zealous devotion to the Patron Saint of their native land.

I was much amused at receiving a letter from an influential member of one of the most prosperous of the temperance societies of New York, in which the writer proudly claimed for his body prominent distinction, on these very cogent grounds—that not only had they a considerable number of members belonging to their society, but that their members owned more property, had more money in the bank and in profitable investments; had built more houses, and of a superior description; had educated their children better, and advanced them more successfully in life, and held a higher social position, than the members of any other society in New York; though the writer had no notion of disparaging any of them whatever. Here was a volume of sermons embodied in these few words; and being the words of a good Irishman, I commend them to his countrymen wherever they may be.

I was thus addressed in a Western city by an Irishman who is himself a credit to his country. Upright, intelligent, and self-respecting, he is one of those men, of whom there are thousands in America, who would not compromise the national honour in his own person for any earthly consideration. He said:—

'I have one request to make of you, and I am certain you will comply with my humble but earnest prayer: and that is, to place before the eyes of the poor intending emigrant, as of those who have their interest at heart, and whose advice is likely to be taken by our people, the terrible dangers of intemperance in this country. Implore of them, in the name of everything pure and lovely in Heaven and on earth, to make up their minds, as good Christians, to leave off the use of intoxicating drinks before starting for this country—otherwise they are not wanted here. Let them stay at home, where, even if of dissipated habits, they can meet some good Samaritan who will extend to them the hand of friendship in distress; for here the man inclined to drink will meet with nothing but bad whisky and a pauper's grave, and not one to say, "Lord have mercy upon him!" This is my request of you, and I make it in the interest of our common country, because I have too good reason to know that drink is the bane of our people.'

With the influence of sound religious teaching, whose tendency leads to self-government and control—the influence of the Church, which is every day drawing her children more within the reach of her salutary authority—the influence of organisations through which even the despairing outcast may learn a lesson of hope, of moral and social redemption,—with these influences steadily acting on the Irish in America, we may look with confidence to the wiping away of a reproach which is due to the folly and madness of the few rather than of the many; as also to the removal from the path of the Irishman of one of the most fatal obstacles to his advancement in a country for which he is eminently suited by qualities that, if not marred or perverted by this one terrible vice, must lead him to success in every walk and department of life, whether public or private.

CHAPTER XV

Poor Irish Gentility—Honest Labour—The Miller's Son—Well-earned Success—No poor Irish Gentility here—A self-made Man—How he became a Master Baker—The Irish don't do themselves Justice—How they are regarded— Scotch-Irish

THERE is another evil which overtakes Irishmen of a certain class in the new world; it may be called the Micawber evil—'waiting for something to turn up.' The delay of a week may be the destruction of the young man who comes out to America with the highest hopes of doing something, he knows not what, and getting on, he knows not how. In mere delay there is danger quite sufficient; but woe to him if he bring with him the faded gentility of poor Ireland to a country utterly without sympathy for such threadbare nonsense. The Irishman who brings with him across the ocean this miserable weakness travels with the worst possible *compagnon de voyage*.

In America there is no disgrace in honest labour. It was labour that made America what she is; it is labour that will make her what she is destined to be—the mightiest power of the earth. But that pestilent Irish gentility, which has never appreciated, perhaps never could appreciate, this grand truth; that Irish gentility, the poorest and proudest, the most sensitive and the most shamefaced, of all such wretched shams—that weakness of indigenous growth has brought many a young Irishman to grief and shame. Advised, by those who knew America well, to 'take anything' or to 'do anything' that offered, poor Irish gentility could not stoop to employment against which its high-stomached pride revolted—poor Irish gentility was 'never used to that kind of thing at home;' so poor Irish gentility wandered hopelessly about, looking in vain for what would suit its notions of respectability; until poor Irish gentility found itself with linen soiled, hat battered, clothes seedy, boots unreliable, and spirits depressed—so down, fatally down, poor Irish gentility sank, until there was not strength or energy to accept the work that offered; and poor Irish gentility faded away in some dismal garret or foul cellar, and dropped altogether out of sight, into the last receptacle of poor gentilities—the grave of a pauper. I heard a good Irish lady describe an awful tragedy of this nature; and as she told the melancholy tale, her face grew pale at its remembrance. Called too late to save one who had been her friend in youth, she was in time to close her eyes as she lay in her last mortal agony on the bare floor of a back room in a tenement house in New York. Meek, gentle, well educated and accomplished, the poor exile who thus died on that bare floor, with scarcely sufficient rags to hide her wasted limbs, was the victim of the husband's false pride and morbid sensitiveness—of his poor Irish gentility. Through every stage of the downward process he rapidly passed, dragging down with him his tenderly-nurtured wife until the sad ending was that death of hunger on those naked boards.

There must be no hesitation, no pause, in a country in which there is no hesitation, no pause, no rest—whose life is movement, whose law is progress. The golden rule to be observed by the new-comer is to accept any employment that offers, and refuse nothing that is honest and not morally degrading: and from the lowest, the humblest, the poorest positions, any commonly well-conducted man can rise, if he only determine to do so. Many of the greatest, highest, proudest men in America have risen from the axe and the spade—from labour of one kind or other; and in the estimation of every honourable mind, they are the greater, the higher, and the prouder, because of their having done so. Americans teach many useful lessons to the nations of the Old World. Progress is not the only principle happily illustrated by them; 'recuperation' is even better understood. If an American fail in business, his failure is no obstacle to his 'trying again;' as if a man happen to fall in the street, there is no reason why he should not pick himself up, rub the dust or mud from his clothes, and continue on his way. The American may fail once, or twice, or even thrice; but he does not therefore sit down in despair—with him, as long as there is life there is hope. It might be curious to speculate how many eminent merchants, now millionaires, or on the high road to that goal of the business man's ambition, owe their present position to the 'never say die' policy—who, so long as they had brains or health, would not give in. To 'begin again' is not the same desperate thing in America that it is in England or Ireland; simply because so many men have begun at the lowest, are beginning at the lowest, must begin at the lowest; and there is no shame attaching to the lowest in a country where honest labour—toil in the sweat of the brow—is honourable, not degrading. To our mind, there is something more than healthful and hopeful in this policy—it is manly and noble. Poor Irish gentility cannot comprehend, or will not accept it; but Irish pluck and energy will. Of this Irish pluck and energy I could give many illustrations; but I must content myself with a few.

I had not been long in the States when, in a Western city, I met the subject of the following true tale.

There landed on the levee of New Orleans on the 26th of January, 1854, a well-built, bright-looking, high-spirited young Irishman, from the neighbourhood of a town in the county Roscommon. The son of a miller, he had received that ordinary kind of education which left much to be done by the pupil in after life. Save health, strength, and a fixed resolution to push his way in the world, the son of the Irish miller had nothing when he stood on the banks of the mighty Mississippi. Young O'B—— did not lose much time, or wear out his boot-leather, in hunting after employment that would harmonise with his notions of Irish gentility—for the simple reason that he had not brought such a commodity with him from Roscommon. Like a sensible young Irishman, who had the world before him, he took the first work that offered. With the savings of a few weeks' labour in his pocket, he paid his passage to St. Louis. Work was scarce in that city at the moment, so he determined not to lose his time there, but push on. From St. Louis he proceeded to the city in which he hoped to find something to do; and as he left the steamer, in which he had taken a deck passage, his entire fortune consisted of three silver dollars. Failing to find work of any kind in this city, he resolved to try what he could make of the country; for being a sober lad, and having his bright Irish wits about him, he determined that he should not 'hang about the town.' He went some eight or ten miles into the country, and found work as a farm hand.

For six weeks he honestly did his best to earn his pay; but his hands becoming sore from the labour, he was forced to give in. Returning to the town, the Roscommon lad was employed by the principal hotel of the place to bring water to the stable with a horse and cart. At this humble employment he was engaged, when, happening to see a small man set upon by a great savage, he came to the rescue of the former, and prostrated the Goliath. The Goliath was treacherous as well as brutal, and rushing into his house, which was near at hand, he possessed himself of a sharp weapon, with which he stabbed the young Irishman, of whom he very nearly made an end. For six months of pain and weariness poor O'B———— was unable to earn a dollar. But he had brought with him from Roscommon a splendid constitution, and 'fine healing flesh.' When he was on his legs again he was taken into the office of the hotel, a position for which his intelligence suited him. The place was a very good one, as a stepping-stone to something better; and when O'B———— quitted it, which he did in twenty months, it was with 900 dollars in his pocket, having saved every cent that he could possibly lay by.

To be a lawyer was his ambition; and he was bright, and quick, and clear, with a fervent tongue, and a good tough brain withal. For two years and three months he studied hard at the desk and in the courts, and was then admitted into the profession after a creditable examination. He then practised with an eminent lawyer in the great city in which he had studied; and with the same eminent lawyer he remained until the summer of 1860. Then he turned his face once more to the smaller city in which be had humbly toiled and faithfully served; and here he determined to set up as an attorney and counsellor. His wealth was then all in the brain and the will, and his exchequer was low indeed. He contrived, however, to get an office, the furniture of which consisted of a small table and a single chair— intended for the joint yet separate use of client and of counsel; while the library was comprehended in a single volume of the statutes, 'loaned' to him by a friend. It was not a very splendid beginning, nor was his office a palace of luxury; but there was the right stuff in the young practitioner. His first case was remarkable, not so much from its being, what it was, a bad one— a 'hard case'—or for its success, as for an incident with which it was attended. The opposing counsel, who knew the history of his 'learned friend,' finding his young antagonist pushing him to the wall, and losing temper, had the good taste and delicacy to suggest that his 'learned friend' was more conversant with the manipulation of a trunk or portmanteau than with the handling of a legal argument; to which taunt the young Irishman replied in a manner at once playful and emphatic—namely, by hurling a great glass inkstand right in the face of his 'learned friend,' down whose obscured features a copious stream of ink, artistically blended with a rosier hue, rolled and lost itself in the full bosom of a shirt which a second before had shone with dazzling lustre. It is not given to every man to make a sensation in court; but the effect of this coup was eminently successful. The judge, representing the majesty of the Law, which affected to be deeply offended and seriously outraged, solemnly imposed a fine of fifty dollars; which fine was less solemnly remitted. The tide of fortune began to set in; and in few days after his double success, alike of ink-bottle and argument, the rising lawyer had the courage to go in debt for four chairs, and to have his office washed out on credit.

But in five years after the delivery of the retort courteous referred to, O'B—— received an absolute fee of 1,000 dollars for the conduct of an important case, and a conditional fee of 5,000 dollars—in other words, one thousand dollars win or lose, and five thousand in case he won; and he did win—that is, he got a young gentleman of good family safely through a little scrape which might have had a fatal termination. The four chairs, long since paid for, are still in the office; and the loaned copy of the statutes, afterwards presented as a tribute of admiration, expanded into a library that is fast encroaching on the last few unoccupied feet of wall. In 1862 and 1863 O'B—— was member of the State Legislature, and at the election for Congress previous to the time I met him, he was a candidate on the Democratic ticket. There is no mystery, no disguise about O'B—— or his career; for at the State Convention the gentleman—a State Senator—who nominated him, made the leading facts which I have now narrated the best claim to the sympathy and respect of his audience, who, like the subject of his eulogium, were, most of them at least, self-made men. I have seen O'B——'s home library, and I can answer that not only is it choice and comprehensive, but that it is well employed by the successful lawyer, who, when a lad of twenty, worked manfully on the levee of New Orleans. Possibly the moral of the story might be found in these words, which I heard him use—'Thank Heaven! I never was drunk in my life.'

One evening in a great Eastern city I met in social intercourse some five-and-twenty or thirty Irishmen from all parts of Ireland, every one of whom was either progressing, prosperous, or rich; and all, without an exception, owed everything they possessed to their own energy and good conduct. During the evening a scrap of paper was handed to me, on which was written the words—'There are more than four millions and a half of dollars represented at this table—all made by the men themselves, and most of it within a few years.' The Irishman who sat next to me was the possessor of a twelfth of the whole. He had not been more than sixteen years in the country, and until some years after he landed in America he had no connection whatever with mercantile affairs. A few dollars and the clothes in which he stood—such was his capital. He had no poor Irish gentility to embarrass him; and at the head of a dray-horse he might be seen soon after his arrival, his frock-coat not altogether suited to his rough employment, and his boots fatally damaged in sole and upper. But in a short time he made and saved money, and he went from one thing to another, mounting step after step of the commercial ladder; until he now is partner in one of the finest concerns of the city, and enjoys the highest repute for probity and enterprise. At the same table sat one who, a native of my own city, had been earning at home four shillings a week—eightpence a day—at a certain employment, but who was then the owner of a prosperous establishment, in which several hundreds were profitably employed. Intelligence, sheer industry, and good conduct,—these the secret of his success.

In the same city I know an Irishman who holds perhaps as prominent and responsible a position as any man within its walls, he having the management of one of the most splendid concerns in America. He had a situation in Ireland of some 100l. a year on a public work; but being a young man of good education, clear brain, and magnificent health, he thought he could do better in America. There was not a bit of false gentility about him, yet he sought to procure a situation at least as respectable as that to which he had been accustomed; but the moment the last sovereign was turned into dollars, and the dollars were rapidly vanishing, he determined he would not be idle a clay longer. 'I saw,' he said, 'there was nothing for it but work, and I was resolved to take anything that offered, I didn't care what. I spent a portion of the morning knocking about here and there, trying to get such employment as I would prefer; but it was not to be had. I was too late, or they didn't want me. 'Come,' said I to myself, 'there must be an end of this kind of thing; the way to get along is to begin with something; so I turned into the first livery-stable I came to, and asked the owner did he require a hand to rub down his horses; he said he did, and that he would willingly employ me. 'All right,' said I; 'so I stripped off my coat, turned up my sleeves, and set to work. And I assure you I slept well that night. I was not long there, having soon found what suited me better—and here I am now, thank God.'

As I was leaving a city 'down South' I was accompanied some way in the 'cars' by a number of my countrymen—every man of them prosperous, respectable, and 'self-made. Near me was a gentleman rather advanced in years, of the kindest expression, the softest voice, and eyes mildly beaming through a pair of gold-rimmed glasses. A thorough American, he was no less a devoted Irishman. I was speaking of the climate, and its effect on the constitution and health of our people, when he said, in his soft voice—'My dear sir, it all depends on a man's prudence or imprudence. The climate is dangerous to those who are foolish—who drink to excess. Any climate would be injurious to them; but this climate, though much talked against, is not dangerous to the sober man. My dear sir, there is an instance of it in my own person —I worked on a canal for three years, often up to my waist in water—'

'You, sir!' I could not help exclaiming.

'Yes, my dear sir'—his eyes mildly beaming at me through the gold-rimmed glasses, and his voice catching a softer intonation—'Yes, my dear sir, I was often up to my hips in water; and at the end of the time I had my health perfectly, and a considerable sum saved—quite enough to begin with. I kept my health, because I never drank—while hundreds of our countrymen were literally dying around me, I may say withering in my sight, all the result of their own folly. Poor fellows! the temptation was great, and the whisky was to be had for next to nothing.'

'But,' I said, 'you surely had not been used to rough work of that kind?'

'Very true, my dear sir; but what was I to do? I knew I had come to a country in which no man—no stranger certainly—could be idle without great injury to himself; and as I had no immediate opportunity of getting such employment as I myself would have preferred, and was accustomed to, why, my dear sir, I took that which offered. And, on the whole, I am not sorry for it.'

My friend then branched off into the adaptability of man to various climates; and, taking a wide and rather comprehensive range of inquiry, he hurried me through several countries of the world, at the same time broaching a number of plausible theories, evidently favourites of his. As I grasped his honest hand, and felt the mild light of those kindly eyes beaming at me through the gold-rimmed spectacles, I pictured to myself that man of soft voice and cultivated mind, working up to his hips in mud and slush, and the Southern sun raining its fierce fire on his head. But there he was, not a bit the worse for his hard work —on the contrary, both personally and philosophically proud of what he had gone through.

Two instances of energy and determination must close a list which could be added to to any extent.

A great strapping Irishman—who would be called at home 'a splendid figure of a man'—landed at Castle Garden about fifteen years since. He neither knew how to write or read, but he was gifted with abundant natural quickness, and he was full of energy and ambition. Work he came for, and work he got—that of a labourer. He was as strong as a horse, but he had not much experience in the management of a hod; and some of the old hands, including one who was inclined to be specially offensive, sneered at the new-comer as a 'greenhorn.' The leader of the old hands was a strong, burly fellow, not bad-natured, but inclined to bully the stranger. Now the stranger was not one of those who liked to be bullied; so the moment he was made fully aware of the meaning and intent of the offensive phrase, he fairly challenged, and in single combat manfully vanquished, his ill-advised assailant. From that moment he lost the verdant tinge which he first wore. So far this was serviceable; but he was not content with so poor a triumph. He saw other men— dull plodders, with 'not half his own gumption,' pushing their way up the social ladder; and why? Because they could read and write,—because they had 'the learning,' which, alas! he had not. But it was not because he had it not at that moment, that he could not have it some time or other. Then he would have it; that he was resolved on. So the large Irishman—who seemed big enough to swallow master and pupils at a meal—sat down on a form in a night school, and commenced to learn his a, b, c; and, with tongue desperately driven against one cheek, struggled with his 'pot-hooks and hangers'—the first efforts of the polite letter writer.

It was hard work, far tougher than that with the spade or the pickaxe. Many a time did the poor fellow's courage begin to fail, and his heart sink, as it were, into his boots; but he would not be beaten—he would not have it said that he failed. He did not fail. With the aid of a fellow-student, more advanced than himself, he drew out his first contract, which was for a few hundred dollars. This was accepted; and being executed in the most satisfactory manner by the young contractor, who himself performed no small part of the task, it was his first great step in life— contracts for thousands of dollars, and hundreds of thousands of dollars, following more rapidly than, in his wildest dreams, he could have imagined possible. This self-made man quickly adapted himself to the manners of the class to which he had so laboriously and creditably raised himself; and no one who converses with the shrewd, genial, off-handed Irishman, who drives his carriage, lives in fine style, and is educating his young family with the utmost care and at great cost, could suppose that he was the same rough giant who a few years before sat upon the form of a night school, wearily plodding at words of two syllables, and, with tongue fiercely driven against his cheek, scrawled on a slate his first lessons in writing.

Any one passing through the fashionable quarter of the capital of a Southern State may see the well-appointed mansion of a worthy Irishman, who was born within the swing of the

Bells of Shandon,
That sound so grand on
The pleasant waters
Of the river Lee.

As a journeyman baker he entered that city in the year 1851. In a few months after, he had saved 200 dollars; and with this, as part payment, he bought a small house and lot of half an acre of ground—the balance to be paid at the covenanted time. Having thus made his first start in life, he then made his second—he married. Besides the half acre in his lot, he rented an additional acre; and this acre was the chief means of his future fortune. His ambition was to be a master baker, 'no man's servant.' How was this to be done? Through the acre of garden. But what time had the journeyman baker, who worked from three o'clock in the morning till four in the evening in the bakery, to spend in cultivating vegetables? Very little time, an ordinary person would suppose; but the Corkman, who had seen how vegetables were grown in the neighbourhood of his native city, and who knew how profitable they would be when raised for his adopted city, was not an ordinary person—on the contrary, he was a determined and energetic person, who was resolved to rise in the world by more than ordinary industry. So, after leaving his day's work at the bakehouse, he would go home and work at his little farm from five o'clock in the afternoon to a late hour in the night—frequently to one o'clock next morning, if the moon served; he would then snatch a couple of hours' rest, and be again in the bakehouse at the regular hour.

Every minute that he could steal from his natural rest, every moment of his leisure time, was devoted by the journeyman baker to the cultivation of his land; and when the bright Southern moon flooded the silent night with its radiance, the Corkman might be seen digging and delving, raking and weeding, planting and sowing; until his farm blossomed as a garden, and bore abundant fruit. By this means he nearly supported his family, and saved his wages. In three years he had 500 dollars in the bank. With this 500 dollars he took his third start in America— he became a master baker. And so well did he succeed in his new capacity that he soon established a good business, saved a considerable sum of money, educated his children, built for them a neat mansion, in which they enjoy every reasonable comfort; and I, who met him, and received much attention at his hands, can state that this self-made man is among the most respected of the Irish-born citizens of the community in whose midst he has established himself so successfully. He had a 'squeeze in his business during the war;' but when I saw him he had got over all his difficulties, and was then sailing before the wind. He is a genuinely sober man, who, to use his own words, 'knows the danger of drink, and never lost an hour by it in his life.'

And here I answer a question which is in every Irishman's mind, on the tip of every Irishman's tongue,—how are the Irish doing in America?—have they bettered their condition, or the contrary?—are they improving or going back? I was nearly six months going from place to place; and during that time, and in the course of that extended journey, I was brought into contact with men of different nationalities, various opinions, and all classes of society. I conversed with Irishmen who took a desponding or a hopeful view of the position of their countrymen, who mourned over their weaknesses and their follies, or were proud of their virtues. I sought to gather information wherever I went, and I had abundant opportunities of doing so. I searched and I sifted with an earnest purpose, and a conscientious desire to come at the truth. I set statement against statement, opinion against opinion, in the spirit of a judge rather than with the feeling of an advocate—though, I honestly confess it, I could not, even for a second, divest myself of a strong wish to hear the best of those of my own race and country. The result, then, of every observation I could make, of every inquiry I instituted, of every information I received, is this,—that while, in some places, there are evils to deplore, but evils which are being remedied, and while many are not doing what they ought or could do for their advancement, on the whole, and dealing with them in mass, the Irish in America are steadily rising, steadily advancing, steadily improving in circumstances and in position; and that, as a rule, they have enormously benefited their condition by having left the old country for the new.

In every walk and department of life they are making their mark. As merchants, bankers, manufacturers—as lawyers, physicians, engineers, architects, inventors—as literary men, as men of science, as artists, as scholars, as teachers of youth—as soldiers, wise in council and terrible in battle—as statesmen, as yet more the sons of Irishmen than Irish born,—the nationality is adequately and honourably represented; while the great bulk—the mass—are felt to be essential to the progress, the greatness, the very life of the American Republic. Where, as must necessarily be the case, the Irish constitute a large proportion of the working population of a great city, they may be looked down upon by the prejudiced or the superfine—those who dislike their religion, or despise homely manners or rude employment; but the toiling, hard-working mass of the Irish are nevertheless rising day by day, not only to greater comfort, but to a fuller appreciation of their duties and their destiny as citizens of America.

The Irish in America injure themselves more than others can or are willing to injure them. They injure themselves seriously by not in all cases putting forward their best men to represent them, whether in municipal or other offices; and by allowing men to speak and act in their name who are not the most qualified, indeed in some, and too many, instances, not in the least qualified to do the one or the other. Thoughtful Irishmen, sensitive and self-respecting, are the very first to deplore this great practical error; and I must say I have been but too sensible of its damaging influence in more than one instance, or one locality. The evil which is done follows as a necessary and inevitable consequence. When the Irish put forward or elect certain men, they are assumed to do so of their own free choice—to select them as the right men, the best men; and, this being so, they must not be surprised if the prejudiced or the censorious are only too willing to accept such ill-chosen and unfit representatives as accurate types and fair exponents of Irish character, Irish genius, or Irish worth. But, on the other hand, when the Irish adopt the right men—men who are upright, honourable, wise—in a word, presentable—men of whom they may say with pride, 'they belong to us; they are of our stock; we are not ashamed to put them forward as our representatives,'—in such case they do not so much do honour to themselves, as simple justice to their country and their race.

I cannot venture to deal otherwise than in generalities; and I shall therefore only add that, while I have frequently witnessed, and always with intense satisfaction, the result of the wise and self-respecting policy of selecting the best, the ablest, and the worthiest Irishmen, or sons of Irishmen, to represent the race, I have had too many occasions to deplore the fatal folly of Irishmen thrusting into public positions, or rather suffering to be thrust into such positions, men who, possibly excellent persons in their own way, and eminently suited for the retirement of domestic life, were not qualified to stand the test of American criticism—that is, as the representatives of a great nationality and a gifted people. There is no lack of the best men for such offices or positions, be they what they may; but it will often happen that the sensitive man of merit has no chance against the vulgar intriguer—and so the Irish are damaged in the public esteem. This, however, is an evil that must cure itself in course of time, when the Irish-American witnesses the happy results of a policy consistent not only with reason and common sense, but with the most ordinary self-respect.

On the whole, then, and notwithstanding this evil, which is more damaging than some will believe, the Irish in America are steadily advancing in social position, as well as improving in material prosperity. They are improving even in the cities in which dangers and temptations are most liable to assail them; they are improving in places in which society is, as it were, only settling down into its legitimate grooves; and in many, many parts of the country they are—taking all circumstances into consideration—progressing more rapidly and more successfully than any other class of the community. The Irish landed on the shores of America poorer—with less money, less means, less capital—than the English, the Scotch, or the Germans; in fact, under less favourable circumstances in almost every respect than the people of any other country. The vast majority of them came in poverty—too many in want and sickness—too many only to find a grave after landing; and, therefore, what the Irish in America have done in their adopted country—their new home—though by no means all, or anything like all, that could be wished of them, is an indisputable proof of the inherent vigour and vitality of their race. This is what may be conscientiously said of them to-day; but how much more may be said of them in ten or twenty years hence belongs to the future and to the goodness of Providence.

And now a word as to the manner in which the Irish are regarded in America. Much necessarily depends upon themselves, but much also depends on the circumstances in which they are placed, or by which they are surrounded. In some places they possibly exercise, or are supposed to exercise, too much influence in elections; and those whose party they happen to oppose, or with whose ambition they interfere, can scarcely be expected to think of them and speak of them in the most friendly or flattering terms. In other places the religious sentiment of a large and powerful class may be so strong as to intensify national prejudice, a jealousy which is common to all countries. Or the majority of the Irish may happen to be humble working people; and even in Republics the rich are like the same class in old-established Monarchies, rather inclined to look down upon those who are not, as themselves, decked in purple and fine linen. I refer in another place to the long and bitter struggle against the Catholic and the foreigner, and I shall only now remark that, whatever prejudice may still exist, it must, to a great extent, be traced to this old feeling, which has manifested itself at various intervals before and since the Revolution; and that, when one may hear or see the Irish spoken of or written of in a harsh or contemptuous spirit, it would be well, before accepting such expressions of opinion as proof of anything more than of a narrow, a malevolent, or an angry mind, to speculate as to the cause, the motive, or the circumstances in which the traducer and the traduced are relatively placed. On the whole, then, and making due allowance for the causes and motives at which I have glanced, the Irish do stand well in the public esteem of America; and in many places in which I have been I know they are not only generally esteemed, but are highly popular.

As to the individual Irishman, he is perhaps more truly popular than any other man in America. His genial qualities and kindly nature, his wit, and humour, and pleasant manners—these render him agreeable as a companion, and sought after in society; and when business ability and rigid conscientiousness are combined with the more social qualities, as they are in numberless instances, then there is no man more admired or respected than the Irishman. I have frequently heard an American say of an Irishman, who would no more think of disguising his nationality than he would of committing a crime, 'Sir, he is a whole-souled Irishman—a high-souled gentleman, sir.'

But there is one class of whom, neither from Irishmen nor Americans, is much said in praise. 'Whole-souled' and 'high-toned' would sound as a sarcasm and a mockery if applied to those Irish, or sons of Irish, *who style themselves* 'Scotch-Irish'—a title or designation so unworthy and so unnatural as to excite the derision of every man of large heart and generous spirit.

The Scotch-Irish! Who are the Scotch-Irish? What does the term mean? Is not the compound of itself a contradiction? Such were the questions which I involuntarily asked when the strange absurdity first met my eye or ear. It was so curious, it comprehended a treason so inconsistent with the ordinary feelings by which men are governed, that I was at first much perplexed when striving to explain its meaning. But now I have no difficulty in understanding and accounting for this most ridiculous compound, this mongrel designation. Scotch-Irish are those Irish, or descendants of Irishmen, who are ashamed of their country, and represent themselves to Americans as other than what they really are. Not only are they ashamed of their country, but, so far as this false feeling influences them, they are its shame. Detested by every true Irishman, they are despised by every genuine American.

It would appear that, though the descendants of settlers who came over, or were sent over, to Ireland in the time of James, or Charles, or Cromwell, and though their families have intermixed with the native population, with whose blood and race theirs has blended during two centuries—in fact, as far back as when the Pilgrim Fathers landed on Plymouth rock—they still are not Irish! This, practically, is what the Scotch-Irish *say of themselves* by the adoption of this unnatural distinction: 'Such is our stubborn hatred of the country on which our remote ancestors were quartered, and from which so many of the rightful owners were driven to make way for us, we could not amalgamate with the Irish nation, or sympathise with its people.' This is a hard judgment for any class to pronounce against itself—and this is unmistakably implied by the mongrel designation of Scotch-Irish. The noble Geraldines soon became more Irish than the Irish themselves. Such is ever the case with a generous race; they will thoroughly identify themselves with the people among whom their lot is cast. Not so with the Scotch-Irish; the longer they dwell in the country, the stronger seems to be their dislike to it, and the greater their anxiety—when abroad—to be recognised as, or mistaken for, something different from that which they are, according to every law of nature. This, practically, is their own story of themselves.

It may be well to inquire why these people call themselves by this unpatriotic title or designation. The reason or cause is based on various motives, not one of which is praiseworthy or ennobling. Cowardice, whether moral or physical, is not a very creditable excuse for the adoption of this description of national masquerade; yet to moral cowardice may be traced this ludicrous disguise. Vanity is not a specially high-toned motive; and vanity has much to do with it. Bigotry is not an ennobling sentiment; and bigotry has also its share in the miserable treason. To conciliate prejudice and gratify dislike—this was the origin of Scotch-Irishism.

The prejudice to be conciliated was twofold—national and religious. But the prejudice against the stranger comprehended all strangers, all Irish, the Northern Protestant no less than the Southern Catholic. Hence then the cry—'I am no mere Irishman; I am Scotch-Irish.' And many of these men—these Irish-born sons of Irish-born fathers, and Irish-born grandfathers, and Irish-born great-grandfathers, and Irish-born great-great-grandfathers, joined in every fierce crusade against Irishmen, or against Irishmen because they were Catholics. There were, no doubt, many more that claimed a remote Scotch ancestry, who, Protestants or Presbyterians as they were, stood by their countrymen on every occasion when either their freedom or their religion was assailed; and these high-minded men would have felt themselves disgraced if they called themselves anything else but what they boasted of being—Irish.

Then the mass of the Irish emigrants were poor, many illiterate, many in a miserable condition, a temporary burden on the charity or the industry of the community. For the moment this Irish emigration was unpopular; it excited apprehension, even hostility, there not being, at least in the minds of some, sufficient confidence either in the energy of the incomers or the resources of the country to which they came. Here again was the occasion for the unnatural Irish to exclaim—'These myriads of penniless adventurers are a different race from us. We, sleek and well fed, have nothing in common with those ill-clad, half-starved creatures; we are not Irish, but Scotch-Irish.' To this pitiable vanity, this abject moral cowardice, there was a splendid contrast in the conduct of Irishmen, who, notwithstanding the old Scotch blood in their veins, welcomed, assisted, and cherished their poor countrymen, with whom they claimed kindred, even though their pockets were empty, their raiment was scanty, and sickness had followed in their track.

Then the vast majority of the Irish emigrants were Catholics; and when the evil spirit of persecution broke out, here was a strong motive for repudiating the country that flooded America with Popery. 'We are of a different race and religion to these people, good Know Nothings! Excellent Native Americans! do not confound us with these Irish Papists. We are Scotch-Irish—Protestant Scotch-Irish. We are as opposed to these Irish Papists as you are; and to prove our sincerity—to prove to you that we are not of the same blood, though we had the misfortune to be born in the same country, we will heartily join you in every effort you may make to put them down.' And they did as they said. They were honest so far.

The literature of England was anti-Catholic, if not anti-Irish; it excited hostility and it deepened prejudice. The literature of England became the literature of America, or it influenced the tone of the literature of native growth,—another reason for the poor-hearted Irishman, while proclaiming his Protestantism, to repudiate his country.

A volume of indignant commentary could not outweigh the force of a few words which I heard uttered by an American, who was much perplexed by the term 'Scotch-Irish:' 'What does Mr. ——— mean? Why should he set himself out as not being an Irishman? What can he mean by this Scotch-Irish? Wasn't he born in Ireland? I was born in America. I am an American. Then why should he pretend he isn't an Irishman? I may prefer an American Protestant to an Irish Catholic, though a man's religion is nothing to me, it's his own affair; but I like the man who stands up for his native land, whatever he is. I don't like a hound that denies the country that gave him birth. It isn't natural.'

Thus it is, whatever their own opinion of their conduct may be, those who proclaim themselves Scotch-Irish gain little in the esteem of the generous and the high-spirited, but, on the contrary, lose much by this shabby absurdity.

I am happy to say that among the most favourable specimens of the country whom I met in British America or the States, whether North or South, were Irish Protestants, from Ulster as well as Munster; but these men were not only known and admired as Irishmen, but they boasted of being Irishmen. 'Whole-souled Irishmen' indeed. I must add, in justice to my countrymen in Canada, that I never heard of the Scotch-Irish until I came to the States.

There may possibly be those in Ireland who in their secret hearts have no love for the country that gave them birth; but there is no open and avowed treason to their nationality. Anything of the kind would only ensure universal contempt, and loss of public honour and private esteem to the person mean enough or rash enough to be guilty of it. Then why should it be pardoned in America?

CHAPTER XVI

Remittances Home—Something of the Angel still—How the Family are brought out—Remittances—A 'Mercenary'—A Young Pioneer—A Poor Irish Widow—Self-sacrifice—The Amount sent

IT is difficult to realise to the mind the magnitude of the pecuniary sacrifices made by the Irish in America, either to bring out their relatives to their adopted country, or to relieve the necessities and improve the circumstances of those who could not leave or who desired to remain in the old country. To say that they have thus disposed of a sum equal to Twenty-four Millions of British money, or, supposing there to have been no depreciation of the currency of the United States, One Hundred and Twenty Millions of Dollars, scarcely conveys the true idea of the vastness of the amount of money sent within a quarter of a century by one branch of the same great family to the other. But if it were asserted—as it might be with the most perfect accuracy—that the amount of money sent across the ocean by the Irish in America and Australia within that time would have paid for more than two-thirds of all the property that passed through the Court of Encumbered Estates in Ireland—property represented by an annual income or rental exceeding 2,000,000l.—the mind might possibly appreciate the prodigious magnitude of this heart-offering of one of the most generous and self-sacrificing of all the families of the human race. As a mere fact, more than 24,000,000l. have been sent by the Irish to pay for passages and outfits and fares to distant places; to enable those 'at home' to pay a high rent, perhaps in a time of scarcity; to support parents too old, or too feeble, or too prejudiced, to venture across the sea; or to secure the safety and education of brothers and sisters yet too young to brave the perils of a protracted voyage and a long journey in a strange country.

There is not a private banker, or passenger broker, or agent in any of the cities of the United States who could not tell of instances of the most extraordinary self-denial practised by the sons and daughters of the Irish race. The entries in their ledgers are prosaic enough—so many dollars sent, on such a day, by a young man or a young woman with an Irish name, to some person in Ireland of a similar name. But were that matter-of-fact entry transfused into its true colours, volumes of poetry might be written of those countless heart-offerings, the fruits of hard self-denial, not merely at the sacrifice of innocent enjoyments, and humble finery, dear to woman's nature, from a natural and graceful instinct, but often at the cost of the fondest hopes of the human heart. How long, for instance, if the accountant troubled himself to consider, may he not have remembered this most regular of his visitors, since when, almost a child in years, she timidly and yet proudly confided to his custody her first earnings, with many an injunction and many a prayer, and—believing she read sympathy in his face—told him for whom it was intended, and how sadly it was wanted by the old people at home, for whom she had risked the dangers of the deep, and the worse perils of a strange land? Did he care to regard her in any other light than as a constant customer, he might have observed how the soft fair face lost its maiden bloom, and hardened into premature age, marked with lines of care and toil, as year after year this unconscious martyr to filial duty surrendered everything —even the vision of a home blessed by the love of husband and the caresses of children—to keep the roof over the head of father or of mother, and provide for their comfort in the winter of their days; or to pay for the support of a young brother or sister, or perhaps the orphan child of a sister who had confided it to her care with her dying breath. I have many times, and always with instinctive reverence, seen such noble Irish women in the act of sending the fortieth or the fiftieth remittance to their relatives in Ireland; and the cool matter-of-fact deliberateness with which the money was deposited, and the order obtained, was an eloquent proof of the frequency of their visits for the same purpose.

The great ambition of the Irish girl is to send 'something' to her people as soon as possible after she has landed in America; and in innumerable instances the first tidings of her arrival in the New World are accompanied with a remittance, the fruits of her first earnings in her first place. Loving a bit of finery dearly, she will resolutely shut her eyes to the attractions of some enticing article of dress, to prove to the loved ones at home that she has not forgotten them; and she will risk the danger of insufficient clothing, or boots not proof against rain or snow, rather than diminish the amount of the little hoard to which she is weekly adding, and which she intends as a delightful surprise to parents who possibly did not altogether approve of her hazardous enterprise. To send money to her people, she will deny herself innocent enjoyments, womanly indulgences, and the gratifications of legitimate vanity; and such is the generous and affectionate nature of these young girls, that they regard the sacrifices they make as the most ordinary matter in the world, for which they merit neither praise nor approval. To assist their relatives, whether parents, or brothers and sisters, is with them a matter of imperative duty, which they do not and cannot think of disobeying, and which, on the contrary, they delight in performing. And the money destined to that purpose is regarded as sacred, and must not be diverted to any object less worthy.

I was told in New York of a young Irish girl, who was only one month in the country, going to the office of the well-known Irish Emigration Society's Bank to send her first earnings to her mother, of course to the care of the parish priest. She brought with her five dollars, which in her simplicity she supposed to be equivalent to the 1l. she intended to transmit. At that time six dollars and fifty cents were required to make up the British pound, and the poor girl's disappointment was intense when she was made to understand that she was deficient a dollar and a half. The friend who accompanied her, and who had been some time longer in the country, lent her a dollar; the clerk advanced her the balance, and the undiminished pound was sent to her ' poor mother, who wanted it badly.' In a few days after, the money advanced by the clerk was paid by the young girl, whose face was soon known in the office, as she came at regular intervals to send remittances, which were gradually increasing in amount. In a very short time she understood the relative value of American 'greenbacks' and British gold, and made no mistake as to the amount of the money-orders she desired to transmit.

It frequently occurred in that office that small sums were advanced to make up the amount required by the person intending to send a remittance; and in no instance was there failure in payment. A debt of the kind is, of all others, the most sacred. The money which the loan thus helps to complete is a filial offering—the gift of a child to a parent; and confidence so reposed is never forfeited. I have heard the same statement made by bankers and brokers in many parts of the United States.

So much is this sending of remittances to Ireland a matter of routine to those engaged in the business, that there must be something special in the circumstance of the case, or in the manner or appearance of the applicant for a bill of exchange, to excite the least attention. But he must have been insensible indeed who was not attracted by the strange aspect and appearance of a regular visitor at the bank in Chambers' Street. So surely as the festivals of Christmas and Easter were approaching, would a man of powerful frame, wild eyes, and dissipated appearance, enter the office, and laying on the counter $15, or $20, ask for an order in favour of an old man away in some country village in Ireland. Not unfrequently would the clothes of the Society's customer bear the marks of abject poverty, and his face evidences of the roughest usage; and were the police asked to give a character of this poor fellow, they would say that, though honest and free from crime, there was not 'a harder case' in New York; and that there were few better known in the Tombs than he was. True, he was a hard case indeed, wasting his strength and energy in folly and dissipation, working now and then as a longshore man, but spending what he earned in drink, and only sober when in prison, paying the penalty of drunkenness or violence, or at the two fixed periods of the year—some time before Christmas and some time before Easter.

While in prison his sobriety was involuntary—at these periods it was voluntary and deliberate. His old father in Ireland expected to hear from 'his boy,' and the letter so anxiously looked for at home should not be empty. So long then as it was necessary to work in order to send a couple of pounds as a Christmas-box or an Easter gift, he would do so, and remain sober during that time; but once the money was sent, and the sacred duty discharged, he would go back to the old course, spending his days partly at work, partly in rows and dissipation, and very constantly in the Tombs, possibly repenting his wanton waste of life. There was no one to tell the old man at home of the wild desperate course of his 'boy' in

America, and he never knew with what heroic self-denial these welcome remittances were earned, or how the one strong affection, the one surviving sense of duty, was sufficient, though unhappily but for a moment, to redeem a reckless but not altogether degraded nature. There was indeed something of the angel left in that victim of the most fatal enemy to the Irish in the New World.

With all banks and offices through which money is sent to Ireland the months of December and March are the busiest portions of the year. The largest amount is then sent; then the offices are full of bustling, eager, indeed clamorous applicants, and then are the clerks hard set in their attempts to satisfy the demands of the impatient senders, who are mostly females, and chiefly 'girls in place.' The great festivals of Christmas and Easter are specially dear to the Irish heart, being associated with the most sacred mysteries of the Christian religion, and likewise with those modest enjoyments with which the family, however humble or poor, seek to celebrate a season of spiritual rejoicing. Then there is joy in the Church, which typifies in the decorations of her altars as in the robes of her ministers the gladness which should dwell in the heart of the Christian. Thus misery, and sorrow, and want, are not in accordance with the spirit of these solemn festivals, nor with the feelings which ought to prevail with those who believe in their teaching. Therefore, to enable the friends at home—the loved ones never forgotten by the Irish exile—to 'keep' the Christmas or the Easter in a fitting manner—in reality, to afford them some little comforts at those grateful seasons of the Christian year—remittances are specially sent; and coming from the source which they do, these comforts, too often sadly needed, are the more prized by those to whom the means for procuring them are forwarded with touching remembrances, and fond prayers and blessings, grateful alike to piety and affection. There is something beautiful in these timely memorials of unabated love; they link still closer hearts which the ocean cannot divide.

What wonderful things have not these Irish girls done! Take a single example—and there is not a State in the Union in which the same does not occur:—Resolving to do something to better the circumstances of her family, the young Irish girl leaves her home for America. There she goes into service, or engages in some kind of feminine employment. The object she has in view—the same for which she left her home and ventured to a strange country —protects her from all danger, especially to her character: that object, her dream by day and night, is the welfare of her family, whom she is determined, if possible, to again have with her as of old. From the first moment, she saves every cent she earns—that is, every cent she can spare from what is absolutely necessary to her decent appearance. She regards everything she has or can make as belonging to those to whom she has unconsciously devoted the flower of her youth, and for whom she is willing to sacrifice her woman's dearest hopes. To keep her place, or retain her employment, what will she not endure?—sneers at her nationality, mockery of her peculiarities, even ridicule of her faith, though the hot blood flushes her cheek with fierce indignation. At every hazard the place must be kept, the money earned, the deposit in the savings-bank increased; and though many a night is passed in tears and prayers, her face is calm, and her eye bright, and her voice cheerful. One by one, the brave girl brings the members of her family about her. But who can tell of her anguish if one of the dear ones goes wrong, or strays from the right path!—who could imagine her rapture as success crowns her efforts, and she is rewarded in the steadiness of the brother for whom she feared and hoped, or in the progress of the sister to whom she has been as a mother! One by one, she has brought them all across the ocean, to become members of a new community, citizens of a great country—it may be, the mothers and fathers of a future race; and knowing the perils which surround youth in a country in which licence is too often—with the unthinking and inexperienced—confounded with liberty, and impatience of control with proper independence of spirit, the faithful girl seeks to draw them within the influence of religion, in which, as in her passionate love of her family, she has found her safeguard and her strength. Probably she has grown old before her time, possibly she realises in a happy marriage the reward of her youth of care and toil; but were the choice to be given her of personal happiness, or all-sacrificing affection, she would choose the hard road rather than the flowery path. Such is the humble Irish girl, who may be homely, who may be deficient in book knowledge, but whose heart is beyond gold in value.

There is no idea of repayment of the money thus expended. Once given, there is an end of it. This is not so with other nationalities. The Germans, a more prudent, are a less generous people than the Irish; and when money is expended in the bringing out of relatives, it is on the understanding that one day or other it will be refunded—that it will become a matter of account, to be arranged as soon as possible, or, at farthest, when convenient. An eminent Irish clergyman, who, from his position, has much to do with the affairs of a large and important diocese, remarked to an Irish girl, one of his penitents, who came to consult him as to the best mode of bringing out her mother and father, she having frequently sent them remittances, and also brought out and provided for a brother and sister,—'Why, Ellen, you are leaving yourself nothing. Now your father, as you tell me, can get on well, and there is work enough for him here; and surely he ought to pay you back something of what I know you have been sending him for years.' The girl looked at her old friend and adviser, first in doubt, then in surprise, then in indignation. When she replied, it was with sparkling eye and flushed cheek—

'What, sir! take back from my father and mother what I gave them from my heart! I could not rest in my bed if I did anything so mean. Never say the like of that to me again, Father, and God bless you!' and the poor girl's voice quivered with emotion, as her eye softened in wistful appeal. 'Don't mind, Ellen,' said the priest, 'I was wrong; I should have known you better.' 'I really,' as he said to me, 'meant to try what answer she would give; for that same day I was cognisant of a very different mode of arranging matters. Sir, let people say what they please of them, the Irish are a grand race, after all, and the Irish women are an honour to their country and their faith.' This was said with an enthusiasm not usual to a man so self-contained as this somewhat Americanised Irish priest.

Instances without number might be adduced in vindication of the eulogium thus pronounced. This year (1867) a young girl landed at Castle Garden, and was fortunate enough to obtain employment the same day. She had in her possession a pound in gold, and some shillings; and finding that she was safely provided for, she determined to send back the money to her mother, to whom it would be of great assistance. Her employer, seeing her so well disposed, advanced her a month's wages, which she was delighted to add to her own money; and a draft was procured and 'mailed' the very first day of her arrival in America!

An Irish girl in Buffalo, who had been but four years in the country, had within that time paid for the passages of two brothers and two sisters, besides sending 40l.; and, when lately sending another remittance through the Irish Emigrant Society of New York, she said she 'would not rest until she brought out her dear father and mother,' which she hoped she would be able to do within the next six months.

In populous cities the women send home more money than the men; in small towns and rural districts the men are as constant in their remittances, and perhaps send larger sums. Great cities offer too many temptations to improvidence or to vice, while in small places and rural districts temptations are fewer, and the occasion for spending money recklessly less frequent; hence it is, that the man who, amidst the whirl and excitement of life in a great city, but occasionally sends $10 or $20 to the old people at home, sends frequent and liberal remittances when once he breathes the purer air of the country, and frees himself from the dangerous fascination of the drinking-saloon.

Whether the money is given as the price of the passage out, or in the form of a ticket paid for in America, and thus forwarded to Ireland, or is sent as a means of supplying some want or relieving a pressing necessity, practically there is no more thought of it by the donor. It not unfrequently happens that tickets are returned to the donors, the persons to whom they were sent having changed their minds, being unwilling or afraid to leave the old country for a new home. But the money—recouped through a friendly agent—is almost invariably sent back, with a remark somewhat in this form: 'I intended it for you any way, either in ticket or in money; and if you won't take it in ticket, why you must in money. It is yours, anyhow, and no one else is to have it.'

A large amount is annually expended in the purchase of tickets at the American side; but this, large as it is, bears only a small proportion when compared with the enormous amount sent in the shape of assistance to relatives at home. For instance, there was sent last year (1866) by one firm in Lowell $44,290; and of this amount $32,000 were for the material assistance of the friends at home, and but $12,000 in passage tickets out. The total amount, though small in comparison to the vast sums sent from the great cities, is still not a little surprising, when it is considered that the Irish population, consisting for the most part of young persons working in mills and factories, is now about 15,000. From another emigration agent in the same place, and who is but recently in the business, a striking instance of liberality is obtained. He says—'The most I received at any one time was 20l., or $140, from an industrious Irish girl in one of our mills.'

The following instance of self-devotion, though not at all of uncommon occurrence, displays in a still more striking manner how ready these humble Irish people—not Scotch-Irish, as the miserable cant of the day has it, but Irish Celts—are to make every sacrifice for those they love. A poor Irish labourer emigrated to America in 1861, in the hope of bettering his condition, and being enabled, by hard work, to bring out his wife and seven children, whom he had been compelled to leave after him in Ireland. It was an unpropitious time for a working man, as the war had just broken out, and employment was scarce in many cities of the Union. All he required was an opportunity to work, his thoughts being for ever turned to the old land in which he left those who, he knew, looked to him as their only hope. For a time he was discouraged and desponding, but he resolved to wait awhile, and take advantage of any opportunity that would offer, through which he might be enabled to achieve his grand object—the bringing out of his wife and family. The opportunity did offer rather unexpectedly, and in this way—a gentleman who preferred the profits of a lucrative business to the risks of war, desired to obtain a substitute, who would take his place, for three years under the banner of the Union; and to secure some one to fight, or possibly die, in his place, he was willing to pay down One Thousand Dollars. The poor Irishman heard of this dazzling offer, and at once accepted it. The money was paid to the substitute, by whom it was thus disposed of: he placed it in the hands of a friend, directing him to send part to Ireland, to bring out his family, and reserve the balance to meet their wants on arrival—saying, if he was killed in battle, or if he died of sickness, he had done the best thing he could for his wife and children. He was quickly marched to the front, where the hot work was going on; but though he was in many a hard-fought battle, and saw death in every shape, he passed scathless through the dread ordeal—steel and lead seemed to have no power to injure him, nor did hunger and hardship break him down. He returned to his family, a bronzed war-worn soldier, and is now a hardworking honest citizen of a New England town. Your scornful 'Special Correspondent' would no doubt have set him down as a base mercenary, who hired himself to butcher his fellow-men; but such was not the opinion of those to whom the facts were known.

The gentleman—an eminent American physician—to whom I am indebted for this strong proof of family affection, says:—'In my professional visits I have met from time to time many instances where a father or a child, a brother or a sister, had made very great efforts and sacrifices to have enough of money to send to Ireland to bring out one or more members of their families. These are noble and beautiful examples of affection and disinterestedness, that have occurred in the obscure and humble life of the Irish emigrant in America, that cannot be surpassed, in my opinion, anywhere by sketches to be found in the biography of individuals or the history of nations.' The civilised world, less scornful or contemptuous than certain traducers of the humble Irish, will endorse that opinion.

Few instances of this 'affection and disinterestedness' could exceed that displayed by a mere child from Kilkenny. Pat —— was but thirteen years old when he determined, if possible, to go to America, having heard that he had an uncle who lived in St. Louis, Missouri. His idea of America was what might be expected from a child of his age,—his notion being, that every boy in that favoured country was his own master, and had a pony to ride whenever he wished for that enjoyment. His motive in urging his father and mother to consent to his perilous enterprise was the desire to make his fortune, and be able to bring out all his family, and make them, according to the story-book formula, 'as happy as the days are long.' The parents of the boy allowed themselves to be persuaded by him, especially as his uncle would be certain to receive and take care of him; and a steerage passage to New Orleans having been procured, the little fellow started on his venturous journey. Landing at New Orleans, he, knowing nothing of the country, imagined that he could easily walk to St. Louis, as he might from Kilkenny to the neighbouring town! Hearing that the goal of his hopes—the city in which his uncle lived—was nearly 2,000 miles distant, he was sorely afflicted. He went from steamboat to steamboat, asking sailor, steward, and captain, 'did they know his uncle? would they take him to St. Louis?' and telling them his name was Pat.

Sailors and stewards and captains of the Mississippi boats are not invariably the mildest of mortals; therefore it must not be a matter of surprise that the eager questions of the poor Irish boy with the beseeching eyes were more often replied to in a rough and surly manner than otherwise. If those to whom he applied troubled themselves to think of him at all, it was as a foolish or importunate cub who had no business to bother them with his stupid nonsense. What was his uncle to them? or did they care a cent whether his name was Pat Blank or Pat anything else? He was bade get about his business, and that quickly too. The child began to sob and pray; and as, sobbing and praying, and sorely bewildered, he was wandering about the levee, he was remarked by a kind-hearted gentleman, who asked him why he cried. He replied that he wanted to go to his uncle in St. Louis, and that no one would take him, and that he would gladly work his way. The meeting was providential, for there was not on the Mississippi a braver, a kinder, or a better man than Captain Durack, the Irish commander of one of the finest steamers that ever ran the risk of a snag or a blow-up. The captain had pity on the helpless child, and took him into his boat, where he at once made himself useful.

In fact, such was the willing spirit and gentle disposition of the little fellow, and such his anxiety to oblige everybody, that he became a general favourite. After a nine days' steaming, the vessel reached St. Louis, where Pat landed, high in hope, his pockets containing more money than he had ever before possessed, the passengers having liberally rewarded his willing services. He found his uncle, but found him—a confirmed drunkard, fast sinking into the grave which his own folly was hourly preparing for him. Cruelly disappointed in the hopes he had so fondly cherished, the boy again sought his friend the captain, who adopted him, and procured for him the appointment of assistant steward in a steamboat on the Upper Mississippi, in which position the young official earned money rapidly, and acquired the good wishes of all who knew him. His friend the captain was made his treasurer, likewise the repository of his hopes and intentions respecting his family at home. For them —his father and mother, his brother and two sisters—the boy offered up many a fervent prayer; and not unfrequently was he observed on his knees under the wheel-house absorbed in his devotions.

The boat, on arriving in port, would remain for an interval of a week or so, and during that time the young Irish lad would attend school, and in this way laid the foundation of his education. While he was thus employed, carefully hoarding his money, and acquiring by snatches some of the learning for which he eagerly strove, he was overwhelmed with the sad news that reached him from home,—that his father and mother were both dead, and that his brother and sisters were in the workhouse! He was so affected by this distressing intelligence, that his health gave way, and his kind protector the captain feared he was falling into a consumption.

The pious boy unburdened his sorrows to a good priest in St. Louis, who cheered him by his advice and sympathy. The vision of his little brother and sisters—the latter only eight and ten years old—in the workhouse, haunted him day and night. To rescue them from that degrading position, and bring them out as soon as possible, was now the great duty of his life; and with this additional motive for economy, every cent he could save was entrusted to the care of his patron and treasurer the captain. He sent 20l. to an uncle in Ireland, to pay for the passages and outfit of his brother and sisters, reserving something for their support on their arrival. Having achieved that first grand work, he next turned his attention to the object of his fondest ambition—the Priesthood; and he resolved, if possible, at once to commence the studies necessary for that sacred calling. He presented himself to the then Superior of the College of St. Mary, of the Barens, Missouri, to whom he confided his touching history and his passionate longing for a religious life. The good Irish priest was deeply impressed by the simple recital, and gave the lad a free place in the seminary. The zealous student soon went through all his studies, was ordained a priest, and became one of the most efficient missionaries of the diocese of St. Louis. The children, whom their brother's love had rescued perhaps from a life of poverty, arrived safely; the infant sisters were adopted by a community of the Sacred Heart in the same diocese, and the brother is a respectable member of one of the learned professions.

An instance of the courage and energy which a mother's affection inspires may be given in the simple language of the poor woman who tells the artless story of her trials. The family were well off so long as the husband lived; but, when he died, the widow was compelled to accept a few pounds in lieu of valuable improvements which her husband had effected on two farms. Left with four children, and seeing her little fund diminishing day by day, and dreading that the poor-house would be their fate if she did not make some desperate effort to save them from such a calamity, she resolved to start for America herself, and there, by hard work, earn as much as would bring them out; and this determination she resolutely acted upon. Telling, in happier times, of her past trials, she used these words:—

'Oh, it would break the heart of a stone to see my four little children on the road, crying after me. My heart, sure enough, was near breaking with the sorrow that day. I ran as hard as I could away from them, for they cried and bawled; and it was "Oh, mammy, mammy! Oh, don't lave us! Oh come back, mammy, mammy!"—it went through and through me like a swoord. I had to look back, no matter though I tried not to do so, and I thought the seven senses would jump out of my two eyes. Poor little Patsey was then about four years old, and he ran after me, and cried "Mammy, mammy!" bigger than the rest. Sure my legs couldn't carry me any farther. He kissed me, and asked me to give him another penny: he didn't know where I was going to, or how long I'd be away, poor darling. This broke my heart entirely—I declare to you I don't know how I got away from them—it was like a bad drame to me. Well, we landed in Quebec, and I didn't know a sowl on God's earth, but a neighbour's boy of my own; and sure I thought that N—— (meaning a place nearly a thousand miles away) was the next ploughland to Quebec! They put me in a boat, and I felt as if it took us months to come to N——, for I was nearly perished with the could and the hunger. Sure the cattle passengers are treated better than the Christians. When I came to N——, I lived with a farmer. I worked hard all the day, and cried the most of the night. No wonder, for I was wanst full and comfortable at home, with my cows, and my pigs, and my horses, till my husband died—God rest his sowl! But, begonnies, in three months I was able to send home for the ouldest little girl—she was only nine years of age. When she came out, it warmed my poor heart; but she was a great care to me—I had to pay $4 a month for her boord, and that was hard enough. After a time I says to myself, "This will never do; paying $4 a month won't help me to bring out the rest of the children, poor things;" so I went and looked out for another place, and God sent me one.

I hired as a cook, and the little girl was taken to nurse the babby for her boord. I took great courage then entirely, and in half a year more I sent for another of the children. But I axed the priest—who was from my own place at home—to lend me the loan of the passages for the other two, and I would pay him, as sure as the Lord was in heaven. He did, sure enough, trust me with the money, and so he might;

and may the Heavens be his bed for that same, amen! The three landed safe into my arms; then I felt I was a happy woman—and I cried that night at my prayers—but it was not like the scalding tears on the road, when I was laving them, and every step was like tearing the heart clane out of me: them tears, that night, did me good. The children were soon able to earn for themselves, and now, thanks be to the Lord! we are all comfortable and happy—no thanks to the villain of a landlord for that same; and the big boy, the Lord mark him to grace! is now able to read his fine books of Greek and Latin, and knows more than Murty Dermody, the schoolmaster in our parts. Oh, the health was a grand thing; that and the help of the Lord, glory be to his holy name! got me through; for, if I had a pain or an ache, the fear would come on me—and what would become of the children? 'Twas hard work enough; but sure the Lord fits the back to the burthen.'

'It would be quite impossible,' said a Sister of Mercy of New York, 'to relate half the instances of heroic sacrifices made for parents or other relatives by Irish girls that come to our knowledge.' Not the less heroic that they are entirely divested of dramatic interest or sensational attraction. Hannah Finn, a poor girl from the county of Limerick, was not just the person or the type a novelist or a poet would have chosen for story or for verse; and yet her life was one of the most complete self-sacrifice. At home she had toiled on a farm, and was therefore unaccustomed to house-work; yet, on her arrival in New York, whither she came in order that she might more effectually assist the old people whom she could not bring with her, she hired herself as 'cook's helper' in one of its hotels, preferring that situation to an easier place, that she might earn higher wages, and thus have more to send to her parents, to whose comfort she devoted her life. Twice a year she sent to them all the money she had saved, and always to the care of the parish priest. In the midst of her hard patient toil she received the sad tidings of her father being obliged 'to leave the land,' at which her heart was sorely troubled. But she only toiled the harder, and saved the more.

On the next occasion she was sending money, the Sister who wrote the letter for her wished to direct it to the place indicated by the girl's mother—the village to which the landless couple had removed; but Hannah persisted in sending it to the care of her former pastor, declaring that she would not send a penny of her money to anyone else. She continued to send her earnings regularly home as long as the old people lived; and soon after their death—her mission being now accomplished—she herself died of dropsy. To the charity of others she was indebted for assistance during her last illness, she having given everything to her parents, and reserved nothing for herself. The story of Hannah Finn, the poor county Limerick girl, the patient drudge in the New York kitchen, is that of many an Irish girl in America, to which they have emigrated rather with the purpose of helping those at home than of advancing their own fortunes.

When a passage is paid for by an Irish emigrant to bring out a member of the family, it is the custom, when sending the ticket, to accompany it with a few pounds to defray incidental expenses.

As a rule, those who are newly come send more and make greater sacrifices to bring out their relatives, or to assist them at home, than those who have been longer in the country: the wants of the family in the old country are more vividly present to the mind of the recent emigrant, and perhaps the affections are warmer and stronger than in after years, when time and distance, and the cares or distractions of a new existence, have insensibly dulled the passionate longings of yore. But thousands—many, many thousands—of Irish girls have devoted, do devote, and will devote their lives, and sacrifice every woman's hope, to the holiest, because the most unselfish, of all affections—that of family and kindred.

'I would say, from my own experience, as agent and otherwise,' remarked an agent in a New England State, 'that emigration will never cease with Irish families as long as any portion of them remain at each side of the Atlantic, and as long as those at this side find means to send for these they left behind—or so long as the Irish nature remains what it is; and I must say I can't see much change in it as yet.'

That the amount of money sent from America, including the British Provinces, to Ireland cannot be far from 24,000,000l. I feel assured. The Commissioners of Emigration, in their Report of 1863, return the amount as 12,642,000l. But they say it would not be unreasonable to estimate the amount, of which there are no returns, at half as much again as that of which there are returns. Taking this rather moderate estimate, the gross amount to the close of 1862 would reach 19,000,000l. That at least a million a year has been sent since then must be assumed. For last year—1866—the Commissioners put down the amount at less than half a million. But I am aware that, for that year, one bank or society in New York—the Irish Emigrant Society—remitted over 100,000l. to Ireland, and that some 130,000l. was sent by agents in Boston whom I could name. Here, then, is more than half the entire amount of which the Commissioners have any official knowledge. In many cities I personally know bankers or agents who sent amounts varying from 20,000l. to 30,000l.; and there is scarcely a place of any importance, or in which there is an Irish population, however inconsiderable, from which some contribution does not go to the old country, for one purpose or another. If, then, we add a million a year to the nineteen millions estimated by the Emigration Commissioners, we have, up to the 1st of January 1868, the amazing sum of 24,000,000l. sent by the Irish abroad to their relatives at home. In the history of the world there is nothing to match this. It is a fact as glorious as stupendous, and may well stand against the sneers and calumnies of a century.

CHAPTER XVII

The Character of Irish Women in America—An Unwelcome Baptism—The Universal Testimony—Shadows—Perils to Female Virtue—Irish Girls; their Value to the Race

A QUESTION of unspeakable importance may be thus put,—is it true that Irish women maintain in America their traditional reputation for virtue? Unhesitatingly, it must be answered in the affirmative. Whatever estimate Americans may form of their Irish fellow-citizens, be that estimate favourable or unfavourable, there is but one opinion as to the moral character of Irish women. Their reputation for purity does not rest on the boastful assertions of those who either regard all matters concerning their race or country from a favourable point of view, or who, to gratify a natural feeling, would wilfully exaggerate, or possibly misstate a fact: it is universally admitted. Were it otherwise—were this reputation not well-founded, sad indeed would be the calamity to the Irish in America, —to their character, position, future—to them and to their descendants. Happily, no such calamity is likely to befall the Irish in America, as the loss to the Irish woman of her pre-eminent reputation for purity and honour. Prejudices, strong prejudices, there are in the States, as in all countries in which diversity of race and religion exists; and where this diversity comprehends race and religion in the same individuals, these prejudices are certain to be the stronger and the more deeply rooted.

The Irish Catholic has to contend against this double prejudice, which nevertheless is not powerful enough to interfere with the conviction, indeed admission, as to the moral character of the women of that country and that faith. The poor Irish emigrant girl may possibly be rude, undisciplined, awkward —-just arrived in a strange land, with all the rugged simplicity of her peasant's training; but she is good and honest. Nor, as she rapidly acquires the refinement inseparable from an improved condition of life, and daily association with people of cultivated manners, does she catch the contagion of the vices of the great centres of wealth and luxury. Whatever her position,—and it is principally amongst the humble walks of life the mass of the Irish are still to be found,—she maintains this one noble characteristic—purity. In domestic service her merit is fully recognised. Once satisfied of the genuineness of her character, an American family will trust in her implicitly; and not only is there no locking up against her, but everything is left in her charge. Occasionally she may be hot-tempered, difficult to be managed, perhaps a little 'turbulent'—especially when her country is sneered at, or her faith is wantonly ridiculed; but she is cheerful and laborious, virtuous and faithful.

An instance of very legitimate 'turbulence' occurred not long since in one of the most rising of the great Western cities. There lived, as a 'help,' in the house of a

Protestant family an intelligent and high-spirited Irish girl, remarkable for her exemplary conduct, and the zeal with which she discharged the duties of her position. Kate acted as a mother to a young brother and sister, whom she was bringing up with the greatest care; and a happy girl was Kate when she received good tidings of their progress in knowledge and piety. Kate, like many other people in the world, had her special torment, and that special torment was a playful-minded preacher who visited at the house, and who looked upon 'Bridget'—he *would* call her Bridget—as a fair butt for the exercise of his pleasant wit, of which he was justly proud. It was Kate's duty to attend table; and no sooner did she make her appearance in the dining-room, than the playful preacher commenced his usual fun, which would be somewhat in this fashion: 'Well, Bridget, my girl! when did you pray last to the Virgin Mary? Tell me, Bridget, when were you with Father Pat? What did you give him, Bridget? What did the old fellow ask for the absolution this time? Now, I guess it was ten cents for the small sins, and $1 for the thumpers! Come now, Bridget, tell me what penance did that priest of yours give you?'

Thus would the agreeable jester pelt the poor Irish girl with his generous pleasantries, to the amusement of the thoughtless, but to the serious annoyance of the fair-minded, who did not like to see her feelings so wantonly wounded. The mistress of the house mildly remonstrated with her servant's lively tormentor, though she did not herself admire 'Bridget's' form of prayer, and was willing to regard 'Father Pat's' absolution as a matter of bargain and sale. But the wit should have his way. 'Bridget' was a handsome girl, and the rogue liked to see the fire kindle in her grey eye, and the hot blood mantle over her fair round cheek; and then the laughter of his admirers was such delightful incense to his vanity, as peal after peal told how successfully the incorrigible wag 'roasted Bridget.' On one memorable day, however, his love of the humorous carried him just too far. A large company was assembled round the hospitable table of the mistress of the house. The preacher was present, and was brimming over with merriment. Kate entered the room, bearing a large tureen of steaming soup in her hands. 'Ho, ho, Bridget!—how are you, Bridget? Well, Bridget, what did you pay Father Pat for absolution this time? Come to me, Bridget, and I will give you as many dollars as will set you all straight with the old fellow for the next six months, and settle your account with purgatory too. Now, Bridget, tell us how many cents for each sin?' The girl had just reached the preacher as he finished his little joke; and if he wished to see the Irish eye flash out its light, and the Irish blood burn in the cheek, he had an excellent opportunity for enjoying that treat.

It was Bridget's turn to be playful. Stopping next to his chair, and looking him steadily in his face, while she grasped the tureen of rich green-pea soup more firmly in her hands, she said: 'Now, sir, I often asked you to leave me alone, and not mind me, and not to insult me or my religion, what no real gentleman would do to a poor girl; and now, sir, as you want to know what I pay for absolution, here's my answer!' and, suiting the action to the word, she flung the hot steaming liquid over the face, neck, breast—entire person —of the playful preacher! A 'header' in one of Mr. Boucicault's dramas could not have produced a more startling effect than did this unexpected baptism. The condition of the preacher may best be described as abject: morally as well as physically, he was overwhelmed. Kate rushed to her room, locked herself in, and relieved her excitement in a cry—'as if her heart would break.' In a short time her mistress tapped at the door, told her to come out, that all was right, and that Mr. Blank was sorry that he had annoyed her—as, no doubt, he was. The sentiment—the generous American sentiment—was in Kate's favour, as she might have perceived in the manner of the guests. For the poor preacher, it may be said that the soup 'spoiled his dinner' for that day. He did not make his appearance again for some time; but when he did, it was as an altered and much-improved gentleman, who appeared to have lost all interest in the religious peculiarities of Kate, whom, strange to say, he never more called by the name of Bridget. The warm bath, so vigorously administered, had done him much service—Kate said, 'a power of good.'

When once her worth is recognised, the most unlimited trust is placed in the Irish girl. There are thousands of houses in the United States in which everything is left to her charge and under her control; and, unless in some rare instances, in which fanaticism is more than a match for common sense, the more devoted she is to the practices of her religion, the more is she respected and confided in by those with whom she lives. Occasional betrayals of trust there may be, for humanity is not perfect; but as a rule, broad and sweeping, confidence and kindness are rewarded with unswerving fidelity.

In the hotels of America the Irish girl is admittedly indispensable. Through the ordeal of these fiery furnaces of temptation she passes unscathed. There, where honesty and good conduct are most essential, she is found equal to the test, while in cheerful willing industry none can surpass her. Such is the testimony which is readily borne to the Irish girl in every State of the Union.

I remember asking one of the best-known hotel proprietors of America, why it was that all the young women in the establishment were Irish, and his replying—'The thing is very simple: the Irish girls are industrious, willing, cheerful, and honest—they work hard, and they are strictly moral. I should say that is quite reason enough.' I agreed with him.

There are testimonies, also, borne to her in a very different spirit, but equally honouring—those extorted from the baffled tempter, who finds all his arts of seduction fail before the seven-fold shield of an austerity as unexpected as unwished-for. Nothing is more common than for one who has failed in his attempts against the honour of an Irish girl to warn his companions from a similar folly—'Oh, hang her!—don't lose your time with *her*; she is one of those d——d Irish girls—the priest has a hold of her—she goes to confession, and all that kind of nonsense —don't lose your time, for it's no use.' Quite true: temptations assail her in vain; in her faith and piety she is invincible.

The Irish woman is naturally religious; the fervent character of her mind is adapted to devotional enthusiasm; and in the practices of her faith she finds occupation for her leisure time, as well as strength for her soul and consolation for her heart. If she happen to be in a new mission, where everything—church, school, asylum, hospital—is to be erected, she enters into the holy task with congenial ardour. To build up, finish, or decorate a church—to her, the House of God and Temple of her Ancient Faith—she contributes with generous hand. It is the same in a long-established parish, whose spiritual necessities keep pace with its growing population; there, also, the Irish girl is unfailing in her liberality. To her there is no idea of making a sacrifice of her means; she gives as well from pleasure as from a feeling of duty. Appeal to her in the name of her religion or country, for the sick or the suffering, and seldom indeed is it that there is no response from her purse and her heart. The Irish girl —whether in store, factory, hotel, or domestic employment—takes pride in renting a seat in her church, which she has so materially helped to erect; and in nearly every city in the Union she may be seen occupying her place in her pew, neat in person, modest in deportment, and collected in manner—as true an honour to her race and country as though the blood of princes flowed in her veins. Thus is maintained over her that religious control which is her own best preservative against danger, and which, while forming and strengthening her character, enables her to bring a salutary influence to bear upon her male relatives, and in case of her marriage—a contingency most probable—upon her husband and children. And this is how the purity and piety of the Irish women are of priceless value to the Irish in America.

To assert that there are no dark shadows to this picture, no murky tints to throw out in stronger relief its prevailing brightness of colour, would be to assert an untruth at once foolish and mischievous. There are dark shadows, there are murky tints—there are exceptions to a rule which is almost universal. Under ordinary circumstances the rule is absolutely in favour of the high moral character of Irish women in America; but there are in some of the great cities circumstances not favourable to female virtue; and these are attended with occasional injury to the reputation of Irish girls.

It is well known that America, while the home of the strong, the adventurous, the honest and industrious of the emigrants from Europe, is also the asylum of the broken-down and the unfortunate. Female frailty seeks refuge from exposure in those convenient hiding-places, the great cities of the Western World. Nor is it always the case that a first fall is atoned for by a future of virtue, or even a career of prudence; and thus the sad wreck which has happened at one side of the ocean is unfairly counted against the moral character of the race at the other. Here then, in the first place, is frailty imported from the old country, and under circumstances not altogether favourable to reformation and moral strength.

Then, without seeking other evidence than may be found in public records, and in the statute-book of the United States, it can be shown how fatal to youth and inexperience has been the long passage in the emigrant sailing ship. As mentioned elsewhere, Congress was compelled, so late as 1860, to pass a law for the protection of female passengers from the foul and systematic attempts of officers and seamen to effect their ruin. Regulations have been made, rules laid down, penalties proclaimed, notices posted, partitions and barriers erected; but all precautionary measures have been, in too many instances, found ineffectual to counteract the watchful wickedness of evil men, and the utter defencelessness of women exposed to the perils of a protracted sea voyage. Even so late as 1866 the Government Commissioner of Emigration reports to the Secretary of State that these protective laws have been systematically violated, and calls for more stringent measures. Nor when the poor Irish girl has escaped her enemy on ship-board, and reached the shelter of Castle Garden, is she entirely in safety; and not rarely has it occurred that the indignant officials have beaten back the prowling wolf, as he sought to get his intended victim within his grasp. Numerous instances, not alone of seduction on board ship, but of lawless violence, are on record; but the Act of 1860 is of itself sufficient evidence of the fact that protection was required, without the necessity of its illustration by harrowing and revolting details.

Terribly suggestive of ruin to female honour were the words addressed by Mr. Thurlow Weed in 1864, on the occasion of laying the foundation, stone of the Emigrant Hospital at Ward's Island. Referring to the helpless condition of the emigrant before the present admirable system was organised in New York, he says: 'Families were frequently plundered of all the money they possessed, and left to the charity of the city. Young and friendless females coming from abroad, to find their friends, or seeking employment, *were not unfrequently outraged.*' Again: 'Thousands of emigrants arrived with railroad tickets purchased abroad, for which they had paid not only double and treble the regular fare, but upon their arrival here, they found themselves with bogus tickets and bogus drafts. *Innocent and unprotected girls came consigned to houses of prostitution.*' Mr. Weed was referring to what frequently occurred some years before; but it is notorious that similar evils have existed at a later period, and are not yet effectually suppressed. The panderers to the lust of great cities are constantly on the watch to drag into their dens of infamy the young, the innocent, and the unsuspecting. There is scarcely a House of Protection under the care of a Religious Order in America, which cannot record cases of young girls snatched from the jaws of danger. Many, it is true, are saved; but what can the helpless do against, the snares and traps and frauds of those who live by the vilest crime? The contest is unequal: the lamb is helpless in the talons of the vulture, or the fangs of the wolf. As a single instance of the peril awaiting the unsuspecting, may be mentioned that of a young and handsome Irish girl who was lately trapped into hiring, in a Western city, with a person of infamous character. She was fortunately observed by a poor old Irish woman, who, knowing the peril in which the young creature stood, boldly rushed to her rescue, and, at personal risk to herself, literally tore the prey from the grasp of the enemy. The rescued girl was taken to the Refuge in the Convent of Mercy, where she was at once in safety; and though she lost all her clothes, save those in which she then stood, she congratulated herself that she had never crossed the threshold of a house of ill-fame.

Perils by sea, and perils by land, is it wonderful that fraud and violence so often triumph over innocence and helplessness?—that human wrecks occasionally strew the highways of the centres of wealth, of luxury, and of vice?

I have in another place referred to the evils of overcrowding, in lowering the tone of the community, and exposing the humbler classes to dangers of various kinds, moral as well as sanitary. Besides the temptations of poverty and passion, of youth and thoughtlessness, there is the terrible mischief of daily and hourly association in the densely-populated lodging-house, in which it too often happens that, even with the best intentions, the most ordinary decency cannot be maintained. There is not a physician or a clergyman in New York who will not say that this system is fraught with danger to the health of soul and body. It is in the last degree unfavourable to the development of virtue; and the same state of things, wherever it is to be found, whether East or West, North or South, must be productive of evil fruits.

There are also the natural consequences of the vicious habits of parents—the drunkenness of the father or the mother, more usually the former—so fatal to the character of their children. This habit alone is quite as destructive in its consequences as orphanage, which, from this more than any other cause, is so prevalent in America, where, at least in the towns, the average duration of human life—especially that of the hard-working classes who are not temperate—is so short. Then there is vanity, love of dress, and perhaps individual perversity, acted upon through all the evil influences of great cities—with the wiles and snares of the fowler ever spread for the destruction of the fluttering bird. These and other causes will explain why it is, that in some, yet comparatively few, places in America a certain percentage of women of bad repute are necessarily of Irish origin.

But, however deplorable that, in any part of the United States, Irish women should form an appreciable percentage of the whole of the class of unfortunates, still, when compared with the Irish female population of those great cities, whether Irish born or of Irish extraction, the number is small indeed. In very many places the proportion is infinitesimal; and there are cities and districts throughout the States in which there has never been known an instance of an Irish girl having come to shame—in which the character of the Irish woman is the pride and glory of all who belong to the old country, or have a drop of genuine Irish blood in their veins.

I have frequently marked with interest, how the countenance of the faithful pastor brightened with enthusiasm as the good conduct of the female portion of his flock was the theme of conversation. I remember an excellent Irish priest—one of those men who are justly looked upon as the fathers of their people—describing the character of his congregation. It was in a town of considerable importance, eminent for its manufacturing industry, and in which the Irish element was particularly strong. 'Good, sir! the Irish girls good! Why, sir,' said their pastor, 'the fall of an Irish girl in this town is as rare as—as—as a white blackbird'—and a pleasant laugh imparted additional raciness to an illustration which its author regarded as both neat and happy. 'Our Irish girls are an honour to their country and their race—they are the glory of the Church; to their influence we look for much of what we hope for in the future. They will yet lift the men to their level by the force of their example.' This was the grave testimony borne by a Western Bishop. 'They are the salvation of their race in this country—the salt of the earth,' said an enthusiastic Southern Prelate. The salt of the earth, indeed; and if the salt should lose its savour, wherewith shall the earth be salted? 'My belief is, that the Holy Ghost has them in special charge, for the good they do, and the evil they prevent.' This was the wind-up of a long eulogium pronounced upon Irish girls by an eminent ecclesiastic, who spoke with all the earnestness and gravity of the most profound conviction.

That would be a sad day for the Irish in America when Irish women lost the reputation which, notwithstanding the evil produced by adverse circumstances and special causes, they universally enjoy. The Irish nature is impetuous and impulsive and passionate, and the young are too often liable to confound license with the display of manly independence; hence even the light yoke of the Church is occasionally too burdensome for the high-mettled Irish youth, in an especial degree the American-born sons of Irish parents. In what, then, if not in the beautiful faith and piety, the unblemished purity of Irish women—in the never-failing example of sister, wife, and mother—are those who love the race to look for a counteracting influence to a freedom fraught with danger, and for that strong yet delicate chain of gold with which to bind the wayward and the headstrong to the Church of their fathers? As yet, as possibly for some time to come, congregations are more numerous than churches, flocks than pastors, children than schools or teachers—such schools and teachers as are most required; and in the meantime, until in churches and pastors, schools and teachers, protection is everywhere afforded to endangered youth, in the piety and purity of the sister and the mother is there the best safeguard against the risk of apostasy, and the deadlier blight of infidelity. Long may the virtue of Irish women constitute one of the noblest claims on the respect and sympathy of the generous-minded people of America!

CHAPTER XVIII

The Catholic Church—The Irish—The Church not afraid of Freedom—A Contrast—Who the Persecutors were—The American Constitution— Washington's Reply to the Catholics—The First Church in New York—Boston in 1790—Universality of the Church—Early Missions—Two Great Orders—Mrs. Seton—Mrs. Seton founds her Order—Early Difficulties and Privations—Irish Sisters

TO their countrymen throughout the world the spiritual condition of the Irish in America cannot be otherwise than a matter of the deepest interest, inasmuch as their material progress in the New World must of necessity, and to a considerable extent, depend on the moral and religious influence brought to bear upon them and their children. The great mass of the Irish in the United States, as in Ireland, are of the Catholic faith: therefore, in order to ascertain what is the spiritual condition of the Irish in America, what the spiritual provision for them, we must enquire as to the position and prospects of the Catholic Church in that country.

But first, before doing so, it is necessary to refer to statements which have been made by some, and relied on by others, as to the alleged falling away of the Irish from the faith of their fathers. Were this statement true, it should be a matter of regret to every Irishman worthy of that name; for nothing could be more calamitous to the race, or more damaging to the honour of their country, than the loss of that which maintains over the Irish heart the most salutary of all influences. Happily for the Irish in America, these statements are the result of exaggerated alarm, or reckless invention.

It has been confidently stated that the moment the Irish touch the free soil of America they lose the old faith—that there is something in the very nature of Republican institutions fatal to the Church of Rome. Admitting, as a fact which cannot he denied, and which Catholics are themselves the first to proclaim, that there have been some, even considerable, falling off from the Church, and no little indifferentism, it must be acknowledged that there has been less of both than, from the circumstances of the country, might have been reasonably expected; and that the same Irish, whose alleged defection en masse has been the theme of ungenerous triumph to those whose 'wish was father to the thought,' have done more to develop the Church, and extend her dominion throughout the wide continent of North America, than even the most devoted of the children of any other of the various races who, with them, are merged in the great American nation. This much may be freely conceded to them, even by those who are most sensitively and justly proud of what their own nationality has done to promote the glory of the Universal Church. Fortified by suffering and trial at home, and inheritors of memories which intensify devotion rather than weaken fidelity, the Irish brought with them a strong faith, the power to resist as well as the courage to persevere, and that generosity of spirit which has ever prompted mankind to make large sacrifices for the promotion of their religious belief.

Those who foolishly think, or pretend to think, that there is something in Republican institutions fatal to the extension and influence of the Catholic Church, must be ignorant of, or wilfully ignore, the evidence of history, or what is going on in the world at the present day; or must have conceived the most erroneous impressions concerning the actual position of the Church in the United States. Not only, throughout her long and chequered history, has the Church flourished under Republican governments, and that at this moment among her faithful subjects are to be found the most strenuous supporters of Republican institutions, as in America and the Catholic Cantons of Switzerland; but it is one of the striking characteristics of the Church—conceded to her even by her enemies—that she has the marvellous faculty of adapting herself to every form of government,, and to every description of human institution. Instinctively conservative—that is, of those great principles which lie at the root of all civil government, and are reverenced in every well-ordered state of society—she fully appreciates the blessings of liberty, and flourishes in vigour under the very freest form of national constitution. In every region she is readily acclimated—in every soil she takes firm hold; nay, even where she is trampled upon and persecuted, the sweeter is the odour she gives forth.

Her progress in the United States has not been over a path bestrewn with roses; but not only are the persecutions and sufferings of other days the glory of the present hour, but they have given her strength to meet with fortitude, and endure with undiminished confidence, those spasmodic outbursts of violence which are born of the mad frenzy of the moment. Under the wise guidance of able and sagacious prelates, no less patriots than churchmen—devoted to the greatness and renown of the noble country of their birth or of their adoption—the Catholic Church is not only adapting herself to the genius of the American people, and in complete harmony with her institutions, but, so far as her influence extends, is one of the most efficient means of maintaining social order and promoting public contentment. And we shall see how, in the moment of the gravest peril that ever overtook a people or tried a Church, when others waved the torch and rang the tocsin peal, she retained her holy serenity in the midst of strife; and while sounds of hate and fury reverberated through so-called temples of religion, she calmly preached her mission of peace on earth, to men of good will.

That there has been falling away, is true—that there is indifference, no one can doubt; but the falling away is not what exaggeration has represented it to be, and is moreover largely compensated by the most valuable acquisitions; and the spirit of indifferentism, which is the form of religious disease most prevalent in the United

States, is steadily yielding to the zeal of the Church, and its fuller and more perfect organisation.

To appreciate rightly what has been accomplished, we must look back; and in order to understand what the Church had to contend with, what obstacles she had to surmount, what she had to create and build up, it is essential that a sketch—for anything more formal would be impossible, and indeed out of place, in this volume—should be given of her position before and at the period when the emigration from Europe began seriously to influence the population of the United States.

So long as England retained her power in her American colonies, persecution and proscription were the lot of her Catholic subjects. It was the same at both sides of the Atlantic—cruel laws and degrading disabilities. If anything, her colonial governors and legislators outdid in violence and malignity the policy of the mother country; for, strange as it must appear, and however dishonouring to our human nature, it is nevertheless the fact, that those who fled from persecution, who braved the stormy ocean in frail vessels, to escape from the tyranny of a sect or a government, became relentless in their persecution of others who, like themselves, had hoped to find a peaceful home and a safe asylum in a new and happy country. The Puritans of New England outdid, in their fierce intolerance, those whose milder tyranny had compelled them to seek relief in exile. The contrast offered by the different policy pursued by Catholic and Puritan colonists should put to shame those who are so lavish in their accusations of Catholic persecution. When the Catholics had power or influence, they proclaimed the broadest toleration, the fullest liberty to every sect of Christians; while, on the contrary, not only were Catholics in a special degree the objects of persecution in every colony, and by every governor or legislature, but the zealots who persecuted them did not refrain from persecuting people of other denominations. We may refer to the conduct of the Catholic settlers of Maryland, and of the Catholics during the only time they ever possessed any influence in the State of New York, and contrast their enlightened policy with the laws against Quakers and Catholics—the latter of which laws were not erased from the statute-book until after America had accomplished her independence.

The code of the New England colonies was conceived in the most ferocious spirit, and was enforced with relentless severity. A single extract from the law passed at Plymouth on the 14th of October 1657, will be sufficient to display the mild and Christian policy of those who themselves had suffered for conscience' sake:—

And it is further enacted, that if any Quaker or Quakers shall presume, after they have once suffered what the law requireth, to come into this jurisdiction, every such male Quaker shall, for the first offence, *have one of his ears cut off*, and be kept at work in the house of correction till he can be sent away at his own charge; and for the second offence, *shall have the other ear cut off*, &c., and be kept at the house of correction as aforesaid. And every woman Quaker that hath suffered the law here, that shall presume to come into this jurisdiction, *shall be severely whipt*, and kept at the house of correction till she be sent away at her own charge, and so also for her coming again she shall be alike used as aforesaid. And for every Quaker, he or she, that shall a third time herein again offend, *they shall have their tongues bored through with a hot iron*, and kept at the house of correction till they be sent away at their own charge.

The offence thus fiendishly punished was the mere coming of any of these harmless people within the jurisdiction of those ardent worshippers of human freedom and religious liberty. It were hard to say whether the Puritan was more ferociously in earnest in his persecution of Quakers and Catholics than in his extermination of witches —for a profound belief in witchcraft was one of the most striking evidences of his enlightenment and good sense.

Bancroft, the historian of America, thus describes the state of things in the Catholic colony of Baltimore:—

Yet the happiness of the colony was enviable. The persecuted and the unhappy thronged to the domains of the benevolent prince. If Baltimore was, in one sense, a monarch—like Miltiades at Chersonnesus, and other founders of colonies of old— his monarchy was tolerable to the exile who sought for freedom and repose. Numerous ships found employment in his harbours. The white labourer rose rapidly to the condition of a free proprietor; the female emigrant was sure to improve her condition, and the cheerful charities of home gathered round her in the New World. ....

Emigrants arrived from every clime; and the colonial legislature extended its sympathies to many nations, as well as to many sects. From France came Huguenots; from Germany, from Holland, from Sweden, from Finland, I believe from Piedmont, *the children of misfortune sought protection under the tolerant sceptre of the Roman Catholic*. Bohemia itself, the country of Jerome and of Huss, sent forth their sons, who at once were made citizens of Maryland with equal franchises. The empire of justice and humanity, according to the light of those days, had been complete but for the sufferings of the people called Quakers. Yet they were not persecuted for their religious worship, which was held publicly, and without interruption. 'The truth was received with reverence and gladness;' and with secret satisfaction George Fox relates that members of the legislature and the council, persons of quality, and justices of the peace, were present at a large and very heavenly meeting.

This was in 1668, but in a few years after the arrival of William Penn, the Quakers had full justice done to them, In Catholic Maryland there had been no ear-cropping, no boring of tongues with hot pokers—such exhibitions of brotherly love and mercy were reserved for the Puritans of Plymouth.

'The apologist of Lord Baltimore,' says Bancroft, 'could assert that his government, in conformity with his strict and repeated injunctions, had never given disturbance to any person in Maryland for matter of religion; that the colonists enjoyed freedom of conscience, not less than freedom of person and estate, as amply as ever any people in any place in the world. The disfranchised friends of prelacy from Massachusetts and the Puritan from Virginia *were welcomed to equal liberty of conscience and political rights in the Roman Catholic province of Maryland.'* These halcyon days did not long continue; for when the Protestants got the upper hand in Maryland, they persecuted the Catholics, who had extended toleration and liberty to all!

We shall now see how Catholics were treated in New York. In 1683 Colonel Thomas Dongan, a Catholic, was sent out as governor, and under his liberal administration the Legislative Assembly—the first which was convoked—proclaimed that 'no person or persons, which profess faith in God by Jesus Christ, shall at any time be any way molested, punished, disquieted, or called in question for any difference of opinion or matter of religious concernment, who do not actually disturb the civil peace of the province; but that all and every such person or persons may, from time to time, and at all times, freely have and fully enjoy his or their judgments or consciences, in matters of religion, throughout all the province—they behaving themselves peaceably and quietly, and not using this liberty to licentiousness, nor to the civil injury, nor outward disturbance of others.' By another article, all denominations then in the province were secured the free exercise of their discipline and forms, and the same privilege extended to such as might come. Bancroft describes this Charter of Liberty as eliminating 'the intolerance and superstition of the early codes of Puritanism.'

The New York Assembly of 1691 declared null and void the acts of the Assembly of 1683, and, instead of the Charter of Liberties, passed a Bill of Rights, which expressly excluded Catholics from all participation in the privileges which it conferred. It had been the same in Maryland, where Catholics had first proclaimed religious liberty, and where the Protestants, who soon gained the ascendancy, proscribed the Papists and their creed.

In 1690 a wicked law was passed, enacting that any priest coming into the colony, or remaining in it after a certain day, should be deemed an incendiary and disturber of the public peace and safety, and an enemy to the true Christian religion, and adjudged to suffer perpetual imprisonment. If he escaped, and were retaken, death was the penalty. And any one who harboured a priest was made liable to a fine of 300l., and to stand three days in the pillory. In 1701 Catholics were excluded from office, and deprived of the right of voting; and in the following year they were specially excluded from sharing in the liberty of conscience granted by Queen Anne to all the inhabitants of New York.

It may be easily imagined that, whatever their condition at home, there was little inducement for Irish Catholics to emigrate to the American colonies while under British rule, and so long as the spirit of their laws was more than a faithful reflection of the odious intolerance breathing in every page of the statute-book of

England. They did come, nevertheless, and, though not in great numbers, they were to be found scattered over the country in various directions, and carrying on business in New York and other of the principal cities.

The Revolution did much for the Catholics of America, if not to change the public sentiment in their favour, at least to afford them relief from positive persecution. No doubt, men of just and generous minds, like Washington, would, without the pressure of special circumstances, have been willing to extend the same liberty to Catholics as to all other religious sects; but had there not existed the necessity of endeavouring to conciliate, or even neutralise, the Catholics of Canada, and of not offending the pride of France, a Catholic nation which had rendered such material assistance to the revolted colonies of England, it is possible they might not so soon have been allowed to participate in the full measure of freedom secured to the citizens of the infant Republic. Even the fact that Catholics—soldiers and merchants, and among them gallant and high-spirited Irishmen—distinguished themselves by their heroism and generosity in the cause of American independence, would not, of itself, have been sufficient to break down the barriers of exclusiveness which intolerance and fanaticism had raised against the just claims of that faithful but persecuted body of Christians.

There is little mention made of religious matters in the Constitution, but what is there proclaimed has often since been appealed to, and will many times again be appealed to, as the solemn declaration of a great and fundamental principle of religious toleration and equality. 'No *religious test shall ever be required as a qualification to any office or public trust under the United States.*' 'Congress *shall make no law respecting an establishment of religion, or prohibiting the free exercise thereof.*' This is the entire; but it was like a grand key-note, to regulate all future legislation, which ought to be in harmony with the principle embodied in these few but memorable words, It rather pointed out to the thirteen States then in the Union what they ought to do, than what they should not do. This broad proclamation notwithstanding, each State was at full liberty to legislate according to its own views, in reference to the important matter of religion. This is put clearly by the authors of 'The *Catholic Church in the United States:*'—

The original thirteen States, one after another, granted to the Catholics liberty of conscience, but many of them long refused the Catholics civil and political rights. Thus it is only since 1806 that Catholics, to hold office in the State of New York, have been dispensed with a solemn abjuration of all obedience to a foreign ecclesiastical power. Down to January 1, 1836, to be an elector and eligible in the State of North Carolina, it was necessary to swear a belief in the truth of the Protestant religion. In New Jersey, a clause excluding Catholics from all offices was only abolished in 1844. And even now (1856), eighty years after the Declaration of the Treaty of Independence, the State of New Hampshire still excludes Catholics from every office, stubbornly resisting all the petitions presented for a removal of this stigma from their statute-book.

As to the States founded on territory ceded by France or Spain, such as Louisiana, Florida, Michigan, Indiana, or severed from Mexico, like Texas and California, the Catholics, original proprietors of the soil, obtained, by the act of cession, the free enjoyment of their worship; and there is on the side of Protestantism mere justice, but no generosity, in keeping the faith of treaties.

In 1790 a remarkable Address was presented to Washington from the Catholics of America, signed by Bishop Carroll, the first Catholic Bishop, on the part of the clergy, and by Charles Carroll of Carrollton, David Carroll, Thomas Fitzsimmons, and Dominick Lynch, on the part of the laity.

Two passages, one from the Address, the other from the reply, may be usefully quoted.

This prospect of national prosperity (say the Catholics) is peculiarly pleasing to us on another account, because, whilst our country preserves her freedom and independence, we shall have a well-founded title to claim from her justice equal rights of citizenship, as the price of our blood spilt under your eyes, and of our common exertions for her defence under your auspicious conduct; rights rendered more dear to us by the remembrance of former hardships.

In his reply, Washington thus referred to that passage in the Catholic Address:—
-

As mankind become more liberal, they will be more apt to allow that all those who conduct themselves as worthy members of the community are equally entitled to the protection of the civil government. I hope ever to see America among the foremost nations in examples of justice and liberality. *And I presume that your fellow-citizens will not forget the patriotic part which you took in the accomplishment of their revolution, and the establishment of their government, or the important assistance they received from a nation in which the Roman Catholic religion is professed.*

To Baltimore we must naturally look for the first establishment of the Catholic Church in America. Members of various religious Orders, especially the illustrious Society of Jesus, those heroic soldiers of the Cross, had shed their blood, or wasted themselves in a life of labour, in the propagation of the faith. Spain, France, England, and Ireland too, had all their share in the glory of those early missions. But, previous to the revolution, the number of those who proclaimed their adherence to the Church was not very considerable. Besides, the priests were few, and many of them worn down by age and hardships. The Catholics of the United States were under the jurisdiction of the Vicar Apostolic of the London district, and during the war there was not the least communication between them and their ecclesiastical superior. Of course, after the termination of the war, which ended in the independence of the American colonies, it was impossible that the Catholics of the United States could any longer remain in subjection to an English bishop; and accordingly the clergy of Maryland and Pennsylvania addressed the Holy See, praying that they themselves might be allowed to choose a spiritual superior, subject to the approbation and confirmation of His Holiness. Dr. Carroll, then the most eminent ecclesiastic in the country, was selected to represent the case of the American Catholics before the Holy See; and in praying that the episcopal power should be placed in the hands of one 'whose virtue, knowledge, and integrity of faith,' should be certified by the clergy of America, he was unconsciously describing his own universally admitted qualification for the high office to which, in the year 1789, he was raised, to the great satisfaction of the clergy and laity of the infant Church, and the approval of the foremost American citizen of that day.

There was a Cardinal Antonelli in those days, as in these; and the Cardinal of that day, when despatching to Dr. Carroll the official documents appointing him to the new see, thus expressed his congratulations and his hopes: 'It is a splendid and glorious office to offer to God, as it were, the first fruits of that portion of the Lord's vineyard. Enjoy, therefore, so great a blessing, not only for the salvation of yourself, but for that of others, and for the increase of the Catholic faith, which we trust will become more and more widely established in that distant region.'

In 1785, when Dr. Carroll submitted the case of his coreligionists to the Propaganda, he estimated the number of Catholics in the United States at 26,000, and thus distributed them—16,000 in Maryland, 7,000 in Pennsylvania, and 2,000 in New York and the other States. This was too low an estimate, as it did not include French and other Catholics living to the west of the Ohio and on the borders of the Mississippi; but the small number attributed to New York, now perhaps the most Catholic of any of the States of the Union, is worthy of notice. It was not until the city of New York was evacuated by the British, in 1783, that the Catholics began to assemble for the open celebration of public worship. They probably might have been content to remain for a longer time without a church of their own, had they been able to obtain any suitable place in which they could decently offer up the Holy Sacrifice; but finding it impossible to accommodate themselves with a building such as they required, they were compelled to commence what must have been in those days a formidable undertaking—the erection of a Catholic church by a small congregation; and in 1786 the Church of St. Peter, the first Catholic Church in the State of New York, was erected—several Irish names being included among its principal benefactors. That there were Irish congregations in the States at that day, and that the New York congregation bore that distinction, we have evidence in a letter quoted by Dr. Bayley in his 'Brief Sketch of the Catholic Church on the Island of New York.' The letter is from Dr. Carroll, dated December 15, 1785, and addressed to his friend the Rev. Charles Plowden:—

The congregation at New York, begun by the venerable Mr. Farmer, of Philadelphia, he has now ceded to an Irish Capuchin resident there. The prospect at that place is pleasing on the whole. The Capuchin is a zealous, pious, and, I think, humble man. He is not indeed so learned, or so good a preacher, as I could wish, which mortifies his congregation: as at New York, and most other places in

America, the different sectaries have scarce any other test to judge of a clergyman than his talent for preaching, and *our Irish congregations, such as New York,* follow the same rule.

Father Whelan had served in a French ship belonging to the fleet of Admiral De Grasse, who was engaged in assisting the cause of American independence; and at the close of the war he selected America as the theatre of his missionary zeal, and became 'the first regularly settled priest in the city of New York.'

By the aid of another letter from the same pen, quoted by Dr. White in his 'Sketch,' we have a glimpse at the state of things at Boston in the year 1790. The description of the feeling of hatred and horror created by 'scandalous misrepresentation' applies, as the reader will have reason to judge, to a period even more than half a century later, and to many parts of America. The name of Carroll was inseparably associated with the successful revolution. When Charles Carroll signed his name to the Declaration of Independence, and added 'of Carrollton,' to his signature, Benjamin Franklin exclaimed—'There goes a cool million!' The new Bishop was therefore certain of being received with distinction even in the capital of the Massachusetts of that day.

It is wonderful (he writes) to tell what great civilities have been done to me in this town, where, a few years ago, a 'Papist priest' was thought to be the grossest monster in the creation. *Many here, even of their principal people, have acknowledged to me, that they would have crossed to the opposite side of the street rather than meet a Roman Catholic some time ago.* The horror which was associated with the idea of a Papist is incredible; and the scandalous misrepresentations by their ministers increased the horror every Sunday. If all the Catholics here were united, their numbers would be about *one hundred and twenty.*

To the revolutionary fury of France, which directed its fiercest rage against the Church, that strongest bulwark of civil government, was America indebted for many eminent scholars and divines—ecclesiastics, pious, zealous, learned, who established seminaries, founded colleges, spread the faith with characteristic ardour, and filled with distinction several of the first sees in the United States. Nowhere is the Catholicity—the Universality of the Church—more strikingly exhibited than in America. Now it is the Spaniard, now it is the Frenchman, now the Englishman, now the Irishman, who preaches the faith or sacrifices his life in its dangerous mission; and, as years roll by, it is the Irish masses, and then, though not to so great an extent, the Germans, who build up her churches, and give strength to her congregations.

The number of Catholics having increased so rapidly, principally through, emigration, the Holy See deemed it advisable to elevate Baltimore into an archbishopric, and to appoint four suffragan Bishops—to Philadelphia, New York, Boston, and Bardstown; and of these four Bishops, two—the Right Rev. Michael Egan and the Right Rev. Luke Concannon—were Irishmen. The new Bishops were consecrated at Baltimore by Archbishop Carroll in 1810, at which period the strength of the Church was represented by seventy priests, eighty churches, and one hundred and fifty thousand laity.

From original documents in his possession, Dr. White gives, in his Appendix to Darras' 'General History of the Church,' some characteristic letters from missionary priests to their Bishop, Dr. Carroll. A passage or two from these letters will afford an idea of missionary life in those days. Considering the sharp provocation to its use, the poor priest's strength of language in the following, written from West Pennsylvania, is but natural. The writer is an Irishman:—

Your reverence (he writes) can have no conception of my distress here, even for the necessaries of life, for really I have not anything like a sufficiency of food such as I get, and, indeed, poor and filthy it is. Most of the Irish, who, though poor, were by far *the most generous*, have now quit this settlement; five or six German families alone remain, whose chaplain I may call myself, since I cannot pretend to travel for want of a horse, and these people, indeed,—abstraction made of religion—are the last of all mankind for sentiments of humanity. The poor man I live with is not paid what was promised for my board, and, whether he intends it or not, he treats me accordingly. Perhaps he can't help it. Bread is the sole support of his family. Morning, noon, and night, flour and water, or bread and water, with a little burnt grease thrown over it, is the support of his starved and almost perfectly naked family. Since my arrival, the only meat they had was a little pig about twenty or thirty pounds, and a calf ten days old, of which we eat this whole week, till it became musty and green for want of salt. . . . Thus have I spent five months of a very rigorous Lent, that threw me into a diarrhoea, that, in such wretchedness and cold, made me pass a most penitential winter.

Another priest writes from Milltown, Pa., in January 1799. After informing his Bishop that he had a large tract of land about twenty miles from there, and that he had placed his sister, a nun, on it, allotting her and her Order five hundred acres, he requests him to send him, in the spring—

Twenty Munster or Connaught men, and if they are poor, I'll pay them as much a year or a day as any other gentleman in the country, provided they are Catholics, because there are plenty of other descriptions here already; but I don't approve of it. Thus you'll free me from a reprobated class of infamous Scotch-Irish, superior in all kinds of wickedness, only in a superlative degree, to the most vile convicts. . . . This before I would not mention to you, until I could be settled, in dread you might suppose interested views might oblige me to exaggerate in my reports. .... In consequence of the cold, I am dislodged from my spring house, and obliged to turn into the pig-sty —that is, the poor honest man's own house, where cats, young dogs, and young fowls, both men and their wives, sons and daughters, all in one store-room comfortably kennel together. But what is more humorous is, that I am kept in pledge, in this sweet-scented situation, for my quarter's diet and lodging.

There is something comical in the bitter wail of distress emanating from poor Father Whelan, who, for many years a missionary in Kentucky, now, January 1805, addresses his Bishop from Clay Creek, Pennsylvania:—

As to Thomas Maguire and his wife, a priest might as well go and lodge in a wolf-pen as with them—he being a wild Irish savage, she being either of the Sambo or Shawnee breed, though some say she is a Hottentot. But, let the case be as it may, she is one whose exterior appearance and interior disposition differ totally from any woman I ever conversed with. At the second word, she will give me the lie to my face. Her husband, though present, would say nothing to all this. . . . No man in Bedlam suffers more than I do, in the company of four wolves. I hope it is a temporal purgatory, and will atone for some of my sins.

Among the many great works associated with the episcopacy of Dr. Carroll, two may be noticed—the foundation of the Jesuit College of Georgetown, and the establishment, under Mrs. Seton, of the Sisters of Charity at Emmettsburg.

From the date of the foundation of the College of Georgetown to the present hour, this parent house of Catholic learning has steadily pursued a noble career of usefulness and honour, educating thousands of the best youth of the country, preparing many of them for the most eminent position in every walk of life, and every department of the public service. And at no period of its splendid career has this first of Catholic American institutions held a higher place in public esteem than it does at this moment. I had the pleasure of walking through its halls, and visiting its rich and varied library, in which there are works of the rarest kind, inestimable in the eyes of a collector. The president is an Irishman, as distinguished for his learning and piety as for his gifts as a preacher.

To two holy women—one a native of America, the other a native of Ireland—is America indebted for a gift beyond measure priceless, and of which no human estimate indeed can be formed—the foundation and introduction of two Religious Orders, which, commencing under circumstances of the greatest difficulty and discouragement, have since spread over the face of the continent, having their branches in every State of the Union, and being in all places where they are established the noblest exemplars of the Catholic religion, because the truest representatives of the Christian virtues. What Mrs. Seton did for the Order of Charity in America, Mrs. M'Auley accomplished for the Order of Mercy in Ireland; and not only was the Order of Mercy introduced from Ireland into the fruitful soil of America, but Ireland—that exhaustless fountain of the faith, whose well-spring is ever full of living waters—contributed to both Orders very many of their most zealous and devoted members.

In founding the Order of the Daughters of Charity in the United States, Mrs. Seton not only rendered a lasting service to religion and humanity, but afforded the honest doubter, as well as the scoffer and the hater of Catholicity, the most convincing proof of what it teaches, what it practises, and what it really is. Born in New York, in the year 1774, of Protestant parents, her father, Dr. Bayley, being an eminent physician of that city, Mrs. Seton was ever remarkable for singular sweetness of disposition, tenderness and compassion for every form of human distress, and a fervent piety, which found the most eloquent expression in her conversation and in her writings. To those who desire to witness, as it were, the struggles of a Christian soul, distracted by doubts springing from the purest conscientiousness, and yet impelled to the light by an invisible influence, we cordially commend the admirable 'Life of Mrs. Seton,' by the Rev. Dr. White; a work that will well repay perusal, whether by the Catholic or the fair-minded Protestant.

It may be remarked, that this holy woman, this model wife and daughter, was deeply impressed with the religious demeanour of the poor Irish emigrants of that day—the opening of the present century—who were detained in quarantine at Staten Island, and attended by her father, as Health Physician to the Port of New York. 'The first thing,' she says, 'these poor people did, when they got their tents, was to assemble on the grass, and all, kneeling, adored our Maker for His mercy; and every morning sun finds them repeating their praises.' The scenes then witnessed at Staten Island remind one of those which were so fatally frequent in subsequent years. Even at that time—1800, and the years following—large numbers of emigrants arrived at the port of New York, suffering from the dreadful scourge of fever, so calamitous to the Irish race. A striking picture of the sufferings of its victims is given in a letter, addressed by Mrs. Seton to her sister-in-law:—

Rebecca, I cannot sleep; the dying and the dead possess my mind —babies expiring at the empty breast of the expiring mother. And this not fancy, but the scene that surrounds me. Father says that such was never known before; that there are actually twelve children that must die from mere want of sustenance, unable to take more than the breast, and, from the wretchedness of their parents, deprived of it, as they have lain ill for many days in the ship, without food, air, or changing. Merciful Father! Oh, how readily would I give them each a turn of my child's treasure, if in my choice! But, Rebecca, they have a provider in Heaven, who will soothe the pangs of the suffering innocent.

She would willingly have become a mother to those helpless little ones, but her father would not permit her to obey the womanly impulse, as her first duty regarded her own child. In 1801 her father fell a victim to his attendance on the Irish emigrants. He had directed the passengers and crew of an Irish emigrant ship, with fever on board, to go on shore to the rooms and tents provided for them, leaving their baggage behind; but on going into the hospital the following morning, he found that his orders, given the evening before, had been disobeyed, and that crew and passengers, men, women, and children, well, sick, and dying, with all their baggage, were huddled together in the same room in which they had passed the night. Into this apartment, before it had been ventilated, he imprudently entered, and remained but a moment, being compelled to retire by deadly sickness of the stomach and intense pain in the head, which seized him immediately on entering within its precincts. From the bed to which he at once retired he never rose again. This was Mrs. Seton's first great grief; but many times, in her after life, was her tender heart wrung by the loss of those whom she loved with all the passionate strength of her nature.

The circumstance of a visit to Italy, whither she went in company with her dying husband, who, as a last resource, sought the mild climate of the South of Europe as his only chance of recovery, not only confirmed her in her previous intention, or desire, to become a Catholic, but acquired for her the enduring friendship of a high-minded and generous family of Leghorn, by name Fellici, to whose munificent assistance in her future work she was under the deepest obligations. At length, and after an exhausting mental conflict, rendered more distressing by the importunities and the anger of her relatives and friends, Mrs. Seton took the final step, and in the church of St. Peter, New York, in March 1805, she joined that Church to which it has been her happiness to render the greatest and most exalted services. By this last act of what her friends regarded as spiritual treason of the most flagrant kind, Mrs. Seton cut herself off for ever from all communion with them; and some time after she established in Baltimore, under the auspices of Bishop Carroll, and with the co-operation of those who knew her story and respected her character, a school for young ladies, in which she soon had the requisite number, including her own daughters, to whom she was the fondest but the wisest of mothers. But she was impelled to a fuller development of her own desire, which was to dedicate herself to the service of the poor; and how this desire was fulfilled is thus told by her biographer:—

About this time another circumstance took place which still more plainly indicated the will of God in reference to the good work. Mr. Cooper, who was then a student in St. Mary's Seminary, at Baltimore, intending, if such were the divine will, to prepare himself for the sacred ministry, possessed some property; and he was desirous of literally following the maxim of the Gospel:—'Go, sell what thou hast, and give it to the poor, and come, follow me.' One morning, immediately after receiving the holy communion, Mrs. Seton felt a strong inclination arise within her to dedicate herself to the care and instruction of poor female children, and to organise some plan for this purpose that might be continued after her death. She communicated this to the Rev. Mr. Dubourg. 'This morning,' she said, 'in my dear communion I thought, Dearest Saviour, if you would give me the care of poor little children, no matter how poor; and Mr. Cooper being directly before me at his thanksgiving, I thought—he has money, if he would but give it for the bringing up of poor little children, to know and love you!' Mr. Dubourg, joining his hands, observed that it was very strange; for Mrs. Seton had not mentioned the subject to anyone else. 'Mr. Cooper,' said he, 'spoke to me this very morning of his thoughts being all for poor children's instruction, and if he had somebody to do it he would give his money for that purpose; and he wondered if Mrs. Seton would be willing to undertake it.' The good priest was struck at the coincidence of their views, and he requested them each to reflect upon the subject for the space of a month, and then to acquaint him with the result. During this time there was no interchange of opinion between Mrs. Seton and Mr. Cooper in relation to their wishes; and at the expiration of it they both returned separately to Mr. Dubourg, renewing the sentiments they had expressed before, one offering a portion of his temporal means, and the other her devoted services for the relief of the poor and suffering members of Christ. The providence of God in behalf of the American Church was so clearly indicated in the circumstances just related that little room was left for deliberation. Bishop Carroll having been informed of the design, gave his warmest approbation to it, in conjunction with the Rev. Francis Nagot, the saintly superior of St. Mary's Seminary; and the only question that now presented itself for consideration was in reference to the locality of the intended establishment.

The two ladies who first joined Mrs. Seton, were Miss Cecilia O'Conway and Miss Maria Murphy; and among those who formed the little community of Emmettsburg—the locality selected for the parent house of the Order in America, we find such names as Maria Burke and Catherine Mullen; proving that, in this infant institution, the Irish element was not wanting. In a miserable little house, of one storey and a garret, sixteen persons, including the female children of Mrs. Seton, were crowded; and here the holy women, who were destined to prove the most eminent benefactors to religion and humanity, suffered hardships and privations which they yet bore with cheerfulness. At times, indeed, they were reduced to a condition of absolute destitution. To supply the place of coffee, they manufactured a beverage from carrots, which they sweetened with molasses; and their rye bread was of the coarsest description. For months they were reduced to such absolute want that they did not know where the next day's meal was to come from. On Christmas-day they considered themselves fortunate in having some smoked herrings for dinner, and a spoonful of molasses for each. By her anti-Catholic friends Mrs. Seton was denounced as 'the pest of society,' and 'a hypocrite and a bigot,' they visiting on her the early death of two loved members of her own family who, braving the trials of her exalted mission, died in the early bloom of youthful womanhood. As, with some modifications to suit the constitution of different religious communities, the objects contemplated by the Daughters of Charity are those common to several Orders in America, it may be well to state their objects, as given by Mrs. Seton's biographer:—

The end which the Sisters of Charity of St. Joseph proposed to themselves was, to honour our Lord Jesus Christ as the source and model of all charity, by rendering to Him every temporal and spiritual service in their power, in the persons of the poor, the sick, prisoners, and others; also to honour the Sacred infancy of Jesus Christ, in the young persons of their sex whom they may be called upon to form to virtue, while they sow in their minds the seeds of useful knowledge. Thus the poor, of all descriptions and ages, the sick, invalids, foundlings, orphans, and even insane persons, were embraced within the sphere of their solicitude and care. Another object of their zeal, no less important at that time in America, was the instruction of young persons of their sex in virtue, piety, and various branches of useful learning.

And these, and such as these, were then, and have been even to this day, described as Mrs. Seton was described by her anti-Catholic friends—'pests of society,' 'hypocrites and bigots!'

Philadelphia was the first place to which a branch of the Order was extended; and the care of the orphans whose parents had perished of yellow fever offered a fitting opportunity for the exercise of their charity. Their's, however, was a hard trial for a considerable time, notwithstanding the sympathy shown to them, and the assistance they received. The Sisters had nothing beyond the coarsest fare, and not always sufficient of that. For three months they had no bread whatever, subsisting wholly on potatoes, which formed their principal article of diet for their first year. Their 'coffee' was made of corn, and their fuel was gathered from the tanyards. 'One day, the Sisters being too much occupied at home, an orphan was despatched to the market with twelve and a half cents, all the money in the house, to buy a shin of beef. A few hours after, the child returned to the asylum with a large piece of meat, telling the Sisters that an old market-woman, finding that she was one of the orphans, had given her the money and meat, and authorised her to call upon her for assistance whenever they were in want. This old woman became a generous friend of the institution. By the benevolence of herself and others it gradually acquired ample resources, and was enabled to maintain under its charitable roof an increasing number of orphans.'

The holy foundress of the Order went to her eternal reward on the 4th January, 1821, in the 47th year of her age, her death being as edifying as her life.

From the very first formation of the Order of Charity in the United States, there were to be found in the infant institution ladies of Irish birth and Irish parentage; and as it gathered strength, and its branches spread from State to State, the Irish element was ever strong in its communities. How attractive the great work of this Order has proved to Irish piety may be learned from a passage in a letter from a Sister of St. Joseph's Academy, Emmettsburg, dated June 3, 1867, and addressed to a reverend friend of mine: 'The number of Irish Sisters now living, and in our community, amounts to *four hundred and ten*. This speaks well of the piety of the Emerald Isle.'

The prosperous branch of the Order in the State of New York, though founded from the mother house at Emmettsburg, and based on the same principles and constitution, and doing the same work, is altogether independent. It numbers several hundred Sisters, the majority of whom are Irish. The Order, wherever it is established, embraces within its ranks a considerable number of Sisters of Irish descent as well as of Irish birth.

CHAPTER XIX

Bishop Connolly's Note-book—'Laity's Directory' for 1822—Dr. Kirwan
previous to his Apostacy—The Church in 1822—Progress in 1834—How the
Faith was Lost

AN extract or two, taken from a note-book, unhappily only a fragment, kept by Dr. Connolly, Bishop of New York, and quoted by Bishop Bayley in his 'Brief Sketch,' will tell us something of the Irish of his day, as also of the condition of his diocese, which comprised the whole of the State of New York and part of New Jersey.

March 10th, 1816.—Wrote to Dr. Troy an account of my voyage to America; illness here for nearly two months. Catholics dispersed through the country parts of the State of Pennsylvania, New York, Jersey, and New England, *where they seldom see a priest*: they are not able to maintain one in any particular district— ambulatory zealous priests, necessary for them to prevent their children from conforming to the persuasions of neighbouring sectaries, who all of them have their respective ministers. *Only four priests in this diocese*, though the Catholics of New York and its district are about seventeen thousand.

Feb. 25th, 1818. .... At present there are here about sixteen thousand Catholics, *mostly Irish*; at least *ten thousand Irish Catholics* arrived at New York only within these last three years. They spread through all the other States of this Confederacy, *and make their religion known everywhere*. Bishops ought to be granted to whatever State here is willing to build a cathedral, as Norfolk has done. The present Dioceses are quite too extensive. Our cathedral owes 53,000 dollars, borrowed to build it, for which it pays interest at the rate of 7 per cent. yearly. This burthen hinders us from supporting a sufficient number of priests, or from thinking to erect a seminary. The American youth have an almost invincible repugnance to the ecclesiastical state.

The names of the priests ordained by Dr. Connolly—O'Gorman, Bulger, Kelly, Brennan, Shanahan, and Conroy —are sufficient evidence of the country from which the infant Church of the United States obtained the greater number of its pastors. Dr. Bayley mentions one of the many amusing incidents in the missionary life of Father Bulger, whose ardent zeal and buoyant spirits enabled him to bear up against many hardships, and not a few insults; for the horror of 'Priests and Popery,' as Bishop Carroll said of Boston, was 'incredible.' Trudging along one day on foot, carrying a bundle, containing his vestments and breviary, under his arm, Father Bulger was overtaken by a farmer and his wife in a wagon. The farmer invited Mr. Bulger to ride; but it having come out in the course of conversation that he was a priest, the wife declared that she would not remain with him in the wagon, and he was obliged to get out and resume his journey on foot. But the strange part of the story is, that the farmer afterwards applied to Father Bulger for instructions, and became a Catholic.

The most authentic and accurate information as to the condition of the American Church towards the latter part of the first quarter of the present century is afforded by the 'Laity's Directory' for 1822, This little compilation deserves notice, not only because of the contrast it offers to the great volume of the present day, but that it enables us to behold how feeble and comparatively insignificant was the Catholic body of the first quarter of this century as compared with its present magnitude and power. At the time it was published, not many pages were required for the ordinary purposes of a directory and calendar; and on analysing the 138 pages of which the little volume is composed, I find there are not more than 50 devoted to such purpose; and of these 50 pages 10 are occupied with obituaries of deceased prelates and priests, and 11 more are devoted to a single institution, and an account of the Society of Jesus in the United States. In fact, less than a dozen pages of Sadlier's voluminous directory of the present year would amply suffice for an epitome of the ecclesiastical intelligence of 1822. But, according to the advertisement, it was intended 'to accompany the Missal, with a view to facilitate the use of the same.' Revised and corrected by an eminent Irish priest—the Rev. John Power of New York—it testifies in every line of its historical and descriptive matter to his piety and eloquence.

Among other offerings to the laity, it contains 'A New Year's Gift for the Year 1822;' and though a somewhat strange New Year's gift, it must have been welcome and valuable at the time. It is a 'Discourse on Religious Innovations,' delivered by the Rev. Walter Blake Kirwan, at the Neapolitan Ambassador's Chapel, in London, on the 20th March, 1786. Having, a short time after the delivery of this remarkable discourse, abandoned the church which in that discourse he so vigorously and, one might say, fiercely defended, his apostacy was a source of great scandal to the faithful, and of corresponding triumph to their opponents. From the published sermons of Mr. Kirwan this discourse was omitted, 'doubtless,' says the Editor of the Directory, 'because his family had no reason to be solicitous to promote its publicity; his fall must to them have been a subject of grief and humiliation: and they felt poignantly that it could not exalt his memory, since the talents and impressive truths it displays are not more conspicuous than that deplorable frailty which so soon afterwards induced himself to become a striking example of what he had therein so wisely and eloquently deprecated.'

The publication of this remarkable discourse was no doubt intended to answer the revilers of that day, and perhaps strengthen faith which was then exposed to many perils. Reading it, one can scarcely avoid arriving at one or other of two conclusions,—either that he was a hypocrite of the most daring description, or that he was seized with some sudden religious vertigo, in which he saw everything through a distorted medium. Thus, for instance, he says, 'Yet in what terms of sufficient indignation shall I speak of that profaneness which has branded her (the Church's) ceremonies and discipline with the foul and opprobrious epithets of pageantry and abuse? I believe, nay, I am confident, when I assert that such ill-founded and scandalous reflections are received, even by those who dissent from us—by the thinking and informed part of the Church of England—with the utmost contempt for the person that utters them, with a perfect detestation of his perfidy.'

Referring to a point of general discipline in the Catholic Church which was then, and has been often since, the subject of comment and attack, that of 'performing the public service in Latin,' he shows how it establishes uniformity, and prevents confusion; 'because natural languages are subject to decay and corruption, and in the space of a century may have undergone a total change as to the meaning and acceptation of words and phrases; the consequence must be that error and obscurity might insensibly steal into the Liturgy. Because,' he adds, 'in the same kingdom, for instance in this island, which is but a speck upon the expanse of Europe, public service would be read in three different tongues, English, Welsh, and Erse. Hence what confusion would arise, even in the Liturgy of this nation, insomuch that were one of you to be present at the Mass in Wales, or in some part of Scotland, not to speak of Ireland, you might as well hear it in the language of Hindostan.' He thus sums up this part of his discourse:

'In whatever point of view I consider this matter, I am persuaded that to alter the present practice would be an unwise and dangerous reform. That such a measure might have been demanded in too insolent a manner may perhaps be true; but that it had not been acceded to, because we are irritated by petulant reflections, or not disposed to pray in the language of a Luther, a Calvin, or an Elizabeth, is not the case; but because the Church judges it expedient to preserve uniformity in her service, and secure it from change, corruption, and confusion.'

With these passages—defending the use of ceremonies—we may turn from the New Year's Gift offered in the 'Laity's Directory' of 1822:—

If there is any faith to be given to the attestations of the primitive writers of Christianity, and usages of the Church, from the earliest ages, most of the ceremonies practised in our public service and administration of sacraments are immediately derived from the Apostles. The Church has judged it expedient to institute additional ones; her power is from Christ.

The use of ceremony is to maintain order, decency, and uniformity in the exterior acts of religion; to raise and elevate the mind to a proper contemplation of our mysteries, and to inspire respect and awe far the supreme majesty of God. How much they conduce to this great object, every one's experience bears ample testimony. The strongest impressions are produced on the mind through the medium of the senses. The animal part of man fetters and clogs the powers of the soul, checks its activity, and blunts the edge of its conception. The sacred pomp of religion was designed, therefore, as an auxiliary to assist the efforts of the mind, and give a spring to its operations.

In 1822 the number of churches throughout the whole of the United States did not much exceed one hundred; and in some of the States not only was there no church, but a priest was never seen by their scattered population: so that if they kept the faith, they did so by a miracle of grace.

The diocese of Baltimore had then more than one-third of all the churches— meaning thereby all the missions—in the States. Baltimore boasted at that time of thirty-nine churches, and several institutions, educational and charitable.

Catholicity had a hard struggle to make any way in the New England States, the historic stronghold of the Puritans. It was nevertheless making progress, but slowly; nor was it until wave after wave of emigration from Ireland was directed to its shores, that these States began to feel the influence of the Catholic element. The diocese of Boston comprehended at that time—1822—the entire of the New England States, including Maine; and in all these States there were but six churches, two of which were in the city of Boston. There was one at Salem, one at New Bedford, and two in the State of Maine, thus leaving districts of enormous extent without church or priest. To two noble French clergymen—Bishop Cheverus and his Vicar-General, Dr. Matignon—was due the exalted merit of having rendered Catholicity respected in Boston. They were learned, pious, zealous, indefatigable, and of the most amiable disposition and conciliatory manners. They failed not, we are told by the Editor of the 'Laity's Directory,' in a short time to win the hearts and gain the affections of their dissenting brethren. 'Prejudices soon began to disappear, inquiries after truth to be made, numbers successively to join their little society; and at this present time the church of Boston forms a very prominent feature in the Catholic body of the United States. O, truly fortunate revolution in France! every true Catholic in this country may exclaim, which has brought so many edifying and enlightened instructors!'

In 1822 the diocese of New York, which comprehended the whole of the State of New York, together with the northern part of Jersey, possessed but seven churches; and including the Bishop, Dr. Connolly, who discharged the ordinary duties of the humblest missionary, the number of priests did not exceed nine. Two of the churches were in New York; the others being in Albany, Utica, Auburn, New Jersey, and Carthage. The clergyman officiating at Albany occasionally visited Troy, Lansingburgh, Johnstown, and Shenectady. Under the head of the 'Clergymen officiating in the diocese,' we find the following items, alike indicative of the laborious duties of the clergy and the spiritual destitution of the scattered flocks:—

'REV. PATRICK KELLY, *Auburn, Rochester, and other districts in the Western part of this State.*

'REV. PHILIP LARISSY *attends regularly at Staten Island, and different other congregations along the Hudson River.*'

Philadelphia, which included Pennsylvania and Delaware, was a comparatively flourishing diocese, with fifteen churches. 'It is pleasing to reflect,' says the Editor of the 'Laity's Directory,' 'that at the present day the professors of Catholicity make up nearly one-fifth of the population of the city.' Even then the Irish were strong in Philadelphia.

The Bishopric of Bardstown was then of 'prodigious extent,' comprehending the States of Kentucky, Tennessee, Ohio, Indiana, and Illinois, with the Michigan and North Western Territories. A few years back all these countries were little better than a wilderness, and with scarcely a Catholic to be seen in them; and though we are told, in the 'Directory,' that they formed, in 1822, 'one of the most populous flourishing portions of Catholic America,' we must only say the Catholics were left very much to themselves; for in the entire of this diocese—we shall not state how many times larger than the United Kingdom—there were but nineteen churches, the majority of them of wood. We are not, therefore, surprised to read a passage like this—'There are yet parts of this country in which many Catholics have settled (chiefly on the borders of the great lakes) *who have not yet seen the face of a Catholic clergyman.*'

The diocese of Louisiana, which included the whole of ancient Louisiana and the Floridas, was then one of the most flourishing of the domains of the Church. It had a considerable staff of priests when compared with the other dioceses, though there were many portions of this extensive region in which the voice of the minister of religion was never heard.

In the diocese of Richmond, which embraced the whole of Virginia, there were but seven churches; and in the famous Bishopric of Charleston, to which Dr. England lent such undying lustre, Catholicity had made but little progress at that time.

The diocese of Charleston included North Carolina, South Carolina, and Georgia. In 1822, or two years after the appointment of Dr. England to the see, there was but one church in the City of Charleston; there was no church in North Carolina, and no church in South Carolina, though churches 'were intended to be;' while in Georgia there were three churches, one in Savannah, one in Augusta, and one at Locust Grove. In this vast diocese there was ample field for the energies of the most zealous missionary: and we shall hereafter see how vigorously the most illustrious Bishop of his day girded his loins to his great work. There were as yet, we are informed, no Catholic schools in any part of the diocese, but active exertions were then being made by Dr. England to diffuse a correct knowledge of the principles of the Catholic Church, through the establishment of societies which had for their object the dissemination of books of piety and instruction.

We now, with the aid of 'The *Metropolitan Catholic Calendar and Laity's Directory* for1834,' pass over a period of twelve years. This little volume, not greater in size than that published at New York in 1822, was printed in Baltimore; and we are not surprised to read in it the following description of the position of the Church in this favoured diocese:—

'Baltimore has, not improperly, been styled the Rome of the United States; and, indeed, whether we consider the monuments of religion, rare and magnificent of their kind, or the splendour of the ceremonies of the Church, or the number, respectability, and piety of those who profess the Catholic faith, there is no one who could question the justice of her claim, or attempt to deprive her of the glory of her title.'

We find four new dioceses in the year 1834, namely, that of Cincinnati, established in 1823, St. Louis in 1827, Mobile in 1825, and Michigan in 1823. Of the old dioceses, we discover more apparent progress in that of Boston, in which twenty-six churches are well distributed through its different States. Thus, while there are nine in Massachusetts, there are three in Rhode Island, two in Connecticut, two in New Hampshire, two in Vermont, and six in Maine. This improved condition of things denotes that the Irish Catholics were even then making their way in the home of the New England Puritan. New York, with a wonderful future before it, has still but nineteen churches throughout its vast diocese; while Charleston, under the vigorous administration of Bishop England, has already twelve, but with only twelve priests for its three States.

The Religious Orders are making themselves known in several of the dioceses, where their value is already thoroughly appreciated. The Sisters of Charity have established twenty-five branches in seven dioceses, these taking the charge and management of academies, free schools, asylums, infirmaries, and hospitals.

In 1829, when the first Provincial Council of Baltimore was held, which was attended by the Archbishop of Baltimore and five Bishops, four being absent, the assembled Prelates expressed their gratitude to God for the increase of the Church, whose position is accurately stated in the following enumeration:—11 dioceses, 10 bishops, 232 priests, 230 churches, 9 ecclesiastical seminaries, 8 colleges, 20 female academies, and a Catholic population of at least half a million. In four of the dioceses, Baltimore, Richmond, New Orleans, and St. Louis, the number of priests was 132, thus leaving but 100 for New York, Boston, Philadelphia, Bardstown, Charleston, Cincinnati, and Mobile. The progress, such as it was, was considerable, taking into account the difficulties with which the infant Church had to contend, especially the want of churches and pastors for fast-growing congregations, and the various hostile influences arrayed everywhere against the faith. In the Directory of 1834, we frequently read such announcements as these— 'Mass occasionally'—'Mass every two months'—'Mass once a month'—'Mass twice a month.' The 'occasionally' was in those times, and for years afterwards, a word of large significance, and might mean once a year, or once in three years, as was in many instances the case. If a certain proportion of the Irish emigrants did lose their faith, the explanation is obvious. It may, however, be given from an authority that cannot be questioned, namely, the Pastoral Letter of the Archbishop and Bishops of the Second Council of Baltimore, dated the 2nd of October, 1833; from which the following passage is taken:—

In viewing the members of our flocks who are spread abroad over the surface of this country, and the comparatively small number of our clergy, we have often been forced to deplore the destitution of spiritual aid under which multitudes labour. God is our witness, that so far as we had the means we have endeavoured to supply the wants of our beloved children. We have not been sparing of ourselves, nor have our brethren in the priesthood been spared. Of this, you, brethren, are also our witnesses. But notwithstanding these efforts, the Catholic has been too frequently removed far from the voice of his pastor, far from the altar of his redeeming Victim, far from the bread of angels, far from the other sacraments and institutions of religion. The emigrant who comes to our shores for the purpose of turning his industry to more profitable account than he could do in regions long and thickly inhabited, has wandered through our forests, our fields, our towns, and some of our cities, in amazement at not being able to find a church in which he could worship according to the rites of his ancestors; he has left our Republic in the bitterness of disappointment, or he has not unfrequently become indifferent. Others have with a firm faith preserved the sacred deposit, and transmitted it to their children, looking forward with hope to that day when they would be cheered by the ancient sounds of a liturgy derived from the Apostolic ages, and known through all the nations of the earth.

From the condition of things in a single diocese, in which, for more than twenty years, the Bishop had to do far more than the hardest work of a missionary priest, the reader may form a notion of the state of Catholicity in many parts of the United States, not alone from the year 1820 to the year 1834, when the Second Council of Baltimore was held, but down to a very recent period indeed — wherever, in fact, the circumstances were at all similar. I have been favoured with a diary kept by Dr. England, Bishop of Charleston, during the first three years of his episcopate; and some extracts from its pages will afford the reader a lively idea, as well of the multiplied work which a Catholic Bishop in those days had to go through, as of certain peculiarities in the religious world of America, for which there is no match to be found in these countries, where the hard line of separation is rigidly defined. Before the Bishop speaks for himself, it may be well to show what manner of man he was, and how far he was fitted for the position to which Providence had called him.

CHAPTER XX

*Dr. England, Bishop of Charleston—Bishop England's Diary—Bishop
England's Missionary Labours—The Bishop's Trials—Bishop England's growing
Fame*

ENDOWED with singular energy of character, and a mind at once vigorous and comprehensive, enriched with information both varied and accurate, John England combined the advantages of a thorough training in all the priestly duties, derived from an active missionary career, first in his native city, and afterwards in the parish of Bandon. To the discharge of his functions as a minister of the Gospel he brought the zeal and piety of an ardent nature, and the promptings of a spirit entirely unselfish, and indeed wholly self-sacrificing. Nor was he unacquainted with those political questions which agitated the public mind of that day.

In Ireland, whatever the disposition of priest or prelate, there happen occasions when he is tempted—nay even compelled—to quit the sacred precincts of the sanctuary for the arena of political strife; and before John England was appointed to the parish of Bandon, even the ecclesiastics who, by character and disposition, were most inclined to shrink from the angry contentions of the outer world, felt themselves compelled by a sense of conscientious obligation to assert their rights as citizens. This was during the long and wearisome struggle for Emancipation, which was mainly carried, as the world knows, by the pluck and determination of the Catholics of Ireland, assisted, no doubt, by the generous and persistent aid of the Liberal Protestants of the United Kingdom. The grand object of the Irish Catholics of that day was to return, as their representatives to Parliament, the friends of Emancipation; and such was the power and influence of those who made a desperate resistance to the just claims of their fellow-countrymen, that it required the utmost effort and the most perfect union on the part of the Catholic body to frustrate the machinations of their wily and relentless opponents.

The Rev. John England was a ready, dashing writer, as bold in attack as skilful in reply; nor as a speaker was he inferior, either in power or brilliancy, to the most gifted orators of a period when men borrowed their best inspiration from the earnest convictions and strong passions of the moment. To him, in no small degree, was owing the courage, the cohesion, and the triumph of the popular party of his native city; and when he left that city for the parish to which, at an unusually early period of life, he was appointed, and afterwards when he quitted the shores of his native land for that great country with which his fame is inseparably associated, he was followed by the best wishes of every friend of freedom, expressed as well by substantial tokens as in eloquent words. Thus was Bishop England especially prepared for the work he had to do in his new field of labour;

his acquaintance with public affairs, and his faculty of dealing with questions other than those within the immediate province of a minister of religion, frequently obtaining for him the most valuable influence with people of position and authority.

We now turn to the diary, which thus opens:—

On Monday, the 10th of July, 1820, I received in Bandon a letter from the Reverend Henry Hughes, dated June 17, 1820, at Rome, informing me that on the preceding Monday I had been appointed Bishop of Charleston, in South Carolina, and requesting of me, for various reasons therein alleged, to accept of this appointment.

September 21st.—I received the grace of Episcopal Consecration in the Catholic Church of St. Finbarr's, in the city of Cork, from the Right Rev. Dr. Murphy, Bishop of the Diocese, assisted by the Right Rev. Dr. Maram, Bishop of Ossory, and Kelly, first Bishop of Richmond (Virginia), whose appointment was subsequent to mine but whose consecration took place at Kilkenny on the 24th of August. There were present, the Most Rev. Dr. Everard, Archbishop of Mytelene, coadjutor of the Most Rev. Dr. Bray, Archbishop of Cashel and the Right Rev. Drs. Coppinger, of Cloyne and Ross, Sughrue of Ardfert and Aghadoe (Kerry), and Tuohy of Limerick. ....

October 11th.—I having many applications from priests and candidates for places on the American mission, I appointed my brother, the Rev. Thomas R. England, and the Rev. Thomas O'Keeffe, my Vicars-General, for the purpose principally of selecting such of those as I may afterwards want, and if necessary having them ordained. This day was the anniversary—twelve years—of my ordination to the priesthood. On this day I parted from my family to go whither I thought God had called me, but whither I had no other desire to go. Should this be read by a stranger, let him pardon that weakness of our common nature which then affected me, and does now after the lapse of three months. . . .

December 26th.—Found soundings in 35 fathoms water, and on the next day saw the Hunting Islands on the coast of South Carolina, after a very tedious and unpleasant passage. On the evening of the 27th came to anchor off Charleston Bar, and on the 28th crossed it, and worked up the channel, and came to anchor in the evening.

December 30th.—Came on shore in Charleston; saw the Rev. Benedict Fenwick, S.O.I., who was Vicar-General of the Archbishop of Baltimore, who exhibited to me his papers. I gave him my Bulls and Certificates, received the resignation of his authority, and renewed his faculties of Vicar-General for my diocese, as Bishop of Charleston, which he accepted.

December 31st.—Being Sunday, I had the happiness of celebrating Mass, took possession of the church, had my Bulls published, and preached.

Dr. England soon made himself acquainted with the condition of his diocese, which in all respects was far from encouraging. Upon inquiry he found that there was a congregation in the City of Savannah (Georgia), but that it had been deserted, and he took into consideration the necessity of having a priest for that mission. He determined to visit Savannah and Augusta, and Warrenton in Georgia, and Columbia in South Carolina, without delay. Appointing the Rev. Mr. Fenwick his Vicar-General, with full powers until his return to Charleston, and requesting him to purchase ground for a second temporary church in that city, and if possible procure a good site for a large cathedral], he went on board the sloop 'Delight,' and sailed for Savannah on the loth of January, 1821. He found there had been no priest in that city since the previous October; and to repair the evil caused by the want of a clergyman for so long a time, he commenced a vigorous course of instruction, followed by the administration of the sacraments. The following entry affords an idea of his energy, and of the attention which he already excited amongst non-Catholics:—

'January 21.—Heard confessions, celebrated the Holy Mass, and administered the Holy Communion to 27 persons. Grave Confirmation to 15 persons. At half-past ten o'clock I spoke on the erection of the See, on my own authority, and publicly committed the flock of Savannah to the care of the Rev. Robert Browne until I should think proper to remove him; and after Mass I preached to a large congregation, amongst whom were the principal lawyers of Savannah, and many other strangers. In the evening I had vespers, and gave an exhortation and benediction—Church crowded and surrounded.'

The next entry records the same round of duty, with this paragraph added: 'Was asked by the Mayor and others to preach in the Protestant Episcopal Church, which I declined for the present.'

Appointing 'John Dillon to read prayers for Mass on Sunday,' until the return of the Rev. Mr. Browne, whom he took with him on his visitation, the Bishop proceeded to Augusta, which place he reached after two days of hard travelling. After a brief but energetic work in this city, where he administered Confirmation 'to John McCormick, Esq., and 48 others,' he set out for Locust Grove, whose Catholic congregation had not had the benefit of a pastor for several years.

Arrived there at nightfall, and was most kindly received by old and young Mrs. Thompson, to the former of whom great merit is due, before God, for preserving the faith in this country. This was the first Catholic congregation in Georgia; it was formed in 1794 or 1795 by the settlement of Mrs. Thompson's family and a few others from Maryland. Bishop Carroll, of Baltimore, sent the Rev. Mr. Le Mercier to attend them. After eighteen months he went to Savannah, and Rev. Mr. Sujet then remained seventeen months, and returned to France. There was no clergyman there until November 1810, when the Rev. Robert Browne came to take charge of Augusta and its vicinity, and remained until 1815. This place was occasionally visited by Rev. Mr. Egan and Rev. Mr. Cooper.

Like all Catholic priests, Bishop England was particularly solicitous for the welfare of the negroes. The policy of the Church was not to oppose an institution which was Altogether beyond its province or jurisdiction; but its ministers nevertheless did what they could to elevate the moral condition of the slave through religious influences, and also sought to improve their temporal condition by inducing their owners to respect the sanctity and validity of the marriage tie. In Locust Grove, Bishop England found several Catholic negroes, amongst whom were some both 'intelligent and well-instructed.'

There he preached his first open-air sermon. 'The church being too small, and several persons having collected from various parts of the neighbourhood, I preached from an elevation outside to about 400 persons.' At Warrenton, he says, 'I met three Cherokee Indians, viz. Colonel Dick, who could speak a little English, John Thompson, and Sampson, to whom I gave their breakfast. I showed the Colonel my ring and cross, of which he took particular notice, and told him I intended visiting his nation; he said he would know me.'

At Columbia he finds a flock consisting 'of about 250 persons, principally Irish labourers employed in making the canal.' There was no church, and the Bishop 'therefore preached in the Court-house that night to a very numerous and respectable congregation,' mostly Protestants. He makes strenuous efforts to commence a church; and on his committee of collection we see such genuine Irish names as Peter M'Guire and John Heffernan.

Returning to Charleston, Dr. England addressed himself, with renewed energy, to his great labours. He now commenced a course of lectures which laid the foundation of a fame that ere long spread through every State in the Union, and attracted the attention of the most thoughtful and intellectual. The first was on the Existence of God; the second on the Nature and Necessity of Religion; the third on the Establishment of the Church by Our Saviour; the fourth on the Marks of the True Church, 'exhibited in the Holy Roman Catholic Church, and in that alone.' These discourses, which were continued during Lent, were not without result; for, under date of April 28, there are recorded in the diary the names of several converts, including that of 'a lawyer of eminence.'

In the last week of Lent the Bishop published a catechism, which, he says, 'I had much labour in compiling from various others, and adding several parts which I considered necessary to be explicitly dwelt upon under the peculiar circumstances of my diocese.'

The number of communicants in Charleston in the Easter fortnight (1821) was 250.

'April 26. Established the Book Society, and had the necessary measures taken to establish a general committee, and to have the Society extended throughout my diocese.'

The following passage, though descriptive of the condition of the Catholics of that day in a Southern State, was just as applicable to most other parts of the Union, save where a priest was regularly stationed. Indeed, it as accurately represented the condition of Catholics in a vast number of places in thirty years after it was written. It was written of Wilmington:—

May 16th.—Celebrated Mass at my lodging, and gave an exhortation to those who attended. After breakfast met the Catholics, about twenty men: not a woman or child of the Catholic faith. No priest had ever been fixed here, nor in the neighbourhood. A Rev. Mr. Burke had spent a fortnight here about twenty-five years before, and a Jesuit going to some Spanish settlement spent two or three days in the town about the year 1815, and baptized the children of Mr. ——; but their mother being a Methodist, they were not educated in the faith. The Catholics who lived here, and they who occasionally came hither, *were in the habit of going to other places of worship—Episcopal Protestant, Methodist, and Presbyterian—and had nearly lost all idea of Catholicity.* I spoke on the necessity of their assembling together on Sundays for prayer and instruction, and of their forming a branch of the Book Society, to both of which they readily agreed, and then recommended their entering into a subscription to procure a lot for a church, and to commence building, as I would take care they should be occasionally visited by a priest. I also exhorted them to prepare for the sacraments.

I received an invitation from the pastor and trustees of the Presbyterian Church to use their building (the best in the town), which upon consideration I accepted. I was waited upon by the Protestant minister, who offered me his church also, which of course I declined, as having accepted of the other. In the evening I preached to a very large congregation, on the nature of the Catholic religion.

Here was a fitting occasion for the zeal of the young Bishop; and we find him daily exhorting his own little flock, and also preaching each evening to large and attentive congregations—'On the nature of Redemption, the Mission of the Apostles, and the Authority of the Church to explain the Scriptures and teach the doctrines of Christ by her traditions.' Nor was his labour without fruit, as he established a branch of the Book Society, raised by subscription 1,160 dollars for a church, and received some converts of note.

Among the entries of May 12th, there is this record: 'Baptized George Washington, aged three years, son of Patrick Murphy and Rebecca Lear; sponsor, J. P. Calhardo.'

'May 20. .... Was requested by some Protestant gentlemen to preach twice this evening, as I was to leave town in the morning. I complied with their request, and preached at half-past three and at seven o'clock, to very full congregations. There was created in Wilmington a spirit of inquiry, and the prejudices which were very general against Catholics were removed.'

In a place near South Washington, we are told that John Doyle, an Irishman, is the only Catholic. In Newbern we find a state of things exactly the reverse of that described in Wilmington. In Wilmington there were twenty Catholic men, and not a single woman or child of the faith; but in Newbern there are 'upwards of twenty

Catholics, principally females.' A priest had visited them seven months previously. Here the Bishop baptized two converts, 'men of colour.'

In North Washington the Catholics were 'few and generally negligent.' No priest since the previous year. 'The Methodists have a meeting-house, the Baptists a temporary place, but there is no other house of worship.' The Bishop not only preached in the Court-house in the evenings, but said Mass in it in the mornings; and the congregations increasing, the converts, including people of colour, coming in, and favourable impressions being made upon others, who took time to consider what they should do, we are not surprised to learn that 'the Baptist and Methodist leaders were drawing off the hearers to the best of their power.'

On his arrival in Plymouth he finds but one Catholic; but in a day after he discovers a second. Still, he is well received, and actually establishes a Book Society. 'Finding,' he says, 'an anxiety to hear me, I consented to remain, and preach twice this day, to about 40 persons at eleven o'clock, and to a much larger congregation at five o'clock, at the Academy, which was the only public building in the town.' For three days he preached, both morning and evening; on the third evening he 'preached to a very crowded congregation in the Academy, after which the Book Society met, and elected their officers.' It was on that evening that the Bishop discovered the second Catholic in the town.

In other places he finds a few Catholics, the greater number attending the Methodist or Baptist places of worship, there being no Catholic church, and the visits of a priest being 'few and far between.' Whatever the nature of the congregation, whatever its admixture of nationalities, Irish are to be found amongst them; thus, next to a high-sounding Spanish name, we alight upon a Daniel Flynn, a Michael Dempsey, or an Ignatius Crowley. Deputations wait upon him to request he will preach in Protestant churches or in Court-houses, which he generally does, and with advantage to the cause of truth. But converts are lukewarm, and Catholics relapse into indifferentism; and priests cannot be had, or are not always reliable, being discouraged by the hardships of a seemingly unpromising mission; and troubles and perplexities plant the Bishop's mitre with plentiful thorns; and rheumatisms rack his bones, and fevers break down his strength; and, to add to his afflictions, poverty oppresses him. 'I was frequently,' says the Bishop of three great States, 'without a dollar, from the wretched state of the income, and the bad disposition of the infidel portion who professed to belong to the flock.' Still, in spite of incessant toil in the mission, and drudgery in his seminary, and the constant pressure of poverty, he continued to extend his Book Society, and establish in Charleston, in 1822, a weekly newspaper, called *The United States Catholic Miscellany*, which, under his management, became one of the most potent means of vindicating the faith, and refuting the calumnies so constantly circulated by its opponents; in fact, it soon grew to be a power in the country.

'December 28th, 1822. Columbia. I preached in the House of Representatives, at the request of the Legislature.'

'April 24th, 1823. Celebrated Mass and exhorted, and after dinner returned to Camden, and stopped by invitation with Mr. Salmond, a Presbyterian.'

'April 24. *Mr. Salmond was kind enough to find the Catholics and to bring them to me.* They consisted of the following persons (French, Spanish, and Irish names), to whom I gave the usual commission. I gave them some books, and heard the confession of one who presented himself. At the request of the inhabitants I preached in the evening, in the new Presbyterian Church, to a very large congregation. I afterwards baptized three children.'

With one other extract we shall conclude a notice of the Bishop's diary, from which sufficient has been given to afford the reader a true picture of a mission throughout which Catholics were thinly scattered, and in which they had to depend, in a very great measure, upon their own steadfastness to retain even a semblance of their faith. In purely country districts—perhaps not visited for years by a clergyman—matters were necessarily worse; notwithstanding which there were many, many instances of Irish Catholics keeping the faith alive under the most discouraging circumstances.

April 29th, 1823.—Fayetteville. Heard confessions, celebrated Mass, and exhorted; had four communicants—baptized a child. I found that the congregation had regularly prayed together on the Sundays and holidays, until the sickly season, when they fell off. I endeavoured to prevail upon them to resume the good practice. Superseded the former commission, and issued a new one to John Kelly, Dillon Jordan, Laurence Fitzharriss, Doctor James Moffet, and Daniel Kenny. Was invited to preach at the State House. In the evening I again saw the Catholics, and exhorted them to persevere—spoke to several individually. At eight o'clock I preached in the State House to a very large and attentive audience.

As years went on, so did the fame of Bishop England increase, until the time came when, from one end of the Union to the other, his name became a household word with Catholics of every nationality, who recognised in him a champion fully equipped, and equal to the good fight. The feeling of his own countrymen towards him cannot be described, so intense was their pride in his great qualities—his power of pen and tongue, his resistless force as a controversialist, his capacity for public affairs—the nobleness and grandeur of his nature, which all men respected, and which made for him the fastest friends among those who were not of his Church. There were other great and good bishops, who by their saintly character and holy lives commanded a respectful toleration for their faith; but Bishop England extorted respect for his religion by the matchless power with which he unfolded its principles to those who crowded round him wherever he went, and refuted the calumnies and misrepresentations that had been the stock-in-trade of the enemies of Catholicity for centuries. Like all Irishmen, of that day as of the present, Bishop England at once became an American citizen, thoroughly identified with his adopted country, proud of her greatness, jealous of her honour, loving her beyond all others, save that old land whose recollection lay warm in his heart.

CHAPTER XXI

Bishop England's diocese—'Music hath Charms'—Preaching by the Wayside—
William George Read—'Mister Paul'—Taking a Fresh Start—Father O'Neill's
Two Hundred Children

BISHOP England's diocese, as we have seen, was sufficiently extensive to satisfy the most insatiate thirst for wide-spread jurisdiction. It extended from Charleston to Elizabeth city, North Carolina, a distance of 450 miles, and from Charleston to within 80 miles of Mobile—about 800 miles in the two directions. It was from 250 to 300 miles broad. Still, extensive as this vast territory was, it was not too much so for the energy of this extraordinary man, and the ardour of his priestly zeal. He would get through his missionary labours in this manner: possessing a little carriage, indifferently described as a 'sulky,' 'buggy,' or 'wagon,' the Bishop endeavoured, perhaps with the aid of one of his few monied friends, to purchase a pair of serviceable horses, or strong ponies, and, accompanied by a negro boy as driver, he would travel from place to place, preaching, instructing, and administering the sacraments; and on his return, it might be in three months, six months, or even nine months, he would readily and even profitably dispose of his cattle, then more valuable than at the commencement of the journey, owing to the training to which they had been subjected.

Many a strange incident, and even startling adventure, occurred to the Bishop during his long and arduous journeyings, at a time when the roads were little better or worse than tracks, the population was thinly scattered, and accommodation, even of the rudest kind, was not always to be had. Frequently, the shelter of the forest was all that could be obtained in those days for the traveller. Once in a city or town, he was sure of being well received; for while prejudice kept some aloof from the 'Popish Bishop,' curiosity, and the irrepressible desire of Americans to listen to sermons, discourses, 'lectures' of any description, impelled numbers to hear a man who was famous for his eloquence. Halls, court-houses, concert-rooms, churches and chapels, would be freely placed at his disposal; and the probability is, that he rarely suffered from lack of hospitality under those circumstances. But there were occasions when the Bishop found it difficult enough to make out a dinner, or secure the shelter of a roof against the night. Even in the Southern States, which are proverbial for the unaffected hospitality of their people, churls were to be met with, at least in Dr. England's time.

One evening the Bishop, who was on this occasion accompanied by one of his few priests—Father O'Neill; it need scarcely be added, a countryman of his own—drew up at a house of rather moderate dimensions, whose master was a marked specimen of the species Surly. Negotiations were entered into for a dinner, which the liberal host was willing to give on certain conditions, somewhat exorbitant in their nature; but there was to be no further accommodation. 'You cannot stop the night, nohow,' said the agreeable owner of the mansion; and his look of dogged dislike was quite as emphatic as his words. After dinner, Dr. England sat on a chair in the piazza, and read his 'office;' while Father O'Neill, having no desire to enjoy the company of his unwilling entertainer, sauntered towards the carriage, a little distance off, where the boy was feeding the horses; and taking his flute from his portmanteau, he sat on a log, and commenced his favourite air, 'The last Rose of Summer,' into which he seemed to breathe the very soul of tenderness. From one exquisite melody to another the player wandered, while the negro boy grinned with delight, and the horses enjoyed their food with a keener relish. That

Music hath charms to soothe the savage breast

was here exemplified. As the sweet notes stole on the soft night air of the South, and reached the inhospitable mansion, a head was eagerly thrust forth, and the projecting ears thereof appeared eagerly to drink in the flood of melody. Another lovely air, one of those which bring involuntary tears to the eyes, and fill the heart with balm, was played with lingering sweetness, when a voice, husky with emotion, was heard uttering these words—'Strangers! don't go!—do stay all night!—don't go; we'll fix you somehow.' It was the voice of the charmed host! That evening the two guests enjoyed the snuggest seats at the hearth, Father O'Neill playing for the family till a late hour. Next morning the master of the house would not accept of the least compensation. 'No, no, Bishop! no, no, Mr. O'Neill! not a cent! You're heartily welcome to it. Come as often as you please, and stay as long as you can. We'll be always glad to see you; but,' specially addressing Father O'Neill, 'be sure and don't forget the flute!'

There were occasions when not even Orpheus himself could have made out a dinner or a bed, had he been, like Bishop England, on the mission in the Southern States. Orpheus would have had to sleep where he could, and carry his dinner with him, as the Bishop very often did. The Bishop was not unfrequently obliged to be his own groom and servant, to look after the comfort of his horse, and see to the cooking of his simple meal. Tying the horse to a stake or a tree, he would brush him down and supply him with corn, and then commence preparations for his own refreshment. One night in the woods, the Bishop and Father O'Neill had taken their frugal supper, read their 'office,' and lain down by the fire to sleep; but they had not been long asleep when they awoke in fright: a few moments more, and the forest would have been on fire, and perhaps the two missionaries 'roasted like chestnuts,' as Father O'Neill afterwards said. The parasite ivy had caught the flame, and it was rapidly encircling a gigantic tree in an embrace of fire. By the most extraordinary exertions, such as fear could alone inspire, the ivy was torn down, the fire extinguished, the forest saved, and the great missionary longer preserved to the American Church.

The desire to hear the Bishop was not confined to any particular class; it was common to all. A somewhat curious instance, illustrative of his popularity as a preacher, occurred during one of his journeys. Arriving at a kind of wayside inn, or what may be described as a carman's stage, the Bishop found himself in the midst of a large convoy of cotton—wagons drawn by horses and mules, with a number of drivers and attendants, white men and negroes. His horses had been fed, and he was about to resume his journey, when a grave elderly man, who seemed to be in command, approached him with every mark of respect, saying—'Stranger, are you Bishop England?' On being answered in the affirmative, he continued— 'Mr. Bishop, we've heerd tell of you much. The folks say you are the most all-fired powerful preacher in this country. I had to leave Washington before you got there, and I can't get to Milledgville till you're gone. Would you, Mr. Bishop, mind giving us a bit of a sermon right here? It'll obleege me and my friends much—do, Mr. Bishop.' 'Do, Mr. Bishop!' was taken up, in full chorus, by the rest. The appeal so urged was irresistible with the zealous missionary, who yielded a ready assent. On the stump of a tree, which had been cut down to widen the road, the Bishop took his stand, the branches of a huge cedar flinging their grateful shadow over the preacher and the reverent group that clustered round him in mute expectation.

It was a scene for a painter—the great overhanging forest, the rude weather-stained log house, the open clearing lit up by a glowing sun, the huge wagons with their horses and mules, the bronzed weather-beaten countenances of the whites, the great eyes and gleaming teeth of negroes of every hue and tint. But the principal figure was not unworthy of its prominence—a man in the prime of life, of powerful well-knit frame, his lower limbs clad in breeches and silk stockings, that exhibited a leg of model symmetry—a face strong, massive, dark, full of power and passion—an eye that looked as if it would search the very soul: this was Bishop England, as he stood upon that tree stump by the way-side. Soon were his willing audience bound by the spell of his eloquence, as he unfolded before them the grand truths of religion, and explained to them their duties to God and their fellow-men. He had been about twenty minutes addressing them, when the leader stepped forward, and raising his hand, said—'That will do, Mr. Bishop, that will do; we're much obleeged to you, Mr. Bishop; it's all just as the folks say—you are an all-fired powerful preacher. We'd like to hear you always, but we musn't stop you now. Thank you, Mr. Bishop, thank you, Mr. Bishop.' 'Thank you, Mr. Bishop,' cried the rest in chorus. And amidst a cheer that would have tried the nerves of horses less trained than his, the Bishop started on his journey.

A brief memoir, or biographical sketch, is given in the first volume of 'The Works of the Right Rev. John England, First Bishop of Charleston,' published by Murphy and Co., of Baltimore. The memoir, too brief for the illustrious subject, is evidently written by one who loved the man, revered the prelate, and thoroughly appreciated his power of intellect, his energy of character, and his boundless zeal.

To an apparently trivial incident was that tribute eventually due. How the Bishop became known to his future biographer happened in this way:

A lady of rank and refinement came to Baltimore with the view of consulting a dentist of repute; whom she accordingly visited shortly after her arrival in that city. The case, though important to the lady, was not of that acute nature which required immediate attention; and the dentist having satisfied himself on this point, asked his visitor to excuse him that day, as he had made an engagement which he was very anxious to keep. 'In fact, madam, Bishop England, the most celebrated preacher in our country, is now in this city, and I had determined to hear him.' 'By all means, sir,' replied the lady, 'do carry out your intention—I can call as conveniently to-morrow.' The lady withdrew: but not well knowing how to dispose of her time, which hung rather heavily on her hands, she thought she could not do better, in order to occupy an hour or so, than go and hear the famous preacher. She went; and so strong was the impression produced on her mind by the Bishop, then in the full vigour of his intellect, that she became half a Catholic on the spot. On her return she confided to her brother—a man of considerable eminence as a scholar, and a gentleman of the highest personal character—the change wrought in her opinions respecting the Catholic Church. The brother received the startling intelligence with feelings of alarm and indignation. But how check the evil?—how draw her back from the fatal goal to which, with all the ardour and impulsiveness of a woman, she was so rapidly hurrying? He should himself undertake the fraternal duty of solving her doubts, and confuting her new-born errors; and the more surely to convince her of her folly, he commenced an earnest course of reading and enquiry—and in order to foil the Bishop with his own weapons, he resolved to hear him preach. He did go; and such was the power of the preacher, and the honest candour of the listener, that the alarmed and indignant brother was actually received into the Church before the sister, who was only on the road to it! And from the date of his conversion, the Catholic Church in America had not a bolder or abler champion than William George Read, the author of the 'Memoir of Bishop England.'

The clenching force of the Bishop's manner of reasoning may be illustrated by the following reply given by an Irishman, who was one of the warmest admirers of his distinguished countryman:—

'Well, Pat,' said a lady to the Irishman, 'what do you think of your bishop?'

'Think of him, ma'am! faith, ma'am, I think a deal of him, and why not? Isn't he grand, ma'am, when he crosses his two arms on his breast, and looks round at them all, after one of his regular smashers, as much as to say—

"Answer me that, and be d——d to you!" '

'Oh Pat!' remonstrated the lady, who, whatever she thought of the criticism, was somewhat startled at the manner in which it was expressed.

To break a lance with the 'Popish Bishop' was an object of no small ambition to the controversialists of his day; and many a fledgling repented his rash attempt to provoke him to an encounter. Animated by the determination to crush the great champion of Rome, a young preacher was unlucky enough to fasten on the Bishop with the pertinacity of a gad-fly. The Bishop happened to be travelling in the same stage with the preacher, and was engaged in an earnest conversation with some of his fellow-passengers, themselves men of mark and position, on a matter which then excited considerable public attention. To the preacher the subject of conversation had no attraction at that moment; he was only thinking of the splendid opportunity which the occasion afforded of striking a blow that would be heard of throughout America, and possibly be felt in the halls of the Vatican. First, he ventured a question, then a sneer, then a challenge, but without effect: the Bishop altogether disregarded his would-be antagonist, and merely waived him off with a careless gesture or a careless phrase.

The spiritual Quixote would not be put down, and would not be waived off; he was resolved on piercing the armour of his scornful foe, and humbling his pride in the presence of chosen spectators of his controversial prowess; and so he persevered, interrupting the conversation, to the annoyance of the other passengers, who preferred the discussion of a topic in which they had a personal and immediate interest, to a bootless polemical disputation. The valiant preacher was not to be extinguished by the cunning evasions or cowardly subterfuges of the faint-hearted Romanist; so he came again and again to the charge, flinging St. Paul at the Bishop with the most destructive intention. It was nothing but 'Paul' here, and 'Paul' there, and how could the champion of the 'Scarlet Woman' get over Paul?—and what answer could 'Antichrist' make to Paul? The nuisance becoming intolerable, the Bishop determined to put an end to it effectually. Confronting the preacher, and directing upon him the blaze of his great eyes, which gleamed with irrepressible fun, he placed his hands with solemn gesture on his knees, and in a deep voice gave utterance to this strange rebuke:—' Young man, young man! if you have not faith and piety sufficient to induce you to call the Apostle "*Saint* Paul*,*" at least have the good manners to call him "*Mister* Paul," and do not be perpetually calling him "Paul," "Paul," as if you considered him no better than a nigger.' The words, assisted by the comical gravity with which they were uttered, and enforced by the roar of laughter with which they were received by the delighted passengers, who had so long suffered from the infliction of his misdirected zeal, extinguished the poor preacher, who rapidly hid himself in the town at which the stage had just arrived. Nor was this the end of the disastrous encounter—for the story having soon got abroad, the unlucky man was interrupted by pome irreverent wag with 'Mister Paul—*Mister* Paul,' while addressing the congregation whom he had come to enlighten and inspire; and he had to leave the place in consequence of the absurdity of the affair.

One of Bishop England's most zealous and efficient clergymen was the Rev. Mr. O'Neill, through the influence of whose melodious flute he obtained, as we have seen, a free dinner and a good bed from one of the rustiest curmudgeons in

South Carolina. Father O'Neill was an Irish priest of the finest type, genial, cheery, and light-hearted, but earnest, and even stern, when the occasion required. Arrived at a patriarchal age, and honoured and respected by all classes of the community, he is still on the mission in the city of Savannah.

Father O'Neill could preach quite as well as he could play, nor was his tongue a less persuasive instrument than his flute. Indeed, it may be doubted if, in his most inspired moment, he could perform as successfully with the former as with the latter, and for the same length of time hold his audience spell-bound with the one as with the other. For Father O'Neill had marvellous powers of endurance as a preacher, or lecturer; and his audience were so 'kept alive' by his manner, in which argument, illustration, wit, and delicate humour were agreeably blended, that they did not perceive the time passing, and were rather sorry than otherwise when 'the Father' gave in.

On one occasion he was preaching somewhere in Georgia, and the country round had assembled to hear him. At the end of two hours and a half, during which there was not the slightest symptom of weariness exhibited by a densely crowded audience, he said that the expiring condition of the candles warned him to bring his remarks to a close. Quick as thought, an Irishwoman, who occupied a conspicuous position among the audience, and who would willingly have sat there till morning, cried out, 'Never mind that, your reverence; sure we brought half-a-box of candles along with us, as we thought you'd need them.' The wise considerateness of the Irishwoman was hailed with general satisfaction, and with brighter auspices the preacher resumed his discourse.

There was one occasion, however, when Father O'Neill surpassed all his former achievements. It was on the reception of a Mrs. Taylor into the Catholic Church.

Mrs. Taylor was a lady of good social position, whose conversion to Catholicism excited much interest among her friends and neighbours. Her reception into the Church was to be made an occasion of some solemnity, and invitations were sent to the gentry for miles round, requesting their attendance at the ceremony, which was to be followed by a banquet of more than usual elegance and profusion. The auspicious morning arrived. In the grand saloon, where an altar had been erected, were assembled sixty or seventy people, and crowding in front of the windows of the apartment were groups of negroes, to whom the day was to be one of welcome rest and rejoicing. At the termination of the Mass, Mrs. Taylor was to be received. Punctual to the appointed hour—eight o'clock in the morning—Father O'Neill commenced. Wearing his soutane, or cassock, he made his appearance at the temporary altar, on which the various robes and vestments worn by a priest in the celebration of Mass were placed. Referring to the purpose of the day's ceremony, he stated the leading reasons why a Protestant should become a Catholic. He then specially explained the doctrine of the Mass, dealing with it as a sacrament and a sacrifice; and having justified the use of the Latin language in its celebration, he said he would represent the symbolical meaning of each vestment as he put it on; which he did in a popular and persuasive manner, that excited the interest and riveted the attention of his audience. Having concluded his series of discourses, and being then fully robed, he turned to the altar to commence; but seeing that one of the candles had been entirely consumed, and that the other was flickering in its socket, he glanced at his watch, and found that the hour was within a quarter to two o'clock! Zealous priest! patient audience! Father O'Neill took the matter coolly, saying, 'My friends, 'I have committed an oversight. According to the ordinary laws of the Church, Mass should commence before twelve o'clock. In a missionary country, like ours, we have the privilege of commencing an hour later—any time up to one. But now it is approaching two, and I cannot proceed with the service. I am sorry for your disappointment this morning; but if you will come to-morrow morning at eight o'clock, we will take a fresh start.' The audience bore the disappointment with perfect equanimity, and were determined to see the ceremony to the end; so they enjoyed the hospitality of Mrs. Taylor for the remainder of the day, and next morning again assembled in the saloon at the appointed hour, when Father O'Neill took his 'fresh start'; this time with such energy that the whole was well finished by twelve o'clock.

But Father O'Neill could be quite as effective in a short speech as in a lengthened discourse; and on an occasion of much interest, and in a time of no small anti-foreign and anti-Catholic excitement, he delivered a few pithy sentences which produced a most salutary effect. It was at a public dinner in Savannah, to celebrate the inauguration of a monument erected to Pulaski, one of the heroes of the Revolution of 1776, who, wounded at the Battle of Savannah, had died a few days after. There had been a procession and an oration in the day, and a grand dinner was to be the agreeable wind-up of an event so dear to the patriotic heart. There could be no public dinner in Savannah that did not include the popular Irish priest as one of the guests, and, as a matter of invariable routine Father O'Neill should have a toast or a sentiment to propose. It was in the time when the wretched 'Know-Nothing' excitement was rife in most parts of America, and the furious cry of 'Down with the foreigner! down with the Papist!' found an echo in the South.

'I have listened,' said Father O'Neill, 'to the oration of the day. It was excellent, so far as it went. But it omitted one most essential point—about Pulaski himself. I will supply the deficiency. Pulaski was a foreigner, who had the extraordinary habit of saying his beads every day. He, a foreigner and a Catholic, shed his blood and sacrificed his life for this country. And I am sure that the monument erected by the grandsons of the heroic men who fought and bled side by side with Pulaski is a proof that they still adhere to the glorious principles of their fathers, who welcomed all brave men—whatever their race or religion—to their country.'

The effect was electrical. The majority of the excited audience exclaimed 'Bravo!' and cheered with ardour; while the few hung their heads with shame, crushed by the implied rebuke, and the courage which inspired its utterance.

Father O'Neill lost and won the good graces of a Protestant lady by an admission of paternity, which, well understood in a Catholic country, was rather startling in the America of that day. He and the Rev. Mr. Byrne, afterwards Bishop of Arkinsau, were travelling from Fayetteville to Cherau, in South Carolina, and stopped for the night at the house of a respectable Protestant lady. The lady being elderly, used the privilege of her sex, and made many enquiries respecting her guests. Having satisfied herself on various points, she at length asked Father O'Neill if he had a family. 'Yes, madam,' replied the priest. 'How many children have you, sir?' enquired the lady. 'Two hundred, madam,' as the astounding answer. 'Two—two—hundred, sir!' gasped the bewildered hostess. 'Yes, madam—two hundred,' coolly replied her guest. Had there been Mormons in those days, she might have imagined she had afforded hospitality to Brigham Young himself; but as Joe Smith had not then made his famous discovery, she possibly had a vague idea of the Grand Turk, or some such polygamous potentate, being beneath her modest roof. She became silent and reserved, displaying an icy civility to the minister with the appallingly large family. On a subsequent occasion Mr. Byrne travelled alone, and stopped at the same house. The old lady rather hesitatingly enquired after 'the other minister,' and then, with more marked hesitation, asked if it were really true that he had so enormous a family as he said he had. Father Byrne laughed heartily at the question, but more at the manner in which it was asked, and explained that Catholic priests did not marry; that by his 200 'children' Father O'Neill meant his congregation—whom he regarded in that light. The old lady's face brightened with pleasure at the explanation of what had been a source of serious and constant perplexity to her ever since she had heard the startling statement from the lips of 'the other minister.' 'Well, sir, he must be a good man!' she said; 'I am sorry I did not understand him at the time. That's just the way a minister should speak and think of his flock. Be sure, sir, to give him my respects when you meet him, and tell him I shall be always happy to have him in this house.' For the future the good old soul felt no embarrassment when enquiring after the two hundred children of the Irish priest.

CHAPTER XXII

Dangers from within and without—The Lay Trustees—A Daring Hoax—
Burning of the Charlestown Convent—A Grateful Ruffian—'Awful Disclosures of
Maria Monk'—Protestant Verdict on Maria Monk

THERE were in those early days of the American Church dangers from within as well as dangers from without, and it may be said that the former were more perilous to the Church, and a more formidable obstacle to her influence and progress, than those which were purely external. These interior causes of difficulty arose mainly from the system of lay trusteeship, which in too many dioceses— notably Philadelphia, New York, and Charleston—were the occasion of long-standing feuds, and of grave public scandal. Certain members of the laity— generally men of little faith, much vanity, and strong self-conceit—braved and defied the authority of their Bishops, treated with contempt the discipline of the Church, and even ventured to appoint and dismiss pastors at their pleasure! The great body of the faithful had no sympathy whatever with the acts of those who, not only by their intrigues and turbulence, but by making their contentions the subject of constant proceedings in courts of law, brought much discredit on Catholicity. It required, on the part of the Bishop who found himself so painfully circumstanced, not merely the greatest prudence and wisdom, but firmness and determination. Occasionally, either through gentleness of nature or utter weariness of soul, or from a spirit of conciliation—in the hope of healing an ugly wound, and preventing further evil—a Bishop consented to surrender some portion of his legitimate authority; but there were others, and those the larger number, who, being of stronger and sterner nature, resolutely set their foot against all and every encroachment on the episcopal functions, and, by sheer force of character, vanquished the intriguers, and crushed schism wherever it showed its head. It would be a profitless task to refer further to events which may be left to merited oblivion, but which planted thorns in the mitre of many an American prelate. There is, however, a circumstance connected with the schism in Philadelphia to which allusion may be made with profit.

To the conduct of a misguided and headstrong priest named Hogan, who afterwards apostatized and took to himself a wife, was due a prolonged scandal in the city of Philadelphia. It is sufficient to state that, although deprived of his faculties by his Bishop, he still continued to perform the priestly functions— openly defying the episcopal authority. The daring contumacy of the unhappy man left no option to the Bishop but at once to cut him off from the Church of which he proved himself so unworthy a minister; and the priest was accordingly excommunicated according to the form prescribed by the Roman pontifical. This necessary act of vigour on the part of the Bishop of Philadelphia was made the occasion of one of the most daring literary frauds probably heard of in America before that date—though, as we shall show a little further on, a second, of more serious consequences, was perpetrated in a few years after. The excommunication being a matter of public notoriety, it was deemed advisable by the enemies of the Church to turn it to the best account against the 'tyranny and despotism of Rome;' and accordingly there was published in a Philadelphia newspaper a form of excommunication which, naturally enough, excited no little horror in the mind of the community. A sample or two of this precious document will afford the reader a sufficient idea of the whole:—

May he be damned wherever he be, whether in the house or in the stable, or the garden, or the field, or the highway, or in the path, or in the wood, or in the water, or in the church; may he be cursed in living and in dying. ....

May he be cursed inwardly and outwardly, may he be cursed in his brains, and in his vertex, in his temples, in his eyes, in his eyebrows, in his cheeks, in his jaw-bones, in his nostrils, in his teeth and grinders, in his lips, in his throat, in his shoulders, in his arms, in his fingers.

May he be damned in his mouth, in his breast, in his heart and purtenance, down to the very stomach.

Even his 'toe-nails' were not spared in this terrible anathema. Those who search for the original of this excommunication in the Roman pontifical would fail to discover it there; but those familiar with light literature may find it in *Tristram Shandy*! In his *Miscellany*, which did so much for the defence of the Church and the cause of religion, Bishop England, who was thoroughly familiar with the writings of Laurence Sterne, promptly exposed the unblushing fraud. But as it is difficult to overtake a lie, let it have never so short a start, many believed in the cursing of the grinders and the toe-nails—perhaps do to this day.

That the spirit of hostility to the Catholic Church was as virulent as ever, we have evidence in the Pastoral Letter of 1833; and an event which followed shortly after—the burning of the convent of Charlestown, Massachusetts—is a proof how successful were the appeals which were then, as in years subsequent, made by malignant sectaries and dishonest politicians to the passions of the unthinking and the brutal. The Bishops say:—

We notice with regret a spirit exhibited by some of the conductors of the press engaged in the interests of those brethren separated from our communion which has within a few years become more unkind and unjust in our regard. Not only do they assail us and our institutions in a style of vituperation and offence, misrepresent our tenets, vilify our practices, repeat the hundred-times-refuted calumnies of days of angry and bitter contention in other lands, but they had even denounced you and us as enemies to the Republic, and have openly proclaimed the fancied necessity of not only obstructing our progress, but of using their best efforts to extirpate our religion; and for this purpose they have collected large sums of money. It is neither our principle nor our practice to render evil for evil, nor railing for railing; and we exhort you rather to the contrary, to render blessing, for unto this you are called, that you by inheritance may obtain a blessing. .... We are too well known to our fellow citizens to render it necessary that we should exhibit the utter want of any ground upon which such charges could rest. We, therefore, advise you to heed them not; but to continue, whilst you serve God with fidelity, to discharge honestly, faithfully, and with affectionate attachment, your duties to the government under which you live, so that we may, in common with our fellow-citizens, sustain that edifice of rational liberty in which we find such excellent protection.

There are in Charlestown—a little outside the City of Boston, which boasts, perhaps with justice, of being the Athens of America—two monuments. One is a monument of glory. The other is a monument of shame. On Bunker's Hill is reared aloft a noble pillar, on which is recorded the triumph of a young nation in the proud assertion of its right to govern itself; and among the names of the heroes who fought and bled in the cause of human liberty are those of Catholics, foreigners and natives. On Mount Benedict, from which the tower of liberty was every day beheld, there remain to this hour the blackened ruins of the Ursuline Convent, destroyed on the night of the 11th of August, 1834, by a ferocious mob, to whose lawless violence neither check nor impediment of any kind was offered. Deceived by reckless falsehood, blinded by the foulest calumnies, their passions infuriated by the harangues of clerical incendiaries, a savage multitude flung themselves upon the dwelling of helpless women and innocent children, and after plundering whatever was portable, and destroying what they could not take away, set fire to it amidst fiendish rejoicings, and with the most complete impunity. What was the origin of this infamous exhibition of ferocity and cowardice? A lie—a fiction—an invention—the coinage of a wicked or a foolish brain. It was the old story, so grateful to the ear of bigotry. A nun was said to be detained in the convent against her will, and was there pining in a subterranean dungeon! The old story, but of marvellous vitality and eternal freshness—told in Boston thirty-three years since—told in Montreal in a few months after—told yesterday or to-day of any convent in England. To this story, old and yet ever new, was added the usual imputation of the systematic infamy of women whose lives were devoted to God's service. On Sunday—the Lord's Day!—the trumpet-note of hate was sounded from more than one pulpit; and on Monday night the fine institution, erected at great cost, was given to destruction.

It would be a malignant slander on the fair fame of Boston to assert that this disgraceful outrage, which sent a thrill of horror and disgust through the civilised world, was sympathised with by any considerable portion of the citizens of that enlightened community. So far from sympathising with a deed which was in the last degree dishonouring to the reputation of their city, a number of Protestant gentlemen, of position and influence, were appointed at a meeting, publicly held the day after in Faneuil Hall, to investigate the circumstances of the outrage, and assist in bringing the perpetrators to justice. A report was presented by that committee, with the signatures of thirty-eight eminent citizens attached to it. Drawn up with singular ability, it put to shame the miserable bigots to whose malice or fanatical credulity the national scandal was entirely owing. The Committee, after describing the Order of Ursulines, their objects, and their institution—of which they state that of sixty pupils, 'for the most part children of those among the most respectable families in the country, of various religious denominations,' not more than ten of whom at any time were Catholics—they present a striking picture of the outrage, which they indignantly denounce. Even at this day—for calumny is still rife, and fanaticism never dies—it may be useful as well as instructive to reproduce this startling description of what men will do when impelled by a blind savage impulse of unchristian hate.

At the time of this attack upon the convent (say the Committee of Protestant gentlemen) there were within its walls about sixty female children and ten adults, one of whom was in the last stage of pulmonary consumption, another suffering under convulsion fits, and the unhappy female who had been the immediate cause of the excitement was, by the agitation of this night, in raving delirium. No warning was given of the intended assault, nor could the miscreants by whom it was made have known whether their missiles might not kill or wound the helpless inmates of this devoted dwelling. Fortunately for them, cowardice prompted what mercy and manhood denied: after the first attack the assailants paused awhile, from the fear that some secret force was concealed in the convent, or in ambush to surprise them; and in the interval the governess was enabled to secure the retreat of her little flock and terrified sisters into the garden. But before this was fully effected, the rioters, finding they had nothing but women and children against them, regained their courage, and, ere all the inmates could escape, entered the building. . .

Three or four torches, which were, or precisely resembled, engine torches, were then brought up from the road; and immediately upon their arrival the rioters proceeded into every room in the building, rifling every drawer, desk, and trunk which they found, and breaking up and destroying all the furniture, and casting much of it from the windows; sacrificing in their brutal fury costly pianofortes, and harps, and other valuable instruments, the little treasures of the children, abandoned in the hasty flight, and even the vessels and symbols of Christian worship.

After having thus ransacked every room in the building, they proceeded, with great deliberation, about one o'clock, to make preparations for setting fire to it. For this purpose, broken furniture, books, curtains, and other combustible materials, were placed in the centre of several of the rooms; and, as if in mockery of God as well as of man, *the Bible was cast, with shouts of exultation, upon the pile first kindled; and as upon this were subsequently thrown the vestments used in religious service, and the ornaments of the altar, those shouts and yells were repeated. Nor did they cease until the cross was wrenched from its place, as the final triumph of this fiendish enterprise.*

But the work of destruction did not end here; for after burning down the Bishop's Lodge, in which there was a valuable library, the rioters proceeded to the farm-house, and gave it also to the flames, and then reduced an extensive barn to ashes. 'And not content with all this,' say the Committee of Protestant gentlemen, 'they *burst open the tomb of the establishment, rifled it of the sacred vessels there deposited, wrested the plates from the coffins, and exposed to view the mouldering remains of their tenants!'*

Nor (say they) is it the least humiliating feature in this scene of cowardly and audacious violation of all that man ought to hold sacred and dear, that it was perpetrated in the presence of men vested with authority, and of multitudes of our fellow-citizens, while not one arm was lifted in defence of helpless women and children, or in vindication of the violated laws of God and man. The spirit of violence, sacrilege, and plunder reigned triumphant. Crime alone seemed to confer courage, while humanity, manhood, and patriotism quailed, or stood irresolute and confounded in its presence.

The report, able and searching, thus stingingly concludes: 'And if this cruel and unprovoked injury, perpetrated in the heart of the commonwealth, be permitted to pass unrepaired, our boasted toleration and love of order, our vaunted obedience to law, and our ostentatious proffers of an asylum to the persecuted of all sects and nations, may well be accounted vainglorious pretensions, or yet more wretched hypocrisy.'

There were trials, no doubt; but, save in one instance, they ended in the acquittal of the accused, of whom the leader was a ferocious savage, who thus addressed his sympathising friends through the public press:—

A CARD.—John R. Buzzell begs leave, through your paper, to tender his sincere thanks to the citizens of Charlestown, Boston, and Cambridge, for the expressions of kindness and *philanthropy* manifested towards him on his acquittal of the charge of aiding in the destruction of the convent; also would gratefully remember the *gentlemanly* deportment of Mr. Watson, while imprisoned in Cambridge Gaol.

The reader may be pardoned for not knowing whether it was the individual complimented for his gentlemanly deportment, or the author of this card—this ludicrous and shameful commentary on the whole proceedings—that was imprisoned. We must assume that Mr. John E. Buzzell, the gallant leader in the outrage on women and children, was the unwilling tenant of the gaol of which Mr. Watson was the custodian of 'gentlemanly deportment.' Before this wretched man Buzzell died, he admitted, what his jury would not, that he was one of the perpetrators of the outrage. And from the day that Mr. Buzzell returned his thanks for the 'kindness and philanthropy' of those who stamped, and yelled, and clapped their hands at his acquittal, and for Mr. Watson's 'gentlemanly deportment' to him while in gaol, that atrocious violation of the laws of God and man is, we shall not say unavenged, but yet unredressed; to this hour, and as it were within the very shadow of the proud record of Boston's glory, lie the blackened evidences of Boston's shame.

Bigotry is the most contagious of all diseases of the human mind, nor is there any moral epidemic whose poison travels more swiftly, or affects more readily or more fatally the sobriety of communities. From Charlestown, Massachusetts, to Charleston, South Carolina, the malignant influence was borne; but had the John K. Buzzells of the latter city attempted to carry their intentions into execution, they would have experienced something less pleasant than 'kindness and philanthropy' and 'gentlemanly deportment;' for at the first hint of danger, a gallant band of Irishmen rallied in defence of the menaced convent of Charleston, and its Irish Bishop coolly examined the flints of their rifles, to satisfy himself that there should be no missing fire—no failure of summary justice. The John E. Buzzells are brave against women; but they care less to see a man's eye gleaming along a musket-barrel, if the ominous-looking tube be pointed at their precious persons. So in South Carolina and in other States, the resolute attitude of those who would have willingly died in defence of the best and noblest of humanity, saved the country at that time from still deeper disgrace.

Shortly after the destruction of the Charlestown Convent by fire, there was perpetrated perhaps the most daring as well as the most infamous swindle upon public credulity ever recorded in the history of fraud; namely, the 'Awful Disclosures of Maria Monk'—the result of a foul conspiracy, of which a dissolute preacher and his miserable tool were among the chief actors. Although that 'damnable invention' was exposed in all its naked vileness; though Maria Monk's mother made solemn oath that the abandoned preacher, her daughter's paramour, had, with another of the conspirators, unavailingly endeavoured to bribe her to support the imposture; though the sect to which the preacher belonged, and whom he had cheated in some money transactions, flung him off with public expressions of loathing; though the conspirators after-wards wrangled about their infamous spoils, and more than one of them admitted the falsehood of the whole story: though, in fact, it was proved that the 'Awful Disclosures' were a verbal copy of a Spanish or Portuguese work which had been translated half a century before; though the monstrous lie was disproved in every form and manner in which a lie could be disproved—still the influence of that lie is felt to this very hour, not only in Canada and in the States, but in Europe. While in Canada, in the autumn of 1866, I read, to my profound astonishment, even more than to my disgust, an article in a Canadian paper said to have influence with a certain class, written in reference to education in convents, and in which article the literary lunatic described those institutions as 'sinks of iniquity.' I might have supposed—did I not know that Maria Monk died in the Tombs of New York, to which prison she had been committed for theft—that the conspiracy was still in full swing, and that the writer—to judge him in the most charitable manner—was one of its besotted dupes. We shall hereafter see how this atrocious book, sworn to by the unscrupulous and believed in by the prejudiced, has poisoned the minds of a generous but credulous people.

We may dismiss this revolting case with a few lines from the statement of Colonel Stone, of New York, who, in company with some half dozen other persons, all of them Protestants, visited and inspected the Hotel Dieu, of Montreal, the scene of the alleged iniquities, which included child massacre scarcely less wholesale than Herod's slaughter of the innocents. It may be remarked that several parties, many of whom were not without faith in the 'Awful Disclosures,' returned from their investigation with the same conviction as that expressed by Colonel Stone, who says:—

I have rarely seen so many ladies together possessing in so great a degree the charm of manner. They were all affability and kindness. Cheerfulness was universal, and very unlike the notions commonly entertained of the gloom of the cloister. Their faces were too often wreathed in smiles to allow us to suppose that they were soon to assist in smothering their own children, or that those sweet spirits were soon to be trodden out of their bodies by the rough-shod priests of the Seminary. .... Indeed, I have never witnessed in any community or family more unaffected cheerfulness and good humour, nor more satisfactory evidence of entire confidence, esteem, and harmony among each other.

Having tested every wall in the building, examined every receptacle for potatoes and turnips, every dungeon devoted to the incarceration of soap and candles or loaf sugar, poked at mortar with an iron-shod stick, peeped into every corner and crevice of the whole establishment, and elaborately traced his progress and its results, the Colonel thus pronounces the judgment of an intelligent and rational mind:—

Thus ended this examination, in which we were most actively engaged for about three hours. The result is the most thorough conviction that Maria Monk is *an arrant impostor—that she never was a nun, and was never within the walls of the Hotel Dieu—and consequently that her disclosures are wholly and unequivocally, from beginning to end, untrue—either the vagaries of a distempered brain, or a series of calumnies unequalled in the depravity of their invention, and unsurpassed in their enormity.* There are those, I am well aware, who will not adopt this conclusion, though one should arise from the dead and attest it—even though 'Noah, Daniel, and Job,' were to speak from the slumber of ages and confirm it.

CHAPTER XXIII

Bishop England's Devotion to the Negro—The Frenchman Vanquished—The Bishop stripped to his Shirt—Bishop England's Death—Spiritual Destitution—As late as 1847—The Sign of the Cross—Keeping the Faith—Bishop Hughes— Bishop Hughes and the School Question—A Lesson for the Politicians—The Riots of Philadelphia—The Native-American Party—The Bishop and the Mayor— Progress of the Church

WE may return to Bishop England, ere, worn out—spent by fatigue and malady—he is snatched from the faithful that loved him as their father, and from the Church which honoured him as one of her stoutest champions and strongest pillars.

Notwithstanding the difficulties of his position, arising in no small degree from the infidel spirit displayed by some unworthy members of his flock, whose vanity and self-sufficiency rendered them impatient of all control, Bishop England prosecuted his mission with characteristic energy. Nor were the three States which constituted his enormous diocese wide enough for the greatness of his zeal. He was to be heard of in most parts of the Union, preaching, lecturing, propagating truth, confounding error; and wherever he went he was surrounded by the leading members of other churches, or those who were of no church, who constitute a rather numerous body in America. He also made frequent visits to Europe; and it is told of him with truth that from a chamber in the Vatican this 'Steam Bishop,' as he was styled in Rome, would announce the day when he was to administer confirmation in the interior of Georgia! This Catholic Bishop found time amidst his pressing avocations, to promote the spread of literary and scientific knowledge in the City of Charleston; and as a minister of peace he fulfilled his vocation by the formation of an anti-duelling association, of which General Thomas Pickney, of revolutionary fame, was the president. As a lecturer, few, if any, equalled Bishop England, and in the pulpit he had no rival in his day in the United States; but it was when the Yellow Fever made havoc among his flock—black as well as white—that the Christian Bishop was seen in all his glory. It was as he hurried from sick bed to sick bed, his charity glowing with an ardour more intense than the sun that seemed to rain down fire on his head, while it scorched the ground beneath his badly-protected feet, that those who were not of his communion thoroughly understood the man. When the poor negro was in health, the Bishop would turn from the wealthy and the learned to instruct him in the truths of religion; and when stricken down by the plague, of which the Black Vomit was the fatal symptom, his first care was for the dying slave. Bishop England did not venture to oppose slavery—few men would have been rash enough even to have hinted at such a policy in his day; but he ever proved himself the truest friend of that unhappy class, and did much to mitigate the hardship of their position. His, indeed, was the policy of his Church in America.

In the diary from which I have quoted, the Bishop more than once makes an entry of this kind: 'Was invited to preach before the Legislature. Preached to a numerous and attentive audience.' Not a word to afford an idea of the effect produced by his discourse. But we have in the brief memoir written by his devoted friend and admirer, William George Read, an account of one of these discourses and its effect:—

An illiberal majority was once organised, in the Lower House of the Legislature of South Carolina, to refuse a charter of incorporation to a community of nuns, whose invaluable services he was desirous to secure for the education of the female portion of his flock at Charleston. They were a branch of that same admirable Ursuline Order whose convent had been pillaged and burned, with such unmanly cruelty, in one of our eastern cities. Some of his friends procured him an invitation to preach before the Senate, and many of the members of the Lower House attended through curiosity. He spoke of religion, its claims, its obligations. He discoursed of toleration. He held up Massachusetts to their scorn. He adverted to the subject of his charter—hurled defiance at them—showed them how he could possess the entire State, for ecclesiastical purposes, had he the means to buy it, despite their narrow-souled policy. He exposed to them the folly of driving those of his communion from the high road of legalised establishments, into the bye-paths of the law. He changed his theme, and told of Catholic charity; arrayed before them her countless institutions for promoting the glory of God and the welfare of man. There was not a dry eye in the house; his Bill was passed without a division on the following day.

It was strange that, although Bishop England's speaking voice was rich and tuneful, equal to the expression of every emotion, he had no faculty whatever for vocal harmony, and lacked the power of turning the simplest air, or singing the least difficult bar of music. His efforts at singing High Mass were pitiable; and, were it not for the solemnity of the occasion, his performance would be more calculated to excite merriment than to inspire devotion. When first appointed to the parish of Bandon, an attempt was made by an excellent and pious man to try and 'hammer' as much music into the new Parish Priest as would enable him to get through his functions as High Priest with some approach to decency; but, though Father England's Bandon instructor was animated by a profound reverence for the dignity of Catholic worship, he failed—miserably failed—in the hopeless attempt. But what all the pious enthusiasm of the honest Bandonian could not accomplish for the ungifted Parish Priest, the vanity of a Frenchman made him believe he could succeed in achieving for the great Bishop of Charleston. The Frenchman felt confident he could make the Bishop sing; the Bishop was certain, and with better reason, that he could not be made to sing. The Professor was positive in his belief and demanded the opportunity of testing his powers, which opportunity was freely afforded to him by the Bishop; and to work they went, the Professor elated with the anticipation of his glorious triumph, the Bishop thoroughly reconciled to his vocal incapacity. They commenced, the teacher ail zeal, the pupil all docility. 'Bravi, bravi!' cried the Professor, as the first note or two rewarded a long and laborious lesson. The world would hear of this splendid achievement; all America would do homage to science in the person of the Professor. The lessons and the practice proceeded; but as they did, so did the Professor's confidence abate. Had the task been simply impossible, it was his duty, as a Frenchman, to accomplish it; but this was something more than impossible. Still the gallant son of Gaul bravely struggled on, hoping against hope—rather, hoping against despair. At length, even the courage of his nation gave way; and thus the crestfallen Professor addressed his doomed but smiling pupil—'Ah, monseigneur! vous prêchez comme un ange, et vous écrivez comme un ange; mais vous chantez diablement!' There is a capital story told of the Bishop doing duty for a Protestant pastor; and it is so characteristic of the liberal side of American Christianity that it may be given in the words of Dr. England's enthusiastic admirer, Mr. Read:—

During one of his visitations he had been obliged with the loan of a Protestant church, for the purpose of delivering a course of lectures on the Catholic religion. On Saturday evening the regular pastor came to him to 'ask a favour.' 'I am sure,' said the Bishop, 'you would not ask what I would not gladly grant.' 'Occupy my pulpit, then, to-morrow! I have been so much engrossed by your lectures through the week, that I have utterly forgotten my own pastoral charge, and am unprepared with a sermon.' 'I should be most happy to oblige you, but are you aware that we can have no partnerships?' 'I have thought of all that—regulate everything as you think proper.' 'At least,' said the Bishop, 'I can promise you that nothing shall be said or done which you or any of your congregation will disapprove.'

On the morrow the novel spectacle was seen of a Catholic Bishop, arrayed in his ordinary episcopal vesture, advancing to the pulpit of this Protestant congregation. He invited them to sing some hymns he had previously selected from those they were accustomed to; read to them from the Douay translation of the Bible; recited appropriate prayers, such as all could freely join in, from a hook of Catholic devotion; preached them a sound practical discourse, and dismissed them with a blessing, wondering if such could be the doctrine and the worship they had so often heard denounced as 'the doctrine of devils.'

It was the custom of the Bishop to wear his ordinary episcopal robes—soutane, rotchet, and short purple cape—whenever he was preaching, whether in a public courthouse or a Protestant church. Many of these latter buildings being in his time rather primitive structures, and affording little accommodation for robing, he was frequently compelled to perform his ecclesiastical toilet behind the pulpit. This happened on one occasion, when his fame was at its height, and people of every creed, as well as class and condition, rushed to hear the famous preacher. One of the robes worn by a Bishop, the rotchet, is a kind of surplice, usually made of muslin or fine linen, and trimmed with lace. Dr. England remained some time hidden from the view of the audience, probably engaged in prayer; and the expectation was somewhat increased in consequence. At length, one, more impatient or more curious than the rest, ventured on a peep, and saw the Bishop in his rotchet, and before he had time to put on his cape; and, rather forgetting the character of the place, and the nature of the occasion, he cried out in a voice that rang throughout the building—'Boys! the Bishop's stripped to his shirt!—he's in earnest, I tell you; and darn me, if he ain't going to give us hell this time.' The Bishop, who, Irishman like, dearly loved a joke, and who frequently told the story, ever with unabated relish, mounted the steps of the pulpit, and looked upon his audience as calmly and with as grave a countenance as if these strange words had never reached his ears.

Too soon, alas! was the life of the great Bishop to come to a close. Returning from Europe in a ship amongst whose steerage passengers malignant dysentery broke out, this noble Christian minister laboured incessantly in the service of the sick. He was at once priest, doctor, and nurse, and during the voyage he scarcely ever slept in his cabin; an occasional doze on a sofa was all that his zeal and humanity would allow him to enjoy. Exhausted in mind and body, and with the seeds of the fatal disease in his constitution, Dr. England landed in Philadelphia; but instead of betaking himself to his bed, and placing himself under the care of a physician, he preached, and lectured, and transacted an amount of business suited only to the most robust health. In Baltimore he stayed four days, and preached five times.

When he arrived here (says Mr. Read) his throat was raw with continued exertion. I discovered the insidious disease that was sapping his strength. I saw his constitution breaking up. He was warned, with the solicitude of the tenderest affection, against continuing these destructive efforts. The weather was dreadful. But he felt it his duty to go on. He said only, 'I hope I shall not drop at the altar— if I do, bring me home.' He wished to do the work he was sent to perform. Exhausted by fatigue, overwhelmed with visitors, he was yet ready at the last moment to give an audience to a stranger who begged admission for the solution of a single doubt; and never did I listen to so precise, so clear, so convincing an exposition of the transubstantiated presence of our Redeemer in the Holy Eucharist. His auditor was a person of intelligence and candour, and the Bishop exhausted, for his instruction, the resources of philosophical objection to the sacred tenet; to show how futile are the cavils of man in opposition to the explicit declaration of God.

His death was worthy of his life. Nothing could be more in keeping with the character of the Christian Bishop. The dying words of this great Prelate of the American Church, addressed to his clergy, who were kneeling round his bed, were noble and impressive, full of paternal solicitude for his flock, and the most complete resignation to the will of his Divine Master. He humbly solicited the forgiveness of his clergy for whatever might at the time have seemed harsh or oppressive in his conduct; but he truly declared that he had acted from a sense of duty, and in the manner best adapted to the end he had in view—their good. 'I confess,' said the dying Prelate, 'it has likewise happened, owing partly to the perplexities of my position, and chiefly to my own impetuosity, that my demeanour has not always been as meek and courteous as it ever should have been; and that you have experienced rebuffs, when you might have anticipated kindness. Forgive me! Tell my people that I love them—tell them how much I regret that circumstances have kept us at a distance from each other. My duties and my difficulties have prevented me from cultivating and strengthening those private ties which ought to bind us together; your functions require a closer and more constant intercourse with them. Be with them—be of them—win them to God. Guide, govern, and instruct them, that you may do it with joy, and not with grief.' In this his last address he did not forget his infant institutions, which were never so dear to his paternal heart as at that moment, when he appealed to his weeping clergy in their behalf; and to the Sisters, who afterwards knelt by his bedside, he bequeathed lessons of wisdom and courage. Almost his last words were, 'I had hoped to rise—but I bow to the will of God, and accept what He appoints.'

By his grave stood the representatives of every sect and communion, offering their last tribute of respect to one who did honour to his native land in the country of his adoption. The press of the United States joined in one universal chorus of sorrow for his loss, and admiration of his exalted merits as a scholar and orator, as a Christian minister, a patriot, and a citizen; for had he been born on her soil, he could not more thoroughly have identified himself with the glory and greatness of America than he did. Even in 1842, when he was lost to the Church, his flock—scattered over three vast States -did not exceed 8,000 souls; but by his matchless zeal and singular power of organisation, and his firmness in dealing with the turbulent and refractory, he succeeded in establishing order in the midst of chaos; and, by his own living example of every virtue which could adorn humanity, even more than by his intellectual power, did the illustrious Bishop England render the name of Catholic respected.

When in 1832 the first Council of Baltimore assembled, the Catholics of the United States numbered not less than half a million. In 1830, according to Bishop Dubois, the Catholic population of the diocese of New York was 150,000, of whom 35,000 were in the city of that name. In 1834 the number in the latter must have been at least 50,000, and in the diocese 200,000, as emigration was steadily setting in; and though the emigration of that day was generally diffused through the country, still the greater portion of this life-current was even then directed to the Empire City. There were at that time—in 1834—in the entire of the State of New York and the portion of New Jersey combined with it in the diocese, but nineteen churches, not a few of which were utterly unworthy of that distinction—being miserable wooden shanties, hastily run up by poor congregations; and the number of priests for this enormous territory, which is now divided into five dioceses, did not exceed five-and-twenty! Too many of the scattered congregations of this vast diocese had not for years seen the face of a priest, or heard the saving truths of religion from a minister of their own faith; and the young people grew up to manhood and womanhood with only such imperfect knowledge of sacred subjects as the scanty information of simple parents could afford them.

One may easily imagine how difficult it was, under those circumstances, for the Irish Catholic to preserve the faith. The Irish Protestant, no matter of what sect or denomination, found a church and a congregation wherever he went, and with him there was neither inducement nor necessity to change. Indeed, the position held then, and for long after, by the Catholics in America, did not offer any special attraction to those of other communions to join their ranks; and while all sects of Protestantism enjoyed comparatively ample means and opportunities for public worship, the Catholic lacked them altogether in too many instances. Save in cities and towns, and not always in these either, the Catholic had no church, no priest, no instruction, no spiritual consolation—nothing, in fact, to depend on for the preservation of the faith, until the coming of the better days for which he ardently longed, but the grace of God and his own steadfastness.

Albany, and Buffalo, and Brooklyn, and Newark, which are now, in a Catholic sense, cathedral cities, and the centres of prosperous dioceses, having a complete ecclesiastical organisation of their own, were each 'served' by a single priest in 1834. When Bishop Dubois visited Buffalo in 1829, he found a congregation of 800 Catholics, about half of whom were Irish, who had been occasionally visited by a clergyman from Rochester; but, previous to that arrangement, they had been for years without having seen a minister of their Church. The first church—a little wooden structure—erected in Buffalo was in the fall of that year. But in 1847, when Buffalo was formed into a diocese, the state of things discovered by Bishop Timon, not only in his first visitation, but on subsequent occasions, was little different from that recorded by Bishop England of his three Southern States; and while there were more Catholics to be found in the towns springing up in the State of New York, the spiritual poverty and destitution were as marked in the North as in the South. Bishop Timon had fifteen priests to assist him, and sixteen churches; but we are told, on the Bishop's authority, that most of them 'might rather be called huts or shanties;' and when there was a church, of whatever kind, there was scarcely a sacred vessel for the use of the altar, and the vestments were 'few and poor.'

There is the strong Catholic likeness in all the Bishops of the American Church—the same energy, the same zeal, the same self-sacrifice, the same disregard of toil or labour; and Bishop Timon's visitation in 1847, or in years after, might be fitly described in the very words employed by Dr. England in 1821.

He preached in Protestant churches, when they were offered, or the Catholics could obtain 'the loan of them,' or in court-houses, or in school-houses; or, when he had none of these at his disposal, in the open air. In his first visitation Bishop Timon confirmed 4,617 of his flock, half of whom were adults—a fact significant of previous spiritual destitution. It is not to be supposed that this state of things is limited to a period so remote as twenty years—it was the same in many of the States so late as a few years back; and even to this day there are Catholic families in America who have rarely entered a church or heard the voice of a priest.

There was never, at any time, on the part of the Irish Catholic, a lack of zeal for religion, or an indifference as to procuring a place for the worship to which, from his infancy, he had been accustomed in his own country. Indeed, one of the inducements which the Irish had to remain in the great cities, instead of pushing on to take possession of the land, was the facility afforded, through their churches and their staff of clergymen, for practising their religion, and of training their children in the knowledge of its principles. Still, better for thousands had they penetrated the remote forest, and there, in the depths of their own hearts, kept alive the love of the faith, and thus lived on in expectation of happier days, than have yielded to a feeling which was commendable rather than blamable. It is true, the children of mixed marriages—especially when the mother was a member of some Protestant body, and where the Catholics were few and thinly scattered amongst persons of other sects—did occasionally adopt the religious belief of their relatives and friends; but in the vast majority of cases the faith was cherished, and kept strong and ardent amidst the gravest discouragements. When the mother was a Catholic, there was little fear for the children; though there have been innumerable instances of fathers resisting the influence of their Baptist or Methodist wives, and bringing up their children in their own faith.

There is not a priest of any experience in the American mission that has not met with the most interesting proofs of the holy flame burning in the hearts of Irish Catholics far removed from a church. The delight of these good people at a visit from one of their own clergymen—the *Sogarth aroon*—is indescribable. A friend, who now holds an eminent position in the ministry, told me how he was affected by the feeling exhibited by an Irish woman whom he visited, as much as by chance as design, in the course of a missionary tour whose extent might be counted by hundreds of miles. He came to a house in the midst of the woods, but surrounded with every appearance of substantial comfort; and on entering through the open doorway he found a number of young people in the principal apartment. He was welcomed, but coldly, by the elder girl, who told him that 'mother' was somewhere about the place with the boys. The clergyman asked some questions, which at first were replied to with evident restraint; but when he said he was a Catholic priest—and an Irish priest, too—there was an end to coldness and reserve. The girl had taken him for a preacher, of one of the many sects to be found in every part of America, and her courtesy was rather scant in consequence.

'Oh, Father, don't go!—I'll run and fetch mother!' cried the girl, as she ran out to impart the joyful tidings to her parent; the priest in the meantime establishing friendly relations with the younger children. Soon were hurried steps heard approaching the house, and one voice, half choked with emotion, saying: 'Mary, Mary, darling, are you serious?—is it the priest?—is it really the priest?' answered by that of the daughter with: ' Yes, mother dear, it is the priest, sure enough.' In rushed a woman of middle age, her arms outstretched, and her face flushed with strong excitement. Falling on her knees on the floor, she exclaimed, with an accent of passionate supplication, that thrilled the priest to his heart—'Oh, Father! for the sake of God and His Blessed Mother, mark me with the sign of the Cross!' Her face, though merely comely at best, was positively beautiful in its expression as her pious request was complied with. The example was contagious.

The entire family were at once on their knees, and 'Me, Father!—don't forget me, Father!—Father, don't forget me,' from the youngest, showed how the mother's spirit pervaded her children. It was some hours before the good woman's excitement subsided; and as she busied herself to do fitting honour to her guest—whom she assured she would rather see in her house than the King on his throne, or the President himself—she constantly broke off into pious ejaculations, full of praise and thanks. The priest remained long enough under her hospitable roof to celebrate Mass, which to her was a source of joy unspeakable, as she looked upon her dwelling as sacred from that moment; and to strengthen by his instruction the strong impression already made upon the minds of her children by their pious mother. This good woman's husband had been carried off by malignant fever, leaving to her care a large and helpless family; but, as she said, 'God gave her strength to struggle on for them,' and she did so, bravely and successfully, until the eldest were able to help her, and abundance and comfort were in her dwelling. For many years she had not seen the face of a priest, or entered the door of a church; but the faith was strong in her Irish heart, and every morning the labours of the day were blessed by the prayers of the family, who repeated them as regularly before they retired to their untroubled rest; and on Sundays the prayers of Mass were read, and the litanies were recited. Thus was the faith kept in the midst of the forest, until the time came when the church was erected, and the congregation knelt beneath its sacred roof, and the voice of praise blended with the swelling peal of the organ, and the exiles really felt themselves 'at home' at last.

When visiting the Hospital of the Good Samaritan in Cincinnati, I was made aware of a remarkable instance of how the faith was kept by the Irish in the days when, from want of priests and churches, the spiritual destitution of Catholics was extreme. In a ward of this splendid hospital, the munificent gift of two Protestant gentlemen to an Irish Sister, a young priest was hurrying fast to the close of his mortal career. He had been a chaplain in the Federal service, in which, as in the ordinary sphere of his ministry, he was much beloved, on account of his great zeal and devotedness; but consumption, the result in a great measure of hardship and exposure, set in, and the termination of a lingering sickness was at hand. His father and mother—the father from Tipperary, the mother from 'the Cove of Cork'—settled amidst the woods of Ohio, about twenty miles from Cincinnati, and not a family within many miles of their home. About that time there were not more than a dozen priests in Ohio, Indiana, Illinois, and Missouri, and but two brick churches in Ohio. This was the state of things when Bishop, now Archbishop, Purcell was consecrated. Little spiritual provision then for the Irish family in the woods. But the faith was strong in the hearts of the Irish parents, and they determined that their children should not be without its knowledge. Every Sunday the father read the prayers of Mass, and then gave an hour or an hour-and-a-half's catechetical instruction to his young flock. Every night the younger children, each in their turn, recited the accustomed prayers; and with the aid of good Catholic books, and a couple of the best of the Catholic newspapers, the right spirit was maintained. The father, who was then in independent circumstances, and is now the owner of 700 acres of land, used to send, four times a year, a 'buggy' for a priest, who celebrated Mass in the house, and explained, in a better manner than the father could have done, the principles of the Catholic religion. The family grew up a credit to their Irish father, himself a credit to his country. One of the sons, thus taught amidst the solitude of the woods, was then closing a noble career of priestly usefulness, and others were exhibiting the influence of their training in various walks of life. The sound Catholic teaching at home counteracted whatever might have been prejudicial in the district school, to which, at a suitable period, the young people were sent. I had the satisfaction of seeing this line old Tipperary man, who, at seventy years of age, had the appearance of one much younger. It was men of his stamp, I felt, that did most honour, in America, to their native land.

Bishop England often mentioned his visit to a family whom he found in the midst of the woods, and who had not seen a priest for forty years! But the faith had been preserved through the piety of the parents. The Bishop described this wonderful fidelity as a miracle of grace.

From the foregoing we learn how the faith has been kept: in the following we have an instance of what a humble man may do for its advancement.

In a rising town of one of the Northern States an Irish priest, actuated by religious zeal, attempted to build a church for the accommodation of his flock, which at that time was small in number and feeble in resources. The task was beyond his and their means, and the work, but partially accomplished, was necessarily suspended. A poor Irishman was passing through the town, on his way to the West, when, attracted by the appearance of the unfinished building, he enquired what it was intended for, and why it was allowed to remain in that incomplete state.

The reply, while it afforded the desired explanation, was mocking and derisive. 'That building! Oh, it was the Papists—them Irish Papists—that tried to get it up; it was too much for them; they couldn't do it, nohow. It does look ridiculous—

don't it, stranger?' 'It does look mighty quare, sure enough,' was the quiet rejoinder of the poor working man, who added, as he first looked at his informant, who had passed on, and then at the incomplete structure; 'but, 'pon my faith, I'll not lave this place 'till it's finished, and I hear Mass said in it, too.' He remained to labour; and being a sober and thrifty man, his labour throve with him. As other emigrants passed through the town, also on their way to the West, he induced several of them to remain, and to these he soon imparted his own spirit. A more vigorous effort was made, and made successfully, mainly owing to this one humble man, who ere long heard Mass in the temple he so effectually helped to raise; and before many years had passed, there were convents and schools, in which his children, and the children of others once as poor as himself, imbibed a thorough knowledge of their religion, and caught the spirit of their fathers. To behold the cross on that church was the object of his ardent desire. He did behold it, and so have many thousands, who worshipped beneath the roof which it adorns.

When, in consequence of the increasing age and infirmities of the sainted Bishop Dubois, one of those holy men whom France had given to the American Church, Dr. Hughes, recently one of the most popular and influential of the working clergy of Philadelphia, assumed, as coadjutor Bishop, the practical administration of the diocese of New York, the state of things was not very hopeful. For this diocese, of 55,000 square miles in extent, there were then but twenty churches and forty priests; with lay trusteeship rampart in its insolence, and disastrous in its mismanagement; the fruits of which were to be witnessed in the condition of the city churches, all of which were in debt, and half at least in a state of bankruptcy. The venerable Bishop Dubois was past the age of dealing successfully with the increasing difficulties of the position. But the man who had been providentially selected for, if not the most important, certainly the most responsible diocese in the United States, soon proved himself to be in every way equal to the emergency.

Bishop Hughes was one of those Irishmen who, loving America as the asylum of their race, rapidly become American citizens in feeling, in spirit, and in thought. Bold, fearless, and independent, he determined to assert his rights of citizenship; and no idea of inferiority to the longest-descended descendant of those who, at one time, were either colonists or exiles, ever crossed the mind of that stout-hearted prelate. As a minister of God, he was ever for peace, and by preference would never have quitted the precincts of the sanctuary; but there were occasions when forbearance would have been criminal, and quiescence or meekness would have been mere abject baseness; and when, for the interests of religion and the safety of his flock, it was his first duty to come forth as a citizen. And when these occasions occurred, his active interference was crowned with success, and productive of the happiest results. Bishop Hughes held the Irish of New York in his hands and under his control by the spell of his eloquence and the genuine ring of his national convictions; and by their aid, and with their fullest sanction—backed by the congregations—he crushed the baneful abuses of the system of trusteeship, and terminated a struggle which had been long a source of interior weakness and external scandal.

To such lengths had the evils of this system arisen under the mild administration of the predecessor of Bishop Hughes, that a committee of the trustees waited upon Bishop Dubois, and with expressions of respect somewhat inconsistent with the object of their mission, informed him that they could not conscientiously vote him his salary, unless he complied with their wishes, and gave them such clergymen as were acceptable to them! The reply given to this cool insolence was characteristic of the holy man. 'Well, gentlemen, you may vote the salary or not, just as seems good to you. I do not need much—I can live in the basement, or in the garret; but whether I come up from the basement, or down from the garret, I will still be your Bishop.'

Bishop Hughes did not destroy the system of lay trusteeship; he purged it of its vicious abuses and defects, such as were opposed to the principles of the Church. There was much in it that was useful, if not absolutely necessary, in the circumstances of the country; but it was essential that it should be regulated according to Catholic principles, and be placed under proper ecclesiastical control. Bishop Bayley, a thoroughly competent authority, thus refers to the services rendered to the Church by Dr. Hughes, whose courage and determination put an end to the scandal, at least in the city of New York:—

Those only who have carefully studied the history of the Church can form any idea of the amount of undeveloped evil that lay hid within that system of uncontrolled lay-administration of ecclesiastical property, and which partially exhibited itself at Charleston, South Carolina, at Richmond, Virginia, in Philadelphia, and more slightly, but still bad enough, here in New York. The whole future of the Church in this country would have been paralysed, if it had been allowed fully to establish itself; and, to my mind, the most important act of Bishop Hughes' life—the one most beneficial to religion—was his thus bringing the whole Catholic community to correct ideas and right principles on this subject.'

Each year strengthened the influence of Bishop Hughes over his flock; and on two remarkable occasions this influence was usefully exerted,—the first, in extinguishing a pestilent danger to faith and morals; the second, in protecting the peace of the city by the firmness of the Catholic attitude.

For nearly two years the School Question, fiercely agitated in New York, attracted the attention of the country at large. The system of education against which the Catholics protested was more than insidiously dangerous—it was actively aggressive; and not merely were the books replete with sneer and libel against that Church which all sects usually delight in assailing, but the teachers, by their explanations, imparted new force to the lie and additional authority to the calumny. Respectful remonstrances were met either with calm disregard or insolent rebuff. Politicians were so confident of having the Irish vote, no matter how they themselves acted, that they supposed they might continue with impunity to go in the very teeth of their supporters, and systematically resist their just claims for redress. But Bishop Hughes read them a salutary lesson, the moral of which it was difficult to forget. With matchless ability he fought the Catholic side in the Municipal Council against all comers, representing every hostile interest; and when justice was denied there and in the Legislature, he resorted to a course of policy which greatly disturbed the minds of the timid, and the sticklers for peace at any price, but which was followed by instantaneous success. Holding his flock well in hand, addressing them constantly in language that, while it convinced their judgment, roused their religious enthusiasm, he advised them to disregard all political ties, and vote only for those who were the friends of the new School system,—which, it may be remarked, was 'Godless' at best,—and the opponents of the old system, which, as we have said, was actively aggressive. The Bishop thus put the case to his flock:—

The question to be decided is not the strength of party, or the emolument and patronage of office, but a question between the helpless and ill-used children and the Public School Society. .... An issue is made up between you and a large portion of the community on the one side, and the monopoly which instils the dangerous principles to which I have before alluded, on the other. The question lies between the two parties, and you are the judges; if you desert the cause, what can you expect from strangers? . . . I have been given to understand that three out of four candidates presented to your suffrages are pledged to oppose your claims. They may perhaps triumph; but all I ask is, that they shall not triumph by the sinful aid of any individual who cherishes a feeling in common with those children. I wish you, therefore, to look well to your candidates; and if they are disposed to make Infidels or Protestants of your children, let them receive no vote of yours.

The advice thus given to them by their Bishop was as consistent with common sense as with decent pride. But something more was required to be done, and that was done. With a few exceptions, the candidates of all parties in the field were pledged to oppose the claims of the Catholics. An independent ticket for members of the Senate and Assembly was therefore suggested and proposed, and this was adopted at a meeting in Carroll Hall, with an enthusiasm which was owing even more to the pluck than to the appeals of the Bishop. Having, by a speech of singular power, put the whole case before his immense audience, he worked them up to a state of extraordinary excitement with the true Demosthenic art, putting to them a series of stinging queries, touching, as it-were, the very life of their honour. 'Will you stand by the rights of your offspring, who have so long suffered under the operation of this injurious system?' 'Will you adhere to the nomination made?' 'Will you be united?' 'Will none of you shrink?' And he thus concludes: 'I ask then, once for all, will this meeting pledge its honour, as the representative of that oppressed portion of the community for whom I have so often pleaded, here as elsewhere—will it pledge its honour, that it will stand by these candidates, whose names have been read, and that no man composing this vast audience will ever vote for any one pledged to oppose our just claims and incontrovertible rights?' The promise, made with a display of feeling almost amounting to frenzy, was fully redeemed; and 2,200 votes, recorded for the candidates nominated only four days before, convinced the politicians, whose promises hitherto had been, as the Bishop said, as large 'as their performances had been lean,' that there was danger in the Catholics—that, in fact, they were no longer to be played with or despised. Notwithstanding the pledges to the contrary, the new system—that of the Common Schools—was carried in the Assembly by a majority of sixty-five to sixteen; and the Senate, apprehending that a similar attempt would be made at an approaching election for the Mayoralty as that which had been made in the elections of candidates for the Senate and the Assembly, passed the measure.

Fiercely assailed by his opponents, bitterly denounced by alarmed and indignant politicians, reviled in every imaginable manner by controversialists of the pulpit and the press, even turned upon by the faint-hearted of his own communion—that decorous and cringing class, to whom anything like vigour, or a departure from rigid rule, is sure, to cause a shudder of the nerves—the Bishop of New York became, at once, one of the best-abused as well as one of the most popular men of the day. His influence over the Irish portion of his flock was unbounded. This flock was rapidly increasing through emigration, which was setting strongly in from the old country, then, for its size, one of the most populous countries of Europe. Bishop Hughes was just the man to acquire influence over an Irish congregation.

That he himself was an Irishman was, of course, no little in his favour; though there are, as I am personally aware, bishops and priests without a drop of Irish blood in their veins, or at best having only some remote connection with the country which has given so many of her children to the American Church, who are beloved and venerated by their Irish flocks—who are referred to in language of the warmest affection, and pointed to with pride, either for their moral excellence or their intellectual endowments. But Bishop Hughes was eminently qualified to gratify the pride of a people who found in him a fearless, a powerful, and a successful champion—one who was afraid of no man, and who was ready, at any moment, not only to grapple with and overthrow the most formidable opponent, but to encounter any odds, and fight under every disadvantage. In his speeches and letters the reader will behold abundant evidence of his boldness in attack, his skill in defence, and his severity in dealing with an enemy, especially one to whom no quarter should be given. When the Bishop struck, it was with no gentle or faltering hand, nor was his weapon a lath or a blunted sword: he struck with the strength of a giant, and the weapon he wielded was bright and trenchant, and never failed to pierce the armour of his closest-mailed foe. With the ablest and most practised writers of the public press, the most accomplished advocates of the bar, the subtlest controversialists, Bishop Hughes had many a fair tilt in the face of an appreciative public; and none of those with whom he was compelled to come into conflict, whether with tongue or pen, speech or letter, who did not acknowledge, or was not obliged to admit, the power of his mind, the force of his reasoning, his happiness of illustration, and his thorough mastery of the English language. It was not, then, to be wondered at that the Irish of New York, as indeed throughout the States, were proud of their great countryman, and looked up to him with confidence and affection. His influence ever his flock was not without being submitted to a severe test.

In 1844 the memorable riots of Philadelphia occurred. It was the old story again. Sectarian bigotry and ignorant prejudice appealed to by reckless firebrands and intriguing politicians; lies, calumnies, and misrepresentations; old falsehoods dug up and furbished afresh, and new falsehoods invented for the occasion; clamour from the press, the platform, and the pulpit—with the grand cry, 'The Bible in danger!—Save it from the Papists!' The only possible ground of this affected alarm for the Bible was the simple fact that the Catholics required that when their children were compelled to read the Bible in the Public Schools, it should be the recognised Catholic version of the Scriptures and not the Protestant version. But the world knows how easy it is to get up a cry, and how it is oftentimes the more effective when based on entire falsehood. Add, then, to this dishonest cry, unreasoning hatred of the foreigner, and bitter hostility to the foreigner's creed, and you have the combustibles, which only required a match and an opportunity, in order to ensure an explosion. And a terrible and savage explosion of human passion it was, scattering confusion and death through one of the fairest cities of the Union, and casting discredit on its boasted civilisation. There was a 'Protestant Association' at its vicious work in those days, and among its most active members were Irishmen, who had brought with them across the ocean the old fierce spirit of Orangeism, which so far blinded their reason and stifled their sense of honour, that they were not ashamed then, as on subsequent occasions, to join with the Native American and Know Nothing party, in their mad crusade against the 'foreigner' — that foreigner their own countryman! During the riots the Orange flag, the symbol of fraternal strife in the old land, in which its children should leave behind them their wicked animosities, was displayed during the shameful riots of 1844. Where there was anything like the semblance of an organisation for defence, the Irish Catholics displayed a courage worthy of their cause; but the means of resistance were not sufficient, nor were they taken in time, and the result is thus described in the words of an excellent Episcopalian clergyman, who felt, with poignant shame, the dishonour cast by national prejudice and brutal fanaticism upon his beautiful city. The author of the 'Olive Branch' thus sums up the wicked deeds of the rioters:—

The Native American party has existed for a period hardly reaching five months, and in that time of its being, what has been seen? Two Catholic churches burnt, one thrice fired and desecrated, a Catholic seminary and retreat consumed by the torches of an incendiary mob, two rectories and a most valuable library destroyed, forty dwellings in ruins, about forty human lives sacrificed, and sixty of our fellow citizens wounded; riot, and rebellion, and treason, rampant, on two occasions, in our midst; the laws set boldly at defiance, and peace and order prostrated by ruffian violence.

From an article on 'The Philadelphia Riots and the Native American Party,' written by Archbishop Spalding, this extract may be quoted:—

For more than ten years previously the 'No-Popery' cry had been raised, from one end of the Union to the other; from the cold and puritanical North, to the warm and chivalrous South. The outcry resounded from the pulpit and the press; its notes were fierce and sanguinary; they were worthy of the palmiest days of Titus Oates and Lord George Gordon, both immortal for the relentless and burning hatred they bore to their Christian brethren of the Roman Catholic Church. Can we wonder, then, that it produced similar results? When we reflect how long that bitter outcry continued; how talented, and influential, and untiring were many of those engaged in raising it; how many different forms and complexions it assumed—now boasting of its zeal for the purity of religion, now parading its solicitude for the preservation of our noble republican institutions threatened with destruction by an insidious foreign influence; when we reflect how very unscrupulous were the men engaged in this crusade against Catholicity, how many glaring untruths they boldly published both from the pulpit and the press, how many base forgeries—subsequently admitted to be such—they unblushingly perpetrated in the full light of day, and with the intelligence of the nineteenth century beaming in their faces; when we reflect that all this warfare against Catholics was openly conducted by a well-concerted action and a regular conspiracy among almost all the rich and powerful Protestant sects of the country, with the avowed purpose of crushing a particular denomination; and that this conspiracy was kept alive by synodical enactments, by Protestant associations, and by the untiring energy and relentless zeal of perhaps the richest and most powerful sect in the country, which ever appeared as the leader of the movement:—when we reflect on all these undoubted facts, can we be any longer surprised at the fearful scenes which lately set the stigma of everlasting disgrace on the second city of the Union?

A strange commentary on this fierce hostility and deadly strife does the position of the Church in Philadelphia offer to-day. As many as five-and-twenty churches, crowded with devout congregations; noble institutions of every description, and intended to minister to every want; a Cathedral of unrivalled grandeur and beauty, reminding one much of St. Peter's; a vast and orderly flock, rising every day in independence and in wealth; and, to crown all, a learned and pious Bishop, who had been a Protestant! Persecution is not a wise game for those who play it; for it almost invariably happens that the persecuted have the best of it in the long run. So does Providence dispose.

Flushed with their unholy triumphs of church-burning, convent-wrecking, and house-pillaging, a chosen band of the Philadelphia rioters were to be welcomed with a public procession by their sympathisers of New York; but the stern attitude of the Catholics, obedient to the voice and amenable to the authority of their Bishop, dismayed the cowardly portion of their enemies, and taught even the boldest that discretion was the better part of valour.

It was not the first time that the Catholics of New York had taken a firm stand against the frenzy of the 'No Popery' faction. Shortly after the burning of the convent in Boston, there was an attempt made to destroy St. Patrick's Cathedral. But the church was put in a state of defence; 'the streets leading to it were torn up, and every window was to be a point whence missiles could be thrown on the advancing horde of sacrilegious wretches; while the wall of the churchyard, rudely constructed, bristled with the muskets of those ready for the last struggle for the altar of their God and the graves of those they loved. So fearful a preparation, unknown to the enemies of religion, came upon them like a thunderclap, when their van had nearly reached the street leading to the Cathedral: they fled in all directions in dismay.'

A meeting of the native Americans of New York was called in the City Hall Park, to give a suitable reception to their brethren from Philadelphia. The time for action had thus arrived. Bishop Hughes had made it known through the columns of the *Freeman's Journal*, then under his entire control, that the scenes of Philadelphia should not be renewed with impunity in New York; and he was known to have said—in reply to a priest who, having escaped from Philadelphia, advised him to publish an address, urging the Catholics to keep the peace—'If a single Catholic church were burned in New York, the city would become a second Moscow.' There was no mistaking his spirit and that of his flock—excepting, of course, the 'good cautious souls who,' as the Bishop wrote, 'believe in stealing through the world more submissively than suits a freeman.' The churches were guarded by a sufficient force of men, resolved to die in their defence, but also resolved to make their assailants feel the weight of their vengeance. By an extra issue of the *Freeman*, the Bishop warned the Irish to keep away from all public meetings, especially that to be held in the Park. He then called upon the Mayor, and advised him to prevent the proposed demonstration.

'Are you afraid,' asked the Mayor, 'that some of your churches will be burned? '

'No, sir; but I am afraid that some of *yours* will be burned. We can protect our own. I come to warn you for your own good.'

'Do you think, Bishop, that your people would attack the procession?'

'I do not, but the native Americans want to provoke a Catholic riot, and if they can do it in no other way, I believe they would not scruple to attack the procession themselves, for the sake of making it appear that the Catholics had assailed them.'

'What, then, would you have me do?'

'I did not come to tell you what to do. I am a churchman, not the Mayor of New York; but if I were the Mayor, I would examine the laws of the State, and see if there were not attached to the police force a battery of artillery, and a company or so of infantry, and a squadron of horse; and I think I should find that there were; and if so, I should call them out. Moreover, I should send to Mr. Harper, the Mayor-elect, who has been chosen by the votes ' of this party. I should remind him, that these men are his supporters; I should warn him, that if they carry out their design, there will be a riot; and I should urge him to use his influence in preventing this public reception of the delegates.'

There was no demonstration. And every right-minded man, every lover of peace in the city, must have applauded the course taken by Dr. Hughes, to whose prudent firmness was mainly attributable the fact that New York was saved from riot, bloodshed, murder, and sacrilege, and, above all, from that dreadful feeling of unchristian hate between man and man, citizen and citizen, neighbour and neighbour, which such collisions are certain for years after to leave rankling in the breast of a community.

We come now to the year 1852, and witness the gigantic stride which the Church has made since 1833, when ten Bishops met at the First Council of Baltimore. Irish and German Catholics had been pouring into the United States by hundreds of thousands; and the 200 Catholics of New York in 1785, and the 35,000 of 1829, had become 200,000 in 1852. Instead of the one archbishop, and ten bishops, of 1833, there were now six archbishops, and twenty-six bishops; while the number of priests, which was about 300 in 1833, had now increased to 1,385, with churches and stations in proportion. We shall see how this advance, great and hopeful as it was, has been far exceeded by the progress made in the short space of the next fourteen years.

Writing of the city of New York of 1853, Bishop Bayley—then Secretary to Archbishop Hughes—says:—'No exertions could have kept pace with the tide of emigration which has been pouring in upon our shores. The number of priests, churches, and schools, rapidly as they have increased, are entirely inadequate to the wants of our Catholic population, and render it imperative that every exertion should be made to supply the deficiency.' Something of the same kind might be said of 1867, though the means are now proportionately greater than they were fifteen years before, not in New York alone, but throughout the United States. Convents, hospitals, asylums, schools, were then, in 1853, rapidly on the increase, the Religious Orders spreading their branches and establishing their houses whenever there was a chance of their bare support, and often, too, braving privations similar to those which Mrs. Seton's infant community endured at Emmettsburg and at Philadelphia in the early days of their existence.

CHAPTER XXIV

The Know Nothing Movement—Jealousy of the Foreigner—Know Nothings
indifferent to Religion—Democratic Orators—Even at the Altar and in the
Pulpit—Almost Incredible—The Infernal Miscreant—A Strange Confession

THE KNOW NOTHING movement of 1854 and 1855 troubled the peace of Catholics, and filled the hearts of foreign-born American citizens with sorrow and indignation. They were made the victims of rampant bigotry and furious political partisanship. There was nothing new in this Know Nothingism. It was as old as the time of the Revolution, being Native Americanism under another name. Its animating spirit was hostility to the stranger—insane jealousy of the foreigner. It manifested itself in the Convention which formed the Constitution of the United States, though the right to frame that Constitution had been largely gained through the valour of adopted citizens, born in foreign countries, and through the aid and assistance of a foreign nation. It manifested itself in the year 1796, in laws passed during the Administration of President Adams, a narrow-minded man, much prejudiced against foreigners. The Alien Act, which was one of the most striking results of the illiberal spirit of that day, provided—'That the President of the United States shall be, and is hereby authorised, in any event aforesaid, *by his proclamation thereof, or other public act*, to direct the conduct to be observed, on the part of the United States, towards aliens .... the manner and degree of the restraint to which they shall be subjected, and in what cases and upon what security their residence shall be permitted, and to provide for the removal of those who, not being permitted to reside in the United States, shall refuse or neglect to depart therefrom.' Here was a despotism marvellously inconsistent with the object and purpose of the struggle which secured freedom and independence to the revolted colonies of England! Here also was folly bordering upon madness, in discouraging that great external resource, through which alone the enormous territory even then comprehended within the limits of the Union could be populated and civilised—namely, the foreign element—those impelled, through various causes and motives, to cross the ocean, and make their home in America.

Remembering the history of the last fifty years, during which thousands, hundreds of thousands, nay millions of the population of Europe have been spreading themselves over the vast American continent, building up its cities, penetrating and subduing its forests, reclaiming its wastes, constructing its great works, developing its resources, multiplying its population—in a word, making America what she is at this day—one does not know whether to laugh at the absurdity of those who imagined that, without injury to the future of the States, they might bar their ports to emigrants from foreign countries; or doubt the sanity of those who could deliberately proclaim, as the Hartford Convention of 1812 did—'That the stock of population already in these States is amply sufficient to render this nation in due time sufficiently great and powerful, is not a controvertible question.' Certainly not controvertible to vanity and folly, which were stimulated by absurd jealousy and causeless apprehension. The generous men who assembled at Hartford were willing to ' offer the rights of hospitality ' to the strangers, under such conditions as those imposed in the Alien Act; but they took care to restrict their munificence to such fair limits as would secure all the honours and emoluments to themselves. Thus: 'No person who shall hereafter be naturalised shall be eligible as a member of the Senate or House of Representatives of the United States, nor capable of holding any office under the authority of the United States.' The Alien and Sedition laws, passed in the Administration of Adams, were repealed, fourteen years afterwards, by the Jefferson Administration. These laws were repugnant to the spirit of the American Constitution; and in opposing such laws, and confronting the narrow and ungrateful policy in which they originated, Jefferson and Maddison were simply treading in the broad footprints of the illustrious Washington.

This hostility to the foreigner, intensified by religious prejudice, exhibited itself on various occasions—notably in the disgraceful riots of 1844; but on no occasion was the feeling so universal, or its display so marked, as in the years 1854 and 1855, when the banner of Know Nothingism was made the symbol of political supremacy. Here was every element necessary to a fierce and relentless strife. The Constitution of Know Nothingism was anomalously adopted on the 17th of June, 1854, the anniversary of the Battle of Bunker's Hill. Strange, that a day> sacred to the freedom of America should be that on which citizens of a free Republic should plot in the dark against the liberties of their fellow men! But so it was. A very few extracts from authentic documents will declare the motives and objects of this organisation:—

ARTICLE II.

A person to become a member of any subordinate council must be twenty-one years of age; he must believe in the existence of a Supreme Being as the Creator and Preserver of the Universe; he must be a native-born citizen; a Protestant, born of Protestant parents, reared under Protestant influence, and not united in marriage with a Roman Catholic, &c. &c. &c.

ARTICLE III.

Sec. 1. The object of this organisation shall be to resist the insidious policy of the Church of Rome, and other foreign influence against the institutions of our country, by placing in all offices in the gift of the people, or by appointment, none but native-born Protestant citizens.

The Know Nothing oath—for the society was not only secret, but bound by oaths—was in accordance with the spirit of the foregoing. It was comprehensive as well as precise, as the following will show:—

You furthermore promise and declare that you will not vote nor give your influence for any man for any office in the gift of the people unless he be an American-born citizen, in favour of Americans ruling America, *nor if he be a Roman Catholic.*

You solemnly and sincerely swear, that if it may be legally, you will, when elected to any office, *remove all foreigners and Roman Catholics from office*; and that you will in no case appoint such to office.

Many who joined this organisation had not the excuse, the bad excuse, of fanaticism for their conduct. Lust of power was their ruling passion; to trample their opponents under foot, and secure everything to themselves, their animating motive. If they could have attained their ends through the Catholic body, they would have employed every art of wile and seduction in the hope of securing their co-operation; but as they deemed it more to their advantage to assail and blacken the Catholics, they accordingly did assail and blacken them to the satisfaction of their dupes. For religion—any form of religion—they did not care a cent; probably they regarded it as so much venerable superstition and priestcraft—a very excellent thing for women and persons of weak mind, but not for men; at any rate, men of their enlightenment. Members of no congregation, these defenders of the faith never 'darkened the door' of a church or meeting-house, and save, like the sailor who did not know of what religion he was, but was 'd——d sure he was not a Papist,' entertaining a blind prejudice against Catholicity, they were as ignorant of Christian belief as any savage of Central Africa.

Happily for the cause of truth and common sense, there were in those days men bold enough to lash hypocrisy and humbug. Henry A. Wise, of Virginia, was one of those bold defenders of the truth, and unmaskers of fraud. His speeches, when canvassing his State on the Democratic ticket for the office of Governor, which he won gallantly, are full of the most stinging rebukes of his opponents, whom he defeated in argument as well as in votes. In his remarkable speech at Alexandria, he thus hit off the religious pretensions of many of this class of Know Nothings, who affected a new-born interest in the Bible:—

They not only appeal to the religious element, but they raise a cry about the Pope. These men, many of whom are neither Episcopalians, Presbyterians, Baptists, Methodists, Congregationalists, Lutherans, or what not—who are men of no religion, who have no church, who do not say their prayers, who do not read their Bible, who live God-defying lives every day of their existence, are now seen with faces as long as their dark-lanterns, with the whites of their eyes turned up in holy fear lest the Bible should be shut up by the Pope! Men who were never known before, on the face of God's earth, to show any interest in religion, to take any part with Christ or His Kingdom, who were the devil's own, belonging to the devil's church, are, all of a sudden, deeply interested for the word of God and against the Pope! It would be well for them that they joined a church which does believe in the Father, and in the Son, and in the Holy Ghost.

As a further specimen of the manner of this famous Democrat, another passage may be quoted from the same speech. He now desires to show the religion of the party, as defined by their Constitution, according to which one of the qualifications of membership is mere belief in the existence of 'a Supreme Being':—

No Christ acknowledged! No Saviour of mankind! No Holy Ghost! No heavenly Dove of Grace! Go, go, you Know Nothings, to the city of Baltimore, and in a certain street there you will see two churches: one is inscribed, 'O Monos Theos'—'to the one God;' on the other is the inscription, 'As for us, we preach Christ crucified —to the Jews a stumbling-block, and to the Greeks foolishness.' The one inscribed, 'O Monos Theos' is the Unitarian church; the other, inscribed, 'We preach Christ crucified' is the Catholic church! Is it—I ask of Presbyterians, Episcopalians, Methodists, and Baptists—is it, I ask, for any orthodox Trinitarian Christian Church to join an association that is inscribed, like the Unitarian church at Baltimore, 'O Monos Theos'—to the one God? Is it for them to join or countenance an association that so lays its religion as to catch men like Theodore Parker and James Freeman Clarke? I put it to all the religious societies—to the Presbyterians, the Episcopalians, the Methodists, and the Baptists—whether they mean to renounce the divinity of Christ and the operation of the Holy Spirit, when they give countenance to this secret society, which is inscribed, 'to the one God?'

A rebuke, milder in tone, and beautiful as a picture, may be taken from a speech delivered at Richmond by Senator R. M. T. Hunter during the Know Nothing campaign:—

But, fellow-citizens, I went a little too far when I said it was proposed to proscribe Catholics for all offices in this country. There are some offices which the sons and daughters of that Church are still considered competent to discharge. I mean the offices of Christian charity, of ministration to the sick. The Sister of Charity may enter yonder pest-house, from whose dread portals the bravest and strongest man quails and shrinks; she may breathe there the breath of the pestilence that walks abroad in that mansion of misery, in order to minister to disease where it is most loathsome, and to relieve suffering where it is most helpless. There, too, the tones of her voice may be heard mingling with the last accents of human despair, to soothe the fainting soul, as she points through the gloom of the dark valley of the shadow of death to the Cross of Christ, which stands transfigured in celestial light, to bridge the way from earth to heaven. And when cholera or yellow fever invades your cities, the Catholic Priest may refuse to take refuge in flight, holding the place of the true Soldier of the Cross to be by the sick man's bed, even though death pervades the air, because he may there tender the ministrations of his holy office to those who need them most.

It is impossible to describe the frenzy that seemed to possess a certain portion of the American people, whose strongest passions and most cherished prejudices were stimulated by appeals from the press and the platform, the pulpit and the street tub. It seized on communities and individuals as a species of uncontrollable insanity. Bitten by the madness of the moment, acquaintance turned savagely on acquaintance, friend upon friend, even relative upon relative. The kindly feelings which it took years to cement were rudely torn asunder and trampled under foot. The Irish Catholic was the chief object of attack. He was guilty of the double crime of being an Irishman and a Catholic; and, to do him justice, he was as ready to proclaim his faith as to boast of his nativity. His enemies were many, his friends few, his defenders less. Poor Pat had indeed a sad time of it.

That the religious feeling added bitterness to the national prejudice was made manifest by the unreasoning fury of those who combined both antipathies in their hostility. Either, however, was quite sufficient to swell the outcry and deepen the hatred against its unoffending objects. Thus the religious prejudice was so bitter, and so violent, that it prevailed against identity of nationality; and the national prejudice was so envenomed that religious sympathy could scarcely restrain its exhibition, and could not prevent its existence. It is not to be wondered at that the genuine Irish Orangeman sided with the persecutors of his Catholic countrymen; and his conduct on many occasions was a sufficient evidence of his unnatural ferocity. Many Irish Protestants, not Orangemen, gave countenance to the Know Nothings, though, according to the Know Nothing code, none but native-born Protestants were held to be eligible for any office or position in the gift of the people, whether by election or appointment. The shabby conduct of this class of Irishmen was the result either of sectarian hate, or a sense of their own helplessness. They were willing to persecute, or they hoped to propitiate; therefore, they too joined in the crusade against their countrymen in a foreign land. But there were many, many glorious exceptions to this unworthy conduct. Irish Protestants—men of strong religious opinions, who opposed Catholicity on principle—boldly took their stand by the oppressed, and resented the policy of the Know Nothing party, as if it were directed exclusively against themselves. Sympathising with their Catholic fellow-countrymen, they met the assailants gallantly, and rebuked their insane folly with the courage and the sense of men. And to Irishmen who thus acted Catholics felt bound by the strongest ties of gratitude and respect. It was a time to test the true merit of the man, and those who stood it triumphantly were deservedly honoured.

Strange as it may appear, this anti-foreign insanity caught hold of the sons of Irish Catholics; nay, its presence was detected at the altar and in the pulpit! It was too base an infirmity to touch a generous mind, and those who were affected by it were weak and vain and foolish, and Americans knew them to be such. Where one is born is a matter of accident. If this be so under ordinary circumstances, it is eminently so with the children of emigrants; they may have been born at either side of the Atlantic, or at sea. Absurd instances might be told of the sons of Irish Catholic emigrants boasting of their American birth, and expressing their sympathy with the Know Nothing's hatred of foreigners. The humble, honest parents, redolent of the soil, endowed with a brogue rich and mellifluous enough to betray their origin, were they met with on the Steppes of Russia or in the desert of Sahara; and the unworthy son railing, with the choicest accent of the country in which he was accidentally 'dropped,' against the land of his fathers! Such spectacles have been witnessed, to the infinite shame of the miserable creatures whose vanity was too much for a weak head and a poor heart. But that such melancholy spectacles were witnessed—were possible—is a proof of the madness that seized on the public mind. The high-minded American Catholic took his stand by hi& Irish co-religionist, to whose fidelity, liberality, and enthusiasm he justly attributed much of the marvellous progress which the Church had made, and was destined to make, in America. There were, among Catholics, a few exceptions to this generous and wise policy; but, on the whole, the religious sympathy held all other feelings in control, or effectually neutralised the poison of the national infection.

Like fever or cholera, this politico-religious epidemic was milder or more virulent in one place than in another. Here it seized hold of the entire community; there it caught but a few individuals. Here it signalised its presence by riots; there by bloodshed. In this city its congenial result was a burning, or a cowardly assassination; in the other, a stand-up fight, in which the Irish Catholic had to encounter enormous odds against him. That comparatively little mischief was done to ecclesiastical property may be accounted for by the manner with which, as by one impulse, the Catholics rallied round churches and convents wherever there was a probability of their being assailed. In New York, Know Nothingism made little external display in mischief and outrage; which fact may be accounted for in two ways—the one, that the Irish population had by this time grown too powerful to be wantonly trifled with; the other, that they listened in an obedient spirit to the advice of the Archbishop, who wisely believed that the madness would speedily die out if left to itself, and if not stimulated by opposition; that it was something similar to a conflagration of flax, violent for the moment, but without any enduring power. The Archbishop was right in his judgment. It was a frenzy of the hour, artfully inflamed by angry sects, and skilfully directed by unscrupulous politicians—men who would stop at nothing which could in any way further the objects of their selfish ambition. The fury of the madness did die out; but the feelings to which it gave rise, or evoked into new life, did not so readily pass away.

I might possibly be accused of romancing if I ventured to describe the feeling of hostility to which abuse and misrepresentation of Catholics—Irish Catholics especially—gave rise in the Protestant mind of America. Horrible as such a confession may sound in the ears of rational men, Protestants of good repute have since declared, that *at one time they believed that to kill a Catholic priest, or burn down a Catholic church, would be doing the most acceptable service to God*! I had heard this from the most reliable sources in more than one State; yet it was so monstrous, I hesitated to give it credence. But while I wavered between doubt and belief, I myself heard from the lips of a Catholic convert—a gentleman of worth and good social position—the same confession, in almost the very same words. I naturally thought, what must have been the sentiment of a low and vulgar mind, when such was the feeling of a man of good character and so-called liberal education? Until I heard him, I did not thoroughly appreciate the moral blindness and savage frenzy of the genuine Know Nothing.

An alderman of a certain city in Tennessee informed a friend of mine that such was his feeling in his youth that 'he considered it doing an honour to the Deity to take his double-barrelled shot-gun, and shoot any Catholic he might meet.' He does not hold that opinion now; as he has been a zealous Catholic since the Christmas of 1865, when he was received into the Church.

In another city of Tennessee an Irishman, named Hefferman, was shot during the Know Nothing excitement; but the three men who were the cause of his death joined the Church which they hated and persecuted in his person.

Indeed, such was the astounding rampancy of assertion—such the omnivorous swallow of public credulity—that when the Catholic Church of Nashville was in the course of erection, it was stated in the newspaper which borrowed its inspiration from the present Governor Brownlow, that the vaults, or basement of the building, were intended for the incarceration of Protestants when the Pope was to come over and take the country! It was also asserted, and rather widely believed, that John Mitchell, who had started the *Citizen* newspaper, was an agent of the Jesuits; in fact, a Jesuit in disguise! I must admit that the credulity which converted basements of churches into dungeons ought not to be quoted as a conclusive proof of the insanity of Know Nothingism; for I have heard much the same thing announced in a solemn place, and with owl-like gravity, not long since, and not in America.

The honest 'No Popery' zealots were not bad but only misguided men; and when they had the opportunity of forming a right judgment—of emancipating themselves from the leading-strings in which interested bigots had held their minds—they unhesitatingly made the fullest and most generous atonement.

One of these furious but honest 'No Popery' zealots was going on a voyage of some days' duration, and happening to come on board the steamer at the last moment before her departure, he found it difficult to procure accommodation. 'Not a cabin, sir—not a berth—all taken,' said the clerk. 'Can't you put me anywhere?' asked the gentleman; 'go I must, though I slept on the floor.' The clerk glanced over his books to see how, if possible, he could accommodate the passenger, who awaited the result with marked anxiety. 'I have discovered a berth, sir—the top berth—in one cabin; the lower berth is occupied by a very quiet person, who won't give you much trouble; he's a Catholic priest.' 'A Catholic priest!—did you say a priest? Why, damn him! I would not stay in the same room with him,' exclaimed the passenger. 'Well, sir, that's your affair, not mine,' replied the clerk; 'it is all I can do for you.' 'Look you!' said the passenger, 'if one of us is missed at the end of the voyage, I tell you it won't be me; for if that fellow dares to address one word to me, out of the window he will go—that I tell you now.' The clerk took the declaration coolly, not being unused to hear strong language, and even occasionally witness strange occurrences. In this happy frame of mind the passenger took possession of his upper berth at night, and growled himself to sleep. When he awoke in the morning, and remembered where he was, and who was his companion, he had the curiosity to ascertain what the 'infernal miscreant was after.' Peeping from his vantage-ground, he beheld the miscreant on his knees, apparently absorbed in prayer. 'Damn you! there you are,' was the benediction muttered in the bed-clothes of the upper berth. Its occupant looked again and again, but the miscreant was still at 'his humbug.' At length the miscreant rose from his knees and left the cabin, thus affording the tenant of the upper berth an opportunity of opening the window, and getting rid of the odour of brimstone which 'the devil' had left after him.

When the pair happened to meet during the day, the lower berth courteously bowed, and said something civil, to which the upper berth responded with something that bore a strange resemblance to an imprecation. 'Is the fellow really serious, or is it all a sham?' thought the Know Nothing, as he witnessed the same piety, the same wrapt devotion, the second morning. Stranger still, if the upper berth happened to visit the cabin during the day, it was ten chances to one that he discovered the 'extraordinary animal' on his knees, or deep in a book of devotion. For days the priest was the object of the most jealous watchfulness, stimulated by suspicion and dislike; but it was ever the same—the same appearance of genuine piety, and the same courtesy of manner. The honest gentleman in the upper berth was staggered, and did not know what to think of it. 'The fellow might possibly be a fool, but certainly was not a humbug.' This was a great concession, a gigantic stride towards liberality of sentiment. At length he spoke with his fellow-passenger, and found him, what others had long before found him to be, intelligent and well-informed. He was not a fool, and not a humbug; then, what was he? The conviction rapidly grew upon the tenant of the upper berth, that his companion was a gentleman and a Christian minister; and, ere the voyage was at an end, the heart of the furious hater of Catholicity was changed; more than that, ere many months had passed, he who threatened to put the priest out of the window on the first provocation, became a practical Catholic, and there is not at this moment in America a stouter defender of the Church than he is!

As a striking contrast to the furious and unreasoning hatred which the incident just narrated represents, one of a different nature may be told. It occurred in the very height of the Know Nothing excitement, during a journey made by a priest, who is now Bishop of a Southern diocese.

The clergyman found himself one of a very miscellaneous company in a public stage. Next to him, as he sat in the front part of the vehicle, was a gentleman of grave and reserved demeanour; while the other passengers appeared to be of the ordinary class to be met with under such circumstances, who freely discussed all manner of topics, whether of a personal or a public nature, and whose language was occasionally sprinkled with profanity. The company had proceeded a considerable way on their journey, when the gentleman who sat next the future Bishop enquired of him if he were not a 'minister?' 'Why do you think so?' asked the priest. 'Well, I don't exactly know; but you say grace before meals, and you don't curse and swear.' 'I am a Catholic priest,' said the gentleman's neighbour. 'I am glad to hear it,' said the gentleman, 'for I desire to ask you a question: and believe me I do not think of asking it from an idle motive, as you will see.' The priest assured him he would be happy to answer any questions which it was in his power to answer. 'Then I wish to know if a Catholic clergyman would hear the confession of a Protestant, if the Protestant wanted to confess?' 'Confession,' replied the priest, 'has two benefits—good advice and absolution. Absolution can only be given to a Catholic, but good advice may be given to a Protestant: and, therefore, for that purpose—the giving of good advice—a priest could hear the confession of a Protestant.' 'I told you,' continued the gentleman, 'I did not ask the question from an idle motive. I am a Protestant, and I wish you to hear my confession, that I may have the benefit of your advice.' The priest consented, using the simple words, 'Very well, begin.' At this moment the passengers, who had left the stage, were walking up a long and steep hill; and while the two men were apparently sauntering, idly up that hill, one of them was pouring into the ear of the other a story of the deepest interest to his peace of soul; and when the passengers again resumed their places in the stage, and while laugh, and jest, and profane remark were heard on every side, that strange confession was continued, as the two men leaned back in the vehicle, and the one listened to the voluntary disclosures of the other. When the story had been told, and the promised advice given, the gentleman said, 'Well, now, I can't understand it! These are matters that I could not tell to my brother—that I would not for the world my wife should know—that I could not confide to my minister, or whisper to my friends, for I would die rather than that the world should know them; and here I have freely told them to you, a stranger, whom I never saw before, and whom I may never see again—and why do I tell all this to you? Because you are a Catholic priest. And what appears to me so strange is the perfect confidence I have in you; for I have not the slightest fear you will ever reveal one word of what I have told you to mortal ears. This is what I cannot understand.'

The seeds of sectarian hatred were scattered broadcast over the land, or wafted, like the thistle-down, on every breeze; and if there has been no recent crop of lusty hate and active frenzy—if there have been no burnings, and wreckings, and outrages, to record up to this time, notwithstanding that the usual period for the outbreak of such semi-religious semi-political epidemics has come and gone, this apparently strange phenomenon may be rationally accounted for. We should be glad to attribute it wholly to the good sense of the American people, who we should desire to think were no longer to be made the dupes of monstrous falsehoods and deliberate misrepresentations, or to be led astray by theories which are not only grossly absurd, but opposed to the progress of the United States. Making, however, every fair allowance for the growing good sense of the American people, we cannot but attribute much of the better feeling which now exists to an event that may be well described as one of the most memorable in the history of the world—the late Civil War. Not only has that war exhibited in the most signal manner the enormous value of the foreign element —its strength, its courage, and its fidelity; but the Catholic Church has had, during that terrible national ordeal, an unlooked-for though Providential opportunity of displaying its true policy, at once Christian and patriotic, and of convincing even the most prejudiced of its purity, its holiness, and its charity.

CHAPTER XXV

The Catholic Church and the Civil War—The True Mission of the Church—The Church speaks for Herself—The 'Sisters' during the War—The Patients could not make them out—The Forgiven Insult—'What the Sister believes I believe'—The Chariot of Mercy—'Am I to forgive the Yankees?'—Prejudices conquered — 'That's she! I owe my Life to her'—An emphatic Rebuke—'We want to become Catholics.'

THE Catholic Church of America, regarding war as a great calamity, and civil war—of State against State, citizen against citizen, even brother against brother—as the direst of all evils, scrupulously abstained from uttering one word that could have a tendency to inflame or exasperate the passions which others were doing their utmost to excite to uncontrollable fury. The mission of the Church was to proclaim glad tidings of peace to man, not to preach strife and hatred amongst brethren. Thus those who visited the Catholic churches of the United States from the Spring of 1861 to the Autumn of that year, would never have supposed, from anything heard within their walls, that the trumpet had sounded through the land; that armies were gathering, and camps were forming; that foundries were at full blast, forging implements of death; that artificers were hard at work, fashioning the rifle and the revolver, sharpening the sword, and pointing the bayonet; that dockyards rang with the clang of hammers, and resounded with the cries of myriads of busy men—that America was in the first throes of desperate strife. Nor, as time went on, and all the pent-up passions of years were unloosed, and a deadly war progressed with varying fortunes, and fury possessed the heart of a mighty people, could the stranger who entered a Catholic temple scarcely believe in the existence of the storm that raged without; the only indications of the tremendous conflict being the many dark robes, the sad livery of woe, worn by women and children—the mothers, wives, or orphans of those who had fallen in battle; for, save in the greater solemnity of the priest, as he raised the hearts of his congregation to the throne of God, there to sue for grace and pardon, there was nothing to imply the existence of a struggle whose gigantic proportions filled the world with amazement.

The Catholic Church was content to preach 'Christ crucified' to its own followers, as to all who came to listen. It regarded its pulpit as a sacred chair, from which it was to teach the knowledge of the truth, how man could best fulfil his duties to his Creator, his country, and his neighbour. It deemed—and the judgment of the wise and good will say it deemed rightly—that if the minister of religion became a firebrand, instead of a preacher of peace, he misunderstood his duty, and prostituted the sanctity of his office: it held, that it was a gross desecration of a temple erected to the worship of the Deity, to suffer it to resound with the language of unholy strife—with eloquent incentives to massacre and desolation. Others might act as they pleased; they might turn their churches into political assemblies, and their pulpits into party platforms—they might rage, and storm, and fulminate—they might invoke the fiercest passions of the human breast, and appeal to the lowest instincts of man's nature—they might stimulate their hearers to a wider destruction of life and property, to sadder and more terrible havoc; others might do this, as others did—but the Catholic Church of America was neither bewildered by the noise and smoke of battle, nor made savage by the scent of blood: she simply fulfilled her mission, the same as that of the Apostles—she preached the Word of God in lovingness and peace.

This was the language and spirit of the Church, as proclaimed in the Pastoral Letter emanating from the Catholic Bishops assembled in the Third Provincial Council of Cincinnati, in May 1861:—

It is not for us to enquire into the causes which have led to the present unhappy condition of affairs. This enquiry belongs more appropriately to those who are directly concerned in managing the affairs of the Republic. The spirit of the Catholic Church is eminently conservative, and while her ministers rightfully feel a deep and abiding interest in all that concerns the welfare of the country, they do not think it their province to enter into the political arena. They leave to the ministers of the human sects to discuss from their pulpits and in their ecclesiastical assemblies the exciting questions which lie at the basis of most of our present and prospective difficulties. Thus, while many of the sects have divided into hostile parties on an exciting political issue, the Catholic Church has carefully preserved her unity of spirit in the bond of peace, literally knowing no North, no South, no East, no West. Wherever Christ is to be preached and sinners to be saved, there she is found with ministrations of truth and mercy. She leaves the exciting question referred to previously where the inspired Apostle of the Gentiles left it, contenting herself, like him, with inculcating on all classes and grades of society the faithful discharge of the duties belonging to their respective states of life, knowing that they will all have to render a strict account to God for the deeds done in the flesh, that this life is short and transitory, and that eternity never ends. Beyond this point her ministers do not consider it their province to go, knowing well that they are the ministers of God, who is not a God of dissension, but of peace and love.

Had this wise and considerate line of conduct been generally followed throughout the country, we are convinced that much of the embittered feeling which now unfortunately exists, would have been obviated, and that brotherly love, the genuine offspring of true Christianity, instead of the fratricidal hatred which is opposed to its essential genius and spirit, would now bless our country, and bind together all our fellow-citizens in one harmonious brotherhood. May God, in his abounding mercy, grant that the sectarianism which divides and sows dissensions, may gradually yield to the Catholic spirit which breathes unity and love!

The startling contrast which the Catholic Church thus presented to most, indeed nearly all, of the other churches during this period of national tribulation, was not without its influence on the public mind of America. It made men think and reflect, and in numberless instances conviction came with thought and reflection. The fervid and furious 'sermons' that were listened to with flashing eyes and quickened pulses by the majority of those to whom they were addressed, excited the sorrow or disgust of not a few. A Protestant gentleman, speaking to a Catholic friend in New York, thus referred to the prevailing topics which inspired the eloquence of his Boanerges:—

'My wife urged me yesterday to accompany her to our church. I refused: she was rather angry. "Well, my dear," I said, "you may go if you please; the pew is there for you—I pay for it. But I shan't go. Whenever I have gone I have never heard but three sermons at the most—Popery, Slavery, and War—War, Slavery, and Popery! These may satisfy you—they don't me. When I go to church I wish to be made better, not worse. Now I think that a little of the Gospel, that tells us something of peace and charity, would do me good—your War, and Slavery, and Popery don't. I repeat, my dear, you may go if you please; but I'm————blessed if I do." '

If the Catholic Church could do nothing to prevent war, she could at least do much to mitigate its horrors; and accordingly she commissioned her noblest representatives—her consecrated daughters—to minister in the public hospitals, in the camp, and in the prisons—wherever wretchedness, and misery, and suffering appealed most powerfully to their Christian duty and womanly compassion.

The events of the war brought out in the most conspicuous manner the merits and usefulness of the Religious Orders, especially those of Charity and Mercy and the Holy Cross, and, spite of prejudice and bigotry, made the name of 'Sister' honoured throughout the land. Prejudice and bigotry are powerful with individuals and communities, powerful, too, in proportion to the ignorance which shrouds the mind of man. Still, these are but relatively strong, and must yield before a force superior to their's—*truth*. And as month followed month, and year succeeded to year, the priceless value of services having their motive in religion and their reward in the consciousness of doing good, were more thoroughly appreciated by a generous people. At their presence in an hospital, whether long established or hastily improvised, order, good management, and economy, took the place of confusion, lax administration, and reckless expenditure, if not worse. Obstacles, in many instances of a serious nature, were placed deliberately in their path; but, with tact, and temper, and firmness, these were encountered by women who had no vanity to wound, no malice to inflame, and whose only object was to relieve the sufferings of the sick and wounded in the most efficacious manner.

It is therefore not to be wondered at that difficulties and obstacles, however apparently formidable at first, vanished before the resistless influence of their sincerity and their goodness, and the quite as conclusive evidence of their usefulness. But the greater their success, the greater the strain on the resources of the principal Orders. Not only did death and sickness thin their ranks, but the war, by adding fearfully to the number of helpless orphans, added likewise to their cares and responsibilities. What with ceaseless duty in the hospitals, teaching in their schools, visiting the sick, providing for the fatherless whom every great battle flung upon their protection, administering the affairs of institutions perilled by the universal disturbance, bringing relief and consolation to the prisoner in the crowded building, or wretched camp to which the chance of war consigned the soldier on either side—the Sisters were tried to the very uttermost. Nothing but the spirit of Religion, together with their womanly compassion for the sick and the suffering, and their interest in the brave fellows who, docile children in their hands, followed them with wistful eyes as, angels of light and mercy, they brought balm to the heart of the wounded,—nothing short of the sublime motives by which these ladies were animated could have sustained them throughout four long years of ceaseless toil and never-ending anxiety.

You may have seen the feeblest bird exhibit unlooked-for courage when danger threatened its young. Maternal instinct renders it almost unrecognisable—the glittering eye, the ruffled plumage, and the bold attitude, make it so unlike the ordinary timid creature. So, gentle, shrinking, timid as the Sister might be under ordinary circumstances, let the least wrong be done to her patients—let even incompetency or neglect be manifested in an hospital under her charge; and that gentle-mannered, soft-spoken Sister would come out instantly in a new character. Many an official—proud, or insolent, or bigoted, or incompetent, or corrupt—has had to bend before the quiet determination expressed in the voice and manner of the Sister inspired by a sense of duty springing alike from humanity and religion. Throughout the country, in almost every State of the Union, are now to be seen Sisters—calm, gentle, soft-voiced women—of whose sturdy energy and resolute courage in defence of their sick charge, or in resistance of abuses, numerous instances are narrated; never by themselves, but by those who, having witnessed them, cherish them in their memory. No officer, no official, ventured to treat the Sister with disrespect, once her value was known; and it was soon made known. The impediments and embarrassments which were occasionally thrown in her way were borne with as far as they possibly might be; but when the time for action arrived, even the youngest Sister was generally equal to the emergency. As the war progressed, so did the influence of the Sisters, until at length there was scarcely a corner of the country into which a knowledge of their services did not penetrate, and there were but few homes in which their name was not mentioned with respect.

At first, the soldiers did not know what to make of them, and could not comprehend who they were, or what was their object. And when the patient learned that the Sister with the strange dress belonged to the Catholic Church— that Church of which so many vile stories had been told him from his childhood— a look of dread, even horror, might be observed in his eyes, as he instinctively recoiled from her proffered services. This aversion rarely continued long; it melted away like ice before the sun; but, unlike the ice, which the winter again brings round, this feeling never returned to the heart of the brave man whom the fortune of war placed under the care of the Sister. Once gone, it was gone for ever. How the prejudice, deep-seated and ingrained, yielded to the influence of the Sisters, may be best exemplified by a few incidents, taken at random from a vast number of a similar nature gathered in many parts of the country.

Seven Sisters of Mercy, belonging to the Houston Street Convent in New York, were sent to an hospital attached to a Federal corps. When they first entered the wards, which were crowded with sick and wounded, the soldiers regarded them with amazement. One of the Sisters, a genial Irishwoman, referring to this her first visit to the hospital, told with much humour how the bewildered patients took the Sisters for seven widows, who were looking for the dead bodies of their husbands!

Among the patients, there was one mere lad—indeed almost a child, scarce fit to leave his mother's guardianship—and he lay with his face on the pillow, as an hospital attendant, not eminent for humanity, carelessly sponged a fearful wound in the back of the poor youth's neck. The hair had been matted with the clotted blood, and the rude touch of the heartless assistant was agony to the miserable patient. 'Let me do it,' said the Sister, taking the instrument of torture from the unsympathising hand; and then, with tepid water, and soft sponge, and woman's delicacy of touch, the hideous sore was tenderly cleansed. 'Oh, who is that?—who are you?—you must be an angel!' cried the relieved youth. The hair was gently separated from the angry flesh, so that the grateful patient could turn his head and glance at the 'angel;' but no sooner did he cast one rapid look at the strange garb and the novel head-dress of the Sister, than he shrieked with terror, and buried his face in the pillow. 'Do not fear me,' said a voice full of sympathy; 'I am only anxious to relieve your sufferings.' The work of mercy was proceeded with, to the ineffable comfort of the wounded boy, who murmured—'Well, no matter what you are, you're an angel anyhow.'

At times there were as many as eighty Sisters in or near Richmond, in active attendance in the hospitals, giving their services alike to the wounded soldiers of both armies. In one of the Richmond hospitals the following took place.

A sick man, looking steadily from his pillow at the Sister, who was busy in her attentions to him, abruptly asked—

'Who pays you?—what do you get a month ?'

'We are not paid: we do not receive salaries,' replied the Sister.

'Then why do you work as you do?—you never cease working.'

'What we do, we do for the love of God—to Him we only look for our reward—we hope He will pay us hereafter.'

The wounded man seemed as if he could not entirely comprehend a devotion so repugnant to the spirit of the Almighty Dollar; but he made no further remark at the time. When he became more confidential with the Sister, the following dialogue was held—

Patient. Well, Sister, there is only one class of people in this world that I hate.

Sister. And who may those be?

Patient. The Catholics.

Sister. The Catholics! Why do you hate them?

Patient. Well, they are a detestable people.

Sister. Did you ever meet with a Catholic that you say that of them?

Patient. No, never; I never came near one.

Sister. Then how can you think so hardly of persons of whom you don't know anything?

Patient. All my neighbours tell me they are a vile and wicked people.

Sister. Now, what would you think and say of me, if I were one of those Catholics?

Patient (indignantly). Oh, Sister! you!—you who are so good! Impossible!

Sister. Then, indeed, I am a Catholic—a Roman Catholic.

The poor fellow, whose nerves were not yet well strung, rose in his bed as with a bound, looked the picture of amazement and sorrow, and burst into tears. He had so lately written to his wife in his distant home, telling her of the unceasing kindness of the Sister to him, and attributing his recovery to her care; and he was now to disclose the awful fact that the Sister was, after all, one of those wicked people of whom he and she had heard such evil things. This was, at first, a great trouble to his mind; but the trouble did not last long, for that man left the hospital a Catholic, of his own free choice, and could then understand, not only that his neighbours had been, like himself, the dupes of monstrous fables, but how the Sister could work and toil for no earthly reward.

A Sister was passing through the streets of Boston with downcast eyes and noiseless step, reciting a prayer or thinking of the poor family she was about to visit. As she was passing on her errand of mercy, she was suddenly addressed, in language that made her pale cheek flush, by a young man of remarkable appearance and free swaggering gait. The Sister, though grievously outraged, uttered no word, but raised her eyes, and looked at the offender with calm steady gaze, in which volumes of rebuke were expressed. Time passed on; the war intervened; and when next they met it was in a ward of a military hospital in Missouri. The once powerful man was now feeble as an infant, and had not many days to live. The Sister, seeing his condition, asked him if he belonged to any Church; and on his replying in the negative, she asked if he would be a Catholic. 'No—not a Catholic—I always hated Catholics,' he replied. 'At any rate, you should ask the pardon of God for your sins, and be sorry for whatever evil you have done in your life,' urged the Sister.

'I have committed many sins in my life, Sister, and I am sorry for them, and hope to be forgiven; but there is one thing that weighs heavy on my mind at this moment —I once insulted a Sister in Boston, and her glance haunted me ever after: it made me ashamed of myself. I knew nothing then of what Sisters were, for I had not known you. But now that I know how good and disinterested you are, and how mean I was, I am disgusted with myself. Oh, if that Sister were here, I could go down on my knees to her and ask her pardon!'

'You have asked it, and received it,' said the Sister, looking full at him, but with a sweet expression of tenderness and compassion.

'What! Are you the Sister I met in Boston? Oh, yes! you are—I know you now. And how could you have attended on me with greater care than on any of the other patients?—I who insulted you so!'

'I did it for our Lord's sake, because He loved His enemies, and blessed those who persecuted Him. I knew you from the first moment you were brought into the hospital, and I have prayed unceasingly for your conversion,' said the Sister.

'Send for the priest!' exclaimed the dying soldier; 'the religion that teaches such charity must be from God.'

And he did die in the Sister's faith, holding in his failing grasp the emblem of man's redemption, and murmuring prayers taught him by her whose glance of mild rebuke had long haunted him like a remorse through every scene of revelry or of peril.

'Do you believe that, Sister? If you believe it, I believe it, too.' There was scarcely an hospital at either side of the line, North or South, of which the Sisters had the care, in which these apparently strange but most significant words were not uttered by the sick and the dying. Many of the poor fellows had not the vaguest notion of religious teaching never having troubled themselves with such matters in the days of their youth and health; and when the experienced eye of the Sister discerned the approach of death, the patient would be asked if he wished to see a clergyman. Frequently the answer would be that he did not belong to any religion. 'Then will you become a Catholic?' would follow as a fair question to one who proclaimed himself not to belong to any Church, or to believe in any form of Christianity. From hundreds, nay thousands of sick beds, this reply was made to that question: 'I don't know much about religion, but I wish to die in the religion of the Sisters.' When asked, for example, if he believed in the Trinity, the dying man would turn to the Sisters who stood by his bedside, and inquire,—'Do you, Sister?' and on the Sister answering, 'Yes, I do,' he would say, 'Then I do— whatever the Sister believes in, I do.' And thus he would make his confession of faith.

A soldier from Georgia, who was tended by the Sisters in an hospital in St. Louis, declared that 'he had never heard of Jesus Christ, and knew nothing about him.' He was asked if he would become a Catholic. 'I have heard of them,' he said; 'I would not be one of them at all—they are wicked people. But I'll be the same as you, Sister; whatever that is, it must be good.'

At the battle of Gettysburg, a number of Sisters joined the camp hospital, bringing with them a considerable quantity of provisions and comforts, procured at their own cost. They even went on the field, bravely conquering the natural reluctance of delicate women to witness scenes of horror such as every inch of a hard-fought battle-field discloses. What services these tender women—some of them young creatures not long professed—rendered to the mangled victims of that furious contest, it were impossible to tell. But so signal was the devotion which they displayed in an emergency of so pressing a nature, that they elicited from a preacher the following strange tribute, published in the newspapers:—'Although I hate their religion, and despise their sectarianism, I must do justice to the self-sacrificing devotion of those pale unmated flowers, that never ripen with fruit.' One, not a preacher, might imagine that the blessings and prayers—the purest offerings of the heart—that sprang up in their path wherever they turned, were fruit the most acceptable to these 'pale unmated flowers;' but the idea would appear fantastical and far-fetched to the material nature of their enlightened panegyrist.

It really matters little, when referring to the services of the Sisters during the war, which army, which State, or which hospital is mentioned as the scene of their labours. Their charity, like their Order, was universal; and whether they ministered to the sick in a Union or Confederate army, or in a Northern or Southern State, it was the same in motive and in object. Next to the sick in the hospital, the prisoner was the dearest object of their solicitude.

The Sisters in Charleston did glorious service during the war—to the sick, the dying, the prisoner, and the needy. At certain times immense numbers of prisoners were camped outside the city. They were in a miserable state. Charleston, partly consumed by the tremendous fire of 1861, by which an enormous amount of property was destroyed, and further assailed by a bombardment scarcely paralleled in modern history, could not afford much accommodation to the captured of the enemy. Penned up together, and scantily fed, the condition of the prisoner was far from enviable; it was indeed deplorable. To these poor fellows the Sisters were in reality what they were styled—'angels of mercy.'

Presented with a universal pass by General Beauregard, the Sisters went everywhere unquestioned, as if they were so many staff officers. The General had likewise presented them with an ambulance and a pair of splendid white horses, remarkable for their beauty, and, on account of their colour, conspicuous at a considerable distance. Many a time has the sight of these horses brought gladness to the heart of the prisoner, as he beheld them turning the corner of the highway leading to the camp. When the white specks were seen some three-quarters of a mile on the road, the word was given, 'The Sisters are coming!' As that announcement was made, the drooping spirit revived, and the fainting heart was stirred with hope; for with the Sisters came food, comforts, presents, perhaps a letter, or at least a message—and always sweet smiles, gentle words, sympathy and consolation. The ambulance, drawn by the gallant white steeds, was usually filled with hundreds of white loaves—in fact, with everything which active charity could procure or generosity contribute. The rations given to the prisoners were about as good as the Confederate soldiers had for themselves; but to the depressed, pent-up prisoner, these were coarse and scanty indeed. 'Sister! Sister of Charity! Sister of Mercy!—put something in this hand!'—'Sister, Sister, don't forget me!'—'Sister, Sister, for the love of God!'—'Oh, Sister, for God's sake!' —such were the cries that too often tortured the tender hearts of the Sisters as they found their stock of provisions fast running out, and knew that hundreds of hungry applicants were still unsatisfied. Many a time did they turn away on their homeward journey with whitened lips and streaming eyes, as they beheld those outstretched hands, and heard those cries of gaunt and famished men ringing in their ears. To the uttermost that they could do, the Sisters did, and this the prisoners knew in their grateful hearts. These horses shed light in their path; the clatter of their feet was as music to the ear of the anxious listener; and the blessings of gallant suffering men followed that chariot of mercy wherever it was borne by its snowy steeds in those terrible days of trial.

Such was the effect produced by the Sisters on the minds of the patients in their charge, that when wounded or sick a second time, they would make every possible effort to go back to the same hospital in which they had been previously cared for. or, if that were not possible, to one under the management of these good women. Instances have been told of wounded men who travelled several hundred miles to come again under the charge of the Sisters; and one, in particular, of two men from Kentucky, who had contrived to make their way to the large hospital at White Sulphur Springs in Virginia, a distance of 200 miles from where they had been wounded. They had been under the care of the Sisters on a former occasion, and had then agreed that should they ever be wounded or fall sick again, they would return to the same hospital, and if they were to die, that they should die in the faith of the Sisters who had been so good to them. Both these men were American Protestants, and had never seen a Catholic priest before they beheld the clergyman who received them into the Church in the Virginian hospital. One of the two men was past cure, and was conscious of his approaching death. 'Ben,' said the dying man to his comrade, 'all is right with me—I am happy; but before I die, let me have the satisfaction of seeing you become a Catholic.' Ben willingly consented to what he had before resolved on doing, and he was received into the Church in the presence of his dying friend, over whose features there stole a sweet smile, that did not depart even in death.

'Oh, my God! what's that? what's that?' shrieked a poor Southern boy, when he first saw a Sister, as she leaned over his hospital pallet. His terror was equalled only by his genuine horror when he discovered she was a Catholic. Soon, however, his eyes would wander round the ward in search of the nurse with the sweet smile, the gentle voice, and the gentler word. Like many of his class, he was utterly ignorant of religion of any description; he disliked 'Papists,' and he thought that sufficed for every spiritual purpose. At length he wished to be baptized in the Sister's faith, and his instruction was commenced. He was told he should forgive his enemies. 'Am I to forgive the Yankees?' he asked, with indignant eagerness. 'Certainly,' replied the Sister, 'you must forgive everybody,' 'Ma'am, no—not the Yankees!—no, ma'am—not the Yankees!—I can't.' 'But you must forgive your enemies, or you can't be a Christian. God forgave those who put Him to death,' persisted the Sister. 'Well, Sister, as *you* ask me to do it, I will forgive the Yankees; but 'tis hard to do it though, I tell you.'

'Before we left Vicksburg to attend the hospitals,' says a Sister, 'many of the Irish soldiers returned dreadfully wounded from the battle of Shiloh, where our pastor, who had gone to assist their dying moments, said they had fought, "not like men, but like indomitable lions." We had many brave Irish patients, but our principal experience in hospital lay amongst Creoles, or soldiers from the country parts of the South, whose horror of Sisters at first (grounded on their ignorance), formed a strange contrast to their subsequent grateful affection.'

'They shrank from us with looks of horror and loathing, as if we were something full of evil,' remarked a Sister, whose name was famous for skill, and an energy that excited the amazement of those who beheld her in the management of a great hospital. Many a letter, replete with gratitude and veneration, came to that Sister from all parts of the States, North and South, and not a few from those who at first regarded her 'with looks of horror and loathing, as if she were full of evil.'

The doctors were not one whit behind the humblest soldiers in ignorant dislike of the Sisters.

A Federal doctor was at first inclined to be rude and uncivil to the Sisters in a crowded Southern hospital, then in possession of the forces of the Union, and occasioned them no little anxiety by his manner, it was so full of evident dislike and suspicion. They wisely took no notice of it, but devoted themselves the more sedulously to their arduous duties. At the end of a few weeks, by which time his manner had become kind and respectful, the doctor candidly confessed to one of the Sisters what his feelings had been, and how completely they were changed. 'I had such an aversion to Catholics,' said he, 'that I would not tolerate one of them in an hospital with me. I had heard of the Sisters, but I was resolved not to have anything to do with them in any place in which I had control. I confess to you my mind is entirely changed; and so far from not wishing to have Sisters in an hospital where I am, I never want to be in an hospital where they are not.'

The officials were, if possible, still more suspicious, still more prejudiced.

'I used to be up at night watching you, when I should have been in my bed. I wanted to see what mischief you were after, for I thought you had some bad motive or object, and I was determined to know what it was. I could find nothing wrong, but it was a long time before I could believe in you, my prejudice against you was so strong. Now I can laugh at my absurd suspicions, and I don't care telling you of my nonsense.' This speech was made by the steward of an hospital to Sisters to whom he had given much trouble by his manner, which seemed to imply—'You are humbugs, and I'll find you out, my ladies! clever as you think you are.' He was a good but prejudiced man; and once that he was convinced how groundless were his suspicions, he not only treated the Sisters with marked respect, but became one of their most strenuous and valuable supporters.

A doctor of the Federal service, who was captured at the battle of Shiloh, said to a Catholic Bishop,—'Bishop, I was a great bigot, and I hated the Catholics; but my opinions are changed since this war. I have seen no animosity, but fraternal love, in the conduct of the priests of both sides. I have seen the same kind offices rendered without distinction to Catholic soldiers of the North and South. The very opposite with Protestant chaplains and soldiers.'

'What conclusion did you draw from this?—these Catholics are not Freemasons,' said the Bishop.

'Well,' replied the doctor, 'I drew this from it—that there must be some wonderful unity in Catholicity which nothing can destroy, not even the passions of war.'

'A very right inference,' was the Bishop's rejoinder.

An officer who was brought in wounded to an hospital at Obanninville, near Pensecola, which was under the care of Sisters, asked a friend in the same hospital what he would call 'those women'—how address them? 'Call them "Sisters,"' replied his friend. 'Sisters! They are no sisters of mine; I should be sorry if they were.' 'I tell you, you will find them as good as sisters in the hour of need.' 'I don't believe it,' muttered the surly patient. Owing, in a great measure, to the care of his good nurses, the officer was soon able to leave the hospital strong in body as well as improved in mind. Before he was well enough to leave, he said to his friend,—'Look here! I was always an enemy to the Catholic Church. I was led to believe by the preachers that these Sisters—both nuns and priests—were all bad. But when I get out of this, I be God darned if I don't knock the first man head over heels who dares say a word against the Sisters in my presence!' He was rough, but thoroughly honest.

During the war, a number of the Sisters were on their way to an hospital, to the care of which they had been urgently called, and, as the train remained stationary at one of the stopping-places on the route, their dress excited the wonder and ridicule of some thoughtless idlers, who entered the car and seated themselves opposite to, but near, the objects of their curiosity, at whom they looked and spoke in a manner far from complimentary. The Sisters bore the annoyance unflinchingly. But there was assistance nearer than they or their cowardly tormentors supposed. A stout man, bronzed and bearded, who had been sitting at one end of the car, quietly advanced, and placing himself in front of the ill-mannered offenders, said, 'Look here, my lads! You don't know who these ladies are; I do. And if you had been, like me, lying sick and wounded on an hospital bed, and been tended night and day by those ladies, as I was, you'd then know them and respect them as well as I do. They are holy women. And now, if you don't, every one of you, at once quit this car, I'll call the conductor, and have you turned out; and if you say one word more, I'll whip you all when I have you outside.' The young fellows shrank away abashed, as much perhaps at the justice of the rebuke as at the evident power by which, if necessary, it would have been rendered still more impressive.

It was a touching sight to witness the manner in which soldiers who had experienced the devotedness of the Sisters to the sad duties of the hospital, exhibited their veneration for these 'holy women.' Did the Sisters happen to be in the same car with the gallant fellows, there was not one of them who did not proffer his place to the Sister, and who did not feel honoured by her acceptance of it. Maimed, lopped of limb, scarcely convalescent, still there was not a crippled brave of them who would not eagerly solicit the Sister to occupy the place he so much required for himself. 'Sister, do take my seat; it is the most comfortable.' 'Oh, Sister, take mine; do oblige me.' 'No, Sister! mine.' Sweet was the Sister's reward as, in their feeble but earnest tones of entreaty, and the smiles lighting up pale wan faces, she read the deep gratitude of the men who had bled for what each deemed to be the sacred cause of country. Wherever the Sister went, she brought with her an atmosphere of holiness. At the first sight of the little glazed cap, or the flapping *cornet*, or the dark robe, or at the whisper that the Sister was coming or present, even the profane and the ribald were hushed into decent silence.

As a company of Confederate prisoners were marched through Washington, a Sister of Mercy who was passing was arrested by the exclamation, 'There she is! That's she! I owe my life to her. She attended me in the hospital. Oh, Sister!' The Sister approached, and as the prisoners were passing, the one who used these words rapidly dropped something into her hand. It was less than the widow's mite—it was a regimental button! But it was accepted in the spirit in which it was offered, as a memorial; and as such, I know, it is cherished.

A Baptist preacher was rather unexpectedly rebuked in the midst of his congregation by one of its members who had experience of the Sisters in the hospital. Addressing his audience, he thought to enliven his discourse with the customary spice—vigorous abuse of the Catholic Church, and a lively description of the badness of nuns and priests; in fact, taking the 'Awful Disclosures of Maria Monk' as his text and inspiration. But just as the preacher, warming with his own eloquence, was heightening his picture with colours borrowed from a rather prurient imagination, these strange words were thundered forth by a sturdy Western farmer, who sprang to his legs in an impulse of uncontrollable indignation,—'Sir, that's a damned lie!' The consternation of the audience was great, the excitement intense. The preacher solemnly reminded his erring brother that that was 'the house of God.' 'Well, sir,' replied the farmer, 'as it is the house of God, it is a lie without the damned.' Then looking round boldly at the meeting, which contained many to whom he was well known, he thus continued: 'I thought and believed the same as you thought and believed, because I was told so, as you were; but I have lived to learn the difference —to know that what we were told, Sunday after Sunday, is not true. I was in the prison at M'Dowall's College; I was there for six months; and I saw the Sisters waiting on the prisoners, and nursing the sick—unpaid and disinterested. I saw them giving up their whole time to doing good, and doing it without fee or reward. I saw the priests, too, constant in their attendance—yes, shaming other ministers by the manner in which they did their duty. That six months cured me of my folly; and I tell you, who know me to be a man of truth, that the Catholic Church is not the thing it is represented to be, and that Sisters and Priests are not what our minister says they are; and that I'll stand to.'

The sympathies of the audience went with the earnestness of the speaker, whose manner carried conviction to their minds; and so strongly did the tide of feeling flow against the preacher, that he dexterously returned to what, in Parliamentary phrase, may be described as 'the previous question.'

Not very long before I visited a place in Tennessee, a 'delegation' from a district in which there was not a single Catholic waited on an Irish priest of my acquaintance; their object being to consult with him as to the feasibility of building a Catholic church in the place. 'A Catholic church!' exclaimed the priest; 'what can you want of a Catholic church, and not a Catholic in the place?" The answer was remarkable: 'We here are all ex-soldiers, and have been in the war; and when we returned, the preachers, —Methodists, Presbyterians, and others—asked us to join their churches, as before. We said nothing at the time, but held a meeting, and sent this reply: "Before the war, you told us that Catholics were capable of committing every crime; that priests and nuns were all bad alike. We went to the war; we were in hospitals, and we met members of our own society there; but the only persons who did anything for us, or cared anything about us, were these same Catholics, the Priests and Sisters that you so represented to us. We were in the prisons of the North, and it was the same. Now what you told us about Catholics was not true. We can't have any further confidence in you, and we will have nothing more to do with you. If we be anything, we will be Catholics." That was our reply; and we now come to consult a Catholic priest, to see how best we may carry out our intentions, and become Catholics.'

The above I give, not because it is the most remarkable of such applications, which are very numerous, and are constantly made in many dioceses throughout the States. The majority of another such 'delegation' told the Bishop on whom they waited that they had been strong Know Nothings before the war; and one of them declared that he had assisted to 'tar and feather' a priest, and that in so doing he thought he was doing service to God!' We don't know what the doctrines of your Church are; these we desire to learn; but though we don't know its doctrines, we have seen its conduct during the war, and that conduct we admired.'

That the Sisters—those truest exponents of Catholic charity—win the respect of Protestants at other times than during war, and in the ordinary discharge of their duty, we have a proof in the following incident:—

The Archbishop of San Francisco and other Catholic Bishops were on their way to the Council of Baltimore; and as the Bishops and the clergy by whom they were accompanied desired to have the use of an apartment or cabin, in which Mass could be daily offered up, the Archbishop made a request to that effect to the Captain of the vessel, who thus replied: 'Archbishop, there are twenty preachers on board who asked me to allow them to preach, and I have refused them, because they would create nothing but confusion. But, Archbishop, though I am an Episcopalian, I am much obliged to you. The yellow fever broke out in my crew, and my ministers deserted me; but you sent the Sisters, and they came and nursed my men all through their sickness. I never can forget it; and whatever I can do for a Catholic Bishop or for the Sisters, I will do most gladly. You shall have the room, Archbishop.'

And as these words are written, the same terrible scourge is thinning the ranks of the Sisters in New Orleans, many of whom have fallen martyrs to their zeal and duty.

A Southern General said to me, 'The war has worn away many a prejudice against Catholics, such was the exemplary conduct of the priests in the camp and the hospital, and the Christian attitude of the Church during the whole of the struggle. Many kind and generous acts were done by the priests to persecuted ladies, who now tell with gratitude of their services. Wherever an asylum was required, they found it for them. I wish all ministers had been like the priests, and we might never have had this war, or it would not have been so bitter as it was.'

elsewhere mentioned the munificent gift made by two Protestant gentlemen to a Sister in Cincinnati; and as that munificent gift—of a splendid hospital—is but one, though a striking proof of the influence which the work of the Sisters has had on the enlightened Protestant mind of America, something may be said of the object of that donation. There is nothing remarkable in the personal appearance of Sister Anthony—nothing of the stately or the majestic—nothing that harmonises with the romantic or the poetical. Sister Anthony is sallow in complexion, worn in feature, but with a bright intelligent look, and an air of genuine goodness. Though thoroughly unaffected in manner, and without the faintest trace of show, every word she utters betrays an animating spirit of piety, an ever-present consciousness of her mission—which is, to do good. One feels better in her presence, lifted up, as it were, into a purer and brighter atmosphere. In accent and manner she is strongly American; and had I not been assured by herself that she was born in Ireland—somewhere, I believe, between Limerick and Tipperary—I should have taken her for a 'full-blooded American,' that is, if Sister Anthony could be taken for a 'full-blooded' anything.

For a considerable time Sister Anthony held a subordinate position, to which she thoroughly adapted herself; but it was impossible she could continue to conceal her great natural ability and talents for organisation and management. Her first important work was the establishment of the Hospital of St. John, which became so famous and so popular under her management, that the most distinguished physicians of Cincinnati sent their patients to her care. In this hospital Sister Anthony made herself perfect in the science of nursing the sick. When the war broke out, she, with twelve Sisters, took charge of the Field Hospital of the Armies of the Cumberland and the Tennessee, and nursed the wounded and the sick in the South and South-West during its continuance. Such was the estimate formed of the services of these and other Sisters of the same institution, as well as of the Catholic Chaplains, that the Generals in command frequently wrote to Archbishop Purcell, asking for 'more Priests and more Sisters, they were so full of devotion to their duty.' Nearly all of those Sisters were, like Sister Anthony, Irish. Her influence was immense. Even the surliest official or stiffest martinet could not resist Sister Anthony. There was a contagion in her goodness. Some years before, when in a subordinate capacity in the Orphan Asylum under the care of her Order, Sister Anthony was in the market, bargaining for chickens to make broth for some sick children, when the salesman, perhaps wearied of her importunity, said—'If you were a pretty woman, I'd talk to you longer; but you are so darnd ugly, you may go your ways, and take the chickens at your own price.'

Sister Anthony, who never gave a thought to her personal appearance, good-humouredly accepted the compliment which ensured her a profitable bargain for her poor little chicks in the asylum. But the wounded soldier on the hospital pallet was not of the fowl-merchant's opinion; the sick man saw everything good and beautiful in the countenance of the nurse who smoothed his pillow with hand light as a feather's weight, and, with voice attuned to the tenderest compassion, won him to hope and resignation. At the mere whisper of the name of Sister Anthony, the eye of the invalid brightened, and a pale flush stole over his wasted cheek; and when it was mentioned in the presence of strong men, it was received with a hearty blessing or a vigorous cheer. Protestant and Catholic alike reverenced Sister Anthony. There was no eulogium too exaggerated for her praise, or for their gratitude. She was styled 'the Ministering Angel of the Army of the Tennessee,' and Protestants hailed her as 'an angel of goodness.' And at a grand reunion, in November 1866, of the generals and officers of the army in whose hospitals Sister Anthony had served, her name was greeted with enthusiastic applause by gallant and grateful men.

The United States Marine Hospital, constructed at a cost of a quarter of a million of dollars, was sold for 70,000 dollars, at which price it was purchased by two Protestant gentlemen, and by them 'donated' to Sister Anthony, and is known by the beautiful and felicitous title 'the Hospital of the Good Samaritan.' This fine institution is now at the service of the sick and suffering of Cincinnati. These generous Protestant gentlemen were known to Sister Anthony, and she to them. Some time before, it was her intention to build, and in the course of a few months she obtained 30,000 dollars to aid her in her task. But, changing her mind, from not wishing to undertake so great a work as she at first contemplated, she determined to refund every dollar of the money. When she came to those two gentlemen, she tendered to them their liberal subscription; but they refused to accept it, saying: 'No; we gave it to God. We cannot take it back.'

Sister Anthony is not insensible to the influence she exercises, as the following brief dialogue will show:—

Sister Anthony (to a friend). I guess I want this hospital painted. I guess Mr. —— —— (mentioning the name of a worthy citizen) will paint it.

Friend. Why, Sister! he is not a painter; he is a grocer.

Sister Anthony. I know that, child; but he is a rich man, and he will have to paint it.

And it was just as Sister Anthony said. He had to paint it, and he felt honoured by the distinction conferred upon him.

One day Sister Anthony was transacting some business in the city with the prosperous owner of a large store. When the business was concluded, the owner said: 'Sister, where is your conveyance—your horse and buggy—to take you up the hill?' 'I have no horse,' replied Sister Anthony. 'Then I will get you a horse and buggy,' said the store-keeper. 'The conveyance I have had for the last fifty years is still very good, but the horses want shoeing,' answered Sister Anthony, pointing to her shoes, which were in the very last stage in which that article of dress could possibly exist. A box of the best shoes was at once supplied to Sister Anthony's well-employed 'horses.'

I present Sister Anthony only as a type, not of her own noble Order, but of all kindred Orders; for, throughout the United States, there are hundreds of Sister Anthonys, who, like her, have been styled 'ministering angels,' and 'angels of goodness;' at the mention of whose honoured names blessings rise from the hearts to the lips of grateful men, and mothers in distant homes pray at night for those who nursed their wounded sons in the hospital, or ministered to them in the prison.

Whether in the hospital and the prison, or on the field of battle, the Catholic Chaplain won the respect of all classes and ranks of men. I have heard soldiers of worldwide fame speak with enthusiasm of the gallantry and devotion of the Catholic Military Chaplains, who calmly performed their duty amidst the fury of conflict, and while bullets whistled by them, and shells shrieked as they passed over their heads. The idea of danger may cross the mind of the Catholic priest, but it never deters him from the discharge of his duty, which is performed as coolly on the battle-field as in the wards of an hospital. Soldier of the Cross, he encounters danger in every form and under every aspect. Without departing in the least from his ordinary course, or making the slightest attempt at display, the Catholic Priest—so long the object of the foulest calumny and the most disgusting ribaldry—found in the events of the war daily opportunities of exhibiting himself in his true light; and soon was suspicion changed into confidence, and prejudice into respect. Unswerving attention to duty is the grand characteristic of the Catholic priest; and when the non Catholic officer or private found the priest always at his post, attending on the sick, raising the drooping spirits of the patient, preparing the dying for their last hour, he could not help contrasting the untiring devotion of the Catholic Chaplain with the lax zeal —if zeal it could be called—of too many of those who assumed that office, or that distinctive title, during the war. When men are stretched on a sick bed, and they depend so entirely for assistance or relief on the attention and kindness of those around them, they form rapid and unerring estimates of merit; and if they cannot be deceived by the sham nurse or the worthless physician, neither can they be hoodwinked by pharisaical cant or religious pretension. The genuine metal was tested in the fire of the crucible, and was admitted to be sterling.

Throughout the war the Catholic priest acted in the spirit of his Church. The Church was a peace-maker, not a partisan. So were her ministers. It little mattered to the priest at which side the wounded soldier had fought, or in what cause the prisoner had been made captive; it was sufficient for him to know that the sick and the imprisoned stood in need of his assistance, which he never failed to afford. The Church deplored the outbreak of war, mourned over its horrors, and prayed for its cessation. As with the Church, so with the priest. It is not in human nature to suppose that the Catholic priests did not feel a sympathy with one side or the other; but no weakness common to humanity could deaden the feeling of charity, which is the living principle of Catholicity; and while the Federal Chaplain ministered to the Confederate soldier or prisoner, the Confederate Chaplain ministered with equal care and solicitude to the soldier who fought under the banner of the Union. This Catholic charity—this spiritual bridging over of the yawning gulf of raging passions—produced a deep impression on the minds of thoughtful men. Many instances might be told of the manner in which this feeling operated on the minds of individuals: one will suffice:

A lawyer of Louisiana was practising in Missouri at the opening of the war; and being known as a Confederate sympathiser, was arrested, and sent as a prisoner to Fort Warren, in Boston Harbour. He had studied law in Boston, where he imagined he had made several lasting friends of members of his profession. Taking means to communicate with some of those on whom he most relied for sympathy, if not for assistance, he informed them of his position, and besought their aid, in the name of friendship and the memory of the pleasant days of the past; but he appealed in vain—fear of being compromised by a suspected rebel, or the bitter prejudice born of the hour, was too strong to be overcome by a momentary impulse; and the prisoner languished in captivity. They—the friends of his youth—came not; but an Irish priest did. Attracted to the prisoner by feelings of compassion, he comforted and consoled him, and assisted him to the utmost of his means and influence. That lawyer learned to love the Church of which that priest was a worthy minister; and his own words may throw light on his conversion, which took place soon after:—'Looking back upon the war, I see that the Protestants of the North were charitable to their own side, and that the Protestants of the South were very charitable to their side; but the Catholics are the only body of Christians who practised charity *for its own sake*, irrespective of politics, and who did so even when it was unpopular, if not dangerous for them to do so.'

The lawyer who languished in the prison of Boston Harbour was not the only one who experienced the value of a charity which has neither sect nor party, and knew no difference between cause or banner in that hour of national convulsion.

There was one other influence, potent in dispelling the dark prejudices imbibed in infancy, and fostered by fanatical teachers; this was the faith, the piety, the resignation of the Irish Catholic soldier, of whatever rank, as he lay wounded or dying in the hospital. In the devotedness of the Sister and the Priest there was a beautiful exemplification of the spirit of Christian Charity; in the unmurmuring resignation of the Catholic Soldier there was the irresistible evidence of Christian Faith. Many a proud scoffer, to whom the very name of Catholic had been odious, received his first impression of the truth from the edifying demeanour of some Irish soldier who lay in anguish by his side, and who, before he rushed into the thickest of the fight, had not been ashamed to crave the blessing of his priest. It was the same in the hospitals of the States as in the hospitals of the Crimea.

CHAPTER XXVI

Catholic Education—The Catholic Church in Advance of the Age—Catholic Teaching favourable to Parental Authority—Protestant confidence in true Catholics—The Liberal American Protestant—Catholic Schools—The Sister in the School and the Asylum—Protestant Confidence in Convent Schools—The Christian Brothers—Other Teaching Orders—From the Camp to the School

FROM the earliest moment that a Catholic community was gathered together in the United States, it sought to train its youth in the principles of religion. The history of Catholic education in America would form a story of the deepest interest to those who reverence steadfastness and courage. It would record privations cheerfully endured, poverty and want heroically disregarded. But the grand object—the moral training of the young—successfully advanced. The efforts of the clergy to promote this essential object have been almost marvellous, considering the difficulties of their position and the smallness of their means, as well as the influences which opposed them; but the result would have been scanty and partial, were there not the devotedness and self-sacrifice of holy women to appeal to. The same spirit that impelled the Sister to brave the perils of the fever shed and cholera ward gave her fortitude to endure the drudgery of teaching in the crowded school; and, thanks alike to the energy of the religious communities throughout the United States, and the respect in which they and their work are held, female education for Catholic youth is now provided for to a very large extent. There is much more to be done, but vast things have been already accomplished.

The Catholic Church holds that religious education is necessary for the children of its communion. Others may hold different notions; but this is its fixed and unalterable belief. Nor is it singular in this respect. If it be a grave error to consider that it is well to form and mould the moral nature of youth, while you develop and strengthen its intellectual faculties, that error is shared in common with the most advanced nations of Europe,—Protestant Prussia and Protestant England—Catholic Austria and Catholic France. Fortunately for the future of the Irish in America, this is the belief of the best and greatest portion of the Catholic population throughout the United States.

To obtain the advantages of strictly religious training for their children, Catholics must of necessity make large sacrifices. They have no option but to pay the tax for the maintenance of the Public Schools, to which all classes have free access, and in which all receive a gratuitous and liberal education; but while Catholics pay their quota of the public rate, they assess themselves voluntarily for the support of the schools of which their Church approves. There have been unavoidable defects in the Catholic schools in some districts, and under certain circumstances; it being difficult for a poor congregation, that has everything to provide, everything to accomplish to vie with the State in the character and material of its schools. Defects there have been, and there must be for a time; but these have been wisely borne with, so long as they were unavoidable; for whatever inferiority there may have been, or may still be, in one respect it has been more than compensated by immeasurably greater advantages. But these defects belong rather to the past, and to parishes still in their first difficulties of church building and other costly undertakings of a kindred nature—not to parishes in which the main wants have been provided for, or where the schools have been any time established. On the contrary, there are numerous instances in which the Catholic school is greatly superior to the Public school, and where the Catholic college puts to shame the most advanced of the educational institutions of the State. Notwithstanding the stupid assertions of the bigoted or the ignorant, the Church never did lag behind in the march of intellect; it has ever put itself in the van of the intellectual movement in every country. It thoroughly comprehends its position, its responsibility, and its duty; and while it is solicitous for the spiritual welfare of its flock, it never disdains the task of fitting youth for the practical business of daily life, and the varied pursuits and duties of citizenship.

How eminently practical is the training given in America under the auspices of the Catholic Church may be understood from the following description of the system adopted in the schools of the Sisters of Mercy. The same system, I may remark, is common to the religious communities of the United States. The writer is a Sister of the Order of Mercy, who thus writes to a friend, from a convent in Missouri. The letter is dated the 3rd of June 1867:—

'Two points of difference between our schools and the Public Schools I will note: with us, children of every class learn to work, devoting nearly two hours a day to it; drawing is also taught in connection with fancy work. We believe it of the greatest importance to bring up our children to industrious habits, especially in a country like this, where reverses are so common, and where people are often so suddenly thrown upon their own resources. The public common schools never teach manual work of any kind—hence their pupils grow up with a sort of contempt for it, and, in case of family reverses, find it difficult to hit upon any honest way of earning a livelihood. They are willing to take professions, but dislike much to apply to trades. Many Protestants of the more sensible classes send their children to us on this account. In some places the school authorities have given several public schools to the Sisters of Mercy, who now teach them in these'—the places mentioned—'and other places.'

The writer explains the other feature of interest, which is of scarcely less importance:—

'We develop in our pupils a taste for useful and elegant reading, not always or necessarily religious, but in all cases perfectly unexceptionable. By thus cultivating their tastes, we hope to give them rational occupation for their leisure, and to hinder them from contracting a liking for foolish or pernicious reading. I need not tell you that the other schools do not take this precaution, and the consequence may be seen in the immense circulation of works of a deleterious character, which are eagerly read, even by children, and to which much of the crime so prevalent may be traced. Circulating libraries are established in common with our schools, sodalities, &c.'

'It is hard to bring up youth, especially boys, in this country,' has been the grave complaint of Irish fathers to whom I spoke on this subject, or who themselves made it one of anxious remark. This is felt more keenly by parents who have reared children in the old country as well as in America. In Ireland the family ties are strong and enduring, while respect for parents and deference to parental authority is the characteristic of the country —of all but the vicious and the worthless.

The mind of Ireland tends to moral conservatism,—it reverences authority, eminently that of the parent or the pastor. It is otherwise in America, whose institutions, no less than the circumstances of a country yet in its early youth, are favourable to the most complete personal independence. When guided by reason, and controlled by the religious principle, nobility of character and dignity of bearing are the natural result of this consciousness of personal as well as public freedom; but without such controlling influences, this independence too often degenerates into a manner and tone of thought which is neither admirable nor attractive. The youth of the country rapidly catch the prevailing spirit, and thus become impatient of restraint at a period of life when restraint is indispensable to their future well-being. This is peculiarly observable in the youth who are educated in the Public Schools. The boy who is trained in these institutions is too apt to disregard, if not altogether despise, that authority which is held so sacred in Ireland; and once this first and holiest of all influences is lost, on goes the headlong youth, reckless of consequences, and the slave of every impulse. There is nothing more graceful than modesty in youth, and that proper respect which it manifests towards age and worth. Self-esteem, not reverence, is the bump which the Public School system of America—a system purely secular—developes; and of all the pupils gathered within the walls of these schools, none are so quick to catch and reflect the prevailing influence as the children of the Irish. The young urchin of eight or ten is not a little proud of the distinction of being a free and independent citizen of the Great Republic; and it may be doubted if the pity which he occasionally feels for his homely and unaffected Irish father is not unconsciously tinctured with Native American contempt for the 'foreigner,' and the 'Pat.'

The Catholic Schools, on the contrary, inculcate obedience to parental authority—respect for the head of the family—reverence for holy things,—for what is great and good and noble; while at the same time they carefully prepare their pupils for the ordinary pursuits of life, and tit them to make their way in the world, by honesty, industry, and intelligence. They send the youth better armed into the world to fight his way against difficulty and temptation, and they give him a resource on which he may fall back at every period of his future career. A sound Catholic education affords the best protection against the blight of indifferentism, which is a dangerous evil to the Irish in America—to that portion of the population whose conduct is most severely scrutinised, or who are regarded, at least by some, and those not a few, with suspicion or dislike.

This system of education extends, while it secures, the legitimate influence of the Church; and that influence is beneficial in a worldly and temporal point of view, as well as in the inner life of the Catholic. Whatever the prejudice of a class of Americans, they are, on the whole, a just and generous people, thoroughly alive to real merit, and ready to appreciate and confide in it. They may not admire the Catholic religion in the abstract; they may object to its tenets, or they may attribute to the Church principles and a policy which have been, times without number, repudiated and disproved; but they instinctively admire and respect a Catholic who is not ashamed to admit his loyalty to his creed, and who exhibits in his life and conduct the influence of its teaching. There are in New York, as in the other cities of America, merchants and bankers and men of business who listen with grave attention, if not warm approval, to inflammatory harangues—one cannot call them sermons, for a sermon suggests the idea of a religious discourse—against 'Popery and its abominations;' who will even join in a crusade against Catholic franchises and freedom—who will contribute largely, and even munificently, to the funds of some aggressive organisation or hostile institution—who will countenance a wrong done, if not to parental authority, at least to religious liberty and Christian charity, in the persons of miserable children, the victims of poverty or neglect;— but the same merchants, bankers, and men of business will place implicit confidence in the honesty and fidelity of Catholics—Irish Catholics too—whom they know to be devoted to their Church, and constant in the performance of their religious duties. Nay, the very men who do not hesitate to indulge in the common cant about priests and confession, will privately enquire whether the Catholic whom they employ attends his church, and complies with its spiritual obligations. These men will place their banks, their warehouses, their offices, their concerns, in the custody of humble Irishmen of the class who consider that true fidelity to their native country includes unswerving devotion to its ancient faith.

In New York there are few places of business which are not confided to the vigilant custody of Irishmen of this stamp; and rarely has this confidence been violated. Money, documents, goods, valuable effects of all kinds, are constantly under their hands, and at their mercy; but no doubt arises as to the trustworthiness of the guardian or the safety of the property. Probably, if the proprietor learned that the guardian of his property had ceased to be a practical Catholic, his confidence would not remain long unshaken: and thus the same man of experience and intellect who allowed himself to be deluded by all manner of anti-Catholic nonsense, would be the first to recognise, in his own interest, how salutary was the influence of the Church over the consciences of those who were faithful to its precepts. And, in their quiet, humble unobtrusive way, the Irish Catholics who live in accordance with the teachings of their Church—who, steady, sober, diligent, faithful, are as solicitous for the welfare of their employers as for their own advancement,—Irishmen of this class not only maintain the honour of their country and the truth of their religion, but do much to remove prejudice, and bring about conversions.

The same applies to Irish Catholics of different classes, and to women as well as men. Even bigoted mistresses and employers will prefer the testimony of the Priest or the Sister to all other testimonies as to the character and conduct of a Catholic girl or woman, and will afford her facilities to 'go to her duty'—will even reproach her if she appear to be lax or indifferent; which, however, is not common with Irish Catholic females. Thus, in a mere worldly or temporal point of view, practical adherence to their Church is beneficial to Catholics in America; and to Catholic teaching alone is this adherence—this noble yet unobtrusive loyalty—to be looked for in the rising generation of that race whose fidelity to their faith has been tested by centuries of persecution.

To provide what they rightly consider to be the best education for their children, Catholics freely tax themselves; but among the generous contributors to Catholic schools are American Protestants, who desire to promote education wherever they can, and who recognise in Catholic teaching a benefit to the community as well as to the individual. They are specially pleased to witness the attention bestowed by the clergy on the schools of their parish, the pride they manifest in their improvement, and the efforts they make to induce cleanliness of person, decency of dress, and propriety of demeanour. It is customary for the priest to refuse admittance to the child unless it is clean and properly clad, the priest knowing well that the vice, not the poverty of the parent, is the cause of the condition of the child; and very often the parent is thus shamed into a sense of decency by the rebuke implied in this refusal, and the child is soon fit to pass muster, and to be received among the other children of the school. The priest also tries to reach the parents through their children, and frequently with signal success; the growing intelligence and modest piety of the child acts as a check on the folly of the parent, and brings the indifferent or the obdurate within the salutary influence of the Church. What most impresses the liberal Protestant in his observation of Catholic schools is the paternal solicitude of the pastor for the welfare of his young flock. And not only will a really enlightened non-Catholic of any denomination rarely refuse an application for assistance towards the extension of Catholic education, should such be made to him, but most frequently are voluntary offerings—and to a considerable amount—made by Protestants who appreciate the conscientious opposition of the Catholic clergy to any system of training of youth which is not based upon religion, and who witness the strenuous efforts they make to raise the standard of teaching in their schools.

An unprejudiced observer—and there are perhaps more of that class in America than in any country in the world—will naturally say: 'The Catholic Church is responsible for the conduct and character of its flock—responsible to the world, as well as to God; it must know what description of education is most suited to its youth—which system will make them better Christians, better men and women, better citizens. It is the oldest Church in the world, therefore the ripest in the wisdom of experience; and that experience convinces it that education based on religion—education which comprehends the spiritual and moral as well as the intellectual nature of the human being—that which strengthens and purifies the heart and moulds the conscience, while it developes the mind and stores the memory of the pupil—is that which is the best preparation for the battle of life. If, then, the Catholic Church is held responsible—as undoubtedly it is—for the character and conduct of those who call themselves Catholics, or are recognised as Catholics, why should it not adopt and insist upon having that system of instruction which it knows to be most conducive to the useful end at which it aims? If we are not yet wise enough, or liberal enough, to assist them through the State, at least we should do so as individuals.'

The educational resources of the Catholic Church of America—meaning thereby the teachers, the buildings, and the pecuniary means—are not as yet equal to the daily-increasing requirements of the country; but though they do not and cannot keep pace with the demand made upon them, they are being steadily and even wondrously developed. The teaching staff is deficient alone in numbers; its energy, its zeal, and its efficiency are equal to every legitimate effort. What can be done under the circumstances is done, and admirably done; but more teachers and more schools and larger means are in many, indeed most instances indispensable. For female schools, and infant schools for both sexes, the American Church can boast of a noble array of the Religious Orders, who are carrying true civilisation into every quarter. Even while an infant city is struggling into existence, beginning to dot itself here and there with an odd building in red brick, you see a convent; and in the school attached you hear the grateful hum of youthful voices. The religious communities in America are numerous, but all are devoted to works of active, practical usefulness, which even the most sceptical must appreciate. Among this glorious army of human benefactors—the most successful civilisers whom the world knows—are the Orders of Charity and Mercy, of Notre Dame, the Sacred Heart, the Ursulines, the Presentation, Benedictines, Dominicans, Franciscans, the Holy Cross, of St. Joseph, of Providence, of the Visitation, of Nazareth, of Loretto, of the Precious Blood, of the Holy Name of Jesus, and others known to the Catholics of America. For male schools, of every class, the Church enjoys the invaluable services of the world-famous Order of Jesus, whose colleges, academies and schools cannot be excelled by any educational establishments in the

United States. To these are added Sulpitians, Franciscans, Vincentians, Redemptorists, the Congregation of the Holy Cross, and the Brothers of the Christian Schools. But these, and others not particularised, though numerous and zealous in the cause of Christian education, bear still but a small proportion to the increasing demand for their teaching.

It is not necessary to give a detailed account of the progress of Catholic education in America. Such is that progress, that the description of to-day would not suffice for to-morrow. Thus in the city of New York there are now about 30,000 children receiving education in Catholic schools; but in all probability 40,000 would not fully represent the number that may be in attendance at the close of 1868. Somewhere about 1833, a single priest was 'attending Brooklyn,' then regarded as a suburb of New York; now there are not fewer than 12,000 Catholic children in Catholic training in that populous city. In places which have grown up within the last twenty years, I found from 12,000 to 15,000 children under various Religious Orders, notwithstanding that the Public Schools were likewise in full and successful activity. And even in small cities there were such numbers as 4,000 and 5,000 and 6,000, while the most strenuous efforts were made by bishops and priests to extend their school accommodation and increase the number of their pupils; and in all cases the majority of the children were Irish—either Irish born or the offspring of Irish parents. The school that commences with 300 soon expands into 500, and the 500 rapidly grow into 1,000—and so on. In New York there are parishes in which the attendance in their Catholic schools is between 2,000 and 3,000; and in these parishes efforts are still made to extend the blessings of the best system of education to those who, perhaps of all other children in the world, are destined to be tried by the most dangerous temptations. I saw throughout the States large and spacious schools growing up in every direction under the auspices of the Church; and I can remember how, when visiting a Southern city, which was slowly rising above the ashes of its desolation, I was impressed with the zeal of the Catholics—mostly Irish—who were erecting a fine female school for 500 pupils, which was to be placed under the care of Sisters.

Without a community of Sisters, no parish, no Catholic community is properly provided for; with Sisters the work of reformation is really begun. Themselves examples of everything good and holy, gentle and refined, they soon exercise a salutary influence over adults as well as children. And what can equal the patience of the Sister in the daily drudgery of the crowded school? It is something wonderful, and can only be accounted for by the light in which she regards her work—as a duty acceptable to God. Whatever she does, her heart is in it; the motive, object, feeling—all exalt and render it sacred in her eyes. It is the consciousness of the sacredness of the nun's vocation that enables her to go through her laborious duties with such unfailing regularity and such matchless cheerfulness and patience. Entering any of the free schools of America, one may see young Sisters, with the bloom of youth's freshness on their cheek, as calm and unmoved amidst the clatter and clamour of a school of some hundred girls or little boys, as if that cheek had grown pale and worn with age. I remember coming into a crowded school in a remote and not over rich district; the teaching staff was miserably small, and each of the two Sisters had to instruct and manage a disproportionately large number of young people.

As I raised the latch of the door of the boys' school—in which there must have been seventy or eighty little fellows of all ages, from four or five to twelve—the clatter was prodigious. But as the door opened, and the stranger entered, the spell of silence—unwonted silence—fell upon the youthful students. The Sister was a young Irishwoman; and notwithstanding the calm serenity of her countenance, and the cheerfulness of her manner, there was something of weariness about her eyes—what one may occasionally remark in the face of a fond mother of a family on whom she doats, but who are nevertheless 'too much for her.' 'I am afraid, Sister,' I remarked, 'these young gentlemen are a little difficult to manage at times?' 'Well, certainly, they are a little troublesome—occasionally,' she replied; 'but,' she added, as her glance roamed round the school, and it rested on the familiar features of so many loved ones, and her voice softened into the sweetest tones, 'poor little fellows, they are very good on the whole—indeed very good.' I did not remain long; and as the door closed after me, I knew, by the splendid clatter which was almost instantaneously renewed, that the trials of the Sister had again begun.

If the patience of the Sister in the school-room is admirable, what can be said of her devotion to the orphan in the asylum? It is the compensation which religion makes to the bereaved one for the loss of a mother's love The waifs and strays of society are cared for, watched over with a solicitude which the natural love of a parent can alone excel. I have seen many such asylums in America—in the British Provinces as in the States Among those helpless little beings there is always one who is sure to be, not better cared for or more beloved, but the 'pet'—a tiny toddler, who will cling in the Sister's robe, or cry itself to sleep in her arms; or the 'prodigy' of the riper age of three or four—a young gentleman who, after conquering his bashfulness, will dance an Irish jig, or a negro breakdown, or recite a pretty pious verse, or sing something comic enough to set all the children in a roar of innocent delight, in which the Sister is sure to join. In one of these asylums I remember to have seen, in the centre of a large apartment, occupied as a day room by the youngest children, a couch, on which lay a helpless and hopeless infant cripple; and how the poor little thing, whose feeble tide of life was slowly ebbing, followed with a look of pleasure and a faint sickly smile, the performance of the infant prodigy. And no mother could have spoken to that stricken child with a gentler voice, or watched over it with a fonder solicitude, than the Sister, whom the inspiration of Faith had given to it as a second parent.

While passing through various institutions under the management of religious communities, the thought has often struck me—that if those who entertain strange notions as to the real character of these communities had the same opportunities as I have had, in Europe as in America, of witnessing the daily drudgery of the Sisters engaged in the laborious and wearisome task of education—the services of the Sisters in the orphan asylum, the prison, the penitentiary, the hospital—in visiting the sick, protecting the unprotected female, teaching habits of industry and neatness, bringing back the erring and the fallen to safety and penitence—in their daily life, in which they exemplify the beauty and holiness of their mission—how prejudice would vanish! And how the good and the enlightened would understand that if society loses the advantage of the presence and influence of these holy women in the ordinary paths of life, as sisters, wives, and mothers, it is compensated a thousand-fold by their services in the training of youth, in the care of the orphan, in the reclamation of the sinner, in the relief of the suffering—nay, in the formation of the female mind on the solid basis of piety, and preparing the young girl, whether the daughter of affluence or the child of the people, for the fulfilment of her future duties, as wife and mother, as companion or as guide.

But whatever the prejudices of the ignorant or the fanatical may be, the enlightened of America recognise the value of the training which young girls receive in schools conducted by members of religious communities—by women who are accomplished, gentle, graceful, and refined—who combine the highest intellectual cultivation with genuine goodness. Protestants of all denominations, and of strong religious convictions too, send their daughters to convent schools; and, strange as it may appear to one who visits America for the first time, more than half of all the pupils educated in such institutions are the children of non-Catholics! Parents know that while under the care of the Sisters their children are not exposed to risk or danger—-that they are morally safe; and one may hear it constantly remarked by Protestants that there is an indefinable 'something' in the manner of girls trained by nuns which is immeasurably superior to the artificial finish of the best secular academy or college. If the young Protestant pupil unwillingly enters the convent school, she leaves it reluctantly; and the influence of the impression it has left upon her mind is never lost in after life—she knows how false are the accusations made against convents and Catholics, and when others are prejudiced or fanatical, she is tolerant and liberal. And for society at large this conversion to common sense is a great gain.

What is true of convent schools is equally true of schools and colleges under the care of the great educational Orders—Jesuits, Sulpitians, Vincentians, Redemptorists, Brothers of the Holy Cross, Christian Brothers, Franciscans, and others. Such indeed is the liberality of some parents, that they formally declare their willingness to have their children brought up in the Catholic faith. This has more generally occurred since the war, which, as I have already shown, triumphantly tested the wisdom of the Church, as well as the nature and results of its teaching.

As the Brothers of the Christian Schools are amongst the most successful promoters of Catholic education in America, something may be said as to their progress. They were first established some thirty years since in Montreal, to which city they were invited by the Sulpitians; and last year, 1866, they had in Canada 19 houses, 170 Brothers, and 9,000 pupils. The first establishment of the Order in the United States was in 1845, the next in 1848; and in 1866 they were to be found in successful operation in the chief cities of the Union—in which there were, that year, 35 houses, 370 Brothers, and more than 20,000 pupils. This year, 1867, there is a considerable increase of houses, brothers, and pupils. The Brothers now exceed 400, and the pupils are fast rising to 30,000.

Besides parochial schools, which they teach with signal success, the Brothers conduct several colleges, including that at Manhattan, in New York; St. Louis, Missouri; Rock Hill, Maryland; and Rass, Mississippi. Of the 370 Brothers who constituted in 1866 the strength of the Order in the United States, 300 were either Irish, or of Irish parents. And of the English-speaking Brothers in Canada, the great majority are of the same race. Probably in 1868 the number of Brothers in the States may be at least 500; but were there 5,000, that number would not be too many for the work to be done. There is in America no lack of appreciation of the educational labours of the Christian Brothers. With bishops and clergy the cry is, 'Give us more Brothers'—'Oh, if we had more Brothers!' These men are the inheritors of one of the best educational systems in the world; and devoting themselves exclusively to their self-imposed task, their success is necessarily great. Their parochial schools vie with the Public Schools in the excellence of their teaching—that is, in mere secular knowledge; and their high schools, academies and colleges rival any corresponding institutions supported by the State. The proficiency of their pupils in the highest branches of polite learning is the theme of admiration in journals of the most marked Protestant character; and enlightened Americans of various denominations admit the services which these men render to society through the influence of their teaching on the rising youth of the country. The Brothers are eminently practical; they thoroughly comprehend the spirit and genius of the American mind; and they so teach their pupils, of whatever class, rich or poor, as to suit them to the position they are to occupy in life.

Perhaps the truest proof of the religious influence which they exercise over their pupils is this—that wherever they are any time established, the Bishop of the diocese has less difficulty in procuring candidates for the ministry. They themselves are examples of self-denial and devotedness. All men of intelligence, many full of energy and genius—all capable of pushing their way in some one walk of life or other—not a few certain to have risen to eminence in the higher departments, had they dedicated themselves to the world and its pursuits; living a life almost of privation, content with the barest pittance—what will, in fact, afford them the merest means of existence—the Brothers labour in their glorious vocation with a zeal and enthusiasm which religion can alone inspire or alone explain. To the mind of generous youth the ambition of rising in the world is natural and laudable, and in a new and vast country like America, and under a constitution which throws open the path of distinction to merit or to courage, the world offers too many tempting attractions to be resisted by the young and the ardent. Hence there is a constant complaint on the part of Bishops of the want of 'vocations' for the priesthood. Indeed the latest utterance on this subject, at once the gravest and most authoritative, proceeds from the Second Plenary Council of Baltimore. The Bishops say:—

We continue to feel the want of zealous priests, in sufficient number to supply the daily increasing necessities of our dioceses. While we are gratified to know that in some parts of our country the number of youths who offer themselves for the ecclesiastical state is rapidly increasing, we are obliged to remark that in other parts, notwithstanding all the efforts and sacrifices which have been made for this object, and the extraordinary encouragements which have been held out to youthful aspirants to the ministry in our Preparatory and Theological Seminaries, the number of such as have presented themselves and persevered in their vocations has hitherto been lamentably small. Whatever may be the cause of this unwillingness to enter the sacred ministry on the part of our youth, it cannot be attributed to any deficiency of ours in such efforts as circumstances have enabled us to make. We fear that the fault lies, in great part, with many parents, who, instead of fostering the desire, so natural to the youthful heart, of dedicating itself to the service of God's sanctuary, but too often impart to their children their own worldly-mindedness, and seek to influence their choice of a state of life by unduly exaggerating the difficulties and dangers of the priestly calling, and painting in too glowing colours the advantage of a secular life.

The 'some parts' referred to in the Pastoral Letter may signify those places in which the best provision has been made for religious teaching, including those in which the Christian Brothers have established their schools, and have had time to exercise their influence on the mind and heart of youth. It has been remarked that the influence of their teaching is not alone manifested in their own immediate pupils; but that many young men who have never frequented their schools have felt themselves impelled to a religious life by the example of a friend or companion educated by the Brothers. Here then are grand results of the successful labours of this Order: youth fitted to make its way in the world, and fortified by the best influences, if not wholly to resist, at least not to be a willing victim to its temptations; and young of higher and nobler purpose induced to sacrifice the glittering attractions of the world, for the self-denying and laborious life of the missionary priest.

The Third Order of St. Francis is rapidly growing in strength and usefulness in the United States. It comprises Priests, Brothers, Sisters, whose ordinary avocation is the training of youth of both sexes, and ministering to the sick and poor in hospitals. To the Archdiocese of Tuam, Ireland, the Catholic Church of America is indebted for the Brothers of this Order, who have established several communities, and conduct with great advantage academies and parochial schools in various dioceses. In 1847, Bishop O'Connor, of Pittsburg, obtained six Brothers, who founded some communities of the Order in his diocese, the principal of which is Loretto, containing about forty Brothers, who conduct an extensive college in that city. This was the origin of this Order in the United States. In 1858, Bishop Loughlin of Brooklyn applied to the Archbishop of Tuam for Brothers, and obtained two; and in the diocese of Brooklyn there are now about thirty of the brotherhood, conducting academies and parochial schools which are largely attended. They have opened a mission in Los Angeles, California, for the last four years; they have founded another in Elizabeth Port, New Jersey; and this year they have established a branch in Erie, Pennsylvania. Thus has the good seed from the old Catholic country fructified in this new domain of the Church.

As the educational necessities of Catholics increase, so in the same or a greater proportion does the Church display greater zeal and greater energy to supply the want. New Orders are constantly springing up for new fields of spiritual and intellectual labour. Thus the Congregation of the Holy Cross, founded in France in 1856, and approved by the Holy See in 1857, has established several flourishing educational institutions in the United States; its teaching ranging from the simplest elementary instruction up to the very highest standard of collegiate requirements. The Priests, who are called Salvatorists, from being specially consecrated to the Sacred Heart of Jesus, devote themselves exclusively to missions and the education of youth. The Brothers are devoted to the great work of religious instruction, with which, according to the circumstances and the necessities of their pupils, is combined practical training in various branches of industry. The Sisters, who are consecrated to the Sacred Heart of Mary, educate female youth of all classes of society, and are also employed in hospitals and asylums. The Sisters already number more than 250 in the States.

Among the most prominent structures in New Orleans are the great schools conducted by the Redemptorist Fathers of that city; and among these good men is one—all zeal, all energy, all ardour—whose name is venerated in the South. Father Sheeran was one of the most devoted, not to say one of the bravest, of the Chaplains of the Southern army. As cool under fire as the oldest campaigner, one glance from Father Sheeran's eye would send the waverer dashing to the front. And now that, happily, the sword is returned to the scabbard, and the generous of North and South can meet again as brethren, if not as friends, Father Sheeran is, with his fellow-priests, actively engaged, indeed almost wholly engrossed, in the noble work of Christian education; which he and they promote with such success, that 1,400 children—the children chiefly of Irish parents—are educated in such a manner as to elicit the warmest and most elaborate praise from Protestant journalists. New Orleans possesses several important educational institutions, academical and parochial; but that of the Redemptorists is remarkable because of the well-known career of the famous Chaplain of the 14th Louisiana Regiment.

CHAPTER XXVII

*Juvenile Reformation—Opposition to Catholic Reformatories—The two Systems
Illustrated—Christianity Meek and Loving—The Work of the Enemy—Solemn
Appeals to Catholic Duty*

IN their various institutions for the protection and reformation of juveniles, the
Americans are keeping pace with the enlightened spirit of European progress.
They wisely believe that prevention is less expensive than cure—that, whatever
their apparent costliness, precaution and prevention are certain to be in the end
more economical and more useful than punishment. They hold, with all sensible
men from the days of Solomon to our own, that it is easier to incline the twig than
bend the tree—to direct the small stream into the right channel, than to deal with
the swollen torrent; that if vice is to be effectually suppressed or diminished, you
must begin with the beginning. This is the belief and the policy of every really
enlightened man or woman of the Old World or the New. In this spirit was
founded the Colony of Mettray, in France, and the juvenile reformatory of the
Vigna Pia in Rome, which, some ten years since, I beheld in active and successful
operation. It is in the same spirit that the Catholic Church, now as in former ages,
in America as in Europe, gathers under her sheltering wing the orphan, and the
'half-orphan,' or the child in danger of ruin. The calendar of the Church is
resplendent with the names of men and women whose lives have been devoted to
the sacred duty which modern philanthropists and social reformers are imitating at
a long distance.

Unfortunately for the success of the Catholics of America in this great work of
juvenile reformation, their resources, at least hitherto, have not been equal to meet
the evils arising from orphanage, or from the poverty, the neglect, or the
viciousness of parents. Thus a wide field was left of necessity to those of a
different communion: but it is much to be deplored that the opportunity of doing
good was not always embraced in the right spirit, and that the gratification of
achieving an unworthy triumph over a rival sect was preferred to the purer delight
of discharging a holy duty in the spirit of Christian charity. In some few cases the
work of reformation was taken up in the right spirit—in a spirit of noble charity,
and in the loftiest sense of justice to one's neighbour; but, alas for poor fallible
human nature! in too many instances it was entered upon as much from a motive
of active hostility, as from a desire to grapple with a social evil of admitted
magnitude and danger. No Catholic—especially no Irish Catholic—could be
insensible to the scandalous nature of the war which, under the mask of
benevolence and philanthropy, was waged against the children of poverty and the
victims of neglect. But, until lately, whether from want of organisation, lack of

means, or the urgency of other claims, little was done, save through religious institutions, to resist the fierce assault or the insidious approach of the proselytiser. In the Pastoral Letter of the Second Plenary Council of Baltimore, the Bishops of the American Church thus refer to this question of vital moment:—

It is a melancholy fact, and a very humiliating avowal for us to make, that a very large proportion of the idle and vicious youth of our principal cities are the children of Catholic parents. Whether from poverty or neglect, the ignorance in which so many parents are involved as to the true nature of education, and of their duties as Christian parents, or the associations which our youth so easily form with those who encourage them to disregard parental admonition; certain it is, that a large number of Catholic parents either appear to have no idea of the sanctity of the Christian family, and of the responsibility imposed on them of providing for the moral training of their offspring, or fulfil this duty in a very imperfect manner. Day after day, these unhappy children are caught in the commission of petty crimes, which render them amenable to the public authorities; and, day after day, are they transferred by hundreds from the sectarian reformatories in which they have been placed by the courts, to distant localities, where they are brought up in ignorance of, and most commonly in hostility to, the Religion in which they have been baptized. The only remedy for this great and daily augmenting evil is to provide Catholic Protectories or Industrial Schools, to which such children may be sent; and where, *under the only influence that is known to have really reached the roots of vice*, the youthful culprit may cease to do evil and learn to do good.

Practical efforts have been made to meet the evil; and in the cities of New York, Boston, and Baltimore, institutions for the protection and reformation of criminal or destitute children have been formed, and, though but a short time in existence, are working with marked success, with the approval of every liberal-minded Protestant of those great centres of American civilisation. The dignified and praiseworthy attitude taken by Catholics, in their efforts to protect the faith of helpless little ones of their own communion, and relieve themselves from a cause of the gravest reproval, excited a storm of opposition from those who had much rather know that Catholics deserted their duty, and thus afforded their enemies the continued power of injuring and right of despising them.

'In obtaining our charter,' say the conductors of the New York institution, of which the late Dr. Ives, a distinguished convert, was president, 'we had to struggle against two objections urged with surprising zeal and pertinacity. The first, that ample provision for vicious and destitute children had already been made by the State, and that an increase would only tend to injure the existing institutions. The second, that these institutions were organised on the fairest and most liberal basis, by excluding all distinctive religion; while the one whose incorporation we sought was professedly sectarian in its character, being placed under the exclusive control of Catholics.' To the first objection they pleaded, what has since been fully admitted, the enormous magnitude of the evil, and the inadequacy of existing means to meet it; and to the second, that if the State had shown its fairness and liberality only by excluding, in fact, all distinctive religion from its institutions, it was high time that one institution, at least, should be organised on a different basis; should professedly and really make distinctive religion its actuating and controlling power, as nothing short of this could so sway the hearts of children as to make them, in the end, good Christians and good men. The absolute falsehood, in fact, of the second objection is thus torn to shreds in the Report:—

But the question was put:—'Has the State succeeded in excluding from its institutions all distinctive religion, and all *sectarian teaching and influence*? Inquire at *"The Juvenile Asylum" "The House of Refuge," "The Children's Aid Society" "The Five Points House of Industry."* Is not the *Protestant* religion inculcated in these institutions, and only the Catholic religion *excluded*? Where, among the managers of all these institutions, is a Catholic to be found? Where, among their superintendents, their teachers, their preachers, do you find a Catholic? Where among their acts of worship is a Catholic act tolerated? While, on the other hand, who does not know, that Protestant worship, in all its various forms, is, without opposition, introduced? And Protestant doctrine, in all its shades and contradictions, is inculcated? Indeed, we did not find it necessary to debate this question. Protestant periodicals not only admitted but gloried in the facts. They boasted that the State is Protestant in all her institutions, and that it is an act of great indulgence on her part that Catholicity is allowed to exist at all; that we, as Catholics, should be grateful that the power of the State has not been invoked to arrest our progress and put an end to our institutions. Can it, therefore, we enquired, be thought unreasonable, while such a spirit actuates the Protestant community, that Catholic parents should be averse to give up their children to Protestant institutions; to institutions, where Protestant dogmas and practices are enforced upon them; and where they are compelled to study books and listen to addresses in which the religion of their fathers is reviled? We pressed the inquiry further, and asked: Whether it was wise and statesman-like to introduce a system of compulsion, where the rights of conscience are concerned? Where the faith of Catholic parents is outraged by forcing Catholic children into Protestant asylums? Whether peace and contentment in the community are likely to be the result of such a system?' This was the line of argument addressed to the Legislature, which, against violent opposition, granted our charter.

One passage from the Report deserves special approval; and were the example which it offers generally adopted, there would remain but little cause for anger or contention: 'A few children belonging to parents not Catholics have been sent to us by the Courts. In such cases the children are received, *if the parents or guardians so request. If they object, the children are returned to the magistrate.* No interference is allowed with the religious tenets of non-Catholics employed at the Protectory.'

One of the institutions referred to in the foregoing Report is the 'New York Juvenile Society.' In its Report for 1863, there is a table stating the 'Religious instruction previous to commitment;' and the result for ten years, from 1853 to the date of publication, is as follows: 'Roman Catholics, 5,210; Protestants, 3,933; Jewish, 67; Unknown, 256—Total, 9,467.' So that the Catholics were in a considerable majority of the whole. Now, what became of these 5,210 Catholic children, in an institution in which, as the Catholics of New York stated before the Legislature, no Catholic manager, superintendent, teacher, or preacher, is tolerated, and from which the Catholic religion is the only one excluded? In page 9 of the same Report, we find these words:—

The benefits of the course of training and education pursued in the institution is seen, not only in the improved character of the children returned to their parents, *but also in that of those sent to the West*. To how many children has been opened there a bright and prosperous future! Scattered among the farm-houses of Illinois, they are members of comfortable households, many of them adopted as sons and daughters, and all in a land where competence is within the reach of all, especially of those who begin there with an education fully equal to that of the average of the farmer's children among whom they dwell, and with whom they are prepared to keep pace.

It is scarcely necessary to enquire how many of the 5,210 Catholic children were 'returned to their parents,' and how many were 'sent to the West.' It may be remarked that the 'Juvenile Asylum' is only one of many similar institutions. Another extract from the Report is most suggestive:—

'But not the least valuable and interesting proofs of success are the letters received from our young Emigrants in their new spheres. These letters are often full of filial love and gratitude *to the teachers*, who have been to them as parents, and under whose kind care and guidance they had their first experience of a happy life.'

There is no word here of the *parent*, possibly the widow of an Irish soldier who died fighting in defence of the Union, and whose boy got beyond her maternal control. But in a letter published in the transactions of another Association—the 'Children's Aid Society' of Baltimore—the following production of a poor perverted child is strangely published. It is here given as it appears in the twenty-sixth page of the Report for 1866:—

'TRANSFERRED.'

'When *my father and my mother forsake me, then the Lord will take me up*.'

'MR. PALMER

JULY 22nd, 1866.

'Respected *Friend*.

'I have been thinking of writing too you for some time, i am well and i hope you are the same i like my home very much i went to school four months last winter and had lots of fun, i had two slay rides i would not be back to Mr. V.'s for any money the country is beautiful up hear we have plenty of black berries, like the country better than the city. *i dont care to know of my parents for i am better off without knowing.* philip and george are well they are both happy and enjoy themselves very mutch in the country we wold all of us like to see you very mutch come see us soon as you can. Philip lives in the same house that i do and George lives right across the road Mrs C has a nice little boy only two years old i love him very mutch i beleave I have told you all at present

    M.'

As a contrast to the teaching which, whatever the intention, had the effect of inducing a wretched child to write that odious sentence—'*i dont care to know of my parents for i am better off without knowing,*'—may be quoted an extract from the first year's Report of the Association established in Boston for the protection of Catholic children. It will commend itself to the mind of the Christian and the heart of the parent:—

Next to their duty to Almighty God, the children are taught to have regard to that which they owe to their parents. Even under the old Law, God not only commanded, as a duty of eternal obligation, that children 'honour and succour their father and mother,' but pronounced a fearful curse upon such as refused to comply! While it is a notorious fact, that in His providence, all those countries which are characterised by a neglect of this command are sunk to the lowest degradation; and that just in proportion as a nation becomes truly civilised, on the basis of Christianity, *are the domestic relations elevated and strengthened.*

It has, therefore, been a matter of deep solicitude with the Managers, so to discharge their duty as that children *may not be alienated from their parents, or led to forget or disregard their obligations to them.* Hence in all those cases where children of parents able to support them have been committed for the minor offences, *we insist upon returning them so soon as, in our judgment, it can safely be done.* In regard to many of this class of young delinquents, a few weeks of strict but kind discipline is found as effectual in subduing their tempers and restoring a spirit of filial obedience, as a much longer period.

This will account for the number which have already been discharged and sent home to their family.

The benefit of this policy is twofold: *it tends to strengthen the family bond*, and to promote the essential virtues of industry and economy. For we have not only to avoid the serious evil of weakening the family tie by unnecessarily separating children from their parents, but also to guard against, what is hardly less pernicious, the mischief of taking away from these parents that main stimulus to exertion, the necessity of providing for their own households.

From a serial, entitled 'The *Little Wanderer's Friend*,' much information may be derived; valuable as indicating the spirit in which not a few of the so-called benevolent institutions are conducted, and the numerical extent of their operations. From the number for May 1865, an interesting paragraph or two may be quoted, in illustration of the liberal and tolerant spirit of those institutions of which that agreeable little publication is the accredited organ. A pleasant article, entitled 'The Heathen of New York,' affords the writer a happy theme for the display of his national feelings and religious convictions. 'The mass of the population,' the writer says, 'consists of the most ignorant, bigoted, degraded foreign Catholics, who know no higher law than the word of their priests. Their Christianity is mere baptized heathenism.' Considering the miserable condition in which the mass of the population are found by the writer, it is fortunate that spiritual succour is so near; for we have this consolatory assurance in the same article:—

'We are in the midst of it. Our mission is in front of one of their large churches—under the shadow of their cross. They listen to our songs, while we witness their idolatry. They curse while we gather in the children, teach them the truth, feed, clothe, and send them to kind Christian homes.'

The missionaries, of whom the writer is the faithful organ and eloquent mouthpiece, are not content with their limited sphere of action in front of one of the large churches of the 'baptized heathen' of New York: they must even meet them on the shore, or on the ship's deck; and thus, if they cannot arrest the in-flowing tide of emigration, at least, by extending the hand of brotherly love and the word of God to their poor misguided brethren who cross the ocean, convert it into a deluge of enriching blessedness. 'Last year 155,223 persons landed here from Europe, of whom 92,861 were from poor, ignorant, bigoted, Catholic-cursed Ireland.' In this manner these unhappy heathens are to be spiritually regenerated: 'Let us meet them ere they leave the ship, and extend to them the kind hand and the word of God. They are our misguided brothers.

Let us be kind and teach them the truth. Let us help the needy and teach them the truth. Let us gather the children in.' The children are always the objects of the pious solicitude of these apostolic missionaries; they first gather them in, and they then send them to 'kind Christian homes,' in which all memory of their former 'heathenism' is lost. The success of their operations is thus detailed in their own words:—

The Home for the Friendless

Led off in this work, and for about thirty years has opened its arms and embraced perishing infancy and neglected childhood. But how little has it done compared with the work yet remaining! Encouraged by its success, a few warm-hearted Methodist ladies organised the

Five Points Mission.

They entered the 'gates of hell' to save the perishing; and a glorious monument to Christianity has been erected. Steadily, earnestly, and successfully do they labour, but want, sin, and woe increase around them.

The Five Points House of Industry

Was originated in 1851 by Rev. Mr. Pease, and 'its fame has gone throughout the country.' After years of struggling he was compelled to seek quiet and rest.

Mr. Barlow took his place, and, with an earnestness which sought to imitate Him, concerning whom it was said 'the zeal of thine house hath eaten me up,' he laboured until called to exchange—'sowing in tears' for 'reaping in joy'—to give up his abode in 'Cow Bay' for the 'place' which Jesus said 'I go to prepare for you.' Each year the work increases, and, although since 1851 over 11,000 *have come under their care*, many of whom have been saved, yet, to a stranger, it seems as if Christianity had done nothing.

The Children's Aid Society,

Under the direction of Mr. Brace, with its Industrial Schools—lodging rooms— boys' meetings—*has gathered in and sent to homes more children than any other institution in the world during the last eight or nine years*, yet a stranger could not perceive a ripple upon the surface of this sea of sin and want.

Our Own Work

Has been so constantly kept before the public that it seems useless to speak of it. Four years ago this *Home for Little Wanderers* was opened, and nearly 1,000 children gathered in the first year. The next year 1,224, and last year 1,543.

With such success attending their efforts, the reader will learn without astonishment that these modern Apostles to the Gentiles are not discouraged; they only want more faithful praying Sunday School teachers, and four more earnest Christian men as Missionaries. 'Our hands are tied,' cries the figurative yet eminently practical organ of the Mission. 'Four *hundred and fifty cords bind us*. Reader, will you cut one of them? We mean, will you be one of the 450 who will give or collect from your Sunday School or friends, and send us $1 per week until May 1866, and thus leave us free from all pecuniary anxiety, *and with nothing to do but to gather the children in?*'

It has been computed that, at a low calculation, 30,000 children of Catholic parents, mostly Irish, have been sent to 'kind Christian homes,' through 'Sectarian Reformatories,' and institutions of a kindred spirit. I have heard 50,000 given as a possible average; and considering that one institution lately boasted of having sent 10,000 Catholic children to the West, the number, though great, is not altogether improbable. Children are at a premium in the West, especially if healthy and robust; and dealing in this description of 'live stock' is not by any means a losing speculation. I was confidently informed that thirty children—one a plump infant of a year and-a-half—had been sold, in Michigan, to the highest bidder, not two years previous to the time at which the circumstance was mentioned to me. The children must be disposed of in one way or other; and if a profit can be made for the institution, or for the individual, through the keen rivalry of Western farmers, who look approvingly at the sturdy thews and sinews and strong limbs of a brawny young 'heathen' of Irish birth or blood, who can be unconscionable enough to object to an operation so legitimate, or so strictly in accordance with the entire system of—kidnapping maybe too rude a term to apply to such institutions and such men,—so we shall say, of gathering little children in?

Whatever this system may be to those engaged in it—a system, we may remark, totally repugnant to the spirit of modern legislation in this country, where there are industrial and reformatory institutions purposely denominational in character, with the view of protecting the faith of the most helpless class of the community—its longer tolerance by the Catholics of America, and in a special manner by those of Irish birth or descent, would be in the last degree shameful and discreditable. Allowance must be made for the difficulties of their position hitherto, owing to the many claims upon their means, and the various works which it was the duty of the Catholic Church to undertake; but they are now too numerous, too powerful, and too influential, to submit to the continuance of that which is degrading to them as Catholics, and deeply dishonouring to them as Irishmen. There can be no mincing terms as to what is their manifest duty. The past, with all its bitterness and shame, is irrevocable; but there is the present as well as the future, and if they cannot restore the faith to those who have lost it—not through the worthiest or most honourable means—they should at least take care themselves to gather in, under the shelter of the Church, the miserable victims of poverty, neglect, and vice, and restore them to society as good Christians and useful citizens. The wide influence of Catholic Schools will do much to counteract the evil; but the general imitation of the good work so auspiciously commenced in New York, and Boston, and Baltimore, will prove the readiest and most direct means of redeeming the honour of the Catholics of America; at the same time affording benevolent people of other communions an undisturbed opportunity of attending to their own criminal or destitute children.

The Pastoral Letter of the Plenary Council of 1866, thus refers to this subject:—

We rejoice that in some of our dioceses—would that we could say in all!—a beginning has been made in this good work, and we cannot too earnestly exhort our Venerable Brethren of the Clergy to bring this matter before their respective flocks, to endeavour to impress on Christian parents the duty of guarding their children from the evils above referred to, and to invite them to make persevering and effectual efforts for the establishment of institutions wherein, under the influence of religious teachers, the waywardness of youth may be corrected and good seed planted in the soil in which, while men slept, the enemy had sowed tares.

These solemn and hopeful words, addressed to a Catholic audience at New York, in 1864, by the late Dr. Ives—one of the most illustrious converts to the Church in America, and the master-spirit of the reformatory movement—may be listened to as to a voice from the tomb: 'But, whatever the State may do, the duty of Catholics is plain, and will be done. The probability of failure in this great undertaking cannot be admitted. Dark as the day is, and heavy as are its burdens, Catholics will be found equal to them. The work in our hands will succeed; it is God's work—dictated by His spirit, demanded by His providence, undertaken in

His name, carried on in His strength and for His glory. I feel that it is no presumption to affirm that it will not fail.'

CHAPTER XXVIII

The Second Plenary Council of Baltimore—Protestant Tribute to the Catholic Church—Progress of Catholicity—Instances of its Progress—The Past and the Present—The Church in Chicago and New York—Catholicity in Boston— Anticipations not realised—Number of Catholics in the States—Circumstances of Protestant and Catholic Emigrant different—Loss of Faith, and Indifferentism

IN the Second Plenary Council of Baltimore the Catholic Church of America presented a singularly grand and imposing spectacle. Rarely has Rome herself witnessed a more august assembly, and, more rarely still, one so remarkable in its character. Even in numbers—according to Archbishop Spalding, its venerable President—it was the largest ever held in Christendom since the Council of Trent, with the exception of two or three held at Rome under the Sovereign Pontiff. But though this assemblage of the Spiritual Chiefs of this young and vigorous branch of the Universal Church consisted of seven Archbishops, thirty-eight Bishops, and three Mitred Abbots—in all, forty-nine Mitred Prelates—it was more remarkable for the wisdom and dignity, and weight of character, of the learned and able men of whom it was composed; and still more so for the unbroken unity which it presented in so brief a period after the termination of the deadliest struggle that ever convulsed a country or rent a people asunder. The wonderful progress of the Church, which this majestic assembly made manifest even to the dull or the unbelieving, was a subject of surprise to friends as to enemies; but its unbroken unity, while a cause of confusion to some, who contrasted with it the severed branches of their own distracted churches, was regarded without astonishment by those who either understood the principles of Catholicity, or watched the conduct of the Church during the war.

Fourteen years before, the First Plenary Council of Baltimore was held; since then there had been added to the Catholic hierarchy one Archbishop and fourteen Bishops; and now, from the Second Plenary Council, there goes forth an appeal to Rome for the creation of fourteen additional Bishops! In the Pastoral Letter they say: 'We have also recommended to the Holy See the erection of several additional Episcopal Sees, and Vicariates Apostolic, which are made necessary by our rapidly increasing Catholic population, and the great territorial extent of many of our present Dioceses.'

In the same Pastoral, the progress of the Church is thus indicated: 'We continue to have great consolation in witnessing the advance of Religion throughout the various dioceses, as shown in the multiplication and improved architectural character of our churches, the increase of piety in the various congregations, and the numerous conversions of so many who have sacrificed early prejudices and every consideration of their temporal interests and human feelings at the shrine of Catholic Truth.'

The constitution of this august assembly of wise and learned men is not without interest, even as affording a further illustration of the universality of the Catholic Church. In the division into nationalities we find the Irish element stronger than would at first appear. Of the forty-nine Mitred Prelates who, with the clergy, composed the Council, sixteen are set down as American, nine Irish, twelve French, two Flemish, three Spanish, two Swiss, one Austrian, and two German. But of the sixteen American Prelates, about one half are of Irish blood—nearly all of these the sons of Irish-born parents. Thus fully two-thirds of the English-speaking Bishops of the American Church owe their origin to that country which is now, as it was in remote ages, the most successful propagandist of Catholicity. Sprung from different branches of the human family, representing different races, speaking in different tongues, gathered together from States and territories separated by thousands of miles, they were animated but by one motive and feeling. When replying to the address presented to him by Archbishop Purcell in the name of the assembled Prelates and Clergy, Archbishop Spalding put this point prominently forward:—

'Here we have venerable Prelates from all parts of this great and vast republic, some of whom have come five or six thousand miles; have come at my voice, because in my voice they recognised the voice of Peter and of Christ.... We came together to devise ways and means to carry out the purpose for which Christ died on the Cross, to save men, to bind them together in unity and charity, and to make them lead holy lives. Absorbed in this great object, we have soared far above the regions of storms and clouds into the pure atmosphere of God, where there is no controversy or contention stirred up by human passion; and men sprung from various nations, in this Council, have lost sight of all differences of nationality and temperament, and have blended in that beautiful unity and harmony which the Catholic Church can alone exhibit.'

The assembling of the Council elicited from an able newspaper of Baltimore a testimony to the conduct of the Catholic Church, which thoroughly represents what I have heard expressed in more than a hundred instances throughout the States. I find it quoted, among other articles from the public press, in the volume containing the official record of this memorable manifestation of the progress of the Church. I know it represents the almost universal feeling of the South, and of all but the extreme or violent of the North:—

But while we do not propose to enter upon a theme so nearly boundless, and involving so many considerations which divide the minds of men, it is but appropriate to the occasion, and it certainly is a pleasure to us to say, that the course of the Clergy of the Roman Catholic Church, during our late civil dissensions, will make this demonstration of its vitality and vigour very welcome to multitudes, who, but a little while ago, would have witnessed it with jealous concern. With but few exceptions—and those chiefly noted for their rarity—the priesthood of the Roman Catholic Communion have kept their hands clean of brothers' blood. They have preached only the Gospel, and the great doctrines of peace and good will on which it rests, and have not sullied their altars with fratricidal emblems, or turned their anthems of praise into songs of hate and war. In the camps of both armies they were ministers of God only, and faithful to their high calling amid the terrors of the battle-field and the dangers of the pest-house and the hospital; they dedicated themselves exclusively to the alleviation of bodily suffering and the gentle and holy ministerings of religious consolation. It is for this that men reverence them to-day, who, ten years ago, would have been prompted by prejudice to revile them. It is for this that the Church, whose ministers they are, is recognised now by thousands who dispute its freed as a worthy depository and teacher of the sacred truths which, in making men Christians, make them love one another. In all the proud annals of the Church of Koine there is no prouder page than that which records her purity and steadfastness and independence—her indifference alike to the threats and seductions of power during the Confederate Revolution.

Seduction could not betray the Church from the straight path of her duty; and to threats, though backed by the power of armed legions, she opposed that same sublime 'Non possumus' by which the Sovereign Pontiff has so persistently baffled the wiles of political intriguers, and resisted the fiercest rage of the enemies of the Papacy. 'We cannot do this evil thing—we cannot prostitute our pulpits to the worst passions of man—we, ministers of peace, cannot preach havoc and slaughter—we cannot desecrate God's temple by substituting for the Cross the banner of human strife.' This was the Non Possumus of the American Church. Two Prelates—one of them of the most eminent rank—were called on during the great struggle to exhibit this courage, in which the Catholic Church has ever excelled. To the order of a general, high in command, that a flag should be displayed on his cathedral, the Archbishop, a meek and saintly man, replied in the spirit of the old Roman—had that old Roman been a Christian—'My banner is there already: that banner is the Cross of Christ—none other shall be there, with my consent.' Coarse threats were used in the second instance, and even personal violence was not altogether improbable; but the undismayed Prelate, a man of lofty stature, drew himself up to his full height, and, as he seemed to fill the entrance to his cathedral with his swelling form, he exclaimed to those who were rudely pushing on—'Then, if you attempt to pass, it must be over my dead body; for so long as I live, no war flag shall desecrate the house of God.' The Clergy caught the spirit of their Bishops, and displayed a quiet resistance to the requirements of vehement partizans which was little short of heroic. Thus, in a moment of the severest trial did the Catholic Church of America maintain a strict neutrality, increase and extend her means of usefulness, and secure the respect of those who admire consistency, or who deplored the disastrous consequence of a war which they were powerless to prevent.

Those who look, as I do, to the present and continuous progress of the Catholic Church as that which most intimately concerns and most deeply involves the future of the Irish in America, cannot but regard that progress with feelings of the keenest satisfaction. Though not yet equal to the unparalleled increase of the Catholic population, it is sufficiently so to prevent that loss of faith of which so much has been said, too often in a spirit of exaggeration, and to counteract that tendency to indifferentism which is unhappily to be met with in the States. Since 1861 the progress of the Church has been literally marvellous. Thus, while in 1861 the number of Priests was 2,317, and the churches 2,519, the number of Priests in 1867 is 3,252. and the number of churches 3,500—an increase of nearly 1,000 priests and 1,000 churches in these few years. In the course of the following year there will be about 60 dioceses in the United States; probably in ten years after there will be a necessity for 20 additional sees; and those who live to the year 1900 may behold 100 Mitred Prelates of the Catholic Church of America assembled, if not in the Cathedral of Baltimore, possibly in one of those gorgeous temples which are now rising in the centres of vast Catholic populations, and for rivals to which one must look to France, or Germany, or Italy—to some of those majestic monuments of piety erected by a Prince or a People, a Monarch or a Pope.

A few examples illustrative of individual Dioceses or States will afford a better idea of the general progress of the Church than a summary of the result conveyed in a mere 'total.' Take, for instance, the Diocese of Milwaukee, comprising the State of Wisconsin.

Up to the year 1834 Milwaukee was the exclusive home of the Red Indian; when in that year a French Canadian, who is now about ten years dead, settled there, as a trader in furs. This first white settler was justly called the father of the city that soon after rose on the shore of Lake Michigan, and the founder of the Church of which he was the earliest and most liberal benefactor. It was not until towards the year 1837 that the Catholics of Milwaukee had the services of a priest permanently settled in that city. The Rev. Patrick Kelly then became the pastor of some thirty souls. In 1839 the first church was erected in Milwaukee, and was the only church in the entire of the Territory, since the State, of Wisconsin. In 1840 the population of the rising city was about 2,000, the Catholics being then one-third of the whole. In March 1844 the diocese of Milwaukee was erected, the Right Rev. John Martin Henni being appointed Bishop. The Bishop found in his vast diocese a Catholic flock of 20,000, scattered in every direction, twenty churches, most of them of the rudest construction, and *two* priests—the Rev. Martin Kundig and the Rev. Thomas Morissey. But behold the wonderful change effected in a few years, the result of European emigration. Where there were 20 so-called churches in 1844, there are now 322 churches, 16 chapels, and 75 stations; and where there were but 2 priests, there are now 163—besides 2 ecclesiastical seminaries, 2 male academies, 6 female academies, 8 religious communities, and 5 charitable institutions, with a Catholic population, mostly Irish and German, of 400,000. As an illustration of the amazing growth of religious institutions in the fruitful soil of the West, the development of a single one,—that of the Order of 'Notre Dame'— might be cited.

It is not more than sixteen years since four Sisters of this famous Order founded a house in Milwaukee,—the first house in the States; and now the Order is represented by 58 convents in different parts of the Union, and nearly 500 Sisters who educate and train more than 20,000 children. In the month of August 1867, 60 ladies received the white veil and 38 received the black veil, in the mother house of Milwaukee. Besides the Order of Notre Dame, the diocese enjoys the services of Sisters of the Dominican and Franciscan Orders. For this wonderful progress of the Church and growth of religious institutions, 'we are, under the blessing of God, indebted to the zeal, untiring energy, and good judgment of our venerable and beloved bishop,' writes an excellent Irishman, who has risen to high honour in the city of his adoption. As a finish to this picture, it may be added, that the assembled bishops of the Council of Baltimore recommended the division of the State of Wisconsin into *three* dioceses, with Milwaukee as an Archiepiscopal see.

Brooklyn, which in 1834 was attended by a single priest, has now twenty-four or twenty-five churches in the city alone, with at least 12,000 children educated under the care of religious Orders—of Mercy, Charity, St. Dominic, the Visitation, St. Joseph, Sisters of the Poor, Christian Brothers, and Brothers of St. Francis. New churches are now being erected throughout the diocese, as well as in the city; and in the latter an entire square is devoted to the site of a magnificent cathedral, which will be a model of architectural splendour. The Irish mainly constitute the Catholic population of Brooklyn, as of New York, and most of the Eastern cities. Still in this, as in other dioceses —indeed, in all dioceses—more priests are required. Of the thirty other churches, besides those of the city, we find that some are attended every two weeks, several once a month, and one only every six weeks. Nevertheless, it is progress—progress—progress—in all directions.

In 1847 Bishop Timon took possession of the see of Buffalo, where, to use his own words, 'in the new diocese there were then sixteen priests and sixteen churches; though most of those churches might rather be called huts or shanties.' That venerable prelate—whom I had the satisfaction of meeting towards the close of 1866—has since gone to receive the reward of a life glorious to religion. That Bishop has left behind him a noble legacy to the Church,—165 churches, including one of the most beautiful cathedrals now in the country; 126 priests; 4 colleges and seminaries; 9 male and 18 female institutions, to which are attached colleges and academies; 16 charitable institutions, 4 being hospitals, and 12 asylums; with 32 parochial schools. And hard work had Bishop Timon for the first years of his mission, in meeting the wants of a fast increasing flock, and resisting the evil spirit of ill-regulated 'trusteeship.' But if his labour was great, so is its result.

When Bishop England terminated his apostolic career, there were in the whole of his diocese, which comprehended the States of North and South Carolina and Georgia, but 8,000 Catholics; and now in Charleston alone there are 12,000 Catholics, 8,000 of whom are Irish-born, or the descendants of Irish, And in the city of Mobile, which bounded the vast diocese of that great prelate, there is now a Catholic population of some 12,000, mostly Irish—a thriving, orderly, prosperous community—presided over by a good and zealous Irish bishop.

Take a Northern city, Manchester, in New Hampshire; and we shall see how the good work proceeds. The case of Manchester is more important, as we may contrast the past—of a few years since—with the present. The existing Catholic church being too small for its growing Catholic congregation, now numbering 8,000, a similar edifice is in the course of erection. Shortly after the existing church had been erected, which it was in evil days, and under circumstances of the greatest discouragement—in fact, of insult and actual outrage—a band of riotous Know Nothings assembled on the Fourth of July, and commenced its destruction. They had succeeded in destroying its windows of stained glass, when a party of Irish Catholics gallantly encountered and dispersed the mob, and saved from further injury the church which had cost them so much sacrifice. To the credit of the local authorities, they not only expressed their regret at the outrage, but offered, as a compensation, to repair all damages. This the Rev. Mr. McDonald declined on behalf of his flock, simply requiring protection from future violence. The attempt on the church was not the only one made against the Catholics in Manchester. The Convent of Mercy, which is adjacent to the church, was near being destroyed by fire at the hands of a fanatical workman who was engaged in its erection. He remained one evening after the other workmen had left, and deliberately set fire to some shavings that he brought with him to the cupola for his nefarious purpose. Fortunately, no sooner had the flames broken out than they were discovered, and the fire was extinguished before any serious injury was done. But since then both church and convent have remained unmolested, and there are few cities in which religious and clergy are now more respected than in Manchester. Since the arrival of the Sisters, in 1858, there have been over 250 converts instructed by them in the faith, and mostly from the wealthier class of society. In the free schools under the charge of the Sisters, there are more than 800 children, all of whom are either Irish-born, or of Irish extraction. Besides the free schools, there are also, under the same management, two pay schools, and a select boarding school.

Twenty-five years since, a room of very moderate size contained all the Catholics that assembled to worship God in the city of Newark. In this temporary chapel the women alone were accommodated with seats, which were formed of rude planks laid across empty boxes. What a change in 1866! A cathedral, with other churches, a church of grand proportions in contemplation, several valuable institutions, an efficient staff of priests, and 13,500 communicants at Christmas!

Then, if we turn our glance Westward, and rest it for a moment on that most marvellous of all modern cities—Chicago—what do we see? A few years ago and Chicago was not heard of; it had no existence. Since then it has risen literally from the swamp, a city of magical growth, yet of full maturity, perhaps the most extraordinary instance of the energy of a people which the world has ever seen. But yesterday a sprinkling of shanties on the flat shore of Lake-Michigan; to-day one of the most famous centres of industry in the States, and known on every public change in Europe. In this marvellous City of the West, in which progress assumes dimensions almost gigantic —with its grain elevators capable of storing twelve million bushels of grain, and lading the largest ship in little more than an hour—its abattoirs, that each slaughter from 1,000 to 2,000 hogs in a single day—its net-work of railways connecting it with every State in the Union—its tunnel running two miles into the lake, to supply pure water for its inhabitants—its machinery for lifting whole blocks of houses, and building additional stories under them without interfering with the business or the comfort of a tenant!—in this marvellous Chicago, the very embodiment of the spirit of go-aheadism, the Catholic Church is not a whit behindhand. It strives, and with cheering success, to keep pace with a progress almost without example in the world. In the city there are about 20 Catholic churches, for a Catholic population of 60,000, of whom 50,000 are Irish; and other churches, including one of considerable grandeur, are either in course of erection or in active contemplation. It has even now 12,000 Catholic children, of all classes and conditions of life, receiving a sound Catholic teaching in academies and parochial schools. And, a not less significant indication of progress, it is receiving daily within its fold converts of the educated classes of society.

In one church, in the year 1866, the Bishop—a most accomplished gentleman and zealous ecclesiastic—administered Confirmation to 500 persons; and of that number over 100 were converts, principally from the middle and upper classes. I met more than one of these converts; and for intelligence, information, and quiet dignity of manner, I have rarely, if ever, seen their superiors. The building of churches and schools is a visible and tangible evidence of progress, and there is abundant evidence of this kind in Chicago; but conversions, and from the educated and enlightened portion of the community, are evidences more important and more conclusive. Even in Chicago, the centre of unceasing movement and constant change, the majestic conservatism of the Catholic Church, its tranquil serenity in the hour of civil strife, its unbroken unity in the midst of dissension and disorder— is a subject of wonder and admiration; and thoughtful earnest men cannot avoid beholding in it an additional proof of its divine mission.

Happily for the interests of religion, happily for the welfare of its enormous Irish population, New York is now devoting all its energies to the construction of a cathedral which will cost three millions of dollars, and will be the pride and glory of the Irish Catholic heart. The Archbishop, one of the ablest of the Prelates of the American Church, is fully alive to the necessity of providing ample accommodation as well for those who have already come, as for those who are certain to come; and by the close of 1868 the churches of the city of New York will have reached the number of forty. But 'more, more, more!' is the cry one hears on every side; and ere the golden cross flashes from the loftiest pinnacle of the Cathedral of St. Patrick, many new churches will have gathered in new congregations, additional thousands and tens of thousands of worshippers. The progress of the Church in this greatest of American cities is hopeful and cheering in the highest degree, and in no city are institutions of all kinds more numerous or more efficient; but the necessity for further efforts is perhaps more pressing, more urgent, and the field for the display of all the resources of zeal and liberality wider and vaster, than in any city within the circle of the Union. Though there is no little poverty and distress in New York, there is also a rich and powerful Catholic community; and though great things have been done, and are every day in progress, still the Catholics of New York are well aware that they must make, and continue to make large sacrifices, in order to meet a state of things which, while exceptional in its character, is the natural and inevitable result of the position of their city—virtually the gate through which the adventurous of the Old World reach the New. And so long as the stream of European emigration flows into and through New York, so long must the spiritual wants of the Church impose an onerous but necessary burden on the generosity of the faithful. From what I have seen of the pastors and the flock, I have no fear as to the result.

But turn to Boston,—Boston, the stronghold of the Puritan—Boston, the nursing-mother of all the 'isms' which in the past proclaimed hostility to the stranger and the Catholic—Boston, which has not to this day obliterated the blackened traces of the fire that, amidst the yells of an infuriated mob, shot up its fierce blaze to the heavens from the burning timbers of the dwelling in which holy women divided their lives between the education of the young and the worship of the Deity,—Boston, whose leading citizens informed Archbishop Carroll that had they, some time before his visit, met a Catholic in the street, they would have crossed to the other side, such was their horror of, or such their aversion to, one of that detested creed. In this same Boston, on Sunday, the 15th of September 1867, Bishop Williams, attended by several other Prelates, and in the presence of an immense multitude, laid the foundation stone of a Cathedral which will be one of the most imposing structures in the country. The vastness of its dimensions fitly typifies the progress of Catholicity in Massachusetts. These are they, at least the principal, given in the words of the architect: 'The extreme length, from the front of the large tower to the rear of the large chapel in East Union Park Street, is 364 feet, while the distance from the front entrance to the rear of the chancel is 295 feet. The breadth of the nave and aisles at the buttresses is 98 feet, the transept is

140 feet. . . . The ridge of the nave roof will be 118 feet above the street, while the nave ceiling will be 87 feet high.' And at an altitude of 300 feet the great tower will rise, crowned with a golden cross. Such are the main dimensions of the Cathedral of the Holy Cross, in whose adornment the best efforts of Christian art and Catholic piety will be enlisted and employed.

Archbishop M'Closky addressed the assembled multitude who witnessed the ceremonial; and his words are at once so authoritative and so descriptive, as well of the progress of the Catholic Church in Massachusetts and the New England States, as of the material and social advance of the 'old world immigrants'—who in these States are principally Irish—that an extract or two from his admirable discourse may fittingly occupy a place in these pages.

Contrasting the past with the present, the Archbishop says :—

There are those most probably now within sound of my voice, who can remember when there was but *one* Catholic church in Boston, and when that sufficed, or had to suffice, not alone for this city, *but for all New England*; and how is it now? Churches and institutions multiplied, and daily continuing to multiply, on every side, in this city, throughout this State, in all, or nearly all, the cities and States of New England; so that, at this day, no portion of our country is enriched with them in greater proportionate numbers, none where they have grown up to a more flourishing condition, none where finished with more artistic skill, or presenting monuments of more architectural taste and beauty.

To God's blessing—not overlooking what may to some appear the natural and obvious reason, namely, 'the never ceasing tide of immigration that has been and still continues to be setting towards the American shores'—the Archbishop attributes this astonishing progress. He accurately represents the anticipations of those, and they were many, who held that the Catholic religion would never take root in the free soil of America—that it would wither and shrivel up in the pure atmosphere of New England enlightenment:—

But with regard to the Catholic portion of these immigrants, must we not bear in mind that their religion was looked on with much disfavour, by some, even with bitter prejudice and inveterate dislike? It was held and represented to be a religion of ignorance and superstition, full of the grossest absurdities and palpable errors. The prediction was confidently made that it could not long endure when once brought face to face with the light and intelligence of this free country—that, at best, it could never make any headway, except in its first migratory character, that it might spread along the surface, but could never take root in the soil; that, in process of time, as it would be brought more in contact with the teachings, as was said, of a purer gospel, it would be subjected more fully to the action of our republican institutions, it would lose its hold on the minds, even of its own followers, and be forced gradually to give way before the progressive and irresistible spirit of the age; and if this would not be true of the old world immigrants, it would be found so, at least, of their descendants. Their children, possessing here the advantages of better education, growing up more intelligent, more inquisitive, more independent, partaking more fully of American life and character, would be too sensible and too shrewd to cling to such an unpopular form of faith; unsuited to the country and the times, that would bring them neither worldly honour nor worldly gain, but, on the contrary, would stand in the way of their temporal interests, would hinder them from rising in the social scale—in a word, would confound them with the vulgar and ignorant horde that still blindly persisted in believing Transubstantiation, and adhering to the Pope of Rome.

The Archbishop eloquently describes the utter falsification of all these hopes and anticipations:—

Well, Beloved Brethren, have these predictions been fulfilled? Certainly there is nothing here that would lead me to think so; and, if not in the past or present, I see less sign of their being so in the future. Many, perhaps most of you, are from a foreign laud. Well, do you love the old faith now less than you did when you first landed on these free shores? Is it less dear to you here, in this home of your adoption, than it was on your native soil in the home of your childhood? Do you cherish it less warmly? do you cling to it less firmly? would you die for it less freely? I think that, with one accord, you will answer No. So, throughout every portion of this great Republic, which you love as ardently as do its own sons, for which you would lay down your lives as generously, to the same question your brethren would give the same response—No! a thousand times No! But your children, how has it been with them?

In their case, assuredly, the test has been a severe, and more dangerous, because a more insidious one. Owing to the causes at which I have already hinted, and to other influences which I need not now enumerate, many indeed have been lost to the household of the faith —more so in times past than in the present—yet nowhere, I venture to affirm, will stauncher or firmer, or more consistent Catholics be found than among these American native born; and while they thus cherish their holy faith, do they not, at the same time, *vie in learning, in intelligence, in spirited enterprise, in patriotism and honest worth, with their fellow citizens in all the various professions and other pursuits of life*? If I needed proof or illustration, I should have only to point to many who are here now before me or at my side, to your own honoured Bishop at their head. But why do I say this? Not surely in any boastful or invidious spirit,—but simply to show that prophecy concerning us has failed—that our holy Catholic faith can take, has taken, root in this free soil; nowhere indeed does it seem to find another more congenial—nowhere does it spread its roots more widely or sink them more deeply—nowhere does it put forth more rapid growth, or flourish with more health and vigour, or give promise of more abundant fruit,—and this, we contend, has come to pass only by God's blessing.

Nor was the Archbishop without referring to the important acquisition to the Church which every day records—of converts of thoughtful and searching minds, blameless lives, and good social position, who have no worldly object to gain, and who perhaps may have much to lose, by embracing a faith against which the passions and prejudices of the world are as yet arrayed.

What may be the number of Catholics in the United States is a question of much interest, respecting which there is considerable difference of opinion—some setting it down as very much less than it really is, others estimating it beyond what it possibly can be. There is little difficulty in proving the number of churches or ecclesiastics to be what is stated; but dealing with a vast proportion of the population, the computation is not so simple a matter. Avoiding anything like an extreme estimate, and taking into account not only the enormous emigration of the last half century, chiefly consisting of Catholics from Ireland and the continent of Europe; considering also that the Irish element is, if not the most, certainly one of the most, fruitful in the world; and not forgetting this fact, that in several parts of the Union, and notably in the New England States, the annual increase of the population is entirely owing to the foreign element—and in most of these States the foreign element is fully five-sixths Irish and Catholic—I am inclined to agree with those who regard from *nine to ten millions of Catholics* as a fair and moderate estimate. They may be more, but it is not probable that there are less than 9,000,000; which is more than one-fourth of the entire population of the United States.

And now, what more need be said of the progress of that Church which has in its charge the spiritual welfare and moral worth of the Irish in America? She has her enemies, and will continue to have them, as she has ever had; and these have been her glory rather than her shame. Sects will assail her, and even parties may league against her; but she will pursue the even tenor of her way, neither looking to the right nor to the left, as indifferent to threat as to seduction—preaching peace and love to all men—lifting up her children, by her holy influence, to a truer appreciation and a more practical fulfilment of their duties as Christians and as citizens—teaching them to love and honour and serve the great country in which, notwithstanding the idle rage of the fanatic and the folly of the shortsighted, she has full freedom of development, of active and noble usefulness.

For this glorious Church of America many nations have done their part. The sacred seed first planted by the hand of the chivalrous Spaniard has been watered by the blood of the generous Gaul; to the infant mission the Englishman brought his steadfastness and his resolution, the Scotchman his quiet firmness, the Frenchman his enlightenment, the Irishman the ardour of his faith; and as time rolled on, and wave after wave of emigration brought with it more and more of the precious life-blood of Europe, from no country was there a richer contribution of piety and zeal, of devotion and self-sacrifice, than from that advanced out-post of the Old World, whose western shores first breast the fury of the Atlantic; to whose people Providence appears to have assigned a destiny grand and heroic—of carrying the civilisation of the Cross to remote lands and distant nations. What

Ireland has done for the American Church every Bishop, every priest can tell. Throughout the vast extent of the Union, there is scarcely a church, a college, an academy, a school, a religious or charitable institution, an asylum, an hospital, or a refuge, in which the piety, the learning, the zeal, the self-sacrifice of the Irish—of the priest or the professor—of the Sisters of every Order and denomination—are not to be traced; there is scarcely an ecclesiastical seminary for English-speaking students in which the great majority of those now preparing for the service of the sanctuary do not belong, if not by birth, at least by blood, to that historic land to which the grateful Church of past ages accorded the proud title—Insula Sanctorum.

A writer who is not remarkable for enthusiasm, and who judges with wisdom and praises with reserve, thus describes to what extent the American Church is indebted for its progress to the Irish population of the United States:—

In recording this consoling advancement of Catholicity throughout the United States, especially in the North and West, justice requires us to state, that it is owing in a great measure to the faith, zeal, and generosity of the Irish people, who have emigrated to these shores, and their descendants. We are far from wishing to detract from the merit of other nationalities; but the vast influence which the Irish population have exerted in extending the domain of the Church is well deserving of notice, because it conveys a very instructive lesson. The wonderful history of the Irish nation has always forced upon us the conviction, that, like the chosen generation of Abraham, they were destined in the designs of Providence to a special mission for the preservation and propagation of the true faith. This faith, so pure, so lively, so generous, displays itself in every region of the globe. To its vitality and energy must we attribute, to a very great extent, the rapid increase in the number of churches and other institutions which have sprung up and are still springing up in the United States, and to the same source are the clergy mainly indebted for their support in the exercise of their pastoral ministry. It cannot be denied, and we bear a cheerful testimony to the fact, that hundreds of clergymen who are labouring for the salvation of souls, would starve, and their efforts for the cause of religion would be in vain, but for the generous aid which they receive from the children of Erin, who know, for the most part, how to appreciate the benefits of religion, and who therefore joyfully contribute of their worldly means, to purchase the spiritual blessings which the Church dispenses.

In concluding this sketch of the progress of the Catholic Church in America, I may refer again, though in a passing manner, to the alleged loss of faith on the part of the Irish. The reader who has gone through the foregoing pages must have found in them sufficient to account, easily and rationally, for whatever loss of faith did occur from the migration of a people without priests, flocks without pastors; while he must have seen no little to admire in the fidelity—the miraculous fidelity—with which the same people kept the faith under circumstances the most unfavourable, and in the face of discouragements of the most formidable nature.

Let it be distinctly borne in mind, that the Irish Catholic had everything against him, nothing in his favour. With the Irish Protestant, of whatever denomination, the case was totally different. The Irish Protestant practically knew nothing of the difficulties by which the Irish Catholic was surrounded, nothing of the trials and temptations to which the Catholic and the family of the Catholic were subjected or exposed. Wherever the Irish Protestant turned his face, there he found a congregation and a church, nay even the people and the very atmosphere to suit him. If he had not, convenient to his dwelling, a church or a congregation of his immediate denomination, there was some kindred church which opened its doors to welcome him, some sect to sympathise with his belief, and receive him in the spirit of religious fraternity. Not so with the Catholic. The multitude of denominations was to him of little avail. There was no friendly sect or kindred communion to receive or sympathise with him. He had to stand alone and aloof, for with none could he amalgamate, or, as Protestant sects might, fuse down in one grand accord every minor difference. Thus, alone and aloof, the Irish Catholic, without church or pastor, had to keep the faith alive in his own breast, and foster it by every parental influence in the breasts of his children; who were exposed to the perilous seductions of association with those young as themselves, but who, unlike them, had a church, a pastor, or a congregation. The wonder is, not that some lost the faith; but the miracle is, that it was so amazingly preserved.

Any speculation as to the number of those who lost the faith would be as idle as profitless. It would require the labour of one of our Royal Commissions, powers well nigh inquisitorial, and a dozen years spent in journeying to and fro, to arrive at anything like an approach to the real number of those who yielded to the force of circumstances, and of those who resisted their influences. The belief of every thoughtful Catholic in the United States with whom I conversed on this subject is, that the loss has been monstrously exaggerated, the statements to that effect partaking more of the nature of an oratorical flourish than of the remotest approach to statistical accuracy—resting upon nothing more solid than a paragraph in a well-meant letter of warning, or a full-swelling passage in a terror-striking discourse. The motive in which these statements had their origin was good, but the language has been sadly reckless. From individual localities, or exceptional circumstances, results sweeping and general have been deduced. Whatever the loss—and it is altogether a thing of the past rather than of the present—there can be no delusion more monstrous, or indeed more unjust to a people or a Church, than that the Irish become, if not actual infidels, at least indifferent, the moment they land in America. Now, were not the character of the Irish—the most retentive and tenacious of all races of the world—a sufficient answer to this absurdity, the proof to the contrary is the present position of the Catholic Church of America. On this head nothing need be added to the force and authority of the passage I have just quoted from a writer so careful and cautious as Dr. White.

Neither is it true that indifferentism, though the all-pervading religious disease of America, is one of the characteristics of Catholicity in that country. The magnitude of the work done, of the vast and splendid things accomplished, is altogether inconsistent with indifferentism. There is as much active zeal, as enthusiastic fervour, as profound piety, in America as even in Ireland; and in many places the organisation for all Church purposes and every spiritual object is more complete than it is in the old country. The ceremonies are conducted with solemnity and dignity, and the congregations are collected and devotional in air and manner; and whenever the Church makes a special appeal to the piety of her children, the religious enthusiasm is fervent and intense. There is one, and that a marked difference between congregations in Catholic churches in America and in Ireland or England; and the difference is too honouring to the American character to be overlooked. In America there is most frequently in Catholic churches a considerable proportion of Protestants —who do not either idly gape about, or exhibit weariness or impatience; but who listen gravely, and conduct themselves with scrupulous decorum. I have been in many of the Catholic churches of America, and I never witnessed on the part of Protestants anything which was not respectful to the place and creditable to them.

Now, at any rate, there is no fear of loss. The day for that is gone. Wherever the axe of the pioneer clears the path in the forest, or the plough of the settler turns up the virgin soil of the prairie, the Church soon follows and erects the Cross; and no sooner does the village begin to assume the outlines of the city than the Religious Orders, those noble standard-bearers and soldiers of the Faith, push on to protect and defend the rising youth of the race and religion of Catholic Ireland. The losses of the past are to be deplored, though they have been exaggerated; but the America of the past is not the America of to-day.

CHAPTER XXIX

The Irish in the War—Irish faithful to either Side—Thomas Francis Meagher—
Why the Irish joined distinct Organisations—Irish Chivalry—The Religious
Influence—Not knowing what he preached on—Cleanliness of the Irish Soldier—
Respect for the Laws of War—A Non-combatant defending his Castle—Defended
with Brickbats—'Noblesse oblige'—Pat's little Game—Irish Devotedness—The
Love of Fight—Testimonies to the Irish Soldier—The handsomest Thing of the
War—Patrick Ronayne Cleburne—His Opinions—In Memoriam—After the
War—The grandest of all Spectacles

FROM the very circumstances of their position, it was almost a matter of inevitable necessity that the Irish citizens of America should ally themselves with that political party which, with respect to the foreigner and the stranger, adopted the liberal and enlightened policy of Jefferson and Madison. The Irish, then, being Democrats, naturally sympathised with the prevailing sentiment of the Southern States, which was strongly Democratic. And yet, notwithstanding this sympathy, the result of a general concurrence of opinion with that of the South, the Irish of the Northern States not merely remained faithful to the flag of the Union, but were amongst the foremost and the most enthusiastic of those who rallied in its defence, and the most steadfast in their support of the Federal cause, from the moment that the first gun, fired in Charleston Harbour, echoed through the land, to the hour when Lee surrendered, and the war was at an end. Whatever their opinions or feelings as to the conduct of those who, justly or unjustly, were held responsible for bringing about or precipitating the contest, and deeply as they felt the injury which war was certain to inflict on the country of their adoption, the Irish-born citizens never wavered in their duty. None more bitterly deplored than they did the sad consequences of civil strife—a conflict which would bring into deadly collision kindred races even of their own people; but once the rupture was irrevocable, they calmly accepted their position. From the first moment to the last, they were animated by a high sense of duty, and an earnest feeling of patriotism. Fortunately for the honour and fame of the Irish, there was in their motives an utter absence of the baneful passions of hatred and revenge, or the least desire to crush or humiliate their opponents.

War with all its tremendous consequences they faced as a stern and terrible necessity; but they entered into it with a chivalrous and Christian spirit, which never deserted them throughout the prolonged struggle. They did not stop to argue or split hairs as to the constitutional rights alleged to be involved; they acted, as they felt, with the community amid whom they lived, and with whom their fortunes were identified. The feeling was the same at both sides of the line. The

Irish in the South stood with the State to which, as they believed, they owed their first allegiance, and, as was the case in the North, they caught the spirit of the community of whom they formed part. They also were profoundly grieved at the necessity for war, and would have gladly avoided the calamity of an open rupture. Southern Irishmen have told me that they shed tears of bitter anguish when, in vindication of what they held to be the outraged independence of their State, which to them was the immediate home of their adoption, they first fired on the flag of that glorious country which had been an asylum to millions of their people. The Northern Irishman went into the war for the preservation of the Union—the Southern Irishman for the independence of his State. And each, in his own mind, was as thoroughly justified, both as to right and duty, principle and patriotism, as the other.

With the political or constitutional question involved at either side I have no business whatever; and were I competent to disentangle it from the maze into which conflicting opinions and subtle disquisitions have brought it, I should still, from a feeling of delicacy, decline dealing with a subject which may not, as yet, be freely handled without exciting anger and irritation. I have heard the undisguised sentiments of Irishmen at both bides of the line—every man of them loving America with a feeling of profound attachment; and I, who stand, as it were, on neutral ground, have as full faith in the patriotism and purity of motive of the Northern as the Southern, the Confederate as the Federal.

In their zeal for the cause which Irishmen on each side mutually and of necessity espoused, they did not at all times, perhaps could not, make due allowance for the feelings and convictions of their countrymen who fought under opposing banners, or fairly consider the position in which they were placed, and the influences by which they were surrounded. Thus, while the Northern Irishman could not comprehend how it was that the Southern Irishman, though sympathising with every passionate throb of the community in which he lived, and whose every feeling or prejudice he thoroughly shared, could possibly take up arms against the Union—against the Stars and Stripes—that 'terror of tyrants and hope of the oppressed;' in the same way, the Southern Irishman could not reconcile it to his notions of consistency, that the very men who sought to liberate their native land from British thraldom should join with those who were doing their utmost to subjugate and trample under foot the liberties of a people fighting for their independence. But, were the struggle to be fought over again, both—Irishmen of the North and Irishmen of the South—would fall inevitably into the same ranks, and fight under the same banner; and though each could not, at least for a time, do justice to the motives of the other, every dispassionate observer, who took their mutual positions into account, should do so. An American general, one of the most thoughtful and intelligent men whom I have ever met, remarked to me one day:—

'Nothing: during the war was more admirable than the fidelity of your countrymen, at both sides, to the State in which they lived. North or South, they were equally devoted, equally faithful, sharing in every emotion of the community of which they formed part. I know that some of your countrymen at our side could not make allowance for those on the other side, and in fact would hear nothing said in their defence; but I always held the conviction that not only could they not have done otherwise, consistently with their duty, but that the manner in which they did it redounds to their lasting honour. The war has tried the Irish, and they stood the test well, as good citizens and gallant soldiers. This has been my opinion from the first; and it is the same now that the war is happily at an end.'

Perhaps to no other man of Irish blood was the Federal government more indebted than to that gifted and gallant Irishman over whom, in the mystery and darkness of the night, the turbid waters of the Missouri rolled in death—Thomas Francis Meagher. Passionately attached to the land which for so many years had been the asylum and the hope of millions of the Irish people, he infused into his brilliant oratory all the ardour of his soul, and the strong fidelity of his heart. The Union was the object of his veneration; its flag the emblem of its greatness and its glory. Meagher 'of the Sword' was in his element at last; and as his fiery words rang through the land, they roused the enthusiasm of a race whose instincts are essentially warlike, and whose fondest aspirations are for military renown. Animated no less by a sense of their duties as citizens, than thrilled by accents that stimulated their national pride, the very flower of the Irish youth of the Northern States rallied under the flag of the Union.

Writers for and in certain journals of the United Kingdom frequently impugned the character and the motives of the Irish who joined the Federal army during the war; and 'mercenary' and 'rowdy' and 'rough' have been the terms too freely employed to express dislike of those who formed so powerful an element of the strength and valour of the Northern army. But never was slander more malignant, or description more entirely inapt. Here, in the words of Thomas Francis Meagher, traced but a few months before his lamentable death, is the simple explanation of the motives and vindication of the character of the men who took up arms for a principle, and who fought with the valour and the chivalry of true soldiers. From a letter dated the 4th of March, 1867, from Virginia City, Montana, I take this sentence: 'A chivalrous—and I may with perfect truth assert a religious—sense of duty, and spirit of fidelity to the Government and Flag of the nation of which they were citizens, alone inspired them to take up arms against the South—and this I well know, that many of my gallant fellows left comfortable homes, and relinquished good wages, and resigned profitable and most promising situations, to face the poor pittance, the coarse rations, the privations, rigours, and savage dangers of a soldier's life in the field.'

The Irish citizens did not enter the army at either side as a matter of calculation and prudence, but as a matter of duty, and from an impulse of patriotism. Yet if they had acted on deliberation, they could not have done more wisely than they did. 'Foreigners and aliens' they would indeed have proved themselves to be, had they stood coldly aloof, or shown themselves insensible to the cause which stirred the heart of the nation to its depths, and, as it were in a moment, made gallant soldiers of peaceful civilians. They vindicated their citizenship not alone by their services, but by their sympathies; and in their terrible sacrifices—on every bloody field and in every desperate assault—in every danger, toil, and suffering—they made manifest their value to the State, no less by their devotion than their valour.

From every State; from every city, town, and village; from the forest and the prairie, the hill and the plain; from the workshop, the factory, and the foundry; from the counter and the desk; from the steam-boat, the wharf, and the river bank—wherever the Irish were, or whatever their occupation, they obeyed the summons of their adopted country, and rushed to the defence of its banner. They either formed organisations of their own, or they fell into the ranks with their fellow-citizens of other nationalities. But special organisations, distinctive and national, had for them peculiar attractions; and once the green flag was unfurled, it acted with magnetic influence drawing to it the hardy children of Erin. There were in both armies, companies, regiments, brigades, exclusively Irish; but whether there was a special organisation or not, there was scarcely a regiment in either service which did not contain a smaller or a greater number of Irish citizens. I cannot venture to particularise or enumerate. The attempt would be idle, if not invidious. But I have spoken to gallant men who led them in action, and were with them amid all the trials and vicissitudes of a soldier's life; and whether they fought under a distinct organisation, or without distinction of national badge or banner, there was only one opinion expressed of their fighting qualities, and their amazing powers of endurance—and that equally in South as in North, in North as well as South. Why the Irish were attracted by distinct organisations was well explained by General Meagher. It was prior to the formation of his famous Brigade that he used the words I am about to quote; but when once the war was in full swing, and the hard work had really commenced, the chief inducement of the Irishman to join either company, regiment, or brigade, was the reputation it had earned, and the glory it had achieved. In the course of his oration on McManus, he referred to the desire even then expressed by the Irish citizen to join a purely Irish regiment or brigade, and said:—

'It is a pardonable prejudice, for the Irishman never fights so well as when he has an Irishman for his comrade. An Irishman going into the field in this cause, has this as the strongest impulse and his richest reward, that his conduct in the field will reflect honour on the old land he will see no more. He therefore wishes that if he falls, it will be into the arms of one of the same nativity, that all may hear that he died in a manner worthy of the cause in which he fell, and the country which gave him birth. This is the explanation why Irishmen desire to be together in the fight for the Stars and Stripes, and I am sure there is not a native-born citizen here who will not confess that it is a pardonable, a generous, and a useful prejudice.'

This tendency of the Irish to join distinct organisations, whether of regiment or brigade, imposed on them more of hard work, more of risk and danger, than fell to the ordinary lot of the soldier. It seemed as if they themselves should do more than others, to sustain the reputation which they had often, in times when civil war was undreamt of, claimed for their race—a reputation that others had freely admitted to be established beyond question. Not only had the Irishman to maintain the honour of his regiment, but he had also to maintain the honour of his country; for if he fought as an American citizen, he also fought as an Irish exile. We have thus, independently altogether of the natural love of fight that seems inherent in the Irish blood, the explanation of the desperate courage displayed on every occasion in which they were engaged, in whatever operation of war, whether as assailants or defenders, steadily resisting or daringly attacking. The character which they soon acquired for courage and devotion, endurance as well as dash, added to their fame; but it was likewise the cause of many a wife being made a widow, many a child an orphan, many a home desolate—of mourning and sorrow at both sides of the Atlantic. When the General had work to do which should be done, he required soldiers on whom he could rely; and whatever other soldiers were selected, there was sure to be an Irish regiment among the rest. And though Irishmen may possibly, at the time, have grumbled at not being given enough to do, they must now, as they calmly recur to the past, admit that they had, to say the very least, their full share of the fight as of the hardship, of the sacrifice as of the glory.

The Irish displayed a still nobler quality than courage, though theirs was of the most exalted nature; they displayed magnanimity, generosity—Christian chivalry. From one end of the South to the other, even where the feeling was yet sore, and the wound of defeat still rankled in the breast, there was no anger against the Irish soldiers of the Union. Whenever the feeble or the defenceless required a protector, or woman a champion, or an endangered church a defender, the protector, the champion, and the defender were to be found in the Irishman, who fought for a principle, not for vengeance or desolation. The evil deeds, the nameless horrors, perpetrated in the fury of passion and in the licence of victory—whatever these were, they are not laid at the door of the Irish. On the contrary, from every quarter are to be heard praises of the Irish for their forbearance, their gallantry, and their *chivalry*—than which no word more fitly represents their bearing at a time when wanton outrages and the most horrible cruelties were too frequently excused or palliated on the absolving plea of stern necessity.

I could fill many pages with incidents illustrative of this noble conduct, did space admit of my doing so. I met, in New Orleans, with a dignitary of the Episcopalian Church, who made the conduct of the Irish in the Northern army the subject of warm eulogium; and in his own words, afterwards written at my request, I shall allow him to tell in what manner the chivalrous Irishman won the respect of the people against whom he fought, but whom he did not hate, and would not willingly humiliate.

It was a cause of real grief to the Southern people when they beheld the Irish nation, in the midst of their great struggle for independence, furnishing soldiers to fight a people who were engaged in a deadly contest for the same boon, and who had never given them cause of offence. This feeling was, however, softened in the progress of the war, when they discovered the generous sympathy yet lurking in the breasts of these misguided men, and which was never invoked in vain. In every assault made upon a defenceless household the Irish soldier was among the first to interpose for the defence of the helpless, to shield them from insult and wrong.

In the march of Sheridan's cavalry through Albemarle county, Virginia, the house of a worthy clergyman was about to be entered by a rude and tumultuous band, when an Irishman rushed forward to protect the family, assumed the place of sentinel and guard, drove the invaders from the threshold, dragged from his hidden retreat, under the portico, a burglar who was breaking into the cellar, and with sword in hand defied any one to violate the sanctity of that home. None dared to resist him, until a company of stragglers following upon the heels of the main body advanced in force, and demanded to know his authority for tarrying there when the troops had left. 'To defend this house from thieves and burglars,' was his reply. Brandishing their weapons, they attempted to drive him from the place, when he looked them quietly in the face and asked, 'How tall are you when you are fat?' The imperturbable coolness of the Irishman was too much for them, and they left him to enjoy the satisfaction of his heroism, and the grateful attentions of the family he had so nobly defended. His mission did not end there, but taking from his knapsack his ration of coffee and sugar, which had not been consumed, he insisted that the good minister and his family should accept it for their own use. The nature of this man's service was the more appreciated when the adjacent plantation was soon after consumed by fire. The husband and father died suddenly from the shock, and the widow and children were left homeless and foodless in the negro cabin, to lament that no Irish soldier was there to shield them from the cruel wrath of their countrymen.

Again, upon the visit of Sherman's army to Mecklenburg co. after the surrender, the estate of Mr. S., the brother of the minister referred to, fell a prey to the same species of violence. His mansion, one of the most magnificent in the State, was despoiled. His wife, being ill, was confined to her chamber, when it was suddenly threatened by an excited group of soldiers maddened with liquor. In vain did the physician who was in attendance remonstrate with the ruffians, who insisted upon forcing the door in search of plunder. At this moment an Irish soldier came to the rescue, took his place as sentinel at the door, hurled back the crowd, and remained there for several hours, the faithful guardian of that sick chamber, until the house was freed from its invaders. Every nook and corner was searched, everything plundered that could be taken away, every apartment rifled save that sheltered under the aegis of the brave-hearted Irish soldier.

The 9th Connecticut, an exclusively Irish regiment, was quartered in New Orleans during its occupation by the force under General Butler. Its officers maintained the chivalrous character of the Irish soldier, who fought for a principle, not for plunder or oppression. They remained in their marquees, and would not take possession of the houses of the wealthy citizens, which, according to the laws of war, they might have done. 'We came to fight men,' said they, 'not to rob women.' They soon won the confidence and respect of the inhabitants.

A soldier of this regiment was placed as sentinel before one of the finest houses in the town, which General Butler intended for his head-quarters; and his orders were that he should allow nothing to be taken out—nothing to pass through that door. The sentinel was suddenly disturbed in his monotonous pacing to and fro before the door of the mansion by the appearance of a smart young girl, who, with an air half timid and half coaxing, said—'Sir, I suppose you will permit me to take these few toys in my apron? surely General Butler has no children who require such things as these?'

'Young woman!' replied the sentry, in a sternly abrupt tone, that quite awed his petitioner, 'my orders are peremptory—not a toy, or thing of any kind, can pass this door while I am here. But, miss,' added the inflexible guardian, in quite a different tone, 'if there is such a thing as another door, or a back window, you may take away as many toys as you can find, or whatever else you wish—I have no orders against it; and the more you take the better I'll be pleased, God knows.' The palpable hint was adopted, and it is to be hoped that something more than the toys was saved to the owners of the mansion.

Even 'Billy Wilson's Zouaves,' a few of whom were admitted to be of the class known to police definition as 'dangerous,' sustained the honourable fame of the Irish soldier, though coming to the South as 'invaders.' These lambs consisted almost exclusively of Irish and the descendants of Irish, and had the reputation of being amongst the roughest of the population of New York. 'They were a hard lot—many a hard case among them lads,' said an Irishman, describing them. Still, such was their good conduct in the South, especially in Louisiana, that the planters regarded them rather as protectors than enemies. A creole lady from Téche county in that State lately wrote to her nephew, who had been on General Dick Taylor's staff, requesting him to hunt up Colonel Wilson, and thank him in her name and his, and to assure him of their continued remembrance of his kindness, and the generous conduct of his men.

I myself heard from the lips of Southerners praises of the gallantry and generosity of these terrible fighters.

The First Division of the Second Corps of the Army of the Potomac was marching, in November 1862, through Lowdon Valley, passing the house of General Ashby, a Confederate officer who had been recently killed. The Irish Brigade was at the head of the column. Orders had been given that property should be respected, that nothing should be touched. As the Brigade was passing the house, a number of chickens, scared by the unusual display, fluttered right into the ranks, and between the feet of the men. The hungry Irishmen looked at each other with a comical expression, as the foolish birds appeared to rush into the very jaws of danger—or the opening of the havresac; and many a poor fellow mentally speculated on the value of each of the flutterers in a stew. The sense of the humorous was speedily dispelled. In the piazza, down on her knees, her hands tossed wildly above her head, was an old woman, thin, stern, white-haired; and as the Brigade were passing she poured—literally shrieked out—curses on all those who fought for the 'murderers of her son.' To Irishmen the curse of the widow or the childless carries with it an awful sound and a terrible import. With averted eyes the gallant men of the Brigade marched past the white-haired mother who, frantic in her bereavement, knew not what she said.

Very frequently the most injurious accounts of the Irish heralded their arrival in a locality; but it invariably happened, wherever they were quartered, that those who regarded their coming with apprehension deplored their departure as a calamity; and numerous instances might be told of communities memorialising the authorities for their continued stay—the people justly considering them as their best protectors amid the insecurity and licence of the moment.

There is a passage in a diary kept by Father Sheeran, which exemplifies the conduct of the Irish soldier better than any description could do. Father Sheeran was one day rebuking a simple Irishman, who with others had been taken prisoner by a surprise attack upon the Federals, for having taken part, as he alleged he had, in the plunder and oppression of the South. The Irishman's reply, while bearing the impress of truth, represents accurately what was the feeling and conduct of his countrymen during the war.

'Well, father,' said he, 'I know they done them things, but I never took part with them. Many a day I went hungry before I would take anything from the people. Even when we had to fall back from Lynchburg under Hunter thro' Western Virginia, and our men were dropping by the roadside with hunger, and some were eating the bark off the trees, I never took a meal of victuals without paying for it.'

The truth is, not only was the Irishman free from the angry passions by which others were animated, but he was constantly impressed by the strongest religious influence; and to this may be ascribed much of the chivalrous bearing which he displayed in the midst of the most trying temptation to licence and excess. The war had in it nothing more remarkable than the religious devotion of the Irish soldier whenever he was within the reach of a chaplain. The practice of their faith, whether before battle or in retreat, in camp or in bivouac, exalted them into heroes. The regiment that, in some hollow of the field, knelt down to receive, bare-headed, the benediction of their priest, next moment rushed into the fray with a wilder cheer and a more impetuous dash. That benediction nerved, not unmanned, those gallant men, as the enemy discovered to their cost. Even in the depth of winter, when the snow lay thick on the earth, the Irish Catholic—Federal or Confederate, it mattered not which—would hear mass devoutly on the bleak plain or the wild hill-side, standing only when that posture was customary, and kneeling in the snow and slush during the greater portion of the time. The same Father Sheeran to whom I have referred, told me how he was impressed with the piety of his poor fellows on one desperate Christmas morning, when so heavy was the snow-storm that he quite lost his way, and did not for a considerable time reach the appointed place where he was to celebrate mass. But there, when he arrived, was a great crowd of whitened figures clustered round the little tent, in which an altar had been erected by the soldiers—the only cleared place being the spot on which the tent was placed. And there, while the storm raged, and sky and earth were enveloped in the whirling snow, the gallant Irishmen prayed with a fervour that was proof against every discouragement.

Before battle, it was not unusual for the Catholic soldiers to go to confession in great numbers, and prepare by a worthy communion to meet whatever fate God might send them in the coming fight. This practice excited the ridicule—the quiet ridicule—of some, but it also excited the respect of others. A distinguished colonel, of genuine American race, who bore on his body the marks of many wounds, life memorials of desperate fights, was speaking to me of the gallantry of the Irish; and he thus wound up: 'Their chaplain—a plucky fellow, sir, I can tell you —had extraordinary influence over them; indeed he was better, sir, I do believe, than any provost-marshal. They would go to mass regularly, and frequently to confession. 'Tis rather a curious thing I'm going to tell you; but it's true, sir. When I saw those Irishmen going to confession, and kneeling down to receive the priest's blessing, I used to laugh in my sleeve at the whole thing. The fact is—you will pardon me—I thought it all so much damned tomfoolery and humbug. That was at first, sir. But I found the most pious of them the very bravest—and that astonished me more than anything. Sir, I saw these men tried in every way that men could be tried, and I never saw anything superior to them. Why, sir, if I wanted to storm the gates of hell, I didn't want any finer or braver fellows than those Irishmen. I tell you, sir, I hated the "blarney" before the war; but now I feel like meeting a brother when I meet an Irishman. I saw them in battle, sir; but I also saw them sick and dying in the hospital, and how their religion gave them courage to meet death with cheerful resignation. Well, sir,'— and the great grim war-beaten soldier softly laughed as he added—'I am a Catholic now, and I no longer scoff at a priest's blessing, or consider confession a humbug. I can understand the difference now, I assure you.'

There were other converts of the battle-field and the hospital, besides my friend the colonel—and of higher rank, too—who, like him, caught their first impression of the truth from the men whom religion made more daring in the fight, more resigned in sickness, more courageous in death.

Archbishop Purcell, the oldest of the bishops of the American Church, was invited to preach in one of the camps of the Army of the Cumberland; and he delivered on that occasion an admirable discourse, which elicited the warm approval of non-Catholics, and excited the enthusiastic admiration of the Irish soldiers; one of whom said to his comrade—'Did you hear that, Mick?' 'To be sure I did,' replied Mick. 'Yes, man; but what did you think of it?—wasn't it the real touch?' 'Well, in my opinion, if I'm to give one—and mind 'twas you asked for it—the Archbishop didn't know what he was preaching on.' 'Why, what the d—l do you mean?—what's come over you?' 'I tell you again—and it's only my opinion—the opinion of a poor gommal, if you like—the Archbishop didn't know what he was preaching on. Look, man, what he was standing on!' Sure enough, the Archbishop did not know what he was preaching on; for there was sufficient in the boxes under his feet to blow up the Vatican and the College of Cardinals.

An Irish soldier, wounded badly, was lying on a hard-fought field in Upper Georgia, towards Chattanooga. He was found by a chaplain attached to his corps in a helpless condition, leaning against a tree. The priest, seeing the case to be one of imminent danger, proposed to hear his confession, but was surprised to hear him say—'Father, I'll wait a little. There's a man over there worse wounded than I am; he is a Protestant, and he's calling for the priest—go to him first.' The priest found the wounded Protestant, received him into the Church, and remained with him till he expired; he then returned to hear the confession of the Irish Catholic, whose first words were —'Well, Father, didn't I tell you true? I knew the poor fellow wanted you more than I did.' The priest and the penitent are still alive to tell the story.

Here is one of a thousand instances of the fact that the religious influence did not impair the martial ardour of the Irish soldier. The colours of a Tennessee regiment were carried into action at Murfreesboro' by a young Irishman named Charles Quinn, of the famous Jackson Guard. In the charge Quinn received a musket wound in the body; but instead of going to the rear, for his injury was desperate, he placed his left hand on his wound, absolutely refusing to give up the colours, until in the thick of the mêlée he was pierced through the head, and fell lifeless. The sole effects of this gallant Irishman came into possession of his heroic captain, afterwards one of the finest colonels in the service; and these were an 'Agnus Dei' and a set of beads!

The fact is incontestable, that the extraordinary health enjoyed by the Irish who fought at either side was owing in a great degree to their remarkable attention to cleanliness. There are obvious reasons to explain why in the old country the constant practice of this homely virtue is not a striking characteristic of the race. Poverty is depressing in its influence, and somewhat neutralises that pride which manifests itself in outward appearance: and, besides, where, as is too often the case in Ireland, the grand battle of life is for a bare subsistence—just as much as keeps body and soul together—cleanliness is too apt to be lost sight of, or regarded as a luxury beyond the possession of the poor. But were one to draw a national inference from the habit of the Irish soldiers in the war, one might fairly assert that cleanliness was one of the marked and special peculiarities of the Irish race. So universal has been the testimony on this point, that doubt would be like wanton scepticism. Whether in barrack, in camp, or on the march, the Irish soldier maintained a reputation for personal cleanliness.

When the war commenced, and while the troops were yet in all the newness of their uniforms, others may have been smarter, or more dandified, than the Irish; but when the stern work commenced in earnest, and uniforms were faded from exposure and hardship, or torn by lead and steel, and when the dandy of the barrack-yard or the garrison town had degenerated into a confirmed sloven, the Irishman was at once neat and jaunty in his war-worn rags. Whatever the length of the day's march, or the severity of the fatigue, if the troops came to a river, or brook, or pond, or even the tiniest trickling rivulet, the Irishman was sure to be at the water, as if with the instinct of a duck. He plunged into the river to enjoy the grand refreshment of a swim, or if it were not deep enough to afford that healthful luxury, he washed himself thoroughly in its shallow stream; and even though his shirt were in ribands, as was too often the lot of the campaigner, it should at least be clean, if water could make it so. I was amused to hear a professor of Georgetown College, himself an Irishman, describe the comical terror of the authorities of that noble institution, when they were informed that the three wells which supplied the establishment were in danger of running dry, owing to the incessant ablutions of a famous Irish regiment—the 69th—quartered there previous to the battle of Bull Run. No cat that ever polished her fur into velvety softness was more careful of her coat than the Irish soldiers—Federal or Confederate—were of the cleanliness of their persons and their clothing, such as it was. In fact, the fiercer the conflict became, the more fully were the soldierly qualities of the Irish developed: and when repeated disasters and reverses produced their demoralising influences on others, the irrepressible buoyancy of the Celtic temperament sustained the spirit and invigorated the frame of the hardy Irishman. But, from first to last, cleanliness was one of their prominent characteristics. And this I state on the highest authority at both sides of the line.

The following may show the value which Irish soldiers attached to their fighting qualities:—

After the famous battle of Manassas, won by the Confederates, the victors were gathering the wounded to convey them to the nearest hospitals. The Confederates were generally the first attended to. But an Irish soldier happening to recognise in a wounded Federal an old acquaintance from his own parish 'in the ould country,' at once raised him from the ground, and placing him tenderly on his shoulder carried his helpless friend to a camp hospital which had been just improvised, and attended to him as well as he could. Next morning, at an early hour, he proceeded to the hospital, to enquire after the patient, and learn how he had got through the night. He found a sentinel at the door, who barred the passage with his bayonet. 'You won't lave me pass, won't ye!—not to see the poor lad from my own parish!' 'Faith, I can't; 'tis again orders,' was the reluctant reply of the Irishman on guard, as he still presented the weapon. 'Yerra, man, stand out of the way with you, and don't bother me!—hav'n't we done the height of the fighting on both sides?' The boastful query, coupled with the good-humoured violence with which the bayonet was shoved aside, were too much for the Hibernian, who, shouldering his rifle, condoled himself with the remark—'Look at that! Faith, one can see that fellow doesn't know much of the laws of war, or he'd respect a sintry. Well, no matter; his intention is good, any way.'

Here is a case where an Irishman emphatically rebuked an adversary on the field of battle, because of his violation of that law of war which prescribes fair fighting as essential.

Early in June 1863 the Federals were advancing to the attack of Secessionville battery, on James's Island, in Charleston Harbour. Their pickets occupied some negro houses and barns at Legree Point. Captain Klyne, of the 100th Pennsylvanians, was in command of the picket. The Charleston battalion and other troops were sent to meet the enemy; and so furious was the dash made by a company of the Old Irish Volunteers, under Captain Ryan, who led his men with characteristic gallantry, that the commander of the Federal picket surrendered as a prisoner of war. As Captain Klyne was in the act of surrendering, a German sergeant was bringing his rifle into position to shoot the Captain of the Volunteers, when one of the Irishmen—Jerry Hurley—who witnessed the motion, flung down his rifle, rushed at the German, caught him by the neck, and, putting his leg dexterously under him, brought him to the ground in the most scientific manner, and then commenced to pummel him unmercifully with his fists, at the same time shouting—'Blast your sowl! you infernal Dutchman! didn't you hear your Captain surrender? Is that what you call fighting in your country? Faith, I'll teach you a lesson that you won't forget in a hurry, my bould boy. Bad luck to you! is it murder you wanted to commit this fine morning? Come along with me, and I'll learn you better manners the next time.' The poor German, who howled tremendously beneath the shower of blows rained on him by the infuriated Irishman, accepted the position, and followed his conqueror, as he and his company rapidly retired after their successful dash.

In the case just mentioned, it was Irishman against German, Confederate against Federal; but here is an instance in which, under rather extraordinary circumstances, it was Irishman against Irishman. During one of the famous battles of the war, a young Irishman named Peter Hughes was wounded in the thigh by a musket ball, and fell helpless on the field. At the same moment, a comrade of his, Michael M'Fadden, received a shot in the groin, and fell prostrate on poor Hughes. Hughes had two infirmities—an irritable temper, and a deplorable stutter; and neither of these was improved by the pain of his wound and the weight of his comrade. He could not shake M'Fadden off, nor could M'Fadden help remaining as he fell; so Hughes remonstrated with the superincumbent mass in this fashion—

'Da—a—a—m—n yo—u—u! isn't this fie—l—ld la—a—rge en—n—o—ough to—to fall in, witho—o—out tum—um—um—bling on m—m—e?' M'Fadden protested his innocence, declaring he was not a free agent in the matter, and that if he had his choice, he would prefer not falling at all; but Hughes would take no excuse, and insisted on M'Fadden tum—um—um—bling off a—a—gain—where, he didn't care. M'Fadden could not stir, but Hughes would not believe in his protestations or his inability to move; so from words they came to blows, and it was in the midst of a regular 'mill' that they were found by the Infirmary corps, by whom the combatants were separated and carried to hospital, where Hughes recovered from his wound, and somewhat improved his temper; but for his stutter there was no hope whatever—that was beyond cure.

The indignation of an Irishman at the injury done to his property by an artillery duel in Charleston Harbour was narrated to me with great relish by a countryman of his. The property consisted of a house and lot for which the owner had paid $1,500 in 'hard cash.' The house was within 150 yards of Fort Moultrie, on Sullivan's Island, and almost in the line of fire from Fort Sumter. The firing was brisk, and many a ball whisked by, one occasionally passing through the tenement, or taking a fragment off a chimney, which seemed to be a favourite target for practice. The owner, who would remain to 'watch his property,' was remonstrated with, and advised to leave the place, and not risk his life. 'Risk my life! I care more about my house; and the devil a one of me will leave it while them blackguards are battering at it this way.' For a day and a night he walked up and down, 'protecting his property,' and occasionally relieving his mind by cursing Major Anderson, to whom he attributed personal spite and malignity of the blackest die. As a tile or a bit of the chimney was carried away, he would exclaim, 'Oh blood! isn't this a mighty hard case? Why then, Major Anderson, may ould Nick fly away with you, and that you may never come back—that's my prayer, sure enough.'—'There again!—there's more of your purty tricks! The devil run buck-hunting with you, Major Anderson.' 'My curse on you, hot and heavy, Major Anderson, that wouldn't leave a decent man's little property alone.' At length, one unlucky shot tore away five feet of the chimney, which came clattering to the ground in a shower of bricks and mortar. 'There now! I said he'd do it, and he's done it without doubt Why then, Major Anderson, may I never be father over my children if I won't make you pay for this work, if there's law to be had for love or money. You're in for it now, my fine joker—and I'm the lad to salt you—see if I don't!'

Fortunately no amount of cannonading could destroy the 'lot,' and the injury to the chimney, with an odd ventilator or two in the shape of shot-holes, were the entire results of Major Andersen's 'mean spite' against the owner of this critically circumstanced property; so, when the chimney was rebuilt, and the holes were filled up, the temper of the proprietor was restored to its accustomed serenity. And the time even came when he could tell with much humour how sturdily he defended his castle from the guns of Fort Sumter.

I was much amused at hearing a crusty American over-seer of the genuine old school tell an anecdote of an Irishman with whom he was well acquainted. At the battle of Manassas, this Irishman, whose name was Morriss, of the 18th Mississippi, when the order was given to his company to lie down and reload, and thus allow the storm of shell and balls to pass over their heads, retained his erect position, crying out—'By japers! I didn't come here to lie down and fight; I came here to stand up and fight like a man.' His clothes were riddled with bullets, and his flesh was torn in a few places, but he escaped all serious injury, as if by a miracle. After a hard chuckle at the fun of the thing, the Southerner added—'From now on, that Irishman could get along without ever doing another lick of work; but Moniss is an industrious man, and a good gardener, and he can help himself quite enough.'

Of the various conflicts of which the harbour of Charleston was the scene, that which took place on the 9th of October 1863, when an attack was made on Fort Sumter, then in the possession of the Confederates, may be mentioned, on account of the rather novel mode of defence successfully adopted by a portion of the garrison. The United States troops, under Gilmore, were at Morriss Island, and the celebrated Dahlgren had command of the fleet. Fort Sumter was defended by Major Elliot; the garrison consisting of the Charleston battalion—which was 'pretty much Irish'—with two companies of Artillery.

The Old Irish Volunteers, the representatives of an organisation dating back more than seventy years, were entrusted with the defence of the east wall or rampart. About one o'clock at night the Captain in command of the Irish Volunteers discovered a small boat evidently reconnoitering, and at once gave the alarm. In a few moments after, a large body of Federals, aided by 600 men from the fleet, commenced a vigorous assault. The fort was not taken by surprise, owing to the vigilance of the Irish Captain, whose command faced the channel; and the enemy were fired upon before they could effect a landing. In a short time a brisk attack was made on the southern and eastern face. The southern face was opposite to Morriss Island, and was attacked by the land force. In little more than a quarter of an hour the Federal fire on the east side slackened, while it was sustained with warmth on the south. This cessation of fire on the eastern side excited the renewed suspicion of the Captain in command; and on reconnoitering, it was found that a number of the attacking force had effected a lodgment on, or rather *in*, the face of the rampart, which in this place had been hollowed out by previous and repeated bombardments. The assailants, who were thus out of the range of fire, and who believed that the fort was almost in their possession, laughed with derisive scorn when called on from above to surrender. Lodged in the very face of the wall or rampart, not only were they thus out of the reach of the guns, but not even a rifle could be conveniently brought to bear against them. What were the defenders to do, in this case? . 'Why, pel them out of that, to be sure.' The men were ordered to lay down their arms, for the moment valueless, and make the best use they could of the fragments of brickwork with which the ramparts were abundantly supplied. The Old Irish Volunteers entered into the fun of the thing amazingly; it was quite an unexpected source of diversion, and so they vigorously proceeded to roll masses of masonry down the face of the rampart, and pelt brickbats at the partly-hidden foe from every possible vantage-ground, while joke and gibe, most galling to the assailants, ran along the line, like a brisk fire of small arms. The amusement was pleasant enough for the gentlemen on the rampart, but not at all so agreeable to their unexpected visitors below; and after enduring the novel species of artillery as long as they possibly could, the latter surrendered. 103 of the enemy, including 10 or 12 officers, yielded to the gentle influence of the brickbats, not being desirous of any longer keeping up the game of 'cock-throw,' of which the fun was altogether one-sided, and against them.

All apprehension of further danger being at an end, the Irishmen made the Federal officers welcome to the best entertainment in their power to afford. But the rough fare did not seem to please the captives, one of whom rather superciliously remarked, that he understood the Southerners had the character of being a hospitable people; but if they treated their guests on other occasions no better than they treated them then, they might possibly forfeit their character for that virtue.

The Irish Captain, after making a punctilious bow, worthy of a Chesterfield, thus replied:—

'Well, sir, I would be sorry that, through me, the State should lose its well-earned reputation for hospitality; but it is usual, even in the South, when visitors, especially a considerable number, as in your case, intend to honour a gentleman by taking up their quarters at his house, that they should give some intimation of their intention; or if they were resolved on making a "surprise party" of it, as was evidently the intention in the present instance, they should provide for themselves.'

The joke was once more against the assailants; but as it was not so bad as the brickbats, it was received in good humour, and captors and captives were soon on the best terms.

The same officer who indulged his men in the exciting game of brickbats on the eastern rampart of Fort Sumter, was in command of a sand-bank battery of three guns, situate between two narrow marshes, the solid land being about eighty yards in front. It was one of the most important positions in the defence of Charleston, and was not taken until the evacuation of the city. On the 16th of June 1862, the Federals made a desperate attempt to take this battery, but were foiled by the pluck with which the Irishmen defended it against overwhelming odds until they were reinforced; the body of the Confederates being 800 yards distant when the attack commenced. And never was pluck more called for than on this occasion, owing to the panic which seized the commander of the picket in front of the fort. That officer suddenly rushed in, right over the battery, having made no resistance to the advancing enemy, whose numbers scared away his wits for the moment.

'What means this conduct? ' sternly enquired the Irishman.

'Oh, you can do nothing—it's impossible—you must retire—the enemy are in overwhelming strength—it's no use—it's madness to resist them—you can do nothing against such desperate odds.'

'You can retire if you please, and nobody will be anything the wiser; but if *I* left my post, the whole world would know of it; and sooner than do anything that would affect the honour and reputation of Irishmen, or of Ireland, I'd stay here till Doomsday.'

This was no vain boast; for, after expending their ammunition, the Irishmen fought with clubbed muskets, and with such savage energy, that the enemy were kept at bay, and the important position held until the body of the Confederates had time to come up. Then commenced a battle which fiercely raged from the early dawn of that summer's morning to half-past 8 o'clock, when the Federals were compelled to retire. It was known as the Battle of Secessionville, and was admitted to be one of the severest of the war in the South.

At one of the battles in Virginia a company of Confederates charged a company of Federals. The latter yielded to the impetuosity of the charge, gave way, and fled, all save one man alone, who said—'You may kill me if you plaze, but not all the rebel army will make me run." The cool courage of the soldier at once disarmed hostility. 'Then will you surrender?' he was asked. 'Oh, yes, there is no disgrace in that,' he replied; 'I surrender.' So long as he remained a prisoner, he was a great favourite with his captors—one of whom I heard narrate the circumstance.

To the quick-wittedness and coolness of an Irishman the Federals were indebted for their preservation from no small disaster, and the Confederates for serious loss and great discouragement. Some time after Fort Pulaski, at the mouth of the Savannah river, had been taken from the Confederates, a small picket boat, steered by a midshipman, and rowed by four sailors—two Georgians and two Irishmen— was making its way cautiously in the direction of the fort, 'to see how the land lay.' The Irishmen were Federalists, who had been pressed into the Confederate navy, and were then, against their inclination, serving on board the 'Atlantic,' a blockade-runner, which had been converted into an iron-clad, and still preserved her fast-steaming qualities. The reconnaissance had been made, and the boat was on her way back, when the officer, taking off his pea-jacket, called out to the bowman—'Here, Pat! catch hold of this, and stow it under the bow;' and he added—'Take care how you handle it, you Irish son of a bitch; there are revolvers in it.' Quick as thought, the pistols were taken from the coat by Pat, who handed one of them to his countryman, and pointed the other at the midshipman, exclaiming in a voice expressive of merriment and triumph—'Now, *you* son of a bitch, steer us straight for Fort Pulaski, and'—turning to the Georgians—'you sons of bitches, pull us there, or we'll blow the tops off your bloody heads!' The gallant young fellow had no option but to do what he was ordered by the possessors of his revolvers, and the boat was rowed right into the landing-place of the enemy. Pat was brought before the officer in command, to whom he imparted the important intelligence that the 'Atlantic,' for which the Federals had been constantly on the look-out, was next morning to pass through St. Augustine's Creek, into Warsaw Sound, thus avoiding the fort, and getting into the open sea, where she was certain to inflict enormous damage on the commerce of the Union, and sink any vessel that did not equal her in speed or in power. This was startling intelligence indeed, for there was but a single gun-boat at the Creek, and this the ' Atlantic ' might disregard, or could destroy. Acting upon the information, an Irish officer of high rank, who happened to be at the time in the fort, at once started on horseback, and never spared whip or spur till he arrived at Port Royal Bay, where a Federal fleet was stationed. In a short time two iron-clads and two heavy transports were steaming for the Creek, where the 'Atlantic' was caught as if in a trap. The 'Irish son of a bitch' had the best of the 'little game.'

I heard an admirable description given by an Irishman in the Confederate service—an officer who had served with great distinction—of his countrymen as soldiers. The portrait is true to the life, and as faithfully represents the soldier of the Union as the champion of the 'Lost Cause.' I heard the same, though not in the same words, from Americans at both sides of the line. My friend thus hits off his compatriots as belligerents:—

'My experience of the Irish in our army was this—that they could endure more than any men on the face of the earth. They would march all day, and the officer in charge would have trouble enough to keep them from playing tricks on one another; and when all others, tired by bodily fatigue, would lie down, indifferent to what would happen, they would be as lively as ever; and if there were a chance of any devilment up, they were bound to be in the midst of it. This is the universal opinion of the officers of the Confederate army with respect to the Irish under their command. They were sometimes difficult to manage, but the fault did not generally lie with them. Their officer should be worthy of their respect. The first condition of their confidence is, that he must be worthy of it—that he is brave and daring—that he can be trusted—that he won't shirk his duty—that he is ready himself to do what he asks them to do. Satisfy them on this essential point, and there is nothing their leader cannot do with them, or that they won't do for him. They would readily die for him; and if there be a bit of fresh meat, or a chicken, or other delicacy to be had by foraging—and they are first-rate at that—he is bound to have his share of it. There are no keener judges of an officer than they are; and woe to the officer who excites their contempt.'

What wonderful devotion to a brave officer by a brave Irish soldier does not the following present! I give it in the words it was told to me —

My brother, Brevet Lieut.-Col. James F. M'Elhone, Regular Army, at Gaines' Mills, Va., while commanding the colour company, 14 Inf. U.S.A., then 1st Lieut., 17 years of age, was wounded late in the day with a Minié ball in the side, at the time supposed to be mortal. His 'striker,' Michael M'Grath by name, who had brought to the 'leftinint' a pot of hot tea during a warm lire from the enemy, had no harsher expression, when a bullet spilled the regretted beverage upon the ground, than 'Damn ye! ye didn't know what a divil's own time I had to get the hot wather, or ye wouldn't have done it.' This noble fellow remained with his officer upon the field, went with him to Savage's Station hospital, was a faithful attendant during the battle that raged there during the ensuing Sunday, accompanied him as prisoner to Richmond, feigning to be wounded so as to prevent separation, built a covering of blankets in the railroad depôt to save him from rain, successfully exerted in every way a fertile ingenuity to get the best in a town crowded to suffocation with wounded of both armies after the seven days' battles: and finally, when my brother was brought on parole to Baltimore by sea, and located in a private house used as a hospital, this Irish soldier I found sitting by his bedside, fanning his fevered brow, and as gentle a nurse almost as any woman could be.

Late in the afternoon of Sunday, 29th June 1862, as I have already said, the battle raged fiercely around the hospital, some being killed and wounded near the building. My brother and M'Grath saw with anxiety the increasing chances of their falling into the hands of the enemy. Up came the 69th New York (an Irish Regiment), to the last charge. My brother, now no more, has related often that, for the time, he forgot his own sad plight and acute suffering. There was a ringing hurrah as the hot Irish closed with the foe. Now the Union flag and the green flag of Ireland are seen to pulsate madly forward; there is a temporary check; the colours stagger, disappear, soon they are again lifted, and sweep onward till they mark a position gained and a battle won. But as the regiment was going into the very 'jaws of death,' one man in the rear rank cried out to the other, 'Toomey, man, step out, and don't he afraid,' to which instantly came the angry reply, 'What, sir! wait till this battle is over, and I'll smash your darn mug for you.'

Innumerable stories are told of the Irishman's irrepressible love of fight. There is not a town that has not its hero of a hundred tales illustrative of this grand passion of the race. There was a soldier in the South who, during a lull, would be 'detailed' to make shoes for the men; but, whenever there was a certainty of Terry Nolan's hearing 'the music'—of the whistling rifle-bullets and the singing shells—then he was seen trotting towards his line, with his rifle on his shoulder, ready to take his part in the concert. Terry's appearance was quite as conclusive as an order of the day, for with infallible scent he sniffed the battle from afar; and as the valiant Crispin took his place in his company he was invariably hailed with a cheer. The men knew they were in for it when Terry showed his Celtic visage, with the light of battle gleaming in his eyes.

'Why then, Captain,' said a great strapping Irishman to the commander of his company, as he scratched his head with a kind of bashfulness that sat rather ill on him,—'why then, Captain, could you tell us when we're going to have something to do? The boys want a fight bad; they hadn't one now for a long time, and sure they can't he always without a scrimmage of some kind or another, just to keep their hand in, as one may say.'

'I tell you, my man,' replied the Captain, 'you'll have quite enough of it soon.'

'Faith, Captain, I'm thinking it's you don't care for it yourself, and that's the raison the poor boys don't get it,' replied the disappointed ambassador, with a look of undisguised contempt.

That captain did not remain long with his company.

A colonel told me that, previous to one of the famous battles of the war, he had given his second horse in care of his orderly, an Irishman, named Moloney, with positive instructions to keep it for him in reserve; but that scarcely had the firing well commenced when he saw Moloney spurring his, the colonel's, horse, brandishing his sword, and rushing into the thick of the fight. The colonel could not sacrifice his horse, even to gratify his orderly's warlike ardour; so poor Moloney was captured, and ingloriously led back. 'How dare you, sir, disobey my orders?' asked the indignant colonel. 'Why, Colonel, I felt I'd be disgraced if I hadn't a dash at them with the boys. Yes, faith, Colonel, I could never hold up my head again.' 'It was a barefaced excuse, sir,' said the colonel, when telling the story,—'it was nothing but sheer love of fight; for Moloney hadn't to make his character then—he had a good record long before.'

Even when wounded and sick in hospital, the 'music' was too attractive to be resisted, if they could contrive to get on their legs at all. An American officer mentioning instances of the kind, said:—

'At the Battle of Shiloh an Irishman of this company received a very severe flesh wound in the shoulder, and was carried back to the Infirmary depôt, as all supposed, disabled for several months. We became hotly engaged soon after, and to my surprise I saw this man in the ranks of his company, fighting like a tiger, the blood running freely from his arm. As soon as I could, I enquired of him why he was not at the hospital. "Oh, Colonel," he said, "when I heard the guns going I was afraid the boys would be lonesome without me, so you see I came to keep them company; besides, my arm is not so bad, after all."'

It would be difficult to say at which side of the line the fighting qualities of the Irish were held in highest esteem by those who were opposed to them; for while the Southern has often said 'Send away your damned Irish, and we'll whip you well,' the Northern as frequently said, 'If all in the South fought like the Irish, Secession would long since be an accomplished fact.' General Patrick Cleburne, confessedly one of the best men of the war, used to say that he never had tougher work than when he met the Northern Irish—that Sweeney gave him the hardest fighting he ever had.

A general who commanded a Southern brigade, in which half—that is 5,000 out of the 10,000 who from time to time recruited its ranks as volunteers—were Irish, thus spoke of them to me:—

'If to-morrow I wanted to win a reputation, I would have Irish soldiers in preference to any others; and I tell you why. First, they have more dash, more *élan* than any other troops that I know of; then they are more cheerful and enduring—nothing can depress them. Next, they are more cleanly. The Irishman never failed to wash himself and his clothes. Not only were they cheerful, but they were submissive to discipline when once broken in—and where they had good officers that was easily done; but once they had confidence in their officers, their attachment to them was unbounded. And confidence was established the moment they saw their general in the fight with them. Afterwards they would say—"You keep back, General—tell us where to go, and we'll be sure to go; but we don't want you to be killed; for, faith, we don't know what would become of us then." They required strict discipline: but they always admitted the justice of their punishment when they believed their commander was impartial; and they never were sullen, or bore malice. There was one great element of strength in these men—they were volunteers, every man of them. Many could have been excused on the ground of their not being American citizens, as not more than one-third of them had a right to vote at the time; but they joined of their own free will—no Irishman was conscripted. I repeat, if I had to take from one to 10,000 men to make a reputation with, I'd take the same men as I had in the war—Irishmen from the city, the levees, the river, the railroads, the canals, or from ditching and fencing on the plantations. They make the finest soldiers that ever shouldered a musket.' And this was the testimony of one of the fiercest fighters of the war.

Another officer of rank says what he thinks of the Irish:—

'My opinion of the Irish is partial. I commanded many of them, and I can appreciate their value. None were more gallant, or none more faithful to our cause; *and it was owing to there being so many of them at the other side that we failed.* Those I commanded were some of the best soldiers I ever saw; but I think they are better when they are by themselves, in companies or regiments. Good soldiers indeed! they worked, and fought, and starved, just as required of them. The feeling of the South is of the warmest character to them. If the war started afresh, I'd raise an entirely Irish regiment, in preference to any other. They would be more under discipline, and could be controlled better than a mixed regiment. I admit that when they are in the camp, and there is nothing for them to do, they may get into mischief; but in the field they are thoroughly reliable.'

Here is the testimony of one who knew the Irish well. It is a chaplain who speaks: and though he saw them in battle, he knew more of them when the fight was over:—

'Commanders prefer them, not only for their bravery, but their cheerfulness, and for their cleanliness and neatness as soldiers. When others would be resting, the

Irishmen would be washing their clothes, and would then play games in their buff till they were dried. They were true soldiers—tigers in battle, lambs after. It was beautiful to witness their conduct to the enemy; they were kind as women to them, assisting the wounded, dividing their rations with them—losing every feeling of anger and hostility.'

Testimonies without number might be quoted; but one from a soldier whose fame is European, may well stand in the place of many. It is General Beauregard who thus gravely records his deliberate and weighty judgment of the Irish: 'Relative to the soldierly qualities of the Irish who 'took a part in our late war, I beg to state, that they displayed the sturdy and manly courage of the English, combined with the impetuous and buoyant character of the French. They required, at times, only discipline, which is always attained under good officers, to be equal to the best soldiers of any country. They always exhibited on the field of battle great gallantry, and during the operations of a campaign showed much patience and fortitude. They joined the Confederate ranks at the first call of the country for volunteers, and remained to the last, devoted and true to the cause they had zealously espoused. They were found to be always the worthy companions of the gallant Confederate soldiers with whom they fought, side by side, during over four years of an internecine struggle.'

'Whichever way,' says a Northern general with a splendid 'record,' 'we turn for the history of Irish Americans, the case is the same; we meet with nothing but cause for honest pride—they are true patriots, good citizens, and splendid soldiers.'

'Ah, sir!' said General Longstreet, whom I met in New Orleans, 'that was one of the handsomest things in the whole war!' What was this handsomest thing of the war? The manner in which the Irish Brigade breasted the death storm from Maire's Heights of Fredericksburg. Six times, in the face of a withering fire, before which whole ranks were mown down as corn before the sickle, did the Irish Brigade rush up that hill—rush to inevitable death. 'I looked with my field-glass,' said the Adjutant-General of General Hancock's staff, 'and I looked for a long time before I was certain of what I saw. I at first thought that the men of the Brigade had lain down to allow the showers of shot and shell to pass over them, for they lay in regular lines. I looked for some movement, some stir—a hand or a foot in motion; but no—they were dead—*dead every man of them*—cut down like grass.' In these six desperate charges that Brigade was almost annihilated. But there was no flinching for a second. Again and again they braved that hell-storm, and would have done so again and again; but of the 1,200 that bore a green badge in their caps that morning, nearly a thousand of them lay on the bloody field, literally mown down in ranks. Little more than 200 rations were that night issued to the remnant of that heroic band. 'It was the admiration of the whole army.' 'Never was there anything superior to it.' But General Longstreet's eulogium—'It was the handsomest thing of the war,' leaves nothing unexpressed.

Behind the stone wall, from which rained the deadliest fire, delivered within range, and with terrible precision, were men of the same blood and race as those who were thus wasting their lives in unavailing devotion. The Georgian regiment which lined that fatal barrier was mostly Irish; and from one of those who took part in that day's terrific strife, I heard some particulars of painful interest. Colonel Robert M'Millan was in command; and though death was in his family, he would not quit his post on that eventful day. When the Brigade was seen advancing from the town, they were at once recognised by their green badge, that sent a thrill to many a brave but sorrowful heart behind that rampart. 'God! what a pity!' said some. 'We're in for it,' said others. 'By heavens! here are Meagher's fellows,' said more. The voice of the Colonel rang clear and shrill—'It's Greek to Greek to-day; boys—give them hell!' And they did. For that deadly fusillade was the genuine *feu d'enfer*. Well might one of the most brilliant of the military historians of the day assert that 'never at Fontenoy, at Albuera, or at Waterloo, was more undoubted courage displayed by the sons of Erin, than during those six frantic dashes which they directed against the almost impregnable position of the foe.' 'It was a sad but glorious day for our country; it made us weep, but it made us proud,' said an Irishman, who helped to lay those thousand dead in their bloody grave.

A German Staff Officer of the Confederates says of the Irish Brigade, how they fought in the memorable seven days' fight in front of Richmond:—

The attack was opened by the columns of Hill (1st), Anderson, and Pickett. These gallant masses rushed forward with thundering hurrahs upon the musketry of the foe, as though it were a joy to them. Whole ranks went down under that terrible hail, but nothing could restrain their courage. The billows of battle raged fiercely onward; the struggle was man to man, eye to eye, bayonet to bayonet. The hostile Meagher's Brigade, composed chiefly of Irishmen, offered heroic resistance. After a fierce struggle our people began to give way, and at length all orders and encouragements were vain—they were falling back in the greatest confusion. Infuriate, foaming at the mouth, bare-headed, sabre in hand, at this critical moment General Cobb appeared upon the field, at the head of his legion, and with the 19th North Carolina and 14th Virginia regiments. At once these troops renewed the attack; but all their devotion and self-sacrifice were in vain. The Irish held their position with a determination and ferocity that called forth the admiration of our officers. Broken to pieces and disorganised, the fragments of that fine legion (Cobb's) came rolling back from the charge.

Almost while I write these words, I read of the death of one who made his name famous in the military annals of America. Stricken by the Yellow Fever,—that grisly king which has slain more victims by many times than fell at Fredericksburg,—now lies in his grave a gallant Irishman, Richard Dowling, of Houston, Texas, who at Sabine Pass performed one of the most extraordinary feats of the whole war. This Lieutenant Richard Dowling,—'Major Dick Dowling,' as he has since then been familiarly styled,—defending this Pass in an earthen fort, protected by a couple of serviceable guns, and manned by 42 Irishmen, crippled an attacking fleet, baffled an important expedition and actually captured of the enemy more than ten times the number of his gallant band! From the despatches of the Federal commanders the world might have imagined that a legion fought behind that rampart: but the astounding victory was entirely owing to the accurate aim, sheer pluck, and matchless audacity of Dick Dowling and his forty-two Irishmen—to whom the Confederate Congress, as well they might, passed a solemn vote of the nation's thanks. Light rest the earth on the breast of all that remains of gallant Dick Dowling!

As I cannot attempt an enumeration of the various Irish organisations that won distinction in the war, neither can I venture on a list of the gallant Irish officers, even of the highest rank, who signalised themselves by their achievements in that memorable struggle. I have before me a long list of men who commanded regiments, brigades, divisions, and corps; but fearing that, from my imperfect knowledge, I should necessarily fall into error, and be guilty perhaps of very serious injustice if I relied upon it, I must adopt the only course left open to me, and deal in generalities. Then, leaving the praises of men like Shiel or Sheridan, the Murat of the Union—Irish by blood, American through birth—to other pens, I shall simply say that the gallantry and skill of the Irish officer, of whatever rank, was quite as conspicuous as the dash and endurance of the rank and file.

But there is a grave amidst the countless graves that mark the scene of one of the deadliest conflicts of the war, on which I would drop a kindly tribute—that is the grave of Patrick Ronayne Cleburne, one of the noblest of the soldiers of the Confederacy.

Patrick Ronayne Cleburne was born within a few miles of the city of Cork. His father—the son of a country gentleman in Tipperary—was for many years physician of the dispensary districts of Ovens and Ballincollig; his mother, Miss Ronayne, was a lady from Queenstown. Patrick, the youngest of three sons, was partly educated for the medical profession; but his tastes, from his earliest youth, tending to a military career, and, owing to his father's second marriage, which resulted in a second and numerous family, not being able to purchase a commission as an officer in the British Army, he in his eighteenth year enlisted in the 41st regiment as a private soldier. He remained in the service until he was twenty-one, when he was purchased out by his friends. But these three years of military training in one of the most thoroughly disciplined armies of Europe was of incalculable advantage to him in after life. He emigrated to America when the war broke out; and it found the young Cork man practising with success as a lawyer in Helena, Arkansas.

I have been favoured with an admirable biographical sketch of General Cleburne by his attached friend and distinguished commander, General W. T. Hardee, one of the most thoroughly accomplished soldiers of either army; and referring the reader to that sketch, which will be found in the Appendix, I shall here simply indicate what manner of man was this Patrick Ronayne Cleburne, who learned his knowledge of military drill and discipline in the ranks of the 41st British regiment of infantry. To begin, then; this heroic Irishman, who was as strong as a wall of granite to the foe, was as simple as a child, and as modest as a girl; and that voice that rang like a trumpet when cannon roared, and balls whistled about his head, was low and gentle and hesitating when he was exposed to the most formidable of all batteries to him, a pair of eyes in the head of any woman of moderate youth or ordinary attractions. His *personnel* is thus sketched by a worthy countryman of his, whom he visited in Mobile, on the occasion of the marriage of his friend General Hardee, whose 'best man' he was on that interesting occasion: 'In person he was about five feet nine or ten inches high, slender in form, with a wiry active look. His forehead was high and broad, with high cheek bones, cheeks rather hollow, and face diminishing in width towards the chin, the upper features being more massive than the lower. The general expression of his countenance in repose was serious and thoughtful; but in conversation he was animated and impressive, while his whole air and manner were remarkably unpretending.'

General Cleburne dining one day with the good Irishman whose words I have quoted, informed him that he had made up his mind during the war to be a total abstainer, because he found that in his pistol practice and in playing chess, of which game he was remarkably fond, even one glass of wine affected his aim, or interfered with his calculation. He determined, therefore, while the war lasted, and he was responsible for the lives of others, and the results consequent on the manner in which he should discharge his duties, that he would abstain altogether from the use of all kinds of liquor.

Cleburne was in favour of arming the negroes as soldiers, conferring upon them and their families freedom as a bounty. He, with several distinguished generals, signed a petition to President Davis to that effect, and he personally offered to take command of a division of such troops, when raised. But the movement failed on account of the opposition which it met with. In private conversation he said that the general sentiment of the world was against the Confederacy on the question of slavery, and that Southerners could look nowhere for active sympathy unless they made some such arrangement as he mentioned: and he unhesitatingly expressed his belief, that the success of the cause depended upon its adoption. He did not pronounce a decided opinion against slavery in the abstract, but he regarded the system in the South as having glaring defects and evils, especially the utter disregard of the married rights of the slaves, which, he said, was enough to deprive the States in which this evil existed of the aid of Providence in the war. The opinions held by General Cleburne were those emphatically expressed in writing and from the pulpit by the Catholic Bishops of Richmond and Savannah.

The opinions of a man of Cleburne's stamp, as to the character of the Irish as soldiers, I give in the words of the friend who heard them expressed by that great General: 'In reference to the relative merits, as soldiers, of the different kind of men in the service, he said he preferred the Irish, not on the ground of their courage, for of that there was no lack in the Confederate service, but for other qualities, highly useful in war. After a long day's march they generally had their tents up first; they were more cleanly in their persons; under the fatigue of hard work, or a heavy march, they showed more endurance, and recovered sooner; they were more cheerful under privation; and above all, they were more amenable to discipline. These, he said, were highly useful qualities in war; and from actual observation he was persuaded the Irish soldiers possessed them in a higher degree than any other people that came under his eye.'

Cleburne was one of those Irishmen who never could understand how it was that his countrymen of the North could join with the 'Yankee' to oppress and crush the South; but had he been a lawyer in a Northern or Northwestern State, he might have been equally surprised if anyone had accused him of turning his military knowledge to the same purpose. His countrymen throughout the Northern States were proud of his splendid reputation; while in the South it was not considered second to that of the very greatest of its commanders. And when he died—struck by a storm of bullets, as the fore feet of his horse were planted on the Federal ramparts—a wail of sorrow and a shudder of despair passed through the land. A tower of strength had fallen. The dauntless soldier sleeps in peace in the cemetery whose solemn beauty elicited the strange remark, as he gazed on it a few days before he gloriously fell, 'It is almost worth dying to rest in so sweet a spot.'

I heard the heroic Irishman thus spoken of by two brave men—General Buckner and General Hood—who had been with him in many a memorable fight, and many a brilliant victory. Referring to his name, the first-named general said:—

And particularly did I recall the virtues of the Irish character, when a few short months ago, I stood, in the twilight hour, over the grave of one of the noblest sons of Ireland. As I looked upon the plain board inscribed with his name in pencil lines, and upon the withered flowers which the fair hands of some of our countrywomen had strewn upon his grave, I wept silent tears to the glorious memory of General Patrick Cleburne. He commanded a brigade in my division, and afterwards succeeded me in the command of troops whom I cannot more highly praise than to say he was one of the few who was worthy to command such men. And conspicuous amongst such gallant men, and worthy soldiers of such a glorious leader, were Irishmen, who illustrated their high military virtues on so many fields, and displayed on so many occasions their fidelity to the cause they had espoused.

And thus spoke General Hood, who bears in many a scar and wound eloquent testimonies to his desperate but unavailing gallantry:—

During the late war it was my fortune to have in my command organisations composed of your countrymen, and it gives me pleasure to assert that they were always at their post. And among these brave men was to be found the gallant Cleburne. His name carries me to the heights near Franklin. And his last remarks, just before moving forward, I shall ever remember. He said: 'General, I have my division in two lines, and am ready. General, I am more hopeful of the success of our cause than I have ever been since the war commenced.' Within twenty-five minutes this brave soldier was no more. Within an hour an army was in mourning over the great loss. Thus ended the career of this distinguished man—hopeful even at the last hour, but doomed to disappointment as all other men.

America is a country of wonders, where things are to be seen of which the Old World mind can have no conception. But nothing that I beheld impressed me with the same admiration, and indeed with the same astonishment, as the manner in which a people, whose tremendous struggle of four long years' duration enchained the attention of every civilised nation, returned to the peaceful pursuits of civil life. To my mind, there was something great beyond description in this unrivalled spectacle. A few months before, and the earth resounded with the clash of armed legions, mightier and more numerous than any which Europe had assembled for centuries; and where is the trace of this colossal conflict in the bearing and deportment of the people? You may behold its marks and traces in the desolated track of the conqueror; in the sedge-broom now usurping the once fruitful soil; in rifled and ruined dwellings abandoned to decay; in burned cities rising anew from their ashes: in crumbling embankments and road-side ramparts, which cost so much blood and so many gallant lives to take or to defend,—but in the calm dignified attitude of the great American people, who have sheathed the sword and laid aside the rifle, you cannot perceive them.

Where, you unconsciously ask, are the soldiers, the fighting men, the heroes, who bore a distinguished part in that protracted contest? Have the brigades, the divisions, the corps, the armies, of which we read in bulletin and report—have they sunk into the earth, or have they vanished in the air? If not, how are these men of war employed?—can they settle down to the ordinary pursuits of life; or have they been fatally intoxicated by the smoke and excitement of battle, and utterly demoralised by the license of the camp? You shall see.

Who is that remarkable-looking man, with something of the clanking sabre in his carriage, yet with nothing more warlike in his hand than a memorandum book, with a bundle of harmless papers protruding from the breastpocket of a coat that seems to cling to his broad chest as if it were a uniform? A commercial agent. Yes, now; but what was he a few months since? One at whose mere mention wives and mothers paled, and with the incantation of whose name nurses hushed their fractious charge—a daring leader of cavalry, whose swoop was as fierce and sudden as the eagle's.

Here, down in this new city, in the midst of the tall pines, you see that coach factory, full of wagons and buggies of all kinds; and what is that bearded man employed at? A sewing-machine? Impossible; it can't be —and yet it is. Yes, it is. That tall bearded man held high rank in his corps; but, the war over, and hating idleness, he established this thriving factory; and with his own hands he is now sewing and embroidering the curtains of that carriage which is to be sent for in a day or two by its purchaser.

At yon lawyer's desk, covered with open or tape-bound documents, an anxious client awaiting his opinion of that knotty case, sits one, now immersed in the intricacy of a legal problem, whose natural element seemed to be amid the thickest press of battle, where squadrons rushed on serried bayonets, or dashed at belching batteries.

Calmly giving some minute instruction to a deferential clerk, respecting a delayed train, or dictating an answer to some impatient enquiry concerning a missing parcel or a bale of dry-goods left behind, is a man whose wisdom and whose courage were the hope of a cause; prudent in council, skilful in strategy, calm and cool in conflict.

Behind that counter, in that store, or perched on that office desk, is he who has done so many brilliant feats, to the wonder of the foe, and the rapture of his friends.

Rushing headlong through the street, in his eagerness to keep some appointment, in which there is to be much talk of bales of cotton, cargoes of corn, or hogsheads of strong wine, is the soldier whose movements were of lightning celerity, who, by right of his lavished blood, had established a kind of vested interest in every desperate undertaking.

And here, at this editor's table, with ink, and paste, and scissors at his elbow, up to his eyes in 'proofs,' and young 'devils' clamorous for 'copy,' you have a dashing colonel, a fortunate general, a famous artillery officer—now as tranquilly engaged in the drudgery of his 'daily' as if he had never led his regiment at the charge, never handled a division or a corps, or never decided a victory with his guns; as if, in fact, he had only learned of war in the pages of Grecian or Roman history, or read of it in one of his European 'exchanges.'

Hush! you are in a seat of learning, in which the hopeful youth of a great country is being trained for its future citizenship. You perceive that quiet-looking elderly gentleman smiling kindly on that bright eager lad, as he speaks to him with gentle voice. That quiet-looking gentleman is the man of men, whose very name was worth an army to the side he espoused. Every home in America, every village in Europe, has heard of that quiet-looking gentleman.

And look again: here is a learned professor instructing his class—not at all a wonderful sight, you may say; but on the wide ocean, in every mart of commerce, on every exchange, in every nook and corner in which the risks of sea, enhanced by the casualties of war, are keenly calculated, there were those who thought by day and dreamed by night of that learned professor.

Go where you will, in field or mine, in workshop, in factory, in store, in counting house, in hotel—at either side of the line—whether on land or water—everywhere—you behold, now absorbed in honest toil and patient industry, the men, high and low, of every rank and grade, and of every nationality too, who, a few months since, were engaged in desperate strife! This spectacle, which the Old World has never seen surpassed, is more wonderful than Niagara, more majestic than the Mississippi, more sublime than the snow-clad pinnacles of the loftiest of the Sierras.

CHAPTER XXX

*Feeling of the Irish in America towards England—A Fatal Mistake—Not
Scamps and Rowdies—Who they really are—Sympathy conquering Irritation—
Indifference to Danger—Down in the Mine—One of the Causes of Anti-English
Feeling—More of the Causes of Bad Feeling—What Grave and Quiet Men
think—If they only could 'see their way'—A Grievance redressed is a Weapon
broken—The Irish Element—Belief in England's Decay—War with England—
Why most Injurious to England—Why loss Injurious to America—The only
Possible Remedy*

IT is a matter of more importance to understand what is the real feeling
entertained by the Irish in America towards England, or the British Government,
than to ascertain the nature or the details of any organisation to which that feeling
may give rise. If the feeling be ephemeral or factitious, the organisation, however
formidable its aspect, resembles a torrent caused by a summer storm, or a tree with
wide branches yet having no hold in the soil. And, on the other hand, though an
organisation may be ill-designed or even ridiculous, or, on account of the folly, or
violence, or treachery, of those who are responsible for its management, may come
to a speedy dissolution, if it have its origin in an earnest and enduring feeling, it is
significant of danger—it represents more than is seen; and die down as it may, it is
sure to spring up again in some new form. Here the abiding life is, as it were, in
the soil, whose vital energy throws these its creations to the surface. The question,
then, should rather be, *what is the feeling in which an organisation*—Fenianism, or
any other 'ism'—*has its origin*, than what is the organisation which springs from
the feeling? With the special organisation, much less with its details, I have no
concern whatever; while with the feeling I cannot, in duty or in honesty, refuse to
deal.

Of the leaders, the real or ostensible leaders, of the existing organisation various
opinions are entertained and freely expressed; and far stronger language has been
used by different sections of the same nominal body with respect to the merits or
demerits of rival chiefs than has been employed by the most indignant and out-
spoken Crown Prosecutor, or the most enthusiastic advocate of British connection.
It is only just, however, to state, that against the personal character, the honour and
integrity, of the present most prominent member of the Fenian organisation I have
never heard a word. Personal ambition, or a desire for display, may have been
urged against him by those who did not agree with his policy, or were opposed to
the movement; but no one, not even a partisan of a rival leader, accuses him of
dishonesty or of treachery.

There cannot be a more fatal mistake, whether fallen into in England or in Ireland, than that which has its origin in the desire to make light of the feeling existing among the Irish in America—namely, of depreciating the position, character, and motives of those who have either joined or aided the present movement, or who sympathise with its objects, whether special or general. It has been frequently asserted that the Fenian organisation embraces within its ranks none but the looser portion of the population—in fact, 'the scum of the great cities,' and that it depends altogether for its support on the contributions extorted from day labourers and servant-girls. That the organisation embraces many young men of loose habits or irregular lives must of necessity be the case—it must be so with every movement or organisation of a similar nature; yet, though such supporters of an organisation may not be the steadiest members of the community, or the most remarkable for self-restraint, they bring to it physical force, courage, and a reckless desperation which no obstacle can daunt or deter. Men of this class, however, do not constitute its strength; they certainly are not its guiding spirits, nor do they form more than a section or percentage of the whole body—they are, in fact, but a mere minority of the rank and file of American Fenianism.

That an individual who takes the lead in a certain locality may be actuated by the lowest motives—vanity, self-interest, or the desire of obtaining influence to be employed for the furtherance of personal objects—is probably true, and it would be strange if such were not the case; but the body, meaning thereby the thousands or the tens of thousands who constitute the strength of the organisation, even in the locality in which there may happen to be a worthless leader, are neither 'roughs' nor 'rowdies,' nor men of irregular or dissipated habits; and the feeling by which these men are animated is as pure as it is unselfish. That what they propose to themselves as their immediate or ultimate object may be as impracticable as mischievous —that it would rather aggravate and intensify the evils which they desire to remedy by sweeping revolution,—this is not properly the question; it is rather, what is their true character?—what is their real feeling? Then, so far as I have been able to learn, my belief is, that among the Fenians in almost every State of the Union there are many thousands of the very cream of the Irish population. Indeed, in several places in which I have been I have learned, on unquestionable authority—very frequently of those who regarded Fenianism with positive dislike, and its leaders with marked mistrust—that the most regular, steady, and self-respecting of the Irish youth, or the immediate descendants of Irish parents, constituted its chief strength.

A few facts, given without method, will best illustrate the real character of those who take part in this organisation, and the feelings by which they are animated.

I happened to be in Buffalo a few months after the famous raid into Canada; and the impression produced by what I then learned was not weakened, but rather confirmed, by every day's additional experience in the United States. I was then brought into contact with persons holding the most opposite opinions as to the character of this raid—those who condemned or those who applauded it; but from the very persons who denounced it, as wanton and wicked, I received as strong testimony in favour of the conduct of the Fenians who took part in it, or who had come to take part in it, as from those who gloried in the attempt, and deplored its failure. It is not necessary to repeat the oft-told story of the Canadian raid, or the part taken by the American Government, under the solemn obligations of international law, to ensure its defeat. Not calculating on the active interference of the authorities, an immense body of Fenians, several thousands in number, concentrated in Buffalo, with the intention of crossing the frontier; and though they were badly provided, if not utterly unprovided, with commissariat, and though, notwithstanding the generosity or the efforts of their friends, they had to subsist on the simplest and even scantiest fare; and though hundreds of these young men were to be seen lying on the side-walks, their only sleeping-places at night (it was in the midst of the summer)—there was not committed by any one of that vast body during the time, fully a fortnight, that they remained in that large and populous city, a single offence against person, or property, or decency, or public order! This fact, so creditable to the Irish character, was admitted, however reluctantly, by the opponents of the Fenians, and was proudly proclaimed by their sympathisers.

In this raid, or ready to take part in it, were men of the best character and the steadiest conduct. Instances were numerous of those who had abandoned well-paid offices, lucrative situations, and valuable appointments—who had given up happy homes and quiet enjoyments, to risk liberty and life in this expedition. Fathers were not restrained from joining in it by family obligations; and those who were beyond the period of active service rather encouraged than checked the ardour of their sons. A striking case in point came under my immediate observation. I visited, on invitation, the store of a respectable man, whom I had known many years before in Ireland, and whose feeling, I knew, had always been strongly 'national.' Speaking of the Canadian raid, in the presence of his wife and children and one or two friends, all grouped round the stove at the far end of his place of business, he pointed to a handsome fresh-coloured young fellow of twenty, and said—'That boy joined them over the way, and with my full consent. His mother there was in a terrible state about him, like all women, I suppose, and wanted not to let him go on any account; but I said to her, "if you do not let him go, I will take his place; and if I say I will go, no power on earth will stop *me*." It was only then she consented—she will tell you so herself. He did go, and he came back, safe too, to his mother and me, thank God!' A deep, heart-felt 'Amen!' was the mother's only response, as she caressed the soft cheek of her youngest child, that, sitting at her feet, rested its head against her knee.

I was passing through an hospital in Buffalo, which was in the charge of a community of Irish Sisters, when the gentleman by whom I was accompanied asked me if I should like to see 'a live Fenian.' I replied that I had seen more than one specimen of the genus Fenian before, and that I had no special curiosity to see one on that occasion. 'Ah,' said he, 'but he was one of the raiders into Canada, and was severely wounded. This case may be interesting to you for this reason—that it affords the best reply to those who, in their eagerness to put down a so-called secret organisation (and, God knows, it puzzles me to discern where the secresy is), represent all who belong to it as infidels and everything bad. This young man, who was wounded at Limestone Ridge, is, to my personal knowledge, one of the best-conducted men in this city. He was and is a monthly communicant, and, I can answer for it, he is exemplary in every relation of life. He is, besides, a man of superior intelligence. Now I am, if anything, an anti-Fenian; yet I tell you it is absurd to suppose that the organisation is what it has been described by your English newspaper correspondents.' The appearance, manner, and bearing of the wounded man, who was sitting on the side of his bed, and who laid down a prayer-book as soon as he saw the visitor approaching, evidently justified the description given of him by my companion.

A distinguished Irish clergyman of the Catholic diocese of Cincinnati, who publicly and privately discouraged the movement, remarked to me:—'It is idle to say that this feeling—call it infatuation if you like—has not a strong hold on our Irish population, or that the organisation does not embrace within it many men of the best character and the purest motives. I have every day ample experience of the fact that this is so. I will give you a case in point. I was sitting at this desk one evening, busily writing, when a visitor was announced. He was a penitent of my own, and I assure you I was very proud of him, for there could not be a more respectable young man, or one who was in every way better conducted. He was likewise singularly thoughtful and intelligent, and held an excellent position, "Father," he said, "I want you to do me a great favour." I told him, what was quite true, that I should be happy to do anything in my power to oblige or serve him. "Well, Father," said he, "I want you to take charge of this little parcel for me—it contains $600. I am going at once on a very important journey, on which much depends. I am not at present at liberty to say anything more, but you shall soon know all about it; but if you don't hear of me in six months, send this money to my parents in Ireland, with this letter." I received the money and the letter from him, and promised strict compliance with his request. I did not press him as to the nature of his journey, for he was studiously reserved on that point; and when he took leave, it was with a display of emotion not very common with him, for he was almost invariably cool and collected in manner. In less than ten days after we parted at that door, I was shocked to read in the morning paper the account of his death,—he was one of the raiders, and he was killed in the fight at Fort Erie.'

From the Southern States—Alabama, Louisiana, the Carolinas, Florida, Texas—young men had come up to the extreme North on this expedition; and had it been even momentarily successful, or had there been the least connivance with the movement on the part of the Government of the United States,—had, in fact, those who first crossed the frontier but the opportunity of making a stand, and holding their own even for a few days, vast numbers would have flocked to the green standard from every State in the Union. That Southern men, or Confederates, should take any active part in the movement was extraordinary, considering the feeling of exasperation that still lingered in the Southern mind, the result of the late war. This feeling was quite as strongly felt by Irishmen in the Confederacy as by Americans; and though there was, of necessity, a sympathy between Irishmen at both sides of the line, still there was a lurking sentiment of irritation not a little aggravated by the policy of the extreme Radical party, as proclaimed through their press, and sought to be enforced by legislation. An incident, which reached me through more than one source, will indicate, better than any description, the feeling of the Irish in the South as to the part taken by their compatriots of the North in the war.

While the contending armies lay in front of each other in the neighbourhood of Chattanooga, a flag of truce brought together several distinguished officers on both sides; amongst them, General Cleburne and General Sweeney—the former fittingly representing the gallantry of the Southern Irish, the latter as fittingly representing the gallantry of the Northern Irish. Friendly greetings and compliments were interchanged, flasks were emptied, and healths were drunk with great cordiality by those who in a few hours after were to meet in deadly strife. On that occasion General Sweeney, addressing himself to General Cleburne, expressed his regret that his countrymen should be found opposed to each other, and fighting on both sides during the war; but he hoped the time would come when they would all be found united, and standing side by side in the effort to recover the independence of their native land. To this Cleburne replied, that to assist in destroying the independence of one people was rather a poor preparation for the work of restoring the independence of another.

This lingering feeling of irritation is, however, rapidly passing away, owing in a great measure not only to the generous bearing of the Federal Irish while as combatants or conquerors in the South, but to the policy generally held by the Irish in the Northern States as to the read-mission of the seceding States into the Union. But, were that sentiment of irritation stronger than it is, it would be absorbed by one far stronger and more intense—'hatred of the common enemy, love of the common country.' I had rather a strange exhibition of the intensity of this feeling in a city in Alabama.

From this city, in which there is a considerable Irish population, there had gone forth, besides other Irish organisations, several companies, all of which distinguished themselves by the most extraordinary daring and intrepidity. In the very thickest of the deadliest struggle these men fought with a desperation that elicited universal admiration. One of these companies lost four out of every five; either they were killed on the field of battle, or they died in the hospital of their wounds. Of 130 men who from time to time joined that company, but 26 survived;

and that gallant remnant of that heroic band limped back to their homes, riddled with shot and shell, and hacked by steel—cripples for life. Those who commanded these heroic men were in every way worthy of those they commanded. Three times this company lost its captain in front of the enemy; and the successor to their honours and responsibilities—an Irishman from Waterford—the fourth who led it into battle—bears on his person terrible evidences of the work in which he had been engaged.

He called on me at my hotel; and the conversation turning on the late civil war, he informed me of many interesting particulars with respect to the part taken in it by Irishmen at both sides. I happened to express a hope that his many wounds, of which I had heard so much from others, did not cause him pain or inconvenience, and my surprise that he survived such grievous injuries in vital parts; when, rather unexpectedly, he said, 'I would like to show you my wounds, if you have no objection; you can then see what narrow escapes I had.' I replied that I could have no objection whatever to behold the marks of a brave man's valour; on which, though not without some difficulty, owing to the helpless condition of one arm, he stripped to the waist. And, poor fellow, he had been riddled and torn indeed. He had been shot through the neck, the ball entering at one side, and going out at the other. Within an inch or two of his spine was a great mark where a rifle bullet had torn through: that bullet, turned by one of those strange eccentric motions which bullets occasionally take, passed out through his side, and shattered his arm. A third had more than grazed the lower stomach—it had literally passed through, leaving its mark of entrance and departure. Then there were scars of minor importance, still eloquent mementos of fierce fights in which he and his noble Irish 'Guard' had taken so conspicuous a part. One arm, as I have mentioned, hung helpless by his side; but I well remember how his eyes sparkled, and his face became suffused with enthusiasm, as, suddenly flinging aloft his other arm, lean and sinewy, he exclaimed in a voice of concentrated passion—'This is the only arm I have left, and, so help me God! I'd give it and every drop of my heart's blood, if I could only strike one blow for Ireland! I'd be satisfied to die of my wounds then, for I'd die happy in her cause.'

I have heard declarations as ardent from Irishmen in other parts of the South— by men who had borne themselves bravely during the war; and though many of them declared their mistrust of certain of the Fenian leaders, and even a dislike to the movement itself, still all expressed themselves in this fashion, 'If I could see my way clearly—if I could only trust the men in New York—if I thought I could do Ireland any good, or give her a chance, I would go in for it at every risk.' Others boasted that they were members of the organisation—that they were ready, at any moment, to unsheath the sword again—that they did not care who or what the leaders were; they were for any organisation that kept alive the national feeling, and prepared Irishmen to avail themselves of the first opportunity for a practical movement in her favour.

So startling and extraordinary were the events in which these men—Northerns and Southerns—were actors, that revolution had become a familiar idea to their minds; and such were the privations and hardships they had endured, such the sacrifices they had made, such the dangers they had gone through almost daily during a protracted war, in sustainment of the cause to which they had been devoted on either side, that the risk of life in the attainment of a great object, or in furtherance of a cherished purpose, is regarded by them as a light matter, if, indeed, it is regarded by them at all. They have been too familiar with Death— have looked the King of Terrors too many times in the face—not to contemplate the possible loss of life with the utmost indifference; added to which, such is the enthusiasm by which they are animated—an enthusiasm at once fierce and exalted, springing from the twofold passion of love and hate, devotion and revenge—that it renders the idea of the sacrifice of life elevating and ennobling rather than discouraging or repelling.

Down in the depths of a mine in Illinois, the workers in which were Irish to a man, I found the same feeling of passionate love, the same feeling of passionate hate. It was a strange scene, and not without its attraction. In one of the central passages of the mine, not more than five feet in height, its prevailing murkiness pierced here and there by the red light of a small lamp, was a truck, in which were four men—two recumbent, as if on a couch; the other two sitting one on each side of that most uncomfortable carriage. The group consisted of the two visitors— myself and a substantial friend, who did not much admire the dark shadows, the low ceiling, and the strange sounds of this underground world; together with one of the 'bosses,' and a remarkably intelligent and younger man.

The miners had each their lamp fastened in front of their caps, while the visitors held theirs in their hands. The galloping mule had been arrested in his course by a stoppage occasioned by something ahead; and for a considerable time—it seemed an age to my stout friend by my side—conversation was the only resource of the party of four. In a company consisting of four Irishmen, it would be strange if the conversation did not fall on Irish affairs, especially at a time when the State-trials in Canada were then going on. My excellent friend, who shared with me the couch of straw, though an ardent Irishman, thought only of how soon he should get out of the mine, and up into the bright world above; and for the moment the Irish Question lost all attraction for his ears. I must confess to having taken the 'legal and constitutional' side in the argument which sprang up; but it found little favour either with the fiery younger man, or with the more sedate 'boss.' Only through courtesy, and that not a little strained either, would they tolerate the mention of moderation, or even admit that an Irishman could love his country sincerely, and even ardently, and yet oppose those who should seek to bring about changes by violence and bloodshed. And as I reclined in my triumphal car, I was harangued in fiery accents by the younger miner, on 'the wrongs of Ireland, and the iniquities of the British Government.' He had the history of the Union and the story of the Irish

Rebellion by heart; and as he referred to some thrilling event, or mentioned some famous name, there was a deep murmur of satisfaction from the 'boss,' whose 'Thrue for you, boy!' seemed to impart an additional swing to the oratory of his companion. They would not believe in the naval or military power of England — that, according to them, as to most others whom I subsequently met, was a thing of the past. 'And, after all, what was it to the power of America?—where were armies like hers?—where iron-clads, and monitors, and turret-ships, such as she could turn out at a moment's notice, as she did during the Rebellion? No; England was to go down, and Ireland was, under Providence, to be the instrument of her ruin.'

Some of the miners had gone before, and others would go again, when the occasion arose, to strike a blow at 'the oppressor of their country;' and there was scarcely a man in the mine that did not joyfully subscribe to the Fenian fund, and would not continue to do so; for though they might not succeed one time, they would another. The 'boss' had not much to say, but that was to the point. 'He didn't care about the money—he could spare that; but he'd give his life if necessary, and gladly too, for the country that he was ever thinking of, and that was dear to his heart.' And the 'boss' looked to be an earnest man, who said what he meant, and would do what he said. The young man made a boast of a fact of which he might well be proud—that, although there were between 200 and 300 Irishmen in the mine, there were not six drunkards among the entire number. They were hard-working, laborious, and zealous, proud of the success of the mine, and not less so of their own well-earned reputation for sobriety and honesty. True, these were humble toilers; but they were the very opposite of the scamps and rowdies who are supposed to constitute the strength of the anti-English organisation in America. Nor had they the remotest intention or hope of ever deriving any personal advantage from the sacrifices they made, or were prepared to make, for 'the cause;'—love of their native land, and the desire to see her 'happy and independent,' were all-sufficient motives with them.

According to a system of logic, with the force and justice of which they are thoroughly satisfied, certain classes of the Irish in America—indeed, the majority of them—hold the British Government responsible for all the evils of Ireland; and at the door of Government and Parliament is also laid the responsibility of the wrongs done by individuals with the sanction of the law, and the passive assent of the Legislature. After all, it is not to be wondered at that Irishmen in America should adopt the logic of Englishmen in Parliament. 'If *a people are discontented, the fault must lie with those who govern them,*' has been more than once heard of late years in the British House of Commons; and though the axiom may have been applied to a foreign people and a foreign government, an Irishman might be excused for holding it of equal force when applied nearer home. I can answer for it, that in this rough-and-ready manner even the humblest men instinctively reason. In fact, the logic is there ready for their use.

Visiting a farm-house in a Western State, I found the owner, a man verging on sixty, in the midst of his family, sons and daughters, fine specimens of the Irish race, with the glow of health on their cheeks, and vigour and life in every movement. A quarter of a century before, the owner of that house and farm was evicted under circumstances of singularly painful severity,—his cottage had been assailed by the 'crowbar brigade,' and he and his wife had barely time to snatch their children from the crashing ruin of what had been their home; and in his heart he cherished a feeling of hatred and vengeance, not so much against the individual by whom the wrong was perpetrated, as against the Government by which it was sanctioned, and under whose authority it was inflicted.

He had not the least objection to tell of his difficulties in the new country, for he had every reason to be proud of his sturdy energy, and his hard struggles for the first few years; but, whatever the subject of which he spoke, he would invariably contrive to wander back to the memorable day of his eviction, when, as he said, 'he and his were turned out like dogs—worse than dogs—on the road-side.' 'See, sir!' he exclaimed, 'I tell you what it is, and you may believe me when I say it, though I love the old country—and God knows I do that same—I would not take a present of 200 acres of the finest land in my own county, and have to live under the British Government.' 'Not if the British Grovernment had anything to do with it, I suppose,' said the wife, as if explaining her husband's assertion, which she seemed to regard as reasonable and natural. 'I'll never forgive that Government the longest day I live.' 'Why then, indeed, Daniel, it's time to forgive them and everybody now,' put in the wife, 'for sure, if that same didn't happen, you would not be here this blessed day, with your 400 acres of fine land, and plenty for all of us, and the schooling for the children, and no one to say "boo" to us, and all our own! May the Lord make us thankful for his mercies!' 'Well, Mary, no thanks to the British Government for that,—'twasn't for my good the blackguards done it— and if you and the children didn't perish that day, 'twas the Lord's will, not theirs.' 'Why then, Daniel, I can't say again that'—and the wife gave in. The sons, one of whom had fought for the Union, sympathised more with the vengeful feeling of their father than with the Christian spirit of their mother.

A similar instance of this holding the British Government responsible for an act of individual cruelty was related to me by an eminent Irish ecclesiastic in one of the Eastern States. In the course of his periodical visitation he became acquainted with a respectable and thriving Irish farmer, who appeared to be in great comfort, his land in fine condition, and his stock of cattle of a good description and abundant. This man was always glad to see the priest coming round, and thought 'he could never make enough of him.' A widower with several children, his house was managed by his wife's sister, who had altogether devoted herself to their welfare. He was a man of abstemious habits, regular life, and inclined to reserve, as if, as the clergyman said, there was some kind of cloud always over his mind. Nothing could exceed his care in the religious training of his young people, in which task he was well seconded by their excellent aunt. But there was this singularity about him,—that, whatever his desire to have his family grow up in the practice of their faith, he never would go to confession.

The priest, as was his duty, spoke to him more than once on the subject; but he was answered evasively, and put off on one plea or another. At length, determined to push the matter home, he said to him—'Now I must speak to you seriously, and you must listen to me as your pastor, who is answerable before God for the welfare of his flock. Your children are now growing up about you, and they will be men and women in a short time, and you should show them an example in your own person of a Catholic father. You are aware how important it is that they should be strong in their faith before they become men and women, and go into the world, where they will no longer be subject to your control, or that of their good pious aunt; but if you don't yourself set them the example, how can you expect they will always continue as they now are—devoted to their religion? Tell me, then, why won't you go to your duty here—where God has prospered your industry—as you did in the old country in former times?' 'Well, Father,' he replied, 'I tell you what it is—I can't go; that's the truth of it, and for a good reason too. I know my religion well enough to tell me I must forgive my enemies, or I can't get absolution—that I know sure enough, for my mother wasn't without telling me as much, and I never forgot it, and 'tis always before me, sleeping and waking. Then, as you must know the truth of it—and 'tis the blessed truth I'm telling you—I can't and I won't forgive them—I never can, and what's more, I never will, to my dying day. Father, that's just the whole of it.' 'Nonsense, man,' said the priest, 'that's not the language of a Christian—an infidel might speak to me in that manner. Why, the Redeemer, who saved you and yours by his blood, forgave his enemies —and you, a Christian man! brought up in a Catholic country, to talk of not forgiving your enemies!' 'True for you, Father—all true—true as the Gospel—I know it; but still there's something in me that I can't get over. I told your reverence I was turned out of my land, where my father and his people before him lived, I don't know how long. Well, sure enough, that same has been many a better man's case, and more's the pity. But that wasn't it. but the way 'twas done. There didn't come out of the heavens a bitterer morning when the sheriff was at my door with the crowbar men, and a power of peelers, and the army too, as if 'twas going to war they were, instead of coming to drive an honest man and his family from house and home. My poor ould father was at his last with rheumatics, and the doctor said 'twas coming to his heart—and my wife too, saving your reverence's presence, was big with child. 'Twas a bad time, God knows, for us to be put out. I asked the agent, who was there, for a week, to see and get a place; but I couldn't get a day—no, not an hour; he said the law should take its coorse, and it did take its coorse, and a bad wicked coorse it was. My mother—she did it, Father, before I could stop her—knelt down to him in her grey hairs; but 'twas no good—you might as well talk to that stone there. I told them the state of my poor ould father—that was no use either; out we should go into the bitter could, and not as much as a place to put our heads! There were others as bad as ourselves, for the whole townland was 'under notice.' I can't tell you all that happened that morning, or that night—I was like a man out of his rayson, that didn't know what he was about, or what was happening to him. But this I know well enough—that my ould father was taken out on the bed he lay on, and he died that night in the gripe of the ditch, under the shelter we made for him with a few bits of boords and sticks and a quilt; and my wife—God rest her blessed sowl this day!—was brought to bed—what a bed it was!—of the youngest child—she you heard just now in her catechism; and my poor wife—my poor girl, Father, died in my arms the next day!'

Here the strong man, with a fierce gesture, dashed the tears from his eyes. 'Well, Father, I went down on my knees, and, the Lord pardon me! I swore I'd never forgive that night and day, and the men that done that wrong—and I never will—and I'll never forgive the bloody English Government that allowed a man to be treated worse than I'd treat a dog, let lone a Christian, and sent their peelers and their army to help them to do it to me and others. No, Father, 'tis no use your talking to me, I can't forgive them; and what's more, I teach my children to hate them too. It would be like turning false to her that's in the grave—the mother of my children—if I ever forgave that bitter day and bitter night.' Again and again, for years, the zealous priest never ceased to urge on that dark spirit the necessity of imitating the Divine example; and it was not until the illness of the daughter whose birthplace was the ditch-side in the bleak winter, softened the father's heart, that he bowed his head in humility, or that the word 'forgiveness' passed his lips. But forgiveness did not necessitate love; and though he had never taken an active part in any organisation, yet whatever was ostensibly adverse to the British Government had his sympathy, and that of his children.

I do not care to speculate as to the number of the class of evicted tenants scattered through the United States, whether, like the men just mentioned, prosperous possessors of land, or adding unduly to the population of some of the great towns; but wherever they exist, there are to be found willing contributors to Fenian funds, and enthusiastic supporters of anti-British organisations.

Then there are the descendants of 'the men of '98,' to whom their fathers left a legacy of hate. Americans these may be, and proud of their birth-right; yet they cherish an affection for the land of their fathers, and a deep-seated hostility to the country which they were taught to regard as its oppressor. From the date of the Irish rebellion to the present hour every successive agitation. or disturbance has driven its promoters, its sympathisers, or its victims, across the ocean; and thus, from year to year, from generation to generation, has an anti-English feeling been constantly quickened into active life, and been widely diffused throughout America; until now, not only does it permeate the whole Irish mass, but it is cherished as fondly and fiercely in the log cabin of the prairie or the forest as it is in the midst of the bustle and movement of the city.

I have met in many parts of the Union grave, quiet men of business—Irishmen who, though holding their opinions with the resolute firmness common to their temperament and tone of thought, rarely take part in public matters, and yet are interested in what is passing around them, especially in whatever concerns the honour of their race and country. From men of this class I heard the most strongly expressed opposition to the Fenian movement, and occasionally the bitterest contempt of its leaders. Jealous of the reputation of their countrymen, and, like all men of high spirit, peculiarly sensitive to ridicule, they were ashamed of the miserable squabbles and dissensions so common among the various branches or sections into which the Irish organisation is, or was then, divided, and they experienced the keenest humiliation as some new disaster rendered the previous boasting more glaring, or more painfully absurd. Yet amongst these grave, quiet men of business—these men of model lives—these men in whose personal integrity any bank in the country would place unlimited trust; amongst these men, England has enemies, not friends. They are opposed to Fenianism, not because it menaces England, but because it compromises Ireland.

So much alike do these men think and express themselves, though perhaps a thousand miles apart, that one would be inclined to suppose them in constant communication and intercourse with each other. Not to say in substance, but almost literally, this is the manner in which I have heard a number of these grave, quiet, steady business men refer to the Fenian movement: 'I strongly object to this Fenian organisation, for many reasons. In the first place, it keeps up a distinct nationality in the midst of the American population, and it is our interest to be merged in this nation as quickly as may be. In the second place, I have no confidence in the men at its head; how can I? Which of them am I to believe? If I believe one, I can't the other. Then what they propose is absurd. They talk nonsense about going to war with England, and England at peace with the world; and every additional disaster only rivets Ireland's chains more strongly. If, indeed, this country were at war with England, that would be quite another thing; and, after all, of what good would that be for Ireland?—would it better her condition?—would it be worth the risk? At any rate, until such an emergency should arise, it is a vexatious thing to see the hard-earned money of our people going to keep up a mischievous delusion. But at the same time, I must say this for myself, if I could see my way clearly—if I thought that a fair chance offered of serving Ireland, and making her happy, I would willingly sacrifice half what I have in the world in the attempt. The opportunity may come, in God's good time; but it has not come yet, and even if it did, the men at the head are not the men to do the work.'

There are others—and they are to be met with in every State of the Union—who are of the O'Connell school; in fact, they are as much of the 'moral force' and 'not a single drop of blood' policy now, as if they were still subscribers to Conciliation Hall, wore the Repeal button, and exhibited a card of membership over the mantel-shelf. They prefer the open ways of the constitution to secret oaths and midnight drillings; and when they read in the Irish news the miserable record of a new failure, they exclaim—'Oh, if these people would only follow O'Connell's advice! He carried Emancipation without the loss of a life, or the spilling of a drop of blood.' And yet these 'moral-force' men are not to be implicitly trusted for consistency: if they, too, 'saw their way,' and matters really came to a crisis, they might be found contributing their $10,000, or their $20,000, or their $50,000 to send a ship to sea with the green flag flying at her peak.

If it be asked, is this anti-British feeling likely to die out? Considering that it has so long existed, and that it is more intense, as well as more active at this day than at any time during the last quarter of a century, it is rather difficult to suppose it would, or will. Emigration is adding yearly, monthly, weekly to its strength. Few who land at Castle Garden that are not prepared by previous sympathy to join or to support whatever anti-British organisation may exist; nor are they long in America before they catch the strong contagion of its bitter hostility—assuming they have not already felt it at home. Every batch of 500 or 1000, every new 50,000, or 100,000, while adding to the Irish population—the Irish Nation—at the American side of the Atlantic, strengthens the Irish element, and deepens and intensifies the anti-English feeling. It may subside—so may the sea; but, like the sea, the first breath will set it again in motion, while a storm would lash it into fury. Thus it is with that vast, deep-lying, all-pervading sentiment which exists in the Irish heart—which is cherished as something holy (and in its unselfish aspirations there is nothing mean or ignoble)—which is fed by tradition, nourished by history, kept alive by instances of legal wrong or sanctioned oppression, stimulated by the musical rhythm and stirring verse of the ballad, roused into a blaze by appeals that flush the cheek and kindle the fire of the eye. It may subside; but it is difficult to think how, without some counteracting cause, it can die out.

The thorough-going Fenians—whether leaders, orators, or rank and file—would, if anything, prefer that the admitted causes of Irish discontent should not be removed; for they naturally argue—'If our hopes of regenerating Ireland be based upon revolution, it is better for our purpose that the various causes and sources of discontent and disaffection should be allowed to exist, and by their prolonged existence irritate and gall the public mind more and more, and thus keep the people in a condition most favourable to revolutionary teaching. Let the sources of discontent be dried up, the causes of anger and irritation be removed, and what can be hoped for then?' If half a dozen new grievances could be improvised to-morrow, their announcement would be hailed with gladness by those who desire to keep alive the Fenian organisation and impart a more vengeful spirit to the feeling against England. A grievance redressed is a weapon broken.

I remember the look of genuine annoyance with which a high-pressure Fenian, who introduced himself to me in a Northern State, received information on a subject having reference to Irish trade and manufactures. He desired to learn—for an oration, as I afterwards understood,—what were the special restrictions which the jealousy of England still imposed on the industry and trade of Ireland. He was filled with the memory of the 'discouragement' of the Irish woollens by that same WILLIAM respecting whose memory so much nonsense is uttered on certain anniversaries; and he glowed as he thought of the indignant oratory of the Irish House of Commons. But he knew little—indeed, he did not desire to know it—of the actual state of things at the present hour; and when I assured him that, so far as the law stood, the merchants, manufacturers, and business men of Ireland were on a complete equality with their brethren in England, he could scarcely bring himself to believe what I said. He was literally disgusted. If he could only have told his eager audience that, at the moment he stood on that platform, Queen Victoria was imitating the example of 'the glorious, pious, and immortal William of Orange,' and 'discouraging' the linen trade of Ireland, as her predecessor had discouraged the woollen trade, what a stroke for the orator! And if he could have added, that the burning words of Grattan had been in vain, and the labelled canon of College Green without their significance, and that the jealousy of the Saxon monopolist was as strong in the Senate of England that day as when a monarch basely listened to the selfish churls who were afraid of Irish competition, he would have convinced his audience that revolution was the only remedy for such oppression. He cherished the belief, that the injustice had only grown more venerable; and I almost sympathised with his distress as I rudely demolished the raw material of his glowing eloquence. Would to Heaven that apathy and folly, timidity and prejudice, had not left so many real grievances still unredressed!

The powerful Public Press of America is favourable, on the whole, to what may be termed 'the Irish cause,' as distinct from any special organisation or movement in its ostensible interest. There are very few journals in the United States that do not either broadly assert or unreservedly admit that Ireland is badly governed—that she is the Poland of England. Some journals vehemently oppose the Fenian movement, and denounce its leaders and their objects in the most unmeasured terms; but the same journals treat the Irish question with sympathy and respect.

The fact is, there are not many journals in the United States which are not, to a certain extent, under the control or influence of Irishmen, or the sons of Irishmen. They are edited, or part edited, or sub-edited, or reported for, by men of Irish birth or blood; and with the birth and the blood come sympathies for the old country, and an unfriendly feeling towards 'her hereditary oppressor.' Then there are papers exclusively Irish in their character, such as the *Boston Pilot*, which I heard described as the *Vade Mecum* of the Irish emigrant—the *Irish American*, or the *Monitor*, a well-written paper in San Francisco; and now John Mitchell is bringing the influence of thorough sincerity, the weight of personal sacrifice, and perhaps one of the ablest pens in America to the anti-British cause: then there are, in almost every direction, journals of various shades of opinion as to policy, but in feeling and principle thoroughly Irish. So that, although there may be decided difference of opinion as to the mode, or the means, or the opportunity of serving Ireland, and a still more strongly marked difference of opinion as to a special organisation, and more so as to its leaders, there is scarcely any difference of opinion as to the existence of Irish wrong, and the justice of the Irish cause. Thus the Public Opinion of the country affords its sanction to the convictions of the Irish in America, and a moral if not an active support to efforts unfriendly and even hostile to England.

The events of the late war have not added, either in the North or in the South, to partisans of England, or to her defenders in the Press. The North blames her for having gone too far in recognition of the South—the South is indignant with her for not having gone farther; and that terrible 'Alabama' has caused many a man in the North to grind his teeth with rage, and fiercely pray fur the opportunity of retaliation. So, altogether independent of whatever sympathy there may be amongst the 'full-blooded' Americans of the Northern States in favour of the Irish cause, the support or sanction, whatever it may be, which the Fenian movement receives from those unconnected with Ireland by birth or blood, is in no small degree the result of the depredations of that famous cruiser. It may be also remarked, that the Irish at both sides of the line won the respect and earned the gratitude of every generous-minded man of Federacy or Confederacy by their dauntless valour and unlimited self-devotion. The Irish have purchased by their blood a claim to the attention of America; and America listens with sympathy to the pleadings of her adopted children, who have made her interests, her honour, and her glory, theirs.

The Irish element being constantly on the increase, it must, as a matter of inevitable necessity, become more influential, more powerful, more to be conciliated and consulted—to be used, or to be abused; and it need scarcely be said, for it is patent and notorious, that there are those who will use and who will abuse it. There is no country in the world in which elections are so frequent as the United States; and the humblest citizen being in possession of the franchise, there are thus afforded almost innumerable opportunities of appealing to the prejudices or pandering to the passions of those in whom is reposed the sovereign power of election, even of raising the successful soldier or the ambitious statesman—nay, the rail-splitter or the journeyman tailor—to the loftiest dignity within the limits of the constitution. Thus we hear of Senators, and members of Congress, and Secretaries of State, and candidates for the Presidency, or even holders of that office, delivering addresses, proposing resolutions, or expressing sentiments favourable to Irish nationality, and tinged with a more or less decided anti-British spirit. Those who thus speak or act may be honest in intention, may really desire to assist Ireland, may believe in the justice of her cause and in the probability of her success; or they may not care a rush about the country of which they so eloquently declaim, and may regard the whole thing as so much moonshine, only useful for the purposes of political capital; but that the speeches are delivered, the resolutions proposed, and the sentiments expressed, is known to the world.

It may become a question—to what lengths will these declarations go?—to what point will these professions of sympathy reach?—how far will these enthusiastic friends of Ireland advance?—or at what line will they halt? Whether they advance, or whether they stop short, the mischief is done in either case—the weight of their name and influence is given in sanction of a sentiment which, so far as the Irish are regarded, is honestly and sincerely entertained. The occasion may arise, sooner or later, when difficulties would spring up between the two great nations at either side of the Atlantic, and these occasions may sorely perplex the men who thus deliberately play with fire; but if they do arise, one thing at least is certain,—the Irish vote will not be cast into the balance on the side of peace, In whatever party England may possibly find a friend, or a peace-maker, it will not be among those who long impatiently for the chance of another Fontenoy.

A strange notion—indeed, downright delusion—exists in the Irish-American mind as to the power of England. One would suppose, from listening to one of her contemners, that England's day was gone—that she was worn out and effete, that the British Lion was fangless, as harmless as a performing poodle, as innocuous as a stuffed specimen in a travelling show. You may tell the scoffer, of her revenue of more than $350,000,000 in gold, and how her people every year ungrudgingly expend $130,000,000 in gold on her army and her fleet; but you are pooh-poohed, and answered, that her day is past, and that she will go to pieces at the first shock. 'Her 100,000, or 150,000 soldiers, scattered over the world; what are they? We had more than a million in arms at the close of the war, besides what the South had. What is she, then, to this great country? We'—the speaker is an Irishman of less than thirty years' standing—'we whipped her in 1776, and we whipped her in 1812, and we'd whip her again; and I wish to God we had the chance to-day before to-morrow —that's all.'

The same belief in the power of America and the decay of England is as strongly entertained by the civilian as by the soldier, by the female contributor to the funds of the local 'circle,' as by the most enthusiastic of its members.

The announcements made through the cable, of the abortive risings in February and March of this year, thrilled the Fenian heart with more of hope than anxiety: they were read through rose-tinted glasses, and translated through the imagination. Not until the very last moment would the admission be made that the whole thing was an utter failure; and even then, there were many who would not, or who could not, regard it as a delusion. I have before me at this moment the calm steady gaze, replete with confidence and enthusiasm, of the Irishman who supplied me with the morning papers, as his first words of salutation were—'Glorious news to-day, sir! The country is up!' I asked, 'What news? what country?' 'Ireland, to be sure.

She's up, sir, thank God!' When I read the telegram, I instinctively exclaimed—'Sad news, indeed—miserable, miserable news.' 'You call it sad and miserable!—I call it glorious.' I told him he would not call it glorious, if he knew the state of things as well as I did; but he regarded me with a look of respectful disdain. He would believe nothing against his hopes. And when, at last, facts were too powerful, even for his seven-fold credulity, he was still unconvinced. It was a mischance, a momentary check, even a blunder; but it would be all right soon; the next time the thing would be done better. And he was only a type of a class—who give, and give largely, of their hard earnings, to sustain a cause on which they have set their heart—a class whom no reverse can discourage, no disaster dismay, no treachery alienate or disgust. This faith is the strength of the organisation—this generous self-sacrifice its unfailing resource. It is idle to say the money is 'extorted,'—*it is freely and gladly given*, with the conviction of its being a holy tribute, offered on the altar of country. The working man takes it perhaps more often from his family than from his pleasures; but he still gives it as a duty as well as a gratification. The female 'help' will deliberately lay down her half-dollar a month, or whole dollar a month, as her fixed contribution to the Fenian funds; and should some sudden emergency arise—some occasion for still greater sacrifice—she will pour her hoarded dollars into her country's exchequer, reserving, it may be, only so much as she intends to send to her parents at home. There is a kind of desperate hopefulness in their faith: 'It may not be this time—perhaps not; but something will be sure to turn up, and that will give us the opportunity we want.'

The something that is sure to turn up is, of course, a war with England—an event which would be hailed with a shout of delight by the Irish in America. Imagination could not conceive the rapture, the frenzy, with which, from every side, the Irish would rush to that war. From the remotest State, from the shores of the Pacific, from the Southernmost limits of Florida, from the heart of the country, from the Far West, from the clearing of the forest, from the home on the prairie—from the mine, the factory, the work-shop—from the river, and from the sea—they would flock to the upraised banners, equally loved and equally sacred—the green flag of Erin, and the Stars and Stripes of the Great Republic. As it were with a bound, and a shriek of exultation, the Irish would rush to meet their enemy—to fight out, on land and ocean, the feud that has survived through centuries—to revenge, if so they could, the wrongs inflicted by monarchs and soldiers and statesmen, by confiscations and by massacres, by penal laws and evil policy. Nay, I solemnly believe they would not desire a greater boon of America than that the fighting should be left entirely to themselves; and never did martyrs more joyfully approach the stake, in which they beheld the gate of Paradise, than would these Irish exiles and their descendants march to battle in a cause that gratified the twin passions of their souls—love and hate. And were the American Government so forgetful of international obligation as to close their eyes to what might be going on, and allow a fortnight, or a month, to pass without any active interference; and were their unwillingness to act a matter thoroughly understood,—in such a case, the frontiers of Canada would be passed with a rush—and then!—why, God knows what then. A rupture with England—to cease when? Is it after a long and terrible or sharp and wicked contest, which would end with the realisation of the American idea of the natural boundaries of the United States at the other side of St. Lawrence and the Lakes, and from Labrador to the Pacific? The future is in the hands of Providence.

Deplorable, indeed, would a deadly struggle be between the two great nations, speaking the same language, inheritors of a common literature, linked together by ties of interest as of blood—deplorable to the dearest interests of humanity and civilisation that such a conflict should occur; that the commerce of each country should be crippled on the high seas, that the sea-board of both should be circled with fire and sword—perhaps still more deplorable to the country which inspires such passionate attachment, and is the cause of such determined hate. Each could and would inflict unspeakable injury on the other; but were a balance of probable evil to be struck, it would be, manifestly must be, on the side of England. This may excite the incredulity or the indignation of the English reader; but there are geographical reasons why it should be so. Assuming the over-sanguine view of the case, and supposing that the title 'United Kingdom' fittingly represented the relations which, in case of war with America, would exist between Great Britain and Ireland, what, after all, is this United Kingdom? A cluster of islands, inhabited, no doubt, by a brave, hardy, high-spirited, energetic, adventurous people, whose greatness rests mainly on their industry, their enterprise, and their skill in the arts of peace,— but not so large in extent as an average State of the Union, which is now typified by the six-and-thirty stars on the banner of the Republic.

These islands are densely populated; but it may be questioned if the same population, which is a source of wealth in peace, when producing at profit for the consumption of the world, would be equally a source of wealth in the time of war, when hostile cruisers infested the seas, and made the path of commerce one of multiplied risk. England cannot feed herself, though her fields are fruitful, and she carries the science of agriculture to a more successful application than any country of Europe: she must depend on foreign sources for her supplies—at least, to supplement her own production. Check and embarrass, not to say cut off, her necessary supply from other countries, and up goes the price of the poor man's loaf to a famine standard! Even high wages would scarcely meet the enhanced price of human food consequent upon a conflict with a maritime nation. But where would the high wages come from, and by whom would they be received? Free and unfettered commerce, which means a safe and unrestricted highway, by land or by sea, is the very life of trade; but only render it necessary for the timid merchantman to cluster round the armed vessel, and seek the protection of her guns, and adieu to free and unfettered commerce, for a safe and uninterrupted highway no longer exists. Why produce calicoes, and linens, and woollens, and laces, and silks, and hardware, if you cannot depend on their reaching your customers in safety?—and if production ceases to be profitable, what is to become of the tens of thousands, the myriads, who now labour in cheerfulness, because their country enjoys the priceless blessings of peace?

The population of Lancashire may have had some idea—a faint idea at best—of the horrors of a universal paralysis of trade; a faint idea, because the country, being generally prosperous, notwithstanding the Cotton Famine caused by the Civil War in America, was able to come, and did promptly come, to their rescue. But were English customers to be reached only by blockade-runners, or by the avoidance of hostile cruisers and daring privateers, or under the protection of iron-clads and monitors, then would bitter poverty and hard privation be brought to the homes of the very workers who, being fully employed in 1862 and 1863, were able to extend the hand of fraternal assistance to the 500,000 sufferers from the failure of a single branch of our multiform national industry. Dear food, and scant wages!—humanly speaking, the most terrible calamities that can befall the working-man, his family, and his home. Those who forged cannon, manufactured rifles, and supplied munitions of war, would flourish; but, with war taxation, and war prices, and war food, and war panic, of what value would be our public securities? Then, suppose the war at an end, providentially in a year, probably in two, how many hundred millions would it have added to the National Debt, which now devours more than one-third of the entire revenue of the State?

And what Irishman can think, than without a shudder of horror, of what his country would have to go through during that tremendous crisis! The pent-up passions of centuries let loose in one wild frenzied outburst—vengeance, long brooded over, stimulated rather than quenched in blood—the hills, and plains, and valleys of that hapless land the theatre of a desperate war, the battle-field not alone of contending armies, but of conflicting races! It requires the insensibility of the Stoic to contemplate the multiplied and complicated horrors which a war with America would entail on Ireland. Turning our eyes from the awful spectacle which the imagination too readily conjures up, let us rather glance across the ocean, and see why the balance would, of necessity, be in favour of the Great Republic.

An enemy might cripple the commerce of the United States, might possibly be able to blockade a few of her harbours, might probably succeed in burning a dockyard, or setting a portion of a maritime city in a blaze; though the bombardment of Charleston does not offer a very hopeful precedent to a foreign foe. But what impression could any English army—any possible army that England, not to say could spare, but could raise—make upon the United States? CURRAN'S image of the child vainly trying to grasp the globe with its tiny hand, affords a not inapt idea of the practical absurdity of an armed invasion of the gigantic territory of the Union by even the mightiest of the military powers of Europe; and England is not that. No foreign nation could reach the heart of

America. The heart of America exists in her natural resources, in her power to feed herself—to sustain her people without the aid of foreign assistance; and her plains, rich with golden grain, lie far away from the reach of charging squadrons and the sound of hostile cannon. War with a European Power would serve rather than injure the manufacturing industry of the United States, employ rather than disemploy her people. Perhaps the evil is, that America continues, even yet, to be too much dependent on the manufacturing industry of Europe for articles of convenience and utility, as well as luxury; and whatever would throw her more on her own resources, natural and created, would, in the long run, be for her benefit. With her mountains of iron, and her enormous regions of coal, with her varied climate, and her infinite natural productions, and the skill, ingenuity, knowledge, and inventive power of a population trained in all the arts of civilisation, and ministering to her wants—she can indeed contemplate without dismay the chances of a war waged against her by any foreign nation, however great, mighty, or formidable that nation may be.

Nor would a foreign war, great calamity as, under the most favourable circumstances, it would be, be altogether unpopular with numbers of the American people, including even the patriotic and the thoughtful; inasmuch as it would most effectually solve the Southern difficulty, settle in a moment the question of reconstruction on the broad basis of mutual amity and reconciliation, and unite under the one banner those who for four long years waged a bitter and relentless war, man against man, and State against State. He must form a strange notion of the relative condition of the two countries, who does not see that, however disastrously Ireland might and would be affected by a war between America and England, the chances would be against England and in favour of America—or, in other words, that England would suffer more and America less from such a contingency.

Assuming, then, that the feeling of the Irish in America against England may possibly or probably, sooner or later, lead to an embroilment, a rupture, war—how is England to reach, influence, or counteract these her eager, watchful, vengeful enemies? But through one channel—*Ireland*. The Irish in America are entirely beyond the reach of England; she can in no possible way control or check the manifestation of their feelings towards her. Nor indeed is it within the power of the Government of the United States to do so, even were it so inclined—which is more than doubtful. By laws and police—physical power, if you will—you may suppress a visible and tangible organisation; but neither by penalty nor punishment, prosecution nor persecution, can you reach a sentiment. It is impervious to lead or steel, and bonds cannot bind it. You must encounter it with a power similar to its own, equally strong, and equally unassailable by mere material force. And the profound belief, which lies at the very root of this hostility, and gives life to every anti-British organisation—that Ireland is oppressed and impoverished by England; that England hates the Irish race, and would exterminate them, were it in her power,—this profound belief can only be conquered by the conviction of the justice and wisdom of England, as exhibited not only in her government and in her legislation, but in the prosperity and contentment of Ireland.

Let Ireland be dealt with in the same spirit, liberal and confiding, with which England has dealt with her colonies—respecting the rights of conscience through the most complete religious equality, and the utmost freedom of education. Let her legislate for a country almost wholly agricultural, and which, from many causes, natural as well as the growth of circumstances, stands in relation to other portions of the United Kingdom in an entirely exceptional position, in somewhat the same spirit which has characterised her policy in reference to the tenure of land in Lower Canada, where she sanctioned the abolition of the Seignorial Rights; in Prince Edward's Island, where, while suppressing an illegal association, the representative of the British Crown proclaimed the wisdom of converting tenure by lease into tenure by freehold, and the determination of the local government to effect that change by the purchase of large estates, principally belonging to absentees, and selling them at low terms to existing occupiers and new settlers; or in India, by affording security of tenure—that most potent of all incentives to human industry—to a race who had previously been trampled upon and oppressed. Let a generous, kindly, and sympathetic spirit breathe in the language of her statesmen and her orators, and mark the writings of her journalists.

Let there be an end, not to say of abuse or denunciation, but of that tone of offensive superiority and still more offensive toleration and condescension which too often characterises British references to Ireland and things Irish. Let it be the honest, earnest desire of the English people to lift Ireland up to their own level of prosperity and contentment; and obliterate, by generous consideration for the wants of her people, the bitter memories and lurking hate which the wrongs of centuries have left in the Irish heart, and which the apathy or neglect of recent times has taken little trouble to recognise. Let statesmen and party-leaders regard this ever present and still unsettled 'Irish Question' as one of the gravest and most solemn that could engage the attention and employ the energies of a wise and patriotic Government and Parliament. To a grander task or a more exalted duty than the solution of this difficulty—the removal of that great scandal which the state of Ireland, political and material, presents to the civilised world—neither minister nor representative could devote his brain and heart. And to a New Parliament, yet to spring, as it were, from the generous impulses of an enfranchised nation, may we hope for an energy and an enthusiasm equal to an emergency whose importance no language can fully represent, much less exaggerate. How this is to be done,—whether by and through the action of the Imperial Legislature, or by entrusting to Ireland a certain local power, by which she might relieve the Parliament of England of serious inconvenience and usefully manage much of her affairs,—it is for the wisdom of statesmen, inspired by a noble sense of duty, to determine. But faltering, and hesitation, and delay will not answer; neither will the old system of wilful blindness and wanton self-delusion suffice in the face of actual and in creasing danger.

The result, if successful, would be worth any effort or any trouble; for once allow the Irish in America to believe that a brighter day has dawned for their brethren in the old country, and that it is for their advantage rather to be linked in affection as in interest with Great Britain, than, by violent effort and tremendous sacrifices, desperately seek to effect a separation of the lesser from the greater country; and the feeling of bitter, rancorous, vengeful hate may gradually soften and die out, and eventually fade into oblivion like a dream of the past. But, on the other hand, let continued wails of distress waft their mournful accents across the ocean, stirring to its depths the heart of a passionate and impulsive race; and though Fenian leaders may quarrel or betray, and Fenian organisations may wither or collapse, there must be perpetual danger to the peace, the honour, if not the safety of England, from a power which it is impossible to ignore, and madness to despise,—

THE IRISH IN AMERICA

APPENDIX A

Bishop Lynch's Letter, Charleston, S. C., Feb. 23,1867.

DEAR SIR,—In compliance with my promise, I undertake to give you a brief statement of what an emigrant may look for who comes to the Southern States, and especially to South Carolina, with the intention of engaging in agriculture.

This State may be divided into several belts, parallel to the sea-coast, each one of which has its peculiarities. The first belt, next to the ocean, is that of the Sea Islands, producing the finest quality of cotton, and, of course, vegetables in abundance. In this belt the heat is great. Frost in winter is almost unknown. Except immediately on the sea-coast, a white man finds himself liable to fever. Lands can be purchased in many places at two pounds sterling an acre; perhaps for less.

A second belt next to this one, is the rice-field belt. It is intersected by a large number of streams, whose waters, though fresh, feel the influence of the tides, and rise high enough to overflow vast bodies of low lands on either side. These lands are devoted to the culture of rice, for which much irrigation is required. Hence, on the whole, this belt is very unhealthy, being subject to malarial fevers.

Both of those belts are, and will, I think, for a long time, be chiefly occupied by negroes, who are exempt from the fevers to which the white man is liable.

A third belt, broader than both of the preceding ones, stretches across the State. The soil is good, but the ground lies level, and is not drained. Hence, at times, the crop is lost by too much water, at other times withers for want of rain; and on the whole, the region is sickly. Were it thoroughly and systematically drained, which, perhaps could only be done under government auspices, it would be the garden of the South.

Here lands may be readily bought for from four to ten shillings an acre.

Another belt follows, of equal width. The land is more rolling, the soil equally sandy, and with less lime. It is considered poor. But when cultivated with ordinary skill, and manures are freely used, it will produce abundant crops of cotton, of Indian corn, of potatoes, and of all root crops and vegetables. It is eminently healthy, and I have seen cases where intelligent and skilful labour reaped a crop of cotton worth ten pounds sterling per acre.

A single man may cultivate four or five acres in cotton; three or four in Indian corn, and half an acre for a kitchen garden. The Americans know little of the use of manures, and much prefer cultivating lands that need none, until they become worn out, when they are left to grow up again in a forest; and other fresh lands are cleared and cultivated.

The lands of this fourth belt vary somewhat in character, in different parts of the State, and vary in prices. But much of it can be bought at from two to ten shillings per acre.

A fifth belt comprises lands that are more hilly and rolling than the preceding, and are nearly all clay lands. They were occupied by a farming population many years ago, and having been long cultivated with little or no manure, and often in a very rude manner, they have lost something of their original fertility. Still the settlers look on them as more productive than the lands I have last spoken of; and doubtless they are so in their hands. There are some portions of them very fertile: and these, of course, are held at high prices. But at present, lands in this belt may be bought at from fifteen to twenty-five shillings an acre.

Beyond this belt, and in the north-west part of the State, comes the mountainous district; which, in soil, is much like mountainous districts of any other country. Meadows and table lands are very rich, yielding excellent crops of Indian corn, of wheat, and other cereals; and the whole country is admirably adapted for grazing. I am not able to say what is the average price of land in this belt. Immigrants would, I think, do better settling on the fourth or fifth belts, where land can easily be procured at the prices indicated, payable on time, after a reasonable credit; and in situations perfectly healthy, and where there is always a demand for agricultural labourers, and a ready access to market for the sale of the crop.

An immigrant coming to this State finds an entirely different climate from that which he has left. In either of the three first belts he will be liable, unless extremely careful not to expose himself, to attacks of fever in autumn; though, even in these belts, some comparatively elevated spots are found which are perfectly healthy.

In the fourth belt there are places near swamps which are likewise unhealthy; and it is to the malaria arising from swamps, and not to the heat of the season, that the fevers are to be attributed. The greater portion of the State is quite healthy; and the heat is by no means so great as to prevent men labouring even twice as long as their crops require. In point of fact, the crop is secure by the labour done during our mild winters, and in spring before the heats of summer set in; and the ordinary crops, if well worked in time, require only a slight attention after the middle of June. I have no doubt that a farmer having one or two sons to aid him, and able to command even a few pounds to start with, would, in a few years, find himself worth hundreds of pounds.

Steps are being taken to invite immigrants to the South, and to present to them at the North and in Ireland the special advantages of the South. Now that negro slavery has been abolished, the negroes are gradually retiring to the sea-coast. The lands in the interior and upper belts, which I have recommended, are being thrown into market, and will be occupied by a white population. It is desirable that the families who emigrate should settle in groups near each other. By so doing, they will secure to themselves a social companionship which they could scarcely have with the inhabitants of the country until several years' acquaintance. They could have a church and priest of their own, and Catholic schools for their children.

This invitation to emigrants from Ireland is but a repetition of what was done over a hundred years ago, when there was a large immigration of Irish Protestant farmers to South Carolina; and with them must have come many Catholics, who, in those days, when there was neither priest nor Catholicity in the country, soon lost the Faith. This Irish immigration almost took possession of the State. Irish family names abound in every rank and condition in life; and there are few men, natives of the State, in whose veins there does not run more or less of Irish blood.

South Carolina is, probably, the most Irish of any of the States of the Union.

While its inhabitants have always had the impetuous character of the Irish race, nowhere has there been a more earnest sympathy for the struggles of Irishmen at home; nowhere will the Irish immigrant be received with greater welcome, or be more generously supported in all his rights; and I do not know any part of the country where *industry and sobriety* would ensure to the immigrant who engages in agriculture an ample competence for himself and family within a briefer number of years.

I believe that all these points will be presented with due details to those who wish to leave Ireland to better their fortunes in America, by a special agent who may be sent out; and also that proper arrangements will likewise be provided for the passage of those who wish to emigrate from Ireland direct to South Carolina.

So far as the ministrations of religion to those who come are concerned, I have hopes that if they settle as I indicated, in groups, they will be fully provided for.

I have the honour to be, my dear Sir, with great respect,

Your obedient, humble servant,

P. N. LYNCH, D.D.,

Bishop of Charleston

J. F. MAGUIRE, Esq., M.P.

Cork, Ireland.

APPENDIX B

Information for Emigrants.
Department of the Interior General Land Office,
Washington, D. C. December 24, 1866.

SIR,—I have the honour to acknowledge the receipt of your letter of the 11th instant, enclosing one of 24th November (ultimo) addressed to you by G. M. Allender, of the Farmers' Club, Salisbury Square, London.

Your correspondent states, that a class of persons in England, consisting of small farmers, or sons of farmers, with small capital, desire to come to America, but are deterred for want of information; that a feeling prevails among this class, that all the best lands and positions are secured by speculators, and that it is only poor lands, badly situated, that can be obtained at the government price of $1.25 per acre—the following questions in this connection being presented:—

1st. In what States can good land, well situated, still be obtained at the price of $1.25 per acre?

I send herewith a map, showing what are called the 'Public Land States,' and territories of the United States, and in reply to this question, state, that such lands may be had east of the Mississippi river, in the upper and lower peninsula of Michigan, in Wisconsin, in the great States west of the Mississippi, of Minnesota, Iowa, Missouri, Kansas, and in Nebraska, and that on the Pacific slope, extensive bodies of public lands have been surveyed and are open to settlement in the States of California, Oregon, and in the territory of Washington. The great mineral bearing State Nevada, lying east of and contiguous to California, is open to actual settlement, and there the public surveys are in progress.

Returning east of the Mississippi, the whole public land surface there will be found surveyed and subdivided in tracts as small as forty acres each, which in eighty-acre tracts can be taken under the Homestead Law, in the States of Florida, Alabama, Mississippi, Louisiana, and Arkansas.

Then the territories of Dakota, Colorado, New Mexico, and Arizona, are open to settlement.

The territory of Idaho has just been organised into a land district, whilst Utah and Montana are yet to be subjected to that organisation.

2nd. Must lands so obtained be paid for immediately?

In order that lands may be placed in the class of those 'subject *to sale at private entry*,' they must have been first offered at public auction, and thereafter, if not disposed of at public sale, are liable at the time of application to be paid for, either in cash, or with military land scrip, or bounty land warrants at the rate of $1.25 per acre, for the number of acres represented on the face of a warrant or scrip.

The minimum price of offered lands is $1.25 per acre, unless that minimum shall have been doubled by reason of the construction of some public work, as an internal improvement such as railroads, and which materially increases the value of the lands in its vicinity; but even where there are United States reserved or $2.50 per acre sections, homestead entries, to the extent of eighty acres each, may be made by citizens or those who have declared their intentions to become such.

3rd. Would a certain adjoining district be reserved, say for a year or two, so that there might be time to call the attention of persons here to that special district?

It is not the policy of the government to withdraw lands once offered at public sale from entry, unless to subserve some important public interest, such as the building of lines of railroads, to connect centres of trade, or some other interest of like importance; nor indeed is it necessary to do so, as tracts varying from forty to one hundred and sixty acres, or even larger size, can be had in some of the land States or territories where the surveys have been extended, and offices are open for the sale of such lands.

In regard to the apprehension that all the best lands and positions had already been disposed of, it is proper to state that in the older settled land States of Ohio, Indiana, and Illinois, the public lands, generally, have been disposed of to actual settlers; but in other States hereinbefore mentioned, tracts to an immense extent of good land well situated may be obtained. In the States of Minnesota, Iowa, Wisconsin, Missouri, and Kansas, in the valley of the Mississippi river, in the State of Michigan, in the vicinity of the great lakes, in California and Oregon on the Pacific, and in the territories of Washington and Nebraska, *large bodies of good land, both prairie and timber, are now subject to sale at private entry at $1.25 per acre*; and in the five first-mentioned States, and in Nebraska, the soil and climate are held to be admirably adapted to the raising of such stock as is alluded to by your correspondent.

There are also good lands well situated in Arkansas, Mississippi, Alabama, Louisiana, and Florida; but in those States, the public lands are only subject to entry under the Homestead Act, approved June 21, 1866.

I am, with great respect,

Your obedient servant,

(Signed) JOS. S. WILSON,

Commissioner.

Hon. E. S. CHILTON,

Commissioner of Immigration,

Washington, D. C.

Department of the Interior General Land Office,

September 25, 1867.

SIR,—Agreeably to the request in your letter of the 17th, I enclose herewith a copy of the Homestead Law. I also send you a list of the local land offices in

Michigan, Wisconsin, Minnesota, Iowa, Missouri, Kansas, and Nebraska, and on application to either of these offices, you will receive all needed information relative to the entry of any lands subject to entry, under the Homestead Law, and situated in the district where the land office to which you apply is located.

Very respectfully,

JOS. SMESIN,

Commissioner.

MICHIGAN

Detroit, East Saginaw, Ionia, Marquette, Traverse City.

WISCONSIN.

Menasha Falls of St. Croix, Stevens' Point, La Crosse, Bayfield, Eau Claire.

MINNESOTA.

Taylor's Falls, St. Cloud, Winnebago City, St. Peter, Greenleaf, Du Luth.

IOWA.

Fort Des Moines, Council Bluffs, Fort Dodge, Sioux City.

MISSOURI.

Boonville, Ironton, Springfield.

KANSAS.

Topeka, Junction City, Humboldt.

ARKANSAS.

Little Rock, Washington, Clarksville.

NEBRASKA T.

Omaha City, Brownsville, Nebraska City, Dakota City.

An Act to secure Homesteads to Actual Settlers on the Public Domain.

Be it enacted by the Senate and House of Representatives of the United States of America in Congress assembled, That any person who is the head of a family, or who has arrived at the age of twenty-one years, and is a citizen of the United States, or who shall have filed his declaration of intention to become such, as required by the naturalization laws of the United States, and who has never borne arms against the United States Government or given aid and comfort to its enemies, shall, from and after the first January, eighteen hundred and sixty-three, be entitled to enter one quarter section or a less quantity of unappropriated public lands, upon which said person may have filed a pre-emption claim, or which may, at the time the application is made, be subject to pre-emption at one dollar and twenty-five cents, or less, per acre; or eighty acres or less of such unappropriated lands, at two dollars and fifty cents per acre, to be located in a body in conformity to the legal subdivisions of the public lands, and after the same shall have been surveyed: *Provided,* That any person owning and residing on land may, under the provisions of this act, enter other land lying contiguous to his or her said land, which shall not, with the land so already owned and occupied, exceed in the aggregate one hundred and sixty acres.

SEC. 2. *And be it further enacted*, That the person applying for the benefit of this act shall, upon application to the register of the land office in which he or she is about to make such entry, make affidavit before the said register or receiver that he or she is the head of a family, or is twenty-one or more years of age, or shall have performed service in the army or navy of the United States, and that he has never borne arms against the Government of the United States or given aid and comfort to its enemies, and that such application is made for his or her exclusive use and benefit, and that said entry is made for the purpose of actual settlement and cultivation, and not, either directly or indirectly, for the use or benefit of any other person or persons whomsoever; and upon filing the said affidavit with the register or receiver, and on payment of ten dollars, he or she shall thereupon be permitted to enter the quantity of land specified: *Provided however*, That no certificate shall be given or patent issued therefor until the expiration of five years from the date of such entry; and if, at the expira tion of such time, or at any other time within two years thereafter, the person make such entry—or if he be dead, his widow; or in case of her death, his heirs or devisee; or in case of a widow making such entry, her heirs or devisee, in case of her death—shall prove by two credible witnesses that he, she, or they have resided upon or cultivated the same for the term of five years immediately succeeding the time of filing the affidavit aforesaid, and shall make affidavit that no part of said land has been alienated, and that he has borne true allegiance to the Government of the United States; then, in such case, he, she, or they, if at any time a citizen of the United States, shall be entitled to a patent, as in other cases provided for by law: *And provided, further*, That in case of the death of both father and mother, leaving an infant child, or children under twenty-one years of age, the right and fee shall enure to the benefit of said infant child or children; and the executor, administrator or guardian may, at any time within two years after the death of the surviving parent, and in accordance with the laws of the State in which such children for the time being have their domicil, sell said land for the benefit of said infants, but for no other purpose; and the purchaser shall acquire the absolute title by the purchase, and be entitled to a patent from the United States, on payment of the office fees and sum of money herein specified.

SEC. 3. *And be it further enacted*, That the register of the land office shall note all such applications on the tract books and plats of his office, and keep a register of all such entries, and make return thereof to the General Land Office, together with the proof upon which they have been founded.

SEC. 4. *And be it further enacted*, That no lands acquired under the provisions of this act shall in any event become liable to the satisfaction of any debt or debts contracted prior to the issuing of the patent therefor.

SEC. 5. *And be it further enacted*, That if at any time after the filing of the affidavit, as required in the second section of this act, and before the expiration of the five years aforesaid, it shall be proven, after due notice to the settler, to the satisfaction of the register of the land office, that the person having filed such affidavit shall have actually changed his or her residence, or abandoned the said land for more than six months at any time, then and in that event the land so entered shall revert to the Government.

SEC. 6. *And be it further enacted,* That no individual shall be permitted to acquire title to more than one quarter section under the provisions of this act; and that the Commissioner of the General Land Office is hereby required to prepare and issue such rules and regulations, consistent with this act, as shall be necessary and proper to carry its provisions into effect; and that the registers and receivers of the several land offices shall be entitled to receive the same compensation for any lands entered under the provisions of this act that they are now entitled to receive when the same quantity of land is entered with money, one half to be paid by the person making the application at the time of so doing, and the other half on the issue of the certificate by the person to whom it may be issued; but this shall not be construed to enlarge the maximum of compensation now prescribed by law for any register or receiver: *Provided,* That nothing contained in this act shall be so construed as to impair or interfere in any manner whatever with existing pre-emption rights: *And provided, further,* That all persons who may have filed their applications for a pre-emption right prior to the passage of this act shall be entitled to all privileges of this act: Provided, further, That no person who has served, or may hereafter serve, for a period of not less than fourteen days in the army or navy of the United States, either regular or volunteer, under the laws thereof, during the existence of an actual war, domestic or foreign, shall be deprived of the benefits of this act on account of not having attained the age of twenty-one years.

SEC. 7. *And be it further enacted,* That the fifth section of the act entitled 'An act in addition to an act more effectually to provide for the punishment of certain crimes against the United States, and for other purposes,' approved the third of March, in the year eighteen hundred and fifty-seven, shall extend to all oaths, affirmations, and affidavits, required or authorised by this act.

SEC. 8. *And be it further enacted,* That nothing in this act shall be so construed as to prevent any person who has availed him or herself of the benefits of the first section of this act from paying the minimum price, or the price to which the same may have graduated, for the quantity of land so entered at any time before the expiration of the five years, and obtaining a patent therefor from the Government, as in other cases provided by law, on making proof of settlement and cultivation as provided by existing laws granting pre-emption rights.

Approved May 20, 1862.

APPENDIX C

It has been frequently said that the Irish in America were, as a rule, in favour of slavery. Were it said that they were, as a rule, against slavery, the statement would be much nearer to the truth. I never heard an Irishman in a Northern State say one word in its favour. Some with whom I spoke were enthusiastic approvers of its extinction at any cost or sacrifice, as purging the country of a great evil, if not a great sin; while others, less enthusiastic, or more reflecting, held that its gradual extinction would have been wiser, more politic, and not likely to produce the difficulties and embarrassments which sudden emancipation was but too certain to create; not alone because the Slave-owning States were unprepared for so sweeping a revolution, but that the slave himself was unsuited to the abrupt cessation of all restriction or control whatever. These Irishmen regretted the existence of slavery, and justly regarded it as a fatal legacy left by England to the people of America; but they were rather in favour of gradual, yet inevitable change, than of violent or reckless revolution. I repeat, I never heard an Irishman in a Northern State speak in favour of slavery as an institution.

Then as to Irishmen in the South; I must equally assert, that I never heard an Irishman in a Southern State, not to say approve of, but justify slavery. Southern Irishmen believed, perhaps more strongly than their countrymen in the North, that neither the circumstances of the country nor the character, capacity nor training of the negro was suited to sudden emancipation; but they at the same time expressed themselves as having always been in favour of gradual and prudent abolition—the final extinction of that which they felt to be a cause of grave social injury and national weakness, and likewise a fruitful source of political trouble, possibly ultimate convulsion. But these Southern Irishmen took their stand on the fundamental principle of State sovereignty, as guaranteed by the Constitution, and denied that Congress had any light whatever to interfere with the institutions of individual States. They held,—and in this they had the sympathy of a vast number of their countrymen in the North,—that the emancipation of the slave, especially regarding it in its present results, was hardly worth the torrents of generous blood shed in its accomplishment. Still, they are satisfied at seeing an end to a cause of weakness and contention between different portions of the Union, though they know the South has to pass through some further tribulation before things can settle down into perfect order and tranquillity.

This is the result of my information on this point, derived from unreserved communication with Irishmen at both sides of the line.

And as to the policy of the Catholic Church with respect to slavery, I cannot do better than subjoin the following interesting communication from an eminent ecclesiastic, who affords as much information upon the subject as I can venture to press into this note.

Bishop England wrote a series of letters on Domestic Slavery, in which he undertakes to show the position of the Catholic Church on that question. The 'abolitionist' party had then caused great excitement at the South. They were resisted on two grounds: first, because the interference of other States, or of Congress, in that question would have been subversive of the American system of government, the question being one of those reserved to the authority of each State, which on such a point was sovereign. To try interference with them from without their own States would have been an invasion of their rights, as much as if it had been done by the British Parliament. Second, because emancipation, even if desirable, should be conducted with precautions which the Abolitionists were unwilling to listen to.

Besides those who resisted him on these grounds, there were, of course, many who defended slavery as in itself a desirable condition of things, especially for the coloured race.

Bishop England did not belong to the latter class; and in a note to the last letter of the series alluded to he defines his position as follows. He was obliged to interrupt the course of letters he intended publishing, and on the 23rd of April 1840, he writes as follows to the editors of the 'United States Catholic Miscellany,' in which they were published:—

'Gentlemen,—My more pressing duties will not permit me for some weeks to continue the letters on the compatibility of domestic slavery with practical religion. I have been asked by many a question which I may as well answer at once, viz. Whether I am friendly to the existence or continuation of slavery? *I am not.* But I also see the impossibility of now abolishing it here. When it can and ought to be abolished, is a question for the legislature, and not for me.' (See his Works, vol. iii. p. 190.)

Anyone acquainted with the state of feeling on this subject in Charleston at the time, cannot but feel that a great amount of courage was necessary to say even that much.

On his return from Europe some time after, he informed one of his most intimate friends that he intended resuming the subject, and showing what were the *rights* of slaves, as Christians and as men, what were the *duties* of masters; and that he intended giving the slaveholders a lecture, such as they never had received before. In the published letters he was anxious to show them that the Catholic Church had never declared the holding of slaves to be in itself sinful; that the Encyclical Letter of Gregory XVI., which had given rise to the controversy, condemned the capture of free men, and taking them unjustly into slavery, as war had done on the coast of Africa, but did not affect domestic slavery under all circumstances. His intention was to show what rights the slave necessarily retained, which masters and legislatures were bound to respect and to protect; and having first cleared himself from the charge of abolitionism in its political meaning as then understood, he intended to be frank and full in this subject. It is to be regretted that sickness, and then death, prevented the carrying out of this idea. I have no doubt that he would have been a powerful advocate of the poor slave in his rights as to personal protection, and religious liberty, and in his family relations, reducing the master's claims merely to his labour, for which compensation was given in food, clothing, &c.; and even the system that denied him the power of disposing of them as he pleased, would have been shown to be fraught with many evils, and a change loudly called for as soon as circumstances would admit of it.

I would refer to two other facts, showing the position of the Catholic Church in the South with regard to slavery. One was a sermon preached, I think, in New Orleans, while the Southern Confederacy was at the moment of its highest prospect of success, by Bishop Verot of Savannah. He first undertook to prove that slavery was not essentially sinful, and he answered the objection made against it. But then he went on to show in what condition it could be tolerated amongst Christians. He showed what were the rights of slaves, and the obligations of masters, in a manner which would have deprived it of its chief horrors. This during the reign of the Confederacy!

During the same time Bishop M'Gill published a book at Richmond, in which he stated it as his opinion, that the calamities under which the country was suffering might be attributed to a chastisement of Heaven for the manner in which the slaves were left unprotected in their marriage relations.

APPENDIX D

It may be of some advantage to exhibit the importance of the foreign element to the American Republic, not alone in developing the general resources of the country, and assisting to occupy and populate, and thus make valuable, new territories; but to preserve from gradual decay, from annual wasting away, from eventual and absolute extinction, communities which were at one time hostile to the foreigner, and even haughtily impatient of his presence. This absurd hostility to the foreigner was more prevalent in the New England States than in any other portion of the Union; and in Massachusetts various 'isms' of the Native-American stamp, almost invariably opposed to the stranger, have had their origin. And yet it is beyond doubt that, only for the foreign element, or the infusion of life-blood into the failing system of this most prominent of these New England States, its population would have dwindled away, and practically would have given up the ghost! This, no doubt, is a very startling announcement, if true. But is it true? It is indisputable. There cannot be a doubt as to its truth.

The Secretary of the Board of State Charities, in his Third Annual Report, dated October 1866, makes use of, and incorporates with the first part of that Report, a document to which he attaches evident importance. It forms a portion of the Fourth Chapter, and is headed 'Inferences from Registration and Census Reports.' The paper in question is thus introduced:—

'In closing this part of my Report, I shall have occasion to avail myself of the studies of a member of this Board, formerly its Chairman, and now the Chairman of its Committee on Statistics. The patient investigations which Dr. Alien has been making for years in regard to the increase of population in Massachusetts have led him to some conclusions which to many appear novel and startling, while others recognise them as familiar to the course of their own thoughts. At my request, he has allowed me to cite from his manuscripts the following passages.'

Unfortunately there is not space remaining to do full justice to one of the most remarkable and suggestive papers ever presented to the American public; but a few extracts from it will be sufficient to show how essential to the progress—*nay, the very life*—of the New England States is their foreign, in other words, their *Irish* population:—

The increase in these ten years of those born in Massachusetts is 110,313, *but a considerable portion are the children of foreigners.* By referring to the table of those born in foreign lands, it will be seen that there was an increase of emigrants from Ireland in these ten years of 69,517. The number must have been considerably larger than this, as many counted foreign born in the Census of 1850 must have died between that date and 1860. The whole increase of foreign born from 1850 to 1860 was 99,205. The foreign element, next largest to the Irish, is 27,069 from British America, including persons of Canadian, French, English, Irish and Scotch extraction. Next in point of numbers are the English, German and Scotch. It should be observed that this second table gives only those born in a foreign land, and not the children of foreigners born in Massachusetts. These are included in the first table, among the 805,549 born within the State.

The remaining extracts, which will be found of very great interest, are now given, and may well stand without note or comment.

II.—*The Foreign Element in Massachusetts.*

But in order to understand correctly the increase and the changes in our population, the history and number of those of a foreign origin must be carefully noted. The rapid increase of this class, and the changes consequent upon its future growth, afford themes which deserve the most grave consideration.

The Census at different periods returns this element as follows:—1830, 9,620; 1840, 34,818; 1850, 164,448; and 1860, 260,114. Here within 30 years, commencing with less than 10,000, we have an increase, by immigration alone, to over 250,000. It should be observed, that this does not include the great number of children born in this State of foreign extraction. The first Registration Report that discriminated in the births as to parentage was that of 1850, returning 8,197 of this class, and 3,278 mixed or not stated. In 1860, the number had increased to 17,549, besides nearly 1,000 not stated. *In 1850, the foreign births were only one-half as many as the American, but they continued to gain every year afterwards upon the American till 1860, when they obtained a majority. This year will ever constitute an important era in the history of Massachusetts when the foreign element, composing only about one-third part of the population of the State, produced more children than the American. Since 1860 they have gained every year upon the American, till in 1865 their births numbered almost 1,000 more than the American.*

From 1850 to 1860, the Registration Reports make the foreign births 137,146, besides 18,598 not stated, a large portion of which undoubtedly was of foreign origin. Then the number of such births from 1830 to 1850 cannot be definitely stated, but, judging by the amount of foreign population at this period and its fruitfulness at other times, the number of births would certainly come up to 50,000 or more. Now what proportion of those of this character born from 1830 to 1860, might have been living when the Census of 1860 was taken, we cannot tell; all that can be determined upon the subject is only an approximation to the truth. It is estimated, where the mortality is largest, that only from two-fifths to one-half of all those born—including both the city and the country—live to reach adult life. After making allowance for this fact, and considering that by far the largest proportion of these births occurred in the years immediately preceding 1860, we think it perfectly safe to say that there must have been over 100,000 persons of this class included in the United States Census returned as native born in

Massachusetts, or, in other words, as American. This fact would change materially the Census report. It would take at least 100,000 from the American portion—970,000—and add 100,000 to the 260,000 reported as born in foreign countries. This result makes at that time *almost one-half of our population strictly of a foreign origin*! It is expressly stated, both in the United States and State Censuses, that the returns are made upon the nativities of the population. Judging by these facts and figures, it would seem *that the foreign population is actually much larger in this State than has generally been considered.*

III.—*Distribution and Employment of the Foreign Population.*

But this class of people do not all live in the cities. They are found scattered in almost every town and neighbourhood in the Commonwealth. The men came first to build railroads, to dig canals, cellars, and aid in laying the foundation of mills, dwellings and public buildings. Then came the women to act as servants and domestics in families, as well as to find useful employment in shops and mills. Then came parents, children and whole families. To such an extent have they increased by immigration and birth, that they now perform a very large portion of the domestic service in all our families; they constitute everywhere a majority of the hired labourers upon the farm; they are found extensively engaged in trade and mechanical pursuits, particularly in the shoe business, and compose by far the largest proportion of all the operatives in the mills.

Within a few years, they have become extensive owners of real estate. In the cities they have built or bought a very large number of small shops and cheap dwellings, and in the rural districts as well as in the farming towns throughout the State, they have purchased very extensively small lots of land, small places, and old farms partially run out; *and (what is significant) they pay for whatever real estate they buy, and are scarcely ever known to sell any.* In fact, it has come to such a pass, that they perform a very large proportion of the physical labour throughout the State, whether it be in the mill or in the shop, whether in the family or upon the farm. As far as muscular exercise is concerned, *they constitute 'the bone and sinew' of the land, and it would be very difficult, if not impossible, to dispense with their services.* Every year the Americans are becoming more and more dependent upon them for manual labour, both in-doors and out-of-doors. Should the foreign population continue to increase as they have in the past twenty or thirty years, and the American portion remain stationary to decrease, a question of no ordinary interest arises, What will be the state of society thirty or fifty years hence in this Commonwealth?

IV.—*Comparative Increase of Natives and Foreigners.*

From 1850 to 1866, the fifteen Registration Reports return 208,730 births of strictly foreign parentage, besides 22,376 not stated, a large portion of which must be foreign. All of these living when the Census is taken, would be considered, according to present usage, American; whereas they should be counted strictly under the foreign head. A careful analysis of the Census and Registration Reports presents the following facts:—

The increase of population in the State has been confined principally to cities and towns where manufacturing, mechanical and commercial business is carried on. In the purely agricultural districts, there has been very little increase of population. Railroads have had a powerful influence in changing the population of the State from the hills and country towns to the valleys and plains. Wherever water-power, or steam-power, has been introduced, or where trade and commerce has found advantages, there population has greatly increased. The eastern section of the State has increased far more than the middle or western districts. Population in manufacturing places has increased about five times more than in agricultural districts. It is found also, *wherever there has been much or a rapid increase of population, it has been made up largely of a foreign element.* Now if a line could be drawn exactly between the American and foreign population, as it respects this increase, it would throw much light upon the subject. According to the Census of 1860, it appears that *two counties*—Dukes and Nantucket—*had actually decreased in population.* There were eighty-six towns also which had *diminished in population* between 1850 and 1860. In a small part of these towns, this change is accounted for by the fact that some section of the place had, in the mean time, been set off to another town. *The places in the State that have increased the least, or declined in population, are found to be settled generally with American stock.*

A serious question here arises, Is there a natural increase in this class of the community? It is generally admitted that foreigners have a far greater number of children, for the same number of inhabitants, than the Americans. It is estimated by some physicians, that the same number of married persons of the former have, on an average, *three times as many children as an equal number of those of the latter.* This gives the foreign element great power of increase of population—derived not so much from emigration as from the births exceeding greatly the deaths.

******

In a report upon the comparative view of the population of Boston in 1849 and 1850, made to the city government, November 1851, Dr. Jesse Chickering, after a most careful analysis of the Births and Deaths in Boston, states that 'the most important fact derived from this view is the result that the whole increase of population arising from the excess of Births over Deaths for these two years has been among the foreign population.' Since 1850 we think it will be very difficult to prove that there has been any *natural* increase of population in Boston with the strictly American population.

Again, many towns in the State have been settled over two hundred years, and their history will include from six to eight generations. The records of several of these towns have been carefully examined with respect to the relative number of children in each generation. It was found that the families comprising the *first* generation had on an average between *eight and ten children*; the *next three generations* averaged between *seven and eight to each family*; the *fifth* generation about *five*, and the *sixth> less than three to each family*. What a change as to the size of the families since those olden times! Then large families were common,— now the exception; then it was rare to find married persons having only one, two or three children; *now it is very common*! Then it was regarded a calamity for a married couple to have no children—*now such calamities are found on every side of us—in fact, they are fashionable.*

It is the uniform testimony of physicians who have been extensively engaged in the practice of medicine, twenty, thirty, forty and fifty years in this State,—and who have the best possible means of understanding this whole subject,—*that there has been gradually a very great falling off in the number of children among American families.*

This decrease of children *is found to prevail in country towns and rural districts almost to the same extent as in the cities, which is contrary to the general impression.* In view of these facts, several questions naturally arise:—If the foreign population in Massachusetts continues to increase as it has, and the American portion remains stationary, or decreases, as the probabilities indicate, what will be the state of society here twenty-five, fifty or a hundred years hence ? How long will it be before the foreign portion will outnumber the American in our principal cities and towns, or constitute even a majority in the whole Commonwealth?

The cause why there should be such a difference in the number of children, between the American families now upon the stage, and those of the same stock, one, two and three generations ago, is a subject of grave inquiry. Again, why should there be such a difference in this respect, between American families and those of the English, German, Scotch and Irish of the present day? Is this difference owing to our higher civilisation or to a more artificial mode of life and the unwholesome state of society? *Or can it be attributed to a degeneracy in the physical condition and organisation of females, or a settled determination with the married to have no children or a very limited number?*

'Such,' says the Secretary, 'are the questions raised by Dr. Allen, and such are some of the facts which their investigation calls forth.'

With the questions raised by Dr. Allen in this Public Document, which Massachusetts has published among its State Papers, I do not attempt to deal; but I may respectfully suggest another,—namely, Does not Native-Americanism, or Know-Nothingism, or any similar 'ism,' appear intensely ridiculous and profoundly absurd, in the face of such facts as these?

APPENDIX E

BIOGRAPHICAL SKETCH OF MAJOR-GENERAL PATRICK RONAYNE CLEBURNE
(BY GENERAL W. T. HARDEE.)

The sketch is necessarily imperfect, from the want of official records. Most of these were lost or destroyed by the casualties attending the close of the late war; and those still in existence are difficult of access. Of Cleburne's early life little is known—the record of his service in the Southern armies belongs to the yet unwritten history of 'the lost cause.' In better days, when the passions and prejudices engendered by civil strife shall have disappeared, and history brings in a dispassionate verdict, the name of Cleburne will appear high in the lists of patriots and warriors. Until then, his best record is in the hearts of his adopted countrymen.

With brief exceptions Cleburne served under my immediate command during his military career. He succeeded first to the brigade, and then to the division which I had previously commanded; and it is to me a grateful recollection, that circumstances enabled me to further his advancement to those important trusts. From personal knowledge, therefore, gained in an intercourse and observation extending through a period of nearly four years, I can give you an outline sketch of Cleburne's character and services.

Patrick Ronayne Cleburne was an Irishman by birth, a Southerner by adoption and residence, a lawyer by profession; a soldier in the British army, by accident, in his youth; and a soldier in the Southern armies, from patriotism and conviction of duty, in his manhood. Upon coming to the United States he located at Helena, Arkansas, where he studied and practised law.

In that profession he had, previous to the great struggle, formed a co-partnership with General T. C. Hindman. His standing as a lawyer was high, as indicated by this association with a gentleman distinguished as an orator and advocate.

It was at this period of his life that, in the unorganised and turbulent condition of society, incident to a newly settled country, he established a reputation for courage and firmness, which was afterwards approved by a still more trying ordeal. In the commencement of the war for Southern independence, he enlisted as a private. He was subsequently made captain of his company, and shortly after was elected and commissioned colonel of his regiment. Thus, from one grade to another, he gradually rose to the high rank he held when he fell. It is but scant praise to say, there was no truer patriot, no more courageous soldier, nor, of his rank, more able commander, in the Southern armies; and it is not too much to add that his fall was a greater loss to the cause he espoused than that of any other Confederate leader, after Stonewall Jackson. In the camp of the army which Albert Sydney Johnston assembled at Bowling Green, Kentucky, in the autumn of 1861, Cleburne had an opportunity in the drill and organisation of the raw troops, of which that army was then composed, of proving his qualifications as a disciplinarian and commander. His natural abilities in this respect had probably been fostered by his early tuition in the British army; and upon his becoming a soldier a second time, were perfected by unremitting study and labour. These qualities secured his promotion to brigadier-general. In April, 1862, Albert Sydney Johnston concentrated his forces at Corinth, Mississippi, to attack General Grant, who had landed an army at Pittsburg, on the Tennessee river, which was now encamped near Shiloh Church, about three miles from the landing. The attack was made on the morning of the 6th of April. Cleburne's brigade was of my corps, which formed the front line of attack. The enemy were steadily driven for three miles through their encampments, past the rich spoils with which a luxurious soldiery had surrounded themselves, and over the heaps of their dead and dying, until the broken and demoralised masses sought the shelter of the river's banks, and the cover of their gunboats. Albert Sydney Johnston had fallen in action about 2 o'clock P.M. His successor in command, General Beauregard, deemed it best, late in the evening, to recall the pursuit. At the moment of recall, Cleburne was pressing on, within 400 yards of Pittsburg Landing, behind the cliffs of which cowered the masses of hopeless and helpless fugitives. That night the enemy were reinforced by the arrival of a fresh army under Buell; and, on the evening of the 7th, the Southern forces, after maintaining, through the day, the now unequal struggle, withdrew, unpursued, to Corinth. In this battle Cleburne's brigade sustained a heavier loss in killed and wounded than any other in the army.

At the initiation of General Bragg's Kentucky campaign, in the summer of 1862, Cleburne's brigade, with one other, was detached and united with Kirby Smith's column, which, starting from Knoxville, Tennessee, was to penetrate Kentucky through Cumberland Gap and form a junction with the main army under General Bragg, which moved from Chattanooga into Kentucky by a different rout. Kirby Smith's forces encountered opposition at Richmond, Kentucky, in September. There Cleburne directed the first day's fighting, and in his first handling of an independent command was mainly instrumental in winning a victory, which, in the number of prisoners and amount of stores captured, and in the utter dispersion and destruction of the opposing force, was one of the most complete of the war. For 'gallant and meritorious service' here, he received an official vote of thanks from the Congress of the Confederate States. In this action he received a singular wound. The missile, a minie rifle ball, entered the aperture of the mouth while his mouth was open, in the act of giving a command to the troops in action, without touching his lips, and passed out of the left cheek, carrying away in its course five lower teeth, without touching or injuring the bone. This wound did not prevent his taking part in the battle of Perryville on the 8th of October following, where he rejoined my command, and was again wounded while leading his brigade in a gallant charge.

An incident occurred in the march out of Kentucky, which will serve to illustrate Cleburne's indomitable will and energy. On the road selected for the passage of ordnance and supply trains of the army, was a very difficult hill, at which the trains unable to pass over it, or to go round it, came to a dead halt. The enemy were pressing the rear, the trains were immovable, and nothing seemed left but to destroy them, to prevent their falling into the hands of the enemy; orders had actually been given for their destruction when Cleburne, who was disabled and off duty on account of his wound, came up. He asked and was given unlimited authority in the premises. He at once stationed guards in the road, arrested every straggler and passing officer and soldier, collected a large force, organised fatigue parties, and literally lifted the trains over the hill. The trains thus preserved contained munitions and subsistence of the utmost value and necessity to the Confederates. It is by no means certain even that the army could have made its subsequent long march through a sterile and wasted country without them.

In December 1862, General Bragg concentrated his army at Murfreesboro, Tennessee, to oppose the Federal forces assembled at Nashville under Rosecranz. At this time, Major-general Buckner, then commanding the division of which Cleburne's brigade formed a part, was transferred to other service, and the President of the Confederate States, who was on a visit to the army at the time, promoted Cleburne to the vacant division. Rosecranz' advance upon Bragg brought on the battle of Murfreesboro, Dec. 31,1862. In the action of this day Cleburne's was one of the two divisions under my command, which attacked the light wing of the Federal army, under M'Cook. This wing was beaten and driven three miles, until its extreme right was doubled back upon the centre of the Federal army. During the day, Cleburne's division in single line of battle, without reinforcement, rest, or refreshment, encountered and drove before it five successive lines of battle, which the Federal commander-in-chief withdrew from his intact centre and left to reinforce his broken right. The general results of the day were not decisive in favour of the Southern arms; but this heightens the achievement of that portion of the army which was successful, and the merit of the officer whose skilful handling of his division contributed materially to that success.

From the battle of Murfreesboro to that of Chickamauga, in September 1863, military operations in the army with which Cleburne was connected were of a desultory and undecisive character. But outpost duty in close proximity to an enemy superior in numbers, afforded Cleburne occasion for the exercise of his high soldierly qualities of vigilance and activity. In the advance from Tullohoma to Wartrace, and the subsequent retirement of the army to Chattanooga, his division habitually formed the vanguard in advance and the rearguard in retreat. The battle of Chickamauga—an Indian name which signifies 'the river cf death'—

wrote the bloodiest page in the history of Western battles. General Bragg, reinforced by Longstreet's corps from Virginia, on the 19th and 20th of September engaged and, after an obstinate contest, defeated, Rosecranz' army, which, routed and demoralised, retreated within its line of works at Chattanooga. In this battle Cleburne's division bore its usual prominent part; a charge made by it, in the struggle for position in the adjustment of lines on the Saturday evening preceding the Sunday's final conflict, is described as especially magnificent and effective.

The Confederate forces soon after occupied Missionary Ridge, and partially invested Chattanooga, with the object of cutting off the supplies of the army within its lines. The attempt was but partially successful. Meantime the Federal government despatched General Grant to succeed Rosecranz in command, and recalled Sherman's army from Mississippi to reinforce him. On the 24th of November, Grant, reinforced by Sherman, attacked Bragg, weakened by the detachment of Longstreet's corps, and carried the position of the Confederate left on Lookout Mountain. On the 25th a general attack was made upon the Confederate line. The right wing, under my command, consisted of four divisions—Cleburne's on the extreme right. The attacking force in this part of the field was commanded by General Sherman. The enemy made repeated and vigorous assaults, which were repelled with heavy loss to the assailants. Cleburne's position on the right was most insecure, from its liability to be turned. He maintained it with his accustomed ability, and upon the repulse of the last assault, directed in person a counter charge, which effected the capture of a large number of prisoners and several stands of colours. The assailants gave up the contest and withdrew from our front. But while the cheers of victory raised on the right were extending down the line, the left of the army had been carried by assault, and the day was lost. All that now remained to the victorious right was to cover the retreat of the army. This it did successfully. It the right, instead of the left of the army, had been carried, it would have given the enemy possession of the only line of retreat, and no organised body of the Confederate army could have escaped. In the gloom of night-fall, Cleburne's division, the last to retire, sadly withdrew from the ground it had held so gallantly, and brought up the rear of the retiring army.

The enemy next day organised a vigorous pursuit; and on the morning of the second day, its advance, Hooker's corps, came up with Cleburne at Ringgold Gap. The enemy moved to attack what they supposed a demoralised force with great confidence. Cleburne had made skilful dispositions to receive the attack, and repulsed it with such serious loss that pursuit was abandoned, and the pursuing force returned to its lines. Here Cleburne again received the thanks of Congress for meritorious conduct.

The Southern army now went into winter quarters at Dalton, in North Georgia. Cleburne's division occupied an outpost at Tunnel Hill. He devoted the winter months to the discipline and instruction of his troops, and revived a previously-adopted system of daily recitations in tactics and the art of war. He himself heard the recitations of his brigade commanders, a quartette of lieutenants worthy their captain—the stately Granberry, as great of heart as of frame, a noble type of the Texan soldier—Govan, true and brave as he was courteous and gentle—Polk, young, handsome, dashing and fearless, and—Lowry, the parson soldier, who preached to his men in camp and fought with them in the field with equal earnestness and effect. These brigadiers heard the recitations of the regimental officers, and they in turn of the company officers. The thorough instruction thus secured, first applied on the drill ground, and then tested in the field, gave the troops great efficiency in action.

About this time the terms of enlistment of the three years' men began to expire. It was of critical importance to the Southern cause that these men should re-enlist. The greater part of Cleburne's division consisted of Arkansans and Texans, who were separated from their homes by the Mississippi river. This river, patroled by Federal gunboats, was an insuperable barrier to communication. Many of these men had not heard from their homes and wives and little ones for three years. To add to this, the occasional reports received from the trans-Mississippi were but repeated narratives of the waste and ravage of their homes by the Federal soldiery. No husband could know that his wife was not homeless—no father, that his children were not starving. Every instinct that appeals most powerfully and most sacredly to manhood, called upon these men to return to their homes as soon as they could do so honourably. Cleburne was a man of warm sympathies, and he felt profoundly the extent of the sacrifice his men were called upon to make; but with Roman virtue he get high above all other earthly considerations the achievement of Southern independence. He adapted himself to the peculiar conditions of a volunteer soldiery, and laying aside the commander, he appealed to his men, as a man and a comrade, to give up everything else and stand by the cause and the country. He succeeded in inspiring them with his own high purpose and exalted patriotism, and the result was the early and unanimous re-enlistment of his division. The Confederate Congress passed later a Conscription Act that retained the three years' men in service; but those whose terms of enlistment expired in the interim would meantime have returned to their homes, and the moral effect of voluntary re-enlistment would have been lost to the cause.

Cleburne fully comprehended the disproportion in the military resources of the North and South, and was the first to point out the only means left the South to recruit her exhausted numbers. In January 1864, he advocated calling in the negro population to the aid of Southern arms. He maintained that negroes accustomed to obedience from youth, would, under the officering of their masters, make even better soldiers for the South than they had been proven to make under different principles of organisation for the North. He insisted that it was the duty of the Southern people to waive considerations of property and prejudices of caste, and bring to their aid this powerful auxiliary. He pointed out further that recruits could be obtained on the borders, who would otherwise fall into the hands of the Federal armies, and be converted into soldiers to swell the ranks of our enemies. His proposition met the disfavour of both government and people. A year later it was adopted by Congress, with the approval of the country, when it was too late.

The following extract of a note written about this time to a lady. a refugee from Tennessee, in reply to some expressions complimentary to himself, and to a hope expressed for the recovery of Tennessee, is markedly characteristic of the man:—

'To my noble division and not to myself belong the praises for the deeds of gallantry you mention. Whatever we have done, however, has been more than repaid by the generous appreciation of our countrymen. I assure you, I feel the same ardent longing to recover the magnificent forests and green valleys of middle Tennessee that you do; and I live in the hope that God will restore them to our arms. I cannot predict when the time will be, but I feel that it is certainly in the future. We may have to make still greater sacrifices—to use all the means that God has given us; but when once our people, or the great body of them, sincerely value independence *above every other earthly consideration*, then I will regard our success as an accomplished fact.

'Your friend,

'P. R. CLEBURNE.'

In a brief absence from Dalton, with one exception his only absence during his service, Cleburne formed an attachment as earnest and true as his own noble nature. The attachment was returned with the fervour and devotion of the daughters of the South. Much might be said of this episode—of its romantic beginning, and its tragic end; but the story of the loved and lost is too sacred to be unveiled to the public eye.

General Bragg had been relieved of the command of the Western army, at his own request, after the battle of Missionary Ridge; subsequently General J. E. Johnston was assigned to the command. To the Federal General Sherman was given the command of the armies assembled at Chattanooga for the invasion of Georgia. The campaign opened on the 7th of May. The history of its military operations, under the conduct of General Johnston, is the record of a struggle against largely superior forces, protracted through a period of seventy days, and extending over a hundred miles of territory. The campaign was characterised by brilliant partial engagements and continuous skirmishing, the aggregate results of which summed up into heavy battles. When the army reached Atalanta, notwithstanding the discouragements of constant fighting, frequent retreats, and loss of territory, it was with unimpaired organisation and *morale*.

In this campaign, Cleburne's division had two opportunities of winning special distinction. At New Hope Church, on the 27th of May. it formed the right of the army in two lines, the first entrenched. In the afternoon of that day the 4th corps of the Federal army advanced as if to pass its right. Cleburne promptly brought his two brigades of the second line into the first, extending it to face the Federal advance. This line received the enemy's attack, made in seven lines, on open ground, with no advantage on our side except a well-chosen position, and after an obstinate fight of an hour-and-a-half repulsed it. Cleburne's troops were not only greatly outnumbered, but were outnumbered by resolute soldiers. At the end of the combat about 700 Federal dead lay within thirty or forty feet of his line. During the action a Federal colour-bearer planted his colours within ten paces of Cleburne's line. He was instantly killed, a second who took his place shared his fate, so with the third and fourth; the fifth bore off the colours.

We read of little more effective fighting than that of Cheatham's and Cleburne's divisions in repelling an assault made upon them by Blair's corps of the Federal army, on the morning of the 27th of June, at Kennesaw. The conduct of the Federal troops on that occasion was as resolute as in the instance above. When they fell back, more than 300 dead bodies were counted within a few yards of Cleburne's entrenchment, some of them lying against it. His loss was two killed and nine wounded, certainly less than 1 to 100 of the enemy. On the 18th of July, Gen. Johnston was removed from the Western army, and Gen. Hood promoted to its command.

On the 21st, while the army was occupying a line encircling the northern front of Atalanta, Cleburne's division was detached to oppose an attempt of a corps of the enemy to turn the Confederate right, and penetrate to Atalanta at an undefended point. His troops, newly arrived at the point of apprehended attack, had no protection, other than the men provided themselves in the brief time allowed for preparation. They were attacked by large odds, in front and on both flanks. At one time Cleburne's line was so completely enfiladed, that a single shot of the enemy killed nineteen men in one company. The position was maintained, the enemy repulsed, and Atalanta preserved. Cleburne described this as the 'bitterest fight' of his life. On the 22nd of July, in carrying out a plan of general attack, my corps, consisting then of Cleburne's and three other divisions, assaulted and carried the entrenched left of the Federal army. The troops opposed to us were McPherson's army, of which Blair's corps formed a part. On the 27th of June, Cleburne had repelled an assault of these troops with a loss signally disproportionate. It bears strong testimony to the soldierly qualities of the Confederate troops, that on the 22nd of July, they, in positions exactly reversed, carried works equally strong manned by the same troops. The loss of twenty-seven of about thirty field officers in Cleburne's division in this action, attests the gallantry of the officers and the severity of the conflict.

On the 26th of August, the Federal commander, Gen. Sherman, commenced to turn the Confederate position at Atalanta. A Federal force made a detour, and occupied a position at Jonesboro, about twenty-five miles south of Atalanta. On the night of the 30th, Gen. Hood, remaining in Atalanta with one corps of his army, sent the remaining two, Lee's and my own, under my command, to dislodge this force. It was found to consist of three corps, strongly entrenched. The attack upon it was unsuccessful. Cleburne commanded my corps in this action, and achieved the only success of the day, the capture of some guns and a portion of the enemy's works. On the night of the 31st, Gen. Hood withdrew Lee's corps towards Atalanta, and the Federal commander was reinforced by three additional corps, so that on the morning of the 1st of September, my corps, in which Cleburne had renewed his place as division-commander, was confronted by six Federal corps. Gen. Sherman had, meantime, arrived on the field, and taken command in person. The enemy at once took the offensive. It was of the last necessity, to secure the safe withdrawal of the remainder of the army from Atalanta, that this Confederate corps should hold its position through the day. The odds were fearful, and the contest that followed was a very trying one; but the position was held against the attacks made upon it through the day, and the remainder of the army retired in safety from Atalanta. Cleburne's services were highly valuable in the operations of this day.

In the fall and winter of 1864, Gen. Hood marched into Tennessee. In this campaign, at the battle of Franklin, November 30th, Cleburne fell at the head of his division. He was one of thirteen general officers killed or disabled in the combat. He had impressed upon his officers the necessity of carrying the position he had been ordered to attack, a very strong one, at all cost. The troops knew from fearful experience of their own, and their enemies, what it was to assault such works. To encourage them, Cleburne led them in person to the ditch of the opposing line. There rider and horse, each pierced by a score of bullets, fell dead against the reverse of the enemy's works.

The death of Cleburne cast a deep gloom over the army and the country. Eight millions of people, whose hearts had learned to thrill at his name, now mourned his loss, and felt there was none to take his place. The division with which his fame was identified merits more particular mention. It was worthy of him, and he had made it so. Its numbers were made up, and its honours were shared, by citizens of five communities—Arkansas, Texas, Alabama, Mississippi, and Tennessee. In it was also one regiment of Irishmen, who, on every field, illustrated the characteristics of the race that furnishes the world with soldiers. No one of its regiments but bore upon its colours the significant device of the 'crossed cannon inverted,' and the name of each battle in which it had been engaged. Prior to the battle of Shiloh, a blue battle flag had been adopted by me for this division; and when the Confederate battle flag became the national colours, Cleburne's division, at its urgent request, was allowed to retain its own bullet-riddled battle flags. This was the only division in the Confederate service allowed to carry into action other than the national colours; and friends and foes soon learned to watch the course of the blue flag that marked where Cleburne was in the battle. Where this division defended, no odds broke its lines; where it attacked, no numbers resisted its onslaught, save only once;—and there is the grave of Cleburne and his heroic division. In this sketch of Cleburne there has been no intention of disparaging, by omission or otherwise, the merits and services of other officers and troops, some of which are eminently worthy of commemoration; but the limits of a sketch, personal in its character, and giving a bare outline of the military operations with which the subject of it was connected, necessarily preclude an account of the services, however great of others, even when rendered in the same action.

Cleburne at the time of his death was about 37 years of age. He was above the medium height, about 5 feet 11 inches, and though without striking personal advantages, would have arrested attention from a close observer as a man of mark. His hair, originally black, became grey under the cares and fatigues of campaigning. His eyes, a clear steel-grey in colour, were cold and abstracted usually, but beamed genially in seasons of social intercourse, and blazed fiercely in moments of excitement. A good-sized and well-shaped head, prominent features, slightly aquiline nose, thin, greyish whiskers worn on the lip and chin, and an expression of countenance when in repose rather indicative of a man of thought than action, completes the picture. His manners were distant and reserved to strangers, but frank and winning among friends. His mind was of a highly logical cast. Before expressing an opinion upon a subject, or coming to a decision in any conjuncture of circumstances, he wore an expression as if solving a mathematical proposition. The conclusion when reached, was always stamped with mathematical correctness. He was modest as a woman, but not wanting in that fine ambition which ennobles men. Simple in his tastes and habits, and utterly regardless of personal comfort, he was always mindful of the comfort and welfare of his troops. An incident which occurred at Atalanta illustrates his habitual humanity to prisoners. A captured Federal officer was deprived of his hat and blankets by a needy soldier of Cleburne's command, and Cleburne, failing to detect the offender or to recover the property, sent the officer a hat of his own, and his only pair of blankets.

Among his attachments was a very strong one for his adjutant, General Captain Irving A. Buck, a boy in years, but a man in all soldierly qualities, who for nearly two years of the war, shared Cleburne's labours during the day and his blankets at night.

He was also much attached to his youngest brother, who was killed in one of Morgan's fights in South-Western Virginia. This brother inherited the brave qualities that belonged to the name, and after being promoted from the ranks for 'distinguished gallantry,' fell in a charge at the head of his regiment.

Cleburne had enough accent to betray his Irish birth. This accent perceptible in ordinary conversation, grew in times of excitement into a strongly marked brogue. He was accustomed to refer to Ireland as the 'old country,' and always in the tone of a son speaking of an absent mother. He possessed considerable powers of wit and oratory, the national heritage of the Irish people; but his wit, perhaps characterised by the stern influences that had surrounded his life, was rather grim than humorous. He had a marked literary turn, and was singularly well-versed in the British poets. Indeed, he had at one period of his life wooed the muse himself, and with no inconsiderable success, as was evidenced by some fragments of his poetical labours which he had preserved.

It was known that he had a brother in the Federal army, but he seldom mentioned his name, and never without classifying him with the mass of the Irish who had espoused the Federal cause, of whom he always spoke in terms of strong indignation. His high integrity revolted at the want of consistency and morality shown in the course of that class of Irish who, invoking the sympathies of the world in behalf of 'oppressed Ireland,' gave the powerful aid of their arms to enslave another people.

Cleburne's remains were buried after the battle of Franklin, and yet rest in the Polk Cemetery, near Columbia, Tennessee, the most beautiful of the many beautiful spots in the valley of the Tennessee. Generals Granberry and Strahl, brave comrades who fell in the same action, were buried at his side. On the march to Franklin, a few days before his death, Cleburne halted at this point, and in one of the gentle moods of the man that sometimes softened the mien of the soldier, gazed a moment in silence upon the scene, and turning to some members of his staff said, 'It is almost worth dying to rest in so sweet a spot.'

It was in remembrance of these words that their suggestion was carried out in the choice of his burial-place. In this cemetery is set apart a division called the 'Bishops' Corner.' Here were buried the remains of the late Right Rev. Bishop Otey of Tennessee—here are to be placed the ashes of the heroic bishop, General Leonidas Polk, and here it is purposed that the tombs of the future bishops of Tennessee shall be ranged beside these illustrious names. In this spot, where nature has lavished her wealth of grace and beauty, in ground consecrated by the dust of illustrious patriots, churchmen, and warriors—in the bosom of the State he did so much to defend, within whose borders he first guided his charging lines to victory, and on whose soil he finally yielded to the cause the last and all a patriot soldier can give—rests what was mortal of Patrick Cleburne, and will rest until his adopted State shall claim his ashes, and raise above them monumental honours to the virtues of her truest citizen, her noblest champion, her greatest soldier.

Cleburne had often expressed the hope that he might not survive the independence of the South. Heaven heard the prayer, and spared him this pang. He fell before the banner he had so often guided to victory was furled—before the people he fought for were crushed—before the cause he loved was lost.

Two continents now claim his name; eight millions of people revere his memory; two great communities raise monuments to his virtues—and history will take up his fame, and hand it down to time for exampling, wherever a courage without stain, a manhood without blemish, an integrity that knew no compromise, and a patriotism that withheld no sacrifice, are honoured of mankind.

SELMA, ALABAMA: *May* 1, 1867.

Made in the USA
Las Vegas, NV
23 November 2021

35065870R00247